JavaScript

David Sawyer McFarland

POGUE PRESS™
O'REILLY®

Beijing · Cambridge · Farnham · Köln · Sebastopol · Taipei · Tokyo

JavaScript: The Missing Manual
by David Sawyer McFarland

Published by O'Reilly Media, Inc., 1005 Gravenstein Highway North, Şebastopol, CA 95472.

O'Reilly books may be purchased for educational, business, or sales promotional use. Online editions are also available for most titles (*safari.oreilly.com*). For more information, contact our corporate/institutional sales department: (800) 998-9938 or *corporate@oreilly.com*.

Printing History:

July 2008:   First Edition.

 This book uses RepKover™, a durable and flexible lay-flat binding.

ISBN: 978-0-596-51589-8
[M]

Table of Contents

Part Two: Building Web Page Features

Chapter 12: Basic Ajax Programming 439

Part Four: Troubleshooting, Tips, and Tricks

Chapter 13: Troubleshooting and Debugging 463

JavaScript: The Missing Manual

The Missing Credits

About the Author

 David Sawyer McFarland is president of Sawyer McFarland Media, Inc., a Web development and training company in Portland, Oregon. He's been building Web sites since 1995, when he designed his first Web site—an online magazine for communication professionals. He's served as webmaster at the University of California at Berkeley and the Berkeley Multimedia Research Center, and oversaw a complete CSS-driven redesign of Macworld.com.

In addition to building Web sites, David is also a writer, trainer, and instructor. He's taught Web design at UC Berkeley Graduate School of Journalism, the Center for Electronic Art, the Academy of Art College, Ex'Pressions Center for New Media, and Portland State University. He's written articles about the Web for *Practical Web Design, MX Developer's Journal, Macworld* magazine, and *CreativePro.com*.

He welcomes feedback about this book by email: *missing@sawmac.com*. (If you're seeking technical help, however, please refer to the sources listed in Appendix A.)

About the Creative Team

Nan Barber (editor) has worked with the Missing Manual series since its inception—long enough to remember booting up her computer from a floppy disk. Email: *nanbarber@oreilly.com*.

Nellie McKesson (production editor) is a graduate of St. John's College in Santa Fe, New Mexico. She currently lives in Jamaica Plain, Mass., and spends her spare time making t-shirts for her friends to wear (*mattsaundersbynellie.etsy.com*). Email: *nellie@oreilly.com*.

Tony Ruscoe (technical reviewer) is a Web developer living in Sheffield, England. His first computer programs were written in Sinclair BASIC on his ZX Spectrum in the mid-1980s. He's been using JavaScript since 1997 when he started to develop websites and web applications. He currently maintains his personal website (*http://ruscoe.net*) and a site dedicated to researching his surname (*http://ruscoe.name*).

Lisa Hasko (technical reviewer) is a nonprofit humanitarian aid worker with a background in project management for an independent film Web site. Aside from freelancing in her spare time, she is a traveler, social connector, and changeaholic. Email: *lisa.hasko@gmail.com*.

Marni Derr (tech reviewer) is a technical writer and Web developer. When not working on computer-related books or client sites, she is madly giving fiction writing a go. She maintains a community blog for technical writers and developers at *http://writingyourdreams.com*. Email: *marni.derr@writerslatte.com*.

Acknowledgements

Many thanks to all those who helped with this book, including Marni Derr, Tanya Symes, Tony Ruscoe, and Lisa Hasko, whose watchful eyes saved me from potentially embarrassing mistakes. Thanks also to my many students at Portland State University who have sat through my long JavaScript lectures and struggled through my programming assignments. Also, we all owe a big debt of gratitude to John Resig and the jQuery team for creating the best tool yet for making JavaScript fun.

Finally, thanks to David Pogue for getting me started; Nan Barber for making my writing sharper and clearer; my wife, Scholle, for putting up with an author's crankiness; and my son, Graham, who's glad I'm done with this book so he and I can finally get back to playing Indiana Jones and the Legos of Doom. (Hey Kate, welcome to the world!)

The Missing Manual Series

Missing Manuals are witty, superbly written guides to computer products that don't come with printed manuals (which is just about all of them). Each book features a handcrafted index; cross-references to specific pages (not just chapters); and RepKover, a detached-spine binding that lets the book lie perfectly flat without the assistance of weights or cinder blocks.

Recent and upcoming titles include:

Access 2007: The Missing Manual by Matthew MacDonald

AppleScript: The Missing Manual by Adam Goldstein

AppleWorks 6: The Missing Manual by Jim Elferdink and David Reynolds

CSS: The Missing Manual by David Sawyer McFarland

Creating Web Sites: The Missing Manual by Matthew MacDonald

Digital Photography: The Missing Manual by Chris Grover and Barbara Brundage

Dreamweaver 8: The Missing Manual by David Sawyer McFarland

Dreamweaver CS3: The Missing Manual by David Sawyer McFarland

eBay: The Missing Manual by Nancy Conner

Excel 2003: The Missing Manual by Matthew MacDonald

Excel 2007: The Missing Manual by Matthew MacDonald

Facebook: The Missing Manual by E.A. Vander Veer

FileMaker Pro 8: The Missing Manual by Geoff Coffey and Susan Prosser

FileMaker Pro 9: The Missing Manual by Geoff Coffey and Susan Prosser

Flash 8: The Missing Manual by E.A. Vander Veer

Flash CS3: The Missing Manual by E.A. Vander Veer and Chris Grover

FrontPage 2003: The Missing Manual by Jessica Mantaro

Google Apps: The Missing Manual by Nancy Conner

The Internet: The Missing Manual by David Pogue and J.D. Biersdorfer

iMovie 6 & iDVD: The Missing Manual by David Pogue

iMovie '08 & iDVD: The Missing Manual by David Pogue

iPhone: The Missing Manual by David Pogue

iPhoto '08: The Missing Manual by David Pogue

iPod: The Missing Manual, Sixth Edition by J.D. Biersdorfer

sMac OS X: The Missing Manual, Tiger Edition by David Pogue

Mac OS X: The Missing Manual, Leopard Edition by David Pogue

Microsoft Project 2007: The Missing Manual by Bonnie Biafore

Office 2004 for Macintosh: The Missing Manual by Mark H. Walker and Franklin Tessler

Office 2007: The Missing Manual by Chris Grover, Matthew MacDonald, and E.A. Vander Veer

Office 2008 for Macintosh: The Missing Manual by Jim Elferdink

PCs: The Missing Manual by Andy Rathbone

Photoshop Elements 6: The Missing Manual by Barbara Brundage

Photoshop Elements 6 for Mac: The Missing Manual by Barbara Brundage

PowerPoint 2007: The Missing Manual by E.A. Vander Veer

QuickBase: The Missing Manual by Nancy Conner

QuickBooks 2008: The Missing Manual by Bonnie Biafore

Quicken 2008: The Missing Manual by Bonnie Biafore

Switching to the Mac: The Missing Manual, Tiger Edition by David Pogue and Adam Goldstein

Switching to the Mac: The Missing Manual, Leopard Edition by David Pogue

Wikipedia: The Missing Manual by John Broughton

Windows XP Home Edition: The Missing Manual, Second Edition by David Pogue

Windows XP Pro: The Missing Manual, Second Edition by David Pogue, Craig Zacker, and Linda Zacker

Windows Vista: The Missing Manual by David Pogue

Windows Vista for Starters: The Missing Manual by David Pogue

Word 2007: The Missing Manual by Chris Grover

Your Brain: The Missing Manual by Matthew MacDonald

Introduction

Not too long ago, the Web was a pretty boring place. Constructed from plain old HTML, Web pages displayed information and not much else. Folks would click a link and then wait for a new Web page to load—and that was about as interactive as it got.

These days, most Web sites are almost as responsive as the programs on a desktop computer, reacting immediately to every mouse-click. And it's all thanks to the subject of the book you're holding—JavaScript.

What Is JavaScript?

JavaScript is a programming language that lets you supercharge your HTML with animation, interactivity, and dynamic visual effects.

JavaScript can make Web pages more useful by supplying immediate feedback. For example, a JavaScript-powered shopping cart page can instantly display a total cost, with tax and shipping, the moment a visitor selects a product to buy. JavaScript can produce an error message immediately after someone attempts to submit a Web form that's missing necessary information.

JavaScript's main selling point is its immediacy. It lets Web pages respond instantly to the actions of someone interacting with a page—clicking a link, filling out a form, or merely moving the mouse around the screen. JavaScript doesn't suffer from the frustrating delay associated with server-side programming languages like PHP, which rely on communication between the Web browser and the Web server.

Because it doesn't rely on constantly loading and reloading Web pages, JavaScript lets you create Web pages that feel and act more like desktop programs than Web pages.

If you've visited Google Maps (*http://maps.google.com/*), you've seen JavaScript in action. Google Maps lets you view a map of your town (or pretty much anywhere else for that matter), zoom in to get a detailed view of streets and bus stops, or zoom out to get a birds-eye view of how to get across town, the state, or the nation. While there were plenty of map sites before Google, they always required reloading multiple Web pages (a usually slow process) to get to the information you wanted. Google Maps, on the other hand, works without page refreshes—it responds immediately to your choices.

The programs you create with JavaScript can range from the really simple (like popping up a new browser window with a Web page in it) to full blown Web applications like Google Docs (*http://docs.google.com/*), which let you create presentations, edit documents, and create spreadsheets using your Web browser with the feel of a program running directly on your computer.

A Bit of History

Invented by Netscape back in 1995, JavaScript is nearly as old as the Web itself. While JavaScript is well respected today, it has a somewhat checkered past. It used to be considered a hobbyist's programming language, used to add less-than-useful effects messages scrolling across the bottom of a Web browser's status bar like a stock-ticker, or animated butterflies following mouse movements around the page. In the early days of JavaScript, it was easy to find thousands of free JavaScript programs (also called *scripts*) online, but many of those scripts frequently didn't work in all Web browsers, and at times even crashed browsers.

Note: JavaScript has nothing to do with the Java programming language. JavaScript was originally named LiveScript, but the marketing folks at Netscape decided they'd get a lot more publicity if they tried to associate the language with the then-hot Java.

In the early days, JavaScript also suffered from incompatibilities between the two prominent browsers, Netscape Navigator and Internet Explorer. Because Netscape and Microsoft tried to outdo each other's browsers by adding newer and (ostensibly) better features, the two browsers often acted in very different ways, making it difficult to create JavaScript programs that worked well in both.

Note: After Netscape introduced JavaScript, Microsoft introduced jScript, their own version of JavaScript included with Internet Explorer.

Fortunately the worst of those days is nearly gone and contemporary browsers like Firefox, Safari, and Internet Explorer 7 have standardized much of the way they handle JavaScript, making it easier to write JavaScript programs that work for most everyone. (There are still a few incompatibilities among current Web browsers, so you'll need to learn a few tricks for dealing with cross-browser problems. You'll learn how to overcome browser incompatibilities in this book.)

In the past several years, JavaScript has undergone a rebirth, fueled by high-profile Web sites like Google, Yahoo, and Flickr, which use JavaScript extensively to create interactive Web applications. There's never been a better time to learn JavaScript. With the wealth of knowledge and the quality of scripts being written, even if you're a beginner you can add sophisticated interaction to your Web site—without becoming a computer scientist.

JavaScript Is Everywhere

JavaScript isn't just for Web pages, either. It's proven to be such a useful programming language that if you learn JavaScript you can create Yahoo Widgets and Apple's Dashboard Widgets, write programs for the iPhone, and tap into the scriptable features of many Adobe programs like Acrobat, Photoshop, Illustrator, and Dreamweaver. In fact, Dreamweaver has always offered clever JavaScript programmers a way to add their own commands to the program.

In addition, the programming language for Flash—ActionScript—is based on JavaScript, so if you learn the basics of JavaScript you'll be well prepared to take on Flash programming projects.

JavaScript Doesn't Stand Alone

JavaScript isn't any good without the two other pillars of Web design—HTML and CSS. Many programmers talk about the three languages as forming the "layers" of a Web page: HTML provides the *structural* layer, organizing content like pictures and words in a meaningful way; CSS (Cascading Style Sheets) provides the *presentational* layer, making the content in the HTML look good; and JavaScript adds a *behavioral* layer, bringing a Web page to life so it interacts with Web visitors.

In other words, to master JavaScript you need to have a good understanding of both HTML and CSS.

Tip: For a full-fledged introduction to HTML and CSS, check out *Head First HTML with CSS and XHTML* by Elisabeth Freeman and Eric Freeman. For an in-depth presentation of the tricky subject of Cascading Style Sheets, pick up a copy of *CSS: The Missing Manual* by David Sawyer McFarland (both O'Reilly).

HTML: The Barebones Structure

HTML (Hypertext Markup Language) uses simple commands called *tags* to define the various parts of a Web page. For example, this HTML code creates a simple Web page:

```
<!DOCTYPE HTML PUBLIC "-//W3C//DTD HTML 4.01//EN" "http://www.w3.org/TR/
html4/strict.dtd">
<html>
<head>
<title>Hey, I am the title of this Web page.</title>
</head>
<body>
Hey, I am some body text on this Web page.
</body>
</html>
```

It may not be exciting, but this example has all the basic elements a Web page needs. This page begins with a few lines that state what type of document the page is and which standards it conforms to. This document type declaration—*doctype* for short—also points the Web browser to a file on the Internet that contains definitions for that type of file. HTML actually comes in different versions, and you use a different doctype with each. In this case, the doctype for this page indicates that the page is an HTML document that uses a "strict" version of HTML 4.01.

In essence, the doctype tells the Web browser how to display the page. In Internet Explorer, the doctype can even affect how CSS and JavaScript work. With an incorrect or missing doctype, you may end up banging your head against a wall as you discover lots of cross-browser differences with your scripts. In other words, always include a doctype in your HTML.

There are four types of HTML commonly used today: HTML 4.01 Transitional, HTML 4.01 Strict, XHTML 1.0 Transitional, and XHTML 1.0 Strict. All four are very much alike, with just slight differences in how tags are written and what tags and attributes are allowed. Most Web page editing programs add an appropriate doctype when you create a new Web page, but if you want examples of how each is written, you can find templates for the different types of pages at *www. webstandards.org/learn/reference/templates.*

It doesn't really matter which type of HTML you use. All current Web browsers understand each doctype and can display Web pages using any of the four document types without problem. Which doctype you use isn't nearly as important as making sure a page *validates* correctly, as described in the box on page 6.

Note: XHTML was once heralded as the next big thing for Web designers. Although you'll still find people who think you should only use XHTML, the winds of change have turned. Most browser manufacturers aren't very excited about the progress (and complexity) of future versions of XHTML, and have instead turned their attention to HTML 5. You can find out more at *www.digital-web.com/articles/html5_xhtml2_and_the_future_of_the_web*.

How HTML Tags Work

In the example on the the previous page, as in the HTML code of any Web page you look at, you'll notice that most commands appear in pairs that surround a block of text or other commands. Sandwiched between brackets, these *tags* are instructions that tell a Web browser how to display the Web page. Tags are the "markup" part of the Hypertext Markup Language.

The starting (*opening*) tag of each pair tells the browser where the instruction begins, and the ending tag tells it where the instruction ends. Ending or *closing* tags always include a forward slash (/) after the first bracket symbol (<). For example, the tag <p> marks the start of a paragraph, while </p> marks its end.

For a Web page to work correctly, you must include at least these three tags:

- The **<html>** tag appears once at the beginning of a Web page (after the doctype) and again (with an added slash) at the end. This tag tells a Web browser that the information contained in this document is written in HTML, as opposed to some other language. All of the contents of a page, including other tags, appear between the opening and closing <html> tags.

  If you were to think of a Web page as a tree, the <html> tag would be its trunk. Springing from the trunk are two branches that represent the two main parts of any Web page—the *head* and the *body*.

- The *head* of a Web page, surrounded by **<head>** tags, contains the title of the page. It may also provide other, invisible information (such as search keywords) that browsers and Web search engines can exploit.

  In addition, the head can contain information that's used by the Web browser for displaying the Web page and for adding interactivity. You put Cascading Style Sheets, for example, in the head of the document. The head of the document is also where you often include JavaScript programming and links to JavaScript files.

- The *body* of a Web page, as set apart by its surrounding **<body>** tags, contains all the information that appears inside a browser window: headlines, text, pictures, and so on.

Within the <body> tag, you commonly find the following tags:

- You tell a Web browser where a paragraph of text begins with a **<p>** (opening paragraph tag), and where it ends with a **</p>** (closing paragraph tag).

- The <strong> tag emphasizes text. If you surround some text with it and its partner tag, </strong>, you get boldface type. The HTML snippet <strong> Warning!</strong> tells a Web browser to display the word "Warning!" in bold type.

- The <a> tag, or anchor tag, creates a *hyperlink* in a Web page. When clicked, a hyperlink—or *link*—can lead anywhere on the Web. You tell the browser where the link points by putting a Web address inside the <a> tags. For instance, you might type *<a href="http://www.missingmanuals.com/">Click here!</a>*.

The browser knows that when your visitor clicks the words "Click here!" it should go to the Missing Manual Web site. The *href* part of the tag is called an *attribute* and the URL (the Uniform Resource Locator or Web address) is the *value*. In this example, *http://www.missingmanuals.com* is the *value* of the *href* attribute.

UP TO SPEED

Validating Web Pages

As mentioned on page 4, a Web page's doctype identifies which type of HTML or XHTML you used to create the Web page. The rules differ subtly depending on type: For example, unlike HTML 4.01, XHTML doesn't let you have an unclosed <p> tag, and requires that all tag names and attributes be lowercase (<a> *not* <A>, for example.) Because different rules apply to each variant of HTML, you should always *validate* your Web pages.

An HTML validator is a program that makes sure a Web page is written correctly. It checks the page's doctype and then analyzes the code in the page to see whether it matches the rules defined by that doctype. For example, the validator flags mistakes like a misspelled tag name or an unclosed tag. The World Wide Web Consortium (W3C), the organization that's responsible for many of the technologies used on the Web, has a free online validator at *http://validator.w3.org*. You can copy your HTML and paste it into a Web form, upload a Web page, or point the validator to an already existing page on the Web; the validator then analyzes the HTML and reports back whether the page is

valid or not. If there are any errors, the validator tells you what the error is and on which line of the HTML file it occurs.

If you use Firefox, you can download the HTML Validator plug-in from *http://users.skynet.be/mgueury/mozilla*. This plug-in lets you validate a page directly in your Web browser; just open a page (even a page directly off of your computer) and the validator will point out any errors in your HTML. There's a similar plug-in for Safari, called Safari Tidy, which you can find at *http://zappatic.net/safaritidy*.

Valid HTML isn't just good form, it's also necessary to make sure your JavaScript programs work correctly. A lot of JavaScript involves manipulating a Web page's HTML: identifying a particular form field, for example, or placing new HTML (like an error message) in a particular spot. In order for JavaScript to access and manipulate a Web page, the HTML must be in proper working order. Forgetting to close a tag, using the same ID name more than once, or improperly nesting your HTML tags can make your JavaScript code behave erratically or not at all.

CSS: Adding Style to Web Pages

HTML used to be the only language you needed to know. You could build pages with colorful text and graphics and make words jump out using different sizes, fonts, and colors. But today, visitors expect more from our Web sites, so you need to turn to a newer, more flexible technology—Cascading Style Sheets (CSS)—to give your pages visual sophistication. CSS is a formatting language that lets you make text look good, build complex page layouts, and generally add style to your site.

Think of HTML as merely the language you use to structure a page. It helps identify the stuff you want the world to know about. Tags like <h1> and <h2> denote headlines and assign them relative importance: a *heading 1* is more important than a *heading 2*. The <p> tag indicates a basic paragraph of information. Other tags provide further structural clues: for example, a <ul> tag identifies a bulleted list (to make a list of recipe ingredients more intelligible, for example).

CSS, on the other hand, adds design flair to well-organized HTML content, making it more beautiful and easier to read. Essentially, a CSS *style* is just a rule that tells a Web browser how to display a particular element on a page. For example, you can create a CSS rule to make all <h1> tags appear 36 pixels tall, in the Verdana font, and the color orange. CSS can do more powerful stuff, too, like add borders, change margins, and even control the exact placement of a page element.

When it comes to JavaScript, some of the most valuable changes you make to a page involve CSS. You can use JavaScript to add or remove a CSS style from an HTML tag, or dynamically change CSS properties based on a visitor's input or mouse clicks. For example, you can make a page element appear or disappear simply by changing the CSS *display* property. To animate an item across the screen, you change the CSS position properties dynamically using JavaScript.

Anatomy of a Style

A single style that defines the look of one element is a pretty basic beast. It's essentially a rule that tells a Web browser how to format something—turn a headline blue, draw a red border around a photo, or create a 150-pixel-wide sidebar box to hold a list of links. If a style could talk, it would say something like, "Hey Browser, make *this* look like *that*." A style is, in fact, made up of two elements: the Web page element that the browser formats (the *selector*) and the actual formatting instructions (the *declaration block*). For example, a selector can be a headline, a paragraph of text, a photo, and so on. Declaration blocks can turn that text blue, add a red border around a paragraph, position the photo in the center of the page—the possibilities are endless.

Note: Technical types often follow the lead of the W3C and call CSS styles *rules*. This book uses the terms "style" and "rule" interchangeably.

Of course, CSS styles can't communicate in nice clear English. They have their own language. For example, to set a standard font color and font size for all paragraphs on a Web page, you'd write the following:

```
p { color: red; font-size: 1.5em; }
```

This style simply says, "Make the text in all paragraphs—marked with <p> tags—red and 1.5 ems tall." (An *em* is a unit or measurement that's based on a browser's normal text size.) As Figure I-1 illustrates, even a simple style like this example contains several elements:

- **Selector.** The selector tells a Web browser which element or elements on a page to style—like a headline, paragraph, image, or link. In Figure I-1, the selector (p) refers to the <p> tag, which makes Web browsers format all <p> tags using the formatting directions in this style. With the wide range of selectors that CSS offers and a little creativity, you can gain fine control of your pages' formatting. (Selectors are so important, you'll find a detailed discussion of them starting on page 172.)

- **Declaration Block.** The code following the selector includes all the formatting options you want to apply to the selector. The block begins with an opening brace ({) and ends with a closing brace (}).

- **Declaration.** Between the opening and closing braces of a declaration, you add one or more *declarations*, or formatting instructions. Every declaration has two parts, a *property* and a *value,* and ends with a semicolon.

- **Property.** CSS offers a wide range of formatting options, called *properties.* A property is a word—or a few hyphenated words—indicating a certain style effect. Most properties have straightforward names like *font-size, margin-top,* and *background-color.* For example, the *background-color* property sets—you guessed it—a background color.

Note: If you need to brush up on your CSS, grab a copy of *CSS: The Missing Manual.*

- **Value.** Finally, you get to express your creative genius by assigning a *value* to a CSS property—by making a background blue, red, purple, or chartreuse, for example. Different CSS properties require specific types of values—a color (like *red,* or *#FF0000*), a length (like *18px, 2in,* or *5em*), a URL (like *images/ background.gif*), or a specific keyword (like *top, center,* or *bottom*).

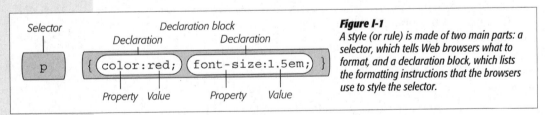

Figure I-1
A style (or rule) is made of two main parts: a selector, which tells Web browsers what to format, and a declaration block, which lists the formatting instructions that the browsers use to style the selector.

You don't need to write a style on a single line as pictured in Figure I-1. Many styles have multiple formatting properties, so you can make them easier to read by breaking them up into multiple lines. For example, you may want to put the selector and opening brace on the first line, each declaration on its own line, and the closing brace by itself on the last line, like so:

```
p {
    color: red;
    font-size: 1.5em;
}
```

It's also helpful to indent properties, with either a tab or a couple of spaces, to visibly separate the selector from the declarations, making it easy to tell which is which. And finally, putting one space between the colon and the property value is optional, but adds to the readability of the style. In fact you can put as much white space between the two as you want. For example *color:red, color: red,* and *color: red* all work.

Software for JavaScript Programming

To create Web pages made up of HTML, CSS, and JavaScript, you need nothing more than a basic text editor like Notepad (Windows) or Text Edit (Mac). But after typing a few hundred lines of JavaScript code, you may want to try a program better suited to working with Web pages. This section lists some common programs, both free and those you can buy.

Note: There are literally hundreds of tools that can help you create Web pages and write JavaScript programs, so the following is by no means a complete list. Think of it as a greatest-hits tour of the most popular programs that JavaScript fans are using today.

Free Programs

There are plenty of free programs out there for editing Web pages and style sheets. If you're still using Notepad or Text Edit, give one of these a try. Here's a short list to get you started:

- **Notepad++** (Windows, *http://notepad-plus.sourceforge.net*) is a coder's friend. It highlights the syntax of JavaScript and HTML code, and lets you save macros and assign keyboard shortcuts to them so you can automate the process of inserting the code snippets you use most.

- **HTML-Kit** (Windows, *www.chami.com/html-kit*) is a powerful HTML/XHTML editor that includes lots of useful features, like the ability to preview a Web page directly in the program (so you don't have to switch back and forth between browser and editor), shortcuts for adding HTML tags, and a lot more.

- **CoffeeCup Free HTML Editor** (Windows, *www.coffeecup.com/free-editor*) is the free version of the commercial ($49) CoffeeCup HTML editor.

- **TextWrangler** (Mac, *www.barebones.com/products/textwrangler*) is free software that's actually a paired down version of BBEdit, the sophisticated, well-known text editor for the Mac. TextWrangler doesn't have all of BBEdit's built-in HTML-tools, but it does include syntax-coloring (highlighting tags and properties in different colors so it's easy to scan a page and identify its parts), FTP support (so you can upload files to a Web server), and more.

Commercial Software

Commercial Web site development programs range from inexpensive text editors to complete Web site construction tools with all the bells and whistles:

- **EditPlus** (Windows, *www.editplus.com*) is an inexpensive ($30) text editor that includes syntax-coloring, FTP, auto-completion, and other wrist-saving features.

- **CoffeCup** (Windows, *www.coffeecup.com*) is a combination text and visual editor ($30). You can either write straight HTML code or use a visual interface to build your pages.

- **skEdit** (Mac, *www.skti.org*) is a cheap ($25) Web page editor, complete with FTP/SFTP support, code hints, and other useful features.

- **textMate** (Mac, *http://macromates.com*) is the new darling of Mac programmers. This text editor ($63) includes many timesaving features for JavaScript programmers like "auto-paired characters," which automatically plops in the second character of a pair of punctuation marks (for example, the program automatically inserts a closing parenthesis after you type an opening parenthesis).

- **BBEdit** (Mac, *www.barebones.com/products/bbedit*). This much-loved Mac text editor ($125) has plenty of tools for working with HTML, XHTML, CSS, JavaScript, and more. Includes many useful Web building tools and shortcuts.

- **Dreamweaver** (Mac and Windows, *www.macromedia.com/software/ dreamweaver*) is a visual Web page editor ($399.) It lets you see how your page looks in a Web browser. The program also includes a powerful text-editor for writing JavaScript programs and excellent CSS creation and management tools. Check out *Dreamweaver: The Missing Manual* for the full skinny on how to use this powerful program.

- **Expression Web Designer** (Windows, *www.microsoft.com*) is Microsoft's new entry in the Web design field ($299). It replaces FrontPage and includes many professional Web design tools, including excellent CSS features.

About This Book

Unlike a piece of software such as Microsoft Word or Dreamweaver, JavaScript isn't a single product developed by a single company. There's no support department at JavaScript headquarters writing an easy-to-read manual for the average Web developer. While you'll find plenty of information on sites like Mozilla.org (see, for example, *http://developer.mozilla.org/en/docs/Core_JavaScript_1.5_ Reference*) or Ecmascript.org (*www.ecmascript.org/docs.php*), there's no definitive source of information on the JavaScript programming language.

Because there's no manual for JavaScript, people just learning JavaScript often don't know where to begin. And the finer points regarding JavaScript can trip up even seasoned Web pros. The purpose of this book, then, is to serve as the manual that should have come with JavaScript. In this book's pages, you'll find step-by-step instructions for using JavaScript to create highly interactive Web pages.

JavaScript: The Missing Manual is designed to accommodate readers who have some experience building Web pages. You'll need to feel comfortable with HTML and CSS to get the most from this book, since JavaScript often works closely with HTML and CSS to achieve its magic. The primary discussions are written for advanced-beginner or intermediate computer users. But if you're new to building Web pages, special boxes called Up to Speed provide the introductory information you need to understand the topic at hand. If you're an advanced Web page jockey, on the other hand, keep your eye out for similar shaded boxes called Power Users' Clinic. They offer more technical tips, tricks, and shortcuts for the experienced computer fan.

Note: This book periodically recommends *other* books, covering topics that are too specialized or tangential for a manual about using JavaScript. Sometimes the recommended titles are from Missing Manual series publisher O'Reilly Media—but not always. If there's a great book out there that's not part of the O'Reilly family, we'll let you know about it.

This Book's Approach to JavaScript

JavaScript is a real programming language: It doesn't work like HTML or CSS, and it has its own set of (often complicated) rules. It's not always easy for Web designers to switch gears and start thinking like computer programmers, and there's no *one* book that can teach you everything there is to know about JavaScript.

The goal of *JavaScript: The Missing Manual* isn't to turn you into the next great programmer. This book is meant to familiarize Web designers with the ins and outs of JavaScript and then move on to advanced tools for adding really useful interactivity to a Web site as quickly and easily as possible.

In this book, you'll learn the basics of JavaScript and programming; but just the basics won't make for very exciting Web pages. It's not possible in 400 pages to teach you everything about JavaScript that you need to know to build sophisticated, interactive Web pages. Instead, this book shows you how to use professional (and free) JavaScript code that will liberate you from all of the minute, time-consuming details of creating JavaScript programs that run well across different browsers.

You'll learn the basics of JavaScript, and then jump immediately to advanced Web page interactivity with a little help—OK, a *lot* of help—from some very sophisticated but easy-to-use JavaScript helper programs. Think of it this way: You could build a house by cutting down and milling your own lumber, constructing your own windows, doors and doorframes, manufacturing your own tile, and so on. That "do it yourself" approach is common to a lot of JavaScript books. But who has that kind of time? This book's approach is more like building a house by taking advantage of already built pieces and putting them together using basic skills. The end result will be a beautiful and functional house built in a fraction of the time it would take you to learn every step of the process.

And even if you want to learn every step of the process, this book is the best place to start. It points out other useful and more advanced JavaScript books so you can continue your programming education after you're done with this book (but only if you want to!).

About the Outline

JavaScript: The Missing Manual is divided into four parts, each containing several chapters:

- **Part 1, Getting Started with JavaScript** starts at the very beginning. You'll learn the basic building blocks of JavaScript as well as get some helpful tips on computer programming in general. This section teaches you how to add a script to a Web page, store and manipulate information, and add smarts to a program so it can respond to different situations. You'll also learn how to communicate with the browser window, store and read cookies, respond to various events like mouse clicks and form submissions, and modify the HTML of a Web page.

- **Part 2, Building Web Page Features,** provides many real-world examples of JavaScript in action. You'll learn how to create pop-up navigation bars, enhance HTML tables, and build an interactive photo gallery. You'll make your Web forms more usable by adding form validation (so visitors can't submit forms missing information), add a calendar widget to make selecting dates easy, and change form options based on selections a Web visitor makes. Finally, you'll create interesting user interfaces with tabbed panels, accordion panels and pop-up dialog boxes that look great and function flawlessly.

- **Part 3, Ajax: Communicating with the Web Server,** covers the technology that single-handedly made JavaScript one of the most glamorous Web languages to learn. In this section, you'll learn how to use JavaScript to communicate with a Web server so your pages can receive information and update themselves based on information provided by a Web server—without having to load a new Web page.

Tip: You'll find step-by-step instructions for setting up a Web server on your computer so you can take advantage of the cool technology (discussed in Part 3) on this book's companion Web page. See "Living Examples" on the next page for details.

• **Part 4, Troubleshooting, Tips, and Tricks,** helps you with those times when nothing seems to be working: your perfectly crafted JavaScript program just doesn't seem to do what you want (or worse, it doesn't work at all!). You'll learn the most common errors new programmers make as well as techniques for discovering and fixing bugs in your programs. In addition, you'll learn a few tips to make your programming more efficient and your scripts run faster.

At the end of the book, an appendix provides a detailed list of references to aid you in your further exploration of the JavaScript programming language.

Living Examples

This book is designed to get your work onto the Web faster and more professionally; it's only natural, then, that half the value of this book also lies on the Web.

As you read the book's chapters, you'll encounter a number of *living examples*—step-by-step tutorials that you can build yourself, using raw materials (like graphics and half-completed Web pages) that you can download from either *www.sawmac.com/javascript/* or from this book's "Missing CD" page at *www.missingmanuals.com/cds*. You might not gain very much from simply reading these step-by-step lessons while relaxing in your porch hammock. But if you take the time to work through them at the computer, you'll discover that these tutorials give you unprecedented insight into the way professional designers build Web pages.

You'll also find, in this book's lessons, the URLs of the finished pages, so that you can compare your work with the final result. In other words, you won't just see pictures of JavaScript code in the pages of the book; you'll find the actual, working Web pages on the Internet.

About MissingManuals.com

At *www.missingmanuals.com*, you'll find articles, tips, and updates to *JavaScript: The Missing Manual*. In fact, we invite and encourage you to submit such corrections and updates yourself. In an effort to keep the book as up to date and accurate as possible, each time we print more copies of this book, we'll make any confirmed corrections you've suggested. We'll also note such changes on the Web site, so that you can mark important corrections into your own copy of the book, if you like. (Go to *http://missingmanuals.com/feedback*, choose the book's name from the pop-up menu, and then click Go to see the changes.)

Also on our Feedback page, you can get expert answers to questions that come to you while reading this book, write a book review, and find groups for folks who share your interest in JavaScript.

While you're there, sign up for our free monthly email newsletter. Click the "Sign Up for Our Newsletter" link in the left-hand column. You'll find out what's happening in Missing Manual land, meet the authors and editors, get bonus video and book excerpts, and so on.

The Very Basics

To use this book, and indeed to use a computer, you need to know a few basics. This book assumes that you're familiar with a few terms and concepts:

- **Clicking.** This book gives you three kinds of instructions that require you to use your computer's mouse or trackpad. To *click* means to point the arrow cursor at something on the screen and then—without moving the cursor at all—to press and release the clicker button on the mouse (or laptop trackpad). To *right-click* means to do the same thing with the right mouse button. To *double-click,* of course, means to click twice in rapid succession, again without moving the cursor at all. And to *drag* means to move the cursor *while* pressing the button.

Tip: If you're on a Mac and don't have a right mouse button, you can accomplish the same thing by pressing the Control key as you click with the one mouse button.

When you're told to ⌘-*click* something on the Mac, or *Ctrl-click* something on a PC, you click while pressing the ⌘ or Ctrl key (both of which are near the Space bar).

- **Menus.** The *menus* are the words at the top of your screen or window: File, Edit, and so on. Click one to make a list of commands appear, as though they're written on a window shade you've just pulled down.

- **Keyboard shortcuts.** If you're typing along in a burst of creative energy, it's sometimes disruptive to have to take your hand off the keyboard, grab the mouse, and then use a menu (for example, to use the Bold command). That's why many experienced computer mavens prefer to trigger menu commands by pressing certain combinations on the keyboard. For example, in the Firefox Web browser, you can press Ctrl-+ (Windows) or ⌘-+ (Mac) to make text on a Web page get larger (and more readable). When you read an instruction like "press ⌘-B," start by pressing the ⌘ key; while it's down, type the letter B, and then release both keys.

- **Operating-system basics.** This book assumes that you know how to open a program, surf the Web, and download files. You should know how to use the Start menu (Windows) and the Dock or menu (Macintosh), as well as the Control Panel (Windows), or System Preferences (Mac OS X).

If you've mastered this much information, you have all the technical background you need to enjoy *JavaScript: The Missing Manual.*

About → These → Arrows

Throughout this book, and throughout the Missing Manual series, you'll find sentences like this one: "Open the System → Library → Fonts folder." That's shorthand for a much longer instruction that directs you to open three nested folders in sequence, like this: "On your hard drive, you'll find a folder called System. Open that. Inside the System folder window is a folder called Library; double-click it to open it. Inside *that* folder is yet another one called Fonts. Double-click to open it, too."

Similarly, this kind of arrow shorthand helps to simplify the business of choosing commands in menus, as shown in Figure I-2.

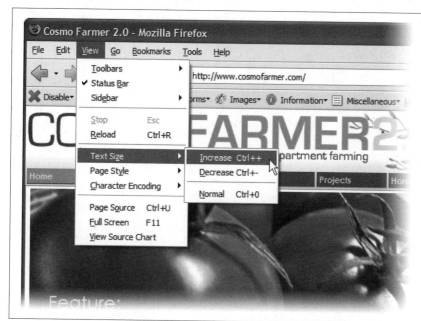

Figure I-2
In this book, arrow notations help simplify menu instructions. For example, View → Text Size → Increase is a more compact way of saying, "From the View menu, choose Text Size; from the submenu that then appears, choose Increase."

Safari® Books Online

When you see a Safari® Books Online icon on the cover of your favorite technology book, that means the book is available online through the O'Reilly Network Safari Bookshelf.

Safari offers a solution that's better than e-Books. It's a virtual library that lets you easily search thousands of top tech books, cut and paste code samples, download chapters, and find quick answers when you need the most accurate, current information. Try it free at *http://safari.oreilly.com*.

Part One: Getting Started with JavaScript

1

Writing Your First JavaScript Program

By itself, HTML doesn't have any smarts: It can't do math, it can't figure out if someone has correctly filled out a form, and it can't make decisions based on how a Web visitor interacts with it. Basically, HTML lets people read text, look at pictures, and click links to move to other Web pages with more text and pictures. In order to add intelligence to your Web pages so they can respond to your site's visitors, you need JavaScript.

JavaScript lets a Web page react intelligently. With it, you can create *smart* Web forms that let visitors know when they've forgotten to include necessary information; you can make elements appear, disappear, or move around a Web page (see Figure 1-1); you can even update the contents of a Web page with information retrieved from a Web server—without having to load a new Web page. In short, JavaScript lets you make your Web sites more engaging and effective.

Introducing Programming

For a lot of people, the word "computer programming" conjures up visions of super-intelligent nerds hunched over keyboards, typing nearly unintelligible gibberish for hours on end. And, honestly, some programming is just like that. Programming can seem like complex magic that's well beyond the average mortal. But many programming concepts aren't difficult to grasp, and as programming languages go, JavaScript is relatively friendly to nonprogrammers.

Figure 1-1:
JavaScript lets Web pages respond to visitors. On Amazon.com, mousing over the "Gifts and Wish Lists" link opens a tab that floats above the other content on the page and offers additional options.

Still, JavaScript is more complex than either HTML or CSS, and programming often is a foreign world to Web designers; so one goal of this book is to help you think more like a programmer. Throughout this book you'll learn fundamental programming concepts that apply whether you're writing JavaScript, ActionScript, or even writing a desktop program using C++. More importantly, you'll learn how to approach a programming task so you'll know exactly what you want to do before you start adding JavaScript to a Web page.

Many Web designers are immediately struck by the strange symbols and words used in JavaScript. An average JavaScript program is sprinkled with symbols ({ } [ ] ; , ( ) !=) and full of unfamiliar words (var, null, else if). It's like staring at a foreign language, and in many ways learning a programming language is a lot like learning another language. You need to learn new words, new punctuation, and understand how to put them together so you can communicate successfully.

In fact, every programming language has its own set of key words and characters, and its own set of rules for putting those words and characters together—the language's *syntax*. Learning JavaScript's syntax is like learning the vocabulary and grammar of another language. You'll need to memorize the words and rules of the language (or at least keep this book handy as a reference). When learning to speak a new language, you quickly realize that placing an accent on the wrong syllable can make a word unintelligible. Likewise, a simple typo or even a missing punctuation mark can prevent a JavaScript program from working, or trigger an error in a Web browser. You'll make plenty of mistakes as you start to learn to program—that's just the nature of programming.

The Client Side vs. The Server Side

JavaScript is a *client-side* language, which (in English) means that it works inside a Web browser. The alternative type of Web programming language is called a *server-side* language, which you'll find in pages built around PHP, .NET, ASP, ColdFusion, Ruby on Rails, and other Web server technologies. Server-side programming languages, as the name suggests, run on a Web server. They can exhibit a lot of intelligence by accessing databases, processing credit cards, and sending email around the globe. The problem with server-side languages is that they require the Web browser to send requests to the Web server, forcing visitors to wait until a new page arrives with new information.

Client-side languages, on the other hand, can react immediately and change what a visitor sees in his Web browser without the need to download a new page. Content can appear or disappear, move around the screen, or automatically update based on how a visitor interacts with the page. This responsiveness lets you create Web sites that feel more like desktop programs than static Web pages. But JavaScript isn't the only client-side technology in town. You can also use plug-ins to add programming smarts to a Web page. Java applets are one example. These are small programs, written in the Java programming language, that run in a Web browser. They also tend to start up slowly and have been known to crash the browser.

Flash is another plug-in based technology that offers sophisticated animation, video, sound, and lots of interactive potential. In fact, it's sometimes hard to tell if an interactive Web page is using JavaScript or Flash. For example, Google Maps could also be created in Flash (in fact, Yahoo Maps was at one time a Flash application, until Yahoo recreated it using JavaScript.) A quick way to tell the difference: Right-click on the part of the page that you think might be Flash (the map itself, in this case); if it is, you'll see a pop-up menu that includes "About the Flash Player."

Ajax, which you'll learn about in Part 3 of this book, brings both client-side and server-side together. Ajax is a method for using JavaScript to talk to a server, retrieve information from the server, and update the Web page without the need to load a new Web page. Google Maps uses this technique to let you move around a map without forcing you to load a new Web page.

At first, you'll probably find JavaScript programming frustrating—you'll spend a lot of your time tracking down errors you made when typing the script. Also, you might find some of the concepts related to programming a bit hard to follow at first. But don't worry: If you've tried to learn JavaScript in the past and gave up because you thought it was too hard, this book will help you get past the hurdles that often trip up folks new to programming. (And if you do have programming experience, this book will teach you JavaScript's idiosyncrasies and the unique concepts involved in programming for Web browsers.)

What's a Computer Program?

When you add JavaScript to a Web page, you're writing a computer program. Granted, most JavaScript programs are much simpler than the programs you use to read email, retouch photographs, and build Web pages. But even though JavaScript programs (also called *scripts*) are simpler and shorter, they share many of the same properties of more complicated programs.

In a nutshell, any computer program is a series of steps that are completed in a designated order. Say you want to display a welcome message using the name of the person viewing a Web page: for example, "Welcome, Bob!" There are several things you'd need to do to accomplish this task:

1. **Ask the visitor his or her name.**

2. **Get the visitor's response.**

3. **Print (that is, display) the message on the Web page.**

While you may never want to print a welcome message on a Web page, this example demonstrates the fundamental process of programming: determine what you want to do, then break that task down into each step that's necessary to get it done. Every time you want to create a JavaScript program, you must go through the process of determining the steps needed to achieve your goal. Once you know the steps, you're ready to write your program. In other words, you'll translate your ideas into programming *code*—the words and characters that make the Web browser behave how you want it to.

FREQUENTLY ASKED QUESTION

Compiled vs. Scripting Languages

JavaScript is called a scripting language. *I've heard this term used for other languages like PHP and ColdFusion as well. What's a scripting language?*

Most of the programs running on your computer are written using languages that are *compiled*. Compiling is the process of turning the code a programmer writes into instructions that a computer can understand. Once a program is compiled, you can run it on your computer, and since a compiled program has been converted directly to instructions a computer understands, it will run faster than a program written with a scripting language. Unfortunately, compiling a program is a time-consuming process: you have to write the program, compile it, then test it. If the program doesn't work, you have to go through the whole process again.

A scripting language, on the other hand, is only compiled when an *interpreter* (another program that can convert the script into something a computer can understand) reads it. In the case of JavaScript, the interpreter is built into the Web browser. So when your Web browser reads a Web page with a JavaScript program in it, the Web browser translates the JavaScript into something the computer understands. As a result, a scripting language operates more slowly than a compiled language, since every time it runs the program must be translated for the computer. Scripting languages are great for Web developers: Scripts are generally much smaller and less complex than desktop programs, so the lack of speed isn't so important. In addition, since they don't require compiling, creating and testing programs that use a scripting language is a much faster process.

How to Add JavaScript to a Page

Web browsers are built to understand HTML and CSS and convert those languages into a visual display on the screen. The part of the Web browser that understands HTML and CSS is called the *layout* or *rendering* engine. But most browsers also have something called a *JavaScript interpreter*. That's the part of the browser that understands JavaScript and can execute the steps of a JavaScript program. Since the Web browser is usually expecting HTML, you must specifically tell the browser when JavaScript is coming by using the <script> tag.

The <script> tag is regular HTML. It acts like a switch that in effect says "Hey Web browser, here comes some JavaScript code; you don't know what to do with it, so hand it off to the JavaScript interpreter." When the Web browser encounters the closing </script> tag, it knows it's reached the end of the JavaScript program and can get back to its normal duties.

Much of the time, you'll add the <script> tag in the <head> portion of the Web page like this:

```
<!DOCTYPE HTML PUBLIC "-//W3C//DTD HTML 4.01//EN" "http://www.w3.org/TR/
html4/strict.dtd">
<html>
<head>
<title>My Web Page</title>
<script type="text/javascript">

</script>
</head>
```

The <script> tag's *type* attribute indicates the format and the type of script that follows. In this case, *type="text/javascript"* means the script is regular text (just like HTML) and that it's written in JavaScript. Theoretically, a Web browser could handle multiple types of scripting languages, but not every browser supports other languages.

Note: Make sure you include *type="text/javascript"* in the opening script tag. If you leave it out, your Web page won't validate (see the box on page 6 for more on validation).

You then add your JavaScript code between the opening and closing <script> tags:

```
<!DOCTYPE HTML PUBLIC "-//W3C//DTD HTML 4.01//EN" "http://www.w3.org/TR/
html4/strict.dtd">
<html>
<head>
<title>My Web Page</title>
<script type="text/javascript">
alert('hello world!');
</script>
</head>
```

You'll find out what this JavaScript actually does in a moment. For now, turn your attention to the opening and closing <script> tags. To add a script to your page, start by inserting these tags. In most cases, you'll put the <script> tags in the page's <head> in order to keep your JavaScript code neatly organized in one area of the Web page.

However, it's perfectly valid to put <script> tags anywhere inside the HTML of the page. In fact, as you'll see later in this chapter, there's a JavaScript command that lets you write information directly into a Web page. Using that command, you place the <script> tags in the location on the page (somewhere inside the body) where you want the script to write its message.

External JavaScript Files

Using the <script> tag as discussed in the previous section lets you add JavaScript to a single page. But many times you'll create scripts that you want to share with all of the pages on your site. For example, you might use a JavaScript program to add animated, drop-down navigation menus to a Web page. You'll want that same fancy navigation bar on every page of your site, but copying and pasting the same JavaScript code into each page of your site is a really bad idea for several reasons.

First, it's a lot of work copying and pasting the same code over and over again, especially if you have a site with hundreds of pages. Second, if you ever decide to change or enhance the JavaScript code, you'll need to locate every page using that JavaScript and update the code. Finally, since all of the code for the JavaScript program would be located in every Web page, each page will be that much larger and slower to download.

A better approach is to use an external JavaScript file. If you've used external CSS files for your Web pages, this technique should feel familiar. An external JavaScript file is simply a text file that ends with the file extension .js—*navigation.js*, for example. The file only includes JavaScript code and is linked to a Web page using the <script> tag. For example, to add a JavaScript file named *navigation.js* to your home page, you might write the following:

```
<!DOCTYPE HTML PUBLIC "-//W3C//DTD HTML 4.01//EN" "http://www.w3.org/TR/
html4/strict.dtd">
<html>
<head>
<title>My Web Page</title>
<script type="text/javascript" src="navigation.js"></script>
</head>
```

The src attribute of the <script> tag works just like the src attribute of an <img> tag, or an <a> tag's href attribute. In other words, it points to a file either in your Web site or on another Web site (see the box on the next page).

Note: When adding the src attribute to link to an external JavaScript file, don't add any JavaScript code between the opening and closing <script> tags. If you want to link to an external JavaScript file and add custom JavaScript code to a page, use a second set of <script> tags. For example:

```
<script type="text/javascript" src="navigation.js"></script>
<script type="text/javascript">
  alert('Hello world!');
</script>
```

URL Types

When attaching an external JavaScript file to a Web page, you need to specify a *URL* for the src attribute of the <script> tag. A URL or *Uniform Resource Locator* is a path to a file located on the Web. There are three types of paths: *absolute path, root-relative path,* and *document-relative path.* All three indicate where a Web browser can find a particular file (like another Web page, a graphic, or a JavaScript file).

An *absolute path* is like a postal address—it contains all the information needed for a Web browser located anywhere in the world to find the file. An absolute path includes http://, the hostname, and the folder and name of the file. For example: *http://www.cosmofarmer.com/scripts/site.js.*

A *root-relative* path indicates where a file is located relative to a site's top-level folder—the site's root folder. A root-relative path doesn't include http:// or the domain name. It begins with a / (slash) indicating the site's root folder—the folder the home page is in. For example, */scripts/site.js* indicates that the file *site.js* is located inside a folder named *scripts*, which is itself located in the site's top-level folder. An easy way to create a root-relative path is to take an absolute path and strip off the http:// and the host name. For example, *http://www.sawmac.com/index.html* written as a root relative URL is */index.html*.

A *document-relative* path specifies the path from the Web page to the JavaScript file. If you have multiple levels of folders on your Web site, you'll need to use different paths to point to the same JavaScript file. For example, suppose you have a JavaScript file named *site.js* located in a folder named *scripts* in your Web site's main directory. The document-relative path to that file will look like one way for the home page—*scripts/site.js*—but for a page located inside a folder named *about*, the path to the same file would be different—*../scripts/site.js*—the *../* means climb up *out* of the *about* folder, while the */scripts/site.js* means go to the *scripts* folder and get the file *site.js*.

Here are some tips on which URL type to use:

- If you're pointing to a file that's not on the same server as the Web page, you *must* use an absolute path. It's the only type that can point to another Web site.

- Root-relative paths are good for JavaScript files stored on your own site. Since they always start at the root folder, the URL for a JavaScript file will be the same for every page on your Web site, even when Web pages are located in folders and subfolders on your site. However, root-relative paths don't work unless you're viewing your Web pages through a Web server—either your Web server out on the Internet, or a Web server you've set up on your own computer for testing purposes. In other words, if you're just opening a Web page off your computer using the browser's File → Open command, the Web browser won't be able to locate, load, or run JavaScript files that are attached using a root relative path.

- Document-relative paths are the best when you're designing on your own computer without the aid of a Web server. You can create an external JavaScript file, attach it to a Web page, and then check the JavaScript in a Web browser simply by opening the Web page off your hard drive. Document-relative paths work fine when moved to your actual, living, breathing Web site on the Internet, but you'll have to rewrite the URLS to the JavaScript file if you move the Web page to another location on the server. In this book, we'll be using document-relative paths, since they will let you follow along and test the tutorials on your own computer without a Web server.

You can (and often will) attach multiple external JavaScript files to a single Web page. For example, you might have created one external JavaScript file that controls a drop-down navigation bar, and another that lets you add a nifty slideshow to a page of photos (you'll learn how to do that on page 263). On your photo gallery page, you'd want to have both JavaScript programs, so you'd attach both files.

In addition, you can attach external JavaScript files and add a JavaScript program to the same page like this:

```
<!DOCTYPE HTML PUBLIC "-//W3C//DTD HTML 4.01//EN" "http://www.w3.org/TR/
html4/strict.dtd">
<html>
<head>
<title>My Web Page</title>
<script type="text/javascript" src="navigation.js"></script>
<script type="text/javascript" src="slideshow.js"></script>
<script type="text/javascript">
alert('hello world!');
</script>
</head>
```

Just remember that you must use one set of opening and closing <script> tags for each external JavaScript file. You'll create an external JavaScript file in the tutorial that starts on page 29.

You can keep external JavaScript files anywhere inside your Web site's root folder (or any subfolder inside the root). Many Web developers create a special directory for external JavaScript files in the site's root folder: common names are *js* (meaning JavaScript) or *libs* (meaning libraries).

Note: Sometimes the order in which you attach external JavaScript files matters. As you'll see later in this book, sometimes scripts you write depend upon code that comes from an external file. That's often the case when using JavaScript libraries (JavaScript code that simplifies complex programming tasks). You'll see an example of a JavaScript library in action in the tutorial on page 29.

Your First JavaScript Program

The best way to learn JavaScript programming is by actually programming. Throughout this book, you'll find hands-on tutorials that take you step-by-step through the process of creating JavaScript programs. To get started, you'll need a text editor (see page 9 for recommendations), a Web browser, and the exercise files located at *www.sawmac.com/javascript* (see the note on the next page for complete instructions).

Note: The tutorials in this chapter require the example files from this book's Web site, *www.sawmac. com/javascript.* Click the "Download tutorials" link to download them. (The tutorial files are stored as a single Zip file.)

Windows users should download the Zip file and double-click it to open the archive. Click the Extract All Files option, and then follow the instructions of the Extraction Wizard to unzip the files and place them on your computer. Mac users, just double-click the file to decompress it. After you've downloaded and decompressed the files, you should have a folder named MM_JAVASCRIPT on your computer, containing all of the tutorial files for this book.

To get your feet wet and provide a gentle introduction to JavaScript, your first program will be very simple:

1. **In your favorite text editor, open the file *1.1.html*.**

   This file is located in the *chapter01* folder in the MM_JAVASCRIPT folder you downloaded from *www.sawmac.com/javascript.* It's a very simple HTML page, with an external cascading style sheet to add a little visual excitement.

2. **Click in the empty line just *before* the closing </head> tag and type:**

   ```
   <script type="text/javascript">
   ```

   This code is actually HTML, not JavaScript. It informs the Web browser that the stuff following this tag is JavaScript.

3. **Press the Return key to create a new blank line, and type:**

   ```
   alert('hello world');
   ```

   You've just typed your first line of JavaScript code. The JavaScript *alert( )* function, is a command that pops open an Alert box and displays the message that appears inside the parentheses—in this case *hello world.* Don't worry about all of the punctuation (the parentheses, quotes, and semicolon) just yet. You'll learn what they do in the next chapter.

4. **Press the Return key once more, and type *</script>*. The code should now look like this:**

   ```
   <link href="../css/global.css" rel="stylesheet" type="text/css">
   <script type="text/javascript">
   alert('hello world');
   </script>
   </head>
   ```

   In this example, the stuff you just typed is shown in boldface. The two HTML tags are already in the file; make sure you type the code exactly where shown.

---

5. **Launch a Web browser and open the *1.1.html* file to preview it.**

A JavaScript Alert box appears (see Figure 1-2). Notice that the page is blank when the alert appears. (If you don't see the Alert box pictured in Figure 1-2, you probably mistyped the code listed in the previous steps. Double-check your typing and read the Tip below.)

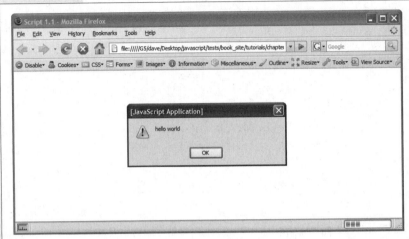

Figure 1-2:
The JavaScript Alert box is a quick way to grab someone's attention. It's one of the simplest JavaScript commands to learn and use.

6. **Click the Alert box's OK button to close it.**

When the Alert box disappears, the Web page appears in the browser window.

Tip: When you first start programming, you'll be shocked at how often your JavaScript programs don't seem to work…at all. For new programmers, the most common cause of nonfunctioning programs is simple typing mistakes. Always double-check to make sure you spelled commands (like *alert* in the first script) correctly. Also, notice that punctuation frequently comes in pairs (the opening and closing parentheses, and single-quote marks from your first script, for example). Make sure you include both opening and closing punctuation marks when they're required.

Although this first program isn't earth-shatteringly complex (or even that interesting), it does demonstrate an important concept: A Web browser will run a JavaScript program the moment it reads in the JavaScript code. In this example, the *alert( )* command appeared *before* the Web browser displayed the Web page, because the JavaScript code appeared *before* the HTML in the <body> tag. This concept comes into play when you start writing programs that manipulate the HTML of the Web page—as you'll learn in Chapter 5.

Note: You'll frequently see the word "execute" used in place of "run." For example, "the Web browser executed the JavaScript program" means the same thing as "the Web browser ran the JavaScript program."

Writing Text on a Web Page

The last script popped up a dialog box in the middle of your monitor. What if you want to print a message directly onto a Web page using JavaScript? There are many ways to do so, and you'll learn some sophisticated techniques later in this book. However, you can achieve this simple goal with a built-in JavaScript command, and that's what you'll do in your second script:

1. **In your text editor, open the file *1.2.html*.**

    While <script> tags usually appear in the <head> of a Web page, you can put them and JavaScript programs directly in the body of the Web page.

2. **Directly below "<h1>Writing to the document window</h1>", type the following code:**

    ```
    <script type="text/javascript">
    document.write('<p>Hello world!</p>');
    </script>
    ```

    Like the *alert( )* function, *document.write( )* is a JavaScript command that literally writes out whatever you place between the opening and closing parentheses. In this case, the HTML *<p>Hello world!</p>* is added to the page: a paragraph tag and two words.

3. **Save the page, and open it in a Web browser.**

    The page opens and the words "Hello world!" appear below the red headline (see Figure 1-3).

Note: The tutorial files you downloaded also include the completed version of each tutorial. If you can't seem to get your JavaScript working, compare your work with the file that begins with *complete_* in the same folder as the tutorial file. For example, the file *complete_1.2.html* contains a working version of the script you added to file *1.2.html*.

The two scripts you just created may leave you feeling a little underwhelmed with JavaScript…or this book. Don't worry. It's important to start out with a full understanding of the basics. You'll be doing some very useful and complicated things using JavaScript in just a few chapters. In fact, in the remainder of this chapter you'll get a taste of some of the advanced features you'll be able to add to your Web pages after you've worked your way through the first two parts of this book.

Attaching an External JavaScript File

As discussed on page 24, you'll usually put JavaScript code in a separate file if you want to use the same scripts on more than one Web page. You can then instruct a Web page to load that file and use the JavaScript inside it. External JavaScript files

---

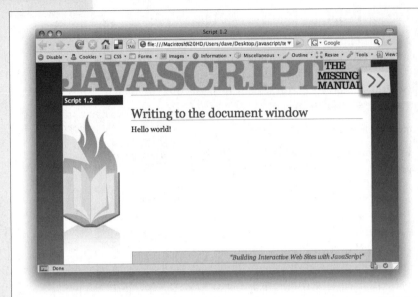

Figure 1-3:
Wow. This script may not be something to document.write home about—ha, ha, JavaScript humor— but it does demonstrate that you can use JavaScript to add content to a Web page, a trick that comes in handy when you want to display messages (like 'Welcome back to the site, Dave') after a Web page has downloaded.

also come in handy when you're using someone else's JavaScript code. In particular, there are collections of JavaScript code called *libraries*, which provide useful JavaScript programming: Usually, these libraries make it easy for you to do something that's normally quite difficult to do. You'll learn more about JavaScript libraries on page 169, and, in particular, the JavaScript library this book uses—jQuery.

But for now, you'll get experience attaching an external JavaScript file to a page, and writing a short program that does some amazing things:

1. **In your text editor, open the file *1.3.html*.**

   This page has a basic HTML table, containing data on a handful of products (see Figure 1-4). HTML tables are like spreadsheets: They organize data into rows and columns. One problem with tables that contain lots of rows and columns is that it's easy to lose your place as you read across a row. One helpful visual effect many designers use is to put a background color on every *other* row, making it much easier to quickly scan across a row of data. To do this, you create a CSS class style that defines a background color or image, then apply that class to every other table row using HTML like this: *<tr class="even">*. Now, that's a lot of repetitive work, and you can ruin it just by inserting a new row in the middle of the table. Fortunately, there's a quick JavaScript solution to this common design problem.

2. **Click in the blank line between the <link> and closing </head> tags near the top of the page, and type:**

   ```
   <script type="text/javascript" src="../js/jquery.js"></script>
   ```

Figure 1-4:
*A plain HTML table can
be hard to read if there
are lots of columns, rows,
and data. While scanning
across a long row of
data, it's easy to lose
your place and view data
from a different row.*

This code links a file named *jquery.js,* that's contained in a folder named *js,* to this Web page. When a Web browser loads this Web page, it also downloads the *jquery.js* JavaScript file and runs the code inside it.

Next, you'll add your own JavaScript programming to this page.

3. **Press Return to create a new blank line, and then type:**

```
<script type="text/javascript">
```

HTML tags usually travel in pairs—an opening and closing tag. To make sure you don't forget to close a tag, it helps to close the tag immediately after typing the opening tag, and then fill in the stuff that goes between the tags.

4. **Press return twice to create two blank lines, and then type:**

```
</script>
```

This ends the block of JavaScript code. Now you'll add some programming.

5. **Click the empty line between the opening and closing script tags and type:**

```
$(document).ready(function( ) {
```

You're probably wondering what the heck that is. You'll find out all the details of this code on page 218, but in a nutshell, this line takes advantage of the programming that's inside the *jquery.js* file to make sure that the browser executes the next line of code at the right time.

6. **Hit return to create a new line, and then type:**

```
$('table.striped tr:even').addClass('even');
```

This line does the magic of adding a background to every other row of the table. Specifically, it does so by adding a CSS class of *.even* to every even row of the table. In the CSS style sheet attached to this page, the *.even* class style sets a blue color for the background property. When you apply this class to a table row, that row gets a blue background.

7. **Hit Return one last time, and then type:**

```
});
```

This code closes up the JavaScript code, much like a closing </script> tag indicates the end of a JavaScript program. Don't worry too much about all those weird punctuation marks—you'll learn how they work in detail later in the book. The main thing you need to make sure of is to type the code exactly as it's listed here. One typo, and the program may not work.

The final code you added to the page should look like the bolded text below:

```
<link href="../css/global.css" rel="stylesheet" type="text/css">
<script type="text/javascript" src="../js/jquery.js"></script>
<script type="text/javascript">
$(function( ) {
$('table.striped tr:even').addClass('even');
});
</script>
</head>
```

8. **Save the HTML file, and open it in a Web browser.**

You should now see a table in which every other row has a blue background (see Figure 1-5).

As you can see, it doesn't take a whole lot of JavaScript to do some amazing things to your Web pages. Thanks to JavaScript libraries like jQuery, you'll be able to create sophisticated, interactive Web sites without being a programming wizard yourself. However, it does help to know the basics of JavaScript and programming. In the next three chapters, we'll cover the very basics of JavaScript so that you're comfortable with the fundamental concepts and syntax that make up the language.

Tracking Down Errors

The most frustrating moment in JavaScript programming comes when you try to view your JavaScript-powered page in a Web browser...and nothing happens. It's one of the most common experiences for programmers. Even very experienced programmers don't always get it right the first time they write a program, so figuring out what went wrong is just part of the game.

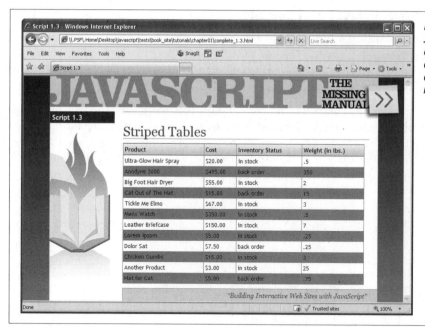

Figure 1-5:
JavaScript can simplify common design tasks like changing the background color of every other table row.

Most Web browsers are set up to silently ignore JavaScript errors, so you usually won't even see a "Hey this program doesn't work!" dialog box. (Generally, that's a good thing, since you don't want a JavaScript error to interrupt the experience of viewing your Web pages.)

So how do you figure out what's gone wrong? There are many ways to track errors in a JavaScript program. You'll learn some advanced *debugging* techniques in Chapter 13, but the most basic method is to consult the Web browser. Most Web browsers keep track of JavaScript errors and record them in a separate window called a *JavaScript console*. When you load a Web page that contains an error, you can then view the console to get helpful information about the error, like which line of the Web page it occurred in and a description of the error.

However, not all consoles are created equal. Internet Explorer's JavaScript console is notoriously cryptic and often misleading. If you suspect errors, you'll find the most helpful JavaScript console in Firefox. Often, you can find the answer to the problem, fix the JavaScript, and then the page will work in Firefox and other browsers as well. The console helps you weed out the basic typos you make when you first start programming, like forgetting closing punctuation, or mistyping the name of a JavaScript command. But since scripts sometimes work in one browser and not another, this section shows you how to turn on the JavaScript console in all major browsers, so you can track down problems in each.

The Firefox JavaScript Console

Firefox's JavaScript console is the best place to begin tracking down errors in your code. Not only does the console provide fairly clear descriptions of errors (no descriptions are ever *that* clear when it comes to programming), it also identifies the line in your code where the error occurred.

For example, in Figure 1-6 the console identifies the error as a missing closing parenthesis after an argument list (you'll learn exactly what an *argument list* is on page 101). The console also identifies the name of the file the error is in (*complete_1.3.html* in this case) and the line number the error occurs (line 9). Best of all, it even indicates the line containing the error with an arrow.

Warning: Although the error console draws an arrow pointing to the location where Firefox encountered the error, that's not always where you made the mistake. Sometimes you need to fix your code before or after that arrow.

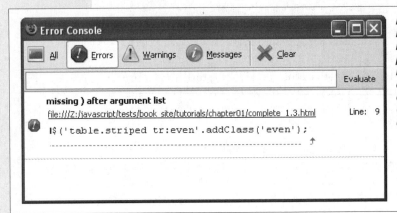

Figure 1-6:
Firefox's JavaScript console identifies errors in your programs. The console keeps a list of errors for previous pages as well, so pretty soon the list can get very long. Just click the Clear button to erase all the errors listed in the console.

To show the JavaScript console, choose Tools → Error Console. The console is a free-floating window that you can move around. It not only displays JavaScript errors but CSS errors as well, so if you've made any mistakes in your Cascading Styles Sheets, you'll find out about those as well. (Make sure you select the Errors button at the top of the console; otherwise you might see warnings and messages that aren't related to your JavaScript error.)

Tip: Since the error console displays the line number where the error occurred, you may want to use a text-editor that can show line numbers. That way, you can easily jump from the error console to your text editor and identify the line of code you need to fix.

Unfortunately, there's a long list of things that can go wrong in a script, from simple typos to complex errors in logic. When you're just starting out with JavaScript programming, many of your errors will be the simple typographic sort. For example, you might forget a semicolon, quote mark, or parentheses, or misspell a JavaScript command. You're especially prone to typos when following examples from a book (like this one). Here are a few errors you may see a lot of when you first start typing the code from this book:

- **Missing) after argument list**. You forgot to type a closing parenthesis at the end of a command. For example in this code—*alert('hello';*—the parenthesis is missing after *'hello'*.

- **Unterminated string literal**. A *string* is a series of characters enclosed by quote marks (you'll learn about these in greater detail on page 41). For example, *'hello'* is a string in the code *alert('hello');*. It's easy to forget either the opening or closing quote.

- **Missing } in compound statement**. In addition to parentheses and quote marks, you'll often use other types of punctuation in your programs, like the *{ }* symbols (which are called *braces*). As with other errors of this kind, you just need to make sure you include both the opening and closing brace.

- **XXX is not defined**. If you misspell a JavaScript command—*aler('hello');*—you'll get an error saying that the (misspelled) command isn't defined: for example, "aler is not defined."

- **Syntax error**. Occasionally, Firefox has no idea what you were trying to do and provides this generic error message. A syntax error represents some mistake in your code. It may not be a typo, but you may have put together one or more statements of JavaScript in a way that isn't allowed. In this case, you need to look closely at the line the error was found on and try to figure out what mistake you made—unfortunately, these types of errors often require experience with and understanding of the JavaScript language to fix.

As you can see from the list above, many errors you'll make simply involve forgetting to type one of a pair of punctuation marks—like quote marks or parentheses. Fortunately, these are easy to fix, and as you get more experience programming, you'll eventually stop making them almost completely (no programmer ever does).

Displaying the Internet Explorer Error Dialog Box

The Internet Explorer console uses a disruptive error dialog box. If you turn the console on, you'll get an annoying error dialog box each time IE encounters an error (see Figure 1-7). To turn it on anyway, choose Tools → Internet Options. Click the Advanced tab, and then turn on the "Display a notification about every script error" checkbox. When you're tired of those annoying error dialogs appearing on every site you visit, repeat these steps to hide the console.

Fortunately, there's a more selective (and less obnoxious) way to view errors in IE: when IE encounters a JavaScript error, a small yellow alert (!) triangle appears in the bottom-left corner of the browser. (It's circled in Figure 1-7.) Just click this icon, and the dialog box appears.

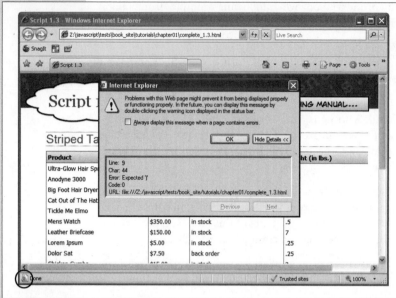

Figure 1-7:
The Internet Explorer error dialog box lists JavaScript errors that occur on a page. Sometimes, the actual error is hidden; if so, click Show Details.

Internet Explorer's error console, unfortunately, is usually not very helpful. Not only are the error messages often cryptic, the line number the console identifies as the location of the error usually isn't correct.

Accessing the Safari Error Console

Safari 3's error console is available from the Develop menu: Develop → Show Error Console (on the Mac you can use the keyboard shortcut Option-⌘-C). However, the Debug menu isn't normally turned on when Safari is installed, so there are a couple of steps to get to the JavaScript console. The process is slightly different, depending on whether you're using the Mac or Windows version of Safari.

On a Mac, choose Safari → Preferences and click the Advanced button. Check the "Show Develop menu in menu bar" box and close the Preferences window.

Note: If you're using Safari 2 on a Mac, the Develop menu is actually called the Debug Menu. To enable this menu for Safari 2, you must launch the Terminal application (Applications → Utilities → Terminal). In the Terminal window, type the following:

```
defaults write com.apple.Safari IncludeDebugMenu 1
```

On Windows, you need to edit a file named Defaults.plist, which is located at *C:\
Program Files\Safari\Safari.Resources\Defaults.plist*. Use a plain text editor, like
WordPad, and add the text shown in bold to the end of the file, just before the
closing </dict> tag. The last four lines of the file should look like the following:

```
<key>IncludeDebugMenu</key>
    <true />
</dict>
</plist>
```

When you restart Safari, the Develop menu will appear between the Bookmarks
and Window menus in the menu bar at the top of the screen. Select Develop →
Show Error Console to open the console (see Figure 1-8).

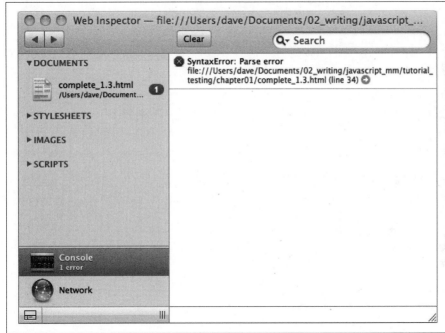

Figure 1-8:
*The Safari Error
Console displays
the name of the
JavaScript error,
the file name (and
location) and the
line on which
Safari
encountered the
error. Each tab or
browser window
has its own error
console, so if
you've already
opened the
console for tab,
you need to
choose Develop →
Error Console if
you wish to see an
error for another
tab or window.*

The Grammar of JavaScript

Learning a programming language is a lot like learning any new language: There are words to learn, punctuation to understand, and a new set of rules to master. And just as you need to learn the grammar of French to speak French, you must become familiar with the grammar of JavaScript to program JavaScript. This chapter covers the concepts that all JavaScript programs rely on.

If you've had any experience with JavaScript programming, many of these concepts may be old hat, so you might just skim this chapter. But if you're new to JavaScript, or you're still not sure about the fundamentals, this chapter introduces you to basic (but crucial) topics.

Statements

A JavaScript *statement* is a basic programming unit, usually representing a single step in a JavaScript program. Think of a statement as a sentence: Just as you string sentences together to create a paragraph (or a chapter, or a book), you combine statements to create a JavaScript program. In the last chapter you saw several examples of statements. For example:

```
alert('Hello World!');
```

This single statement opens an alert window with the message "Hello World!" in it. In many cases, a statement is a single line of code. Each statement ends with a semicolon—it's like a period at the end of a sentence. The semicolon makes it clear that the step is over and that the JavaScript interpreter should move onto the next action.

Note: Officially, putting a semicolon at the end of a statement is optional, and some programmers leave them out to make their code shorter. Don't be one of them. Leaving off the semicolon makes reading your code more difficult and, in some cases, causes JavaScript errors. If you want to make your JavaScript code more compact so that it downloads more quickly, see page 502.

The general process of writing a JavaScript program is to type a statement, enter a semicolon, press Return to create a new, blank line, type another statement, followed by a semicolon, and so on and so on until the program is complete.

Commands

JavaScript and Web browsers let you use various commands to make things happen in your programs and on your Web pages. For example, the *alert( )* command you encountered earlier makes the Web browser open a dialog box and display a message. These commands are usually called *functions* or *methods,* and are like verbs in a sentence. They get things done.

Some commands, like *alert( )* or *document.write( )*, which you encountered on page 29, are specific to Web browsers. In other words, they only work with Web pages, so you won't find them when programming in other environments that use JavaScript (like, for example, when scripting Adobe applications like Acrobat or Dreamweaver or in Flash's JavaScript-based ActionScript).

Other commands are universal to JavaScript and work anywhere JavaScript works. For example, *isNaN( )* is a command that checks to see if a particular value is a number or not—this command comes in handy when you want to check if a visitor has correctly supplied a number for a question that requires a numerical answer (for example, "How many widgets would you like?"). You'll learn about *isNaN( )* and how to use it in Chapter 4 on page 137.

JavaScript has many different commands, which you'll learn about throughout this book. One quick way to identify a command in a program is by the use of parentheses. For example, you can tell *isNaN( )* is a command, because of the parentheses following *isNaN*.

In addition, JavaScript lets you create your own functions, so you can make your scripts do things beyond what the standard JavaScript commands offer. You'll learn about functions in Chapter 3, starting on page 97.

Types of Data

You deal with different types of information every day. Your name, the price of food, the address of your doctor's office, and the date of your next birthday are all information that is important to you. You make decisions about what to do and how to live your life based on the information you have. Computer programs are no different. They also rely on information to get things done. For example, to calculate the total for a shopping cart, you need to know the price and quantity of each item ordered. To customize a Web page with a visitor's name ("Welcome Back, *Kotter*"), you need to know his or her name.

Programming languages usually categorize information into different types, and treat each type in a different way. In JavaScript, the three most common types of data are *number, string,* and *Boolean.*

Numbers

Numbers are used for counting and calculating; you can keep track of the number of days until summer vacation, or calculate the cost of buying two tickets to a movie. Numbers are very important in JavaScript programming: you can use numbers to keep track of how many times a visitor has visited a Web page, to specify the exact pixel position of an item on a Web page, or to determine how many products a visitor wants to order.

In JavaScript, a number is represented by a numeric character; *5*, for example, is the number five. You can also use fractional numbers with decimals, like 5.25 or 10.3333333. JavaScript even lets you use negative numbers, like –130.

Since numbers are frequently used for calculations, your programs will often include mathematical operations. You'll learn about *operators* on page 48, but just to provide an example of using JavaScript with numbers, say you wanted to print the total value of 5 plus 15 on a Web page; you could do that with this line of code:

```
document.write(5 + 15);
```

This snippet of JavaScript adds the two numbers together and prints the total (20) onto a Web page. There are many different ways to work with numbers, and you'll learn more about them starting on page 134.

Strings

To display a name, a sentence, or any series of letters, you use strings. A *string* is just a series of letters and other symbols enclosed inside of quote marks. For example, *'Welcome Hal'*, and "You are here" are both examples of strings. You used a string in the last chapter with the alert command—*alert('Hello World!');*.

A string's opening quote mark signals to the JavaScript interpreter that what follows is a string—just a series of symbols. The interpreter accepts the symbols literally, rather than trying to interpret the string as anything special to JavaScript like a command. When the interpreter encounters the final quote mark, it understands that it has reached the end of the string and continues onto the next part of the program.

You can use either double quote marks (*"hello world"*) or single quote marks (*'hello world'*) to enclose the string, but you must make sure to use the *same type* of quote mark at the beginning and end of the string (for example, *"this is not right'* isn't a valid string because it begins with a double-quote mark but ends with a single-quote.)

So, to pop-up an alert box with the message *Warning, warning!* you could write:

```
alert('Warning, warning!');
```

or

```
alert("Warning, warning!");
```

You'll use strings frequently in your programming—when adding alert messages, when dealing with user input on Web forms, and when manipulating the contents of a Web page. They're so important that you'll learn a lot more about using strings starting on page 116.

FREQUENTLY ASKED QUESTION

Putting Quotes into Strings

When I try to create a string with a quote mark in it, my program doesn't work. Why is that?

In JavaScript, quote marks indicate the beginning and end of a string, even when you don't want them to. When the JavaScript interpreter encounters the first quote mark, it says to itself, "Ahh, here comes a string." When it reaches a matching quote mark, it figures it has come to the end of the string. That's why you can't create a string like this: "He said, "Hello."". In this case, the first quote mark (before the word "He") marks the start of the string, but as soon as the JavaScript interpreter encounters the second quote mark (before the word "Hello"), it figures that the string is over, so you end up with the string *"He said, "* and the *Hello.* part, which creates a JavaScript error.

There are a couple of ways to get around this conundrum. The easiest method is to use single quotes to enclose a string that has one or more double quotes inside it. For example, *'He said, "Hello."'* is a valid string—the single quotes create the string, and the double quotes inside are a *part* of the string. Likewise, you can use double quotes to enclose a string that has a single quote inside it: "This isn't fair" for example.

Another method is to tell the JavaScript interpreter to just treat the quote mark inside the string literally—that is, treat the quote mark as part of the string, not the end of the string. You do this using something called an *escape character*. If you precede the quote mark with a backward slash (\), the quote is treated as part of the string. You could rewrite the above example like this: *"He said, "Hello.\ "".* In some cases, an escape character is the only choice. For example: *'He said, "This isn\'t fair."'* Because the string is enclosed by single quotes, the lone single quote in the word "isn't" has to have a forward slash before it: *isn\'t.*

You can even escape quote marks when you don't necessarily have to—as a way to make it clear that the quote mark should be taken literally. For example. *'He said, "Hello."'.* Even though you don't need to escape the double quotes (since single quotes surround the entire string) some programmers do it anyway so that it's clear to them that the quote mark is just a quote mark.

Booleans

Whereas numbers and strings offer infinite possibilities, the Boolean data type is simple. It is either one of two values: *true* or *false*. You'll encounter Boolean data types when you create JavaScript programs that respond intelligently to user input and actions. For example, if you want to make sure a visitor supplied an email address before submitting a form, you can add logic to your page by asking the simple question: "Did the user type in a valid email address?" The answer to this question is a Boolean value: either the email address is valid (true) or it's not (false). Depending on the answer to the question, the page could respond in different ways. For example, if the email address is valid (true), then submit the form; if it is not valid (false), then display an error message and prevent the form from being submitted.

You'll learn how Boolean values come into play when adding logic to your programs in the box on page 80.

Variables

You can type a number, string, or Boolean value directly into your JavaScript program, but these data types work only when you already have the information you need. For example, you can make the string "Hi Bob" appear in an alert box like this:

```
alert('Hi Bob');
```

But that statement only makes sense if everyone who visits the page is named Bob. If you want to present a personalized message for different visitors, the name needs to be different depending on who is viewing the page: 'Hi Mary,' 'Hi Joseph,' 'Hi Ezra,' and so on. Fortunately, all programming languages provide something known as a *variable* to deal with just this kind of situation.

A variable is a way to store information so that you can later use and manipulate it. For example, imagine a JavaScript-based pinball game where the goal is to get the highest score. When a player first starts the game, her score will be zero, but as she knocks the pinball into targets, the score will get bigger. In this case, the *score* is a variable since it starts at 0 but changes as the game progresses—in other words, a variable holds information that can *vary*. See Figure 2-1 for an example of another game that uses variables.

Think of a variable as a kind of basket: you can put an item into a basket, look inside the basket, dump out the contents of a basket, or even replace what's inside the basket with something else. However, even though you might change what's inside the basket, it still remains the same basket.

Creating a Variable

Creating a variable is a two-step process that involves *declaring* the variable and naming it. In JavaScript to create a variable named *score* you would type:

```
var score;
```

The first part, *var*, is a JavaScript keyword that creates, or, in programming-speak, *declares* the variable. The second part of the statement, *score*, is the variable's name.

Figure 2-1:
The game Real World Racer (www.thomasscott. net/realworldracer) merges JavaScript with Google Maps technology to let you race your way along any road in the world. The game tracks your speed, time, and the number of checkpoints you've crossed (in the top-right box). These are all examples of variables since they change value as the game goes on.

What you name your variables is up to you, but there are a few rules you must follow when naming variables:

- **Variable names must begin with a letter, $, or _.** In other words, you can't begin a variable name with a number or punctuation: so *1thing*, and *&thing* won't work, but *score*, *$score*, and *_score* are fine.

- **Variable names can only contain letters, numbers, $, and _.** You can't use spaces or any other special characters anywhere in the variable name: *fish&chips* and *fish and chips* aren't legal, but *fish_n_chips* and *plan9* are.

- **Variable names are case-sensitive.** The JavaScript interpreter sees uppercase and lowercase letters as distinct, so a variable named *SCORE* is different from a variable named *score*, which is also different from variables named *sCoRE* and *Score*.

- **Avoid keywords.** Some words in JavaScript are specific to the language itself: *var* for example is used to create a variable, so you can't name a variable *var*. In addition, some words, like *alert, document,* and *window,* are considered special properties of the Web browser. You'll end up with a JavaScript error if you try to use those words as variable names. You can find a list of some reserved words in Table 2-1. Not all of these reserved words will cause problems in all browsers, but it's best to steer clear of these names when naming variables.

Table 2-1. *Some words are reserved for use by JavaScript and the Web browser. Avoid using them as variable names.*

JavaScript keywords	Reserved for future use	Reserved for browser
break	abstract	alert
case	boolean	blur
catch	byte	closed
continue	char	document
default	class	focus
delete	const	frames
do	debugger	history
else	double	innerHeight
finally	enum	innerWidth
for	export	length
function	extends	location
if	final	navigator
in	float	open
instanceof	goto	outerHeight
new	implements	outerWidth
return	import	parent
switch	int	screen
this	interface	screenX
throw	long	screenY
try	native	statusbar
typeof	package	window
var	private	
void	protected	
while	public	
with	short	
	static	
	super	
	synchronized	
	throws	
	transient	
	volatile	

In addition to these rules, aim to make your variable names clear and meaningful. Naming variables according to what type of data you'll be storing in them makes it much easier to look at your programming code and immediately understand what's going on. For example, *score* is a great name for a variable used to track a player's game score. The variable name *s* would also work, but the single letter "s" doesn't give you any idea about what's stored in the variable.

Likewise, make your variable names easy to read. When you use more than one word in a variable name, either use an underscore between words or capitalize the first letter of each word after the first. For example, *imagepath* isn't as easy to read and understand as *image_path* or *imagePath*.

Tip: If you want to declare a bunch of variables at one time, you can do it in a single line of code like this:

```
var score, players, game_time;
```

This line of code creates three variables at once.

Using Variables

Once a variable is created, you can store any type of data that you'd like in it. To do so, you use the = sign. For example, to store the number 0 in a variable named *score*, you could type this code:

```
var score;
score = 0;
```

The first line of code above creates the variable; the second line stores the number 0 in the variable. The equal sign is called an *assignment operator*, because it's used to assign a value to a variable. You can also create a variable and store a value in it with just a single JavaScript statement like this:

```
var score = 0;
```

You can store strings, numbers and Boolean values in a variable:

```
var firstName = 'Peter';
var lastName = 'Parker';
var age = 22;
var isSuperHero = true;
```

Tip: To save typing, you can declare multiple variables with a single *var* keyword, like this:

```
var x, y, z;
```

You can even declare and store values into multiple variables in one JavaScript statement:

```
var isSuperHero=true, isAfraidOfHeights=false;
```

Once you've stored a value in a variable, you can access that value simply by using the variable's name. For example, to open an alert dialog box and display the value stored in the variable *score*, you'd type this:

```
alert(score);
```

Notice that you don't use quotes with a variable—that's just for strings, so the code *alert('score')* will display the word "score" and not the value stored in the variable *score*. Now you can see why strings have to be enclosed in quote marks: the JavaScript interpreter treats words without quotes as either special JavaScript objects (like the *alert( )* command) or a variable name.

Spaces, Tabs, and Carriage Returns in JavaScript

JavaScript seems so sensitive about typos. How do I know when I'm supposed to use space characters, and when I'm not allowed to?

You must put a space between keywords: *varscore=0*, for example, doesn't create a new variable named *score*. The JavaScript interpreter needs the space between *var* and *score* to identify the *var* keyword: *var score=0*. However, space isn't necessary between keywords and symbols like the assignment operator (=) or the semicolon that ends a statement.

JavaScript interpreters ignore extra space, so you're free to insert extra spaces, tabs and carriage returns to format your code. For example, you don't need a space on either side of an assignment operator, but you can add them if you find it easier to read. Both of the lines of code below work:

```
var formName='signup';
var formRegistration = 'newsletter' ;
```

In fact, you can insert as many spaces as you'd like, and even insert carriage returns within a statement. So both of the following statements also work:

```
var formName        =      'signup';
var formRegistration
                =
        'newsletter';
```

Of course, just because you can insert extra space, doesn't mean you should. The last two examples are actually harder to read and understand because of the extra space. So the general rule of thumb is add extra space if it makes your code easier to understand. You'll see examples of how space can make code easier to read with arrays (page 58) and with JavaScript Object Literals (page 188).

One important exception to the above rules: you can't insert a carriage return inside a string; in other words you can't split a string over two lines in your code like this:

```
var name = 'Bob
            Smith';
```

Inserting a carriage return (pressing the Enter or Return key) like this produces a JavaScript error and your program won't run.

Note: You only need to use the *var* keyword once—when you first create the variable. After that, you're free to assign new values to the variable without using *var*.

Working with Data Types and Variables

Storing a particular piece of information like a number or string in a variable is usually just a first step in a program. Most programs also manipulate data to get new results. For example, add a number to a score to increase it, multiply the number of items ordered by the cost of the item to get a grand total, or personalize a generic message by adding a name to the end: "Good to see you again, Igor." JavaScript provides various *operators* to modify data. An operator is simply a symbol or word that can change one or more values into something else. For example, you use the + symbol—the addition operator—to add numbers together. There are different types of operators for the different data types.

Basic Math

JavaScript supports basic mathematical operations such as addition, division, subtraction, and so on. Table 2-2 shows the most basic math operators and how to use them.

Table 2-2. Basic math with JavaScript

Operator	What it does	How to use it
+	Adds two numbers	5 + 25
–	Subtracts one number from another	25 – 5
*	Multiplies two numbers	5 * 10
/	Divides one number by another	15/5

You may be used to using an x for multiplication (4×5, for example), but in JavaScript, you use the * symbol to multiply two numbers.

You can also use variables in mathematical operations. Since a variable is only a container for some other value like a number or string, using a variable is the same as using the contents of that variable.

```
var price = 10;
var itemsOrdered = 15;
var totalCost = price * itemsOrdered;
```

The first two lines of code create two variables (*price* and *itemsOrdered*) and store a number in each. The third line of code creates another variable (*totalCost*) and stores the results of multiplying the value stored in the *price* variable (10) and the value stored in the *itemsOrdered* variable. In this case, the total (150) is stored in the variable *totalCost*.

This sample code also demonstrates the usefulness of variables. Suppose you write a program as part of a shopping cart system for an e-commerce Web site. Throughout the program, you need to use the price of a particular product to make various calculations. You could code the actual price throughout the program (for example, say the product cost 10 dollars, so you type 10 in each place in the program that price is used). However, if the price ever changes, you'd have to locate and change each line of code that uses the price. By using a variable, on the other hand, you can set the price of the product somewhere near the beginning of the program. Then, if the price ever changes, you only need to modify the one line of code that defines the product's price to update the price throughout the program:

```
var price = 20;
var itemsOrdered = 15;
var totalCost = price * itemsOrdered;
```

There are lots of other ways to work with numbers (you'll learn a bunch starting on page 134), but you'll find that you most frequently use the basic math operators listed in Table 2-2.

The Order of Operations

If you perform several mathematical operations at once—for example, you total up several numbers then multiply them all by 10—you need to keep in mind the order in which the JavaScript interpreter performs its calculations. Some operators take precedence over other operators, so they're calculated first. This fact can cause some unwanted results if you're not careful. Take this example:

```
4 + 5 * 10
```

You might think this simply is calculated from left to right: 4 + 5 is 9 and 9 * 10 is 90. It's not. The multiplication actually goes first, so this equation works out to 5 * 10 is 50, plus 4 is 54. Multiplication (the * symbol) and division (the / symbol) take precedence over addition (+) and subtraction (-).

To make sure that the math works out the way you want it, use parentheses to group operations. For example, you could rewrite the equation above like this:

```
(4 + 5) * 10
```

Any math that's performed inside parentheses happens first, so in this case the 4 is added to 5 first and the result, 9, is then multiplied by 10. If you do want the multiplication to occur first, it would be clearer to write that code like this:

```
4 + (5*10);
```

Combining Strings

Combining two or more stings to make a single string is a common programming task. For example, if a Web page has a form that collects a person's first name in one form field and his last name in a different field, you need to combine the two fields to get his complete name. What's more, if you want to display a message letting the user know his form information was submitted, you need to combine the generic message with the person's name: "John Smith, thanks for your order."

Combining strings is called *concatenation*, and you accomplish it with the + operator. Yes, that's the same + operator you use to add number values, but with strings it behaves a little differently. Here's an example:

```
var firstName = 'John';
var lastName = 'Smith';
var fullName = firstName + lastName;
```

In the last line of code above, the contents of the variable *firstName* are combined (or concatenated) with the contents of the variable *lastName*—the two are literally joined together and the result is placed in the variable *fullName*. In this example, the resulting string is "JohnSmith"—there isn't a space between the two names, since concatenating just fuses the strings together. In many cases (like this one), you need to add an empty space between strings that you intend to combine:

```
var firstName = 'John';
var lastName = 'Smith';
var fullName = firstName + ' ' + lastName;
```

The ' ' in the last line of this code is a single quote, followed by a space, followed by a final single quote. This code is simply a string that contains an empty space. When placed between the two variables in this example, it creates the string "John Smith". This last example also demonstrates that you can combine more than two strings at a time; in this case, three strings.

Combining Numbers and Strings

Most of the mathematical operators only make sense for numbers. For example, it doesn't make any sense to multiply 2 and the string 'eggs'. If you try this example, you'll end up with a special JavaScript value *NaN*, which stands for "not a number." However, there are times when you may want to combine a string with a number. For example, say you want to present a message on a Web page that specifies how many times a visitor has been to your Web site. The number of times she's visited is a *number*, but the message is a *string*. In this case, you use the + operator to do two things: convert the number to a string and concatenate it with the other string. Here's an example:

```
var numOfVisits = 101;
var message = 'You have visited this site ' + numOfVisits + ' times.';
```

In this case, *message* contains the string "You have visited this site 101 times." The JavaScript interpreter recognizes that there is a string involved, so it realizes it won't be doing any math (no addition). Instead, it treats the + as the concatenation operator, and at the same time realizes that the number should be converted to a string as well.

This example may seem like a good way to print words and numbers in the same message. In this case, it's obvious that the number is part of a string of letters that makes up a complete sentence, and whenever you use the + operator with a string value and a number, the JavaScript interpreter converts the number to a string.

That feature, known as *automatic type conversion,* can cause problems, however. For example, if a visitor answers a question on a form ("How many pairs of shoes would you like?") by typing a number (*2*, for example), that input is treated like a string—*'2'*. So you can run into a situation like this:

```
var numOfShoes = '2';
var numOfSocks = 4;
var totalItems = numOfShoes + numOfSocks;
```

You'd expect the value stored in *totalItems* to be 6 (2 shoes + 4 pairs of socks). Instead, because the value in *numOfShoes* is a string, the JavaScript interpreter converts the value in the variable *numOfSocks* to a string as well, and you end up with the string '24' in the *totalItems* variable. There are a couple of ways to prevent this error.

First, you add + to the beginning of the *string* that contains a number like this:

```
var numOfShoes = '2';
var numOfSocks = 4;
var totalItems = +numOfShoes + numOfSocks;
```

Adding a + sign before a variable (make sure there's no space between the two) tells the JavaScript interpreter to try to convert the string to a number value—if the string only contains numbers like '2', you'll end up with the string converted to a number. In this example, you end up with 6 (2 + 4). Another technique is to use the *Number( )* command like this:

```
var numOfShoes = '2';
var numOfSocks = 4;
var totalItems = Number(numOfShoes) + numOfSocks;
```

Number( ) converts a string to a number if possible. (If the string is just letters and not numbers, you get the *NaN* value to indicate that you can't turn letters into a number.)

In general, you'll most often encounter numbers as strings when getting input from a visitor to the page; for example, when retrieving a value a visitor entered into a form field. So, if you need to do any addition using input collected from a form or other source of visitor input, make sure you run it through the *Number( )* command first.

Changing the Values in Variables

Variables are useful because they can hold values that change as the program runs—a score that changes as a game is played, for example. So how do you change a variable's value? If you just want to replace what's contained inside a variable, assign a new value to the variable. For example:

```
var score = 0;
score = 100;
```

However, you'll frequently want to keep the value that's in the variable and just add something to it or change it in some way. For example, with a game score you never just give a new score, you always add or subtract from the current score. To add to the value of a variable, you use the variable's name as part of the operation like this:

```
var score = 0;
score = score + 100;
```

That last line of code may appear confusing at first, but it uses a very common technique. Here's how it works: All of the action happens to the right of the = sign first; that is, the *score + 100* part. Translated, it means "take what's currently stored in *score* (0) and then add 100 to it." The result of that operation is *then* stored back into the variable *score*. The final outcome of these two lines of code is that the variable score now has the value of 100.

The same logic applies to other mathematical operations like subtraction, division, or multiplication:

```
score = score - 10;
score = score * 10;
score = score / 10;
```

In fact, performing math on the value in a variable and then storing the result back into the variable is so common that there are shortcuts for doing so with the four main mathematical operations, as pictured in Table 2-3.

Table 2-3. Shortcuts for performing math on a variable

Operator	What it does	How to use it	The same as
+=	Adds value on the right side of equal sign to the variable on the left.	score += 10;	score = score + 10;
-=	Subtracts value on the right side of the equal sign from the variable on the left.	score -= 10;	score = score - 10;
*=	Multiples value on the right side of the equal sign to the variable on the left.	score *= 10;	score = score * 10
/=	Divides the value in the variable by the value on the right side of the equal sign.	score /= 10	score = score / 10
++	Placed directly after a variable name, ++ adds 1 to the variable.	score++	score = score + 1
--	Placed directly after a variable name, -- subtracts 1 from the variable.	score--	score = score - 1

The same rules apply when concatenating a string to a variable. For example, say you have a variable with a string in it and want to add another couple of strings onto that variable:

```
var name = 'Franklin';
var message = 'Hello';
message = message + ' ' + name;
```

As with numbers, there's a shortcut operator for concatenating a string to a variable. The += operator adds the string value to the right of the = sign to the end of the variable's string. So the last line of the above code could be rewritten like this:

```
message += ' ' + name;
```

You'll see the += operator frequently when working with strings, and throughout this book.

Tutorial: Using Variables to Create Messages

In this tutorial, you'll use variables to print (that is, write) a message onto a Web page.

Note: To follow along with the tutorials in this chapter you need to download the tutorial files from this book's companion Web site: *www.sawmac.com/missing/js*. See the note on page 27 for details.

---

1. **In a text editor, open the file *2.1.html* in the *chapter02* folder.**

   This page is just a basic HTML file with a simple CSS-enhanced design. It doesn't yet have any JavaScript. You'll use variables to write a message onto a Web page.

2. **Locate the <h1> tag (a little over half way down the file) and add the opening and closing <script> tags, so that the code looks like this:**

   ```
   <h1>Using a Variable</h1>
   <script type="text/javascript">

   </script>
   ```

   This HTML should be familiar by now: it simply sets the page up for the script you're about to write.

3. **In between the <script> tags type:**

   ```
   var firstName = 'Cookie';
   var lastName = 'Monster';
   ```

   You've just created your first two variables—*firstName* and *lastName*—and stored two string values into them. Next you'll add the two strings together, and print the results to the Web page.

4. **Below the two variable declarations type:**

   ```
   document.write('<p>');
   ```

   As you saw in Chapter 1, the *document.write( )* command adds text directly to a Web page. In this case, you're using it to write HTML tags to your page. You supply the command a string—'<p>'—and it outputs that string just as if you had typed it into your HTML code. It's perfectly OK to supply HTML tags as part of the *document.write( )* command. In this case, the JavaScript is adding the opening tag for a paragraph to hold the text you're going to print on the page.

Note: There are more efficient methods than *document.write( )* to add HTML to a Web page. You'll learn about them on page 181.

---

5. **Press Return and type the following JavaScript:**

   ```
   document.write(firstName + ' ' + lastName);
   ```

Here you use the values stored in the variables you created in step 3. The + operator lets you put several strings together to create one longer string, which the *document.write( )* command then writes to the HTML of the page. In this case, the value stored in firstName—'Cookie'—is added to a space character, and then added to the value of lastName—'Monster'. The results are one string: 'Cookie Monster'.

6. **Press return again and type** *document.write('</p>');*.

   The finished script should look like this:

   ```
   <script type="text/javascript">
   var firstName = 'Cookie';
   var lastName = 'Monster';
   document.write('<p>');
   document.write(firstName + ' ' + lastName);
   document.write('</p>');
   </script>
   ```

7. **Preview the page in a Web browser to enjoy the fruits of your labor (see Figure 2-2).**

   The words "Cookie Monster" should appear below the headline "Using a Variable." If you don't see anything, there's probably a typo in your code. Compare the script above with what you typed and check page 34 for tips on debugging a script using Firefox.

8. **Return to your text editor and change the second line of the script to read:**

   ```
   var lastName = 'Jar';
   ```

   Save the page and preview it in a Web browser. Voila, the message now reads: Cookie Jar. (The file *complete_2.1.html* has a working copy of this script.)

Tutorial: Asking for Information

In the last script, you saw how to create variables, but you didn't get to experience how variables can respond to the user and produce unique, customized content. In this next tutorial, you'll learn how to use the *prompt( )* command to gather input from a user and change the display of the page based on that input.

1. **In a text editor, open the file** *2.2.html* **in the** *chapter02* **folder.**

   To make your programming go faster, the <script> tags have already been added to this file. You'll notice that there are two sets of <script> tags: one in the head and one in the body. The JavaScript you're about to add will do two things. First, it will open up a dialog box that asks the user to type in an answer to a question; second, in the body of the Web page, a customized message using the user's response will appear.

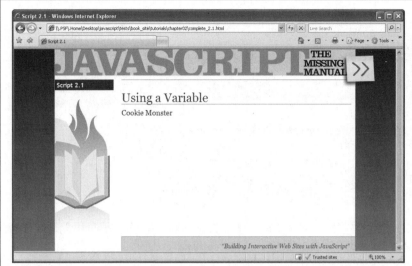

Figure 2-2:
While writing "Cookie Monster" might not exactly be the reason you picked up a book on JavaScript, this script does demonstrate an important concept: how to create and use variables in JavaScript.

2. Between the first set of <script> tags in the document head, type the bolded code:

```
<script type="text/javascript">
var name = prompt('What is your name?', '');
</script>
```

The *prompt( )* command produces a dialog box similar to the *alert( )* command. However, instead of just displaying a message, the *prompt( )* command can also retrieve an answer (see Figure 2-3). In addition, to use the *prompt( )* command, you supply two strings separated by a comma between the parentheses. Figure 2-3 shows what happens to those two strings: the first string appears as the dialog's question ("What is your name?" in this example).

The second string appears in the field the visitor types into. This example uses what's called an *empty string*, which is just two single quote marks (' ') and results in a blank text field. However, you can supply a useful instruction like "Please type both your first and last names" for the second string, and it will appear in the field. Unfortunately, a visitor will need to first delete that text from the text field before entering his own information.

The *prompt( )* command returns a string containing whatever the visitor typed into the dialog box. In this line of JavaScript code, that result is stored into a new variable named *name*.

Note: Many commands *return* a value. In plain English, that just means the command supplies some information after it's done. You can choose to ignore this information or store it into a variable for later use. In this example, the *prompt( )* command returns a string that you store in the variable *name*.

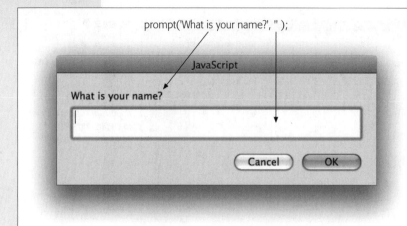

prompt('What is your name?', '');

JavaScript

What is your name?

Cancel   OK

Figure 2-3:
The prompt( ) *command is one way to retrieve user input. It works by providing two strings to the command— one to appear as the question, and another that pre-fills the prompt box with text.*

3. **Save the page and preview it in a Web browser.**

   When the page loads, you'll see a dialog box. Notice that nothing else happens—you don't even see the Web page—until you fill out the dialog box and click OK. You'll also notice that nothing much happens after you click OK— that's because, at this point, you've merely collected and stored the response; you haven't used that response on the page. You'll do that next.

4. **Return to your text editor. Locate the second set of <script> tags and add the code in bold:**

   ```
   <script type="text/javascript">
   document.write('<p>Welcome ' + name +  '</p>');
   </script>
   ```

   Here you take advantage of the information supplied by the visitor. As with the script on page 53, you're combining several strings—an opening paragraph tag and text, the value of the variable, and a closing paragraph tag—and printing the results to the Web page.

5. **Save the page and preview it in a Web browser.**

   When the Prompt dialog appears, type in a name and click OK. Notice that the name you type appears in the Web page (Figure 2-4). Reload the Web page and type a new name—it changes! Just like a good variable should.

Arrays

Simple variables, like the ones you learned about in the previous section, only hold one piece of information, such as a number or a string value. They're perfect when you only need to keep track of a single thing like a score, an age, or a total cost. However, if you need to keep track of a bunch of related items—like the names of all of the days in a week, or a list of all of the images on a Web page—simple variables aren't very convenient.

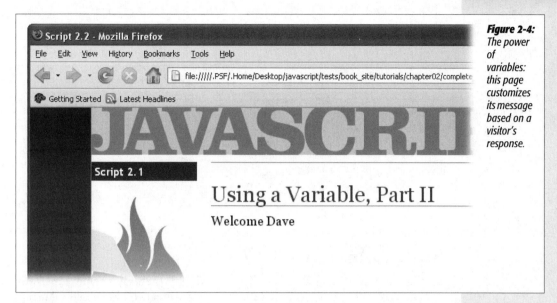

Figure 2-4:
The power of variables: this page customizes its message based on a visitor's response.

For example, say you've created a JavaScript shopping cart system that tracks items a visitor intends to buy. If you wanted to keep track of all of the items the visitor adds to her cart using simple variables you'd have to write code like this:

```
var item1 = 'Xbox 360';
var item2 = 'Tennis shoes';
var item3 = 'Gift certificate';
```

But what if they wanted to add more items than that? You'd have to create more variables—item4, item5, and so on. And, because you don't know how many items the visitor might want to buy, you really don't know how many variables you'll have to create.

Fortunately, JavaScript provides a better method of tracking a list of items, called an *array*. An array is a way of storing more than one value in a single place. Think of an array like a shopping list. When you need to go to the grocery store, you sit down and write a list of items to buy. If you just went shopping a few days earlier, the list might only contain a few items; but if your cupboard is bare, your shopping list might be quite long. Regardless of how many items on the list, though, there's still just a single list.

Without an array, you have to create a new variable for each item in the list. Imagine, for example, that you couldn't make a list of groceries on a single sheet of paper, but had to carry around individual slips of paper—one for each item that you're shopping for. If you wanted to add another item to buy, you'd need a new slip of paper; then you'd need to keep track of each slip as you shopped (see Figure 2-5). That's how simple variables work. But with an array you can create a single list of items, and even add, remove, or change items at anytime.

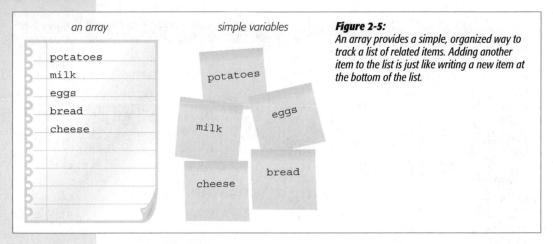

Figure 2-5:
An array provides a simple, organized way to track a list of related items. Adding another item to the list is just like writing a new item at the bottom of the list.

Creating an Array

To create and store items in an array, you first declare the array's name (just as you would a variable) and then supply a list of comma separated values: each value represents one item in the list. As with variables, what you name your array is up to you, but you need to follow the same naming rules listed on page 44. To indicate an array, you put the list of items between opening and closing brackets—[ ]. For example, to create an array containing abbreviations for the seven days of the week, you could write this code:

```
var days = ['Mon', 'Tues', 'Wed', 'Thurs', 'Fri', 'Sat', 'Sun'];
```

The brackets—[ ]—are very important; they tell the JavaScript interpreter that it's dealing with an array. You can create an empty array without any elements like this:

```
var playList = [];
```

Creating an empty array is the equivalent of declaring a variable as described on page 43. You'll create an empty array when you don't add items to the array until the program is running. For example, the above array might be used to track songs that someone selects from a list on a Web page—you don't know ahead of time which songs the person will choose, so you declare an empty array and later fill it with items as the person selects music. (Adding items to an array is described on page 61.)

Note: When looking through other people's JavaScript programs (or other JavaScript books), you may encounter another way to create an array using the *Array* keyword, like this:

```
var days = new Array('Mon', 'Tues', 'Wed');
```

This method is valid, but the method used in this book (called an *array literal*) requires less typing and less code.

You can store any mix of values in an array. In other words, numbers, strings, and Boolean values can all appear in the same array:

```
var prefs = [1, 223, 'www.oreilly.com', false];
```

Note: You can even store arrays and other objects as elements inside an array. This can help store complex data. You'll see an example of this advanced topic on page 108.

The array examples above show the array created on a single line. However, if you've got a lot of items to add, or the items are long strings, trying to type all of that on a single line can make your program difficult to read. Another option many programmers use is to create an array over several lines, like this:

```
var authors = [ 'Ernest Hemingway',
                'Charlotte Bronte',
                'Dante Alighieri',
                'Emily Dickinson'
              ];
```

As mentioned in the box on page 47, a JavaScript interpreter skips extra space and line breaks, so even though this code is displayed on five lines, it's still just a single statement, as indicated by the final semicolon on the last line.

Tip: To make the names line up as above, you'd type the first line – *var authors = ['Ernest Hemingway',* –hit Return, then press the space key as many times as it takes to line up the next value–*'Charlotte Bronte',*.

Accessing Items in an Array

You can access the contents of a simple variable just by using the variable's name. For example *alert(lastName)* opens an alert box with the value stored in the variable *lastName*. However, because an array can hold more than one value, you can't just use its name alone to access the items it contains. A unique number, called an *index*, indicates the position of each item in an array. To access a particular item in an array, you use that item's index number. For example, say you've created an array with abbreviations for the days of the week, and want to open an alert box that displayed the first item. You could write this:

```
var days = ['Mon', 'Tues', 'Wed', 'Thurs', 'Fri', 'Sat', 'Sun'];
alert(days[0]);
```

This code opens an alert box with 'Mon' in it. Arrays are *zero-indexed,* meaning that the *first* item in an array has an index value of 0, and the *second* item has an index value of 1: in other words, subtract one from the item's spot in the list to get its index value—the fifth item's index is 5 − 1; that is 4. Zero-indexing is pretty confusing when you first get started with programming, so Table 2-4 shows how the array *days* (from the above example) is indexed, the values it contains and how to access each value.

Table 2-4. *Items in an array must be accessed using an index number that's the equivalent to their place in the list minus 1*

Index value	Item	To access item
0	Mon	days[0]
1	Tues	days[1]
2	Wed	days[2]
3	Thurs	days[3]
4	Fri	days[4]
5	Sat	days[5]
6	Sun	days[6]

You can change the value of an item in an array by assigning a new value to the index position. For example, to put a new value into the first item in the array *days*, you could write this:

```
days[0] = 'Monday';
```

Because the index number of the last item in an array is always one less than the total number of items in an array, you only need to know how many items are in an array to access the last item. Fortunately, this is an easy task since every array has a length property, which contains the total number of items in the array. To access the length property, add a period followed by *length* after the array's name: for example, *days.length* returns the number of items in the array named *days* (if you created a different array, *playList*, for example, you'd get its length like this: *playList.length*). So you can use this tricky bit of JavaScript to access the value stored in the last item in the array:

```
days[days.length-1]
```

This last snippet of code demonstrates that you don't have to supply a literal number for an index (for example, the 0 in *days[0]*). You can also supply an equation that returns a valid number: in this case *days.length − 1* is a short equation: it first retrieves the number of items in the *days* array (that's 7 in this example) and subtracts 1 from it. So, in this case, *days[days.length-1]* translates to *days[6]*.

You can also use a variable containing a number as the index:

```
var i = 0;
alert(days[i]);
```

The last line of code is the equivalent of *alert(days[0]);*. You'll find this technique particularly useful when working with loops as described in the next chapter (page 90).

Adding Items to an Array

Say you've created an array to track items that a user clicks on a Web page. Each time the user clicks the page, an item is added to the array. JavaScript supplies several ways to add contents to an array.

Adding an item to the end of an array

To add an item to the end of an array, you can use the index notation from page 59, using an index value that's one greater than the last item in the list. For example, say you've have created an array named *properties*:

```
var properties = ['red', '14px', 'Arial'];
```

At this point, the array has three items. Remember that the list item is accessed using an index that's one less than the total number of items, so in this case, the last item in this array is properties[2]. To add another item, you could do this:

```
properties[3] = 'bold';
```

This line of code inserts *'bold'* into the fourth spot in the array, which creates an array with four elements: *['red', '14px', 'Arial', 'bold']*. Notice that when you add the new item, you use an index value that's equal to the total number of elements currently in the array, so you can be sure you're always adding an item to the end of an array by using the array's *length* property as the index. For example, you can rewrite the last line of code like this:

```
properties[properties.length] = 'bold';
```

You can also use an array's *push( )* command, which adds whatever you supply between the parentheses to the end of the array. As with the *length* property, you apply *push( )* by adding a period to the array's name followed by *push( )*. For example, here's another way to add an item to the end of the *properties* array:

```
properties.push('bold');
```

Whatever you supply inside the parentheses (in this example the string *'bold'*) is added as a new item at the end of the array. You can use any type of value, like a string, number, Boolean, or even a variable.

One advantage of the *push( )* command is that it lets you add more than one item to the array. For example, say you want to add three values to the end of an array named *properties*, you could do that like this:

```
properties.push('bold', 'italic', 'underlined');
```

Note: *Push( )*, *unshift( )*, and the other commands associated with arrays are technically called array *methods*. In this book, when you see the word *method*, you can just think of it as a command that accomplishes a task.

Adding an item to the beginning of an array

If you want to add an item to the beginning of an array, use the *unshift( )* command. Here's an example of adding the 'bold' value to the beginning of the *properties* array:

```
var properties = ['red', '14px', 'Arial'];
properties.unshift('bold');
```

After this code runs, the array *properties* contains four elements: *['bold', 'red', '14px', 'Arial']*. As with *push( )*, you can use *unshift( )* to insert multiple items at the beginning of an array:

```
properties.unshift('bold', 'italic', 'underlined');
```

Note: Make sure you use the *name* of the array followed by a period and the method you wish to use. In other words, *push('new item')* won't work. You must first use the array's name (whatever name you gave the array when you created it) followed by a period, then the method like this: *authors.push('Stephen King');*.

Choosing how to add items to an array

So far, this chapter has shown you three ways to add items to an array. Table 2-5 compares these techniques. Each of these commands accomplishes similar tasks, so the one you choose depends on the circumstances of your program. If the order that the items are stored in the array doesn't matter, then any of these methods work. For example, say you have a page of product pictures, and clicking one picture adds the product to a shopping cart. You use an array to store the cart items. The order the items appear in the cart (or the array) doesn't matter, so you can use any of these techniques.

However, if you create an array that keeps track of the order in which something happens, then the method you choose does matter. For example, say you've created a page that lets visitors create a playlist of songs by clicking song names on the page. Since a playlist lists songs in the order they should be played, the order is important. So if each time the visitor clicks a song, the song's name should go at the end of the playlist (so it will be the last song played), then use the *push( )* method.

Table 2-5. *Various ways of adding elements to an array*

Method	Original array	Example code	Resulting array	Explanation
.length property	var p = [0,1,2,3]	p[p.length]=4	[0,1,2,3,4]	Adds one value to the end of an array.
push( )	var p = [0,1,2,3]	p.push(4,5,6)	[0,1,2,3,4,5,6]	Adds one or more items to the end of an array.

Table 2-5. *Various ways of adding elements to an array (continued)*

Method	Original array	Example code	Resulting array	Explanation
unshift()	var p = [0,1,2,3]	p.unshift(4,5)	[4,5,0,1,2,3]	Adds one or more item to the beginning of an array.

The *push( )* and *unshift( )* commands return a value (see the Note on the previous page). To be specific, once *push( )* and *unshift( )* complete their tasks, they supply the number of items that are in the array. Here's an example:

```
var p = [0,1,2,3];
var totalItems = p.push(4,5);
```

After this code runs, the value stored in *totalItems* is 6, because there are six items in the *p* array.

POWER USERS' CLINIC

Creating a Queue

The methods used to add items to an array—*push( )* and *unshift( )*—and the methods used to remove items from an array—*pop( )* and *shift( )*—are often used together to provide a way of accessing items in the order they were created. A classic example is a musical playlist. You create the list by adding songs to it; then, as you play each song, it's removed from the list. The songs are played in the order they appear in the list, so the first song is played and then removed from the list. This arrangement is similar to a line at the movies. When you arrive at the movie theater, you take your place at the end of the line; when the movie's about to begin, the doors open and the first person in line is the first to get in.

In programming circles, this concept is called FIFO for "First In, First Out." You can simulate this arrangement using arrays and the *push( )* and *shift( )* commands. For example say you had an array named *playlist*. To add a new song to the end of the list you'd use *push( )* like this:

```
playlist.push('Yellow Submarine');
```

To get the song that's supposed to play next, you get the first item in the list like this:

```
nowPlaying = playlist.shift( );
```

This code removes the first item from the array and stores it in a variable named *nowPlaying*. The FIFO concept is useful for creating and managing queues such as a playlist, a to-do list, or a slideshow of images.

Deleting Items from an Array

If you want to remove an item from the end or beginning of an array, use the *pop( )* or *shift( )* commands. Both commands remove one item from the array: the *pop( )* command removes the item from the end of the array, while *shift( )* removes one item from the beginning. Table 2-6 compares the two methods.

Table 2-6. *Two ways of removing an item from an array*

Method	Original array	Example code	Resulting array	Explanation
pop()	var p = [0,1,2,3]	p.pop()	[0,1,2]	Removes the last item from the array.
shift()	var p = [0,1,2,3]	p.shift()	[1,2,3]	Removes the first item from the array.

As with *push( )* and *unshift( )*, *pop( )* and *shift( )* return a value once they've completed their tasks of removing an item from an array. In fact, they return the value that they just removed. So, for example, this code removes a value and stores it in the variable *removedItem*:

```
var p = [0,1,2,3];
var removedItem = p.pop( );
```

The value of *removedItem* after this code runs is 3 and the array *p* now contains [0,1,2].

Note: This chapter's files include a Web page that lets you interactively test out the different array commands. It's named *array_methods.html* and it's in the *tutorials* → *chapter02* folder. Open the file in a Web browser and click the various buttons on the Web page to see how the array methods work. (By the way, all the cool interactivity of that page is all thanks to JavaScript.)

Adding and Deleting with *splice( )*

The techniques in the previous sections for adding and removing array items only work for the beginning and end of arrays. What if you want to insert an item in the middle of an array, or remove the item that's in the third position in the array? For example, say you write a program that lets visitors create slideshows by selecting images from a Web page. You could store their selections (for example, information about each image such as the *src* attribute) in an array. However, the visitor may want to edit his selections—perhaps remove one of the pictures he previously selected.

JavaScript provides one command—*splice( )*—that lets you add items to an array and delete items from an array. It's a powerful command and a little hard to understand, so we'll explain it in stages.

Deleting items with splice( )

To remove items from an array, tell the *splice( )* command where it should begin deleting (the index number of the first item to remove) and how many items it should delete. For example, say you create an array named fruits like this:

```
var fruit=['apple','pear','kiwi','pomegranate'];
```

This code creates an array of four items. To remove 'pear' and 'kiwi' from the array, you need to tell *splice( )* to begin with the second item (which has an index of 1, remember) and delete two items like this:

```
fruit.splice(1,2);
```

The result as diagrammed in Figure 2-6, is an array with just two strings—'apple' and 'pomegranate'—left.

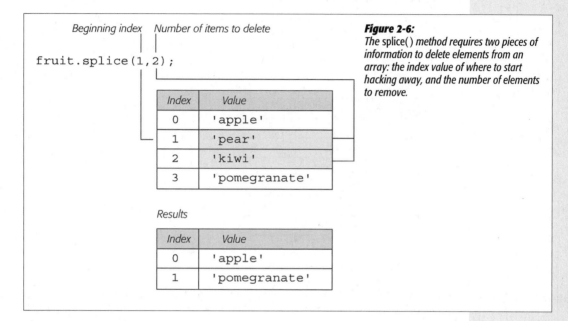

Figure 2-6:
The splice( ) method requires two pieces of information to delete elements from an array: the index value of where to start hacking away, and the number of elements to remove.

Adding items with splice( )

The *splice( )* command does double duty: it can also add items in the middle of an array. To use *splice( )* in this way, provide the index value where the new items should be located, 0 to indicate that you don't want to delete any items, then the list of items to insert: one or more values separated by commas. For example, say you start out with the *fruit* array again:

```
var fruit=['apple','pear','kiwi','pomegranate'];
```

If you want to add two items in between 'pear' and 'kiwi' in this list, you can use *splice( )* like this:

```
fruit.splice(2,0,'grape','orange');
```

This code adds two strings—'grape' and 'orange'—starting at index 2. In other words, 'grape' becomes the third item in the list, 'orange' the fourth, and 'kiwi' and 'pomegranate' are moved to the end. You can see this diagrammed in Figure 2-7.

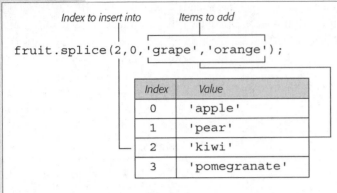

Index to insert into   Items to add

```
fruit.splice(2,0,'grape','orange');
```

Index	Value
0	'apple'
1	'pear'
2	'kiwi'
3	'pomegranate'

Results

Index	Value
0	'apple'
1	'pear'
2	'grape'
3	'orange'
4	'kiwi'
5	'pomegranate'

Figure 2-7:
Add items in the middle of an array using splice( ). The first number you provide splice( ) represents the index position in the array where the new items will go. Make sure the second number is a 0; otherwise, you'll also delete elements from the array as you insert new items.

Replacing items with splice( )

If you want to get really tricky, you can add and delete elements from an array in a single operation. This maneuver can come in handy when you want to replace one or more elements in an array with new items, for example, if someone wants to replace one song in a playlist with another song.

The process is the same as for adding an item, but instead of specifying 0 for the second piece of information that you supply *splice( )*, you indicate the number of items you wish to remove. So, if you start with the fruit array again:

```
var fruit=['apple','pear','kiwi','pomegranate'];
```

Say you want to replace both 'kiwi' and 'pomegranate' with 'grape' and 'orange', you can write this statement:

```
fruit.splice(2,2,'grape','orange');
```

In this case, the first 2 identifies which index position to start at, the second 2 specifies how many items to remove, and the other items indicate what should replace the deleted items. See Figure 2-8 for a clear picture of the process.

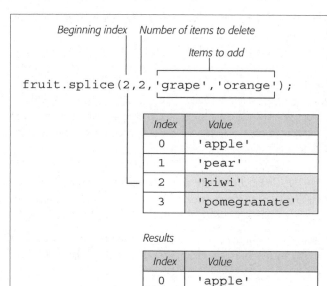

Beginning index   Number of items to delete

Items to add

Figure 2-8:
*When you want to replace items in an array with
new items, you can turn to the splice( ) method.*

```
fruit.splice(2,2,'grape','orange');
```

Index	Value
0	'apple'
1	'pear'
2	'kiwi'
3	'pomegranate'

Results

Index	Value
0	'apple'
1	'pear'
2	'grape'
3	'orange'

Tutorial: Writing to a Web Page Using Arrays

You'll use arrays in many of the scripts in this book, but to get a quick taste of creating and using arrays, try this short tutorial.

Note: See the note on page 27 for information on how to download the tutorial files.

---

1. In a text editor, open the file *2.3.html* in the *chapter02* folder.

   You'll start by simply creating an array containing four strings. As with the previous tutorial, this file already contains <script> tags in both the head and body regions.

2. Between the first set of <script> tags, type the bolded code:

```
<script type="text/javascript">
var authors = [ 'Ernest Hemingway',
                'Charlotte Bronte',
                'Dante Alighieri',
                'Emily Dickinson'
            ];
</script>
```

This code comprises a single JavaScript statement, but it's broken over five lines. To create it, type the first line—*var authors = ['Ernest Hemingway',*—hit Return, then press the Space bar until you line up under the ' (about 16 spaces), and then type *'Charlotte Bronte',*.

Note: Most HTML editors use a *monospaced* font like Courier or Courier New for your HTML and JavaScript code. In a monospaced font, each character is the same width as every other character, so it's easy to line up columns (like all the author names in this example). If your text editor doesn't use Courier or something similar, you may not be able to line up the names perfectly.

As mentioned on page 59, when you create an array with lots of elements, you can make your code easier to read if you break it over several lines. You can tell it's a single statement since there's no semicolon until the end of line 5.

This line of code creates an array named *authors* and stores the names of 4 authors (4 string values) into the array. Next, you'll access an element of the array.

3. **Locate the second set of <script> tags, and add the code in bold:**

```
<script type="text/javascript">
document.write('<p>The first author is <strong>');
document.write(authors[0] + '</strong></p>');
</script>
```

The first line starts a new paragraph with some text and an opening <strong> tag—just plain HTML. The next line prints the value stored in the first item of the authors array and prints the closing </strong> and </p> tags to create a complete HTML paragraph. To access the first item in an array, you use a 0 as the index—*authors[0]*—instead of 1.

At this point, it's a good idea to save your file and preview it in a Web browser. You should see "The first author is **Ernest Hemingway**" printed on the screen. If you don't, you may have made a typo either when you created the array in step 2 or 3.

Note: Remember to use the Firefox Error Console described on page 34 to help you locate the source of any JavaScript errors.

---

4. **Return to your text editor and add the two lines of bolded code below to your script:**

```
document.write('<p>The last author is <strong>');
document.write(authors[4] + '</strong></p>');
```

This step is pretty much the same as the previous one, except that you're printing a different array item. Save the page and preview it in a browser. You'll see "undefined" in place of an author's name (see Figure 2-9). Don't worry; that's intentional. Remember that an array's index values begin at 0, so the last item is actually the total number of items in the array minus 1. In this case, there are four strings stored in the authors array, so that last item would actually be accessed with *authors[3]*.

Note: If you try to read the value of an item using an index value that doesn't exist, you'll end up with the JavaScript "undefined" value. All that means is that there's no value stored in that index position.

Fortunately, there's an easy technique for retrieving the last item in an array no matter how many items are stored in the array.

Figure 2-9:
If you try to access an array element that doesn't exist, then you'll end up with the value "undefined."

5. **Return to your text editor and edit the code you just entered. Erase the *4* and add the bolded code in its place:**

```
document.write('<p>The last author is <strong>');
document.write(authors[authors.length-1] + '</strong></p>');
```

As you'll recall from page 60, an array's length property stores the number of items in the array. So the total number of items in the *authors* array can be found with this code *authors.length*. At this point in the script, that turns out to be 4.

Knowing that the index value of the last item in an array is always 1 less than the total number of items in an array, you just subtract one from the total to get the index number of the last item: *authors.length-1*. You can provide that little equation as the index value when accessing the last item in an array: *authors[authors.length-1]*.

You'll finish up by adding one more item to the beginning of the array.

---

6. **Add another line of code after the ones you added in step 5:**

```
authors.unshift('Stan Lee');
```

As you read on page 62, the *unshift( )* method adds one or more items to the beginning of an array. After this line of code runs the authors array will now be *['Stan Lee', 'Ernest Hemingway',*

Finally, you'll print out the newly added item on the page.

7. **Add the three more lines (bolded below) so that your final code looks like this:**

```
document.write('<p>The first author is <strong>');
document.write(authors[0] + '</strong></p>');
document.write('<p>The last author is <strong>');
document.write(authors[authors.length-1] + '</strong></p>');
authors.unshift('Stan Lee');
document.write('<p>I almost forgot <strong>');
document.write(authors[0]);
document.write('</strong></p>');
```

Save the file and preview it in a Web browser. You should see something like Figure 2-10. If you don't, remember the error console in Firefox can help you locate the error (page 34).

Figure 2-10:
OK, Stan Lee may not be your idea of a literary giant, but at least he's helping you learn how arrays work.

Comments

There are times when you're in the midst of programming and you feel like you understand everything that's going on in your program. Every line of code makes sense, and better yet, it works! But a month or two later, when your boss or a client asks you to make a change or add a new feature to that cool script you wrote, you might find yourself scratching your head the moment you look at your once-familiar JavaScript: what's that variable for? Why'd I program it like that? What's going on in this section of the program?

It's easy to forget how a program works and why you wrote your code the way you did. Fortunately, most programming languages provide a way for programmers to leave notes for themselves or other programmers who might look through their code. JavaScript lets you leave *comments* throughout your code. If you've used HTML or CSS comments, these should feel familiar. A comment is simply a line or more worth of notes: the JavaScript interpreter ignores them, but they can provide valuable information on how your program works.

The syntax for JavaScript comments is the same as for CSS. To create a single line comment, precede the comment with double forward slashes:

```
// this is a comment
```

You can also add a comment after a JavaScript statement:

```
var price = 10; // set the initial cost of the widget
```

The JavaScript interpreter executes everything on this line until it reaches the //, and then it skips to the beginning of the next line.

You can also add several lines worth of comments by beginning the comments with /* and ending them with */. The JavaScript interpreter ignores all of the text between these two sets of symbols. For example, say you want to give a description of how a program works at the beginning of your code. You can do that like this:

```
/*
    JavaScript Slideshow:
    This program automates the display of
    images in a pop-up window.
*/
```

You don't need to leave the /* and */ on their own lines, either. In fact, you can create a single line JavaScript comment with them:

```
/* this is a single line comment */
```

In general, if you want to just write a short, one-line comment, use //. For several lines of comments, use the /* and */ combination.

When to Use Comments

Comments are an invaluable tool for a program that's moderately long or complex and that you want to keep using (and perhaps changing) in the future. While the simple scripts you've learned so far are only a line or two of code, you'll eventually be creating longer and much more complex programs. To make sure you can quickly figure out what's going on in a script, it's a good idea to add comments to help you understand the overall logic of the program and to explain any particularly confusing or complex bits.

Tip: Adding lots of comments to a script makes the script larger (and slower to download). However, as you'll learn on page 502, there are ways to make JavaScript files smaller and faster.

Many programmers add a block of comments at the beginning of an external JavaScript file. These comments can explain what the script is supposed to do, identify the date the script was created, include a version number for frequently updated scripts, and provide copyright information.

For example, at the beginning of a the jQuery library's JavaScript file, you'll find this comment:

```
/*
 * jQuery 1.2.6 - New Wave Javascript
 *
 * Copyright (c) 2008 John Resig (jquery.com)
 * Dual licensed under the MIT (MIT-LICENSE.txt)
 * and GPL (GPL-LICENSE.txt) licenses.
 *
 * $Date$
 * $Rev: 5685 $
 */
```

At the beginning of the script, you might also include instructions on how to use the script: variables that might need to be set, anything special you might need to do to your HTML to make the script work, and so on.

You should also add a comment before a series of complex programming steps. For example, say you write a script that animates an image across a visitor's browser window. One part of that script is determining the image's current position in the browser window. This can take several lines of complex programming; it's a good idea to place a comment before that section of the program, so when you look at the script later, you'll know exactly what that part of the program does:

```
// determine x and y positions of image in window
```

The basic rule of thumb is to add comments anywhere you'll find them helpful later. If a line of code is painfully obvious, you probably don't need a comment. For example, there's no reason to add a comment for simple code like *alert('hello')*, because it's pretty obvious what it does (opens an alert box with the word "hello" in it).

Comments in this Book

Comments are also very helpful when explaining JavaScript. In this book, comments frequently explain what a line of programming does or indicate the results of a particular statement. For example, you might see a comment like the following to show the results of an alert statement:

```
var a = 'Bob';
var b = 'Smith';
alert( a + ' ' + b); // 'Bob Smith';
```

The third line ends with a comment that indicates what you should see when you preview this code in a Web browser. If you want to test the code that you read in this book by adding it to a Web page and viewing it in a Web browser, you can leave out comments like these when typing the code into a Web page. These types of comments are intended simply to help you understand what's happening in the code as you read along with the book.

As you start to learn some of the more complex commands available in JavaScript, you'll begin to manipulate the data in variables. You'll often see comments in this book's code to display what should be stored in the variable after the command is run. For example, the *charAt( )* command lets you select a character at a specific point in a string. When you read about how to use that command in this book, you might see code like this:

```
var x = "Now is the time for all good programmers.";
alert(x.charAt(2)); // 'w'
```

The comment *// 'w'* that appears at the end of the second line indicates what you should see in an alert dialogue if this code were actually run in a Web browser. (And, yes, 'w' is correct. Strings are like arrays in that the first letter in a string has an index position of 0. So *charAt(2)* retrieves the *third* character from the string. Sometimes programming just hurts your brain.)

Adding Logic and Control to Your Programs

So far you've learned about some of JavaScript's basic building blocks. But simply creating a variable and storing a string or number in it doesn't accomplish much. And building an array with a long list of items won't be very useful unless there's an easy way to work your way through the items in the array. In this chapter, you'll learn how to make your programs react intelligently and work more efficiently by using conditional statements, loops, and functions.

Making Programs React Intelligently

Our lives are filled with choices: "What should I wear today?", "What should I eat for lunch?", "What should I do Friday night?", and so on. Many choices you make depend on other circumstances. For example, say you decide you want to go to the movies on Friday night. You'll probably ask yourself a bunch of questions like "Are there any good movies out?", "Is there a movie playing at the right time?", "Do I have enough money to go to the movies (and buy a $17 bag of popcorn)?"

Suppose there *is* a movie that's playing at just the time you want to go. You then ask yourself a simple question: "Do I have enough money?" If the answer is yes, you'll head out to the movie. If the answer is no, you won't go. But on another Friday, you do have enough money, so you go to the movies. This scenario is just a simple example of how the circumstances around us affect the decisions we make.

JavaScript has the same kind of decision-making feature called *conditional statements*. At its most basic, a conditional statement is a simple yes or no question.

If the answer to the question is yes, your program does one thing; if the answer is no, it does something else. Conditional statements are one of the most important programming concepts: they let your programs react to different situations and behave intelligently. You'll use them countless times in your programming, but just to get a clear picture of their usefulness here are a few examples of how they can come in handy:

- **Form validation.** When you want to make sure someone filled out all of the required fields in a form ("Name," "Address," "E-mail", and so on), you'll use conditional statements. For example, if the Name field is empty, don't submit the form.

- **Drag and drop.** If you add the ability to drag elements around your Web page, you might want to check where the visitor drops the element on the page. For example, if he drops a picture onto an image of a trash can, you make the photo disappear from the page.

- **Evaluating input.** If you pop-up a window to ask a visitor a question like "Would you like to answer a few questions about how great this Web site is?", you'll want your script to react differently depending on how the visitor answers the question.

Figure 3-1 shows an example of an application that makes use of conditional statements.

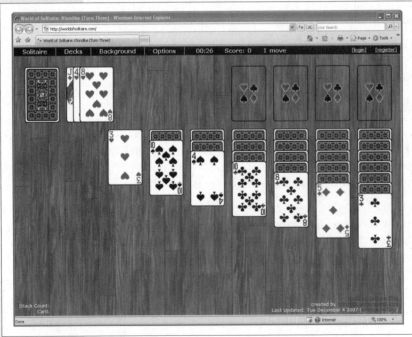

Figure 3-1:
It takes a lot of work to have fun. A JavaScript-based game like Solitaire (http://worldofsolitaire. com) demonstrates how a program has to react differently based on the conditions of the program. For example, when a player drags and drops a card, the program has to decide if the player dropped the card in a valid location or not, and then perform different actions in each case.

Conditional Statement Basics

Conditional statements are also called "if/then" statements, because they perform a task only if the answer to a question is true: "*If* I have enough money *then* I'll go to the movies." The basic structure of a conditional statement looks like this:

```
if ( condition ) {
    // some action happens here
}
```

There are three parts to the statement: *if* indicates that the programming that follows is a conditional statement; the parentheses enclose the yes or no question, called the *condition* (more on that in a moment); and the curly braces ({ }) mark the beginning and end of the JavaScript code that should execute if the condition is true.

Note: In the code listed above, the "// some action happens here" is a JavaScript comment. It's not code that actually runs; it's just a note left in the program, and, in this case, points out to you, the reader, what's supposed to go in that part of the code. See page 71 for more on comments.

In many cases, the condition is a comparison between two values. For example, say you create a game that the player wins when the score is over 100. In this program, you'll need a variable to track the player's score and, at some point, you need to check to see if that score is more than 100 points. In JavaScript, the code to check if the player won could look like this:

```
if (score > 100) {
  alert('You won!');
}
```

The important part is *score > 100*. That phrase is the condition, and it simply tests whether the value stored in the *score* variable is greater than 100. If it is, then a "You won!" dialog box appears; if the player's score is less than or equal to 100, then the JavaScript interpreter skips the alert and moves onto the next part of the program. In addition to > (greater than), there are several other operators used to compare numbers (see Table 3-1).

Tip: Type two spaces (or press the tab key once) before each line of JavaScript code contained within a pair of braces. The spaces (or tab) indent those lines and makes it easier to see the beginning and ending brace and to figure out what code belongs inside the conditional statement. Two spaces is a common technique, but if four spaces make your code easier for you to read, then use four spaces. The examples in this book always indent code inside braces.

More frequently, you'll test to see if two values are equal or not. For example, say you create a JavaScript-based quiz, and one of the questions asks, "How many moons does Saturn have?" The person's answer is stored in a variable named *answer*. You might then write a conditional statement like this:

```
if (answer == 31) {
  alert('Correct. Saturn has 31 moons.');
}
```

The double set of equal signs (==) isn't a typo; it instructs the JavaScript interpreter to compare two values and decide whether they're equal. Remember, in JavaScript, a single equal sign is the *assignment operator* that you use to store a value into a variable:

```
var score = 0; //stores 0 into the variable score
```

Because the JavaScript interpreter already assigns a special meaning to a single equal sign, you need to use two equal signs whenever you want to compare two values to determine if they're equal or not.

You can also use the == (called the *equality operator*) to check to see if two strings are the same. For example, say you let the user type a color into a form, and if they type *'red'*, then you change the background color of the page to red. You could use the conditional operator for that:

```
if (enteredColor == 'red') {
  document.body.style.backgroundColor='red';
}
```

Note: In the code above, don't worry right now about how the page color is changed. You'll learn how to dynamically control CSS properties using JavaScript on page 186.

You can also test to see if two values aren't the same using the *inequality* operator:

```
if (answer != 31) {
  alert("Wrong! That's not how many moons Saturn has.");
}
```

The exclamation mark translates to "not", so != means "not equal to." In this example, if the value stored in *answer* is not 31, then the poor test taker would see the insulting alert message.

Table 3-1. Use these comparison operators to test values as part of a conditional statement

Comparison operator	What it means
==	**Equal to.** Compares two values to see if they're the same. Can be used to compare numbers or strings.
!=	**Not equal to.** Compares two values to see if they're *not* the same. Can be used to compare numbers or strings.

Table 3-1. *Use these comparison operators to test values as part of a conditional statement (continued)*

Comparison operator	What it means
>	**Greater than.** Compares two numbers and checks if the number on the left side is greater than the number on the right. For example, 2 > 1 is true, since 2 is a bigger number than 1, but 2 > 3 is false, since 2 isn't bigger than 3.
<	**Less than.** Compares two numbers and checks if the number on the left side is less than the number on the right. For example, 2 < 3 is true, since 2 is a smaller number than 3, but 2 < 1 is false, since 2 isn't less than 1.
>=	**Greater than or equal to.** Compares two numbers and checks if the number on the left side is greater than or the same value as the number on the right. For example, 2 >= 2 is true, since 2 is the same as 2, but 2 >= 3 is false, since 2 isn't a bigger number 3, nor is it equal to 3.
<=	**Less than or equal to.** Compares two numbers and checks if the number on the left side is greater than or the same value as the number on the right. For example, 2 <= 2 is true, since 2 is the same as 2, but 2 <= 1 is false, since 2 isn't a smaller number than 1, nor is 2 equal to 1.

The code that runs if the condition is true isn't limited to just a single line of code as in the previous examples. You can have as many lines of JavaScript between the opening and closing curly braces as you'd like. For example, as part of the Java-Script quiz example, you might keep a running tally of how many correct answers the test-taker gets. So, when the Saturn question is answered correctly, you also want to add 1 to the test-taker's total. You would do that as part of the conditional statement:

```
if (answer == 31) {
  alert('Correct. Saturn has 31 moons.');
  numCorrect = numCorrect + 1;
}
```

And you could add additional lines of JavaScript code between the braces as well—any code that should run if the condition is true.

Adding a Backup Plan

But what if the condition is false? The basic conditional statement in the previous section doesn't have a backup plan for a condition that turns out to be false. In the real world, as you're deciding what to do Friday night and you don't have enough money for the movies, you'd want to do something *else*. An *if* statement has its own kind of backup plan, called an *else clause*. For example, say as part of the

The Return of the Boolean

On page 42, you learned about the Boolean values—*true* and *false*. Booleans may not seem very useful at first, but you'll find out they're essential when you start using conditional statements. In fact, since a condition is really just a yes or no question, the answer to that question is a Boolean value. For example, check out the following code:

```
var x = 4;
if ( x == 4 ) {
    //do something
}
```

The first line of code stores the number 4 into the variable *x*. The condition on the next line is a simple question: is the value stored in *x* equal to 4? In this case, it is, so the JavaScript between the curly braces runs. But here's what really happens in between the parentheses: the JavaScript interpreter converts the condition into a Boolean value; in programming-speak, the interpreter *evaluates* the condition. If the condition evaluates to *true* (meaning the answer to the question is yes), then the code between the braces runs. However, if the condition evaluates to *false*, then the code in the braces is skipped.

One common use of Booleans is to create what's called a *flag*—a variable that marks whether something is true. For example, when validating a form full of visitor submitted information, you might start by creating a *valid* variable with a Boolean value of *true*—this means you're assuming, at first, that they filled out the form correctly. Then, you'd run through each form field, and if any field is missing information or has the wrong type of information, you change the value in *valid* to *false*. After checking all of the form fields, you test what's stored in *valid*, and if it's still true, you submit the form. If it's not true (meaning one or more form fields were left blank), you display some error messages and prevent the form from submitting:

```
var valid = true;
// lot of other programming gunk happens
in here
// if a field has a problem then you set
valid to false
if (valid) {
  //submit form
} else {
  //print lots of error messages
}
```

JavaScript testing script, you want to notify the test-taker if he gets the answer right, or if he gets it wrong. Here's how you can do that:

```
if (answer == 31) {
  alert('Correct. Saturn has 31 moons.');
  numCorrect = numCorrect + 1;
} else {
  alert("Wrong! That's not how many moons Saturn has.");
}
```

This code sets up an either/or situation; only one of the two messages will appear. If the number 31 is stored in the variable *answer*, then the "correct" alert appears; otherwise, the "wrong" alert appears.

To create an *else* clause, just add "else" after the closing brace for the conditional statement followed by another pair of braces. You add the code that should execute if the condition turns out to be false in between the braces. Again, you can have as many lines of code as you'd like as part of the *else* clause.

Testing More Than One Condition

Sometimes you'll want to test several conditions and have several possible outcomes: think of it like a game show where the host says, "Would you like the prize behind door #1, door #2, or door #3?" You can only pick one. In your day-to-day activities, you also are often faced with multiple choices like this one.

For example, return to the "What should I do Friday night?" question. You could expand your entertainment options based on how much money you have and are willing to spend. For example, you could start off by saying, "If I have more than $50 I'll go out to a nice dinner and a movie (and have some popcorn too)." If you don't have $50, you might try another test: "If I have $35 or more, I'll go to a nice dinner." If you don't have $35, then you'd say, "If I have $12 or more, I'll go to the movies." And finally, if you don't have $12, you might say, "Then I'll just stay at home and watch TV." What a Friday night!

JavaScript lets you perform the same kind of cascading logic using *else if* statements. It works like this: you start with an *if* statement, which is option number 1; you then add one or more *else if* statements to provide additional questions that can trigger additional options; and finally, you use the *else* clause as the fallback position. Here's the basic structure in JavaScript:

```
if (condition) {
  // door #1
} else if (condition2) {
  // door #2
} else {
  // door #3
}
```

This structure is all you need to create a JavaScript "Friday night planner" program. It asks visitors how much money they have, and then determines what they should do on Friday (sound familiar?). You can use the *prompt( )* command that you learned about on page 55 to collect the visitor's response and a series of if/else if statements to determine what he should do:

```
var fridayCash = prompt('How much money can you spend?', '');
if (fridayCash >= 50) {
  alert('You should go out to a dinner and a movie.');
} else if (fridayCash >= 35) {
  alert('You should go out to a fine meal.');
} else if (fridayCash >= 12) {
  alert('You should go see a movie.');
} else {
  alert('Looks like you'll be watching TV.');
}
```

Here's how this program breaks down step-by-step: The first line opens a prompt dialog asking the visitor how much he can spend. Whatever the visitor types is stored in a variable named *fridayCash*. The next line is a test: Is the value the visitor typed 50 or more? If the answer is yes, then an alert appears telling him to go get a meal and see a movie. At this point, the entire conditional statement is done. The JavaScript interpreter skips the next *else if* statement, the following *else if* statement, and the final *else* clause. With a conditional statement, only one of the outcomes can happen, so once the JavaScript interpreter encounters a condition that evaluates to *true*, then it runs the JavaScript code between the braces for that condition and skips everything else within the conditional statement.

Suppose the visitor typed 25. The first condition, in this case, wouldn't be true, since 25 is a smaller number than 50. So the JavaScript interpreter skips the code within the braces for that first condition and continues to the *else if* statement: "Is 25 greater than or equal to 35?" Since the answer is no, it skips the code associated with that condition and encounters the next *else if*. At this point, the condition asks if 25 is greater than or equal to 12; the answer is yes, so an alert box with the message, "You should go see a movie" appears and the program ends, skipping the final *else* clause.

Tip: There's another way to create a series of conditional statements that all test the same variable, as in the *fridayCash* example. *Switch* statements do the same thing, and you'll learn about them on page 499.

More Complex Conditions

When you're dealing with many different variables, you'll often need even more complex conditional statements. For example, when validating a required email address field in a form, you'll want to make sure both that the field isn't empty and that the field contains an email address (and not just random typed letters). Fortunately, JavaScript lets you do these kinds of checks as well.

Making sure more than one condition is true

You'll often need to make decisions based on a combination of factors. For example, you may only want to go to a movie if you have enough money *and* there's a movie you want to see. In this case, you'll go only if two conditions are true; if either one is false, then you won't go to the movie. In JavaScript, you can combine conditions using what's called the *logical AND operator*, which is represented by two ampersands (&&). You can use it between the two conditions within a single conditional statement. For example, if you want to check if a number is between 1 and 10, you can do this:

```
if (a < 10 && a > 1) {
//the value in a is between 1 and 10
alert("The value " + a + " is between 1 and 10");
}
```

In this example, there are two conditions: $a < 10$ asks if the value stored in the variable a is less than 10; the second condition, $a > 1$, is the same as "Is the value in a greater than 1?" The JavaScript contained between the braces will run only if *both* conditions are true. So if the variable a has the number 0 stored in it, the first condition ($a < 10$) is true (0 is less than 10), but the second condition is false (0 is not greater than 1).

You're not limited to just two conditions. You can connect as many conditions as you need with the && operator:

```
if (b>0 && a>0 && c>0) {
  // all three variables are greater than 0
}
```

This code checks three variables to make sure all three have a value greater than 0. If just one has a value of 0 or less, then the code between the braces won't run.

Making sure at least one condition is true

Other times you'll want to check a series of conditions, but you only need one to be true. For example, say you've added a keyboard control for visitors to jump from picture to picture in a photo gallery. When the visitor presses the N key, the next photo appears. In this case, you want her to go to the next picture when she types either *n* (lowercase) or, if she has the Caps Lock key pressed, *N* (uppercase). You're looking for a kind of either/or logic: either this key *or* that key was pressed. The *logical OR operator*, represented by two pipe characters (||), comes in handy:

```
if (key == 'n' || key == 'N') {
  //move to the next photo
}
```

Tip: To type a pipe character, press Shift-\. The key that types both backslashes and pipe characters is usually located just above the Return key.

With the OR operator, only one condition needs to be true for the JavaScript that follows between the braces to run.

As with the AND operator, you can compare more than two conditions. For example, say you've created a JavaScript racing game. The player has a limited amount of time, a limited amount of gas, and a limited number of cars (each time he crashes he loses one car). To make the game more challenging, you want it to come to an end when any of these three things runs out:

```
if (gas <= 0 || time <= 0 || cars <= 0) {
  //game is over
}
```

When testing multiple conditions, it's sometimes difficult to figure out the logic of the conditional statement. Some programmers group each condition in a set of parentheses to make the logic easier to grasp:

```
if ((key == 'n') || (key == 'N')) {
//move to the next photo
}
```

To read this code, simply treat each grouping as a separate test; the results of the operation between parentheses will always turn out to be either true or false.

Negating a condition

If you're a Superman fan, you probably know about Bizarro, an anti-hero who lived on a cubical planet named Htrae (Earth spelled backwards), had a uniform with a backwards S, and was generally the opposite of Superman in every way. When Bizarro said "Yes," he really meant "No"; and when he said "No," he really meant "Yes."

JavaScript programming has an equivalent type of character called the *NOT* operator, which is represented by an exclamation mark (*!*). You've already seen the NOT operator used along with the equal sign to indicate "not equal to": !=. But the NOT operator can be used by itself to completely reverse the results of a conditional statement; in other words, it can make false mean true, and true mean false.

You use the NOT operator when you want to run some code based on a negative condition. For example, say you've created a variable named *valid* that contains a Boolean value of either *true* or *false* (see the box on page 80). You use this variable to track whether a visitor correctly filled out a form. When the visitor tries to submit the form, your JavaScript checks each form field to make sure it passes the requirements you set up (for example, the field can't be empty and it has to have an email address in it). If there's a problem, like the field is empty, you could then set *valid* to false (*valid = false*).

Now if you want to do something like print out an error and prevent the form from being submitted, you can write a conditional statement like this:

```
if (! valid) {
//print errors and don't submit form
}
```

The condition *! valid* can be translated as "if not valid," which means if *valid* is false, then the *condition* is *true*. To figure out the results of a condition that uses the NOT operator, just evaluate the condition without the NOT operator, then reverse it. In other words, if the condition results to *true*, the ! operator changes it to *false*, so the conditional statement doesn't run.

As you can see the NOT operator is very simple to understand (translated from Bizarro-speak: it's very confusing, but if you use it long enough, you'll get used to it).

JAVASCRIPT: THE MISSING MANUAL

Nesting Conditional Statements

In large part, computer programming entails making decisions based on information the visitor has supplied or on current conditions inside a program. The more decisions a program makes, the more possible outcomes and the "smarter" the program seems. In fact, you might find you need to make further decisions *after* you've gone through one conditional statement.

Suppose, in the "What to do on Friday night?" example, you want to expand the program to include every night of the week. In that case, you need to first determine what day of the week it is, and then figure out what to do on that day. So you might have a conditional statement asking if it's Friday, and if it is, you'd have another series of conditional statements to determine what to do on that day:

```
if (dayOfWeek == 'Friday') {
 var fridayCash = prompt('How much money can you spend?', '');
 if (fridayCash >= 50) {
  alert('You should go out to a dinner and a movie.');
 } else if (fridayCash >= 35) {
  alert('You should go out to a fine meal.');
 } else if (fridayCash >= 12) {
  alert('You should go see a movie.');
 } else {
  alert('Looks like you'll be watching TV.');
 }
}
```

In this example, the first condition asks if the value stored in the variable *dayOf-Week* is the string 'Friday'. If the answer is yes, then a prompt dialog appears, gets some information from the visitor, and another conditional statements is run. In other words, the first condition (*dayOfWeek == 'Friday'*) is the doorway to another series of conditional statements. However, if *dayOfWeek* isn't 'Friday', then the condition is false and the nested conditional statements are skipped.

Tips for Writing Conditional Statements

The example of a nested conditional statement in the last section may look a little scary. There are lots of ( ), {}, elses, and ifs. And if you happen to mistype one of the crucial pieces of a conditional statement, your script won't work. There are a few things you can do as you type your JavaScript that can make it easier to work with conditional statements.

- **Type both of the curly braces before you type the code inside them.** One of the most common mistakes programmers make is forgetting to add a final brace to a conditional statement. To avoid this mistake, type the condition and the braces first, then type the JavaScript code that executes when the condition is true. For example, start a conditional like this:

```
if (dayOfWeek=='Friday') {

}
```

In other words, type the *if* clause and the first brace, hit Return twice, and then type the last brace. Now that the basic syntax is correct, you can click in the empty line between the braces and add JavaScript.

- **Indent code within braces.** You can better visualize the structure of a conditional statement if you indent all of the JavaScript between a pair of braces:

```
if (a < 10 && a > 1) {
   alert("The value " + a + " is between 1 and 10");
}
```

By using several spaces (or pressing the Tab key) to indent lines within braces, it's easier to identify which code will run as part of the conditional statement. If you have nested conditional statements, indent each nested statement:

```
if (a < 10 && a > 1) {
   //first level indenting for first conditional
   alert("The value " + a + " is between 1 and 10");
     if (a==5) {
     //second level indenting for 2nd conditional
     alert(a + " is half of ten.");
   }
}
```

- **Use == for comparing equals.** When checking whether two values are equal, don't forget to use the equality operator, like this:

```
if (name == 'Bob') {
```

A common mistake is to use a single equal sign, like this:

```
if (name = 'Bob') {
```

A single equal sign stores a value into a variable, so in this case, the string 'Bob' would be stored in the variable *name*. The JavaScript interpreter treats this step as true, so the code following the condition will always run.

Tutorial: Using Conditional Statements

Conditional statements will become part of your day-to-day JavaScript toolkit. In this tutorial, you'll try out conditional statements to control how a script runs.

Note: See the note on page 27 for information on how to download the tutorial files.

---

1. **In a text editor, open the file *3.1.html* in the *chapter03* folder.**

   You'll start by simply prompting the visitor for a number. This file already contains <script> tags in both the head and body regions.

2. **Between the first set of <script> tags, in the page's <head> section, type the code in bold:**

   ```
   <script type="text/javascript">
   var luckyNumber = prompt('What is your lucky number?','');
   </script>
   ```

   This line of code opens a JavaScript prompt dialog box, asks a question, and stores whatever the visitor typed into the *luckyNumber* variable. Next, you'll add a conditional statement to check what the visitor typed into the prompt dialog box.

3. **Locate the second set of <script> tags down in the body of the page, and add the code in bold:**

   ```
   <script type="text/javascript">
   if (luckyNumber == 7 ) {
   </script>
   ```

   Here's the beginning of the conditional statement; it simply checks to see if the visitor typed *7*.

4. **Press Return twice and type the closing brace, so that the code looks like this:**

   ```
   <script type="text/javascript">
   if (luckyNumber == 7 ) {


   }
   </script>
   ```

   The closing brace ends the conditional statement. Any JavaScript you add between the two braces will only run if the condition is true.

Tip: As mentioned on page 85, it's a good idea to add the closing brace before writing the code that runs as part of the conditional statement.

---

5. **Click into the empty line above the closing brace. Hit the Space bar twice and type:**

   ```
   document.write("Hey, 7 is my lucky number too!");
   ```

   The two spaces before the code indent the line so you can easily see that this code is part of the conditional statement. The actual JavaScript here should feel familiar by now—it simply writes a message to the page.

---

6. **Save the file and preview it in a Web browser. Type *7* when the prompt dialog appears.**

   You should see the message "Hey, that's my lucky number too!" below the headline when the page loads. If you don't, go over your code and make sure you typed it correctly (see page 32 for tips on dealing with a broken script). Reload the page, but this time type a different number. This time, nothing appears underneath the headline. You'll add an *else clause* to print another message.

7. **Return to your text editor, and add the bolded text to your page:**

```
<script type="text/javascript">
if (luckyNumber == 7 ) {
  document.write("Hey, 7 is my lucky number too!");
} else {
  document.write("The number " + luckyNumber + " is lucky for you!");
}
</script>
```

   The *else* clause provides a backup message, so that if the visitor doesn't type *7*, she'll see a different message that includes her lucky number. To round out this exercise, you'll add an *else if* statement to test more values and provide another message.

8. **Add the two bolded lines below to your script:**

```
<script type="text/javascript">
if (luckyNumber == 7 ) {
  document.write("Hey, 7 is my lucky number too!");
} else if (luckyNumber == 13 || luckyNumber == 24) {
  document.write("Wooh. " + luckyNumber + "? That's an unlucky number!");
} else {
  document.write("The number " + luckyNumber + " is lucky for you!");
}
</script>
```

   At this point, the script first checks to see if 7 is stored in the variable *luckyNumber*; if *luckyNumber* holds a value other than 7, then the *else if* kicks in. This conditional statement is made up of two conditions, *luckyNumber == 13* and *luckyNumber == 24*. The ||, called the logical OR operator, makes the entire conditional statement turn out to be true if either of the conditions are true. So if the visitor types in 13 *or* 24, a "That's an unlucky number" message is printed to the page.

Tip: You add the logical OR operator by typing Shift-\ twice to get ||.

Preview the page in a Web browser, and type 13 when the prompt dialogue appears. Press the browser's reload button, and try different numbers as well as letters or other characters. You'll notice that if you type a word or other non-number character the final *else* clause kicks in, printing a message like, "The number asdfg is lucky for you!" Since that doesn't make a lot of sense, you'll pop up another prompt dialog box if your visitor enters a nonnumber the first time.

9. **Return to your text editor, and locate the first set of <script> tags in the <head> of the page. Add the code in bold:**

```
<script type="text/javascript">
var luckyNumber = prompt('What is your lucky number?','');
luckyNumber = parseInt(luckyNumber, 10);
</script>
```

This line of code runs the value of *luckyNumber* through a function named *parseInt( )*. This JavaScript command takes a value and tries to convert it to an integer, which is a whole number like 1, 5, or 100. You'll learn about this command in the next chapter, on page 135, but for now just realize that if the visitor types in text like "ha ha," the *parseInt( )* command won't be able to convert that to a number; instead, the command will provide a special JavaScript value, *NaN*, which stands for "not a number." You can use that information to pop-up another prompt dialog box if a number isn't entered the first time.

10. **Add the bolded code to your script:**

```
<script type="text/javascript">
var luckyNumber = prompt('What is your lucky number?','');
luckyNumber = parseInt(luckyNumber);
if (isNaN(luckyNumber)) {
 luckyNumber = prompt('Please, tell me your lucky number.','');
}
</script>
```

Here again, a conditional statement comes in handy. The condition *isNaN(luckyNumber)* uses another JavaScript command that checks to see if something is a number. Specifically, it checks to see if the value in *luckyNumber* is *not* a number. If the value isn't a number (for example, the visitor types *askls-dkl*), a second prompt appears and asks the question again. If the visitor did type a number, the second prompt is skipped.

Save the page and preview it in a Web browser again. This time, type a word and click OK when the prompt dialog box appears. You should then see a second prompt. Type a number this time. Of course, this script assumes the visitor made an honest mistake by typing a word the first time, but won't make the same mistake twice. Unfortunately, if the visitor types a word in the second prompt, you end up with the same problem—you'll learn how to fix that in the next section.

Note: You'll find a completed version of this tutorial in the *chapter03* tutorial folder: *complete_3.1.html*.

Handling Repetitive Tasks with Loops

Sometimes a script needs to repeat the same series of steps over and over again. For example, say you have a Web form with 30 text fields. When the user submits the form, you want to make sure that none of the fields are empty. In other words, you need to perform the same set of actions—check to see if a form field is empty—30 times. Since computers are good at performing repetitive tasks, it makes sense that JavaScript includes the tools to quickly do the same thing repeatedly.

In programming-speak, performing the same task over and over is called a *loop*, and because loops are so common in programming JavaScript offers several different types. All do the same thing, just in slightly different ways.

While Loops

A *while loop* repeats a chunk of code as long as a particular condition is true; in other words, *while* the condition is true. The basic structure of a while loop is this:

```
while (condition) {
 // javascript to repeat
}
```

The first line introduces the *while* statement. As with a conditional statement, you place a condition between the set of parentheses that follow the keyword *while*. The condition is any test you'd use in a conditional statement, such as *x > 10* or *answer == 'yes'*. And just like a conditional statement, the JavaScript interpreter runs all of the code that appears between the opening and closing braces *if* the condition is true.

However, unlike a conditional statement, when the JavaScript interpreter reaches the closing brace of a *while* statement, instead of continuing to the next line of the program, it jumps back to the top of the *while* statement and tests the condition a second time. If the condition is again true, the interpreter runs JavaScript between the braces a second time. This process continues until the condition is no longer true; then the program continues to the next statement following the loop (see Figure 3-2).

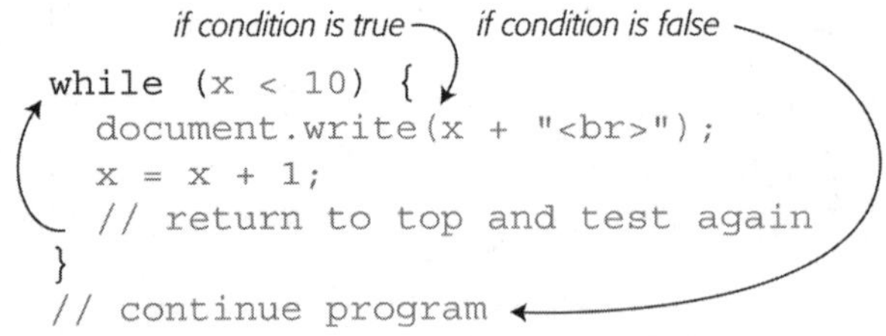

```
        if condition is true ⌐     if condition is false ⌐
  while (x < 10) {
    document.write(x + "<br>");
    x = x + 1;
    // return to top and test again
  }
  // continue program ◄
```

Figure 3-2:
A while *loop runs the JavaScript code between curly braces as long as the test condition (x < 10 in this case) is true.*

Say you want to print the numbers 1 to 5 on a page. One possible way to do that is like this:

```
document.write('Number 1 <br>');
document.write('Number 2 <br>');
document.write('Number 3 <br>');
document.write('Number 4 <br>');
document.write('Number 5 <br>');
```

Notice that each line of code is nearly identical: only the number changes from line to line. In this situation, a loop provides a more efficient way to achieve the same goal:

```
var num = 1;
while (num <= 5) {
 document.write('Number ' + num + '<br>');
 num = num + 1;
}
```

The first line of code—*var num = 1;*—isn't part of the while loop: it sets up a variable to hold the number to be printed to the page. The second line is the start of the loop. It sets up the test condition. As long as the number stored in the variable *num* is less than or equal to 5, the code between the braces runs. When the test condition is encountered for the first time, the value of num is 1, so the test is true (1 is less than 5), and the *document.write( )* command executes, writing 'Number 1
' to the page (the <br> is just an HTML line break to make sure each line prints onto a separate line on the Web page).

Tip: A more compact way to write *num = num +1* (which just adds one to the current number stored in the variable num) is like this:

```
num++
```

This shorthand method also adds one to the variable *num* (see Table 2-3 on page 52 for more information.)

The last line of the loop—*num = num + 1*—is very important. Not only does it increase the value of *num* by 1 so the next number (2, for example) will print, but it also makes it possible for the test condition to eventually turn out to be false. Because the JavaScript code within a *while* statement repeats as long as the condition is true, you must change one of the elements of the condition so that the condition eventually becomes false in order to stop the loop and move onto the next part of the script. If the test condition never turns out to be false, you end up with what's called an *infinite loop*—a program that never ends. Notice what would happen if you left that line out of the loop:

```
var num = 1;
while (num <= 5) { // this is an endless loop
 document.write('Number ' + num + '<br>');
}
```

The first time through this loop, the test would ask: Is 1 less than or equal to 5? The answer is yes, so *document.write( )* runs. At the end of the loop (the last brace), the JavaScript interpreter goes back to the beginning of the loop and tests the condition again. At this point, *num* is still 1, so the condition is true again and the *document.write( )* executes. Again, the JavaScript interpreter returns to the beginning of the loop and tests the condition a third time. You can see where this goes: an endless number of lines that say "Number 1."

This simple example also shows some of the flexibility offered by loops. Say, for example, you wanted to write the numbers 1–100, instead of just 1–5. Instead of adding lots of additional lines of *document.write( )* commands, you just alter the test condition like this:

```
var num = 1;
while (num <= 100) {
  document.write('Number ' + num + '<br>');
  num = num + 1;
}
```

Now the loop will execute 100 times, writing 100 lines to the Web page.

Loops and Arrays

You'll find loops come in handy when dealing with a common JavaScript element—an array. As you recall from page 56, an array is a collection of data. You can think of an array as a kind of shopping list. When you go shopping, you actually perform a kind of loop: You walk around the store looking for an item on your list and, when you find it, you put it into your cart; then you look for the next item on your list, put it into the cart, and so on, and so on until you've gone through the entire list. Then you're done (this is the same as exiting the loop) and go to the check out counter (in other words, move to the next step of your "program").

You can use loops in JavaScript to go through items in an array and perform a task on each item. For example, say you're building a program that generates a calendar (see Figure 3-3). The calendar is completely generated using JavaScript, and you want to print the name of each day of the week on the calendar. You might start by storing the names of the weeks into an array like this:

```
var days = ['Monday', 'Tuesday', 'Wednesday', 'Thursday', ↵
      'Friday', 'Saturday', 'Sunday'];
```

Note: The ↵ symbol that appears in the code above indicates that this line of JavaScript code belongs on a single line. Since the width of this book's pages sometimes prevents a single line of code from fitting on a single printed line, this book uses the ↵ symbol to indicate code that should appear together on a single line. If you were going to type this code into a text editor, you'd type it as one long line (and leave out the ↵).

Figure 3-3:
*MooMonth is a free,
open-source JavaScript
calendar system:* www.
moomonth.com/demo.

You can then loop through each item in the array and print it to the page. Remember that you access one item in an array using the item's index value. For example, the first item in the *days* array above (Monday), is retrieved with *days[0]*. The second item is *days[1]*, and so on.

Here's how you can use a *while* loop to print each item in this array:

```
var counter = 0;
while (counter < days.length) {
  document.write(days[counter] + ', ');
  counter++;
}
```

The first line—*var counter = 0*—sets up (or *initializes* in programmer-speak) a counter variable that's used both as part of the test condition, and as the index for accessing array items. The condition—*counter < days.length*—just asks if the current value stored in the counter variable is less than the number of items in the array (remember, as described on page 60, the number of items in an array is stored in the array's *length* property). In this case, the condition checks if the counter is less than 7 (the number of days in the week). If *counter* is less than 7 then the loop begins, the day of the week is written to the page (followed by a comma and a period), and the counter is incremented by 1 (*counter++* is the same as *counter = counter + 1* [see the Tip on page 91]). After the loop runs, it tries the test again; the loop continues to run until the test turns out to be false. This process is diagrammed in Figure 3-4.

```
var counter = 0;
while (counter < days.length) {
    document.write(days[counter] + ', ');
    counter++;
}
```

counter *value* before test	condition	loop?	days[counter]	counter *value* after counter++
0	0 < 7	yes	days[0]	1
1	1 < 7	yes	days[1]	2
2	2 < 7	yes	days[2]	3
3	3 < 7	yes	days[3]	4
4	4 < 7	yes	days[4]	5
5	5 < 7	yes	days[5]	6
6	6 < 7	yes	days[6]	7
7	7 < 7	no		

Figure 3-4:
For this loop, the condition is tested 8 times. The last test asks if 7 is less than 7. It isn't, so the while statement is completed, and the JavaScript interpreter skips the loop and continues with the next part of the script. The final result of this script will be "Monday, Tuesday, Wednesday, Thursday, Friday, Saturday, Sunday".

For Loops

JavaScript offers another type of loop, called a *for loop*, that's a little more compact (and a little more confusing). *For* loops are usually used for repeating a series of steps a certain number of times, so they often involve some kind of counter variable, a conditional test, and a way of changing the counter variable. In many cases, a *for* loop can achieve the same thing as a *while* loop, with fewer lines of code. For example, here's the *while* loop shown on page 92:

```
var num = 1;
while (num <= 100) {
  document.write('Number ' + num + '<br>');
  num = num + 1;
}
```

You can achieve the same effect using a *for* loop with only three lines of code:

```
for (var num=1; num<=100; num++) {
  document.write('Number ' + num + '<br>');
}
```

At first, *for* loops might look a little confusing, but once you figure out the different parts of the for statement, they aren't hard. Each *for* loop begins with the keyword *for*, followed by a set of parentheses containing three parts, and a pair of curly braces. As with *while* loops, the stuff inside curly braces (*document. write('Number ' + num + '<br>');* in this example) is the JavaScript code that executes as part of the loop.

Table 3-2 explains the three parts inside the parentheses, but in a nutshell, the first part (*var num=1;*) initializes a counter variable. This step only happens once at the very beginning of the statement. The second part is the condition, which is tested to see if the loop is run; the third part is an action that happens at the end of each loop—it usually changes the value of the counter, so that the test condition eventually turns out to be false and the loop ends.

Table 3-2. *Understanding the parts of a* for *loop*

Parts of loop	What it means	When it's applied
`for` `var num = 1;`	Introduces the for loop Set variable num to 1	Only once; at the very beginning of the statement.
`num <= 100;`	Is num less than or equal to 100? If yes, then loop again. If not, then skip loop and continue script	At beginning of the statement and before each time through the loop
`num++`	Add 1 to variable num. Same as num = num + 1	At end of each time through loop

Since *for* loops provide an easy way to repeat a series of steps a set number of times, they work really well for working through the elements of an array. The *while* loop in Figure 3-4, which writes each item in an array to the page, can be rewritten using a *for* loop, like this:

```
var days = ['Monday', 'Tuesday', 'Wednesday', 'Thursday', ↵
    'Friday', 'Saturday', 'Sunday'];
for (var i=0; i<days.length; i++) {
    document.write(days[i] + ', ');
}
```

Tip: Seasoned programmers often use a very short name for counter variables in *for* loops. In the code above, the letter *i* acts as the name of the counter. A one-letter name (i, j, and z are common) is fast to type; and since the variable isn't used for anything except running the loop, there's no need to provide a more descriptive name like *counter*.

The examples so far have counted up to a certain number and then stopped the loop, but you can also count backwards. For example, say you want to print the items in an array in reverse order (in other words, the last item in the array prints first). You can do this:

```
var example = ['first','second','third','last'];
for (var j = example.length ; j > 0; j--) {
    document.write(example[j-1] + '<br>');
}
```

In this example, the counter variable *j* starts with the total number of items in the array (4). Each time through the loop, you test to see if the value in *j* is greater than 0; if it is, the code between the curly braces is run. Then, 1 is subtracted from *j* (*j--*), and the test is run again. The only tricky part is the way the program accesses the array item (*example[j-1]*). Since arrays start with an index of 0, the last item in an array is one less than the total number of items in the array (as explained on page 59). Here *j* starts with the total number of items in the array, so in order to access the last item, you must subtract 1 from *j* to get the proper item.

Do/While Loops

There's another, less common type of loop, known as a *do/while loop*. This type of loop works nearly identically to a *while* loop. Its basic structure looks like this:

```
do {
 // javascript to repeat
} while (condition) ;
```

In this type of loop, the conditional test happens at the *end*, after the loop has run. As a result, the JavaScript code within the curly braces always run *at least once*. Even if the condition isn't ever true, the test isn't run until after the code runs once.

There aren't too many cases where this comes in handy, but it's very useful when you want to prompt the user for input. The tutorial you did earlier in this chapter (page 86) is a good example. That script asks visitors to type in a number. It includes a bit of a fail-safe system, so that if they don't type a number, the script asks them one more time to type a number. Unfortunately, if someone's really stubborn and types something other than a number the second time, a nonsensical message is printed to the page.

However, with a *do/while loop*, you can continually prompt the visitor for a number until she types one in. To see how this works, you'll edit the page you completed on page 89:

1. **In a text editor, open the *3.1.html* page you completed on page 89.**

   (If you didn't complete that tutorial, you can just open the file *complete_3.1. html*.) You'll replace the code near the top of the page with a *do/while* loop.

2. **Locate the code between the <script> tags in the <head> of the page, and delete the code in bold below:**

   ```
   var luckyNumber = prompt('What is your lucky number?','');
   luckyNumber = parseInt(luckyNumber, 10);
   if (isNaN(luckyNumber)) {
    luckyNumber = prompt('Please, tell me your lucky number.','');
   }
   ```

   The code you deleted provided the second prompt dialog box. You won't need that anymore. Instead, you'll wrap the code that's left inside a *do/while* loop.

3. Place the cursor before the first line of code (the line that begins with *var luckyNumber*) and type:

```
do {
```

This code creates the beginning of the loop. Next, you'll finish the loop and add the test condition.

4. Click at the end of the last line of JavaScript code in that section and type: *} while (isNaN(luckyNumber));*. The completed code block should look like this:

```
do {
var luckyNumber = prompt('What is your lucky number?','');
luckyNumber = parseInt(luckyNumber, 10);
} while (isNaN(luckyNumber));
```

Save this file and preview it in a Web browser. Try typing text and other non-numeric symbols in the prompt dialog. That annoying dialog continues to appear until you actually type a number.

Here's how it works: the *do* keyword tells the JavaScript interpreter that it's about to enter a *do/while* loop. The next two lines are then run, so the prompt appears and the visitor's answer is converted to a whole number. It's only at this point that the condition is tested. It's the same condition as the script on page 89: it just checks to see if the input retrieved from the visitor is "not a number." If the input isn't a number, the loop repeats. In other words, the prompt will keep reappearing as long as a nonnumber is entered. The good thing about this approach is that it guarantees that the prompt appears at least once, so if the visitor does type a number in response to the question, there is no loop.

Functions: Turn Useful Code Into Reusable Commands

Imagine that at work you've just gotten a new assistant to help you with your every task (time to file this book under "fantasy fiction"). Suppose you got hungry for a piece of pizza, but since the assistant was new to the building and the area, you had to give him detailed directions: "Go out this door, turn right, go to the elevator, take the elevator to the first floor, walk out of the building…" and so on. The assistant follows your directions and brings you a slice. A couple hours later you're hungry again, and you want more pizza. Now, you don't have to go through the whole set of directions again— "Go out this door, turn right, go to the elevator…". By this time, your assistant knows where the pizza joint is, so you just say, "Get me a slice of pizza," and he goes to the pizza place and returns with a slice.

In other words, you only need to provide detailed directions a *single time*; your assistant memorizes those steps and with the simple phrase "Get me a slice" he instantly leaves and reappears a little while later with a piece of pizza. JavaScript has an equivalent mechanism called a *function*. A function is a series of programming steps that you set up at the beginning of your script—the equivalent of providing detailed directions to your assistant. Those steps aren't actually run when you create the function; instead, they're stored in the Web browser's memory, where you can call upon them whenever you need those steps performed.

Functions are invaluable for efficiently performing multiple programming steps repeatedly: for example, say you create a photo gallery Web page filled with 50 small thumbnail images. When someone clicks one of the small photos, you might want the page to dim, a caption to appear, and a larger version of that image to fill the screen (you'll learn to do just that on page 254). Each time someone clicks an image, the process repeats, so on a Web page with 50 small photos, your script might have to do the same series of steps 50 times. Fortunately, you don't have to write the same code 50 times to make this photo gallery work. Instead, you can write a function with all the necessary steps, and then, with each click of the thumbnail, you run the function. You write the code once, but run it any time you like.

The basic structure of a function looks like this:

```
function functionName() {
  // the JavaScript you want to run
}
```

The keyword *function* lets the JavaScript interpreter know you're creating a function—it's similar to how you use *if* to begin an *if/else* statement or *var* to create a variable. Next you provide a function name; as with a variable, you get to choose your own function name. Follow the same rules listed on page 44 for naming variables. In addition, it's common to include a verb in a function name like *calculateTax, getScreenHeight, updatePage,* or *fadeImage.* An active name makes it clear that it does something and makes it easier to distinguish between function and variable names.

Directly following the name, you add a pair of parentheses, which are another characteristic of functions. After the parentheses, there's a space followed by a curly brace, one or more lines of JavaScript and a final, closing curly brace. As with *if* statements, the curly braces mark the beginning and end of the JavaScript code that make up the function.

Tip: As with *if/else* statements, functions are more easily read if you indent the JavaScript code between the curly braces. Two spaces (or a tab) at the beginning of each line are common.

Here's a very simple function to print out the current date in a format like "Sun May 12 2008":

```
function printToday() {
  var today = new Date();
  document.write(today.toDateString());
}
```

The function's name is *printToday*. It has just two lines of JavaScript code that retrieve the current date, convert the date to a format we can understand (that's the *toDateString( )* part), and then print the results to the page using our old friend the *document.write( )* command. Don't worry about how all of the date stuff works—you'll find out in the next chapter.

Programmers usually put their functions at the beginning of a script, which sets up the various functions that the rest of the script will use later. Remember that a function doesn't run when it's first created—it's like telling your assistant how to get to the pizza place without actually sending him there. The JavaScript code is merely stored in the browser's memory, waiting to be run later, when you need it.

But how do you run a function? In programming-speak you *call* the function whenever you want the function to perform its task. Calling the function is just a matter of writing the function's name, followed by a pair of parentheses. For example, to make our *printToday* function run, you'd simply type:

```
printToday();
```

As you can see, making a function run doesn't take a lot of typing—that's the beauty of functions. Once they're created, you don't have to add much code to get results.

Note: When calling a function, don't forget the parentheses following the function. That's the part that makes the function run. For example, *printToday* won't do anything, but *printToday( )* executes the function.

Mini-Tutorial

Because functions are such an important concept, here's a series of steps for you to practice creating and using a function on a real Web page:

1. **In a text editor, open the file *3.2.html*.**

   You'll start by adding a function in the head of the document.

2. **Locate the code between the <script> tags in the <head> of the page, and type the following code:**

   ```
   function printToday( ) {
    var today = new Date( );
    document.write(today.toDateString( ));
   }
   ```

   The basic function is in place, but it doesn't do anything yet.

3. **Save the file and preview it in a Web browser.**

   Nothing happens. Well, actually something does happen; you just don't see it. The Web browser read the function statements into memory, and was waiting for you to actually call the function, which you'll do next.

---

4. Return to your text editor and the *3.2.html* file. Locate the <p> tag that begins
   with "Today is", and between the two <strong> tags, add the following bolded
   code:

   ```
   <p>Today is <strong><script type="text/javascript">printToday( );⏎
   </script></strong></p>
   ```

Note: Remember, when you see the ⏎ character, that just means the full line of code wouldn't fit across
the page of this book. You just type the code on one line in your text editor. Don't start a new line, and
don't attempt to type a ⏎ character.

Save the page and preview it in a Web browser. The current date is printed to the
page. If you wanted to print the date at the bottom of the Web page as well, all
you'd need to do is call the function a second time.

Giving Information to Your Functions

Functions are even more useful when they receive information. Think back to your
assistant—the fellow who fetches you slices of pizza. The original "function"
described on page 97 was simply directions to the pizza parlor and instructions to
buy a slice and return to the office. When you wanted some pizza, you "called" the
function by telling your assistant "Get me a slice!" Of course, depending on how
you're feeling, you might want a slice of pepperoni, cheese, or olive pizza. To make
your instructions more flexible, you can tell your assistant what type of slice you'd
like. Each time you request some pizza, you can specify a different type.

JavaScript functions can also accept information, called *parameters*, which the
function uses to carry out its actions. For example, if you want to create a function
that calculates the total cost of a person's shopping cart, then the function needs to
know how much each item costs, and how many of each item was ordered.

To start, when you create the function, place the name of a new variable inside the
parentheses—this is the *parameter*. The basic structure looks like this:

```
function functionName(parameter) {
  // the JavaScript you want to run
}
```

The parameter is just a variable, so you supply any valid variable name (see page 44
for tips on naming variables). For example, let's say you want to save a few key-
strokes each time you print something to a Web page. You create a simple function that lets you replace the Web browser's *document.write( )* function with a
shorter name:

```
function print(message) {
  document.write(message);
}
```

The name of this function is *print* and it has one parameter, named *message*. When this function is called, it receives some information (the message to be printed) and then it uses the *document.write( )* function to write the message to the page. Of course, a function doesn't do anything until it's called, so somewhere else on your Web page, you can call the function like this:

```
print('Hello world.');
```

When this code is run, the print function is called and some text—the string 'Hello world.'—is sent to the function, which then prints "Hello World." to the page. Technically, the process of sending information to a function is called "passing an argument." In this example, the text—'Hello world.'—is the *argument*.

Even with a really simple function like this, the logic of when and how things work can be a little confusing if you're new to programming. Here's how each step breaks down, as shown in the diagram in Figure 3-5:

1. **The function is read by the JavaScript interpreter and stored in memory. This step just prepares the Web browser to run the function later.**

2. **The function is called and information—"Hello world."—is passed to the function.**

3. **The information passed to the function is stored in a new variable named *message*. This step is equivalent to *var message = 'Hello World.';***

4. **Finally, the function runs, printing the value stored in the variable *message* to the Web page.**

```
   3
❶ function print(message) {
     document.write(message); ❹
   }


❷ print( 'Hello world!' );
```

Figure 3-5:
When working with functions, you usually create the function before you use it. The print( ) function here is created in the first three lines of code, but the code inside the function doesn't actually run until the last line.

A function isn't limited to a single parameter, either. You can pass any number of arguments to a function. You just need to specify each parameter in the function, like this:

```
function functionName(parameter1, parameter2, parameter3) {
  // the JavaScript you want to run
}
```

And then call the function with the same number of arguments in the same order:

```
functionName(argument1, argument2, argument3);
```

In this example, when *functionName* is called, *argument1* is stored in *parameter1*, *argument2* in *parameter2,* and so on. Expanding on the print function from above, suppose in addition to printing a message to the Web page, you want to specify an HTML tag to wrap around the message. This way, you can print the message as a headline or a paragraph. Here's what the new function would look like:

```
function print(message,tag) {
  document.write('<' + tag + '>' + message +'</' + tag + '>');
}
```

The function call would look like this:

```
print('Hello world.', 'p');
```

In this example, you're passing two arguments—'Hello world.' and 'p'—to the function. Those values are stored in the function's two variables—*message* and *tag.* The result is a new paragraph—*<p>Hello world.</p>*—printed to the page.

You're not limited to passing just strings to a function either: you can send any type of JavaScript variable or value to a function. For example, you can send an array, a variable, a number, or a Boolean value as an argument.

Retrieving Information from Functions

Sometimes a function simply does something like write a message to a page, move an object across the screen, or validate the form fields on a page. Other times, you'll want to get something back from a function: after all, the "Get me a slice of pizza" function wouldn't be much good if you didn't end up with some tasty pizza at the end. Likewise, a function that calculates the total cost of items in a shopping cart isn't very useful unless the function lets you know the final total.

Some of the built-in JavaScript functions we've already seen return values. For example the *prompt( )* command (see page 55) pops up a dialog box with a text field, whatever the user types in to the box is returned. As you've seen, you can then store that return value into a variable and do something with it:

```
var answer = prompt('What month were you born?', '');
```

The visitor's response to the prompt dialog is stored in the variable *answer;* you can then test the value inside that variable using conditional comments or do any of the many other things JavaScript lets you do with variables.

To return a value from your own functions, you use *return* followed by the value you wish to return:

```
function functionName(parameter1, parameter2) {
  // the JavaScript you want to run
  return value;
}
```

For example, say you want to calculate the total cost of a sale including sales tax. You might create a script like this:

```
var TAX = .08; // 8% sales tax
function calculateTotal(quantity, price) {
 var total = quantity * price * (1 + TAX);
 var formattedTotal = total.toFixed(2);
 return formattedTotal;
}
```

The first line stores the tax rate into a variable named *TAX* (which lets you easily change the rate simply by updating this line of code). The next three lines define the function. Don't worry too much about what's happening inside the function—you'll learn more about working with numbers in the next chapter. The important part is the fourth line of the function—the return statement. It returns the value stored in the variable *formattedTotal*.

To make use of the return value you usually store it inside a variable, so in this example, you could call the function like this:

```
var saleTotal = calculateTotal(2, 16.95);
document.write('Total cost is: $' + saleTotal);
```

In this case, the values 2 and 16.95 are passed to the function. The first number represents the number of items purchased, and the second their individual cost. The result is returned from the function and stored into a new variable—*saleTotal*—which is then used as part of a *document.write( )* command to print the total cost of the sale including tax.

You don't have to store the return value into a variable, however. You can use the return value directly within another statement like this:

```
document.write('Total: $' + calculateTotal(2, 16.95));
```

In this case, the function is called and its return value is added to the string 'Total: $', which is then printed to the document. At first, this way of using a function may be hard to read, so you might want to take the extra step of just storing the function's results into a variable and then using that variable in your script.

Tip: A function can only return one value. If you want to return multiple items, store the results in an array and return the array.

Keeping Variables from Colliding

One great advantage of functions is that they can cut down the amount of programming you have to do. You'll probably find yourself using a really useful function time and time again on different projects. For example, a function that helps calculate shipping and sales tax could come in handy on every order form you create, so you might copy and paste that function into other scripts on your site or on other projects.

One potential problem arises when you just plop a function down into an already created script. What happens if the script uses the same variable names as the function? Will the function overwrite the variable from the script, or vice versa? For example:

```
var message = 'Outside the function';
function warning(message) {
    alert(message);
}
warning('Inside the function'); // 'Inside the function'
alert(message); // 'Outside the function'
```

Notice that the variable *message* appears both outside the function (the first line of the script) and as a parameter in the function. A parameter is really just a variable that's filled with data when the function's called. In this case, the function call—*warning('Inside the function');*—passes a string to the function and the function stores that string in the variable *message*. It looks like there are now two versions of the variable *message*. So what happens to the value in the original *message* variable that's created in the first line of the script?

You might think that the original value stored in *message* is overwritten with a new value, the string 'Outside the function'; it's not. When you run this script, you'll see two alert dialogues: the first will say "Inside the function" and the second "Outside the function." There are actually two variables named *message*, but they exist in separate places (see Figure 3-6).

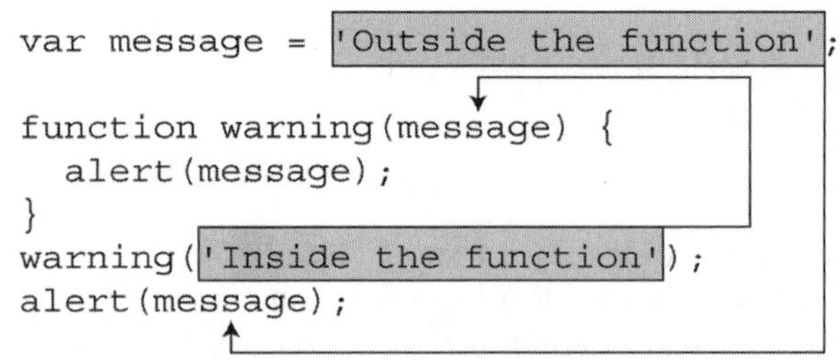

Figure 3-6:
A function parameter is only visible inside the function, so the first line of this function—function warning(message)—will create a new variable named message that can only be accessed inside the function. Once the function is done, that variable disappears.

The JavaScript interpreter treats variables inside of a function differently than variables declared and created outside of a function. In programming-speak, each function has its own *scope*. A function's scope is like a wall that surrounds the function—variables inside the wall aren't visible to the rest of the script outside the wall. Scope is a pretty confusing concept when you first learn about it, but it's very useful. Because a function has its own scope, you don't have to be afraid that the names you use for parameters in your function will overwrite or conflict with variables used in another part of the script.

So far, the only situation we've discussed is the use of variables as parameters. But what about a variable that's created inside the function, but not as a parameter, like this:

```
var message = 'Outside the function';
function warning( ) {
 var message ='Inside the function';
 alert( message );
}
warning( ); // 'Inside the function'
alert( message ); //'Outside the function'
```

Here, the code creates a *message* variable twice—in the first line of the script, and again in the first line inside the function. This situation is the same as with parameters—by typing *var message* inside the function, you've created a new variable inside the function's scope. This type of variable is called a *local variable*, since it's only visible within the walls of the function—the main script and other functions can't see or access this variable.

However, variables created in the main part of a script (outside a function) exist in *global scope*. All functions in a script can access variables that are created in its main body. For example, in the code below, the variable message is created on the first line of the script—it's a *global variable*, and it can be accessed by the function.

```
var message = 'Global variable';
function warning( ) {
 alert( message );
}
warning( ); // 'Global variable'
```

This function doesn't have any parameters and doesn't define a *message* variable, so when the *alert(message)* part is run, the function looks for a global variable named *message*. In this case, that variable exists, so an alert dialog with the text "Global variable" appears.

There's one potential gotcha with local and global variables—a variable only exists within the function's scope if it's a parameter, or if the variable is created inside the function with the *var* keyword. Figure 3-7 demonstrates this situation. The top chunk of code demonstrates how both a global variable named *message* and a function's local variable named *message* can exist side-by-side. The key is the first line inside the function—*var message ='Inside the function';*. By using *var*, you create a local variable.

Compare that to the code in the bottom half of Figure 3-7. In this case, the function doesn't use the *var* keyword. Instead, the line of code *message='Inside the function';* doesn't create a new local variable; it simply stores a new value inside the global variable *message*. The result? The function clobbers the global variable, replacing its initial value.

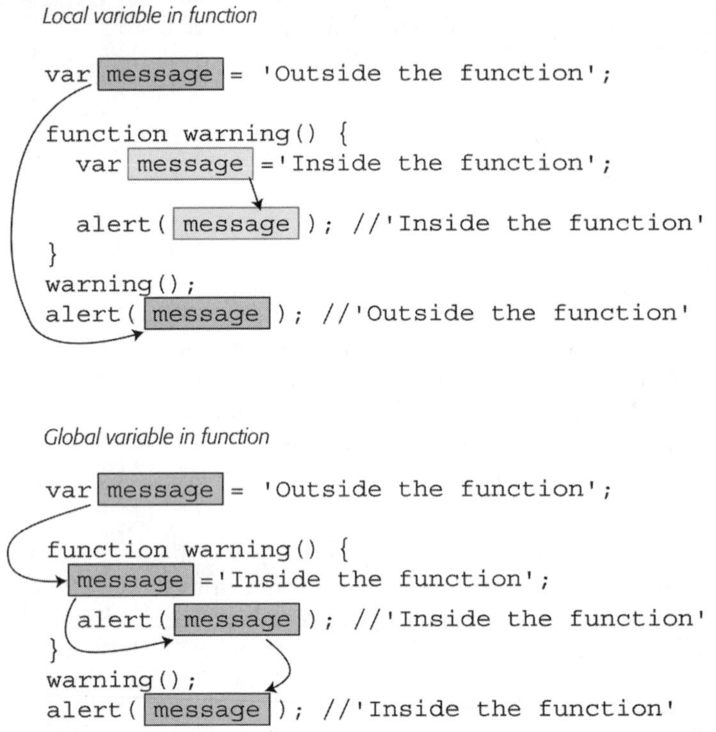

Figure 3-7:
There's a subtle yet crucial difference when assigning values to variables within a function. If you want the variable to only be accessible to the code inside the function, make sure to use the var keyword to create the variable inside the function (top). If you don't use var, you're just storing a new value inside the global variable (bottom).

Local variable in function

```
var message = 'Outside the function';

function warning() {
  var message ='Inside the function';

  alert( message ); //'Inside the function'
}
warning();
alert( message ); //'Outside the function'
```

Global variable in function

```
var message = 'Outside the function';

function warning() {
  message ='Inside the function';

  alert( message ); //'Inside the function'
}
warning();
alert( message ); //'Inside the function'
```

The notion of variable scope is pretty confusing, so the preceding discussion may not make a lot of sense for you right now. But just keep one thing in mind: if the variables you create in your scripts don't seem to be holding the values you expect, you might be running into a scope problem. If that happens, come back and reread this section.

Tutorial: A Simple Quiz

Now it's time to bring together the lessons from this chapter and create a complete program. In this tutorial, you'll create a simple quiz system for asking questions and evaluating the quiz-taker's performance. First, this section will look at a couple of ways you could solve this problem, and discuss efficient techniques for programming.

As always, the first step is to figure out what exactly the program should do. There are a few things you want the program to accomplish:

• **Ask questions.** If you're going to quiz people, you need a way to ask them questions. At this point, you know one simple way to get feedback on a Web page: the *prompt( )* command. In addition, you'll need a list of questions; since arrays are good for storing lists of information, you'll use an array to store your quiz questions.

- **Let quiz-taker know if she's right or wrong.** First, you need to determine if the quiz-taker gave the right answer: a conditional statement can take care of that. Then, to let the quiz taker know if she's right or wrong, you can use the *alert( )* command.

- **Print the results of the quiz.** You need a way to track how well the quiz-taker's doing—a variable that keeps track of the number of correct responses will work. Then, to announce the final results of the quiz, you can either use the *alert( )* command or the *document.write( )* method.

There are many ways to solve this problem. Some beginning programmers might take a blunt-force approach and repeat the same code to ask each question. For example, the JavaScript to ask the first two questions in the quiz might look like this:

```
var answer1=prompt('How many moons does Earth have?','');
if (answer1 == 1 ) {
 alert('Correct!');
} else {
 alert('Sorry. The correct answer is 1');
}
var answer2=prompt('How many moons does Saturn have?','');
if (answer2 == 31) {
 alert('Correct!');
} else {
 alert('Sorry. The correct answer is 31');
}
```

This kind of approach seems logical, since the goal of the program is to ask one question after another. However, it's not an efficient way to program. Whenever you see the same steps written multiple times in a program, it's time to consider using a loop or a function instead. We'll create a program that does both: uses a loop to go through each question in the quiz, and a function that performs the question asking tasks:

1. **In a text editor, open the file *3.3.html*.**

   You'll start by setting up a few variables that can track the number of correct answers and the questions for the quiz.

2. **Locate the code between the <script> tags in the <head> of the page, and type the following code:**

   ```
   var score = 0;
   ```

   This variable stores the number of answers the quiz-taker gets right. At the beginning of the quiz, before any questions have been answered, you set the variable to 0. Next, you'll create a list of questions and their answers.

3. **Hit Return to add a new line and type *var questions* = [.**

   You'll be storing all of the questions inside an array, which is really just a variable that can hold multiple items. The code you just typed is the first part of an array statement. You'll be typing the array over multiple lines as described on page 59.

4. **Press Return twice to add two new lines and type *];. Your code should now look like this:**

   ```
   var score = 0;
   var questions = [


   ];
   ```

   Since the quiz is made up of a bunch of questions, it makes sense to store each question as one item in an array. Then, when you want to ask the quiz questions, you simply go through each item in the list and ask the question. However, every question also has an answer, so you need a way to keep track of the answers as well.

   One solution is to create another array—*answers[]*, for example—that holds all of the answers. To ask the first question, look for the first item in the questions array, and to see if the answer is correct, look in the first item of the answers array. However, this has the potential drawback that the two lists might get out of sync: for example, you add a question in the middle of the questions array, but put the answer at the beginning of the answers array. At that point, the first item in the questions array no longer matches the first item in the answers array.

   A better alternative is to use a *nested array* or (if you really want to sound scary and out-of-this-world) a *multidimensional array*. All this really means is that you create an array that includes the question *and* the answer, and you store that array as one item in the questions array. In other words, you create a list where each item in the list is another list.

5. **Click in the empty line between the [and *]; and add the code in bold below:**

   ```
   var questions = [
     ['How many moons does Earth have?', 1],
   ];
   ```

   The code *['How many moons does Earth have?', 1]* is an array of two items. The first item is a question, and the second item is the answer. This array is the first item in the array *questions*. You don't give this array a name, since it's nested inside another array. The comma at the end of the line marks the end of the first item in the questions array and indicates that another array item will follow.

6. **Hit Return to create a new, empty line and add the following two bolded lines to the script:**

```
var questions = [
 ['How many moons does Earth have?', 1],
 ['How many moons does Saturn have?',31],
 ['How many moons does Venus have?', 0]
 ];
```

These are two more questions for the quiz. Note that after the last item in an array, you *don't* type a comma. Setting up all of your questions in a single array provides for a lot of flexibility. If you want to add another question to the list, just add another array containing a new question and answer.

Now that the basic variables for the quiz are set up, it's time to figure out how to ask each question. The questions are stored in an array, and you want to ask each question in the list. As you'll recall from page 92, a loop is a perfect way to go through each item in an array.

7. **Click after the *];* (the end of the *answers* array) and hit Return to create a new, empty line and add the following code:**

```
for (var i=0; i<questions.length; i++) {
```

This line is the first part of a *for* loop (page 94). It does three things: First, it creates a new variable named *i* and stores the number 0 in it. This variable is the counter that keeps track of the number of times through the loop. The second part—*i<questions.length*—is a condition, as in an *if/else* statement. It tests to see if the value in *i* is less than the number of items in the *questions* array—if that's true, the loop runs again. As soon as *i* is equal to or greater than the total number of items in the array, the loop is over. Finally, *i++* changes the value of *i* each time through the loop—it adds 1 to the value of *i*.

Now it's time for the core of the loop—the actual JavaScript that's performed each time through the loop.

8. **Hit Return to create a new, empty line and add the following line of code:**

```
askQuestion(questions[i]);
```

Instead of putting all of the programming code for asking the question in the loop, you'll merely run a function that asks the questions. The function (which you'll create in a moment) is named *askQuestion( )*. Each time through the loop, you'll send one item from the questions array to the function—that's the *questions[i]* part. Remember that you access an item in an array using an index value, so *questions[0]* is the first item in the array, *questions[1]* is the second item, and so on.

By creating a function that asks the questions, you make a more flexible program. You can move and reuse the function to another program if you want. Finally, you'll finish the loop code.

9. Hit Return to create a new, empty line and type } to indicate the end of the loop. The finished loop code should look like this:

```
for (var i=0; i<questions.length; i++) {
askQuestion(questions[i]);
}
```

Yes, that's all there is to it—just a simple loop that calls a function with every question in the quiz. Now, you'll create the heart of the quiz, the *askQuestion( )* function.

10. Create an empty line before the *for* loop you just added.

In other words, you'll add the function between the two statements that define the basic variables at the beginning of the script and the loop you just added. It's OK to define functions anywhere in your script, but most programmers place functions near the beginning of the program. In many scripts, global variables—like *score* and *questions* in this script—are defined first, so that you can see and change those easily; functions appear next, since they usually form the core of most scripts; and finally the step-by-step actions like the loop appear last.

11. Add the following code:

```
function askQuestion(question) {

}
```

This code indicates the body of the function—it's always a good idea to type both the beginning and ending curly braces of a function and then add the script within them. That way, you won't accidentally forget to add the closing curly brace.

This function receives a single argument and stores it in a variable named *question*. Note that this isn't the same as the *questions[]* array you created in step 6. In this case, the *question* variable will actually be filled by one item from the *questions[]* array. As you saw in step 8, one item from that array is actually another array containing two items, the question and the answer.

12. Add the line in bold below:

```
function askQuestion(question) {
var answer = prompt(question[0],'');
}
```

This should look familiar—your old friend the *prompt( )* command. The only part that might feel new is *question[0]*. That's how you access the first element in the array *question*. In this example, the function receives one array, which includes a question and answer: for example, the first array will be *['How many moons does Earth have?', 1]*. So *question[0]* accesses the first item—'How many moons does Earth have'—which is passed to the *prompt( )* command as the question that will appear in the prompt dialog box.

Your program stores whatever the quiz-taker types into the prompt dialog in the variable *answer*. Next, you'll compare the quiz-taker's response with the question's actual answer.

13. **Complete the function by adding the code in bold below:**

```
function askQuestion(question) {
 var answer = prompt(question[0],'');
    if (answer == question[1]) {
        alert('Correct!');
        score++;
    } else {
        alert('Sorry. The correct answer is ' + question[1]);
    }
}
```

This code is just a basic *if/else* statement. The condition—*answer == question[1]*— checks to see if what the user entered (*answer*) is the same as the answer, which is stored as the second item in the array (*question[1]*). If they match, then the quiz-taker was right: an alert appears to let her know she got it right, and her score is increased by one (*score++*). Of course, if she doesn't answer correctly, an alert appears displaying the correct answer.

At this point, the quiz is fully functional. If you save the file and load it into a Web browser, you'll be able to take the quiz. However, you haven't yet provided the results to the quiz-taker so she can see how many she got correct. You'll add a script in the <body> of the Web page to print out the results.

14. **Locate the second pair of <script> tags near the bottom of the Web page and type:**

```
var message = 'You got ' + score;
```

Here, you create a new variable and store the string 'You got ' plus the quiz-taker's score. So if she got all three right, the variable *message* would be 'You got 3'. To make the script easier to read, you'll build up a longer message over several lines.

15. **Press return and type:**

```
message += ' out of ' + questions.length;
```

This adds ' out of ' and the total number of questions to the message string, so at this point, the message will be something like "You got 3 out of 3". Now to finish up the message and print it to the screen.

16. **Add the bolded lines of code to your script:**

```
var message = 'You got ' + score;
message += ' out of ' + questions.length;
message += ' questions correct.';
document.write(message);
```

Save the page, and open it in a Web browser. Take the quiz and see how well you do (see Figure 3-8). If the script doesn't work, remember to try some of the troubleshooting techniques mentioned on page 32. You can also compare your script with a completed, functional version in the file *complete_3.3.html*.

Try adding additional questions to the *questions[]* array at the beginning of the script to make the quiz even longer.

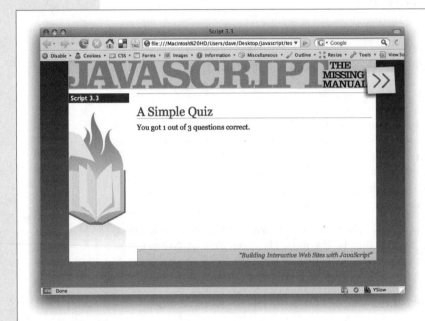

Figure 3-8:
The results of your simple quiz program. After you learn more about how to manipulate a Web page on page 155, try to rewrite this quiz program so that the questions appear directly within the web page, and the score is dynamically updated after each answer. In other words, you'll soon learn how to ditch that clunky prompt( ) command.

Working with Words, Numbers, and Dates

Storing information in a variable or an array is just the first step in effectively using data in your programs. As you read in the last chapter, you can use data to make decisions in a program ("Is the score 0?"). You'll also frequently manipulate data by either searching through it (trying to find a particular word in a sentence, for example), manipulating it (rounding a number to a nearest integer), or reformatting it to display properly (formatting a number like 430 to appear in the proper monetary format, like $430.00).

This chapter will show you how to accomplish common tasks when working with strings and numbers. In addition, it'll introduce the JavaScript Date object, which lets you determine the current date and time on a visitor's computer.

A Quick Object Lesson

So far in this book, you've learned that you can write something to a Web page with the *document.write( )* command, and to determine how many items are in an array, you type the name of the array followed by a period and the word "length," like so: *days.length*. You're probably wondering what those periods are about. You've made it through three chapters without learning the particulars of this feature of JavaScript syntax, and it's time to address them.

You can conceptualize many of the elements of the JavaScript language, as well as elements of a Web page, as *objects*. The real world, of course, is filled with objects too, such as a dog or a car. Most objects are made up of different parts: a dog has a tail, a head, and four legs; a car has doors, wheels, headlights, a horn, and so on. An object might also do something—a car can transport passengers, a dog can bark. In fact, even a part of an object can do something: for example, a tail can wag, and a horn can honk. Table 4-1 illustrates one way to show the relationships between objects, their parts, and actions.

Table 4-1. *A simplified view of the world*

Object	Parts	Actions
dog		bark
	tail	wag
car		transport
	horn	honk

The world of JavaScript is also filled with objects: a browser window, a document, an array, a string, and a date are just a few examples. Like real-world objects, JavaScript objects are also made up of different parts. In programming-speak, the parts of an object are called *properties*. The actions an object can perform are called *methods*, which are basically functions (like the ones you created in the previous chapter) that are specific to an object (see Table 4-2).

Note: You can always tell a method from a property because methods end in parentheses: *write( )*, for example.

Each object in JavaScript has its own set of properties and methods. For example, the array object has a property named *length*, and the document object has a method named *write( )*. To access an object's property or execute one of its methods, you use *dot-syntax*—those periods! The dot (period) connects the object with its property or method. For example, *document.write( )* means "run the *write( )* method of the document object." If the real world worked like that, you'd have a dog wag his tail like this: *dog.tail.wag( )* (of course, in the real world, a doggy treat works a lot better).

Table 4-2. *Some methods and properties of an array object (see page 56 for more information on arrays)*

An array object	Property	Method
['Bob', 'Jalia', 'Sonia']	length	
		push( )
		pop( )
		shift( )

And just as you might own several dogs in the real world, your JavaScript programs can have multiple versions of the same kind of object. For example, say you create two simple variables like this:

```
var first_name = 'Jack';
var last_name = 'Hearts';
```

You've actually created two different *string* objects. Strings (as you'll see in this chapter) have their own set of properties and methods, which are different from the methods and properties of other objects, like arrays. When you create an object (also called creating an *instance* of that object) you can access all of the properties and methods for that object. You've actually been doing that in the last few chapters without even realizing it. For example, you can create an array like this:

```
var names = ['Jack', 'Queen', 'King'];
```

The variable *names* is an instance of an array object. To find out the number of items in that array, you access that array's *length* property using dot notation:

```
names.length
```

Likewise, you can add an item to the end of that array by using the array object's *push( )* method like this (see page 61 for a refresher on array methods):

```
names.push('Ace');
```

Whenever you create a new variable and store a value into it, you're really creating a new instance of a particular type of object. So each of these lines of JavaScript create different types of JavaScript objects:

```
var first_name = 'Bob'; // a string object
var age = 32; // a number object
var valid = false; // a Boolean object
var data = ['Julia', 22, true]; // an array object composed of other objects
```

In fact, when you change the type of information stored in a variable, you change the type of object it is as well. For example, if you create a variable named *data* that stores an array, then store a number in the variable, you've changed that variable's type from an array to a number object:

```
var data = ['Julia', 22, true]; // an array object composed of other objects
data = 32; //changes to number object
```

The concepts of objects, properties, methods, and dot-syntax may seem a little weird at first glance. However, since they are a fundamental part of how JavaScript works, you'll get used to them pretty quickly.

Tip: As you continue reading this book, keep in mind these few facts:

- The world of JavaScript is populated with lots of different types of objects.
- Each object has its own properties and methods.
- You access an object's property or activate an object's method using dot-syntax: *document.write( )*, for example.

Strings

Strings are the most common type of data you'll work with: input from form fields, the path to an image, a URL, and HTML that you wish to replace on a page are all examples of the letters, symbols, and numbers that make up strings. Consequently, JavaScript provides lot of methods for working with and manipulating strings.

Determining the Length of a String

There are times when you want to know how many characters are in a string. For example, say you want to make sure that when someone creates an account on your top secret Web site, they create a new password that's more than 6 letters but no more than 15. Strings have a *length* property that gives you just this kind of information. Add a period after the name of the variable, followed by *length* to get the number of characters in the string: *name.length*.

For example, to make sure a password has the proper number of characters, you could use a conditional statement to test the password's length like this:

```
var password = 'sesame';
if (password.length <= 6) {
  alert('That password is too short.');
} else if (password.length > 15) {
  alert('That password is too long.');
}
```

Note: In the above example, the password is just directly assigned to the variable *var password = 'sesame'*. In a real world scenario, you'd get the password from a form field, as described on page 312.

Changing the Case of a String

JavaScript provides two methods to convert strings to all uppercase or all lowercase, so you can change 'hello' to 'HELLO' or 'NOT' to 'not'. Why, you might ask? Converting letters in a string to the same case makes comparing two strings easier. For example, say you created a Quiz program like the one from last chapter (see page 106) and one of the questions is "Who was the first American to win the Tour De France?" You might have some code like this to check the quiz-taker's answer:

```
var correctAnswer = 'Greg LeMond';
var response = prompt('Who was the first American to win the Tour De↵
France?', '');
if (response == correctAnswer) {
  // correct
} else {
  // incorrect
}
```

The answer is Greg LeMond, but what if the person taking the quiz typed Greg Lemond? The condition would look like this: 'Greg Lemond' == 'Greg LeMond'. Since JavaScript treats uppercase letters as different than lowercase letters, the lowercase 'm' in Lemond wouldn't match the 'M' in LeMond, so the quiz-taker would have gotten this question wrong. The same would happen if her key-caps key was down and she typed GREG LEMOND.

To get around this difficulty, you can convert both strings to the same case and then compare them:

```
if (response.toUpperCase() == correctAnswer.toUpperCase()) {
  // correct
} else {
  // incorrect
}
```

In this case, the conditional statement converts both the quiz-taker's answer and the correct answer to uppercase, so 'Greg Lemond' becomes 'GREG LEMOND' and 'Greg LeMond' becomes 'GREG LEMOND'.

To get the string all lowercase, use the *toLowerCase( )* method like this:

```
var answer = 'Greg LeMond';
alert(answer.toLowerCase()); // 'greg lemond'
```

Note that neither of these methods actually alters the original string stored in the variable—they just return that string in either all uppercase or all lowercase. So in the above example, *answer* still contains 'Greg LeMond' even after the alert appears. (In other words, these methods work just like a function that returns some other value as described on page 102.)

Searching a String: *indexOf( )* Technique

JavaScript provides several techniques for searching for a word, number, or other series of characters inside a string. Searching can come in handy, for example, if you want to know which Web browser a visitor is using to view your Web site. Every Web browser identifies information about itself in a string containing a lot of different statistics. You can see that string for yourself by adding this bit of JavaScript to a page and previewing it in a Web browser:

```
<script type="text/javascript">
alert(navigator.userAgent);
</script>
```

Navigator is one of a Web browser's objects, and *userAgent* is a property of the navigator object. The *userAgent* property contains a long string of information; for example, on Internet Explorer 7 running on Windows XP, the *userAgent* property is: Mozilla/4.0 (compatible; MSIE 7.0; Windows NT 5.1). So, if you want to see if the Web browser was IE 7, you can just search the *userAgent* string for "MSIE 7".

One method of searching a string is the *indexOf( )* method. Basically, after the string you add a period, *indexOf( )* and supply the string you're looking for. The basic structure looks like this:

```
string.indexOf('string to look for')
```

The *indexOf( )* method returns a number: if the search string isn't found, the method returns −1. So if you want to check for Internet Explorer, you can do this:

```
var browser = navigator.userAgent; // this is a string
if (browser.indexOf('MSIE') != -1) {
  // this is Internet Explorer
}
```

In this case, if *indexOf( )* doesn't locate the string 'MSIE' in the *userAgent* string, it will return −1, so the condition tests to see if the result is not (*!=*) −1.

When the *indexOf( )* method *does* find the searched for string, it returns a number that's equal to the starting position of the searched for string. The following example makes things a lot clearer:

```
var quote = 'To be, or not to be.'
var searchPosition = quote.indexOf('To be'); // returns 0
```

Here, *indexOf( )*searches for the position of 'To be' inside the string 'To be, or not to be.' The larger string begins with 'To be', so *indexOf( )* finds 'To be' at the first position. But in the wacky way of programming, the first position is considered 0, the second letter (o) is at position 1, and the third letter (a space in this case) is 2 (as explained on page 59, arrays are counted in the same way).

The *indexOf( )* method searches from the beginning of the string. You can also search from the end of the string by using the *lastIndexOf( )* method. For example, in the Shakespeare quote, the word 'be' appears in two places, so you can locate the first 'be' using *indexOf( )* and the last 'be' with *lastIndexOf( )*:

```
var quote = "To be, or not to be."
var firstPosition = quote.indexOf('be'); // returns 3
var lastPosition = quote.lastIndexOf('be'); // returns 17
```

The results of those two methods are pictured in Figure 4-1. In both cases, if 'be' didn't exist anywhere in the string, the result would be −1, and if there's only one instance of the searched-for word, *indexOf( )* and *lastIndexOf( )* will return the same value—the starting position of the searched for string within the larger string.

Extracting Part of a String with *slice( )*

To extract part of a string, use the *slice( )* method. This method returns a portion of a string. For example, say you had a string like "http://www.sawmac.com" and

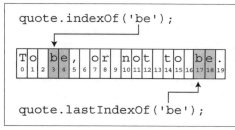

Figure 4-1:
The indexOf( ) *and* lastIndexOf( ) *methods search for a particular string inside a larger string. If the search string is found, its position in the larger string is returned.*

you wanted to eliminate the http:// part. One way to do this is to extract every character in the string that follows the http:// like this:

```
var url = 'http://www.sawmac.com';
var domain = url.slice(7); // www.sawmac.com
```

The *slice( )* method requires a *number* that indicates the starting *index* position for the extracted string (see Figure 4-2). In this example—*url.slice(7)*—the 7 indicates the eighth letter in the string (remember, the first letter is at position 0). The method returns all of the characters starting at the specified index position to the end of the string.

Figure 4-2:
If you don't supply a second argument to the slice( ) *method, it just extracts a string from the specified position (7 in this example) all the way to the end of the string.*

You can also extract a specific number of characters within a string by supplying a second argument to the *slice( )* method. Here's the basic structure of the *slice( )* method:

```
string.slice(start, end);
```

The *start* value is a number that indicates the first character of the extracted string; the end *value* is a little confusing—it's not the position of the last letter of the extracted string; it's actually the position of the last letter + 1. For example, if you wanted to extract the first five letters of the string 'To be, or not to be.', you would specify 0 as the first argument, and 5 as the second argument. As you can see in Figure 4-3, 0 is the first letter in the string, and 5 is the sixth letter, but the last letter specified is not extracted from the string. In other words, the character specified by the second argument is *never* part of the extracted string.

Tip: If you want to extract a specific number of characters from a string, just add that number to the starting value. For example, if you want to retrieve the first 10 letters of a string, the first argument would be 0 (the first letter) and the last would be 0 + 10 or just 10: *slice(0,10)*.

You can also specify negative numbers, for example *quote.slice(-6,-1)*. A negative number counts backwards from the end of the string, as pictured in Figure 4-3.

CHAPTER 4: WORKING WITH WORDS, NUMBERS, AND DATES

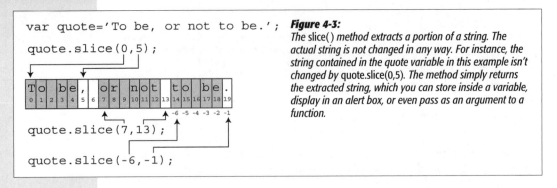

Figure 4-3:
The slice( ) method extracts a portion of a string. The actual string is not changed in any way. For instance, the string contained in the quote variable in this example isn't changed by quote.slice(0,5). The method simply returns the extracted string, which you can store inside a variable, display in an alert box, or even pass as an argument to a function.

Tip: If you want, say, to extract a string that includes all of the letters from the 6th letter from the end of the string all the way to the end, you leave off the second argument:

```
quote.slice(-6);
```

Finding Patterns in Strings

Sometimes you wish to search a string, not for an exact value, but for a specific pattern of characters. For example, say you want to make sure when a visitor fills out an order form, he supplies a phone number in the correct format. You're not actually looking for a specific phone number like 503-555-0212. Instead you're looking for a general pattern: 3 numbers, a hyphen, three numbers, another hyphen, and four numbers. You'd like to check the value the visitor entered, and if it matches the pattern (for example, it's 415-555-3843, 408-555-3782, or 212-555-4828, and so on) then everything's OK. But if it doesn't match that pattern (for example, the visitor typed 823lkjxdfglkj) then you'd like to post a message like "Hey buddy, don't try to fool us!"

JavaScript lets you use *regular expressions* to find patterns within a string. A regular expression is a series of characters that define a pattern that you wish to search for. As with many programming terms, the name "regular expression" is a bit misleading. For example, here's what a common regular expression looks like:

```
/^[-\w.]+@([a-zA-Z0-9][-a-zA-Z0-9]+\.)+[a-zA-Z]{2,4}$/
```

Unless you're a super-alien from Omicron 9, there's nothing very *regular*-looking about a regular expression. To create a pattern you use characters like *, +, ?, and \ *w*, which are translated by the JavaScript interpreter to match real characters in a string like letters, numbers, and so on.

Note: Pros often shorten the name regular expression to *regex*.

Creating and Using a Basic Regular Expression

To create a regular expression in JavaScript, you must create a regular expression object, which is a series of characters between two forward slashes. For example, to create a regular expression that matches the word 'hello', you'd type this:

```
var myMatch = /hello/;
```

Just as an opening and closing quote mark creates a string, the opening / and closing / create a regular expression.

There are several string methods that take advantage of regular expressions (you'll learn about them starting on page 131), but the most basic method is the *search( )* method. It works very much like the *indexOf( )* method, but instead of trying to find one string inside another, larger string, it searches for a pattern (a regular expression) inside a string. For example, say you want to find 'To be' inside the string 'To be or not to be.' You saw how to do that with the *indexOf( )* method on page 117, but here's how you can do the same thing with a regular expression:

```
var myRegEx = /To be/; // no quotes around regular expression
var quote = 'To be or not to be.';
var foundPosition = quote.search(myRegEx);  // returns 0
```

If the *search( )* method finds a match, it returns the position of the first letter matched, and if it doesn't find a match, it returns –1. So in the above example, the variable *foundPosition* is 0, since 'To be' begins at the very beginning (the first letter) of the string.

As you'll recall from page 117, *indexOf( )* method works in the same way. You might be thinking that if the two methods are the same, why bother with regular expressions? The benefit of regular expressions is that they can find patterns in a string, so they can make much more complicated and subtle comparisons than the *indexOf( )* method, which always looks for a match to an exact string. For example, you could use the *indexOf( )* method to find out if a string contains the Web address *http://www.missingmanuals.com/*, but you'd have to use a regular expression to find any text that matches the format of a URL—exactly the kind of thing you want to do when verifying if someone supplied a Web address when posting a comment to your blog.

However, to master regular expressions, you need to learn the often confusing symbols required to construct a regular expression.

Building a Regular Expression

While a regular expression can be made up of a word or words, more often you'll use a combination of letters and special symbols to define a pattern that you hope to match. Regular expressions provide different symbols to indicate different types of characters. For example, a single period (.) represents a single character, any character, while \w matches any letter or number (but not spaces, or symbols like $ or %). Table 4-3 provides a list of the most common pattern-matching characters.

Note: If this entire discussion of "regular" expressions is making your head hurt, you'll be glad to know this book provides some useful regular expressions (see page 126) that you can copy and use in your own scripts (without really knowing how they work).

Learning regular expressions is a topic better presented by example, so the rest of this section walks you through a few examples of regular expressions to help you wrap your mind around this topic. Assume you want to match five numbers in a row—perhaps to check if there's a U. S. Zip code in a string:

1. **Match one number.**

   The first step is simply to figure out how to match one number. If you refer to Table 4-3, you'll see that there's a special regex symbol for this, \d, which matches any single number.

2. **Match five numbers in a row.**

   Since \d matches a single number, a simple way to match five numbers is with this regular expression: \d\d\d\d\d. (Page 124, however, covers a more compact way to write this.)

3. **Match only five numbers.**

   A regular expression is like a precision-guided missile: It sets its target on the first part of a string that it matches. So, you sometimes end up with a match that's part of a complete word or set of characters. This regular expression matches the first five numbers in a row that it encounters. For example, it will match 12345 in the number 12345678998. Obviously, 12345678998 isn't a Zip code, so you need a regex that targets just five numbers.

   The \b character (called the *word boundary* character) matches any nonletter or nonnumber character, so you could rewrite your regular expression like this: \b\d\d\d\d\d\b. You can also use the ^ character to match the beginning of a string and the $ character to match the end of a string. This trick comes in handy if you want the entire string to match your regular expression. For example, if someone typed "kjasdflkjsdf 88888 lksadflkjsdkfjl" in a Zip code field on an order form, you might want to ask the visitor to clarify (and fix) their Zip code before ordering. After all, you're really looking for something like 97213 (with no other characters in the string). In this case, the regex would be ^\d\d\d\d\d$.

Note: Zip codes can have more than five numbers. The ZIP + 4 format includes a dash and four additional numbers after the first five, like this: 97213-1234. For a regular expression to handle this possibility, see page 126.

---

4. **Put your regex into action in JavaScript.**

Assume you've already captured a user's input into a variable named *zip*, and you want to test to see if the input is in the form of a valid five-number Zip code:

```
var zipTest = /^\d\d\d\d\d$/; //create regex
if (zip.search(zipTest) == -1) {
  alert('This is not a valid zip code');
} else {
  // is valid format
}
```

Table 4-3.

Character	Matches
.	Any one character—will match a letter, number, space, or other symbol
\w	Any word character including a–z, A–Z, the numbers 0–9, and the underscore character: _.
\W	Any character that's not a word character. It's the exact opposite of \w.
\d	Any digit 0–9.
\D	Any character except a digit. The opposite of \d.
\s	A space, tab, carriage return, or new line.
\S	Anything but a space, tab, carriage return, or new line.
^	The beginning of a string. This is useful for making sure no other characters come before whatever you're trying to match.
$	The end of a string. Use $ to make sure the characters you wish to match are at the end of a string. For example, /com$/ matches the string "com", but only when it's the last three letters of the string. In other words, /com$/ would match "com" in the string "Infocom," but not 'com' in 'communication'.
\b	A space, beginning of the string, end of string, or any nonletter or number character such as +, =, or '. Use \b to match the beginning or ending of a word, even if that word is at the beginning or ending of a string.
[ ]	Any one character between the brackets. For example, [aeiou] matches any one of those letters in a string. For a range of characters, use a hyphen: [a-z] matches any one lower case letter; [0-9] matches any one number (the same as \d.)
[^]	Any character except one in brackets. For example, [^aeiouAEIOU] will match any character that isn't a vowel. [^0-9] matches any character that's not a number (the same as \d).
|	Either the characters before or after the | character. For example, a|b will match either *a* or *b*, but not both. (See page 130 for an example of this symbol in action.)
\	Used to escape any special regex symbol (*,.,\,/, for instance) to search for a literal example of the symbol in a string. For example, . in regex-speak means "any character," but if you want to really match a period in a string you need to escape it, like this: \. .

The regex example in these steps works, but it seems like a lot of work to type \d five times. What if you want to match 100 numbers in a row? Fortunately, JavaScript includes several symbols that can match multiple occurrences of the same character. Table 4-4 includes a list of these symbols. You place the symbol directly *after* the character you wish to match.

For example, to match five numbers, you can write \d{5}. The \d matches one number, then the {5} tells the JavaScript interpreter to match five numbers. So \d{100} would match 100 digits in a row.

Let's go through another example. Say you wanted to find the name of any GIF file in a string. In addition, you want to extract the file name and perhaps use it somehow in your script (for example, you can use the *match( )* method described on page 131). In other words, you want to find any string that matches the basic pattern of a GIF file name, such as *logo.gif, banner.gif* or *ad.gif*.

1. **Identify the common pattern between these names.**

   To build a regular expression, you first need to know what pattern of characters you're searching for. Here, since you're after GIFs, you know all the file names will end in .gif. In other words, there can be any number of letters or numbers or other characters before .gif.

2. **Find .gif.**

   Since you're after the literal string '.gif', you might think that part of the regular expression would just be *.gif*. However, if you check out Table 4-3, you'll see that a period has special meaning as a "match any character" character. So *.gif* would match ".gif," but it would also match "tgif." A period matches any single character so in addition to matching a period, it will also match the "t" in tgif. To create a regex with a literal period, add a slash before it; so \. translates to "find me the period symbol". So the regex to find .gif would be \.*gif*.

3. **Find any number of characters before .gif.**

   To find any number of characters, you can use .*, which translates to "find one character (.) zero or more times (*)." That regular expression matches all of the letters in any string. However, if you used that to create a regular expression like .*\.*gif*, you could end up matching more than just a file name. For example, if you have the string 'the file is logo.gif', the regex .*\.*gif* will match the entire string, when what you really want is just logo.gif. To do that, use the \S character, which matches any nonspace character: \S*\.*gif* matches just logo.gif in the string.

4. **Make the search case-insensitive.**

   There's one more wrinkle in this regular expression: it only finds files that end in .gif, but .GIF is also a valid file extension, so this regex wouldn't pick up on a name like logo.GIF. To make a regular expression ignore the difference between upper and lowercase letters, you use the *i* argument when you create the regular expression:

```
/\S*\.gif/i
```

Notice that the *i* goes outside of the pattern and to the right of the / that defines the end of the regular expression pattern.

5. **Put it into action:**

```
var testString = 'The file is logo.gif'; // the string to test
var gifRegex = /\S*\.gif/i; // the regular expression
var results = testString.match(gifRegex);
var file = results[0]; // logo.gif
```

This code pulls out the file name from the string. (You'll learn how the *match( )* method works on page 131.)

Grouping Parts of a Pattern

You can use parentheses to create a subgroup within a pattern. Subgroups come in very handy when using any of the characters in Table 4-4 to match multiple instances of the same pattern.

Table 4-4. Characters used for matching multiple occurrences of the same character or pattern

Character	Matches
?	Zero or one occurrences of the previous item, meaning the previous item is optional, but if it does appear, it can only appear once. For example the regex *colou?r* will match both "color" and "colour," but not "colouur."
+	One or more occurrences of the previous item. The previous item must appear at least once.
*	Zero or more occurrences of the previous item. The previous item is optional and may appear any number of times. For example, .* matches any number of characters.
{n}	An exact number of occurrences of the previous item. For example \d{3} only matches three numbers in a row.
{n, }	The previous item *n* or more times. For example, a{2,} will match the letter "a" two or more times: that would match "aa" in the word "aardvark" and "aaaa" in the word "aaaahhhh."
{n,m}	The previous item at least *n* times but no more than *m* times. So \d{3,4} will match three or four numbers in a row (but not two numbers in a row, nor five numbers in a row).

For example, say you want to see if a string contains either "Apr" or "April"—both of those begin with "Apr," so you know that you want to match that, but you can't just match "Apr," since you'd also match the "Apr" in "Apricot" or "Aprimecorp." So, you must match "Apr" followed by a space or other word ending (that's the \b regular expression character described in Table 4-3) or April followed by a word ending. In other words, the "il" is optional. Here's how you could do that using parentheses:

```
var sentence = 'April is the cruelest month.';
var aprMatch = /Apr(il)?\b/;
if (sentence.search(aprMatch) != -1) {
  // found Apr or April
} else {
  //not found
}
```

The regular expression used here—/Apr(il)?\b/—makes the "Apr" required, but the subpattern—(il)—optional (that ? character means zero or one time). Finally, the \b matches the end of a word, so you won't match "Apricot" or "Aprilshowers." (See the box on page 133 for another use of subpatterns.)

Tip: You can find a completely library of regular expressions at *www.regexlib.com*. At this Web site, you'll find a regular expression for any situation.

Useful Regular Expressions

Creating a regular expression has its challenges. Not only do you need to understand how the different regular expression characters work, but you then must figure out the proper pattern for different possible searches. For example, if you want to find a match for a Zip code, you need to take into account the fact that a Zip code may be just five numbers (97213) or 5+4 (97213-3333). To get you started on the path to using regular expressions, here are a few common ones.

Note: If you don't feel like typing these regular expressions (and who could blame you), you'll find them already set up for you in a file named *example_regex.txt* in the *chapter04* folder that's part of the tutorial download. (See page 27 for information on downloading the tutorial files.)

U.S. Zip code

Postal codes vary from country to country, but in the United States they appear as either five numbers, or five numbers followed by a hyphen and four numbers. Here's the regex that matches both those options:

```
\d{5}(-\d{4})?
```

Tip: For regular expressions that match the postal codes of other countries visit *http://regexlib.com/Search.aspx?k=postal+code*.

That regular expression breaks down into the following smaller pieces:

• \d{5} matches five digits, as in 97213.

- *( )* creates a subpattern. Everything between the parentheses is considered a single pattern to be matched. You'll see why that's important in a moment.

- *-\d{4}* matches the hyphen followed by four digits, like this: -1234.

- *?* matches zero or one instance of the preceding pattern. Here's where the parentheses come in: *(-\d{4})* is treated as a single unit, so the *?* means match zero or one instance of a hyphen followed by four digits. Because you don't have to include the hyphen + four, that pattern might appear zero times. In other words, if you're testing a value like 97213, you'll still get a match because the hyphen followed by four digits is optional.

Tip: To make sure an entire string matches a regular expression, begin the regex with ^ and end it with $. For example, if you want to make sure that someone only typed a validly formatted Zip code into a Zip code form field, use the regex ^\d{5}(-\d{4})?$. to prevent a response like "blah 97213 blah blah."

U.S. phone number

U.S. phone numbers have a three-digit area code followed by seven more digits. However, people write phone numbers in many different ways, like 503-555-1212, (503) 555-1212, 503.555.1212, or just 503 555 1212. A regex for this pattern is:

    \(?(\d{3})\)?[-.](\d{3})[-.](\d{4})

Tip: For regular expressions that match the phone number format of other countries, visit *http://regexlib. com/Search.aspx?k=phone+number*.

This regex looks pretty complicated, but if you break it down (and have a good translation like the following) it comes out making sense:

- *\(* matches a literal opening parenthesis character. Because parentheses are used to group patterns (see the Zip code example previously), the opening parentheses has special meaning in regular expressions. To tell the JavaScript interpreter to match an actual opening parenthesis, you need to escape the character (just like escaping the quotes discussed on page 42) with the forward slash character.

- *?* indicates that the *(* character is optional, so a phone number without parentheses like 503-555-1212 will still match.

- *(\d{3})* is a subpattern that matches any three digits.

- *\)?* matches an optional closing parenthesis.

- *[-.]* will match either a space, hyphen, or period. (Note that normally you have to escape a period like this \. in order to tell the JavaScript interpreter that you want to match the period character and not treat it as the special regular expression symbol that matches *any* character; however, when inside brackets, a period is always treated literally.)

- *(\d{3})* is another subpattern that matches any three digits.

- *[-.]* will match either a space, hyphen or period.

- *(\d{4})* is the last subpattern, and it matches any four digits.

Note: Subpatterns are patterns that appear inside parentheses, as in *(\d{3})* in the phone number regular expression above. They come in very handy when you use the *replace( )*, method as described in the box on page 133.

Email address

Checking for a valid email address is a common chore when accepting user input from a form. A lot of people try to get away without trying to provide a valid email using a response like "none of your business," or people just mistype their email address (*missing@sawmac.commm* for example). The following regex can check to see if a string contains a properly formatted email address:

```
[-\w.]+@([A-z0-9][-A-z0-9]+\.)+[A-z]{2,4}
```

Note: This regex doesn't check to see if an address is somebody's real, working email address, it just checks that it's *formatted* like a real email address.

This regex breaks down like this:

- *[-\w.]+* matches a hyphen, any word character, or a period one or more times. So it will match "bob," "bob.smith," or "bob-smith."

- *@* is the @ sign you find in an email address: *missing@sawmac.com*.

- *[A-z0-9]* matches one letter or number.

- *[-A-z0-9]+* matches one or more instances of a letter, number, or hyphen.

- *\.* is a period character so it would match the period in *sawmac.com*.

- *+* matches one or more instances of the pattern that includes the above three matches. This character allows for subdomain names like *bob@mail.sawmac.com*.

- *[A-z]{2,4}* is any letter 2, 3, or 4 times. This matches the com in .com, or uk in .uk.

Note: The email regex listed above doesn't match *all* technically valid email addresses. For example, *!#$%&'*+-/=?^_`{|}~-@example.com* is technically a valid email address, but the regex described here won't match it. It's designed to find email addresses that people would actually use. If you really want to be accurate, you can use the following regex. Type this expression on a single line:

```
/^[\w!#$%&\'*+\/=?^`{|}~.-]+@(?:[a-z\d][a-z\d-]*(?:\.[a-z\d][a-z\d-]*)?)+\.
(?:[a-z][a-z\d-]+)$/i
```

Date

A date can be written in many different ways; for example, 09/28/2008, 9-28-2007, 09 28 2007, or even 09.28.2007. (And those are just formats for the United States. In other part of the world, the day appears before the month like 28.09.2007.) Because your visitors may enter a date in any one of these formats, you need a way to check to see if they supplied a validly formatted date. (In the box on page 133, you'll learn how to convert any of these formats into a single, standard format, so that you can make sure all the dates you receive on a form are formatted correctly.)

Here's the regex that checks for a correctly entered date:

```
([01]?\d)[-\/ .]([0123]?\d)[-\/ .](\d{4})
```

- *( )* surrounds the next two regex patterns to group them. Together they form the number for the month.

- *[01]?* matches either 0 or 1 and the ? makes this optional. This is for the first number in a month. Obviously it can't be bigger than 1—there's no 22 month. In addition, if the month is January through September, you might just get 5 instead of 05. That's why it's optional.

- *\d* matches any number.

- *[-\/ .]* will match a hyphen, a backslash, a period, or a space character. These are the acceptable separators between the month and day, like 10/21, 10 21, 10.21, or 10-21.

- *( )* is the next subpattern, which is meant to capture the day of the month.

- *[0123]?* matches either 0, 1, 2, or 3 zero or more times. Since there's no 40th day of the month, you limit the first number of the month to one of these four digits. This pattern is optional (as determined by the ? character), because someone might just type 9 instead of 09 for the ninth day of the month.

- *\d* matches any digit.

- *[-\/ .]* is the same as above.

- *( )* captures the year.

- *\d{4}* matches any four digits, like 1908 or 2880.

Web address

Matching a Web address is useful if you're asking a visitor for his Web site address and you want to make sure he's supplied one, or if you want to scan some text and identify every URL listed. A basic regular expression for URLs is:

```
((\bhttps?:\/\/)|(\bwww\.))\S*
```

This expression is a little tricky because it uses lots of parentheses to group different parts of the expression. Figure 4-4 can help guide you through this regular

---

expression. One set of parentheses (labeled 1) wraps around two other parenthetical groups (2 and 3). The | character between the two groups represents "or". In other words, the regular expression needs to match either 2 or 3.

- *(* is the start of the outer group (1 in Figure 4-4).

- *(* is the start of inner group (2 in Figure 4-4).

- *\b* matches the beginning of a word.

- *http* matches the beginning of a complete Web address that begins with *http*.

- *s?* is an optional *s*. Since a Web page may be sent via a secure connection, a valid Web address may also begin with *https*.

- *:\/\/* matches *://*. Since the forward slash has meaning in regular expressions, you need to precede it by a backslash to match the forward slash character.

- *)* is the end of the inner group (2 in Figure 4-4). Taken all together, this group will match either *http://* or *https://*.

- *|* matches either one or the other group (2 or 3 in Figure 4-4).

- *(* is the start of second inner group (3 in Figure 4-4).

- *\b* matches the beginning of a word.

- *www\.* matches *www.*.

- *)* is the end of the second inner group (3 in Figure 4-4). This group will capture a URL that is missing the *http://* but begins with *www*.

- *)* is the end of the outer group (1 in Figure 4-4). At this point, the regular expression will match text that begins with *http://*, *https://*, or *www*.

- *\S** matches zero or more nonspace characters.

This expression isn't foolproof (for example, it would match a nonsensical URL like http://#$*%&*@*), but it's relatively simple, and will successfully match real URLs like *http://www.sawmac.com/missing/js/index.html*.

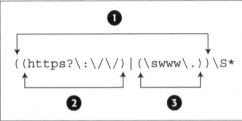

Figure 4-4:
You can group expressions using parentheses and look for either one of two expressions by using the | (pipe) character. For example, the outer expression (1) will match any text that matches either 2 or 3.

Tip: To see if a string only contains a URL (nothing comes before or after the URL), use the ^ and $ characters at the beginning and end of the regular expression and remove the *\b* characters: *^((https?:\/\/)|(www\.))\S*$*.

Matching a Pattern

The *search( )* method described on page 121 is one way to see if a string contains a particular regular expression pattern. The *match( )* method is another. You can use it with a string to not only see if a pattern exists within the string, but to also capture that pattern so that you can use it later in your script. For example, say you have a text area field on a form for a visitor to add a comment to your site. Perhaps you want to check if the comments include a URL, and if so, get the URL for further processing.

The following code finds and captures a URL using *match( )*:

```
// create a variable containing a string with a URL
var text='my web site is www.missingmanuals.com';
// create a regular expression
var urlRegex = /((\bhttps?:\/\/)|(\bwww\.))\S*/
// find a match for the regular expression in the string
var url = text.match(urlRegex);
alert(url[0]); // www.missingmanuals.com
```

First, the code creates a variable containing a string that includes the URL *www. missingmanuals.com*. Next, a regular expression matches a URL (see page 129 for the details on this regex). Finally, it runs the *match( )* method on the string. The *match( )* function is a string method, so you start with the name of a variable containing a string, add a period, followed by *match( )*. You pass the *match( )* method a regular expression to match.

In the above example, the variable *url* holds the results of the match. If the regular expression pattern isn't found in the string, then the result is a special JavaScript value called *null*. If there is a match, the script returns an array—the first value of the array is the matched text. For instance, in this example, the variable *url* contains an array, with the first array element being the matched text. In this case, *url[0]* contains *www.missingmanuals.com* (see page 56 for more on arrays).

Tip: In JavaScript, a *null* value is treated the same as false, so you could test to see if the *match( )* method actually matched something like this:

```
var url = text.match(urlRegex);
if (! url) {
  //no match
} else {
  //match
}
```

Matching every instance of a pattern

The *match( )* method works in two different ways, depending on how you've set up your regular expression. In the above example, the method returns an array with the first matched text. So, if you had a long string containing multiple URLs, only the first URL is found. However, you can also turn on a regular expression's *global* search property to search for more than one match in a string.

You make a search global by adding a *g* at the end of a regular expression when you create it (just like the *i* used for a case-insensitive search, as discussed on page 125):

```
var urlRegex = /((\bhttps?:\/\/)|(\bwww\.))\S*/g
```

Notice that the *g* goes outside of the ending / (which is used to enclose the actual pattern). This regular expression performs a global search; when used with the *match( )* method, it searches for every match within the string and will return an array of all matched text—a great way to find every URL in a blog entry, for example, or every instance of a word in a long block of text.

You could rewrite the code from page 131 using a global search, like this:

```
// create a variable containing a string with a URL
var text='there are a lot of great web sites like ↵
         www.missingmanuals.com and http://www.oreilly.com';
// create a regular expression with global search
var urlRegex = /((\bhttps?:\/\/)|(\bwww\.))\S*/g
// find a match for the regular expression in the string
var url = text.match(urlRegex);
alert(url[0]);
alert(url[1]); // http://www.oreilly.com
```

You can determine the number of matches by accessing the *length* property of the resulting array: *url.length*. This example will return the number 2, since two URLs were found in the tested string. In addition, you access each matched string by using the array's index number (as described on page 59); so in this example, *url[0]* is the first match and *url[1]* is the second.

Replacing Text

You can also use regular expression to replace text within a string. For example, say you have a string that contains a date formatted like this: 10.28.2008. However, you want the date to be formatted like this: 10/28/2008. The *replace( )* method can do that. It takes this form:

```
string.replace(regex,'replace');
```

The *replace( )* method takes two arguments: the first is a regular expression that you wish to find in the string; the second is a string that replaces any matches to the regular expression. So, to change the format of 10.28.2008 to 10/28/2008, you could do this:

```
1   var date='10.28.2008'; // a string
2   var replaceRegex = /\./g // a regular expression
3   var date = date.replace(replaceRegex, '/'); // replace . with /
4   alert(date); // 10/28/2008
```

Line 1 creates a variable and stores the string '10.28.2008' in it. In a real program, this string could be input from a form. Line 2 creates the regular expression: the / and / marks the beginning and end of the regular expression pattern; the \. indicates a literal period; and the *g* means a global replace—every instance of the period will be replaced. If you left out the *g*, only the first matched period would be replaced, and you'd end up with '10 /28.2008'. Line 3 performs the actual replacement—changing each . to a /, and stores the result back into the date variable. Finally the newly formed date—10/28/2008—is displayed in an alert box.

POWER USERS' CLINIC

Using Subpatterns to Replace Text

The *replace( )* method not only can replace matched text (like the . in 10.28.2008) with another string (like /), but it can also remember *subpatterns* within a regular expression and use those subpatterns when replacing text. As explained in the Note on page 128, a subpattern is any part of a regular expression enclosed in parentheses. For example the *(il)* in the regular expression */Apr(il)?\b/* is a subpattern.

The use of the *replace( )* method demonstrated on page 132 changes 10.28.2008 to 10/27/2008. But what if you also want to put other formatted dates like 10 28 2008 or 10-28-2008 into the same 10/27/2008 format? Instead of writing multiple lines of JavaScript code to replace periods, spaces, and hyphens, you can create a general pattern to match any of these formats:

```
var date='10-28-2008';
var regex = /([01]?\d)[-\/ .]([0123]?\d)[-
\/ .](\d{4})/;
date = date.replace(regex, '$1/$2/$3');
```

This example uses the regular expression described on page 129 to match a date. Notice the groups of patterns within parentheses—for example, *([01]?\d)*. Each subpattern matches one part of the date. The *replace( )* method remembers matches to those subpatterns, and can use them as part of the replacement string. In this case, the replacement string is *'$1/$2/$3'*. A dollar sign followed by a number represents one of the matched subpatterns. $1, for example, matches the first subpattern—the month. So this replacement string translates to "put the first subpattern here, followed by a /, followed by the second subpattern match, followed by another /, and finally followed by the last subpattern."

Trying Out Regular Expressions

As mentioned on page 126, you'll find sample regular expressions in the *example_ regex.txt* file that accompanies the Chapter 4 tutorial files. In addition, you'll find a file named *regex_tester.html*. You can open this Web page in a browser and try your hand at creating your own regular expressions (see Figure 4-5). Just type the string you'd like to search in the "String to Search" box, and then type a regular expression in the box (leave out the beginning and ending / marks used when creating a regex in JavaScript and just type the search pattern). You can then select the method you'd like to use—Search, Match, or Replace—and any options, like case-insensitivity or global search. Click the Run button and see how your regex works.

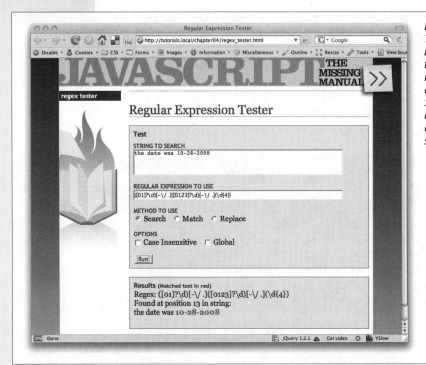

Figure 4-5:
This sample page, included with the tutorial files, lets you test out regular expressions using different methods—like Search or Match—and try different options such as case-insensitive or global searches.

Numbers

Numbers are an important part of programming. They let you perform tasks like calculating a total sales cost, determining the distance between two points, or simulating the roll of a die by generating a random number from 1 to 6. JavaScript gives you many different ways of working with numbers.

Changing a String to a Number

When you create a variable, you can store a number in it like this:

```
var a = 3.25;
```

However, there are times when a number is actually a string. For example, if you use the *prompt( )* method (page 55) to get visitor input, even if someone types 3.25, you'll end up with a string that contains a number. In other words, the result will be '3.25' (a string) and not 3.25 (a number). Frequently, this method doesn't cause a problem, since the JavaScript interpreter usually converts a string to a number when it seems like a number is called for. For example:

```
var a = '3';
var b = '4';
alert(a*b); // 12
```

In this example, even though the variables *a* and *b* are both strings, the JavaScript interpreter converts them to numbers to perform the multiplication (3×4) and return the result: 12.

However, when you use the + operator, the JavaScript interpreter won't make that conversion, and you can end up with some strange results:

```
var a = '3';
var b = '4';
alert(a+b); // 34
```

In this case, both *a* and *b* are strings; the + operator not only does mathematical addition, it also combines (concatenates) two strings together (see page 49). So instead of adding 3 and 4 to get 7, in this example, you end up with two strings fused together: 34.

When you need to convert a string to a number, JavaScript provides several ways:

• *Number( )* converts whatever string is passed to it into a number, like this:

```
var a = '3';
a = Number(a); // a is now the number 3
```

So the problem of adding two strings that contain numbers could be fixed like this:

```
var a = '3';
var b = '4';
var total = Number(a) + Number(b); // 7
```

A faster technique is the + operator, which does the same thing as *Number( )*. Just add a + in front of a variable containing a string, and the JavaScript interpreter converts the string to a number.

```
var a = '3';
var b = '4';
var total = +a + +b // 7
```

The downside of either of these two techniques is that if the string contains anything except numbers, a single period or a + or − sign at the beginning of the string, you'll end up with a nonnumber, or the JavaScript value *NaN*, which means "not a number" (see page 50).

• *parseInt( )* tries to convert a string to a number as well. However, unlike *Number( )*, *parseInt( )* will try to change even a string with letters to a number, as long as the string begins with numbers. This command can come in handy when you get a string like '20 years' as the response to a question about someone's age:

```
var age = '20 years';
age = parseInt(age,10); //20
```

The *parseInt( )* method looks for either a number or a + or – sign at the beginning of the string and continues to look for numbers until it encounters a non-number. So in the above example, it returns the number 20 and ignores the other part of the string, ' years'.

Note: You're probably wondering what the 10 is doing in *parseInt(age,10);*. JavaScript can handle Octal numbers (which are based on 8 different digits 0-7, unlike decimal numbers which are based on 10 different digits 0-9); when you add the *,10* to *parseInt( )*, you're telling the JavaScript interpreter to treat whatever the input is as a decimal number. That way, JavaScript correctly interprets a string like '08' in a prompt window or form field—decimally. For example, in this code *age* would be equal to 0:

```
var age = '08 years';
age = parseInt(age);
```

However, in the following code the variable *age* would hold the value 8:

```
var age = '08 years';
age = parseInt(age,10);
```

In other words, always add the *,10* when using the *parseInt( )* method.

This method is also helpful when dealing with CSS units. For example, if you want to find the width of an element on a page (you'll learn how to do that on page 186), you often end up with a string like this: '200px' (meaning 200 pixels wide). Using the *parseInt( )* method, you can retrieve just the number value and then perform some operation on that value.

- *parseFloat( )* is like *parseInt( )*, but you use it when a string might contain a decimal point. For example, if you have a string like '4.5 acres' you can use *parseFloat( )* to retrieve the entire value including decimal places:

```
var space = '4.5 acres';
space = parseFloat(space); // 4.5
```

If you used *parseInt( )* for the above example, you'd end up with just the number 4, since *parseInt( )* only tries to retrieve whole numbers (integers).

Which of the above methods you use depends on the situation: If your goal is to add two numbers, but they're strings, then use *Number( )* or + operator. However, if you want to extract a number from a string that might include letters, like '200px' or '1.5em', then use *parseInt( )* to capture whole numbers (200, for example) or *parseFloat( )* to capture numbers with decimals (1.5, for example).

Testing for Numbers

When using JavaScript to manipulate user input, you often need to verify that the information supplied by the visitor is of the correct type. For example, if you ask for people's years of birth, you want to make sure they supply a number. Likewise, when you're performing a mathematical calculation, if the data you use for the calculation isn't a number, then your script might break.

To verify that a string is a number, use the *isNaN( )* method. This method takes a string as an argument and tests whether the string is "not a number." If the string contains anything except a plus or minus (for positive and negative numbers) followed by numbers and an optional decimal value, it's considered "not a number," so the string '-23.25' is a number, but the string '24 pixels' is not. This method returns either *true* (if the string is not a number) or *false* (if it is a number). You can use *isNaN( )* as part of a conditional statement like this:

```
var x = '10'; // is a number
if (isNaN(x)) {
  // is NOT a number
} else {
  // it is a number
}
```

Rounding Numbers

JavaScript provides a way to round a fractional number to an integer—for example, rounding 4.5 up to 5. Rounding comes in handy when you're performing a calculation that must result in a whole number. For example, say you're using JavaScript to dynamically set a pixel height of a <div> tag on the page based on the height of the browser window. In other words, the height of the <div> is calculated using the window's height. Any calculation you make might result in a decimal value (like 300.25), but since there's no such thing as .25 pixels, you need to round the final calculation to the nearest integer (300, for example).

You can round a number using the *round( )* method of the Math object. The syntax for this looks a little unusual:

```
Math.round(number)
```

You pass a number (or variable containing a number) to the *round( )* method, and it returns an integer. If the original number has a decimal place with a value below .5, the number is rounded down; if the decimal place is .5 or above, it is rounded up. For example, 4.4 would round down to 4, while 4.5 rounds up to 5.

```
var decimalNum = 10.25;
var roundedNum = Math.round(decimalNum); // 10
```

Note: JavaScript provides two other methods for rounding numbers *Math.ceil( )* and *Math.floor( )*. You use them just like *Math.round( )*, but *Math.ceil( )* always rounds the number up (for example, *Math.ceil(4.0001)* returns 5), while *Math.floor( )* always rounds the number down: *Math.floor(4.99999)* returns 4. To keep these two methods clear in your mind, think a *ceil*ing is up, and a *floor* is down.

Formatting Currency Values

When calculating product costs or shopping cart totals, you'll usually include the cost, plus two decimals out, like this: 9.99. But even if the monetary value is a whole number, it's common to add two zeros, like this: 10.00. And a currency

---

value like 8.9 is written as 8.90. Unfortunately, JavaScript doesn't see numbers that way: it leaves the trailing zeros off (10 instead of 10.00, and 8.9 instead of 8.90, for example).

Fortunately, there's a method for numbers called *toFixed( )*, which lets you convert a number to a string that matches the number of decimal places you want. To use it, add a period after a number (or after the name of a variable containing a number), followed by *toFixed(2)*:

```
var cost = 10;
var printCost = '$' + cost.toFixed(2); // $10.00
```

The number you pass the *toFixed( )* method determines how many decimal places to go out to. For currency, use 2 to end up with numbers like 10.00 or 9.90; if you use 3, you end up with 3 decimal places, like 10.000 or 9.900.

If the number starts off with more decimal places than you specify, the number is rounded to the number of decimal places specified. For example:

```
var cost = 10.289;
var printCost = '$' + cost.toFixed(2); // $10.29
```

In this case, the 10.289 is rounded up to 10.29.

Note: The *toFixed( )* method only works with numbers. So if you use a string, you end up with an error:

```
var cost='10';//a string
var printCost='$' + cost.toFixed(2);//error
```

To get around this problem, you need to convert the string to a number as described on page 134, like this:

```
var cost='10';//a string
cost = +cost;
var printCost='$' + cost.toFixed(2);//$10.00
```

Creating a Random Number

Random numbers can help add variety to a program. For example, say you have an array of questions for a quiz program (like Script 3.3 on page 106). Instead of asking the same questions in the same order each time, you can randomly select one question in the array. Or, you could use JavaScript to randomly select the name of a graphic file from an array and display a different image each time the page loads. Both of these tasks require a random number.

JavaScript provides the *Math.random( )* method for creating random numbers. This method returns a randomly generated number between 0 and 1 (for example .9716907176080688 or .10345038010895868). While you might not have much need for numbers like those, you can use some simple math operations to generate a whole number from 0 to another number. For example, to generate a number from 0 to 9, you'd use this code:

```
Math.floor(Math.random( )*10);
```

This code breaks down into two parts. The part inside the *Math.floor( )* method—*Math.random( )*10*—generates a random number between 0 and 10. That will generate numbers like 4.190788392268892; and since the random number is *between* 0 and 10, it never *is* 10. To get a whole number, the random result is passed to the *Math.floor( )* method, which rounds any decimal number down to the nearest whole number, so 3.4448588848 becomes 3 and .1111939498984 becomes 0.

If you want to get a random number between 1 and another number, just multiply the *Random( )* method by the uppermost number and add one to the total. For example, if you want to simulate a die role to get a number from 1 to 6:

```
var roll = Math.floor(Math.random( )*6 +1); // 1,2,3,4,5 or 6
```

Randomly selecting an array element

You can use the *Math.random( )* method to randomly select an item from an array. As discussed on page 59, each item in an array is accessed using an index number. The first item in an array uses an index value of 0, and the last item in the array is accessed with an index number that's 1 minus the total number of items in the array. Using the *Math.random( )* method makes it really easy to randomly select an array item:

```
var people = ['Ron','Sally','Tricia','Bob']; //create an array
var random = Math.floor(Math.random( ) * people.length);
var rndPerson = people[random]; //
```

The first line of this code creates an array with four names. The second line does two things: First, it generates a random number between 0 and the number of items in the array (*people.length*)—in this example, a number *between* 0 and 4. Then it uses the *Math.floor( )* method to round down to the nearest integer, so it will produce the number 0, 1, 2, or 3. Finally, it uses that number to access one element from the array and store it in a variable named *rndPerson*.

A function for selecting a random number

Functions are a great way to create useful, reusable snippets of code (page 97). If you use random numbers frequently, you might want a simple function to help you select a random number between any two numbers—for example, a number between 1 and 6, or 100 and 1,000. The following function is called using two arguments; The first is the bottom possible value (1 for example), and the second is the largest possible value (6 for example):

```
function rndNum(from, to) {
  return Math.floor((Math.random( )*(to - from + 1)) + from);
}
```

To use this function, add it to your Web page (as described on page 98), and then call it like this:

```
var dieRoll = rndNum(1,6); // get a number between 1 and 6
```

Dates and Times

If you want to keep track of the current date or time, turn to JavaScript's *Date* object. This special JavaScript object lets you determine the year, month, day of the week, hour, and more. To use it, you create a variable and store a new *Date* object inside it like this:

```
var now = new Date( );
```

The *new Date( )* command creates a *Date* object containing the current date and time. Once created, you can access different pieces of time and date information using various date-related methods as listed in Table 4-5. For example, to get the current year use the *getFullYear( )* method like this:

```
var now = new Date( );
var year = now.getFullYear( );
```

Note: *new Date( )* retrieves the current time and date as determined by each visitor's computer. In other words, if someone hasn't correctly set their computer's clock, then the date and time won't be accurate.

Table 4-5. Methods for accessing parts of the Date object

Method	What it returns
getFullYear( )	The year: 2008, for example.
getMonth( )	The month as an integer between 0 and 11: 0 is January and 11 is December.
getDate( )	The day of the month—a number between 1 and 31.
getDay( )	The day of the week as a number between 0 and 6. 0 is Sunday, and 6 is Saturday.
getHours( )	Number of hours on a 24-hour clock (i.e. a number between 0 and 23). For example, 11p.m. is 23.
getMinutes( )	Number of minutes between 0 and 59.
getSeconds( )	Number of seconds between 0 and 59.
getTime( )	Total number of seconds since January 1, 1970 at midnight (see box on page 142).

Getting the Month

To retrieve the month for a *Date* object, use the *getMonth( )* method, which returns the month's number:

```
var now = new Date( );
var month = now.getMonth( );
```

However, instead of returning a number that makes sense to us humans (as in 1 meaning January), this method returns a number that's one less. For example,

January is 0, February is 1, and so on. If you want to retrieve a number that matches how we think of months, just add 1 like this:

```
var now = new Date();
var month = now.getMonth()+1;//matches the real month
```

There's no built-in JavaScript command that tells you the name of a month. Fortunately, JavaScript's strange way of numbering months comes in handy when you want to determine the actual name of the month. You can accomplish that by first creating an array of month names, then accessing a name using the index number for that month:

```
var months = ['January','February','March','April','May',
              'June','July','August','September',
              'October','November','December'];
var now = new Date();
var month = months[now.getMonth()];
```

The first line creates an array with all twelve month names, in the order they occur (January–December). Remember that to access an array item you use an index number, and that arrays are numbered starting with 0 (see page 59). So to access the first item of the array *months*, you use *months[0]*. So, by using the *getMonth()* method, you can retrieve a number to use as an index for the *months* array and thus retrieve the name for that month.

Getting the Day of the Week

The *getDay()* method retrieves the day of the week. And as with the *getMonth()* method, the JavaScript interpreter returns a number that's one less than what you'd expect: 0 is considered Sunday, the first day of the week, while Saturday is 6. Since the name of the day of the week is usually more useful for your visitors, you can use an array to store the day names and use the *getDay()* method to access the particular day in the array, like this:

```
var days = ['Sunday','Monday','Tuesday','Wednesday',
            'Thursday','Friday','Saturday'];
var now = new Date();
var dayOfWeek = days[now.getDay()];
```

In the tutorial on page 146, you'll see use both the *getDay()* and *getMonth()* techniques to create a useful function for creating a human-readable date.

Getting the Time

The *Date* object also contains the current time, so you can display the current time on a Web page or use the time to determine if the visitor is viewing the page in the a.m. or p.m. You can then do something with that information, like display a background image of the sun during the day, or the moon at night.

Dates and Times

POWER USERS' CLINIC

The Date Object Behind the Scenes

JavaScript lets you access particular elements of the *Date* object, such as the year or the day of the month. However, the JavaScript interpreter actually thinks of a date as the number of *milliseconds* that have passed since midnight on January 1, 1970. For example, Wednesday, July 2, 2008 is actually 1214982000000 to the JavaScript interpreter.

That isn't a joke: As far as JavaScript is concerned, the beginning of time was January 1, 1970. That date (called the "Unix epoch") was arbitrarily chosen in the 70s by programmers creating the Unix operating system, so they could all agree on a way of keeping track of time. Since then, this way of tracking a date has become common in many programming languages and platforms.

Whenever you use a *Date* method like *getFullYear( )*, the JavaScript interpreter does the math to figure out (based on how many seconds have elapsed since January 1, 1970) what year it is. If you want to see the number of milliseconds for a particular date, you use the *getTime( )* method:

```
var sometime = new Date( );
var msElapsed = sometime.getTime( );
```

Tracking dates and times as milliseconds makes it easier to calculate differences between dates. For example, you can determine the amount of time until next New Year's day by first getting the number of milliseconds that will have elapsed from 1/1/1970 to when next year rolls around and then subtracting the number of milliseconds that have elapsed from 1/1/1970 to today:

```
// milliseconds from 1/1/1970 to today
var today = new Date( );
// milliseconds from 1/1/1970 to next new
year
var nextYear = new Date(2009, 1, 1);
// calculate milliseconds from today to
next year
var  timeDiff = nextYear - today;
```

The result of subtracting two dates is the number of milliseconds difference between the two. If you want to convert that into something useful, just divide it by the number of milliseconds in a day (to determine how many days) or the number of milliseconds in an hour (to determine how many hours), and so on.

```
var second = 1000; // 1000 milliseconds in
a second
var minute = 60*second; // 60 seconds in a
minute
var hour = 60*minute; // 60 minutes in an
hour
var day = 24*hour; // 24 hours in a day
var totalDays = timeDiff/day; // total
number of days
```

(In this example, you may have noticed a different way to create a date: *new Date(2009,1,1)*. You can read more about this method on page 145.)

You can use the *getHours( )*, *getMinutes( )*, and *getSeconds( )* methods to get the hours, minutes, and seconds. So to display the time on a Web page, add the following in the HTML where you wish the time to appear:

```
var now = new Date( );
var hours = now.getHours( );
var minutes = now.getMinutes( );
var seconds = now.getSeconds( );
document.write(hours + ":" + minutes + ":" + seconds);
```

This code produces output like 6:35:56 to indicate 6 a.m., 35 minutes, and 56 seconds. However, it will also produce output that you might not like, like 18:4:9 to indicate 4 minutes and 9 seconds after 6 p.m. One problem is that most people

142   JAVASCRIPT: THE MISSING MANUAL

reading this book, unless they're in the military, don't use the 24-hour clock. They don't recognize 18 as meaning 6 p.m. An even bigger problem is that times should be formatted with two digits for minutes and seconds (even if they're a number less than 10), like this: 6:04:09. Fortunately, it's not difficult to adjust the above script to match those requirements.

Changing hours to a.m. and p.m.

To change hours from a 24-hour clock to a 12-hour clock, you need to do a couple of things. First, you need to determine if the time is in the morning (so you can add 'am' after the time) or in the afternoon (to append 'pm'). Second, you need to convert any hours greater than 12 to their 12-hour clock equivalent (for example, change 14 to 2 p.m.).

Here's the code to do that:

```
1    var now = new Date();
2    var hour = now.getHours();
3    if (hour < 12) {
4       meridiem = 'am';
5    } else {
6       meridiem = 'pm';
7    }
8    hour = hour % 12;
9    if (hour==0) {
10      hour = 12;
11   }
12   hour = hour + ' ' + meridiem;
```

Note: The column of numbers at the far left is just line numbering to make it easier for you to follow the discussion below. Don't type these numbers into your own code!

Lines 1 and 2 grab the current date and time and store the current hour into a variable named *hour*. Lines 3–7 determine if the hour is in the afternoon or morning; if the hour is less than 12 (the hour after midnight is 0), then it's the morning (a.m.); otherwise, it's the afternoon (p.m.).

Line 8 introduces a mathematical operator called *modulus* and represented by a percent (%) sign. It returns the remainder of a division operation. For example, 2 divides into 5 two times (2×2 is 4), with 1 left over. In other words, 5 % 2 is 1. So in this case, if the hour is 18, 18 % 12 results in 6 (12 goes into 18 once with a remainder of 6). 18 is 6 p.m., which is what you want. If the first number is smaller than the number divided into it (for example, 8 divided by 12), then the result is the original number. For example, 8 % 12 just returns 8; in other words, the modulus operator doesn't change the hours before noon.

Lines 9–11 take care of two possible outcomes with the modulus operator. If the hour is 12 (noon) or 0 (after midnight), then the modulus operator returns 0. In this case, *hour* is just set to 12 for either 12 p.m. or 12 a.m.

Finally, line 12 combines the reformatted hour with a space and either "am" or "pm", so the result is displayed as, for example, "6 am" or "6 pm".

Padding single digits

As discussed on page 142, when the minutes or seconds values are less than 10, you can end up with weird output like 7:3:2 p.m. To change this output to the more common 7:03:02 p.m., you need to add a 0 in front of the single digit. It's easy with a basic conditional statement:

```
1   var minutes = now.getMinutes();
2   if (minutes<10) {
3      minutes = '0' + minutes;
4   }
```

Line 1 grabs the minutes in the current time, which in this example could be 33 or 3. Line 2 simply checks if the number is less than 10, meaning the minute is a single digit and needs a 0 in front of it. Line 3 is a bit tricky, since you can't normally add a 0 in front of a number: 0 + 2 equals 2, not 02. However, you can combine strings in this way so *'0' + minutes* means combine the string '0' with the value in the *minutes* variable. As discussed on page 50, when you add a string to a number, the JavaScript interpreter converts the number to a string as well, so you end up with a string like '08'.

You can put all of these parts together to create a simple function to output times in formats like 7:32:04 p.m., or 4:02:34 a.m., or even leave off seconds altogether for a time like 7:23 p.m.:

```
function printTime(secs) {
    var sep = ':'; //seperator character
    var hours,minutes,seconds,time;
    var now = new Date();
    hours = now.getHours();
    if (hours < 12) {
        meridiem = 'am';
    } else {
        meridiem = 'pm';
    }
    hours = hours % 12;
    if (hours==0) {
        hours = 12;
    }
```

```
        time = hours
        minutes = now.getMinutes( );
        if (minutes<10) {
            minutes = '0' + minutes;
        }
        time += sep + minutes;
        if (secs) {
            seconds = now.getSeconds( );
            if (seconds<10) {
                seconds = '0' + seconds;
            }
            time += sep + seconds
        }
        return time + ' ' + meridiem;
    }
```

You'll find this function in the file *printTime.js* in the *chapter04* folder in the Tutorials. You can see it in action by opening the file *time.html* (in that same folder) in a Web browser. To use the function, either attach the *printTime.js* file to a Web page (see page 23), or copy the function into a Web page or another external JavaScript file (page 22). To get the time, just call the function like this: *printTime( )*, or, if you want the seconds displayed as well, *printTime(true)*. The function will return a string containing the current time in the proper format.

Creating a Date Other Than Today

So far, you've seen how to use *new Date( )* to capture the current date and time on a visitor's computer. But what if you want to create a *Date* object for next Thanksgiving or New Year's? JavaScript lets you create a date other than today in a few different ways. You might want to do this if you'd like to do a calculation between two dates: for example, "How many days until the new year?" (Also see the box on page 142.)

When using the *Date( )* method, you can also specify a date and time in the future or past. The basic format is this:

```
new Date(year,month,day,hour,minutes,seconds,milliseconds);
```

For example, to create a *Date* for noon on New Year's Day 2010, you could do this:

```
var ny2010 = new Date(2010,0,1,12,0,0,0);
```

This code translates to "create a new Date object for January 1, 2010 at 12 o'clock, 0 minutes, 0 seconds, and 0 milliseconds." You must supply at least a year and month, but if you don't need to specify an exact time, you can leave off milliseconds, seconds, minutes, and so on. For example, to just create a date object for January 1, 2010, you could do this:

```
var ny2010 = new Date(2010,0,1);
```

Note: Remember that JavaScript uses 0 for January, 1 for February, and so on, as described on page 141.

Creating a date that's one week from today

As discussed in the box on page 142, the JavaScript interpreter actually treats a date as the number of milliseconds that have elapsed since Jan 1, 1970. Another way to create a date is to pass a value representing the number of milliseconds for that date:

```
new Date(milliseconds);
```

So another way to create a date for January 1, 2010 would be like this:

```
var ny2010 = new Date(1262332800000);
```

Of course, since most of us aren't human calculators, you probably wouldn't think of a date like this. However, milliseconds come in very handy when you're creating a new date that's a certain amount of time from another date. For example, when setting a cookie using JavaScript, you need to specify a date at which point that cookie is deleted from a visitor's browser. To make sure a cookie disappears after one week, you need to specify a date that's one week from today.

To create a date that's one week from now, you could do the following:

```
var now = new Date( ); // today
var nowMS = now.getTime( ); // get # milliseconds for today
var week = 1000*60*60*24*7; // milliseconds in one week
var oneWeekFromNow = new Date(nowMS + week);
```

The first line stores the current date and time in a variable named *now*. Next, the *getTime( )* method extracts the number of milliseconds that have elapsed from January 1, 1970 to today. The third line calculates the total number of milliseconds in a single week (1000 milliseconds * 60 seconds * 60 minutes * 24 hours * 7 days). Finally, the code creates a new date by adding the number of milliseconds in a week to today.

Tutorial

To wrap up this chapter, you'll create a useful function for outputting a date in several different human-friendly formats. The function will be flexible enough to let you print out a date, as in "January 1, 2009," "1/1/09," or "Monday, February 2, 2009." In addition, you'll use some of the date and string methods covered in this chapter to build this function.

Overview

As with any program you write, it's good to start with a clear picture of what you want to accomplish and the steps necessary to get it done. For this program, you want to output the date in many different formats, and you want the function to be easy to use.

In other programming languages (like PHP or .NET), it's common to use special characters or *tokens* to symbolize elements of a date that are formatted in a specific way. In PHP, for example, a lowercase *l* used with that language's date function outputs the name of a month, like "January."

In this program, you'll use a similar approach by assigning special tokens to different parts of a date (see Table 4-6). The function will accept a date and a string containing these tokens, and return a human-friendly date.

For example, you'll be able to call your function like this:

```
dateString(new Date( ), '%N/%D/%Y');
```

This code returns a string, like '01/25/2009'. In other words, the function replaces each token in the supplied string with a properly formatted part of the date. Note that the tokens listed in Table 4-6 aren't any special JavaScript mojo; they're just arbitrary characters that the author decided to use. You could just as easily change the function in this tutorial to accept different formatted tokens, like *#YEAR#* instead of *%Y*, or *#DAY#* instead of *%D*.

Table 4-6. *Tokens for the date-formatting function*

Token	Replaced with
%Y	Four digit year: 2009
%y	Last two digits of year: 09
%M	Full month name: January
%m	Abbreviated month name: Jan
%N	Number of month, with leading zero if necessary: 01
%n	Number of month without leading zero: 1
%W	Full name of weekday: Monday
%w	Abbreviated name of weekday: Mon
%D	Day of month with leading zero if necessary: 05
%d	Day of month without leading zero: 5

Writing the Function

Now it's time to get down to coding and create your function. If you're still a little unsure of what a function is and how it works, turn to page 97 for a refresher.

Note: See the note on page 27 for information on how to download the tutorial files.

---

1. **In a text editor, open the file *4.1.html* in the *chapter04* folder.**

   You'll start by beginning the function definition.

---

2. **Between the first set of <script> tags in the page's <head> section, type the code in bold:**

```
<script type="text/javascript">
function dateString(date,string) {
</script>
```

This code creates a new function named *dateString( )*, which accepts two pieces of information (arguments) and stores them in variables named *date* and *string* (see page 99 for more on creating functions). The *date* variable will hold a JavaScript *Date* object, while the *string* variable will hold a string containing the special tokens like *%D*.

It's always a good idea to close any opening braces immediately, so you don't forget later.

3. **Press Return twice to create two empty lines, and then type *}*.**

This closing brace marks the end of the function. All the code you enter between the braces makes up the steps in the function.

This function will have two parts: the first part will get the different parts of the date in the proper formats; the second part of the function will then replace any tokens in the supplied string with correctly formatted parts of the date. First, you'll determine the year.

4. **Click in the empty line above the closing brace you just typed and add the code in bold below:**

```
<script type="text/javascript">
function dateString(date,string) {
 var year=date.getFullYear( );
}
</script>
```

This creates a new variable and stores the date's full, four-digit year in it. Next you'll get the date's month and modify it for a few different format options.

5. **Hit Return to create a new, blank line, and then add the following code:**

```
var month=date.getMonth( );
var realMonth=month+1;
```

The first line of code retrieves the number of the date's month. Remember that JavaScript assigns a number that's one less than you'd normally use for a month. For example, January is 0. So, the next line creates a variable named *realMonth*, which is simply the month plus 1. In other words, if the month is January, the *realMonth* variable will hold the number 1. Next, you'll take care of the case when the month has to be two digits long: 11 or 08, for example.

6. **Press Return, and type:**

```
var fillMonth = realMonth;
if (realMonth<10) {
  fillMonth = '0' + realMonth;
}
```

First, you declare a new variable named *fillMonth*, and store the current month's value in it. This conditional statement adds zero in front of the value in *realMonth*, if *realMonth* is less than 10 and stores that value in *fillMonth*. This is the variable you'll use if you want to format a date like this: 08/10/2008.

Now you'll get the name of the month.

7. **Hit Return and then add the following code:**

```
var months = ['January','February','March','April','May',
              'June','July','August','September',
              'October','November','December'];
var monthName=months[month];
```

The first line creates an array that stores the name of each month of the year. To get the proper name, you can use the value stored in the *month* variable as the index. For example, if the month is January, then the *month* variable will be 0: *months[0]* is the first item in the array, or the string 'January' (see page 141 for a detailed explanation).

Next, you'll retrieve the day of the month.

8. **Hit Return and then type:**

```
var day=date.getDate();
var fillDate=day;
if (day<10) {
  fillDate='0' + day;
}
```

The first line just gets the day of the month: if it's January 5, then the date will be 5. The rest of the code above works like step 6, and adds a zero in front of any date that is less than 10, so 5 becomes 05.

Now you'll get the day of the week.

9. **Hit Return, and then add the following code:**

```
var weekday=date.getDay();
var weekdays = ['Sunday','Monday','Tuesday','Wednesday', ↵
                'Thursday','Friday','Saturday'];
var dayName=weekdays[weekday];
```

These three lines of code retrieve the name of the date's day of the week. The method is similar to step 7: the names of the days of the week are stored in an array, then the correct name is retrieved using an index value retrieved from the *getDay( )* method. For example, if the day of the week is Sunday, *getDay( )* returns 0, and *weekdays[0]* returns the string 'Sunday'.

At this point, the function has collected all of the different parts of a date that you might need (year, month, and so on) and stored them into separate variables. Now, you'll replace the tokens inside the string that was passed to the function with properly formatted date elements. First, you'll tackle the year.

10. **Hit Return, and then type:**

```
string = string.replace(/%Y/g,year);
```

Remember that *string* is a variable that's created at the beginning of the function (see step 2), and it's filled with a string full of tokens that the function will replace with formatted date parts. The heart of the process of replacing those tokens is the *replace( )* method, which takes a regular expression and replaces any matches with another string (see page 132). So *string.replace( )* tells the JavaScript interpreter to execute the *replace( )* method on the contents contained in the *string* variable.

The first argument sent to *replace( )* is a regular expression: */%Y/g*. The first / marks the beginning of the regular expression pattern; *%Y* is the pattern to match. In other words, if the string contains the two characters *%Y* anywhere inside it, then there's a match. The second / marks the end of the regex pattern, and the final *g* indicates that the replacement should be global. In other words, every instance of *%Y* should be replaced, not just the first one (see page 132 for a discussion of the *g* flag in regular expressions). The second argument—*year*—is the variable created in step 4.

To break down this code into plain English: Replace every instance of *%Y* with the value stored in the variable *year* and store the results back into *string*. In other words, this line will replace *%Y* with something like 2009. If the characters *%Y* aren't found in the string, then the string remains unchanged.

Next, you'll insert an abbreviated two-digit year when requested.

11. **Hit Return, and type:**

```
string = string.replace(/%y/g,year.toString( ).slice(-2));
```

The token *%y* is to be replaced with just the last two digits of the year: 08, for example. This line of code uses the same *replace( )* method described in step 10, but the replacement string (the year) is reduced to the last two digits using the *slice( )* method described on page 118.

The rest of the lines of code in this function are all just variations on this theme: replace a token with one of the parts of the date.

12. **Hit Return and then type this code:**

```
string = string.replace(/%M/g,monthName);
string = string.replace(/%m/g,monthName.slice(0,3));
string = string.replace(/%N/g,fillMonth);
string = string.replace(/%n/g,realMonth);
string = string.replace(/%W/g,dayName);
string = string.replace(/%w/g,dayName.slice(0,3));
string = string.replace(/%D/g,fillDate);
string = string.replace(/%d/g,day);
```

These lines of code replace various tokens with the different formatted date elements created in the first part of this function. Once the program does all of the replacing, it returns the revised string.

13. **Press Return, and then type** *return string;*

The complete function should look like this:

```
function dateString(date,string) {
  var year=date.getFullYear();
  var month=date.getMonth();
  var realMonth=month+1;
  if (realMonth<10) {
    fillMonth = '0' + realMonth;
  } else {
    fillMonth = realMonth;
  }
  var months = ['January','February','March','April','May',
                'June','July','August','September',
                'October','November','December'];
  var monthName=months[month];
  var day=date.getDate();
  if (day<10) {
    fillDate='0' + day;
  } else {
    fillDate=day;
  }
  var fillDate = (day<10) ? '0' + day : day;
  var weekday=date.getDay();
  var weekdays = ['Sunday','Monday','Tuesday','Wednesday', ↵
                  'Thursday','Friday','Saturday'];
  var dayName=weekdays[weekday];
  string = string.replace(/%Y/g,year);
  string = string.replace(/%y/g,year.toString().slice(-2));
  string = string.replace(/%M/g,monthName);
  string = string.replace(/%m/g,monthName.slice(0,3));
  string = string.replace(/%N/g,fillMonth);
```

```
string = string.replace(/%n/g,realMonth);
string = string.replace(/%W/g,dayName);
string = string.replace(/%w/g,dayName.slice(0,3));
string = string.replace(/%D/g,fillDate);
string = string.replace(/%d/g,day);
return string;
}
```

Now that the function is complete, you can use it to print many differently formatted dates to a page.

14. **Locate the second set of <script> tags down in the body of the page, and add the code in bold:**

```
<script type="text/javascript">
var today = new Date();
</script>
```

This code creates a new variable named *today* and stores a *Date* object with the current date and time in it. You'll use that *Date* object to call the newly created function

15. **Press Return and then type:**

```
var message = dateString(today, 'Today is %W, %M %d, %Y');
```

Here you call the function by passing the *Date* object created previously as well as the string *'Today is %W, %M %d, %Y'*. Basically, the function takes the date, extracts different parts of the date, and then looks for and replaces any special token values in the string. You can refer to Table 4-6 to see what each of these tokens is replaced with, but, in a nutshell, this line of code will return a string like 'Today is Sunday, January 6, 2008' and store it into the variable *message*. Finally, you just need to print that string to the page.

16. **Hit Return one last time, and then type *document.write(message);***

The final script should look like this.

```
<script type="text/javascript">
var today = new Date();
var message = dateString(today, 'Today is %W, %M %d, %Y');
document.write(message);
</script>
```

Save the file and preview it in a Web browser. The result should look something like Figure 4-6. The file *complete_4.1.html* contains the finished version of this tutorial. In addition, you'll find a slightly more advanced version of this function in the file *dateString.js*. That function supports one other token, %O, which returns the date plus the correct ordinal for the date: 1st, 2nd, or 3rd, instead of 1, 2, or 3.

Figure 4-6:
The dateString( ) *function
you created in this
tutorial lets you output a
date in many different
formats. Try rewriting the
code in step 16 using
different tokens listed in
Table 4-6 to produce
dates in different
formats.*

Dynamically Modifying Web Pages

JavaScript gives you the power to change a Web page before your very eyes. Using JavaScript, you can add pictures and text, remove content, or change the appearance of an element on a page instantly. In fact, dynamically changing a Web page is the hallmark of the newest breed of JavaScript-powered Web sites. For example, Google Maps (*http://maps.google.com/*) provides access to a map of the world; when you zoom into the map or scroll across it, the page gets updated without the need to load a new Web page. Similarly, when you mouse over a movie title at Netflix (*www.netflix.com*) an information bubble appears on top of the page providing more detail about the movie (see Figure 5-1). In both of these examples, JavaScript is changing the HTML that the Web browser originally downloaded.

The first four chapters of this book covered many of the fundamentals of the Java-Script programming language—the keywords, concepts, and syntax of JavaScript. Now that you have a handle on how to write a basic JavaScript program and add it to a Web page, it's time to see what JavaScript programming is all about. This chapter, and the next one on JavaScript events, together show you how to create the great interactive effects you see on the Web these days.

Modifying Web Pages: An Overview

In this chapter, you'll learn how to alter a Web page using JavaScript. You'll add new content, HTML tags and HTML attributes, and also alter content and tags that are already on the page. In other words, you'll use JavaScript to generate new HTML and change the HTML that's already on the page.

Figure 5-1:
JavaScript can make Web pages simpler to scan and read, by only showing content when it's needed. At Netflix.com, movie descriptions are hidden from view, but revealed when the mouse travels over the movie title or thumbnail image.

Whenever you change the content or HTML of a page—whether you're adding a navigation bar complete with pop-up menus, creating a JavaScript-driven slide show, or simply adding alternating stripes to table rows (like you did in the tutorial in Chapter 1)—you'll perform two main steps.

1. **Identify an element on a page.**

   An element is any existing tag, and before you have to do anything with that element, you need to *identify* it in your JavaScript (which you'll learn how to do in this chapter). For example, to add a color to a table row, you first must identify the row you wish to color; to make a pop-up menu appear when you mouse over a button, you need to identify that button. Even if you simply want to use JavaScript to add text to the bottom of a Web page, you need to identify a tag to insert the text either inside, before, or after that tag.

2. **Do something with the element.**

   OK, "do something" isn't a very specific instruction. That's because there's nearly an endless number of things you can *do* with an element to alter the way your Web page looks or acts. In fact, most of this book is devoted to teaching you different things to do to page elements. Here are a few examples:

   • **Add/remove a class attribute.** In the example on page 30, you used Java-Script to assign a class to every other row of a table. The JavaScript didn't actually "color" the row; it merely applied a class, and the Web browser used the information in the CSS style sheet to change the appearance of the row.

   • **Change a property of the element.** When animating a <div> across a page, for example, you change that element's position on the page.

- **Add new content.** If, while filling out a Web form, a visitor incorrectly fills out a field, it's common to make an error message appear—"Please supply an email address," for example. In this case, you're adding content somewhere in relation to that form field.

- **Remove the element.** In the Netflix example pictured in Figure 5-1, the pop-up bubble disappears when you mouse off the movie title. In this case, Java-Script removes that pop-up bubble from the page.

- **Extract information from the element.** Other times, you'll want to know something about the tag you've identified. For example, to validate a text field, you need to identify that text field, then find out what text was typed into that field—in other words, you need to get the value of that field.

The first step above—identifying an element on a page—is mainly what this chapter is about. To understand how to identify and modify a part of a page using Java-Script you first need to get to know the *Document Object Model*.

Understanding the Document Object Model

When a Web browser loads an HTML file, it displays the contents of that file on the screen (appropriately styled with CSS, of course). But that's not all the Web browser does with the tags, attributes, and contents of the file: it also creates and memorizes a "model" of that page's HTML. In other words, the Web browser remembers the HTML tags, their attributes, and the order in which they appear in the file—this representation of the page is called the *Document Object Model*, or DOM for short.

The DOM provides the information needed for JavaScript to communicate with the elements on the Web page. The DOM also provides the tools necessary to navigate through, change, and add to the HTML on the page. The DOM itself isn't actually JavaScript—it's a standard from the World Wide Web Consortium (W3C) that most browser manufacturers have adopted and added to their browsers. The DOM lets JavaScript communicate with and change a page's HTML.

To see how the DOM works, take look at this very simple Web page:

```
<!DOCTYPE HTML PUBLIC "-//W3C//DTD HTML 4.01//EN" "http://www.w3.org/TR/
html4/strict.dtd">
<html>
<head>
<title>A web page</title>
</head>
<body class="home">
<h1 id="header">A headline</h1>
<p>Some <strong>important</strong> text</p>
</body>
</html>
```

On this and all other Web sites, some tags wrap around other tags—like the <html> tag, which surrounds all other tags, or the <body> tag, which wraps around the tags and contents that appear in the browser window. You can represent the relationship between tags with a kind of family tree (see Figure 5-2). The <html> tag is the "root" of the tree—like the great-great-great granddaddy of all of the other tags on the page—while other tags represent different "branches" of the family tree; for example, the <head> and <body> tags, which each contain their own set of tags.

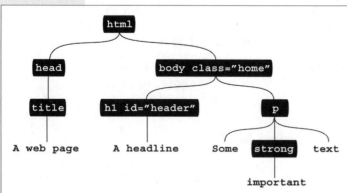

Figure 5-2:
The basic nested structure of an HTML page, where tags wrap around other tags, is often represented in the form of a family tree, where tags that wrap around other tags are called ancestors, and tags inside other tags are called descendents.

In addition to HTML tags, Web browsers also keep track of the text that appears inside a tag (for example, "A headline" inside the <h1> tag in Figure 5-2), as well as the *attributes* that are assigned to each tag (the class attribute applied to the <body> and <h1> tags in Figure 5-2). In fact, the DOM treats each of these—tags (also called *elements*), attributes, and text—as individual units called *nodes*.

Selecting a Page Element

A Web browser thinks of a Web page simply as an organized collection of tags, tag attributes, and text, or, in DOM-talk, a bunch of *nodes*. So for JavaScript to manipulate the contents of a page, it needs a way to communicate with a page's nodes. There are two main methods for selecting nodes: *getElementById( )* and *getElementsByTagName( )*.

getElementById()

Getting an element by ID means locating a single node that has a unique ID applied to it. For example, in Figure 5-2, the <h1> tag has an ID attribute with the value of *header*. The following JavaScript selects that node:

```
document.getElementById('header')
```

In plain English, this line means, "Search this page for a tag with an ID of 'header' assigned to it." The *document* part of *document.getElementById('header')* is a keyword that refers to the entire document. It's not optional, so you can't type *getElementById( )* by itself. The command *getElementById( )* is the method name (a command for the document) and the *'header'* part is simply a string (the name of the ID you're looking for) that's sent to the method as an argument. (See page 101 for the definition of an argument.)

Note: The *getElementById( )* method requires a single string–the name of a tag's ID attribute. For example:

```
document.getElementById('header')
```

However, this doesn't mean you have to provide a literal string to the method: you can also pass a variable that contains a string with the sought after ID:

```
var lookFor = 'header';
var foundNode = document.getElementById(lookFor);
```

Frequently, you'll assign the results of this method to a variable to store a reference to the particular tag, so you can later manipulate it in your program. For example, say you want to use JavaScript to change the text of the headline in the HTML pictured on page 157. You can do this:

```
var headLine = document.getElementById('header');
headLine.innerHTML = 'JavaScript was here!';
```

The *getElementById( )* command returns a reference to a single node, which in this example is stored in a variable named *headline*. Storing the results of *getElementById( )* in a variable is very convenient; it lets you refer simply to the variable name each time you wish to manipulate that tag, rather than the much more longwinded *document.getElementById('idName')*. For example, the second line of code uses the variable to access the tag's *innerHTML* property: *headline. innerHTML* (you'll learn what *innerHTML* is on page 163).

getElementsByTagName( )

Sometimes, you'll want more than just the single element that *getElementById( )* provides. For example, maybe you'd like to find every link on a Web page and do something to those links—like force every link that points outside your site to open in a new window. In that case, you need to get a list of elements, not just one element marked with an ID. The command *getElementsByTagName( )* does the trick.

This method works similarly to *getElementById( )* but instead of providing the name of an ID, you supply the name of the tag you're looking for. For example, to find all of the links on a page, you write this:

```
var pageLinks = document.getElementsByTagName('a');
```

Translated, this means, "Search this document for every <a> tag and store the results in a variable named *pageLinks*." The *getElementsByTagName( )* method returns a list of nodes, instead of just a single node. In that sense, the list acts a lot like an array: You can access a single node using the same index notation, find the total number of elements using the *length* property, and loop through the list of elements using a *for* loop (see page 94).

For example, the first item in the *pageLinks* variable from the code above is *pageLinks[0]*—the first <a> tag on the page—and *pageLinks.length* is the total number of <a> tags on the page.

Tip: It's easy to make a typo with these two methods. Most commonly, beginners (and pros) will capitalize both letters of *Id*. Only the first letter is capitalized. Likewise, *Elements* is plural in *getElementsByTagName( )*–don't forget the *s*:

```
document.getElementById('banner');
document.getElementsByTagName('a');
```

You can also use *getElementById( )* and *getElementsByTagName( )* together. For example, say you have a Web page containing a <div> tag, and that <div> tag has an ID of 'banner' applied to it. If you want to find out how many links were in just that <div>, you can use *getElementById( )* to retrieve the <div>, and then use *getElementsByTagName( )* to search the <div>. Here's how it works:

```
var banner = document.getElementById('banner');
var bannerLinks = banner.getElementsByTagName('a');
var totalBannerLinks = bannerLinks.length;
```

While searching for an element with an ID is one method of searching within the document (*document.getElementById( )*), you can find tags of a particular type by searching the entire document (*document.getElementsByTagName( )*) or by searching the tags within a particular node. For example, in the above code, the variable *banner* contains a reference to a <div> tag, so the code *banner.getElementsByTagName('a')* only searches for <a> tags *inside* that <div>.

Selecting nearby nodes

As mentioned earlier, text is also considered a node, so the text "A headline" inside the <h1> tag on page 157 is a separate node from the <h1> tag that surrounds it. In other words, if you select that <h1> tag using the techniques you've just learned, you've just selected that tag and not the text inside. So, what if you want to get at that text? Unfortunately, the way the DOM provides to do so involves a rather roundabout technique: You have to start at the <h1> node, move to the text node, and then get the value of the text node.

To understand how this process works, you need to understand how tags are related to each other. If you've spent some time working with Cascading Style Sheets, you're probably familiar with *descendent* selectors—one of the most powerful tools in CSS. In a nutshell, a descendent selector lets you format a particular tag based on its relationship to another tag. Thus, using a descendent selector, you can make a paragraph (<p>) tag look one way when it's in the sidebar of a page, and look another way when that same tag is in the footer of the page.

Descendent selectors rely on the kind of relationship pictured in Figure 5-2; if a tag is inside another tag, it's called a descendent. The <h1> tag in the sample HTML on page 157 is a descendent of the <body> tag, and, because it's also inside the <html> tag, it's a descendent of that tag as well. Tags that wrap around other tags are called *ancestors*; so in Figure 5-2, the <p> tag is an ancestor of the <strong> tag.

The DOM also thinks of tags that wrap around other tags as being related, but the DOM only provides access to the "immediate family." That is, the DOM can access a "parent" node, "child" node, or "sibling" node. Figure 5-3 demonstrates these relationships: If a node is directly inside another node, like the text "Some" inside the <p> tag, then it's a *child*; a node that directly surrounds another node, like the <strong> tag surrounding the text "important", is a *parent*. Nodes that share the same parent, like the two text nodes—"Some" and "strong"—and the <strong> tag are like brothers and sisters, so they're called *siblings*.

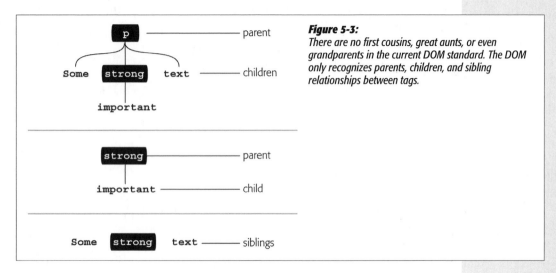

Figure 5-3:
There are no first cousins, great aunts, or even grandparents in the current DOM standard. The DOM only recognizes parents, children, and sibling relationships between tags.

The DOM provides several methods of accessing nearby nodes:

- *.childNodes* is a property of a node. It contains a list of all nodes that are direct children of that node. The list of nodes works just like the list that's returned by the *getElementsByTagName( )* method (see page 159). For example, suppose you add the following JavaScript to the HTML file on page 157:

```
var headline = document.getElementById('header');
var headlineKids = headline.childNodes;
```

The variable *headlineKids* will contain a list of all nodes that are children of the tag that has the ID of 'headline' (the <h1> tag in this example). In this case, there's only one child, the text node containing the text "A headline." So, if you want to know what the text inside that node is, add an additional line of code, like this:

```
var headlineText = headlineKids[0].nodeValue;
```

The first child in the list is *headlineKids[0]*—since there is only one child for the headline (see Figure 5-2), it's also the only node in the list. To get the text inside a text node, you access the *nodeValue* property. (On the other hand, there's also an easier way to do so, as you'll see on page 181.)

- *.parentNode* is a node property that represents the direct parent of a particular node. For example, if you wanted to know what tag wraps around the <h1> tag in Figure 5-2, you could write this:

```
var headline = document.getElementById('header');
var headlineParent = headline.parentNode;
```

The variable *headlineParent* is a reference to the <body> tag in this case.

- *.nextSibling* and *.previousSibling* are properties that point to the node that comes directly after the current node, or the node that comes before. For example, in Figure 5-2, the <h1> and <p> tags are siblings: the <p> tag comes directly after the ending </h1> tag.

```
var headline = document.getElementById('header');
var headlineSibling = headline.nextSibling;
```

The variable *headlineSibling* is a reference to the <p> tag that follows the <h1> tag. If you try to access a sibling node that doesn't exist, JavaScript returns the value of *null* (see the Tip on page 131). For example, you can check to see if a node has a *previousSibling* like this:

```
var headline = document.getElementById('header');
var headlineSibling = headline.prevSibling;
if (! headlineSibling) {
  alert('This node does not have a previous sibling!');
} else {
  // do something with the sibling node
}
```

As you can see, it takes a fair amount of gymnastics to move around a page's DOM structure. For instance, to get all of the text inside the <p> tag in Figure 5-2, you'd have to get a list of all of the <p> tags children, and then go through each child node and look for text. In the case of the <strong> tag pictured in Figure 5-2, you'd have to look at its child nodes to get the text inside it! Fortunately, there's a much easier way to work with the DOM, as you'll see on page 169.

Adding Content to a Page

JavaScript programs frequently need to add, delete, or change content on a page. For example, in the quiz program you wrote in Chapter 3 (page 106), you used the *document.write( )* method to add the test-taker's final score to the page. On the Netflix site (Figure 5-1), a description appears on the page when a visitor mouses over a movie title.

Note: In earlier chapters you used the *document.write( )* command to add JavaScript-generated content to a page (see page 29 for an example). That command is easy to learn and use, but very limited in what it can do–for example, *document.write( )* lets you add new content, but not alter what's already on the page. Furthermore, that command works when the page loads, so you can't use it to add content to a page later (for example, when a visitor clicks a button or types into a form field).

Adding content using the DOM is a big chore. It involves creating each node of the content you require, and then injecting the results into the page. In other words, if you want to add a <div> tag with a couple of other tags and some text, you have to create each node individually and place them in the proper relation to each other. Fortunately, browser manufacturers have provided a much simpler method: the *innerHTML* property.

The *innerHTML* property isn't a standard part of the DOM. It was first implemented in Internet Explorer, but all current, JavaScript-savvy Web browsers support it. Basically, *innerHTML* represents all of the HTML inside of a node. For example, if you look at the HTML code on page 157, the <p> tag wraps around other HTML. So the *innerHTML* for that <p> tag node is *Some important text*. Here's how you use JavaScript to access that HTML:

```
//get a list of all <p> tags on page
var pTags = document.getElementsByTagName('p');
//get the first <p> tag on page
var theP = pTags[0];
alert(theP.innerHTML);
```

In this case, the variable *theP* represents the node for the first paragraph on the page. The last line of code opens an alert box that displays all of the code inside that tag. For example, adding this JavaScript to the HTML on page 157 would make an alert box appear with the text "Some important text".

Note: *innerHTML* is a proposed part of the new HTML 5 standard that is being developed at the W3C (see *www.w3.org/TR/html5*).

Not only can you find out what's inside a node using *innerHTML*, you can also change the contents inside the node by setting the *innerHTML* property:

```
var headLine = document.getElementById('header');
headLine.innerHTML = 'JavaScript was here!';
```

In this example, the contents inside the tag with an ID of 'header' is changed to "JavaScript was here!" You aren't limited to just text either: you can set the *innerHTML* property to complete chunks of HTML, including tags and tag attributes. You'll see an example of this in the next section.

The Moon Quiz Revisited

In Chapter 3, you created a JavaScript program that used the *prompt( )* command to ask quiz questions, and the *document.write( )* command to write the test-taker's results to the page. In this short tutorial, you'll rewrite that script to take advantage of the DOM techniques you've learned in this chapter.

Note: See the note on page 27 for information on how to download the tutorial files.

---

1. **In a text editor, open the file *5.1.html* in the *chapter05* folder.**

   This file is the completed version of tutorial 3.3 from page 112. The first step is to get rid of the JavaScript in the body of the page.

2. **Locate the HTML, and delete the JavaScript that's bolded in this code:**

   ```
   <p>
     <script type="text/javascript">
       var message = 'You got ' + score;
       message += ' out of ' + questions.length;
       message += ' questions correct.';
       document.write(message);
     </script>
   </p>
   ```

   You're left with an empty paragraph. When the quiz program runs, the test-taker's results will appear inside this paragraph. To make it easy to later select this tag, you'll add an ID attribute to the <p> tag.

3. **Add *id="quizResults"* to the <p> tag. The final HTML should look like this:**

   ```
   <h1>A Simple Quiz Revisited</h1>
   <p id="quizResults"></p>
   </div>
   ```

   Next, you'll create a function that goes through the list of questions, and then prints the results on the page.

4. **Locate the *for* loop in the block of JavaScript near the top of the page. Add the following bolded code around the loop:**

   ```
   function doQuiz() {
     //go through the list of questions and ask each one
     for (var i=0; i<questions.length; i++) {
       askQuestion(questions[i]);
     }
   }
   ```

Don't forget the closing brace on the last line; it marks the end of the new function. At this point, you've just turned the original *for* loop (which looped through each item in the questions array) into a function. You'll find out why you want a function here in a moment.

Next, you'll build the results message; it's the same code as in the finished *3.3.html* tutorial.

5. **Between the closing brace for the loop and the closing brace of the new function, add the following three lines of JavaScript:**

```
var message = 'You got ' + score;
message += ' out of ' + questions.length;
message += ' questions correct.';
```

This code is straight from Tutorial 3.3, so, if you don't feel like typing, you can copy from that tutorial and past the code into this page. At this point, you haven't done much different from Tutorial 3.3—give your visitor a quiz and report the results. Now it's time to use the DOM. You'll start by getting a reference to the empty <p> tag on the page.

6. **Hit Return to add a new blank after the three lines of code you just added, and then type:**

```
var resultArea = document.getElementById('quizResults');
```

This line searches the document for a tag with an ID of 'quizResults'—you created that in step 3—and stores a reference to that tag in a variable named *resultArea*. Now you can place the results message there.

7. **Hit Return again, and type *resultArea.innerHTML = message;*. The complete code for the function should now look like this:**

```
function doQuiz( ) {
  //go through the list of questions and ask each one
  for (var i=0; i<questions.length; i++) {
      askQuestion(questions[i]);
  }
  var message = 'You got ' + score;
  message += ' out of ' + questions.length;
  message += ' questions correct.';
  var resultArea = document.getElementById('quizResults');
  resultArea.innerHTML = message;
}
```

This final line of the function assigns the contents of the variable *message* to the *innerHTML* property of the <p> tag. In other words, it simply writes the message into that paragraph just like the *document.write( )* command. The *innerHTML* approach is simpler, since you don't need to add a second block of JavaScript code in the main body of the page as you do when using the *document.write( )* command.

Remember, functions don't run until the program calls them (see page 99). So even though you've finished setting up a function that asks the quiz questions and writes the test-taker's results onto the page, your program won't actually ask the questions until the *doQuiz( )* function runs. You'll add the code for that now.

8. **Locate the closing </script> tag (below all of the JavaScript code on this page, inside the <head>) and add the code in bold below:**

```
window.onload=doQuiz;
</script>
```

Welcome to the wonderful world of JavaScript events. The line of code you added in this step instructs the JavaScript interpreter to run the *doQuiz( )* function *after* the page finishes loading. The *onload* part is what's called an *event handler*. An event is the moment when something happens in the Web browser or on the page. When the page finishes loading, for example, the load event happens. When a visitor moves her mouse over a link, a mouseover event occurs. An event handler assigns a function to the event—in other words, tells the browser what to do when the event occurs. You'll learn all about events in the next chapter.

So, why can't you just run the quiz before the page loads? After all, that's what you did in Tutorial 3.3 on page 106. If you open your completed *3.3.html* file (or the supplied *complete_3.3.html* file in the *chapter03* tutorial folder) in a Web browser, you'll see something different about how that quiz works. Notice that the page is completely blank while the quiz questions are being asked (top image in Figure 5-4). That's because the JavaScript code on that page runs as soon as the JavaScript interpreter encounters the *for* loop. It doesn't wait until the HTML is read and displayed by the Web browser, so the Web browser has to wait until all of the questions have been asked and answered before displaying the HTML.

Now, save the *5.1.html* file you've just finished, and preview it in a Web browser. See how the browser draws the page before the questions are asked (bottom image in Figure 5-4)? That's what the *window.onload=doQuiz* does. It instructs the JavaScript interpreter to wait until the page is loaded and drawn to the screen before running the quiz. Not only does this method look a bit better—a completely blank Web page is a little distracting—but you must do it this way when you use the DOM to manipulate a page's content.

Think of it this way: the JavaScript code comes *before* the HTML on the page. When the code is loaded, the browser is unaware of any of the HTML that follows it. So the paragraph tag into which the program writes the final results—"You got 3 out of 3 questions right"—doesn't yet exist for the Web browser. If you tried to run the JavaScript code *immediately* (before the HTML is loaded), the Web browser would spit out an error at the moment the program tried to get the <p> tag and write the message into it—again, because that <p> tag doesn't yet exist to the JavaScript interpreter.

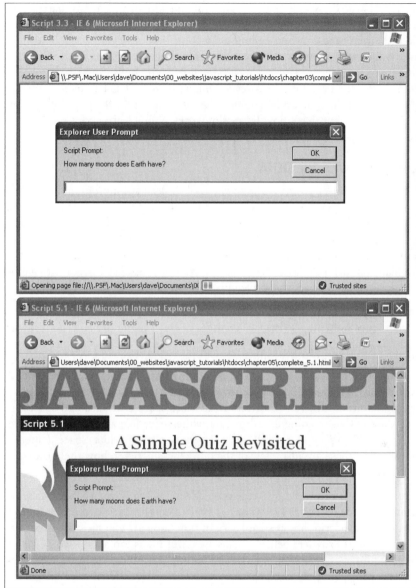

Figure 5-4:
When you run a JavaScript program before a page loads, the page won't appear until after the program is completed. In the page pictured at the top of this image, the JavaScript must finish asking each question of the quiz before the browser displays any of the Web page. However, if you use the onload event, you can have the Web browser load and display a Web page and then run your JavaScript program (bottom image).

That's why, in step 4, you put the loop, the results message, and the steps that select the <p> tag and write the message into that paragraph into a function. The function lets you wait until Web browser has read and stored the Web page and its HTML into its memory and only *then* execute all of the steps that create the quiz.

Finally, you may be wondering why the function doesn't have any parentheses after it in the line *window.onload=doQuiz*. As you read on page 98, you always include the parentheses when calling a function, like this: *doQuiz( )*. The short answer is that when you include the ( ), the function runs *immediately*—in other words, if you had typed *window.onload=doQuiz( )*, the quiz would run immediately, not after the page loads. However, *window.onload=doQuiz* merely points to the function and doesn't run it. The function only runs after the page loads. Confusing? Certainly, but that's how JavaScript works. You'll learn about this topic in more depth on page 218.

The Problem with the DOM

The Document Object Model is a powerful tool for JavaScript programmers, but it has some shortcomings. As you saw on page 160, moving from node to node in the DOM is a time-consuming process. Also, the DOM only supplies a couple of ways to get to tags—by ID name and by tag name. It doesn't provide an easy way, for example, to find all tags with a specific class name—a useful task if you want to manipulate a bunch of related elements (for example, make all images with a class of *slideshow* part of a JavaScript-driven photo slideshow).

A further complication is that the major browsers interpret the DOM differently. The techniques presented in the earlier pages of this chapter are all cross-browser compatible, but other parts of the DOM standard aren't. For example, Internet Explorer handles events differently from other browsers; the same HTML can produce more text nodes in Firefox and Safari than in Internet Explorer; and IE doesn't always retrieve HTML tag attributes in the same way as Firefox, Safari, or Opera. In addition, different browsers treat white space (like tabs and spaces) in HTML differently—in some cases treating white space like additional text nodes (Firefox and Safari) and in other cases ignoring that white space (Internet Explorer). And those are just a few of the differences between how the most common Web browsers handle the DOM.

Overcoming cross-browser JavaScript problems is such a huge task for JavaScript programmers that an entire (very boring) book could be dedicated to the subject. In fact, many JavaScript books spend a lot of time showing you the code needed to make the various browsers behave themselves. But life is too short—you'd rather be building interactive user interfaces and adding cool effects to your Web sites, instead of worrying about how to get your script to work identically in Internet Explorer, Firefox, Safari, and Opera. That's why this book skips a lot of the mind-numbing details required to make basic DOM functions work across browsers. Instead, it takes advantage of some very advanced, free JavaScript programming that you can use to build JavaScript-driven pages that will work well in all browsers in a fraction of the time. You'll start learning where to find this free JavaScript in the next section.

Introducing JavaScript Libraries

Many JavaScript programs have to deal with the same set of Web page tasks again and again: selecting an element, adding new content, hiding and showing content, modifying a tag's attributes, determining the value of form fields, and making programs react to different user interactions. The details of these basic actions can turn out to be quite complicated—especially if you want the program to work in all major browsers. Fortunately, JavaScript *libraries* offer a way to leap-frog past many time-consuming programming details.

A JavaScript library is simply a collection of JavaScript code that provides simple solutions to many of the mundane, day-to-day details of JavaScript. You can think of a library as a collection of prewritten JavaScript functions that you add to your Web page. These functions make it easy to complete common tasks. In many cases, you can replace many lines of your own JavaScript programming (and the hours required to test them) with a single function from a JavaScript library. A sizable chunk of your programming has already been done for you! There are lots of Java-Script libraries out there and many of them are in use on major Web sites such as Yahoo, NBC, Amazon, Digg, CNN, Apple, Microsoft, Twitter, and many more.

This book uses the popular jQuery library (*www.jquery.com*). There are other Java-Script libraries (see the box on page 170), but jQuery has many advantages:

- **Relatively small file size.** A minimized version of the library is only 55K, and a more fully compressed version weighs in at only 30K.

- **Friendly to Web designers.** jQuery doesn't assume you're a computer scientist. It takes advantage of knowledge about CSS that most Web designers already have.

- **It's tried and true.** jQuery is used on thousands of sites, including many popular, highly trafficked Web sites like Digg, Dell, the Onion, Warner Bros. Records, NBC, and Newsweek. Even Google uses it in some places. The fact that jQuery is so popular is a testament to how good it is.

- **It's free.** Hey, you can't beat that!

- **Large developer community.** As you read this, scores of people are working on the jQuery project—writing code, fixing bugs, adding new features, and updating the Web site with documentation and tutorials. A JavaScript library created by a single programmer (or one supplied by a single author) can easily disappear if the programmer (or author) grows tired of the project. jQuery, on the other hand, should be around a long time, supported by the efforts of programmers around the world. It's like having a bunch of JavaScript programmers working for you for free.

- **Plug-ins, plug-ins, plug-ins.** jQuery lets other programmers create *plug-ins*—add-on JavaScript programs that work in conjunction with jQuery to make certain tasks, effects, or features incredibly easy to add to a Web page. In this book, you'll learn about plug-ins that make validating forms, adding drop-down navigation menus, and building interactive slideshows a half-hour's worth of work, instead of a two-week project. There are literally hundreds of other plug-ins available for jQuery.

You've actually used jQuery in this book already. In the tutorial for Chapter 1 (page 30), you added just a few lines of JavaScript code to quickly and easily add stripes to alternating rows in a table.

UP TO SPEED

Other Libraries

jQuery isn't the only JavaScript library in town. There are many, many others. Some are designed to perform specific tasks, and others are all-purpose libraries aimed at solving every JavaScript task under the sun. Here are a few of the most popular:

Yahoo User Interface Library (*http://developer.yahoo.com/yui/*) is a project of Yahoo, and indeed the company uses it throughout its site. Yahoo programmers are constantly adding to and improving the library, and they provide very good documentation on the YUI site.

Prototype (*http://www.prototypejs.org/*) was one of the first JavaScript libraries available. Weighing in at a hefty 124K, it lets you do all sorts of things from selecting making

manipulating the DOM easier, to simplifying the task of communicating with a Web server using Ajax. It's often used in combination with a visual effects library named *scriptaculous* (*http://script.aculo.us/*), which adds animation and other user interface goodies.

Dojo Toolkit (*http://dojotoolkit.org/*) is another library that's been around a long time. It's a very powerful and very large collection of JavaScript files that tackle nearly every JavaScript task around.

Mootools (*http://mootools.net/*) is another popular library with good documentation and a great looking Web site.

Getting Started with jQuery

The first step in using jQuery is downloading it—the *jquery.js* file is a single JavaScript file that you link to a Web page to use. The tutorial files you downloaded for this book at *www.sawmac.com/js/* include the jQuery library file, but since the jQuery team updates the library on a regular basis, you can always find the latest version at *http://docs.jquery.com/Downloading_jQuery*, listed under the Current Release headline (circled in Figure 5-5).

The jQuery file comes in three versions on the download site. Which file you pick depends on how you want to use it:

- **Uncompressed.** The uncompressed jQuery file has the largest file size (the uncompressed version of jQuery 1.2.6, for example, is 97.8K) You shouldn't use this file on your Web site, but it's helpful if you want to learn how the jQuery library is put together. The code includes lots of comments (page 71) that help make clear what the different parts of the file do. (But in order to understand the comments, you need to know *a lot* about JavaScript.)

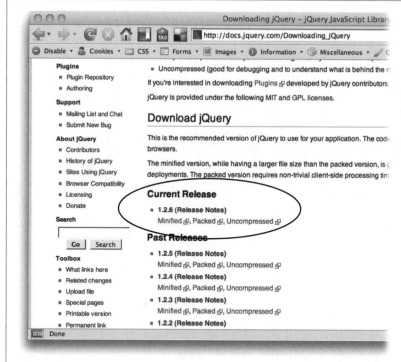

Figure 5-5:
*The external JavaScript file for
the jQuery library comes in
three flavors. Make sure to
download the minified
version; it offers the best
combination of file size and
performance.*

- **Packed.** The packed version of jQuery provides the smallest file size (the packed version of jQuery 1.2.6 is only 30.3K). It provides all the same functions as the uncompressed version, but the JavaScript code has been put through a clever compression program (*http://dean.edwards.name/packer/*) that's reduced the number of characters needed in the file. The downside of a packed JavaScript file is that the visitor's Web browser has to "unpack" the file each time it's run—meaning it's slightly slower than an unpacked version.

- **Minified.** The minified jQuery file uses a simpler compression method than a *packed* file, but the file is a bit larger (the minified version of jQuery 1.2.6 is 54. 5K). However, since the minified version doesn't need to be unpacked each time it's run, this file (once it's downloaded) performs a bit faster than the packed version. Also, since a Web browser usually caches the downloaded jQuery file, file size isn't the most important issue. The Web browser only needs to download the file from your site once, then, when a visitor goes to another page on your site, the browser simply uses the previously downloaded jQuery file. Because the minified version has fairly small file size and runs quickly, this book uses it in the tutorials.

Once you download the jQuery file, put it somewhere in your site, such as the site's root folder. Some Web designers create a separate folder just for JavaScript files (*js* or *libs* are common names) and store the jQuery file as well as any other .js files in it.

Tip: The jQuery file you download from jQuery.com includes the version number and compression type–for example, *jquery-1.2.6.min.js* is the minified version of *jQuery 1.2.6.* You can rename this to something simpler like *jquery126.js* or just *jquery.js.*

To use the file, you must attach it to your Web page. It's just an external .js file, so you attach it just like any external JavaScript file, as described on page 24. For example, say you've stored the *jquery.js* file in a folder named *js* in your site's root folder. To attach the file to your home page, you'd add the following script tag to the head of the page:

```
<script type="text/javascript" src="js/jquery.js"></script>
```

Once you've attached the jQuery file, you're ready to add your own scripts that take advantage of jQuery's advanced functions. For example, you can attach another external JavaScript file with your own programming in it, or add a second <script> tag to the Web page and start programming:

```
<script type="text/javascript" src="js/jquery.js"></script>
<script type="text/javascript">
   // your script goes here
</script>
```

Selecting Page Elements (Revisited)

As you saw on page 158, the DOM provides two primary methods for selecting an element on a Web page—*document.getElementById( )* and *document. getElementsByTagName( )*. Unfortunately, these two methods don't provide the control needed to make more subtle kinds of selections. For example, if you want to select every <a> tag with a class of *navButton*, you first need to select every tag, and then go through each and find only the ones that have the proper class name. Or (as you did in the tutorial in Chapter 1) you may want to select every *other* row in a table.

Fortunately, jQuery offers a very powerful technique for selecting and working on a collection of elements—CSS Selectors. That's right, if you're used to using Cascading Style Sheets to style your Web pages, you're ready to use jQuery. A CSS selector is simply the instruction that tells a Web browser which tag the style applies to. For example, *h1* is basic element selector, which applies a style to every <h1> tag, while *.copyright*, is a class selector, which styles any tag that has a class attribute of copyright like this:

```
<p class="copyright">Copyright, 2009</p>
```

With jQuery, you select one or more elements using a special command called the *jQuery object*. The basic syntax is like this:

```
$('selector')
```

You can use nearly all CSS 2.1 and many CSS 3 selectors when you create a jQuery object (even if the browser itself doesn't understand the particular selector—like IE with certain CSS 3 selectors). For example, if you want to select a tag with a specific ID of *banner* in jQuery, you can write this:

```
$('#banner')
```

The *#banner* is the CSS selector used to style a tag with the ID name *banner*—the # part indicates that you're identifying an ID. Of course, once you select one or more elements, you'll want to do something with them—jQuery provides many tools for working with elements. For example, say you want to change the HTML inside an element; you can write this:

```
$('#banner').html('<h1>JavaScript was here</h1>');
```

You'll learn more about how to work with page elements using jQuery starting on page 181, and throughout the rest of this book. But first, you need learn more about using jQuery to select page elements.

Basic Selectors

Basic CSS *selectors* like IDs, classes, and element selectors make up the heart of CSS. They're a great way to select a wide range of elements using jQuery.

Because reading about selectors isn't the best way to gain an understanding of them, this book includes an interactive Web page so you can test selectors. In the *chapter05* folder of the book's tutorial files, you'll find a file named *selectors.html*. Open the file in a Web browser. You can test various jQuery selectors by typing them into the selector box and clicking Apply (see Figure 5-6).

Note: See page 27 for information on where to find the tutorial files for this book.

ID selectors

You can select any page element that has an ID applied to it using jQuery and a CSS ID selector. For example, say you have the following HTML in a Web page:

```
<p id="message">Special message</p>
```

To select that element using the old DOM way, you'd write this:

```
var messagePara = document.getElementById('message');
```

The jQuery method looks like this:

```
var messagePara = $('#message');
```

Unlike with the DOM method, you don't just use the ID name (*'message'*); you have to use the CSS-syntax for defining an ID selector (*'#message'*). In other words, you include the pound sign before the ID name, just as if creating a CSS style for that ID.

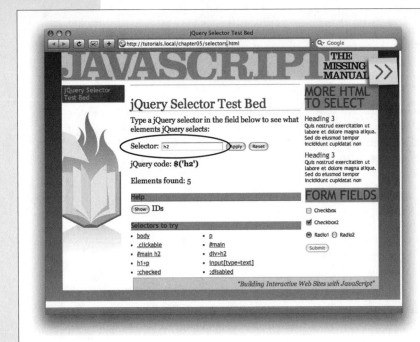

Figure 5-6:
The file selectors.html, provided with this book's tutorial files, lets you try out jQuery selectors. Just type a selector in the Selector form field (circled), and then click Apply. The page converts your selector into a jQuery object, and any elements that match the selector you typed turn red. Below the field is the jQuery code used to select the item, as well as the total number or elements selected. In this case, h2 is the selector, and all <h2> tags on the page (there are five on this page) are highlighted in red (which looks surprisingly like grey here).

Element selectors

jQuery also has its own replacement for the *getElementsByTagName( )* method. Just pass the tag's name to jQuery. For example, using the old DOM method to select every <a> tag on the page, you'd write this:

```
var linksList = document.getElementsByTagName('a');
```

With jQuery, you'd write this:

```
var linksList = $('a');
```

Note: jQuery supports an even wider range of selectors than are listed here. Although this book lists many useful ones, you can find a complete list of jQuery selectors at *http://docs.jquery.com/Selectors*.

Class selectors

The DOM doesn't have any built-in method to find all elements with a particular class attribute, which unfortunately is a common task for JavaScript programmers. For example, suppose you want to create a navigation bar that includes drop-down menus; when a visitor mouses over one of the main navigation buttons, you want a drop-down menu to appear. You need to use JavaScript to control those menus, and you need a way to program each of the main navigation buttons to open a drop-down menu when someone mouses over the button.

Note: Because finding all elements with a particular class name is such a common task, some browsers (like the latest versions of Firefox and Safari) have added that feature. But since not all browsers have a built-in way to find elements of a specific class, a library like jQuery, which takes the different browsers into account, is invaluable.

One technique is to add a class—like *navButton*—to each of the main navigation bar links, and then use JavaScript to search for links with *just* that class name and apply all of the magical menu-opening power to those links (you'll learn how to do that, by the way, on page 300). This scheme may sound confusing now, but the important point for now is that to make this navigation bar work, you need a way to select only the links with a specific class name.

Fortunately, jQuery provides an easy method to select all elements with the same class name. Just use a CSS class selector like this:

```
$('.submenu')
```

Again, notice that you write the CSS class selector just like, well, a CSS class selector, with the period before the class name. Once you select those tags, you can manipulate them using jQuery. For example, to hide all tags with the class name of *.submenu*, you'd write this:

```
$('.submenu').hide();
```

You'll learn more about the jQuery *hide( )* function on page 243, but for now this example gives you a bit of an idea of how jQuery works.

UP TO SPEED

Understanding CSS

Cascading Style Sheets are a big topic in any discussion of JavaScript. To get the most out of this book, you need to have at least some background in Web design and know a bit about CSS and how to use it. CSS is the most important tool a Web designer has for creating beautiful Web sites, so if you don't know much about it, now's the time to learn. Not only will CSS help you use jQuery, but you'll find that you can use JavaScript in combination with CSS to easily add interactive visual effects to a Web page.

If you need some help getting up to speed with CSS, there are plenty of resources at your disposal:

For a basic overview on CSS, try the HTML Dog CSS Tutorials *www.htmldog.com/guides/*. You'll find basic, intermediate, and advanced tutorials at the site.

You can also pick up a copy of *CSS: The Missing Manual,* which provides thorough coverage of CSS (including many hands-on tutorials just like the ones in this book).

Most of all, when working with jQuery, it's very important to understand *CSS selectors*—the instructions that tell a Web browser which tag a CSS rule applies to. To get a handle on selectors, the resources in this box are very good. There are also a few places to go if you just want a refresher on the different selectors that are available:

- *http://css.maxdesign.com.au/selectutorial/*

- *http://www.456bereastreet.com/archive/200601/
  css_3_selectors_explained/*

Advanced Selectors

jQuery also lets you use more complicated CSS selectors to accurately pinpoint the tags you wish to select. Don't worry too much about mastering these right now: Once you've read a few more chapters and gained a better understanding of how jQuery works and how to use it to manipulate a Web page, you'll probably want to turn back to this section and take another look.

- **Descendent selectors** provide a way to target a tag inside another tag (see "Selecting nearby nodes" on page 160). For example, say you've created an unordered list of links and added an ID name of *navBar* to the list's <ul> tag like this: *<ul id="navBar">*. The jQuery expression *$('a')* selects all <a> tags on the page. However, if you want to select only the links inside the unordered list, you use a descendent selector like this:

  ```
  $('#navBar a')
  ```

  Again, this syntax is just basic CSS: a selector, followed by a space, followed by another selector. The selector listed last is the target (in this case, *a*), while each selector to the left represents a tag that wraps around the target.

- **Child selectors** target a tag that's the child of another tag. A child tag is the direct descendent of another tag. For example, in the HTML diagrammed in Figure 5-2, the <h1> and <p> tags are children of the <body> tag, but the <strong> tag is not (since it's wrapped by the <p> tag). You create a child selector by first listing the parent element, followed by a >, and then the child element. For example, to select <p> tags that are the children of the <body> tag, you'd write this:

  ```
  $('body > p')
  ```

- **Adjacent sibling** selectors let you select a tag that appears directly after another tag. For example, say you have an invisible panel that appears when you click a tab. In your HTML, the tab might be represented by a heading tag (say <h2>), while the hidden panel is a <div> tag that follows the header. To make the <div> tag (the panel) visible, you'll need a way to select it. You can easily do so with jQuery and an adjacent sibling selector:

  ```
  $('h2 + div')
  ```

  To create an adjacent sibling selector, just add a plus sign between two selectors (which can be any type of selector: IDs, classes, or elements). The selector on the right is the one to select, but only if it comes directly after the selector on the left.

- **Attribute selectors** let you select elements based on whether the element has a particular attribute, and even check to make sure the attribute matches a specific value. With an attribute selector, you can find <img> tags that have the alt attribute set, or even match an <img> tag that has a particular alt text value. Or you could find every link tag that points outside your site, and add code to just those links, so they'll open in new windows.

You add the attribute selector after the name of the element whose attribute you're checking. For example, to find <img> tags that have the alt attribute set, you write this:

```
$('img[alt]')
```

There are a handful of different attribute selectors:

- *[attribute]* selects elements that have the specified attribute assigned in the HTML. For example, *$(a[href])* locates all <a> tags that have an *href* attribute set. Selecting by attribute lets you exclude named anchors—*<a name="placeOnPage"></a>*—that are simply used as an in-page link.

- *[attribute=value]* selects elements that have a particular attribute with a specific value. For example, to find all text boxes in a form, you can use this:

```
$('input[type=text]')
```

Since most form elements share the same tag—<input>—the only way to tell the type of form element is to check its type attribute (selecting form elements is so common that jQuery includes specific selectors just for that purpose, as described on page 311).

- *[attribute^=value]* matches elements with an attribute that *begins* with a specific value. For example, if you want to find links that point outside your site, you can use this code:

```
$('a[href^=http://]')
```

Notice that the entire attribute value doesn't have to match just the beginning. So *href^=http://* matches links that point to *http://www.yahoo.com*, *http://www.google.com*, and so on. Or you could use this selector to identify *mailto:* links like this:

```
$('a[href^=mailto:]')
```

- *[attribute$=value]* matches elements whose attribute ends with a specific value, which is great for matching file extensions. For example, with this selector you can locate links that point to PDF files (maybe to use JavaScript to add a special PDF icon, or dynamically generate a link to Adobe.com so your visitor can download the Acrobat Reader program). The code to select links that point to PDF files looks like this:

```
$('a[href$=.pdf]')
```

- *[attribute*=value]* matches elements whose attribute contains a specific value anywhere in the attribute. For example, you can find any type of link that points to a particular domain. For example, here's how to find a link that points to missingmanuals.com:

```
$('a[href*=missingmanuals.com]')
```

This selector provides the flexibility to find not only links that point to *http://www.missingmanuals.com*, but also *http://missingmanuals.com* and *http://www.missingmanuals.com/library.html*.

Note: jQuery has a set of selectors that are useful when working with forms. They let you select elements such as text fields, password fields, and selected radio buttons. You'll learn about these selectors on page 311.

---

jQuery Filters

jQuery also provides a way to filter your selections based on certain characteristics. For example, the *:even* filter lets you select every even element in a collection of elements (you used this filter in the tutorial on page 30 to highlight every other row in a table). In addition, you can find elements that contain particular tags, specific text, elements that are hidden from view, and even elements that do *not* match a particular selector. To use a filter, you add a colon followed by the filter's name after the main selector. For example, to find every even row of a table, write your jQuery selector like this:

```
$('tr:even')
```

This code selects every even <tr> tag. To narrow down the selection, you may want to just find every even table row in a table with class name of *striped*. You can do that like this:

```
$('.striped tr:even')
```

Here's how *:even* and other filters work:

- *:even* and *:odd* select every *other* element in a group. These filters work a little counter-intuitively; just remember that a jQuery selection is a list of all elements that match a specified selector. In that respect, they're kind of like arrays (see page 56). Each element in a jQuery selection has an index number—remember that index values for arrays always start at 0 (see page 59). So, since *:even* filters on even index values (like 0, 2, and 4), this filter actually returns the first, third, and fifth items (and so on) in the selection—in other words, it's really selecting every other odd element! The *:odd* filter works the same except it selects every odd index number (1, 3, 5, and so on).

- You can use *:not( )* to find elements that *don't* match a particular selector type. For example, say you want to select every <a> tag except ones with a class of *navButton*. Here's how to do that:

```
$('a:not(.navButton)');
```

You give the *:not( )* function the name of the selector you wish to ignore. In this case, *.navButton* is a class selector, so this code translates to "not with the class of *.navButton*." You can use *:not( )* with any of the jQuery filters and with most jQuery selectors; so, for example, to find every link that doesn't begin with http://, you can write this:

```
$('a:not([href^=http://])')
```

- *:has( )* finds elements that contain another selector. For example, say you want to find all <li> tags, but only if they have an <a> tag inside them. You'd do that like this:

```
$('li:has(a)')
```

This setup is different from a descendent selector, since it doesn't select the <a>; it selects <li> tags, but only those <li> tags with a link inside them.

- *:contains( )* finds elements that contain specific text. For example, to find every link that says "Click Me!" you can create a jQuery object like this:

```
$('a:contains(Click Me!)')
```

- *:hidden* locates elements that are hidden, which includes elements that either have the CSS *display* property set to *none* (which means you won't see them on the page), elements you hide using jQuery's *hide( )* function (discussed on page 243), or hidden form fields. (This selector doesn't apply to elements whose CSS *visibility* property is set to *invisible*.) For example, say you've hidden several <div> tags; you can find them and then make them visible using jQuery, like this:

```
$('div:hidden').show( );
```

This line of code has no effect on <div> tags that are currently visible on the page. (You'll learn about jQuery's *show( )* function on page 243.)

- *:visible* is the opposite of *:hidden*. It locates elements that are visible on the page.

Understanding jQuery Selections

When you select one or more elements using the jQuery object—for example *$('#navBar a')*—you don't end up with a traditional list of DOM nodes, like the ones you get if you use *getElementById( )* or *getElementsByTagName( )*. Instead, you get a special jQuery-only selection of elements. These elements don't understand the traditional DOM methods; for example, you can't use the *innerHTML* property (page 163) with a jQuery object like this:

```
$('#banner').innerHTML = 'New text'; // won't work
```

In fact, if you learned about DOM methods in another book, you'll find that none of them work with the jQuery object as-is. That may seem like a major drawback, but nearly all of the properties and methods of a normal DOM node have jQuery equivalents, so you can do anything the traditional DOM can do—only usually much faster and with fewer lines of code.

There are, however, two big conceptual differences between how the DOM works and how jQuery selections work. jQuery was built to make it a lot easier and faster to program JavaScript. One of the goals of the library is to let you do a lot of stuff with as few lines of code as possible. To achieve that, jQuery uses two unusual principles.

Automatic loops

Normally, when you're using the DOM and you select a bunch of nodes, you then need to create a loop (page 90) to go through each node selected and do something to that node. For example, if you want to select all the images in a page then hide them—something you might do if you want to create a JavaScript-driven slideshow—you must first select the images and then create a loop to go through the list of images.

Because looping through a collection of elements is so common, jQuery functions have that feature built right in. In other words, when you apply a jQuery function to a selection of elements, you don't need to create a loop yourself, since the function does it automatically.

For example, to select all images inside a <div> tag with an ID of *slideshow* and then hide those images, you write this in jQuery:

```
$('#slideshow img').hide();
```

The list of elements created with *$('#slideshow img')* might include 50 images. The *hide( )* function automatically loops through the list, hiding each image individually. This setup is so convenient (imagine the number of *for* loops you won't have to write) that it's surprising that this great feature isn't just part of the DOM.

Chaining functions

Sometimes you'll want to perform several operations on a selection of elements. For example, say you want to set the width and height of a <div> tag (with an ID of *popUp*) using JavaScript. Normally, you'd have to write at least two lines of code. But jQuery lets you do so with a single line:

```
$('#popUp').width(300).height(300);
```

jQuery uses a unique principle called *chaining*, which lets you add functions one after the other. Each function is connected to the next by a period, and operates on the same jQuery collection of elements as the previous function. So the code above changes the width of the element with the ID *popUp*, *and* changes the height of the element. Chaining jQuery functions lets you concisely carry out a large number of actions. For example, say you not only want to set the width and height of the <div> tag but also want to add text inside the <div> and make it fade into view (assuming it's not currently visible on the page). You can do that very succinctly like this:

```
$('#popUp').width(300).height(300).text('Hi!').fadeIn(1000);
```

This code applies four jQuery functions (*width( )*, *height( )*, *text( )*, and *fadeIn( )*) to the tag with an ID name of *popUp*.

Tip: A long line of chained jQuery functions can be hard to read, so some programmers break it up over multiple lines like this:

```
$('#popUp').width(300)
     .height(300)
     .text('Message')
     .fadeIn(1000);
```

As long as you only add a semicolon on the *last line* of the chain, the JavaScript interpreter treats the lines as a single statement.

The ability to chain functions is pretty unusual and is a specific feature of jQuery—in other words, you can't add non-jQuery functions (either ones you create or built-in JavaScript functions) in the chain.

Adding Content to a Page

jQuery provides many functions for manipulating elements and content on a page, from simply replacing HTML, to precisely positioning new HTML in relation to a selected element, to completely removing tags and content from the page.

Note: An example file, *content_functions.html*, located in the *chapter05* tutorial folder lets you take each of these jQuery functions for a test drive. Just open the file in a Web browser, type some text in the text box, and click any of the "Run It" boxes to see how each function works.

To study the following examples of these functions, assume you have a page with the following HTML:

```
<div id="container">
  <div id="errors">
    <h2>Errors:</h2>
  </div>
</div>
```

- *.html( )* works like the DOM's *innerHTML* property. It can read the current HTML inside an element as well as replace the current contents with some other HTML. You use the *html( )* function in conjunction with a jQuery selection.

  To retrieve the HTML currently inside the selection, just add *.html( )* after the jQuery selection. For example, you can run the following command using the HTML snippet at the beginning of this section:

  ```
  alert($('#errors').html());
  ```

This code creates an alert box with the text "*<h2>Errors:</h2>*" in it. When you use the *html( )* function in this way, you can make a copy of the HTML inside a specific element and paste it into another element on a page.

- If you supply a string as an argument to *.html( )*, you replace the current contents inside the selection:

```
$('#errors').html('<p>There are four errors in this form</p>');
```

This line of code replaces all of the HTML inside an element with an ID of *errors*. It would change the example HTML snippet to:

```
<div id="container">
  <div id="errors">
    <p>There are four errors in this form</p>
  </div>
</div>
```

Notice that it replaces the <h2> tag that was already there. You can avoid replacing that HTML using other functions listed below.

Note: jQuery also has a function named *text( )* that works just like *html( )*, except that any HTML tags that are passed to *text( )* are encoded so that <p> is translated to *<p>*—use it if you want you to actually display the brackets and tag names *on* the page. For example, you can use it to display example HTML code for other people to view.

- *append( )* adds HTML as the last child element of the selected element. For example, say you select a <div> tag, but instead of replacing the contents of the <div>, you just want to add some HTML before the closing </div> tag. The *.append( )* function is a great way to add an item to the end of a bulleted (<ul>) or numbered (<ol>) list. As an example, say you run the following code on a page with the HTML listed at the beginning of this section:

```
$('#errors').append('<p>There are four errors in this form</p>');
```

After this function runs, you end up with HTML like this:

```
<div id="container">
  <div id="errors">
    <h2>Errors:</h2>
    <p>There are four errors in this form</p>
  </div>
</div>
```

Notice that the original HTML inside the <div> remains the same, and the new chunk of HTML is added after it.

- *prepend( )* is just like *append( )*, but adds HTML directly after the opening tag for the selection. For example, say you run the following code on the same HTML listed previously:

```
$('#errors').prepend('<p>There are four errors in this form</p>');
```

After this *prepend( )* function, you end up with the following HTML:

```
<div id="container">
  <div id="errors">
    <p>There are four errors in this form</p>
    <h2>Errors:</h2>
  </div>
</div>
```

Now the newly added content appears directly after the <div>'s opening tag.

- If you want to add HTML just *outside* of a selection, either before the selected element's opening tag or directly after the element's closing tag, use the *before( )* or *after( )* functions. For example, it's common practice to check a text field in a form to make sure that the field isn't empty when your visitor submits the form. Assume that the HTML for the field looks like the following before the form is submitted:

```
<input type="text" name="userName" id="userName">
```

Now suppose that when the visitor submits the form, this field is empty. You can write a program that checks the field and then adds an error message after the field. To add the message after this field (don't worry right now about how you actually check that the contents of form fields are correct—you'll find out on page 330), you can use the *.after( )* function like this:

```
$('userName').after('<span class="error">User name required</span>');
```

That line of code makes the Web page show the error message, and the HTML component would look like this:

```
<input type="text" name="userName" id="userName">
<span class="error">User name required</span>
```

The *.before( )* function simply puts the new content before the selected element.

Replacing and Removing Selections

At times you may want to completely replace or remove a selected element. For example, say you've created a pop-up dialog box using JavaScript (not the old-fashioned *alert( )* method, but a more professional-looking dialog box that's actually just an absolutely-positioned <div> floating on top of the page). When the visitor clicks the "Close" button on the dialog box, you naturally want to remove the dialog from the page. To do so, you can use the jQuery *remove( )* function. Say the pop-up dialog had an ID of *popup*; you can use the following code to delete it:

```
$('#popup').remove();
```

The *.remove( )* function isn't limited to just a single element. Say you want to remove all <span> tags that have a class of *error* applied to them; you can do this:

```
$('span.error').remove();
```

View Source Chart Provides Clear View

One problem with using JavaScript to manipulate the DOM by adding, changing, deleting, and rearranging HTML code is that it's hard to figure out what the HTML of a page looks like when JavaScript is finished. For example, the View Source command available in every browser only shows the Web page file as it was downloaded from the Web server. In other words, you see the HTML *before* it was changed by JavaScript, which can make it very hard to figure out if the JavaScript you're writing is really producing the HTML you're after. For example, if you could see what the HTML of your page looks like after your JavaScript adds 10 error messages to a form page, or after your JavaScript program creates an elaborate pop-up dialog box complete with text and form fields, it would be a lot easier to see if you're ending up with the HTML you want.

Fortunately, there are a couple of Firefox extensions that can help with this dilemma. The *View Source Chart* extension (*http://jennifermadden.com/scripts/ViewRenderedSource.html*) shows you the current state of the DOM whenever you open the View Source Chart window. In other words, if you open the View Source Chart window after JavaScript has added or changed a bunch of HTML, you'll see the new JavaScript-enhanced HTML.

To use the extension, open Firefox, visit the URL above, and install the extension. Then, when you want to view the current state of a page's HTML, choose *View Source Chart* from Firefox's View menu. When you open the window, it shows the current state of the HTML. If you then do something on the Web page that once again changes the DOM using JavaScript (like click an image or try to submit a form), you need to close the View Source Chart window and open it again to see the just-created HTML.

Another extension, the Web Developer Toolbar (*http://chrispederick.com/work/web-developer/*), provides a similar tool. Using Firefox, visit the URL listed and install the extension. After Firefox restarts, you'll see a new toolbar of options (there are *lots* of useful tools for Web developers). If you choose View Source → View Generated Source, you'll see the JavaScript-modified DOM. However, the HTML this tool displays isn't as well formatted as the View Source Chart extension, so it's a bit harder to read.

You can also completely replace a selection with new content. For example, suppose you have a page with photos of the products your company sells. When a visitor clicks on an image of a product, it's added to a shopping cart. You might want to replace the <img> tag with some text when the image is clicked ("Added to cart," for example). You'll learn how to make particular elements react to events (like an image being clicked) in the next chapter, but for now just assume there's an <img> tag with an ID of *product101* that you wish to replace with text. Here's how you do that with jQuery:

```
$('#product101').replace('<p>Added to cart</p>');
```

This code removes the <img> tag from the page and replaces it with a <p> tag.

Note: jQuery also includes a function named *clone( )* that lets you make a copy of a selected element. You'll see this function in action in the tutorial on page 199.

Setting and Reading Tag Attributes

Adding, removing, and changing elements isn't the only thing jQuery is good at—and it's not the only thing you'll want to do with a selection of elements. You'll often want to change the value of an element's attribute—add a class to a tag, for example, or change a CSS property of an element. You can also get the value of an attribute—for instance, what URL does a particular link point to?

Classes

Cascading Style Sheets are a very powerful technology, letting you add all sorts of sophisticated visual formatting to your HTML. One CSS rule can add a colorful background to a page, while another rule might completely hide an element from view. You can create some really advanced visual effects simply by using JavaScript to remove, add, or change a class applied to an element. Because Web browsers process and implement CSS instructions very quickly and efficiently, simply adding a class to a tag could complete change that tag's appearance—even make it disappear from a page.

For example, in the tutorial on page 30, you wrote a JavaScript program that changed the background color of every other row in a table. Well, actually what you did was write a program that added a particular class to every other row in the table. CSS actually handled the coloring of the row's background.

jQuery provides several functions for manipulating a tag's class attribute:

• *addClass( )* adds a specified class to an element. You add the *addClass( )* after a jQuery selection and pass the function a string, which represents the class name you wish to add. For example, to add the class *externalLink* to all links pointing outside your site, you can use this code:

```
$('a[href^=http://]').addClass('externalLink');
```

This code would take HTML like this:

```
<a href="http://www.oreilly.com/">
```

And change it to the following:

```
<a href="http://www.oreilly.com/" class="externalLink">
```

For this function to be of any use, you'll need to create a CSS class style beforehand and add it to the page's style sheet. Then, when the JavaScript adds the class name, the Web browser can apply the style properties from the previously defined CSS rule.

Note: When using the *addClass( )* and *removeClass( )* functions, you only supply the class name–leave out the period you normally use when creating a class selector. For example, *addClass('externalLink')* is correct, but *addClass('externalLink')* is wrong.

This jQuery function also takes care of issues that arise when a tag already has a class applied to it—the *addClass( )* function doesn't eliminate the old classes already applied to the tag; the function just adds the new class as well.

Note: Adding multiple class names to a single tag is perfectly valid and frequently very helpful. Check out *http://webdesign.about.com/od/css/qt/tipcssmulticlas.htm* for more information on this technique.

• *removeClass( )* is the opposite of *addClass( )*. It removes the specified class from the selected elements. For example, if you wanted to remove a class named *highlight* from a <div> with an ID of *alertBox*, you'd do this:

```
$('#alertBox').removeClass('highlight');
```

• Finally, you may want to *toggle* a particular class—meaning add the class if it doesn't already exist, or remove the class if it does. Toggling is a popular way to show an element in either an on or off state. For example, when you click a radio button, it's checked (on); click it again, and the checkmark disappears (off).

Say you have a button on a Web page that, when clicked, changes the <body> tag's class. By so doing, you can add a complete stylistic change to a Web page by crafting a second set of styles using descendent selectors. When the button is clicked again, you want the class removed from the <body> tag, so that the page reverts back to its previous appearance. For this example, assume the button the visitor clicks to change the page's style has an ID of *changeStyle* and you want to toggle the class name *altStyle* off and on with each click of the button. Here's the code to do that:

```
$('#changeStyle').click(function() {
    $('body').toggleClass('altStyle');
});
```

At this point, don't worry about the first and third lines of code above; those have to do with events (Chapter 6), which let scripts react to actions—like clicking the button—that happen on a page. The bolded line of code demonstrates the *toggleClass( )* function; it either adds or removes the class *altStyle* with each click of the button.

Reading and Changing CSS Properties

jQuery's *css( )* function also lets you directly change CSS properties of an element, so instead of simply applying a class style to an element, you can immediately add a border or background-color, or set a width or positioning property. You can use the *css( )* function in three ways: to find the current value for an element's CSS property, to set a single CSS property on an element, or to set multiple CSS properties at once.

To determine the current value of a CSS property, pass the name of the property to the *css( )* function. For example, say you want to find the background color of a <div> tag with an ID of *main*:

```
var bgColor = $('#main').css('background-color');
```

After this code runs, the variable *bgColor* will contain a string with the element's background-color value (jQuery returns either *'transparent'* if no color is set, or an RGB color value like this: *'rgb(255, 255, 0)'*).

Note: jQuery may not always return CSS values the way you expect. For example, jQuery doesn't understand shorthand CSS properties like *font*, *margin*, *padding*, or *border*. Instead, you have to use the specific CSS properties like *font-face*, *margin-top*, *padding-bottom*, or *border-bottom-width* to access styles that can be combined in CSS shorthand. In addition, jQuery translates all unit values to pixels, so even if you use CSS to set the <body> tag's font-size to 150%, jQuery returns a pixel value when checking the *font-size* property.

The *css( )* function also lets you set a CSS property for an element. To use the function this way, you supply two arguments to the function: the CSS property name and a value. For example, to change the font size for the <body> tag to 200% size, you can do this:

```
$('body').css('font-size', '200%');
```

The second argument you supply can be a string value, like '200%', or a numeric value, which jQuery translates to pixels. For example, to change the padding inside all of the tags with a class of *.pullquote* to 100px, you can write this code:

```
$('.pullquote').css('padding',100);
```

In this example, jQuery sets the padding property to 100 pixels.

Note: When you set a CSS property using jQuery's *.css()* function, you can use the CSS shorthand method. For example, here's how you could add a black, one-pixel border around all paragraphs with a class of *highlight*:

```
$('p.highlight').css('border', '1px solid black');
```

It's often useful to change a CSS property based on its current value. For example, say you want to add a "Make text bigger" button on a Web page, so when a visitor clicks the button, the page's font-size doubles. To make that happen, you read the value, and then set a new value. In this case, you first determine the current font-size and then set the font-size to twice that value. It's little trickier than you might think. Here's the code, and a full explanation follows:

```
var baseFont = $('body').css('font-size');
baseFont = parseInt(baseFont,10);
$('body').css('font-size',baseFont * 2);
```

The first line retrieves the <body> tag's font-size value—the returned value is in pixels and is a string like this: *'16px'*. Since you want to double that size—multiplying it by 2—you must convert that string to a number by removing the "px" part of the string. The second line accomplishes that using the JavaScript *parseInt( )* method discussed on page 135. That function essentially strips off anything following the number, so after line two *baseFont* contains a number, like 16. Finally, the third line resets the *font-size* property by multiplying the *baseFont* value by 2.

Note: This code affect the page's type size only if the other tags on the page—paragraphs, headlines, and so on—have their font-size set using a relative value like ems or percentages. If the other tags use absolute values like pixels, changing the <body> tag's font size won't affect them.

Changing Multiple CSS Properties at Once

If you want to change more than one CSS property on an element, you don't need to resort to multiple uses of the *.css( )* function. For example, if you want to dynamically highlight a <div> tag (perhaps in reaction to an action taken by a visitor), you can change the <div> tag's background color *and* add a border around it, like this:

```
$('#highlightedDiv').css('background-color','#FF0000');
$('#highlightedDiv').css('border','2px solid #FE0037');
```

Another way is to pass what's called an *object literal* to the *.css( )* function. Think of an object literal as a list of property name/value pairs. After each property name, you insert a colon (:) followed by a value; each name/value pair is separated by a comma, and the whole shebang is surrounded by braces—{}. Thus, an object literal for the two CSS property values above looks like this:

```
{ 'background-color' : '#FF0000', 'border' : '2px solid #FE0037' }
```

Because an object literal can be difficult to read if it's crammed onto a single line, many programmers break it up over multiple lines. The following is functionally the same as the previous one-liner:

```
{
  'background-color' : '#FF0000',
  'border' : '2px solid #FE0037'
}
```

The basic structure of an object literal is diagrammed in Figure 5-7.

Warning: When creating an object literal, make sure to separate each name/value pair by adding a comma after the value (for instance, in this example the comma goes after the value '#FF0000'. However, the last property/value pair should *not* have a comma after it, since no property/value pair follows it. If you do add a comma after the last value, some Web browsers (including Internet Explorer) will generate an error.

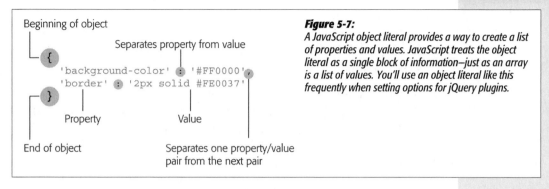

Figure 5-7:
A JavaScript object literal provides a way to create a list of properties and values. JavaScript treats the object literal as a single block of information—just as an array is a list of values. You'll use an object literal like this frequently when setting options for jQuery plugins.

To use an object literal with the *css( )* function, just pass the object to the function like this:

```
$('#highlightedDiv').css({
  'background-color' : '#FF0000',
  'border' : '2px solid #FE0037'
});
```

Study this example closely, because it looks a little different from what you've seen so far, and because you'll be encountering lots of code that looks like it in future chapters. The first thing to notice is that this code is merely a single JavaScript statement (essentially just one line of code)—you can tell because the semicolon that ends the statement doesn't appear until the last line. The statement is broken over four lines to make the code easier to read.

Next, notice that the object literal is an argument (like one piece of data) that's passed to the *css( )* function. So in the code *css({*, the opening parenthesis is part of the function, while the opening *{* marks the beginning of the object. The three characters in the last line break down like this: *}* is the end of the object and the end of the argument passed to the function; *)* marks the end of the function, the last parenthesis in *css( )*; and *;* marks the end of the JavaScript statement.

And if all this object literal stuff is hurting your head, you're free to change CSS properties one line at a time, like this:

```
$('#highlightedDiv').css('background-color','#FF0000');
$('#highlightedDiv').css('border','2px solid #FE0037');
```

Reading, Setting, and Removing HTML Attributes

Since changing classes and CSS properties using JavaScript are such common tasks, jQuery has built-in functions for them. But the *addClass( )* and *css( )* functions are really just shortcuts for changing the HTML *class* and *style* attributes. jQuery includes general-purpose functions for handling HTML attributes—the *attr( )* and *removeAttr( )* functions.

The *attr( )* function lets you read a specified HTML attribute from a tag. For example, to determine the current graphic file a particular <img> points to, you pass the string 'src' (for the <img> tag's *src* property) to the function:

```
var imageFile = $('#banner img').attr('src');
```

The *attr( )* function returns the attributes value as it's set in the HTML. This code returns the *src* property for the first <img> tag inside another tag with an ID of *banner*, so the variable *imageFile* would contain the path set in the page's HTML: for instance, 'images/banner.png' or 'http://www.thesite.com/images/banner.png'.

Note: When passing an attribute name to the *.attr( )* function, you don't need to worry about the case of the attribute name—href, HREF, or even HrEf will work.

If you pass a second argument to the *attr( )* function, you can set the tag's attribute. For example, to swap in a different image, you can change an <img> tag's *src* property like this:

```
$('#banner img').attr('src','images/newImage.png');
```

If you want to completely remove an attribute from a tag, use the *removeAttr( )* function. For example, this code removes the *bgColor* property from the <body> tag:

```
$('body').removeAttr('bgColor');
```

Creative Headlines

In this tutorial, you'll use jQuery in combination with CSS to create a unique headline effect (see Figure 5-8). The basic concept is to overlay a transparent PNG image on top of each headline. The PNG acts as a kind of mask that covers parts of the headlines. In this example, an image made of fading horizontal lines will lie over several headlines to give the appearance that the text itself has stripes.

The key to this effect is to add an empty <span> tag inside each headline's tag. Using CSS, you can format this <span> tag so that it sets on top of the headline and displays a transparent image inside it.

Note: See the note on page 27 for information on how to download the tutorial files.

---

1. **In a text editor, open the file *5.2.html* in the *chapter05* folder.**

   The first step is to link to the jQuery library file.

2. **In the empty line, just before the closing </head> tag, add:**

   ```
   <script type="text/javascript" src="../js/jquery.js"></script>
   ```

Figure 5-8:
With some clever CSS and a little JavaScript, it's easy to add visual flair to headlines and text. To see more examples of this effect and read more about how it works, check out www.webdesignerwall.com/tutorials/css-gradient-text-effect *and* http://cssglobe.com/lab/textgradient.

This line of code loads the jQuery library file. This line must appear *before* any other JavaScript code that uses a jQuery function, so it's a good idea to always list this line before any other <script> tags on the page.

Next, you'll start your own JavaScript.

3. **Press return to create a new blank line and type:**

```
<script type="text/javascript">
```

While you're here, it's a good idea to close the <script> tag as well.

4. **Press return twice and type** *</script>*.

Now you'll get started with some jQuery.

5. **Add the code that's bolded below to your page:**

```
<script type="text/javascript" src="../js/jquery.js"></script>
<script type="text/javascript">
$(document).ready(function( ) {

});
</script>
```

You encountered this code before in the tutorial on page 30. You'll learn about this strange-looking stuff in detail in the next chapter, but in a nutshell, this code makes sure that the HTML for the page has loaded before your JavaScript program runs. That's very important when using JavaScript to manipulate a Web page, because if JavaScript tries to add, delete, or rearrange HTML before the page's HTML has loaded, you'll end up with an error.

Now you'll create a jQuery selection object.

6. **Between the two lines of code you just added, type $('#main h2') so your code now looks like this:**

```
<script type="text/javascript" src="../js/jquery.js"></script>
<script type="text/javascript">
$(document).ready(function( ) {
  $('#main h2')
});
</script>
```

The *#main h2* is a CSS descendent selector that matches every <h2> tag that appears inside another tag with an ID of *#main*, so this code selects every <h2> tag within the main area of the page. Now you'll do something with those tags.

7. **Type .prepend('<span class="headEffect"></span>'); so that your finished code looks like this:**

```
<script type="text/javascript" src="../js/jquery.js"></script>
<script type="text/javascript">
$(document).ready(function( ) {
 $('#main h2').prepend('<span class="headEffect"></span>');
});
</script>
```

The *.prepend( )* function adds content just after the opening tag of the matched element. In other words, this code will add an empty <span> tag inside each <h2> tag, transforming the HTML from, for example, *<h2>A Mysterious Head-line</h2>* to *<h2><span class="headEffect"></span>A Mysterious Headline</h2>*.

8. **Save the page and preview it in a Web browser.**

The three big, bold, and blue headlines should look like Figure 5-8 (you can find all of the finished code in the file *complete_5.2.html*). The real secret of this technique isn't really JavaScript or jQuery, but the CSS. In a nutshell, each <span> tag added to the headlines has a CSS style applied to it that turns the span into a 36-pixel-tall box that floats above and over the headlines. A transparent image is tiled inside that box, creating a mask that blocks part of each headlines text (note the *.headEffect* class style defined in the internal style sheet near the top of the document).

So, you may be asking, if the effect is really a CSS effect, why use JavaScript? Without JavaScript, you'd need to manually add the <span> tags inside each headline you wanted the effect for. That's a lot of extra work, not to mention extra code added to your Web page. What's more, if you grew tired of this effect (is that even possible?), you'd have to search all of your pages and remove the no-longer-needed <span> tags. This way, you just have a little JavaScript code to remove.

Acting on Each Element in a Selection

As discussed on page 180, one of the unique qualities of jQuery is that most of its functions automatically loop through each item in a jQuery selection. For example, to make every <img> on a page fade out, you only need one line of JavaScript code:

```
$('img').fadeOut();
```

The *.fadeOut( )* function causes an element to disappear slowly, and when attached to a jQuery selection containing multiple elements, the function loops through the selection and fades out each element. There are plenty of times when you'll want to loop through a selection of elements and perform a series of actions on each element. jQuery provides the *.each( )* function for just this purpose.

For example, say you want to list of all of the external links on your page in a bibliography box at the bottom of the page, perhaps titled "Other Sites Mentioned in This Article." (OK, you may not ever want to do that, but just play along.) Anyway, you can create that box by:

1. **Retrieving all links that point outside your site.**

2. **Getting the HREF attribute of each link (the URL).**

3. **Adding that URL to the other list of links in the bibliography box.**

jQuery doesn't have a built-in function that performs these exact steps, but you can use the *each( )* function to do it yourself. It's just a jQuery function, so you slap it on at the end of a selection of jQuery elements like this:

```
$('selector').each();
```

Anonymous Functions

To use the *each( )* function, you pass a special kind of argument to it—an *anonymous function*. The anonymous function is simply a function containing the steps that you wish to perform on each selected element. It's called *anonymous* because, unlike the functions you learned to create on page 97, you don't give it a name. Here's an anonymous function's basic structure:

```
function() {
  //code goes here
}
```

Because there's no name, you don't have a way to call the function. Instead, you use the anonymous function as an argument that you pass to another function (strange, confusing, but true!). Here's how you incorporate an anonymous function as part of the *each( )* function:

```
$('selector').each(function() {
   // code goes in here
});
```

Figure 5-9 diagrams the different parts of this construction. The last line is particularly confusing, since it includes three different symbols that close up three parts of the overall structure. The *}* marks the end of the function (that's also the end of the argument passed to the *each( )* function); the *)* is the last part of the *each( )* function; and *;* indicates the end of a JavaScript statement. In other words, the JavaScript interpreter treats all of this code as a single instruction.

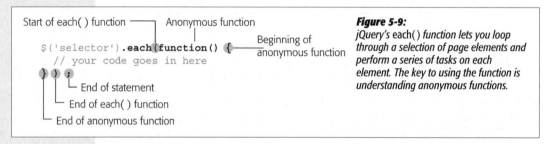

Figure 5-9:
jQuery's each( ) *function lets you loop through a selection of page elements and perform a series of tasks on each element. The key to using the function is understanding anonymous functions.*

Now that the outer structure's in place, it's time to put something inside the anonymous function: all of the stuff you want to happen to each element in a selection. The *each( )* function works like a loop—meaning the instructions inside the anonymous function will run once for each element you've retrieved. For example, say you have 50 images on a page and add the following JavaScript code to one of the page's scripts:

```
$('img').each(function() {
   alert('I found an image');
});
```

Fifty alert dialog boxes with the message "I found an image" would appear. (That'd be really annoying, so don't try this at home.)

this and *$(this)*

When using the *each( )* function, you'll naturally want to access or set attributes of each element—for example, to find the URL for each external link. To access the current element through each loop, you use a special keyword called *this*. The *this* keyword refers to whatever element is calling the anonymous function. So the first time through the loop, *this* refers to the first element in the jQuery selection, while the second time through the loop, *this* refers to the second element.

The way jQuery works, *this* refers to a traditional DOM element, so you can access traditional DOM properties like *innerHTML* (page 163) or *childNodes* (page 161). But, as you've read in this chapter, the special jQuery selection lets you tap into all of the wonderful jQuery functions. So to convert *this* to its jQuery equivalent, you write *$(this)*.

At this point, you're probably thinking that all of this *this* stuff is some kind of cruel joke intended to make your head swell. It's not a joke, but it sure is confusing. To help make clear how to use *$(this)*, take another look at the task described at the beginning of this section—creating a list of external links in a bibliography box at the bottom of a page.

Assume that the page's HTML already has a <div> tag ready for the external links. For example:

```
<div id="bibliography">
<h3>Web pages referenced in this article</h3>
<ul id="bibList">
</ul>
</div>
```

The first step is to get a list of all links pointing outside your site. You can do so using an attribute selector (page 177):

```
$('a[href^=http://]')
```

Now to loop through each link, we add the *each( )* function:

```
$('a[href^=http://]').each( )
```

Then add an anonymous function:

```
$('a[href^=http://]').each(function( ) {

});
```

The first step in the anonymous function is to retrieve the URL for the link. Since each link has a different URL, you must access the current element each time through the loop. The *$(this)* keyword lets you do just that:

```
$('a[href^=http://]').each(function( ) {
   var extLink = $(this).attr('href');
});
```

The code in the middle, bolded line does several things: First, it creates a new variable (*extLink*) and stores the value of the current element's *href* property. Each time through the loop, *$(this)* refers to a different link on the page, so each time through the loop, the *extLink* variable changes.

After that, it's just a matter of appending a new list item to the <ul> tag (see the HTML on page 195), like this:

```
$('a[href^=http://]').each(function( ) {
  var extLink = $(this).attr('href');
  $('#bibList').append('<li>' + extLink + '</li>');
});
```

You'll use the *$(this)* keyword almost every time you use the *each( )* function, so in a matter of time, *$(this)* will become second nature to you. To help you practice this concept, you'll try it out in another tutorial.

Note: The example script used in this section is a good way to illustrate the use of the *$(this)* keyword, but it probably isn't the best way to accomplish the task of writing a list of external links to a page. First, if there are no links, the <div> tag (which was hardcoded into the page's HTML) will still appear, but it'll be empty. In addition, if someone visits the page without JavaScript turned on, he won't see the links, but will see the empty box. A better approach is to use JavaScript to create the enclosing <div> tag as well. You can find an example of that in the file *bibliography.html* accompanying the tutorials for this chapter.

Automatic Pull Quotes

In the final tutorial for this chapter, you'll create a script that makes it very easy to add pull quotes to a page (like the one pictured in Figure 5-10). A *pull quote* is a box containing an interesting quote from the main text of a page. Newspapers, magazines, and Web sites all use these boxes to grab readers' attention and emphasize an important or interesting point. But adding pull quotes manually requires duplicating text from the page and placing it inside a <div> tag, <span> tag, or some other container. Creating all that HTML takes time and adds extra HTML and duplicate text to the finished page. Fortunately, with JavaScript you can quickly add any number of pull quotes to a page, adding just a small amount of HTML.

Overview

The script you're about to create will do several things:

1. **Locate every <span> tag containing a special class named *pq* (for pull quote).**

   The only work you have to do to the HTML of your page is to add <span> tags around any text you wish to turn into a pull quote. For example, suppose there's a paragraph of text on a page and you want to highlight a few words from that paragraph in pull quote box. Just wrap that text in the <span>, tag like this:

   ```
   <span class="pq">...and that's how I discovered the Loch Ness monster.</span>
   ```

Figure 5-10:
Adding pull quotes manually to the HTML of a page is a pain. Especially when you can just use JavaScript to automate the process.

2. **Duplicate each <span> tag.**

   Each pull quote box is essentially another span tag with the same text inside it, so you can use JavaScript to just duplicate the current <span> tag.

3. **Remove the *pq* class from the duplicate <span> and add a new class *pullquote*.**

   The formatting magic—the box, larger text, border, and background color—that makes up each pull quote box isn't JavaScript's doing. The page's style sheet contains a CSS class selector, *.pullquote*, that does all of that. So by simply using JavaScript to change the duplicate tags' class name, you completely change the look of the new <span> tags.

4. **Add the duplicate <span> tag to the page.**

   Finally, you add the duplicate <span> tag to the page. (Step 2 just makes a copy of the tag in the Web browser's memory, but doesn't actually add that tag to the page yet. This gives you the opportunity to further manipulate the duplicated tag before displaying it for the person viewing the page.)

Programming

Now that you have an idea of what you're trying to accomplish with this script, it's time to open a text editor and make it happen.

Note: See the note on page 27 for information on how to download the tutorial files.

---

1. In a text editor, open the file *5.3.html* in the *chapter05* folder.

   The page already contains the code to link the *jquery.js* file to the page, as well as a <script> tag, including that strange *$(document).ready* stuff you encountered in step 5 on page 191.

2. Click in the empty line between after the *$(document).ready* stuff, and then add the code that's in bold below:

```
1   <script type="text/javascript" src="../js/jquery.js"></script>
2   <script type="text/javascript">
3   $(document).ready(function( ) {
4       $('span.pq')
5
6   });
7   </script>
```

Note: The line numbers to the left of each line of code are just for your reference. Don't actually type them as part of the script on the Web page.

The *$('span.pq')* is a jQuery selector that locates every <span> tag with a class of *pq* applied to it. Next you'll add the code needed to loop through each of these <span> tags and do something to them.

3. Add the bolded code below on lines 4 and 6:

```
1   <script type="text/javascript" src="../js/jquery.js"></script>
2   <script type="text/javascript">
3   $(document).ready(function( ) {
4       $('span.pq').each(function( ) {
5
6       });
7   });
8   </script>
```

As discussed on page 193, *.each( )* is a jQuery function that lets you loop through a selection of elements. The function takes one argument, which is itself a function.

Next you'll start to build the function that will apply to each matching <span> tag on this page: the first step is creating a copy of the <span>.

4. Add the code listed in bold on line 5 below to the script:

```
1   <script type="text/javascript" src="../js/jquery.js"></script>
2   <script type="text/javascript">
3   $(document).ready(function( ) {
4       $('span.pq').each(function( ) {
5           var quote=$(this).clone( );
6       });
7   });
8   </script>
```

This function starts by creating a new variable named *quote*, which contains a "clone" (just a copy) of the current <span> (see page 194 if you forgot what *$(this)* means). The jQuery *.clone( )* function duplicates the current element, including all of the HTML within the element. In this case, it makes a copy of the <span> tag, including the text inside the <span> that will appear in the pull quote box.

Cloning an element copies everything, including any attributes applied to it. In this instance, the original <span> had a class named *pq*. You'll remove that class from the copy.

5. **Add the two lines of code listed in bold on lines 6 and 7 below to the script:**

```
1    <script type="text/javascript" src="../js/jquery.js"></script>
2    <script type="text/javascript">
3    $(document).ready(function( ) {
4      $('span.pq').each(function( ) {
5        var quote=$(this).clone( );
6        quote.removeClass('pq');
7        quote.addClass('pullquote');
8      });
9    });
10   </script>
```

As discussed on page 186, the *removeClass( )* function removes a class name from a tag, while the *.addClass( )* function adds a class name to a tag. In this case, we're replacing the class name on the copy, so you can use a CSS class named *.pullquote* to format the <span> as a pull quote box.

Finally, you'll add the <span> to the page.

6. **Add the bolded line of code (line 8 below) to the script:**

```
1    <script type="text/javascript" src="../js/jquery.js"></script>
2    <script type="text/javascript">
3    $(document).ready(function( ) {
4      $('span.pq').each(function( ) {
5        var quote=$(this).clone( );
6        quote.removeClass('pq');
7        quote.addClass('pullquote');
8        $(this).before(quote);
9      });
10   });
11   </script>
```

This line is the final piece of the function—up until this line, you've just been manipulating a copy of the <span> in the Web browser's memory. No one viewing the page would see it until the copy is actually added to the DOM.

In this case, you're inserting the copy of the <span> tag, just before the one in your HTML. In essence, the page will end up with HTML sort of like this:

```
<span class="pullquote">...and that's how I discovered the Loch Ness monster.
</span> <span class="pq">...and that's how I discovered the Loch Ness
monster.</span>
```

Although the text looks like it will appear duplicated side by side, the CSS formatting makes the pull quote box float to the right edge of the page.

Note: To achieve the visual effect of a pull quote box, the page has a CSS style that uses the CSS *float* property. The box is moved to the right edge of the paragraph in which the text appears, and the other text in the paragraph wraps around it. If you're unfamiliar with this technique, you can learn about the CSS *float* property at *http://css.maxdesign.com.au/floatutorial/*.

At this point, all of the JavaScript is complete. However, you won't see any pull quote boxes until you massage the HTML a bit.

7. **Find the first <p> tag in the page's HTML. Locate a sentence and wrap *<span class="pq"> </span>* around it. For example:**

```
<span class="pq">Nullam ut nibh sed orci tempor rutrum.</span>
```

You can repeat this process to add pull quotes to other paragraphs as well.

8. **Save the file and preview it in a Web browser.**

The final result should look something like Figure 5-10. If you don't see a pull quote box, make sure you added the <span> tag in step 12 correctly. Also, check out the tips on page 32 for fixing a malfunctioning program. You can find a completed version of this tutorial in the file *complete_5.3.html*.

Action/Reaction: Making Pages Come Alive with Events

When you hear people talk about JavaScript, you usually hear the word "interactive" somewhere in the conversation: "JavaScript lets you make interactive Web pages." What they're really saying is that JavaScript lets your Web pages react to something a visitor does: moving a mouse over a navigation button produces a menu of links; selecting a radio button reveals a new set of form options; clicking a form's submit button alerts you to form fields that were left blank.

All the different visitor actions that a Web page can respond to are called *events*. JavaScript is an *event-driven* language: without events, your Web pages wouldn't be able to respond to visitors or do anything really interesting. It's like your desktop computer. Once you start it up in the morning, it doesn't do you much good until you start clicking files, making menu selections, and moving your mouse around the screen.

What Are Events?

Web browsers are programmed to recognize basic actions like the page loading, someone moving a mouse, typing a key, or resizing the browser window. Each of the things that happens to a Web page is an *event*. To make your Web page interactive, you write programs that respond to events. In this way, you can make a <div> tag appear or disappear when a visitor clicks the mouse, a new image appear when she mouses over a link, or check the contents of a text field when she clicks a form's Submit button.

An event represents the precise moment when something happens. For example, when you click a mouse, the precise moment you release the mouse button, the Web browser signals that a *click event* has just occurred. The moment that the Web browser indicates that an event has happened is when the event *fires*, as programmers put it.

Web browsers actually fire several events whenever you click the mouse button. First, as soon as you press the mouse button, the mousedown event fires, then when you let go of the button the mouseup event fires, and finally the click event fires (see Figure 6-1).

Note: Understanding when and how these events fire can be tricky. To let you test out different event types, this chapter includes a demo Web page with the tutorial files. Open *events.html* (in the *chapter06* folder) in a Web browser. Then move the mouse, click, and type to see some of the many different events that constantly occur on a Web page (see Figure 6-1).

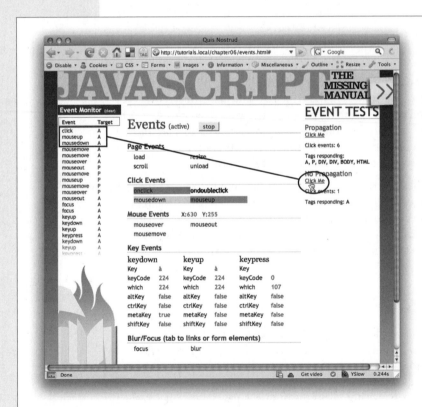

Figure 6-1:
While you may not be aware of it, Web browsers are constantly firing off events whenever you type, mouse around, or click. The events.html *file (included with the tutorial files for this chapter) shows you many of these events in action. For example, clicking a link (circled) fires the mousedown, mouseup, and click events.*

Preparing a Web page to respond to an event is a two-stage process:

1. **Identify the page element that you wish to respond to an event.**

   While the entire document can respond to a mouse click anywhere on a Web page, it's more common to attach events to particular page elements like specific links, form fields, or even a particular paragraph of text. For example, if you want a menu to pop up when a visitor moves his mouse over a navigation link, you need to attach the mouseover event to that particular link. After all, it wouldn't make much sense for the pop-up menu to appear whenever the mouse passes over just *any* part of the page.

   This step of the process—selecting a page element—is easy (you learned how to do it in the last chapter).

2. **Assign an event and define a function to run when the event occurs.**

   There are several methods of assigning a function to respond to an event (as you'll learn starting on page 207). But the basic idea is that you create a function that runs whenever the event fires. For example, you can write a function that makes a previously hidden <div> appear (a <div> containing links that are part of a menu, for example), and then assign that function to respond to the mouseover event of a particular link. Then, when the visitor mouses over the link, the function runs and makes the <div> appear.

You'll learn how to assign events to page elements on page 207, but before you do, you should learn about the events available to most Web browsers. The following sections cover events that work in all currently shipping browsers.

Mouse Events

Ever since Steve Jobs introduced the Macintosh in 1984, the mouse has been a critical device for all personal computers. Folks use it to open applications, drag files into folders, select items from menus, and even to draw. Naturally, Web browsers provide lots of ways of tracking how a visitor uses a mouse to interact with a Web page:

- **click.** The *click* event fires after you click and release the mouse button. You'll commonly assign a click event to a link: for example, a link on a thumbnail image when clicked can display a larger version of that image. However, you're not limited to just links. You can also make any tag on a page respond to an event—even just clicking anywhere on the page.

Note: The click event can also be triggered on links via the keyboard. If you tab to a link, then press the Enter (Return) key, the click event fires.

- **dblclick.** When you press and release the mouse button twice, a double-click (*dblclick*) event fires. It's the same action you use to open a folder or file on your desktop. Double-clicking a Web page isn't a usual Web-surfer action, so if you use this event, you should make clear to visitors where they can double-click and what will happen after they do. Also note that a double-click event is the same thing as two click events, so don't assign click and double-click events to the same tag. Otherwise, the function for the click will run twice before the double-click function runs.

- **mousedown.** The *mousedown* event is the first half of a click—the moment when you click the button before releasing it. This event is handy for dragging elements around a page. You can let visitors drag items around your Web page just like they drag icons around their desktop—by clicking on them (without releasing the button) and moving them, then releasing the button to drop them.

- **mouseup.** The *mouseup* event is the second half of a click—the moment when you release the button. This event is handy for responding to the moment when you drop an item that has been dragged.

- **mouseover.** When you move your mouse over an element on a page, a *mouseover* event fires. You can assign an event handler to a navigation button using this event and have a submenu pop up when a visitor mouses over the button. (If you're used to the CSS *:hover* pseudo-class, then you know how this event works.)

- **mouseout.** Moving a mouse off an element triggers the *mouseout* event. You can use this event to signal when a visitor has moved her mouse off the page, or to hide a pop-up menu when the mouse travels outside the menu.

- **mousemove.** Logically enough, the *mousemove* event fires when the mouse moves—which means this event fires all of the time. You use this event to track the current position of the cursor on the screen. In addition, you can assign this event to a particular tag on the page—a <div> for example—and respond only to movements within that tag.

Note: Some Web browsers, like Internet Explorer support many events (*http://msdn2.microsoft.com/en-us/library/ms533051(VS.85).aspx*), but most browsers share just a handful of events.

Document/Window Events

The browser window itself understands a handful of events that fire from when the page loads to when the visitor leaves the page:

- **load.** The *load* event fires when the Web browser finishes downloading all of a Web page's files: the HTML file itself, plus any linked images, Flash movies, and external CSS and JavaScript files. Web designers have traditionally used this event to start any JavaScript program that manipulated the Web page. However, loading a Web page and all its files can take a long time if there are a lot of graphics or other large linked files. In some cases, this meant the JavaScript didn't run for quite some time after the page was displayed in the browser. Fortunately, jQuery offers a much more responsive replacement for the load event, as described on page 218.

- **resize.** When you resize your browser window by clicking the maximize button, or dragging the browser's resize handle, the browser triggers a *resize* event. Some designers use this event to change the layout of the page when a visitor changes the size of his browser. For example, after a visitor resizes his browser window, you can check the window's width—if the window is really wide, you could change the design to add more columns of content to fit the space.

Note: Internet Explorer, Opera, and Safari fire multiple resize events as you resize the window, whereas Firefox only fires the resize event a single time after you've let go of the resize handle.

- **scroll.** The *scroll* event is triggered whenever you drag the scroll bar, or use the keyboard (up/down/home/end and so on keys) or mouse scroll wheel to scroll a Web page. If the page doesn't have scrollbars, no scroll event is ever triggered. Some programmers use this event to help figure out where elements (after a page has scrolled) appear on the screen.

- **unload.** When you click a link to go to another page, close a browser tab, or close a browser window, a Web browser fires an *unload* event. It's like the last gasp for your JavaScript program and gives you an opportunity to complete one last action before the visitor moves on from your page. Nefarious programmers have used this event to make it very difficult to ever leave a page. Each time a visitor tries to close the page, a new window appears and the page returns. But you can also use this event for good: for example, a program can warn a visitor about a form they've started to fill out but haven't submitted, or the program could send form data to the Web server to save the data before the visitor exits the page.

Note: Safari and Internet Explorer fire unload events whenever you click a link to leave a page or even just close a window or tab with the page. Opera and Firefox let you click the window's close button without firing the unload event.

Form Events

In the pre-JavaScript days, people interacted with Web sites mainly via forms created with HTML. Entering information into a form field was really the only way for visitors to provide input to a Web site. Because forms are still such an important part of the Web, you'll find plenty of form events to play with.

- **submit.** Whenever a visitor submits a form, the *submit* event fires. A form might be submitted by clicking the Submit button, or simply by hitting the Enter (Return) key while the cursor is in a text field. You'll most frequently use

---

the submit event with form validation—to make sure all required fields are correctly filled out *before* the data is sent to the Web server. You'll learn how to validate forms on page 330.

• **reset.** Although not as common as they used to be, a Reset button lets you undo any changes you've made to a form. It returns a form to the state it was when the page was loaded. You can run a script when the visitor tries to reset the form by using the *reset* event. For example, if the visitor has made some changes to the form, you might want to pop up a dialog box that asks "Are you sure you want to delete your changes?" The dialog could give the visitor a chance to click a "No" button and prevent the process of resetting (erasing) the form.

• **change.** Many form fields fire a *change* event when their status changes: for instance, when someone clicks a radio button, or makes a selection from a drop-down menu. You can use this event to immediately check the selection made in a menu, or which radio button was selected.

• **focus.** When you tab or click into a text field, it gives the field *focus*. In other words, the browser's attention is now focused on that page element. Likewise, selecting a radio button, or clicking a checkbox, gives those elements focus. You can respond to the focus event using JavaScript. For example, you could add a helpful instruction inside a text field —"Type your full name." When a visitor clicks in the field (giving it focus), you can erase these instructions, so he has an empty field he can fill out.

• **blur.** The *blur* event is the opposite of focus. It's triggered when you exit a currently focused field, by either tabbing or clicking outside the field. The blur event is another useful time for form validation. For example, when a person types her email address in a text field, then tabs to the next field, you could immediately check what she's entered to make sure it's a valid email address.

Note: Focus and blur events also apply to links on a page. When you tab to a link, a focus event fires; when you tab (or click) off the link, the blur event fires.

Keyboard Events

Web browsers also track when visitors use their keyboard, so you can assign commands to keys or let your visitors control a script by pressing various keys. For example, pressing the Space bar could start and stop a JavaScript animation.

Unfortunately, the different browsers handle keyboard events differently, even making it hard to tell which letter was entered! (You'll find one technique for identifying which letter was typed on a keyboard in the tip on page 223.)

• **keypress.** The moment you press a key, the *keypress* event fires. You don't have to let go of the key, either. In fact, the keypress event continues to fire, over and over again, as long as you hold the key down.

- **keydown.** The *keydown* event is like the keypress event—it's fired when you press a key. Actually, it's fired right *before* the keypress event. In Firefox and Opera, the keydown event only fires once. In Internet Explorer and Safari, the keydown event behaves just like the keypress event—it fires over and over as long as the key is pressed.

- **keyup.** Finally, the *keyup* event is triggered when you release a key.

Using Events with Functions

To take advantage of events, you need to tell the Web browser to run a function when a particular event happens to a specific tag. For example, to make a row in a table change color when a visitor mouses over it, you attach a mouseover event to the table row and assign a function to the event (the function provides the instructions to change the row's color). There are several ways to accomplish this.

Inline Events

The simplest way to run a function when an event fires is called *inline event registration.* If you've ever tried JavaScript programming before, you're probably familiar with this technique, which lets you assign an *event handler* directly to the HTML of your page. For example, to make an alert box appear when you mouse over a particular link, you write this:

```
<a href="page.html" onmouseover="alert('this is a link');">A link</a>
```

In this case, the event is mouseover and the event handler is called *onmouseover*. You add the event handler directly to the HTML of the tag and assign a command to the handler (in this example, an *alert( )* command). Event handler names are created by simply adding the word *on* to the beginning of the event, so a mouseover event handler is written as *onmouseover*, a click event handler as *onclick*, and so on.

Note: You can think of *on* as "when" so *onmouseover* just means "when the mouse moves over" the element.

You can even use the inline technique to call a previously created function, like this:

```
<body onload="startSlideShow( )">
```

The line of code above calls a function (that's been defined somewhere else on the page) named *startSlideShow( )* after the page and all its required files have loaded.

Adding an event handler directly to a HTML tag is certainly convenient, and lots of programmers use this technique. However, it's not the best way to go. When you add inline event handlers, you end up sprinkling JavaScript throughout your HTML. For example, if you have several buttons that each do something when clicked, you need to manually add inline event handlers to the each button in the

---

HTML. This arrangement can make future updates to your site a real chore, since you'll have to scan your HTML carefully to find all of the JavaScript code you need to update. Most professional JavaScript programmers aim to separate JavaScript from HTML as much as possible (see the box below). You'll learn how to do this next.

UP TO SPEED

Don't Let JavaScript Get in the Way

If you've been building Web pages for a long time, you'll remember that in the days before CSS, you had to style all of your pages using various HTML tags. So to change the look of text, you'd add additional HTML to a page like this:

```
<font face="Arial, Helvetica, sans-serif"
size="2" color="#EEFF00">
The stylish text.
</font>
```

When CSS came around, you learned how to put all of your style information in a style sheet located in either the <head> of the page or in a separate, external CSS file. Suddenly, your HTML was free from a lot of extra markup. HTML was reserved for content and structure, while formatting was controlled by CSS that was defined in a single location (a style sheet).

Most professional JavaScript programmers argue that putting your JavaScript code directly inside a tag—for example, *<a href="page.html" onmouseover="alert('where you going?');">a link</a>*—is akin to those bad old days before CSS. It clutters up your HTML with JavaScript, adding extra code to your HTML and making it hard to separate out the content and structure (HTML) from the page's behavior (JavaScript).

Fortunately, without much effort you can keep all of your JavaScript code confined to an external file or just inside <script> tags in the <head> of the page. jQuery's event functions (page 210) or even the so-called "traditional model" of event handlers (below) are much better than using inline event registration.

The Traditional Model

Any Web browser that understands JavaScript can take advantage of another technique for assigning an event handler to a tag. There's no official name for this technique, but most programmers call it the *traditional model*. It lets you assign an event handler to a page element without having to muck around in the HTML within the body of a page. This method involves identifying the page element you wish to add the event to, then assigning an event handler to the element.

Note: You used the traditional model of assigning an event to an element in one of the tutorials from the previous chapter. See step 8 on page 166.

For example, say you wanted to have an alert box appear after the page loads. You could do that by adding the following code either within <script> tags in the <head> of the page or in an external JavaScript file (page 24).

```
function message( ) {
  alert("Welcome...");
}
window.onload=message;
```

The first three lines create a simple function named *message*. When a program calls this function, it opens an alert box with "Welcome…" inside it. The event magic happens in line four, where the *onload* event handler is assigned to the window object—that is, when the page loads (see page 204 for more on the load event), the function is called.

Notice that the function is assigned to the *onload* event handler much like a value is assigned to a variable. The equal sign in *window.onload=message;* essentially stores a reference to the function in the event handler. That's why there are no parentheses after the function's name: *message* instead of *message( )*. When parentheses appear after a function name, you're telling the function to run immediately. So the code *window.onload=message( )* actually calls the function *before* the page loads. By omitting the parentheses, you're letting the *onload* event handler know which function to call when the time comes—when the page finishes loading.

The Modern Way

The two previously described methods of responding to events on a Web page have been around since Netscape Navigator 3 (that's a long time), and all Web browsers understand them. There's one main drawback to those techniques, though—you can only assign a single function per event per tag. For example, only one function can respond to the *onload* event handler, so in the code below the second event handler essentially erases the first:

```
window.onload=message;
window.onload=setUpPage;
```

In this example, only the *setUpPage( )* function will run when the page loads. This gotcha may not sound like too big a problem, since you can just combine the commands in the two functions into a single function. But when you're placing scripts on pages that already have JavaScript on them, scripts can easily end up erasing each other's event handlers. The danger gets worse when you start to include scripts from other programmers—like JavaScript libraries or the cool jQuery plugins you'll be learning about in future chapters.

To deal with this and other problems associated with the old event handler methods, the W3C introduced a new innovation called *event listeners*. The underlying concept is pretty much the same as event handlers: select an element (a link, for example), and assign a function that runs when a particular event (like mouseover) occurs. Any page element can have multiple event listeners, so you can assign multiple functions to the same event for the same tag.

Firefox, Safari, and Opera all use the W3C's event listener model…and then there's Microsoft Internet Explorer, which long ago went off on its own path for dealing with events. Internet Explorer has a completely different model for how events work and a unique syntax for assigning functions to respond to events. For the longest time, this meant that if a JavaScript programmer wanted her programs to work in all browsers, she had to learn two different techniques for handling the same task, and write different sets of code to make sure a site worked in all browsers.

Fortunately, you don't have to worry about browser differences when using events *if* you use a JavaScript library, like jQuery, which creates a single way for handling events that works in all current Web browsers.

UP TO SPEED

The Mixed-Up World of Events

Much to the frustration of Web programmers everywhere, Internet Explorer implements events in a way that's very different from all other Web browsers. This situation has forced JavaScript programmers to come up with two different methods to get the same job done.

Most Web browsers let you assign an *event listener* to an element using the method supported by the W3C. Using the *addEventListener( )* method, you can assign both an event and a function to respond to the event to any element on a Web page. Internet Explorer, on the other hand, has *attachEvent( )* method to accomplish the same thing.

In addition, while all browsers let you *inspect* an event—that is, find out information about the event, such as whether a key was pressed or the mouse position when the event fired—IE handles the *event object* (see page 222) differently than everybody else.

Fortunately, when you use a JavaScript library like jQuery, you don't usually have to worry about any of these differences—all the cross-browser madness is resolved by the programming in the library, so you only have to learn one way to accomplish the same goal for all browsers.

The jQuery Way

Many JavaScript books spend a lot of time talking about how Internet Explorer handles events differently than Firefox, Safari, and Opera. In fact, a lot of JavaScript books dedicate an entire chapter to dealing with the way IE and other browsers handle events. In the end, most JavaScript books just provide boilerplate code to make events work across browsers, and this book won't bore you with the details of the two different event models—see the box above for some information if you're curious. This section cuts to the chase, providing a simple, cross-browser compatible method for attaching events to elements using jQuery.

As you learned in the last chapter, JavaScript libraries like jQuery solve a lot of the problems with JavaScript programming—including pesky browser incompatibilities. In addition, libraries often simplify basic JavaScript-related tasks. jQuery makes assigning events and *event helpers* (the functions that deal with events) a breeze. Here's the basic process:

1. **Select one or more elements.**

   The last chapter explained how jQuery lets you use CSS selectors to choose the parts of the page you want to manipulate. When assigning events, you want to select the elements that the visitor will interact with. For example, what will a visitor click—a link, a table cell, an image? If you're assigning a mouseover event, what page element does a visitor mouse over to make the action happen?

2. **Assign an event.**

In jQuery, most DOM events have an equivalent jQuery function. So to assign an event to an element, you just add a period, the event name, and a set of parentheses. So, for example, if you want to add a mouseover event to every link on a page, you can do this:

```
$('a').mouseover( );
```

To add a click event to a element with an ID of *menu*, you'd write this:

```
$('#menu').click( );
```

You can use any of the event names listed on pages 203-207 (and a couple of jQuery-only events discussed on page 220).

After adding the event, you still have some work to do. In order for something to happen when the event fires, you must provide a function for the event.

3. **Pass a function to the event.**

Finally, you need to define what happens when the event fires. To do so, you pass a function to the event. The function contains the commands that will run when the event fires: for example, making a hidden <div> tag visible or highlighting a moused-over element.

You can pass a previously defined function's name like this:

```
$('#start').click(startSlideShow);
```

As mentioned on page 209, when you assign a function to an event, you omit the ( ) that you normally add to the end of a function's name to call it. In other words, the following won't work:

```
$('#start').click(startSlideShow())
```

You can also pass an *anonymous function* to the event. You read about anonymous functions on page 193—they're basically a function without a name. The basic structure of an anonymous function looks like this:

```
function( ) {
// your code here
}
```

The basic structure for using an anonymous function with an event is pictured in Figure 6-2.

Note: To learn more about how to work with jQuery and events, visit *http://docs.jquery.com/Events*.

Here's a simple example. Assume you have a Web page with a link that has an ID of *menu* applied to it. When a visitor moves his mouse over that link, you want a hidden list of additional links to appear—assume that the list of links has an ID of

---

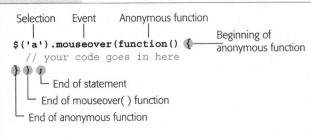

Figure 6-2:
In jQuery, an event works like a function, so you can pass an argument to the event. You can think of an anonymous function, then, as really just an argument—like a single piece of data that's passed to a function. If you think of it that way, it's easier to see how all of the little bits of punctuation fit together. For example, in the last line, the } marks the end of the function (and the end of the argument passed to the mouseover function); the) is the end of the mouseover( ) function; and the semicolon is the end of the entire statement that began with the selector $('a').

submenu. So what you want to do is add a mouseover event to the menu, and then call a function that shows the submenu. The process breaks down into four steps:

1. **Select the menu:**

   ```
   $('#menu')
   ```

2. **Attach the event:**

   ```
   $('#menu').mouseover();
   ```

3. **Add an anonymous function:**

   ```
   $('#menu').mouseover(function() {

   });
   ```

4. **Add the necessary actions (in this case, it's showing the submenu):**

   ```
   $('#menu').mouseover(function() {
    $('#submenu').show();
   });
   ```

A lot of people find the crazy nest of punctuation involved with anonymous functions very confusing (that last *});* is always a doozy). And it *is* confusing, but the best way to get used to the strange world of JavaScript is through lots of practice, so the following hands-on tutorial should help reinforce the ideas just presented.

Note: The *show( )* function is discussed on page 243.

Tutorial: Highlighting Table Rows

So far the tutorials you've completed for this book have been almost entirely free of events (although in the first tutorial in Chapter 5 (page 164), you used the load event to trigger a function). In this chapter, you finally get to pull out the techniques that let your pages take the most advantage of JavaScript and really respond to visitors.

In this tutorial, you'll expand on the exercise from Chapter 1, in which you used JavaScript to add alternating colored rows to a table. Now you'll add some interactivity to the table, so that when a visitor mouses over a row, that row is highlighted (see Figure 6-3). In essence, you have to do two things:

1. **Add a mouseover event to each row in the table.**

2. **Assign a function to that event that changes the background color of that row.**

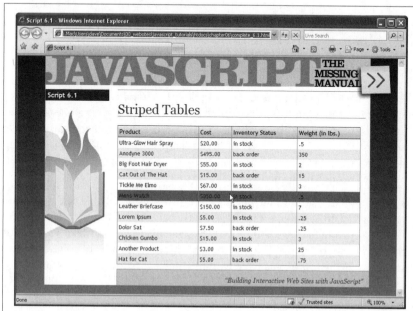

Figure 6-3:
While Web browsers offer lots of different events, responding to a mouseover event is one of the most common.

You'll use jQuery to tackle this problem, following the three-step process outlined on page 210.

Note: See the note on page 27 for information on how to download the tutorial files.

---

1. **In a text editor, open the file *6.1.html* in the *chapter06* folder.**

   This file is the completed version of the *1.3.html* file you created on page 30. It already has the *jQuery.js* file linked to it, and the <script> tags to which you'll add more programming:

   ```
   <script type="text/javascript" src="../js/jquery.js"></script>
   <script type="text/javascript">
   $(document).ready(function( ) {
       $('table.striped tr:even').addClass('even');

   });
   </script>
   ```

The first step is to create a jQuery selector to identify the elements to which you wish to add the mouseover event. In this case, that action will happen when a visitor mouses over one of the table rows, so you need to create a selector to target those rows.

2. **Add the code in bold below to the script:**

```
<script type="text/javascript" src="../js/jquery.js"></script>
<script type="text/javascript">
$(document).ready(function( ) {
    $('table.striped tr:even').addClass('even');
    $('table.striped tbody tr')
});
</script>
```

The particular CSS selector used here—*table.striped tbody tr*—certainly isn't the only selector you could use. A far simpler selector would be *tr* alone, like this: *$('tr')*. That would work fine with the HTML on this page; however, the simple *tr* selector selects *every* table row, so if you happen to have other tables on the page (for a calendar, for example, or even for your page layout) the rows in those tables would also be highlighted!

The selector you use here targets only the rows inside a table with the class *striped* applied to it—that's the *table.striped* part. In addition, you limit the selection to just table rows within a *tbody* tag. This way, you make sure to not highlight a table row that appears in the table head, so the row of column names that appear at the top of this table won't be highlighted when you mouse over them.

Next, you'll add the event.

3. **Directly after the code you just entered, type** *.mouseover( );* **so the code looks like this:**

```
$('table.striped tbody tr').mouseover( );
```

As described under "Automatic Loops" on page 180, jQuery has a nifty feature built into each of its functions—like the *mouseover( )* function here. Every jQuery function automatically loops through all of the elements in the selection, so in this case, the *mouseover* event will be attached to every table row in the jQuery selection.

Note: Step 3 is deceptively simple...thanks to jQuery. Without jQuery, you'd first have to write a really complicated function to retrieve each of the table rows. You'd then have to create a loop (see page 90) to attach the event to each element—and remember, you'd have to attach the event differently depending upon whether the Web browser was Internet Explorer or Firefox, Safari, or Opera (page 210). In other words, this one line of code represents the dozens of lines you don't have to write yourself.

Next you'll add an anonymous function as an argument for the *mouseover( )* function.

4. **Click between the two parentheses in *mouseover( )* and type *function( ) {*. Hit Return (or Enter) twice, and then type a *}*. The code should now look like this:**

```
$('table.striped tbody tr').mouseover(function() {

});
```

The anonymous function holds the actual programming that the browser will run when the event is triggered—highlighting a table row, the heart of the effect we're after.

5. **Click in the empty line between the anonymous function's opening and closing brace, hit the Space bar twice, and then type *$(this)*.**

The two spaces, while not required, indent the code and help indicate that this line of code is a part of the anonymous function, making the code easier to read.

As mentioned on page 194, *$(this)* is a way to refer to the page element that's currently being worked on. Since this code is looping through a long list of table rows, you need a way to assign an action to each particular row so you can tell the Web browser "when a visitor mouses over *this* specific row, highlight *this* specific row."

6. **Directly after *$(this)*, type *.addClass('highlight');* so the code looks like this:**

```
$('table.striped tbody tr').mouseover(function() {
  $(this).addClass('highlight');
});
```

You can read more about jQuery's *addClass( )* function on page 185. On page 32, you used the same function to stripe table rows; it simply applies a CSS class to the element. If you want, you can use JavaScript to add some crazy highlight effect, but it's usually faster to simply assign a CSS style that you've previously created. In this case, the page has a CSS style sheet with a class style named *highlight*, with a yellow background color. So when you mouse over a row, its background color changes to yellow.

Tip: The nice thing about using a CSS class style instead of just pure JavaScript to highlight the table row is that if you want to change the appearance of the highlight–for example, use a different font, change the font color or size–you simply add additional CSS formatting properties to the style. You don't have to do anything at all to the JavaScript.

---

7. **Save the page and preview it in a Web browser. When you do, make sure you move your mouse over the table rows.**

The rows' background color should change to a yellowish color when you mouse over them; if it doesn't, double-check your code for any typos. The only problem is that the yellowish background color doesn't go away! To make the row revert back to its old background color, you must add a mouseout event.

8. **Add the bolded code (shown on lines 6–8 below), so the finished script looks like this:**

```
1   $(document).ready(function( ) {
2     $('table.striped tr:even').addClass('even');
3     $('table.striped tbody tr').mouseover(function( ) {
4       $(this).addClass('highlight');
5     });
6     $('table.striped tbody tr').mouseout(function( ) {
7       $(this).removeClass('highlight');
8     });
9   });
```

This new code should look familiar now—it's basically the opposite of the mouseover function. That is, the class is removed when you move your mouse off the row.

Save the page and preview it in a Web browser. The rows should now revert to their old style when you mouse off them. The program works fine, but it's slightly inefficient. Notice that for both the mouseover and mouseout functions you have the same jQuery object: *$('table.striped tbody tr')*.

The jQuery object is really a kind of function that runs through the HTML of a page and finds all elements that match the given CSS selector. Each time you call the jQuery object, jQuery has to search the page. Depending on how complicated a CSS selector you use, creating the jQuery object can take some time, and while jQuery is fast, there's no need to waste time creating the same selection twice. A method that's more efficient (meaning your script will be a tad faster) is to store any jQuery object you use multiple times into a variable. The next steps show you how.

9. **Insert a blank line just *below* line 2 (see numbered code in step 8 above), and type:**

```
var rows = $('table.striped tbody tr');
```

This line of code creates a variable, *rows*, which holds a jQuery object containing all of the rows you want to add events to. All you need to do is replace two other jQuery objects with the variable name.

10. On lines 4 and 8, replace *$('table.striped tbody tr')* with *rows*. The finished code should look like this:

```
1   $(document).ready(function( ) {
2     $('table.striped tr:even').addClass('even');
3     var rows =    $('table.striped tbody tr')
4   rows.mouseover(function() {
5       $(this).addClass('highlight');
6     });
7   rows.mouseout(function() {
8       $(this).removeClass('highlight');
9     });
10  });
```

Now jQuery has to search the page's HTML only once to find the desired table rows; the results get stored in a variable that can be used any number of times. (jQuery provides another technique for applying multiple functions to the same jQuery object, called *chaining*. See the box below for more detail.)

Save the page and preview it in a Web browser.

Efficient Programming with jQuery Chaining

As discussed on page 180, jQuery lets you use a technique known as *chaining* to string together a series of functions and apply them to a single jQuery object. For example, say you want to change the text inside a currently hidden DIV with an ID of *popup*, and make the DIV fade into view. You can do that with two lines of code like these:

```
$('#popUp').text('Hi!');
$('#popUp').fadeIn(1000);
```

Or, using chaining, on a single line, like this:

```
$('#popUp').text('Hi!').fadeIn(1000);
```

Chaining also means you don't have to use a temporary variable like you did in step 10 above to store a jQuery object that you want to apply several functions to. Instead, you can simply chain the two events from that example—mouseover and mouseout—onto the single jQuery object.

You can replace lines 3–9 in step 10 with code like this:

```
$('table.striped tbody tr')
  .mouseover(function() {
    $(this).addClass('highlight');
  })
  .mouseout(function() {
    $(this).removeClass('highlight');
  });
```

This code is a little scary looking, for sure, but, believe it or not, it works. Even though the code spans seven lines, it's really just a single JavaScript statement (notice the semicolon at the end). To make reading the statement clearer, the events *.mouseover( )* and *.mouseout( )* are placed on their own lines. Since JavaScript mostly ignores white space (see page 47), breaking the code into multiple lines is perfectly legal (see the Tip on page 181 for more on this technique).

More jQuery Event Concepts

Because events are a critical ingredient for adding interactivity to a Web page, jQuery includes some special jQuery-only functions that can make your programming easier and your pages more responsive.

Waiting for the HTML to Load

When a page loads, a Web browser tries immediately to run any scripts it encounters. So scripts in the head of a page might run before the page fully loads—you saw an example of this in the last chapter in the top image of Figure 5-4. Unfortunately, this phenomenon often causes problems. Since a lot of JavaScript programming involves manipulating the contents of a Web page—displaying a pop-up message when a particular link is clicked, hiding specific page elements, adding stripes to the rows of a table, and so on—you'll end up with JavaScript errors if your program tries to manipulate elements of a page that haven't yet been loaded and displayed by the browser.

The most common way to deal with that problem has been to use the load event to wait until a page is fully downloaded and displayed before executing any JavaScript. You used that technique in the last chapter in the revised quiz program: In step 8 on page 166, you added the *onload* event handler to the page to make sure the function *doQuiz* didn't run until the page had loaded.

Unfortunately, waiting until a page fully loads before running JavaScript code can create some pretty strange results. The load event only fires *after* all of a Web page's files have downloaded—meaning all images, movies, external style sheets, and so on. As a result, on a page with lots of graphics, the visitor might actually be staring at a page for several seconds while the graphics load *before* any JavaScript runs. If the JavaScript makes a lot of changes to the page—for example, styles table rows, hides currently visible menus, or even controls the layout of the page—visitors will suddenly see the page change before their very eyes. ·

Fortunately, jQuery comes to the rescue. Instead of relying on the load event to trigger a JavaScript program, jQuery has a special function named *ready( )* that waits just until the HTML has been loaded into the browser and then runs the page's scripts. That way, the JavaScript can immediately manipulate a Web page without having to wait for slow-loading images or movies. (That's actually a complicated and useful feat—another reason to use a JavaScript library.)

You've already used the *ready( )* function in a few of the tutorials in this book. The basic structure of the function goes like this:

```
$(document).ready(function( ) {
  //your code goes here
});
```

Basically, all of your programming code goes inside this function. In fact, the *ready( )* function is so fundamental, you'll probably include it on every page on which you use jQuery. You only need to include it once, and it's usually the first and last line of a script. You must place it within a pair of opening and closing <script> tags (it is JavaScript, after all) and after the <script> tag that adds jQuery to the page.

So, in the context of a complete Web page, the function looks like this:

```
<!DOCTYPE HTML PUBLIC "-//W3C//DTD HTML 4.01//EN" "http://www.w3.org/TR/
html4/strict.dtd">
<html>
<head>
<meta http-equiv="Content-Type" content="text/html; charset=UTF-8">
<title>Page Title</title>
<script type="text/javascript" src="js/jquery.js"></script>
<script type="text/javascript">
$(document).ready(function( ) {

    // all of your JavaScript goes in here.

}); // end of ready( ) function
</script>
</head>
<body>
The Web page content...
</body>
</html>
```

As you've already seen, the *});* appears frequently when using anonymous functions (page 193). See step 4 on page 215 for an example. Trying to figure out which statement a particular *});* belongs to can be tricky, so it's a good idea to add a comment at the end makes of the *ready( )* function to easily identify it:

```
}); // end of ready( ) function
```

Tip: Because the *ready( )* function is used nearly anytime you add jQuery to a page, there's a shorthand way of writing it. You can remove the *$(document).ready* part, and just type this:

```
$(function( ) {

});
```

jQuery Events

jQuery also provides special events for dealing with two very common interactivity issues—moving the mouse over and then off of something, and switching between two actions when clicking.

The hover() event

The mouseover and mouseout events are frequently used together. For example, when you mouse over a button, a menu might appear; move your mouse off the button, and the menu disappears. Because coupling these two events is so common, jQuery provides a shortcut way of referring to both. jQuery's *hover( )* function works just like any other event, except that instead of taking one function as an argument, it accepts two functions. The first function runs when the mouse travels over the element, and the second function runs when the mouse moves off the element. The basic structure looks like this:

```
$('#selector').hover(function1, function2);
```

You'll frequently see the *hover( )* function used with two anonymous functions. That kind of code can look a little weird; the following example will make it clearer. Suppose when someone mouses over a link with an ID of *menu*, you want a (currently invisible) DIV with an ID of *submenu* to appear. Moving the mouse off of the link hides the submenu again. You can use *hover( )* to do that:

```
$('#menu').hover(function() {
    $('#submenu').show();
}, function() {
    $('#submenu').hide();
});
```

To make a statement containing multiple anonymous functions easier to read, move each function to its own line. So a slightly more readable version of the code above would look like this:

```
$('#menu').hover(
    function() {
      $('#submenu').show();
    },
    function() {
    $('#submenu').hide();
    }
);
```

Figure 6-4 diagrams how this code works for the mouseover and mouseout events.

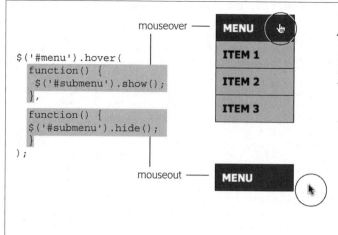

```
$('#menu').hover(
   function() {
     $('#submenu').show();
   },
   function() {
     $('#submenu').hide();
   }
);
```

mouseover —— MENU

ITEM 1

ITEM 2

ITEM 3

mouseout —— MENU

Figure 6-4:
jQuery's hover( ) *function lets you assign two
functions at once. The first function is run
when the mouse moves over the element,
while the second function runs when the
mouse moves off the element.*

If the anonymous function method is just too confusing, you can still use plain old
functions (page 97) to get the job done. First, create a named function to run when
the mouseover event triggers; create another named function for the mouseout
event; and finally, pass the names of the two functions to the *hover( )* function. In
other words, you could rewrite the code above like this:

```
function showSubmenu( ) {
   $('#submenu').show( );
}
function hideSubmenu( ) {
   $('#submenu').hide( );
}
$('#menu').hover(showSubmenu, hideSubmenu);
```

If you find this technique easier, then use it. There's no real difference between the
two, though some programmers like the fact that by using anonymous functions
you can keep all of the code together in one statement, instead of spread out
amongst several different statements.

The toggle() Event

jQuery's *toggle( )* event works identically to the *hover( )* event, except that instead
of responding to mouseover and mouseout events, it responds to clicks. One click
triggers the first function; the next click triggers the second function. Use this event
when you want to alternate between two states using clicks. For example, you
could make an element on a page appear with the first click and disappear with the
next click. Click again, and the element reappears.

For example, say you want to make the *submenu* <div> (from the *hover( )* examples above) appear when you first click the link, then disappear when the link is next clicked. Just swap "toggle" for "hover" like this:

```
$('#menu').toggle(
  function() {
   $('#submenu').show();
  },
  function() {
  $('#submenu').hide();
  }
);
```

Or, using named functions, like this:

```
function showSubmenu() {
  $('#submenu').show();
}
function hideSubmenu() {
  $('#submenu').hide();
}
$('#menu').toggle(showSubmenu, hideSubmenu);
```

The Event Object

Whenever a Web browser fires an event, it records information about the event and stores it in what's called an *event object.* The event object contains information that was collected when the event occurred, like the vertical and horizontal coordinates of the mouse, the element on which the event occurred, or whether the Shift key was pressed when the event was triggered.

In jQuery, the event object is available to the function assigned to handling the event. In fact, the object is passed as an argument to the function, so to access it, you just include a parameter name with the function. For example, say you want to find the X and Y position of the cursor when the mouse is clicked anywhere on a page.

```
$(document).click(function(evt) {
  var xPos = evt.pageX;
  var yPos = evt.pageY;
  alert('X:' + xPos + ' Y:' + yPos);
});
```

The important part here is the *evt* variable. When the function is called (by clicking anywhere in the browser window) the event object is stored in the *evt* variable. Within the body of the function, you can access the different properties of the event object using dot syntax—for example, *evt.pageX* returns the horizontal location of the cursor (in other words, the number of pixels from the left edge of the window). (The *chapter06* tutorials folder contains a file named *coordinates.html*, which will let you see a version of this code in action.)

Note: In this example, *evt* is just a variable name supplied by the programmer. It's not a special Java-Script keyword, just a variable used to store the event object. You could use any name you want such as *event* or simply *e*.

The event object has many different properties, and (unfortunately) the list of properties varies from browser to browser. Table 6-1 lists some common properties.

Table 6-1. *Every event produces an event object with various properties that you can access within the function handling the event*

Event property	Description
pageX	The distance (in pixels) of the mouse pointer from the left edge of the browser window.
pageY	The distance (in pixels) of the mouse pointer from the top edge of the browser window.
screenX	The distance (in pixels) of the mouse pointer from the left edge of the monitor.
screenY	The distance (in pixels) of the mouse pointer from the top edge of the monitor.
shiftKey	Is *true* if the shift key is down when the event occurs.
which	Use with the keypress event to determine the numeric code for the key that was pressed (see tip below).
target	The object that was the "target" of the event—for example, for a *click()* event, the element that was clicked.
data	A jQuery object used with the *bind()* function to pass data to an event handling function (see page 225).

Tip: If you access the event object's *which* property with the *keypress()* event, you'll get a numeric code for the key pressed. If you want the specific key that was pressed (a, K, 9, and so on), you need to run the *which* property through a JavaScript method that coverts the key number to the actual letter, number, or symbol on the keyboard:

```
String.fromCharCode(evt.which)
```

Stopping an Event's Normal Behavior

Some HTML elements have preprogrammed responses to events. A link, for example, when clicked usually loads a new Web page; a form's Submit button when clicked sends the form data to a Web server for processing. Sometimes you don't want the Web browser to go ahead with its normal behavior. For example, when a form is submitted (the *submit()* event), you might want to stop the form data from being sent if the person filling out the form left out important data.

You can prevent the Web browser's normal response to an event with the *preventDefault()* function. This function is actually a part of the event object (see the previous section), so you'll access it within the function handling the event. For example, say a page has a link with an ID of *menu*. The link actually points to another menu page (so that visitors with JavaScript turned off will be able to get to the menu page). However, you've added some clever JavaScript, so when a visitor clicks the link, the menu appears right on the same page. Normally, a Web browser would follow the link to the menu page, so you need to prevent its default behavior, like this:

```
$('#menu').click(function(evt){
  // clever javascript goes here
  evt.preventDefault(); // don't follow the link
});
```

Another technique is simply to return the value false at the end of the event function. For example, the following is functionally the same as the code above:

```
$('#menu').click(function(evt){
  // clever javascript goes here
  return false; // don't follow the link
});
```

Removing Events

At times, you might want to remove an event that you had previously assigned to a tag. jQuery's *unbind( )* function lets you do just that. To use it, first create a jQuery object with the element you wish to remove the event from. Then add the *unbind( )* function, passing it a string with the event name. For example, if you want to prevent all tags with the class *tabButton* from responding to any click events, you can write this:

```
$('.tabButton').unbind('click');
```

Take a look at a short script to see how the *unbind( )* function works.

```
1  $('a').mouseover(function() {
2    alert('You moved the mouse over me!');
3  });
4  $('#disable').click(function() {
5    $('a').unbind('mouseover');
6  });
```

Lines 1–3 add a function to the mouseover event for all links (<a> tags) on the page. Moving the mouse over the link opens an alert box with the message "You moved your mouse over me!" However, because the constant appearance of alert messages would be annoying, lines 4–6 let the visitor turn off the alert. When the visitor clicks a tag with an ID of *disable* (a form button, for example), the mouseover events are unbound from all links, and the alert no longer appears.

Note: For more information on jQuery's *unbind( )* function, visit *http://docs.jquery.com/Events/unbind*.

Stopping an Event in Its Tracks

Both Internet Explorer and the W3C event model supported by Firefox, Safari, and Opera let an event pass beyond the element that first receives the event. For example, say you've assigned an event helper for click events on a particular link; when you click the link, the click event fires and a function runs. The event, however, doesn't stop there. Each ancestor tag can also respond to that same click. So if you've assigned a click event helper for a <div> tag that the link is inside, the function for that <div> tag's event will run as well.

This concept, known as *event bubbling*, means that more than one element can respond to the same action. Here's another example: say you add a click event to an image so when the image is clicked, a new graphic replaces it. The image is inside a <div> tag to which you've also assigned a click event. In this case, an alert box appears when the <div> is clicked. Now when you click the image, both functions will run. In other words, even though you clicked the image, the <div> also receives the click event.

You probably won't encounter this situation too frequently, but when you do, the results can be disconcerting. Suppose in the example in the previous paragraph, you don't want the <div> to do anything when the image is clicked. In this case, you have to stop the click event from passing on to the

<div> tag without stopping the event in the function that handles the click event on the image. In other words, when the image is clicked, the function assigned to the image's click event should swap in a new graphic, but then stop the click event.

jQuery provides a function called *stopPropagation( )* that prevents an event from passing onto any ancestor tags. The function is a method of the event object (see page 222), so you access it within an event-handling function:

```
$('#theLink').click(function(evt) {
  // do something
  evt.stopPropagation(); // stop the
event from continuing
});
```

You can see how event bubbling works in the *events.html* file in the *chapter06* tutorial folder. The right sidebar has two links. One, when clicked, doesn't stop the event, so you'll see a list of all of the tags that receive the click event and can respond to the event. The second link uses the *stopPropagation( )* function, so the click event only affects that one link. For more information on controlling event bubbling with jQuery, visit *http://docs.jquery.com/Events_%28Guide*.

Advanced Event Management

You can live a long, happy programming life using just the jQuery event methods and concepts discussed on the previous pages. But if you really want to get the most out of jQuery's event-handling techniques, then you'll want to learn about the *bind( )* function.

Note: If your head is still aching from the previous section, you can skip ahead to the tutorial on page 227 until you've gained a bit more experience with event handling.

The *bind( )* method is a more flexible way of dealing with events than jQuery's event-specific functions like *click( )* or *mouseover( )*. It not only lets you specify an event and a function to respond to the event, but also lets you pass additional data for the event-handling function to use. This lets different elements and events (for example a click on one link, or a mouseover on another image) pass different information to the same event-handling function—in other words, one function can act differently based on which event is triggered.

The basic format of the *bind( )* function is the following:

```
$('#selector').bind('click', myData, functionName);
```

The first argument is a string containing the name of the event (like click, mouseover, or any of the other events listed on page 204). The second argument is the data you wish to pass to the function—either an object literal or a variable containing an object literal. An object literal (discussed on page 188) is basically a list of property names and values:

```
{
    firstName : 'Bob',
    lastName : 'Smith'
}
```

You can store an object literal in a variable like so:

```
var linkVar = {message:'Hello from a link'};
```

The third argument passed to the *bind( )* function is another function—the one that does something when the event is triggered. The function can either be an anonymous function or named function—in other words, this part is the same as when using a regular jQuery event, as described on page 211.

Note: Passing data using the *bind( )* function is optional. If you want to use *bind( )* merely to attach an event and function, then leave the data variable out:

```
$('selector').bind('click', functionName);
```

This code is functionally the same as:

```
$('selector').click(functionName);
```

Suppose you wanted to pop up an alert box in response to an event, but you wanted the message in the alert box to be different based on which element triggered the event. One way to do that would be to create variables with different object literals inside, and then send the variables to the *bind( )* function for different elements. Here's an example:

```
var linkVar = { message:'Hello from a link'};
var pVar = { message:'Hello from a paragraph};
function showMessage(evt) {
    alert(evt.data.message);
}
$('a').bind('click',linkVar,showMessage);
$('p').bind('mouseover',pVar,showMessage);
```

Figure 6-5 breaks down how this code works. It creates two variables, *linkVar* on the first line and *pVar* on the second line. Each variable contains an object literal, with the same property name, *message*, but different message text. A function, *showMessage( )*, takes the event object (see page 222) and stores it in a variable named *evt*. That function runs the *alert( )* command, displaying the *message* property (which is itself a property of the event object's *data* property). Keep in mind that *message* is the name of the property defined in the object literal.

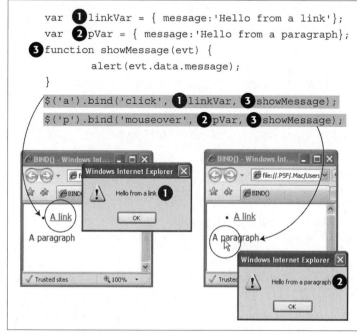

Figure 6-5:
jQuery's bind( ) *function lets you pass data to the function responding to the event. That way, you can use a single named function for several different elements (even with different types of events), while letting the function use data specific to each event helper.*

Tutorial: A One-Page FAQ

"Frequently Asked Questions" pages are a common sight on the Web. They can help improve customer service by providing immediate answers 24/7. Unfortunately, most FAQ pages are either one very long page full of questions and complete answers, or a single page of questions that link to separate answer pages. Both solutions slow down the visitors' quest for answers.

In this tutorial, you'll solve this problem by creating a JavaScript-driven FAQ page. All of the questions will be visible when the page loads, so it's easy to locate a given question. The answers, however, are hidden until the question is clicked—then the desired answer fades smoothly into view (see Figure 6-6).

Overview of the Task

The JavaScript for this task will need to accomplish several things:

• When a question is clicked, the corresponding answer will appear.

• When a question whose answer is visible is clicked, then the answer should disappear.

In addition, you'll want to use JavaScript to hide all of the answers when the page loads. Why not just use CSS? For example, setting the CSS *display* property to *none* for the answers is another way to hide the answers. The problem with this technique is what happens to visitors who don't have JavaScript turned on: They won't see the answers when the page loads, nor will they be able to make them visible by clicking the questions. To make your pages viewable to both those with JavaScript enabled and those with JavaScript turned off, it's best to use JavaScript to hide any page content.

Note: See the note on page 27 for information on how to download the tutorial files.

The Programming

1. **In a text editor, open the file *6.2.html* in the *chapter06* folder.**

   This file already contains a link to the jQuery file, and the *$(document).ready( )* function (page 218) is in place. First, you'll hide all of the answers when the page loads.

2. **Click in the empty line after the *$(document).ready( )* function, and then type *$('.answer').hide( );*.**

   The text of each answer is contained within a <div> tag with the class of *answer* applied to it. This one line of code selects each <div> and hides it (the *hide( )* function is discussed on page 243). Save the page and open it in a Web browser. The answers should all be hidden.

   The next step is determining which elements you need to add an event listener to. Since the answer appears when a visitor clicks the question, you must select every question in the FAQ. On this page, each question is a <h2> tag in the page's main body.

3. **Press return to create a new line and add the code in bold below to the script:**

   ```
   <script type="text/javascript" src="../js/jquery.js"></script>
   <script type="text/javascript">
   $(document).ready(function( ) {
     $('.answer').hide( );
    $('#main h2')
   }); // end of ready( )
   </script>
   ```

That's a basic descendent selector used to target every <h2> tag inside an element with an ID of *main* (so it doesn't affect the <h2> tag in the left sidebar). Now it's time to add an event. The click event is a good candidate; however, you can better meet your requirements—that clicking the question either shows or hides the answer—using the jQuery *toggle( )* function (see page 221). This function lets you switch between two different functions with each mouse click.

4. **Immediately following the code you typed in step 2 (on the same line), type** *.toggle(.*

This code marks the beginning of the *toggle( )* function, which takes two anonymous functions (page 193) as arguments. The first anonymous function runs on the first click, the second function runs on the next click. You'll get the basic structure of these functions in place first.

5. **Press Return to create a new line, and then type:**

```
function( ) {

}
```

This code is the basic shell of the function and represents the first argument passed to the *toggle( )* function. You'll add the basic structure for the second function next.

6. **Add the code in bold, so that your script looks like this:**

```
1   <script type="text/javascript" src="../js/jquery.js"></script>
2   <script type="text/javascript">
3   $(document).ready(function( ) {
4     $('.answer').hide( );
5     $('#main h2').toggle(
6       function( ) {
7
8       },
9       function( ) {
10
11      }
12    ); // end of toggle( )
13  }); // end of ready( )
14  </script>
```

Be sure you don't leave out the comma at the end of line 8 above. Remember that the two functions here act like arguments passed to a function (page 100). When you call a function, you separate each argument with a comma, like this: *prompt('Question', 'type here')*. In other words, the comma on line 8 separates the two functions. (You can leave out the comment on line 12—*// end of toggle*—if you want. It's just there to make clear that that line marks the end of the *toggle( )* function.)

CHAPTER 6: ACTION/REACTION: MAKING PAGES COME ALIVE WITH EVENTS

Now it's time to add the effect you're after: the first time the <h2> tag is clicked, the associated answer needs to appear. While each question is contained in a <h2> tag, the associated answer is in a <div> tag immediately following the <h2> tag. In addition, the <div> has a class of *answer* applied to it. So what you need is a way to find the <div> tag following the clicked <h2>.

7. **Within the first function (marked as line 6 in step 5 above), add** *$(this)* *.next('.answer').fadeIn( ); to the script.*

As discussed on page 194, *$(this)* refers to the element currently responding to the event—in this case, a particular <h2> tag. jQuery provides several functions to make moving around a page's structure easier. The *.next( )* function finds the tag immediately following the current tag. In other words, it finds the tag following the <h2> tag. You can further refine this search by passing an additional selector to the *.next( )* function—the code *.next('answer')* finds the first tag following the <h2> that also has the class *answer* applied to it. Finally, *.fadeIn( )* gradually fades the answer into view (the *fadeIn( )* function is discussed on page 244).

Note: The *.next( )* function is just one of the many jQuery functions that help you navigate through a page's DOM. To learn about other helpful functions, visit *http://docs.jquery.com/Traversing*.

Now's a good time to save the page and check it out in a Web browser. Click one of the questions on the page—the answer below it should open (if it doesn't, double-check your typing and refer to the troubleshooting tips on page 32).

In the next step you'll complete the second half of the toggling effect—hiding the answer when the question is clicked a second time.

8. **Add the code bolded on line 10 below:**

```
1    <script type="text/javascript" src="../js/jquery.js"></script>
2    <script type="text/javascript">
3    $(document).ready(function( ) {
4      $('.answer').hide( );
5      $('#main h2').toggle(
6        function() {
7          $(this).next('.answer').fadeIn( );
8        },
9        function() {
10          $(this).next('.answer').fadeOut( );
11        }
12      ); // end of toggle( )
13    }); // end of ready( )
14    </script>
```

Now the answer fades out on a second click. Save the page and give it a try. While the page functions fine, there's one nice design touch you can add. Currently, each question has a small plus sign to the left of it. The plus sign is a common icon used to mean, "Hey, there's more here." To indicate that a visitor can click to hide the answer, replace the plus sign with a minus sign. You can do it easily by just adding and removing classes from the <h2> tags.

9. **Add two final lines of code (lines 8 and 12 below). The finished code should look like this:**

```
1    <script type="text/javascript" src="../js/jquery.js"></script>
2    <script type="text/javascript">
3    $(document).ready(function( ) {
4      $('.answer').hide( );
5      $('#main h2').toggle(
6        function( ) {
7          $(this).next('.answer').fadeIn( );
8          $(this).addClass('close');
9        },
10       function( ) {
11         $(this).next('.answer').fadeOut( );
12         $(this).removeClass('close');
13       }
14     ); //end toggle
15   });
16   </script>
```

This code simply adds a class named *close* to the <h2> tag when it's clicked the first time, then removes that class when it's clicked a second time. The minus sign icon is defined within the style sheet as a background image. (Once again, CSS makes JavaScript programming easier.)

Save the page and try it out. Now when you click a question, not only does the answer appear, but the question icon changes (see Figure 6-6).

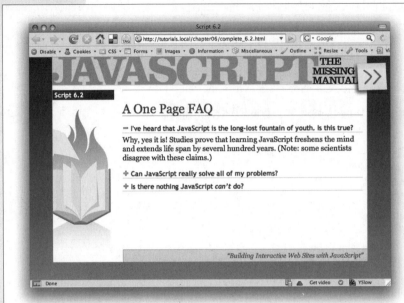

Figure 6-6:
*With just a few lines of
JavaScript, you can make
page elements appear or
disappear with a click of
the mouse.*

Improving Your Images

Web designers use images to improve a page's design, decorate navigation bars, highlight elements on a page—and to show the world what fun they had on their last vacation. Adding an image to a Web page immediately adds interest and visual appeal. When you add JavaScript to the mix, however, you can really add excitement by dynamically changing images on a page, presenting an animated photo gallery, or showing off a series of photos in a self-running slideshow. In this chapter, you'll learn a slew of tricks for manipulating and presenting images on your Web site.

Swapping Images

Probably the single most common use of JavaScript is the simple *image rollover*: when move your mouse over an image, it changes to another image. This basic technique has been used since the dawn of JavaScript to create interactive navigation bars whose buttons change appearance when the mouse hovers over them.

But in the past couple of years, more and more designers have turned to CSS to achieve this same effect (for example, see *www.monkeyflash.com/css/image-rollover-navbar/*). However, even if you're using CSS to create interactive navigation bars, you still need to understand how to use JavaScript to swap one image for if you want to create slide shows, image galleries, and adding other types of interactive graphic effects to a Web page.

Changing an Image's *src* Attribute

Every image displayed on a Web page has a *src* (short for *source*) attribute that indicates a path to a graphic file; in other words, it points to an image on a Web server. If you change this property to point to a different graphic file, the browser displays the new image instead. Say you have an image on a page and you assign it an ID of *photo*. Using the traditional DOM (page 157), you can store a reference to that image in a variable like this:

```
var photo = document.getElementById('photo');
```

In this example, the variable *photo* is a DOM object—the actual <img> tag in the page's HTML. The object has all of the properties of a normal <img> tag, so to change the *src* attribute, you can do the following:

```
photo.src = 'images/newImage.jpg';
```

This line of code makes the Web browser download the file *newImage.jpg* and replace the current image on the page with it.

Using jQuery, you can achieve the same effect like this:

```
$('#photo').attr('src','images/newImage.jpg');
```

Note: When you change the *src* property of an image using JavaScript, the path to the image file is based on the page location, *not* the location of the JavaScript code. This point can be confusing when you use an external JavaScript file (page 24) located in a different folder. In the example above, the Web browser would try to download the file *newImage.jpg* from a folder named *images*, which is located in the same folder as the Web page. That method works even if the code is included in an external file located in another folder elsewhere on the site. Accordingly, it's often easier to use root relative links inside external JavaScript files (see the box on page 25 for more information on the different links types).

Changing an image's *src* attribute doesn't change any of the <img> tag's other attributes, however. For example, if the *alt* attribute is set in the HTML, the swapped-in image has the same *alt* text as the original. In addition, if the *width* and *height* attributes are set in the HTML, changing an image's *src* property makes the new image fit inside the same space as the original. If the two graphics have different dimensions, then the swapped-in image will be distorted.

In a situation like rollover images in a navigation bar, the two images will most likely be the same size and share the same *alt* attribute, so you don't get that problem. But you can avoid the image distortion problem entirely by simply leaving off the *width* and *height* property of the original image in your HTML. Then when the new image is swapped in, the Web browser displays the image at the dimensions set in the file.

Another solution is to first download the new image, get its dimensions, then change the *src*, *width*, *height*, and *alt* attributes of the <img> tag:

```
1   var newPhoto = new Image( );
2   newPhoto.src = 'images/newImage.jpg';
3   var photo = document.getElementById('photo');
4   photo.src = newPhoto.src;
5   photo.width = newPhoto.width;
6   photo.height = newPhoto.height;
```

Note: The line numbers on the left aren't part of the code, so don't type them. They're just to make the code easier to read.

The key to this technique is line 1, which creates a new image object. To a Web browser, the code *new Image( )* says, "Browser, I'm going to be adding a new image to the page, so get ready." The next line tells the Web browser to actually download the new image. Line 3 gets a reference to the current image on the page, and lines 4–6 swap in the new image and change the width and height to match the new image.

In jQuery, the code would look like this:

```
1   var newPhoto = new Image( );
2   newPhoto.src = 'images/newImage.jpg';
3   var photo = $('#photo');
4   photo.attr('src',newPhoto.src);
5   photo.attr('width',newPhoto.width);
6   photo.attr('height',newPhoto.height);
```

Tip: The jQuery *attr( )* function can set multiple HTML attributes at once. Just pass an object literal (see page 188) that contains each attribute name and new value. You could write the jQuery code from above more succinctly, like this:

```
var newPhoto = new Image( );
newPhoto.src = 'images/newImage.jpg';
$('#photo').attr({
   src: newPhoto.src,
   width: newPhoto.width,
   height: newPhoto.height
});
```

Preloading Images

There's one problem with swapping in a new image using the techniques listed above: when you swap the new file path into the *src* attribute, the browser has to download the image. If you wait until someone mouses over an image before downloading the new graphic, there'll be an unpleasant delay before the new image appears. In the case of a navigation bar, the rollover effect will feel sluggish and unresponsive.

To avoid that delay, preload any images that you want to immediately appear in response to an action. For example, when a visitor mouses over a button on a navigation bar, the rollover image should appear instantly. *Preloading* an image simply means forcing the browser to download the image before you plan on displaying it. When the image is downloaded, it's stored in the Web browser's cache so that any subsequent requests for that file are served from the visitor's hard drive instead of downloaded a second time from the Web server.

Preloading an image is as easy as creating a new image object and setting the object's *src* property. In fact, you already know how to do that:

```
var newPhoto = new Image();
newPhoto.src = 'images/newImage.jpg';
```

What makes this preloading is that you do it before you need to replace an image currently on the Web page. One way to preload is to create an array at the beginning of a script containing the paths to all graphics you wish to preload, then loop through that list, creating a new image object for each one:

```
1   var preloadImages = ['images/roll.png',
2                        'images/flower.png',
3                        'images/cat.jpg'];
4   var imgs = [];
5   for (var i=0; i<preloadImages.length;i++) {
6     imgs[i] = new Image();
7     imgs[i].src = preloadImages[i];
8   }
```

Lines 1–3 are a single JavaScript statement that creates an array named *preloadImages*, containing three values—the path to each graphic file to preload. (As mentioned on page 59, it's often easier to read an array if you place each array item on its own line.) Line 4 creates a new empty array, *imgs*, which will store each of the preloaded images. Lines 5–8 show a basic JavaScript *for* loop (see page 94), which runs once for each item in the array *preloadImages*. Line 6 creates a new image object, while line 7 retrieves the file path from the *preloadImages* array—that's the magic that causes the image to download.

Rollover Images

A *rollover image* is just an image swap (as discussed on page 234) triggered by the mouse moving over an image. In other words, you simply assign the image swap to the mouseover event. For example, say you have an image on the page with an ID of *photo*. When the mouse rolls over that image, you want the new image to appear. You can accomplish that with jQuery like this:

```
1   <script type="text/javascript" src="jquery.js"></script>
2   <script type="text/javascript">
3   var newPhoto = new Image();
4   newPhoto.src = 'images/newImage.jpg';
```

```
5   $(document).ready(function() {
6     $('#photo').mouseover(function() {
7         $(this).attr('src', newPhoto.src);
8     });
9   });
10  </script>
```

Lines 3 and 4 preload the image that you want to swap in. Line 5 waits until the HTML has loaded, so the JavaScript can access the HTML for the current photo. The rest of the code assigns a mouseover event to the image, with a function that changes the image's *src* attribute to match the new photo.

Since rollover images usually revert back to the old image once you move the mouse off the image, you need to also add a mouseout event to swap back the image. As discussed on page 220, jQuery provides its own event, called *hover( )*, which takes care of both the mouseover and mouseout events:

```
1   <script type="text/javascript" src="jquery.js"></script>
2   <script type="text/javascript">
3   var newPhoto=new Image();
4   newPhoto.src='images/newImage.jpg';
5   $(document).ready(function() {
6     var oldSrc=$('#photo').attr('src');
7     $('#photo').hover(
8       function() {
9           $(this).attr('src', newPhoto.src);
10      },
11      function() {
12          $(this).attr('src', oldSrc);
13    });
14  });
15  </script>
```

The *hover( )* function takes two arguments: the first argument is a function telling the browser what to do when the mouse moves over the image; the second argument is a function telling the browser what to do when the mouse moves off the image. This code also adds a variable, *oldSrc*, for tracking the original *src* attribute—the path to the file that appears when the page loads.

You aren't limited to rolling over just an image, either. You can add a *hover( )* function to any tag—a link, a form element, even a paragraph. In this way, any tag on a page can trigger an image elsewhere on the page to change. For example, say you want to make a photo swap out when you mouseover a page's <h1> tag. Assume that the target image is the same as the previous example. You just change your code as shown here in bold:

```
1   <script type="text/javascript" src="jquery.js"></script>
2   <script type="text/javascript">
3   var newPhoto = new Image();
```

```
4    newPhoto.src = 'images/newImage.jpg';
5    $(document).ready(function() {
6      var oldSrc = $('#photo').attr('src');
7      $('h1').hover(
8        function() {
9            $('#photo').attr('src', newPhoto.src);
10       },
11       function() {
12          $('#photo').attr('src', oldSrc);
13     });
14   });
15   </script>
```

Tutorial: Adding Rollover Images

In this tutorial, you'll add a rollover effect to a series of images (see Figure 7-1). You'll also add programming to preload the rollover images in order to eliminate any delay between mousing over an image and seeing the rollover image. In addition, you'll learn a new a technique to make the process of preloading and adding the rollover effect more efficient.

Figure 7-1:
Make a navigation bar, link, or simply a photo more visually interactive with rollovers.

Overview of the Task

The tutorial file *7.1.html* (located in the *chapter07* tutorial folder) contains a series of six images (see Figure 7-2). Each image is wrapped by a link that points to a larger version of the photo, and all of the images are wrapped in a <div> tag with an ID of *gallery*. Basically, you're trying to achieve two things:

• Preload the rollover image associated with each of the images inside the <div>.

- Attach a *hover( )* function to each image inside the <div>. The *hover( )*function swaps the rollover image when the mouse moves over the image, then swaps back to the original image when the mouse moves off.

From this description, you can see that both steps are tied to the images inside the <div>, so one way to approach this problem is to first select the images inside the <div>, then loop through the selection, preloading each images' rollover and attaching a *hover( )* function.

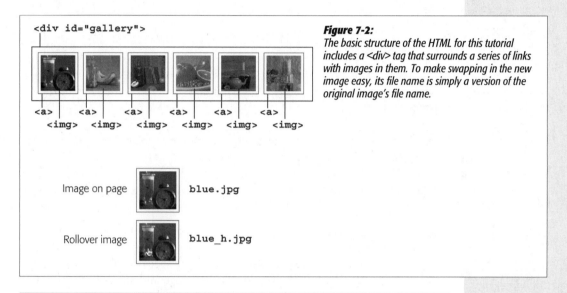

Figure 7-2:
The basic structure of the HTML for this tutorial includes a <div> tag that surrounds a series of links with images in them. To make swapping in the new image easy, its file name is simply a version of the original image's file name.

Note: See the note on page 27 for information on how to download the tutorial files.

The Programming

1. **In a text editor, open the file *7.1.html* in the *chapter07* folder.**

   This file already contains a link to the jQuery file, and the *$(document).ready( )* function (page 218). The first step is to select all of the images within the <div> tag and set up a loop with the jQuery *each( )* function discussed on page 193.

2. **Click in the empty line after the *$(document).ready( )* function and type *$('#gallery img').each(function( ) {.***

   The selector *#gallery img* selects all <img> tags within a tag that has the ID *gallery*. jQuery's *each( )* function provides a quick way to loop through a bunch of page elements, performing a series of actions on each element. The *each( )* function takes an anonymous function (page 193) as its argument. It's a good idea to provide the code that completes the function, so you'll do that next.

3. Press Return twice, and then type *}); // end each* to close the anonymous function, end the call to the *each( )* function, and terminate the JavaScript statement. Your code should now look like this:

```
1    <script type="text/javascript" src="../js/jquery.js"></script>
2    <script type="text/javascript">
3    $(document).ready(function( ) {
4    $('#gallery img').each(function( ) {
5
6    }); // end each
7    }); // end ready
```

At this point, the script loops through each of the images in the gallery, but doesn't actually do anything yet. The first order of business is to capture the image's *src* property and store it in a variable that you'll use later on in the script.

Note: The JavaScript comments–*// end each* and *// end ready*–aren't required for this script to work. However, they do make it easier to identify what part of the script the line goes with.

---

4. Click inside the empty line (line 5 in step 3) and type *var imgFile = $(this).attr('src');*.

As described on page 194, you can use *$(this)* to refer to the current element in the loop; in other words, *$(this)* will refer to each of the image tags in turn. The jQuery *attr( )* function (see page 189) retrieves the specified HTML attribute. In this case, it retrieves the *src* property of the image and stores it in a variable named *imgFile*. For example, for the first image, the *src* property is *images/small/blue.jpg*, which is the path to the image that appears on the page.

You can use that very *src* value to preload the image.

5. Hit Return to create a blank line, and then add the following two lines of code:

```
var preloadImage = new Image( );
var imgExt = /(\.\w{3,4}$)/;
preloadImage.src = imgFile.replace(imgExt,'_h$1');
```

As described on page 236, to preload an image you must first create an image object. In this case, the variable *preloadImage* is created to store the image object. Next, we preload the image by setting the Image object's *src* property.

One way to preload images (as discussed on page 235) is to create an array of images you wish to preload, then loop through each item in the array, creating an image object and adding the image's source to the object.

In this example, you'll use a more creative (and less labor-intensive method) to preload images. You just have to make sure you store the rollover image in the same location as the original image and name it similarly. For this Web page, each image on the page has a corresponding rollover image with an _h added to the end of the image name. For example, for the image *blue.jpg*, there's a rollover image named *blue_h.jpg*. Both files are stored in the same folder, so the path to both files is the same.

Here's the creative part: Instead of manually typing the *src* of the rollover to preload it like this, *preloadImage.src='images/small/blue_h.jpg'*, you can let JavaScript figure out the *src* by simply changing the name of the original image's source so it reflects the name of the rollover. That's what the other two lines of code do. The first line—*var imgExt = /(\.\w{3,4}$)/;*—creates a regular expression (see page 121) that matches a period followed by three or four characters at the end of a string. For example, it will match both *.jpeg* in */images/small/blue.jpeg* and *.gif* in */images/orange.gif*.

The next line—*preloadImage.src = imgFile.replace(imgExt,'_h$1');*—uses the *replace( )* method (see page 132) to replace the matched text with something else. Here a *.jpg* in the path name will be replaced with *_h.jpg*, so *images/small/blue.jpg* is changed to *images/small/blue_h.jpg*. This technique is a little tricky since it uses a regular expression subpattern (see the box on page 133 for full details), so you may want to reread the regular expression section of Chapter 4 (page 121).

Now that the rollover image is preloaded you can assign the *hover( )* event to the image.

6. **Hit Return and then add the code listed on lines 9–11 below:**

```
1    <script type="text/javascript" src="../js/jquery.js"></script>
2    <script type="text/javascript">
3    $(document).ready(function( ) {
4    $('#gallery img').each(function( ) {
5      var imgFile = $(this).attr('src');
6      var preloadImage = new Image( );
7      var imgExt = /(\.\w{3,4}$)/;
8      preloadImage.src = imgFile.replace(imgExt,'_h$1');
9      $(this).hover(
10
11     ); // end hover
12   }); // end each
13   }); // end ready
```

jQuery's *hover( )* function is just a shortcut method of applying a mouseover and mouseout event to an element (see page 220). To make it work, you pass two functions as arguments. The first function runs when the mouse moves over the element—in this case, the image changes to the rollover. The second function runs when the mouse moves off the element—here, the rollover image swaps back to the original image.

7. In the empty line (line 9 in step 6), add the following three lines of code:

```
function( ) {
  $(this).attr('src', preloadImage.src);
},
```

This first function simply changes the *src* property of the current image to the *src* of the rollover image. The comma at the end of the last line is required because the function you just added is acting as the first argument in a call to the *hover( )* function—a comma separates each argument passed to a function.

8. Finally, add the second function (lines 12–14 below). The finished script should look like this:

```
1   <script type="text/javascript" src="../js/jquery.js"></script>
2   <script type="text/javascript">
3   $(document).ready(function( ) {
4   $('#gallery img').each(function( ) {
5     var imgFile = $(this).attr('src');
6     var preloadImage = new Image( );
7     var imgExt = /(\.\w{3,4}$)/;
8     preloadImage.src = imgFile.replace(imgExt,'_h$1');
9     $(this).hover(
10      function( ) {
11        $(this).attr('src', preloadImage.src);
12      },
13      function( ) {
14      $(this).attr('src', imgFile);
15      }
16    ); // end hover
17  }); // end each
18  }); // end ready
```

This second function simply changes the *src* attribute back to the original image. In line 5, the path to the image originally on the page is stored in the variable *imgFile*. In this function (line 13), you access that value again to set the *src* back to its original value. Save the page, view it in a Web browser, and mouse over each of the black and white images to see them pop into full color.

jQuery Effects

Making elements on a Web page appear and disappear is a common JavaScript task. Drop-down navigation menus, pop-up tooltips, and automated slideshows all rely on the ability to show and hide elements when you want to. jQuery supplies a handful of functions that achieve the goal of hiding and showing elements.

To use each of these effects, you apply them to a jQuery selection, like any other jQuery function. For example, to hide all tags with a class of *submenu,* you can write this:

```
$('.submenu').hide();
```

Each effect function also can take an optional speed setting and a *callback* function. The speed represents the amount of time the effect takes to complete, while a callback is a function that runs when the effect is finished. (See the box on page 246 for details on callbacks.)

To assign a speed to an effect, you supply one of three string values—*'fast'*, *'normal'*, or *'slow'*—or a number representing the number of milliseconds the effect takes (1,000 is 1 second, 500 is half of a second, and so on). For example, the code to make an element fade out of view slowly would look like this:

```
$('element').fadeOut('slow');
```

Or if you want the element to fade out *really* slowly, over the course of 10 seconds:

```
$('element').fadeOut(10000);
```

When you use an effect to make an element disappear, the element isn't actually removed from the DOM. Its code is still in the browser's memory, but its *display* setting (same as the CSS display setting) is set to *none*. Because of that setting, the space taken up by the element is removed, so other content on the page may move into the position previously taken up by the hidden element. You can see all of the jQuery effects in action on the *effects.html* file include in the *chapter07* tutorial folder (see Figure 7-3).

Note: jQuery's User Interface library (see the box on page 361) includes an official set of add-on effects. It builds on jQuery's basic features and offers more eye-catching effects, like scaling an item, shaking an element, bouncing an element, and so on. You can learn more about these additional effects at *http://docs.jquery.com/UI/Effects*.

Basic Showing and Hiding

jQuery provides three functions for basic hiding and showing of elements:

- *show( )* makes a hidden element visible. It doesn't have any effect if the element is already visible on the page. If you don't supply a speed value, the element appears immediately. However, if you supply a speed value—*show(1000)*, for example—the element animates from the top-left corner down to the bottom-left corner.

- *hide( )* hides a visible element. It doesn't have any effect if the element is already hidden, and as with the *show( )* function, if you don't supply a speed value, the element immediately disappears. However, with a speed value the element animates out of view in a kind of shrinking motion.

• *toggle( )* switches an element's current display value. If the element is currently visible, *toggle( )* hides the element; if the element is hidden, then *toggle( )* makes the element appear. This function is ideal when you want to have a single control (like a button) alternately show and hide an element.

In the tutorial on page 228 of the previous chapter, you saw both the *hide( )* and *toggle( )* functions in action. That script uses *hide( )* to make all of the answers on an FAQ page disappear when the page's HTML loads, then uses *toggle( )* to alternately show and hide those answers when you click the question.

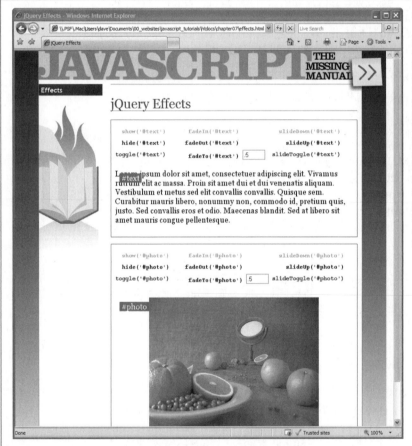

Figure 7-3:
You can test out jQuery's visual effects on the effects.html file located in the chapter07 tutorials file. Click the function text–fadeOut('#photo'), for example–to see how text and images look when they fade out, slide up, or appear. Some effects will appear in grey to indicate that they don't apply to the element. For example, it doesn't make much sense for the code to make a photo appear if it's already visible on the page.

Fading Elements In and Out

For a more dramatic effect, you can fade an element out or fade it in—in either case, you're just changing the opacity of the element over time. jQuery provides three fade-related functions:

• *fadeIn( )* makes a hidden element fade into view. First, the space for the element appears on the page (this may mean other elements on the page move out of the way); then the element gradually becomes visible. This function doesn't have any effect if the element is already visible on the page. If you don't supply a speed value, the element fades in using the *'normal'* setting (400 milliseconds).

- *fadeOut( )* hides a visible element by making it fade out of view like a ghost. It doesn't have any effect if the element is already hidden, and like the *fadeIn( )* function, if you don't supply a speed value, the element fades out over the course of 400 milliseconds.

- *fadeTo( )* works slightly differently than other effect functions. It fades an image to a specific opacity. For example, you can make an image fade so that it's semi-transparent. Unlike other effects, you must supply a speed value. In addition, you supply a second value from 0 to 1 that indicates the opacity of the element. For example, to fade all paragraphs to 75% opacity, you'd write this:

```
$('p').fadeTo('normal',.75);
```

This function changes an element's opacity regardless of whether the element is visible or invisible. For example, say you fade a currently hidden element to 50% opacity. If you then show that element using *show( )* or *fadeIn( )*, the element will appear at 50% opacity. Likewise, if you hide a semitransparent element and then make it reappear, its opacity setting is recalled.

If you fade an element to 0 opacity, the element is no longer visible, but the space it occupied on the page remains. In other words, unlike the other disappearing effects, fading to 0 will leave an empty spot on the page where the element is.

Tip: Firefox sometimes makes text on a page temporarily change appearance during a fade-in or -out. To stop this distraction, you need to set the opacity of the page to just less than 100%. A simple way to do that is to add a body tag style to a page's style sheet, like this:

```
body {
    -moz-opacity:.999;
}
```

Sliding Elements

For a little more visual action, you can also slide an element in and out of view. The functions are similar to the fading elements in that they make page elements appear and disappear from view, and may have a speed value:

- *slideDown( )* makes a hidden element slide into view. First, the top of the element appears and anything below the element is pushed down as the rest of the element appears. It doesn't have any effect if the element is already visible on the page. If you don't supply a speed value, the element slides in using the *'normal'* setting (400 milliseconds).

Performing an Action After an Effect Is Completed

Sometimes you want to do something once an effect is complete. For example, suppose that when a particular photo fades into view, you want a caption to appear. In other words, the caption must pop onto the page after the photo finishes fading into view. Normally, effects aren't performed one after the other; they all happen at the same time they're called. So if your script has one line of code to fade the photo into view, and another line of code to make the caption appear, the caption will appear while the photo was still fading in.

To get around this dilemma, you can pass a *callback function* to any effect; that's a function that runs only after the effect is completed. The callback function is passed as the second argument to most effects (the third argument for the *fadeTo( )* function).

For example, say you have an image on a page with an ID of *photo*, and a paragraph below it with an ID of *caption*. To fade the photo into view and then make the caption appear, you can use a callback function like this:

```
$('#photo').fadeIn(1000, function() {
  $('#caption').show();
});
```

Of course, if you want to run the function when the page loads, you'd want to hide the photo and caption first, then do the *fadeIn* effect:

```
$('#photo, #caption').hide();
$('#photo').fadeIn(1000, function() {
  $('#caption').show();
});
```

You'll see an example of a callback in step 8 of the tutorial on page 252.

- *slideUp( )* removes the element from view by hiding the bottom of the element and moving anything below the element up until the element disappears. It doesn't have any effect if the element is already hidden, and as with the *slideDown( )* function, if you don't supply a speed value, the element slides out over the course of 400 milliseconds.

- *slideToggle( )* applies the *slideDown( )* function if the element is currently hidden, and the *slideUp( )* function if the element is visible. This function lets you have a single control (like a button) both show and hide an element.

Animation

jQuery also provides an *animate( )* function that lets you animate any CSS property that accepts pixel, em, or percentage values. For example, you can animate the size of text, the position of an element on a page, the opacity of an object, or the width of a border.

Note: jQuery, by itself, can't animate color—for example, the color of text, the background color, or border color. However, the jQuery UI library (see the box on page 170) builds on jQuery's basic *animate( )* function and, among other cool additions, includes the ability to animate color. See *http://docs.jquery.com/UI/Effects/ColorAnimations* for more information.

To use this function, you must pass an object literal (page 188) containing a list of CSS properties you wish to change and the values you wish to animate to. For example, say you want to animate an element by moving it 650 pixels from the left edge of the page, changing its opacity to 50%, and enlarging its font size to 24 pixels. The following code creates an object with those properties and values:

```
{
  left: '650px';
  opacity: .5,
  fontSize: '24px';
}
```

Note: JavaScript doesn't accept hyphens for CSS properties. For example, *font-size* is a valid CSS property, but JavaScript doesn't understand it because the hyphen has special meaning (it's JavaScript's minus operator). When using CSS properties in JavaScript, remove the hyphen and capitalize the first letter of the word following the hyphen. For example, *font-size* becomes *fontSize*, and *border-width* becomes *borderWidth*.

Suppose you want to animate an element with an ID of *message* using these settings. You can use the *animate( )* function like this:

```
$('#message').animate(
{
  left: '650px';
  opacity: .5,
  fontSize: '24px';
},
1500
);
```

The *animate( )* function can take several arguments. The first is an object literal containing the CSS properties you wish to animate. The second is the duration (in milliseconds) of the animation. In the above example, the animation lasts 1,500 milliseconds, or 1.5 seconds. Finally, you can pass a third argument: a callback function to run after the animation is complete (see the box on page 246).

You can also set a property relative to its current value using += or -= as part of the animation options. For example, say you want to animate an element by moving it 50 pixels to the right each time you click on it. Here's how:

```
$('#moveIt').click(function( ) {
  $(this).animate({left:'+=50px'},1000);
});
```

Note: In order to animate a position of an element using the CSS *left, right, top,* or *bottom* properties, you must set that element's CSS *position* property to either *absolute* or *relative*. Those are the only two positioning properties that let you assign positioning values to them.

Tutorial: Photo Gallery with Effects

Now you'll expand on the last tutorial to create a single-page photo gallery. You'll be able to load a larger image onto the page when a visitor clicks a thumbnail image (see Figure 7-4). In addition, you'll use a couple of jQuery's effect functions to make the transition between larger images more visually interesting.

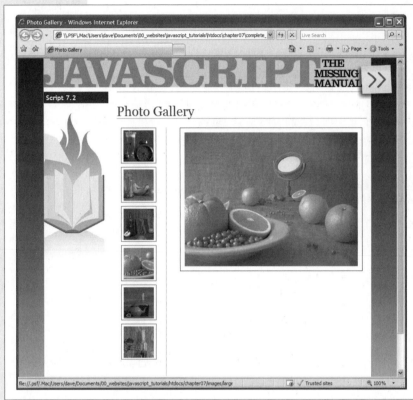

Figure 7-4:
The finished photo gallery page. Clicking a thumbnail makes a larger image fade into view and the current image fade out. The completed version of this tutorial file, completed_7.2.html, is in the chapter07 *folder. In the same folder, you'll find a more advanced version (*complete_7.2_advanced.html*) that highlights the currently selected thumbnail.*

Overview of Task

The way the gallery works is pretty straightforward—click a thumbnail to see a larger image. However, this tutorial shows you how to add a few features that make the presentation more interesting by using fade effects to swap larger images in and out of the page.

Another important technique you'll use here is *unobtrusive JavaScript*. That simply means that users who have JavaScript turned off will still be able to access the larger versions of the photos. To achieve that, each thumbnail image is wrapped in a link that points to the larger image file (see Figure 7-5). For those without Java-Script, clicking the link exits the current Web page and follows the link to load the larger image file. It won't look fantastic, since the visitor has to exit the gallery page and will see just the single larger image, but the photos will at least be accessible. For folks who have JavaScript turned on, clicking a link will make the larger image fade into view on the page.

All of the action occurs when the link is clicked, so this script uses the link's click event to achieve the following steps:

- **Stop the default behavior of the link.** Normally, clicking a link takes you to another page. On this page, clicking the link around a thumbnail exits the Web page and displays a larger image. Since you'll use JavaScript to display the image, you can add some JavaScript code to prevent the browser from following that link.

- **Get the href value of the link.** The link actually points to the larger image, so by retrieving the link's *href*, you're also getting the path to the larger image file.

- **Create a new image tag to insert into the page.** This image tag will include the path from the *href* value.

- **Fade the old image out while fading the new image in.** The current image fades out of view as the large version of the clicked thumbnail fades into view.

The tutorial includes a few additional nuances, but these four steps cover the basic process.

The Programming

This tutorial expands on the previous one, but the starting Web page has been reorganized a little: the thumbnails are now in a left column, and a <div> tag with an ID of *photo* has been added to the page (see Figure 7-5).

Note: See the note on page 27 for information on how to download the tutorial files.

---

1. **In a text editor, open the file *7.2.html* in the *chapter07* folder.**

   This file contains the programming from the previous tutorial, plus a new <div> tag to display the large version of each thumbnail image. Since the process of displaying a gallery image is triggered by clicking one of the links wrapped around the thumbnail images, the first step is to create a selection of those links and add the click event to each.

2. **Locate the JavaScript comment that reads "insert script 7.2 below this line" and add the following code:**

   ```
   $('#gallery a').click(function(evt) {

   }); // end click
   ```

   The selector *#gallery a* selects all link tags inside another tag with the ID *gallery*. The *.click* is a jQuery function for adding an event handler (see page 210 if you

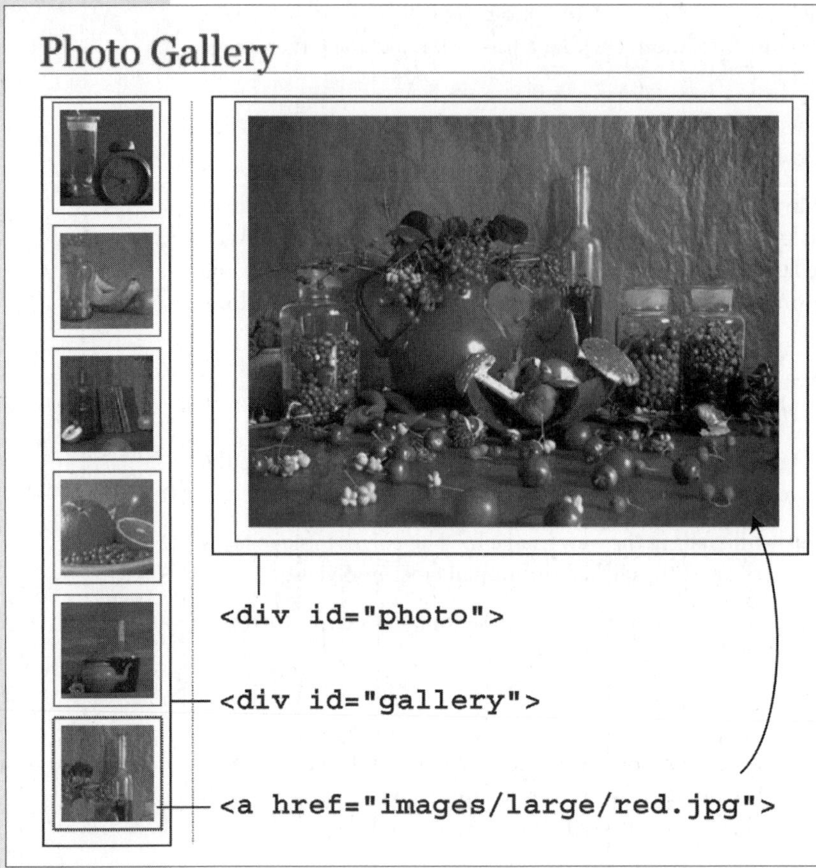

Photo Gallery

Figure 7-5:
*The basic structure of the
photo gallery. All of the
thumbnail images are
wrapped in links that
point to the larger
version of the photo.
Clicking each link will
load the larger image
inside a <div> tag with
the ID of photo.*

```
<div id="photo">

<div id="gallery">

<a href="images/large/red.jpg">
```

need a refresher on events). Also, the code passes an anonymous function to the
click event (as mentioned on page 222, functions that are executed in response
to an event automatically have the event object passed to them). In this case, the
variable *evt* stores that event object. You'll use it in the next step to stop the
browser from following the clicked link.

3. **Between the two lines of code you added in step 2, type *evt.preventDefault( );*.**

Normally, clicking a link makes the Web browser load whatever the link points
to (a Web page, graphic file, PDF document, and so on). In this case, the link is
just there so that people who don't have JavaScript turned on will be able to go
to a larger version of the thumbnail image. To prevent the Web browser from
following the link for those who have JavaScript enabled, you run the event
object's *preventDefault( )* function (see page 223).

Next, we'll get the *href* attribute for the link.

4. **Hit Return to create a new, blank line, and then type** *var imgPath = $(this).attr('href');*

```
$('#gallery a').click(function(evt) {
  evt.preventDefault();
  var imgPath = $(this).attr('href');
}); // end click
```

Here, *$(this)* refers to the element that's clicked—in other words, a link. A link's *href* attribute points to the page or resource the link goes to. In this case, each link contains a path to the larger image. That's important information, since you can use it to add an image tag that points to the image file. But before you do that, you need to get a reference to the large image that's currently displayed on the page. After all, you need to know what it is so you can fade it out of view.

Tip: You'll see that each line of code inside the *click( )* event in step 4 is indented. That's optional, but it helps make the code more readable, as described in the box on page 47. Many programmers use two spaces (or a tab) for each level of indentation.

---

5. **Hit Return and type** *var oldImage = $('#photo img');*.

The variable *oldImage* holds a jQuery selection containing the <img> tag inside the photo <div> (see Figure 7-5). Now it's time to create a tag for the new image.

6. **Hit Return again and add** *var newImage = $('<img src="' + imgPath +'">'); * **to the script.**

There are quite a few things going on here. jQuery lets you select an element that's in the page's DOM. For example, *$('img')* selects all images on the page. In addition, the jQuery object can add a *new* element to the DOM. For example, *$('<p>Hello</p>')* creates a new paragraph tag containing the word Hello. This line creates a new <img> tag and stores it in a variable named *newImage*.

Since the jQuery object expects a string as an argument (*'<p>Hello</p>'*, for example), this line of code *concatenates* or *combines* several strings to make one. The first string (surrounded by single quotes) is *<img src="*; the second string is stored in the variable *imgPath* (which you created in step 4) and is the path to the image file (for example, *images/large/red.jpg*); the third string (also surrounded by single quotes) is *">*. Taken altogether, they add up to an HTML tag: *<img src="images/large/red.jpg">*. When the script passes it to the jQuery object like this, *$('<img src="images/large/red.jpg">')*, the browser creates a DOM element. It isn't displayed on the page yet, but the browser is ready to add it to the page at anytime.

7. **Add the code listed below on lines 6–8, so the code you've added so far looks like this:**

```
1    $('#gallery a').click(function(evt) {
2        evt.preventDefault();
3        var imgPath = $(this).attr('href');
4        var oldImage = $('#photo img');
5        var newImage = $('<img src="' + imgPath +'">');
6        newImage.hide();
7        $('#photo').prepend(newImage);
8        newImage.fadeIn(1000);
9    }); // end click
```

In line 6, the newly created image (which is stored in the variable *newImage*) is hidden using the *hide()* function described on page 243. This step is necessary because if you just added the image tag created in line 5, the image would be immediately visible on the page—no cool fade in effect. So you first hide the image, and then add it to the page inside the photo <div> (line 7). The *prepend()* function (described on page 182) adds HTML inside a tag. Specifically, it adds the HTML at the very beginning of the tag. At this point, there are two images on the page inside the photo <div>—Figure 7-6 shows how one image can sit on top of the other. The image on top is invisible, but in line 8, the *fadeIn()* function makes the image slowly fade in over the course of 1,000 milliseconds (1 second).

Now it's time to make the original image fade out.

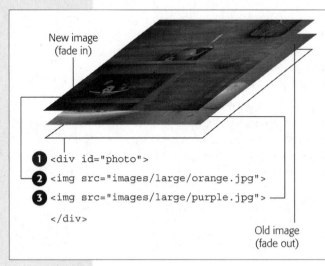

New image (fade in)

```
1  <div id="photo">
2    <img src="images/large/orange.jpg">
3    <img src="images/large/purple.jpg">
   </div>
```

Old image (fade out)

Figure 7-6:
To achieve the effect where two photos appear in the same spot on the page, but one photo fades in and another fades out, you need to use some creative CSS. Absolute positioning lets an element sit above the page, and even on top of another element. In this case, both images are absolutely positioned within the <div> tag, making them float one on top of the other. The style sheet gallery.css included in the chapter07 folder has all the CSS required—make sure to check out the #photo img style.

8. **Press Return and then add these three lines of code:**

```
oldImage.fadeOut(1000,function(){
    $(this).remove();
});
```

In step 5, you created a variable named *oldImage* and stored a reference to the original image on the page into it. That's the image we want to fade out, so you apply the *fadeOut( )* function. You pass two arguments to the function: The first is the duration of the effect—1,000 milliseconds (1 second); and the second is a callback function (as described in the box on page 246). The callback function runs *after* the fade out effect finishes, and removes the <img> tag for that image.

Note: The *remove( )* function is discussed on page 183. It actually removes the tag from the DOM, which erases the HTML from the browser's memory, freeing up computer resources. If you didn't take this step, each time your visitor clicks a thumbnail, a new <img> tag would be added (see step 7), but the old one would simply be hidden, not deleted. You'd end up with lots and lots of hidden <img> tags still embedded in the Web page, slowing down the responsiveness of the Web browser.

There's one final step—loading the first image. Currently the <div> tag where the photo goes is empty. You could type an <img> tag in that spot, so when the page loads there'd be a larger image for, say, the first thumbnail. But why bother—you've got JavaScript!

9. **Add one last line after the end of the** *click( )* **function (line 13 below), so your completed code looks like this:**

```
1    $('#gallery a').click(function(evt) {
2       evt.preventDefault( );
3       var imgPath = $(this).attr('href');
4       var oldImage = $('#photo img');
5       var newImage = $('<img src="' + imgPath +'">');
6       newImage.hide( );
7       $('#photo').prepend(newImage);
8       newImage.fadeIn(1000);
9       oldImage.fadeOut(1000,function( ){
10          $(this).remove( );
11      });
12   }); // end click
13   $('#gallery a:first').click( );
```

This last statement has two parts. First the selector—*#gallery a:first*—selects just the first link only in the gallery <div>. Next is the *click( )* function. So far, you've used jQuery's *click( )* function to assign a function that runs when the event occurs. However, if you don't pass any arguments to an event function, jQuery simply triggers that event, causing any previously defined event handlers to run. So, this line triggers a *click* on the first link that makes the Web browser run the function that you created earlier in lines 1–11. That is, it makes the larger image for the first thumbnail fade into view when the page loads.

Save the page and preview it in a Web browser. Not only do the thumbnails change color when you mouse over them, clicking a thumbnail makes its associated large image fade into view. (If you're having trouble with your code, the file *complete_7.2.html* contains a working copy of the script.)

Advanced Gallery with jQuery lightBox

Displaying a gallery of photos is such a common task that you'll find dozens of different ways to show off your imagery. One very popular technique dims the Web page and displays the larger version of the thumbnail as if it were floating on top of the browser window (see Figure 7-7). The most well known version of this method is a JavaScript program called Lightbox (*www.huddletogether.com/projects/lightbox2/*). There have been many imitations of the original, as well as one script created to work with jQuery. jQuery lightBox (*http://leandrovieira.com/projects/jquery/lightbox/*) is a jQuery plug-in that, with just a single line of code, creates a spectacular way to present images as part of a portfolio, gallery, or slideshow.

Note: Before continuing, you might want to open the file *complete_7.3.html* in the *chapter07* folder included with this book's tutorial files. It has a working demo of jQuery lightBox. Watching it in action first will probably make the rest of this section easier to understand.

Figure 7-7:
The jQuery lightBox plug-in, created by Leandro Vieira Pinho, is a very easy way to create an attractive, single-page photo gallery. You can navigate through a series of photos by clicking a Next or Previous button that appears when you mouse over the image. In addition, the left and right arrow keys, as well as the P and N keys, let you navigate through the gallery of large images.

The Basics

jQuery lightBox is very easy to use—you just need to set up your Web page with links to the images you wish to display, attach .css and .js files to the page, and add one line of code to call the light box into action.

1. **Set up your gallery page.**

   There's not really much you need to do—just add links to the larger images you wish to display on the page. These could be links added to thumbnail images, so when the thumbnail is clicked the larger image appears (that's how the gallery you programmed in the previous tutorial worked). The important thing to remember is that the link points to a graphic file—a .png, .jpeg, or .gif file—not to a Web page.

   In addition, you need a way to identify just the gallery links (as opposed to other links on the page). One way is to wrap the links in a <div> tag with a specific ID—*gallery*, for example. Then you can target just those links with a selector like '*#gallery a'*. Another approach is to add specific class names to each gallery link: for example, *<a href="images/potato.jpg" class="gallery">*. Then you can target those links with a selector like '*a.gallery'*. This last method is handy if the links are scattered around the page and aren't contained in a single <div>.

   Tip: To add a caption to a photo, just supply a *title* attribute to the <a> tag that links to the large image. For example:

   ```
   <a href="images/potato.jpg" title="A handsome potato">
   ```

   ---

2. **Download the jQuery lightBox files and put them into your site.**

   You can find the files at *http://leandrovieira.com/projects/jquery/lightbox/*. They're also provided with the tutorial files for this book. There are a handful of files you'll need: a JavaScript file, a CSS file, and several graphics files:

   - The JavaScript file is named something like *jquery.lightbox-0.5.js*, where 0.5 represents a version number. Your best bet is the minified version—*jquery. lightbox-0.5.min.js*—which is a compressed version of the file. A version of the file, *jquery.lightbox.js*, is located in the *js* folder of the tutorial files for this book. You can place this file anywhere in your site, though a common approach is to put external JavaScript files in a folder (named something like *js* or *libs*) in the root folder of your site.

   - The CSS file, *jquery.lightbox-0.5.css*, can also go anywhere in your site. You might want to put this in a folder where you keep all of your external CSS files, or, if you're just adding the light box effect to a single page on your site, you can put the file in the same folder as the light box enhanced Web page. You'll also find the CSS file in a folder named *css* in the *chapter07* tutorial folder, where it's named *lightbox.css*.

- jQuery lightBox depends on five graphic files: *lightbox-blank.gif*, *lightbox-btn-close.gif*, *lightbox-btn-next.gif*, *lightbox-btn-prev.gif*, and *lightbox-ico-loading.gif*. Some of these images are buttons for moving between images and closing the large image overlay. All five files should be located in a folder named *images*, which is located in the same folder as your lightBox-enhanced Web page. In other words, the jQuery lightBox plug-in expects the images to be in a specific location (you'll learn how to change the location, if you wish, on page 259).

3. **Attach the external style sheet to your page.**

   jQuery lightBox uses some fancy CSS to achieve the dark, transparent overlay effect and display the pop-up image. Attach this file as you would any CSS file. For example:

   ```
   <link href="css/lightbox.css" rel="stylesheet" type="text/css">
   ```

   Most JavaScript programmers place any style sheet information before their JavaScript programming—some JavaScript programs depend on having the style sheet information available first, in order for the program to work correctly. That's especially true of many jQuery plug-ins, so get in the habit of placing all style sheets before JavaScript files and programs.

4. **Attach the JavaScript files.**

   jQuery lightBox gets most of its power from the jQuery library (no surprise), so you must first attach the jQuery file to the page (see page 172 for a recap of this procedure). Also, the lightBox JavaScript file (like any JavaScript that uses jQuery) must be attached after the jQuery file. For example:

   ```
   <script type="text/javascript" src="js/jquery.js"></script>
   <script type="text/javascript" src="js/jquery.lightbox.js"></script>
   ```

5. **Add a <script> tag, the jQuery *ready( )* function, and call lightBox.**

   Believe it or not, steps 1–4 above are the hardest part of the whole process. Getting lightBox to work requires just a single line of JavaScript. Of course, as you read on page 218, you should put that code inside a jQuery *ready( )* function, so the browser has processed the HTML and is ready to manipulate the DOM. For example:

   ```
   <script type="text/javascript">
   $(document).ready(function() {
     $('#gallery a').lightBox();
   });
   </script>
   ```

   The *lightBox( )* function must be applied to just the links that point to the image files you wish to display. You use a jQuery selector (*$('#gallery a')*, for example) to tell lightBox which links to use: in this example, any <a> tag inside another tag with an ID of *gallery* becomes part of the lightBox effect. As mentioned in step 1, you need to set up your HTML so you can use jQuery to identify the specific links that make up your light box.

Tip: lightBox works really well with a gallery of thumbnails to create a slideshow effect where a visitor can click a Next button to step through each photo in the gallery. However, you can also use it to display a single image on a page. Or you can apply lightBox to different images on a page so they aren't part of the same "gallery." In other words, each image will open independently, so the images aren't connected with Next or Previous buttons. You just need to supply a jQuery selector to select a single image—for example, apply an ID to a link, then call lightBox on just that one link:

```
$('#soloImage').lightBox();
```

And that's it. Now, when you click each of the gallery links, a transparent background appears over the page, and a large version of the image appears in the middle of the window.

Customizing lightBox

While the general look of the lightBox effect is really nice, you may want to tinker a bit with its appearance. You can customize a variety of different parts of the light-Box look, including the buttons that let you close the lightBox window or navigate to the previous and next images; you can also change the color and opacity of the transparent background that overlays the page or change the background color of the caption box and picture frame.

lightBox options

The lightBox plug-in lets you supply custom options that affect the appearance of the light box effect. Basically, you pass a JavaScript object literal (see page 188) to the lightBox function containing the names of the options you wish to set and the values you wish to set them to. For example, to change the background color and opacity of the background placed over the page, you can create a variable containing your new settings and pass that to lightBox like this:

```
var lbOptions = {
  overlayBgColor: '#FF0033',
  overlayOpacity: .5
}
$('#gallery a').lightBox(lbOptions);
```

In this example, the color of the overlay is set to a bright red (#FF0033), and its opacity is set to 50% (.5). jQuery lightBox accepts a lot of different options (visit *http://leandrovieira.com/projects/jquery/lightbox/* for the complete list), but here are the most useful:

- **overlayBgColor.** The background color that covers the page while lightBox displays an image. This option accepts a hex color value like #FF0033, which must be inside quotes: *overlayBgColor: '#FF0033'*.

- **overlayOpacity.** The opacity of the overlay. This option sets how much of the page below the overlay should show through. You specify a number from 0 to 1: .5, for example, is 50% opacity. If you don't want to be able to see through the overlay—for example, you want to completely black out the rest of the Web page while the image appears—set this option to 1.

- **containerResizeSpeed.** When you move from image to image in a lightBox-powered page, the box containing the image is animated as it changes size from the dimensions of the current image to match the dimensions of the next image. You can control the speed of this transition by setting this option. The default is 400, meaning 400 milliseconds, or slightly less than half of a second.

- **txtImage.** When displaying multiple images, a message appears below the current image announcing which image you're viewing and the total number of images. For example, "Image 1 of 20." You can change the default word "Image" to something else (like "Photo") by setting this option.

- **txtOf.** Same as *txtImage*, but replaces the default "of" with the word of your choice. Changing this setting comes in handy if the page uses a language other than English, or you want the message to read something universal, like "Photo 1/6".

- **imageBtnClose.** The path to the image used for the Close button on the pop-up image window. Normally, this option points to *images/lightbox-btn-close.gif*, but you can change that setting to point to a different location, or to a different file name or type (for example, a PNG file).

- **imageBtnPrev.** The path to the image used for the Previous button on the pop-up image window: normally *images/lightbox-btn-prev.gif*.

- **imageBtnNext.** The path to the image used for the Close button on the pop-up image window: normally *images/lightbox-btn-next.gif*.

- **imageLoading.** The path to the image used for the Close button on the pop-up image window. Normally this points to *images/lightbox-ico-loading.gif*, but you can change the setting to point to a different location, or to a different file name or type (for example, a PNG file).

- **imageBlank.** Internet Explorer 6 needs a special image that allows it to respond correctly to the mouse hovering over the image to display Next and Previous buttons. Normally, this option points to *images/lightbox-blank.gif*. There's really no reason to change this setting, unless you want to move the image to a different folder, thus changing the path.

Here's an example of how you might set these options. Say you want to change the caption text to read "Photo 1/6" and the speed at which the images change size while navigating through the gallery, and you want to use PNG files for the Close,

Previous, and Next buttons. Just set up an object literal with those values and pass it to the lightBox function like this:

```
var lbOptions = {
  txtImage: 'Photo',
  txtOf: '/',
  containerResizeSpeed: 1000,
  imageBtnClose: 'images/close.png',
  imageBtnPrev: 'images/previous.png',
  imageBtnNext: 'images/next.png'
}
$('#gallery a').lightBox(lbOptions);
```

In this example, the lightBox options are stored in a variable (*lbOptions* in this case) and then passed to the *lightBox( )* function. You can also simply pass the object literal to the function (and skip the creating a variable step). For example, the above code could also be written like this:

```
$('#gallery a').lightBox({
  txtImage: 'Photo',
  txtOf: '/',
  containerResizeSpeed: 1000,
  imageBtnClose: 'images/close.png',
  imageBtnPrev: 'images/previous.png',
  imageBtnNext: 'images/next.png'
});
```

Both examples work exactly the same way, so use the method that's easiest for you. In the tutorial on page 261, you'll use the second approach—just passing the object literal directly to the function.

lightBox images

As mentioned in the previous section, you can use any images you'd like to replace the ones supplied with the lightBox plug-in. You only need to set the proper options (like *imageBtnClose* or *imageBtnPrev*) to point to your new image files.

Another method to use your own images is to simply name your images identically to the ones supplied with the plug-in and put your new images into the *images* folder. That way you don't need to change any of the plug-in's default settings.

However, the images you use should be close in size to the ones supplied with the plug-in, as shown in Figure 7-8. The Close, Previous, and Next buttons are all 63 pixels wide by 32 pixels tall, while the loading image is 32 pixels square.

Tip: Create your own "This image is now loading" icon at the hip, Web 2.0, Ajax icon generator: *www. ajaxload.info*. At this site, you can choose from over 20 different animated designs, and even choose background and foreground colors for the icon.

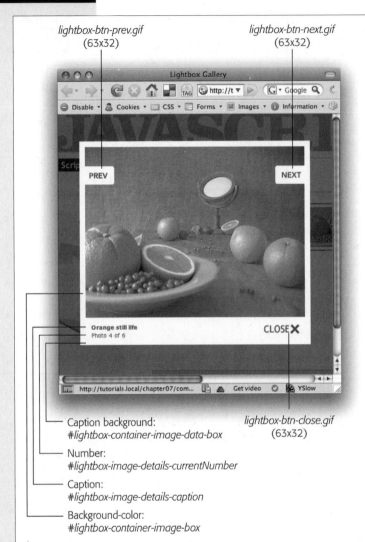

lightbox-btn-prev.gif
(63x32)

lightbox-btn-next.gif
(63x32)

Figure 7-8:
*You don't need to use lightBox's option
settings to customize the look of your
lightBox. Simply replacing the supplied
graphics and altering the CSS file lets
you tweak the design to better match
your site.*

Caption background:
#lightbox-container-image-data-box

lightbox-btn-close.gif
(63x32)

Number:
#lightbox-image-details-currentNumber

Caption:
#lightbox-image-details-caption

Background-color:
#lightbox-container-image-box

lightBox CSS

A few of lightBox's visual elements can only be controlled via CSS. For example, to change the font used for captions, you have to edit the *#lightbox-image-details-caption* style in the CSS file supplied with lightBox (see Figure 7-8).

In addition, to change the:

- **Background color of the frame** surrounding the pop-up image, edit the background-color property of the *#lightbox-container-image-box* style.

- **Background color of the caption box**, edit the *#lightbox-container-image-data-box* style.

- **Text formatting for the caption,** edit the *#lightbox-image-details-caption* style.

- **Text formatting for the photo numbers,** edit the *#lightbox-image-details-currentNumber* style.

Tutorial: lightBox Photo Gallery

Although jQuery lightBox is really easy to use, it's always helpful to have a step-by-step tutorial showing you how it's done. In this tutorial, you'll take a page with a basic set of thumbnail images and turn it into a fancy lightBox slide show.

Note: See the note on page 27 for information on how to download the tutorial files.

---

1. **In a text editor, open the file *7.3.html* in the *chapter07* folder.**

   This file is the same as the one you started with for the first tutorial in this chapter—a simple group of thumbnail images. Each image is linked to a larger version of the photo, and all of the thumbnails are contained within a <div> tag with an ID of *gallery*.

   The first step is to attach the CSS file used by lightBox.

2. **In the <head> of the document, locate the empty line below the <link> tag, which attaches the *gallery.css* style sheet file (it's the blank line that appears directly above the first <script> tag). On that line, type:**

   ```
   <link href="css/lightbox.css" rel="stylesheet" type="text/css">
   ```

   The *lightbox.css* file contains all of the styles used to format the background that lies over the Web page, the pop-up image, and the photo caption text. Next, you need to attach the plug-in's JavaScript file.

3. **On the blank line immediately after the <script> tag that attaches the *jquery.js* file to this page, type:**

   ```
   <script type="text/javascript" src="../js/jquery.lightbox.js"></script>
   ```

   All of the JavaScript files supplied with the tutorials are kept in a folder named *js*, which is located in the main tutorial folder. Remember that you need to load any jQuery plug-in files after the *jquery.js* file itself.

   This page already has another <script> tag, complete with the jQuery *ready( )* function and the preloading/rollover magic you created in the first tutorial in this chapter. You just need to add the lightBox function and you're good to go.

4. **Click in blank line directly below *$(document).ready(function( ),* and type:**

   ```
   $('#gallery a').lightBox();
   ```

All of the links that point to larger images are contained inside a <div> tag with the ID *gallery*, so *$('#gallery a')* selects those, and the *.lightBox( )* function applies the lightBox effect to the page.

Believe it or not, you're done! Save the page and preview it in a Web browser. Click one of the thumbnail images to see the magic happen (Figure 7-7). Now you can see why plug-ins are so useful—you don't really have to do any programming to get some fantastic effects!

One thing that's missing however, are captions for each photo. To add a caption, you don't need any JavaScript, just an HTML *title* attribute added to an <a> tag.

5. **In the <body> of the page, locate** *<a href="images/large/blue.jpg">* **and add** *title="Blue still life"* **to the tag, so it looks like this:**

```
<a href="images/large/blue.jpg" title="Blue still life">
```

Save the file and preview it in a Web browser. Click the first thumbnail on the left—voila, the caption appears. Add title attributes to the other <a> tags in this <div>. Now, you'll tweak some of lightBox's default settings to customize its look.

6. **Change the code you added in step 4 by adding an object literal between the** *lightBox( )* **function's parentheses. The new code is bolded below:**

```
$('#gallery a').lightBox({
  txtImage: 'Photo',
  overlayOpacity: .5,
  overlayBgColor: '#003376'
});
```

This code passes an object literal (page 188) to the *lightBox( )* function. An object literal is made up of a property name, followed by a colon and then a value. So *txtImage* is the name of an option for lightBox (see page 257), and you're setting its value to *'Photo'*. This particular option changes the default text that appears in a pop-up box ("Image 1 of 6") to read "Photo 1 of 6." The next two options change the opacity to 50% and assign a different background color for the overlay on the page.

Note: Object literals look kind of weird and have some strange rules. Make sure to add a comma after each property/value pair for each pair except the last one. For example, the last line *above overlayBg-Color: '#003376'* must not have a comma at the end. You'll find more information about object literals on page 188.

7. **Save the page and preview it in a Web browser.**

Who says JavaScript is hard! The file *complete_7.3.html* is a completed, working version of the tutorial.

Animated Slideshows with Cycle

The slideshow galleries presented earlier in this chapter provide a great way to display a series of images. However, none of them are self-running—the visitor has to click to see each photo—and the effect as one image transitions to the next is limited. Another jQuery plug-in, Cycle, solves both of these problems.

The Cycle plug-in, written by Mike Alsup, lets you automatically cycle through a series of images using one of the plug-in's many transition effects such as zoom, fade out, scroll right, and shuffle (as in a deck of cards). In addition, the plug-in lets you add "paging" controls so you can jump immediately to a given image, and even pause and restart the slideshow (see Figure 7-9).

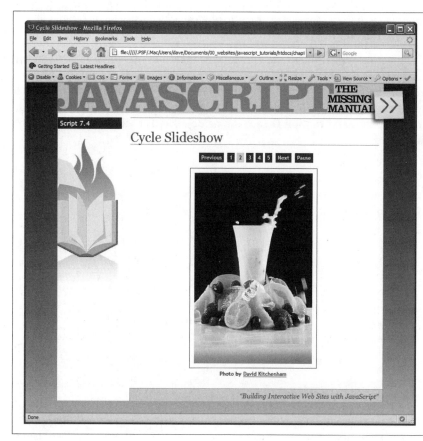

Figure 7-9:
Unfortunately, a book can't adequately demonstrate the great animation effects available with the Cycle plug-in. To see the plug-in in action, open the file complete_7.4.html in a Web browser, or visit the Cycle Web site at www.malsup.com/jquery/cycle/.

The Basics

As with the lightBox plug-in, using the Cycle plug-in isn't all that hard. Here's an overview of the steps required (you'll put this knowledge into action in the tutorial on page 267).

1. **Set up the gallery Web page.**

   Unlike the other gallery pages mentioned in this chapter, the Cycle plug-in is intended to show a series of larger images without the need for clicking a smaller, thumbnail image. You must enclose the images inside of a <div> tag with an ID, like this:

   ```
   <div id="photos">
   <img src="elephant.jpg" alt="Elephant" width="150" height="150">
   <img src="tiger.jpg" alt="Tiger" width="150" height="150">
   <img src="lion.jpg" alt="Lion" width="150" height="150">
   </div>
   ```

   If you view the page in a Web browser at this point, all of these images will appear together on the page. The Cycle plug-in adds the magic that hides all but one image at a time.

   The plug-in cycles through the immediate children of the <div> tag, so you can even enclose the images in another <div> tag and include a caption with each image. The plug-in will then show each photo and caption. In other words, it cycles through each <div> before transitioning to the next <div> containing another photo and caption (hence the name). The HTML for that might look like this:

   ```
   <div id="photos">
     <div>
       <img src="elephant.jpg" alt="Elephant" width="150" height="150">
       <p>An elephant!</p>
     </div>
     <div>
       <img src="tiger.jpg" alt="Tiger" width="150" height="150">
       <p>An elephant!</p>
     </div>
     <div>
       <img src="lion.jpg" alt="Lion" width="150" height="150">
       <p>An elephant!</p>
     </div>
   </div>
   ```

2. **Set up the CSS for the container and images.**

   The Cycle plug-in does some pretty fancy on-the-fly manipulation of the images, including animating them on the screen. This process involves changing the images' CSS position property to *absolute*. Absolute positioning can do some funny things to a page layout, so it's recommended that you set a specific width and height for both the container and the elements you're cycling through. For example, the CSS for the first example in step 1 might look like this:

   ```
   #photos { width: 150px; height: 150px }
   #photos img { width: 150px; height: 150px}
   ```

The plug-in works best with images that are all the same size. But you can still use images of different sizes successfully—just wrap each image in a <div> and set a specific width and height for those <div> tags. The tutorial on page 267, for example, uses different-size photos.

3. **Attach the Cycle plug-in JavaScript file to the page.**

   You can download the Cycle file from *www.malsup.com/jquery/cycle/download. html*. Version 2.22 of the plug-in is included with the tutorial files: it's named *jquery.cycle.js* and is located in the *js* folder in the tutorial files folder. Make sure to attach this file after the *jquery.js* file:

   ```
   <script type="text/javascript" src="js/jquery.js"></script>
   <script type="text/javascript" src="js/jquery.cycle.js"></script>
   ```

4. **Add a <script> tag, the jQuery *ready( )* function (page 218), and call the *cycle( )* function.**

   Apply the *cycle( )* function to the containing <div>. You only need to specify the type of transition you want to appear between slides, such as *fade*, *scrollRight*, and the others listed on page 244. For example, for the HTML in step 1, the containing <div> tag has an ID of *photos*, so the code to start the Cycle slideshow might look like this:

   ```
   <script type="text/javascript">
   $(document).ready(function( ) {
     $('#photos').cycle('fade');
   });
   </script>
   ```

In addition to the type of transition effect, there are a ton of other preferences you can set to make this plug-in act the way you want it to. Read on.

Customizing the Cycle Plug-in

As with the jQuery lightBox plug-in (see page 254), the *cycle( )* function accepts an object literal containing the names of options and their settings. You can tweak the performance and look of the plug-in by passing in new values for any of the many options the plug-in supports. You can find a complete list of options at *www. malsup.com/jquery/cycle/options.html*, but here are some of the most useful.

Effects

The Cycle plug-in actually comes in two forms. The basic plug-in has a single effect (fade) but lets you define your own custom effects. The complete package includes 15 additional effects such as *fadeZoom*, *scrollLeft*, *slideX*, and more. You can find a complete list at *www.malsup.com/jquery/cycle/download.html*. You should experiment with the different effect types to see which ones work for you.

To apply an effect to the slideshow, you can just pass the effect's name as a string to the plug-in like this:

```
$('#photos').cycle('shuffle');
```

If you want to set other options for the plug-in, you must include the effect inside an object literal using the assigned property name *fx*. For example, you can rewrite the code above this way using an object literal:

```
$('#photos').cycle({
   fx: 'shuffle'
});
```

Note: You can create your own transition effects for the Cycle plug-in. For more info, visit *www.malsup. com/jquery/cycle/adv.html*.

Speed

Several options control the speed at which transition and effects occur.

- **timeout.** Each slide in the slideshow stays visible for four seconds before the next slide begins to appear. If four seconds is too long or too short, you can set your own timing by supplying the number of milliseconds you want the image to stay visible. For example, 1,000 is 1 second, while 6,000 is 6 seconds.

- **speed.** This option controls the slide transition's duration. Normally, the transition between one slide and another is one second (1,000 milliseconds). To make the effect go faster or slower, supply a number in milliseconds for this option.

- **delay.** When the Web page first loads, the initial slide stays on the screen a bit longer than the *timeout* setting, giving the visitor a bit more time to view the entire page and image before the slideshow begins. The delay setting controls how long to pause before starting the slideshow. The normal setting is 0, so if you want the initial image to stay visible for a longer time before the slideshow begins, set this option to a positive number (1,000, for example, makes the first slide stay on the page for 1 second longer than normal). You can also supply a negative number to get the show started more quickly (for example, −2,000 makes the slideshow begin 2 seconds sooner than it normally would).

For example, say you want the slides to move more quickly, the transition between slides to be slower, and the delay before the slideshow starts to go away. You can call the *cycle( )* function with those options like this:

```
$('#photos').cycle({
   timeout: 3000,
   speed: 2000,
   delay: -1000
});
```

Navigating slides

A regular Cycle slideshow steps through each slide in the order they appear in the page's HTML. You can offer visitors more control by letting them skip immediately to the next or previous slide, or by providing one button for each slide which, when clicked, immediately displays the associated slide.

To add a "Previous slide" and "Next slide" buttons, you need to do two things:

1. **Add HTML to the page where the buttons should go, and identify those buttons with unique IDs.**

   For example, you could add the following HTML to create side-by-side "Previous slide" and "Next slide" buttons:

   ```
   <span id="previous">Previous slide</span>
   <span id="next">Next slide</span>
   ```

   You can put the HTML anywhere you want the buttons to appear.

2. **Pass the IDs of the buttons to the *cycle( )* function.**

   The Cycle plug-in supports two options—*prev* and *next*—that let you specify which elements should become the Previous and Next links. For example, using the HTML from above, you could add Previous and Next links like this:

   ```
   $('#photos').cycle({
     prev: '#previous',
     next: '#next'
   });
   ```

The Cycle plug-in provides another method of navigating a slideshow—slide *paging*. Paging simply refers to the ability to jump to any slide by clicking a button associated with the particular slide (see Figure 7-9). To add pager buttons to a slideshow:

1. **Add an empty tag to the page's HTML. The tag should have a unique ID, and should appear in the spot where you want the buttons to appear.**

   For example, you could insert a <div> tag with an ID like this:

   ```
   <div id="pager"></div>
   ```

Tip: It needn't be a <div> tag. You could just as easily add an ID to a <span> tag or <td> tag. Just make sure there's no other content inside the tag—otherwise, the pager won't function correctly.

---

2. **Pass the tag's ID to the *cycle( )* function.**

   The Cycle plug-in's pager option lets you specify which element the pager buttons should appear in. For example, using the HTML from above, you can add paging to a slideshow like this:

   ```
   $('#photos').cycle({
     pager: '#pager'
   });
   ```

You can combine any or all of these options. For example, on page 270 of the next tutorial, you'll add pager buttons, as well as Previous and Next links.

You can also use CSS to style the buttons the Cycle plug-in creates. The pager buttons are simply <a> tags inside the element you specified as the pager box, so a descendent selector would work well. For example, say you add the pager links to a <div> tag with an ID of pager; you can then use the CSS selector *#pager a* to style those buttons. In addition, the plug-in adds a class, *activeSlide*, to the button associated with the currently displayed slide. To style that button, just create a style named *#pager a.activeSlide* (assuming, of course, that the wrapper <div> has the ID *pager*).

Starting and stopping the slideshow

Although a Cycle slideshow automatically starts when the page loads, you can pause and resume the slideshow after it has begun by re-calling the *cycle( )* function and passing the string *'pause'* to stop the slideshow or *'resume'* to start it again. For example, suppose when the page loads you want the slideshow to pause and only start again when you click a Play button. You can do that with the following code:

```
$('#gallery').cycle(); //start slideshow
$('#gallery').cycle('pause'); //stop slideshow
$('#play').click(function() { // add click event
  $('#gallery').cycle('resume'); //start slideshow
});
```

In this example, the play button is assumed to be some tag with an ID of *play*. The actual tag could be a form button, an anchor, or simply a <span> tag that you attach a click event to.

In addition, you can combine the pause and resume functions into a single button that toggles the automated slideshow so that you can pause it, then start it again. You'll see an example of that in the tutorial below.

Tip: The Cycle plug-in isn't really limited to just photos. In fact, you don't need to use photos at all. For example, you can have a page with a series of <div> tags containing other kinds of material that cycle like a slideshow. Or, you can control them using navigation buttons.

Tutorial: An Automated Slideshow

In this tutorial, you'll use the jQuery Cycle plug-in to create an automated slideshow. To allow some user control, you'll also add buttons to move around the slides or pause the slideshow (see Figure 7-9).

Note: See the note on page 27 for information on how to download the tutorial files.

---

1. **In a text editor, open the file *7.4.html* in the *chapter07* folder.**

   If you look at the HTML, you'll see that there's a <div> tag with an id of *gallery*. Inside that <div> are five other <div> tags, each with an image and a paragraph of text. You'll use the Cycle plug-in to display the <div> tags one at a time.

   Another thing to note is that in the CSS file for the slideshow (*slideshow.css* in the *css* folder), two styles define a specific height and width for the container <div> and the <div> tags inside it (see the styles *#gallery* and *#gallery div* in the style sheet). As mentioned on page 264, because the Cycle plug-in manipulates the positioning of the slides, you need specific dimensions for the animated slide transitions to work properly.

   The first step is to attach the plug-in's JavaScript files.

2. **On the blank line immediately after the <script> tag for the *jquery.js* file, type:**

   ```
   <script type="text/javascript" src="../js/jquery.cycle.js"></script>
   ```

   This page already has a <script> tag and jQuery's *.ready( )* function added, so you just need to add the code to call the cycle plug-in.

3. **Click in the blank line below *$(document).ready( )* and type *$('#gallery').cycle('fade');*. The code at this point should look like this:**

   ```
   <script type="text/javascript" src="../js/jquery.js"></script>
   <script type="text/javascript" src="../js/jquery.cycle.js"></script>
   <script type="text/javascript">
   $(document).ready(function( ) {
     $('#gallery').cycle('fade');
   }); // end ready( )
   </script>
   ```

   You apply the *cycle( )* function to the container <div>. In this case, since the <div> has the ID name *gallery*, the jQuery selector *$('#gallery')* will select that <div>. Passing the *cycle( )* function to the string *'fade'* sets the type of transition effect, so that each photo will fade into view.

   There's more to do, but if all you want is for the slideshow to work, you can stop now. Save the page and preview it in a Web browser. (It takes a few seconds for the first image to disappear and the next to appear.)

   The fade effect isn't too inspiring, especially since the Cycle plug-in provides many more visually interesting effects. In addition, the slideshow gets off to a slow start, and it runs a bit slowly. By supplying a few optional settings, you can tweak the plug-in to fix these problems.

4. **Edit the line you added in the previous step, so it looks like this:**

   ```
   $('#gallery').cycle({
     fx: 'scrollRight',
   ```

```
    timeout: 3000,
    speed: 500,
    delay: -2000
});
```

You've just passed an object literal (page 188) to the *cycle( )* function (don't forget the opening *{* and closing *}*). The object literal contains four option settings: *fx* controls the type of effect (in this case, the images slide off towards the right edge of the screen); the *timeout* option sets the time each slide stays on the screen (each image appears for three seconds before the next slide moves into place); the *speed* setting controls the speed at which the images slide through the transition (in this example, it takes just half a second, or 500 milliseconds, for an image to slide across the screen and out of view); finally, setting the *delay* option to –2,000 makes the slideshow begin 2 seconds earlier.

Save the page and test this new version out in a Web browser.

To make the slideshow more functional for those viewing it, you'll next add buttons that let a visitor jump immediately to any one of the photos. To do this, you first need to add some HTML to the page.

5. **On the blank line underneath the HTML *<h1>Cycle Slideshow</h1>*, add the following HTML:**

```
<div id="controls">
  <span id="pager"></span>
</div>
```

This new <div> holds several different buttons for controlling how the slideshow plays. The first controller will be a set of numbered buttons—one for each photo—that let you jump to an photo in the slideshow. The <span> tag with the ID of *pager* will hold those buttons. Fortunately, you don't have to do anything else to add those buttons except tell the Cycle plug-in where to put them.

6. **In the object literal you added in step 4, add a comma after *delay: -2000*, hit return and type *pager: '#pager'*.**

As mentioned on page 268, the Cycle plug-in's *pager* option lets you specify the ID of an element on the page (in this case, the empty <span> tag you added in the last step), where the plug-in inserts buttons to navigate the slideshow. If you save the page now and view it in a Web browser, you'll see five numbered buttons. Click them to move to specific slides.

It would also be handy to have Previous and Next buttons as well.

7. **Directly before the <span> tag you added in step 5, type *<span id="prev" class="control">Previous</span>*. Directly after the closing </span>, type *<span id="next" class="control">Next</span>*.**

In other words, you've just inserted two spans on either side of the paging buttons you added in the previous two steps. These two spans will be the Previous and Next buttons—you just have to tell the *cycle( )* function about them. The ID for each <span> tag lets the Cycle plug-in identify them (the classes on each span are just for formatting the buttons with CSS).

8. **Edit the JavaScript you've added to the page so it looks like this:**

```
$('#gallery').cycle({
  fx: 'scrollRight',
  timeout: 3000,
  speed: 500,
  delay: -2000,
  pager: '#pager',
  next: '#next',
  prev: '#prev'
});
```

In other words, add a comma after *pager: '#pager'* and add two new options to the object literal. Save the file and preview it in a Web browser.

For a final touch, you'll add a button that lets you stop and start the slideshow. First, you need to add the HTML for the button.

9. **Add** *<span id="playControl" class="control">Pause</span>* **just before the closing** *</div>* **you added in step 5. The HTML for that** *<div>* **should now look like this:**

```
<div id="controls">
  <span id="prev" class="control">Previous</span>
  <span id="pager"></span>
  <span id="next" class="control">Next</span>
  <span id="playControl" class="control">Pause</span>
</div>
```

You can't add the ability to stop and start simply by adding another option to the object literal passed to the *cycle( )* function. You'll have to add some custom programming for that.

10. **Insert a blank line** *after* **the** *cycle( )* **function and add** *$('#playControl').toggle( );* **to the script.**

The *$('#playControl')* selects the <span> you added in the last step, while *toggle( )* adds event magic to that <span>. As discussed on page 221, the *toggle( )* function requires two functions, which are alternately triggered by each mouse click—for example, the first mouse click on the element runs the first function, while the next mouse click runs the second function. For this page, since the slideshow automatically starts when the page loads, the first click on the Pause button pauses the slideshow, the second click starts it up again, the third click pauses it again, and so on.

11. **Click between the *toggle( )* function's opening and closing parentheses. Press Return, and then type:**

```
function() {
  $('#gallery').cycle('pause');
  $(this).text('Play');
}
```

The first function does two things: pauses the slideshow and changes the text on the button from Pause to Play. As mentioned on page 268, you can pause the slideshow by applying the *cycle( )* function to the <div> containing the slideshow slides and passing the string *'pause'*. Since clicking the Pause button stops the slideshow, it makes sense to change the text on that button to Play so visitors will know they can click the same button to make the slideshow start again. The *$(this)* refers to the element being clicked—in this case, the <span> tag—while the *text( )* function changes the text inside that <span> to Play (see the note on page 182 for more on the *text( )* function).

12. **Add the second function, so the complete code for the *toggle( )* is:**

```
1  $('#playControl').toggle(
2    function() {
3      $('#gallery').cycle('pause');
4      $(this).text('Play');
5    },
6    function() {
7      $('#gallery').cycle('resume');
8      $(this).text('Pause');
9  });
```

Make sure to include the comma (line 5) and make sure the functions close properly (line 9). The second function just undoes the first function: starts the slideshow and changes the button's text back to Pause.

13. **Save the page and preview it in a Web browser.**

The finished page should look like Figure 7-9. Try out all the buttons and make sure they work. You'll find a finished version of the tutorial in the *chapter07* folder (*complete_7.4.html*).

Part Two: Building Web Page Features

2

Improving Navigation

Links make the Web go around. Without the instant access to information provided by linking from page to page and site to site, the Web wouldn't have gotten very far. In fact, it wouldn't be a *web* at all. Since links are one of the most common and powerful pieces of HTML, it's only natural that there are lots of JavaScript techniques for enhancing how links work. In this chapter, you'll learn the basics of using JavaScript to control links, and how to open links in new windows and in windows within a page. In addition, you'll learn how to make links more usable by creating larger link targets and navigation bars with multiple levels of menus.

Some Link Basics

You undoubtedly know a lot about links already. After all, they're the heart of the Web, and the humble <a> tag is one of the first pieces of HTML a Web designer learns. Adding JavaScript to a page can turn a basic link into a supercharged gateway of interactivity...but only if you know how to use JavaScript to control your links. Once you've got the basics, later sections of this chapter will give you real-world techniques for controlling links with JavaScript.

Selecting Links with JavaScript

To do anything with a link on a Web page, you must first select it. You can select all of the links on a page, just one, or a particular group of related links—for example, links that are grouped together in the same part of a page, or that share a certain characteristic such as external links that point to other Web sites.

As discussed on page 159, all Web browsers let you select every instance of a particular tag using the *getElementsByTagName( )* method, so you can create an array containing all links on a page like this:

```
var allLinks = document.getElementsByTagName('a');
```

Of course, you've hopefully learned by now that a JavaScript library like jQuery gives you greater flexibility in selecting document elements. For example, the code *$('a')* creates a jQuery selection of all links on a page. Furthermore, jQuery lets you refine your selections, so you can quickly select all the links within a particular area of a page. For example, you can select all of the links contained inside a bulleted list with an ID of *mainNav* like this: *$('#mainNav a')*. Likewise, you can use attribute selectors (page 177) to select links whose HREF values (the paths to the files they point to) match a certain pattern such as links that point to other sites, or which point to PDF files (see "Opening External Links in a New Window" on page 278 for an example).

And once you've used jQuery to select those links, you can use the jQuery functions to work with those links. For example, you can loop through each link using the *each( )* function (page 193), apply a class to those links (page 174), or add event functions to them (page 207). You'll see many examples of what you can do to links later in this chapter.

Determining a Link's Destination

After you've selected one or more links, you may be interested in where they lead. For example, in the slideshow you built on page 268 each link pointed to a larger image; by retrieving the path, you used JavaScript to display that larger image. In other words, you extracted the link's *href* value and used that path to create a new <img> tag on the page. Likewise, you can retrieve the *href* value that leads to another Web page and, instead of going to that page when you click the link, you can actually display the new Web page on top of the current page. (See page 286 to learn how to do that.)

In each case, you need to access the *href* attribute, which is an easy process using jQuery's *attr( )* function (page 189). For example, say you've applied an ID to the link that leads back to a site's home page. You can retrieve that link's path like this:

```
var homePath = $('#homeLink').attr('href');
```

You'll find this information handy in many instances. For example, say you want to add the full URL of a link pointing outside of your site next to the link text itself. In other words, suppose you have a link with the text "Learn more about bark beetles" that points to *http://www.barkbeetles.org/*. Now suppose you'd like to change the text on the page to read "Learn more about bark beetles (www.barkbeetles.org)" (so when people print the page they'll know where that link leads to).

You can do that easily with the following JavaScript:

```
1   $('a[href^=http://]').each(function() {
2       var href = $(this).attr('href');
3       href = href.replace('http://','');
4       $(this).after(' (' + href + ')');
5   });
```

Note: The line numbers at left aren't part of the code, so don't type them. They're just for examining the code line by line.

Line 1 selects all external links (page 177) then runs the *each( )* function (page 193), which simply looks through each link and applies a function to it. In this case, lines 2–4 make up the function body. Line 2 retrieves the link's *href* of the link (for example, *http://www.barkbeetles.org*). Line 3 is optional—it just simplifies the URL for display purposes by removing the *http://*, so the *href* variable now holds something like *www.barkbeetles.org*. Finally, line 4 adds the contents of the variable *href* (wrapped in parentheses) after the link: (*www.barkbeetles.org*), and line 5 closes the function.

Don't Follow That Link

When you add a click event to a link, you may not want the Web browser to follow its normal behavior of exiting the current page and loading the link's destination. For example, in the image gallery on page 248, when you click a link on a thumbnail image, the page loads a larger image. Normally, clicking that link would exit the page and show the larger image by itself on a blank page. However, in this case, instead of following the link to the image, you stay on the same page, where the larger image is loaded.

There are a couple of ways you can stop a link in its tracks—you can return a *false* value or use jQuery's *preventDefault( )* function (page 223). For example, say you have a link that takes a visitor to a login page. To make your site feel more responsive, you want to use JavaScript to show a login form when the visitor clicks that link. In other words, if the visitor's browser has JavaScript turned on, when he clicks that link a form will appear on the page; if the browser has JavaScript turned off, clicking the link will take the visitor to the login page.

There are several steps to achieve this goal:

1. **Select the login link.**

   See the first part of this section on the previous page, if you need ideas for how to do this.

2. **Attach a click event.**

   You can use jQuery's *click( )* function (page 222) to do so. The *click( )* function takes another function as an argument. That function contains the steps that happen when a user clicks the link. In this example only two steps are required.

3. Show the login form.

The login form might be hidden from view when the page loads—perhaps an absolutely positioned <div> tag directly under the link. You can show the form using the *show( )* function or one of jQuery's other show effects (see page 243).

4. Stop the link!

This step is the most important. If you don't stop the link, the Web browser will simply leave the current page and go to the login Web page.

Here's how to stop the link using the "return false" method. Assume that the link has an ID of *showForm* and the hidden <div> tag with the login form has an ID of *loginForm*:

```
1    $('#showForm').click(function( ) {
2      $('#loginForm').fadeIn('slow');
3      return false;
4    });
```

Line 1 accomplishes both steps 1 and 2 on page 277; line 3 displays the hidden form. Line 3 is the part that tells the Web browser "Stop! Don't follow that link." You must put the *return false;* statement as the last line of the function, because once the JavaScript interpreter encounters a return statement, it exits the function.

You can also use jQuery's *preventDefault( )* function, like this:

```
1    $('#showForm').click(function(evt) {
2      $('#loginForm').fadeIn('slow');
3      evt.preventDefault( );
4    });
```

The basic details of this script are the same as the one before it. The main difference is that the function assigned to the click event now accepts an argument—*evt*—which represents the event itself (the event object is described on page 222). The event has its own set of functions and properties—the *preventDefault( )* function simply stops any default behavior associated with the event: for a click on a link, that's loading a new Web page.

Opening External Links in a New Window

Losing visitors is one of the great fears for any site that depends on readership. Online magazines that make money from ad revenue don't want to send people away from their site if they can help it; an e-commerce site doesn't want to lose a potential customer by letting a shopper click a link that leaves the site behind; and while displaying a portfolio of completed Web sites, a Web designer might not want to let a potential client leave her site while viewing one of the designer's finished projects.

Many sites deal with these fears by opening a new window whenever a link to another site is clicked. That way, when the visitor finishes viewing the other site and closes its window, the original site is still there. HTML has long provided a method of doing that using a link's *target* attribute—if you set that attribute to *_blank*, a Web browser knows to open that link in a new window (or, with browsers that use tabs, open the link a new tab).

Note: There's a quite a bit of debate amongst Web usability experts about whether the strategy of opening new windows is a good or bad idea. For example, see *www.useit.com/alertbox/990530.html*.

Unfortunately, the HTML *target* attribute isn't valid HTML for the strict versions of HTML 4.01 and XHTML 1.0, so including that attribute in your HTML can mean your Web pages won't pass validation (see the box on page 6). An even bigger pain, however, is having to manually place the *target* attribute on each link that points to a page outside your own Web site—a time-consuming process that's prone to error.

Fortunately, using JavaScript and jQuery, there's a quick, easy method to force Web browsers to open external links (or really any links you want) in a new window or browser tab. The basic process is simple:

1. **Identify the links you wish to open in a new window.**

   In this chapter, you'll use a jQuery selector (page 172) to identify those links.

2. **Add the *target* attribute with a value of *_blank* to the link.**

   You might be thinking, "Hey, that's invalid HTML, I can't do that." Well, first it's only invalid for the strict versions of HTML 4.01 and XHTML 1.0, so it's fine for any other document type. Second, your page will still validate, since an HTML validator (for example, *http://validator.w3.org/*) only analyzes the actual HTML code in the Web page file and not any HTML that JavaScript adds. And, lastly, every browser understands the *target* attribute, so you know that the link will open in a new window, regardless of the standards for strict document types. While, in general, you don't want your JavaScript to produce invalid HTML, in this case it won't cause any harm, and will work in all browsers.

Note: The HTML 5 standard that's currently under development returns the *target* attribute to the <a> tag. In other words, *target* will, in the not-to-distant future, again be legal to use on links.

In jQuery you can complete the previous two steps in one line of code:

```
$('a[href^=http://]').attr('target','_blank');
```

The jQuery selector—*$('a[href^=http://]')*—uses an attribute selector (page 177) to identify <a> tags that begin with *http://* (for example, *http://www.yahoo.com*). The selector identifies all of these types of links and then uses the jQuery *attr( )* function (page 189) to set the *target* attribute to *_blank* for each link. And that's it!

If you use absolute paths to specify links to files on your own site, you need one more step. For example, if your site's address is *www.your_site.com*, and you link to other pages or files on your site like this: *http://www.your_site.com/a_page.html*, then the previous code also forces those links to open in a new window. If you don't want to open up a new window for every page of your site (your poor visitors), you need code like the following:

```
var myURL = location.protocol + '//' + location.hostname;
$('a[href^=http://]').not('[href^='+myURL+']').attr('target','_blank');
```

This code first specifies the URL for your site and assigns it to a variable—*myURL*. The URL of your site is accomplished with a little bit of help from the browser's window object. A browser knows the protocol used for accessing a URL—*http:*, or for secured sites *https:*. It's stored in the location object's *protocol* property. Likewise, the name of the site—*www.sawmac.com*, for example—is stored in the *hostname* property. So the JavaScript *location.protocol + '//' + location.hostname* generates a string that looks like *http://www.sawmac.com*. Of course, the hostname in this case changes depending upon where the page with this JavaScript code comes from. For example, if you put this code on a page that comes from *http://www.your_site.com*, then when someone views the page from that site *location.hostname* would be *www.your_site.com*.

The second line of code, starts with a jQuery selector which retrieves all links that start with *http://*. Then, the *not( )* function removes any links start with your URL—in this example, for example links that point to *http://www.sawmac.com*. (The *not( )* function is a useful way of excluding some elements from a jQuery selection—to learn about it, visit *http://docs.jquery.com/Traversing/not#expr*.)

So to actually use this code on a page, you just link to the jQuery file, add the *$(document).ready( ) function* (page 218), and then insert the previous code inside like this:

```
<script type="text/javascript" src="js/jquery.js"></script>
<script type="text/javascript">
$(document).ready(function( ) {
  var myURL = location.protocol + '//' + location.hostname;
  $('a[href^=http://]').not('[href^='+myURL+']').attr('target','_blank');
});
</script>
```

Another approach would be to create an external JavaScript file (see page 24); in that file, create a function that runs the code to make external links open in a new window; attach that file to the page; and then call the function on that page.

For example, you could create a file named *open_external.js* with the following code:

```
function openExt( ) {
  var myURL = location.protocol + '//' + location.hostname;
  $('a[href^=http://]').not('[href^='+myURL+']').attr('target','_blank');
}
```

Then add the following code to each page on your site that you'd like to apply this function to:

```
<script type="text/javascript" src="js/jquery.js"></script>
<script type="text/javascript" src="js/open_external.js"></script>
<script type="text/javascript">
$(document).ready(function( ) {
  openExt( );
  // add any other JavaScript code to the page
});
</script>
```

The benefit of using an external file is that if you've used this function throughout your site on hundreds of pages, you can easily update the script so it's fancier—for example, you can later change the *openExt( )* function to open external pages in a frame within the current page (see page 286 for how to do that). In other words, an external *.js* file makes it easier for you to keep your scripts consistent across your entire site.

Creating New Windows

Web browsers let you open new windows and customize many of their properties, like width and height, onscreen placement, and even whether they display scrollbars, menus, or the location (address) bar. The basic technique uses the *open( )* method, which follows this basic structure:

```
open(URL, name, properties)
```

The *open( )* method takes three arguments. The first is the URL of the page you wish to appear in the new open window—the same value you'd use for the *href* attribute for a link (*http://www.google.com*, */pages/map.html*, or *../../portfolio.html*, for example). The second argument is a name for the window, which can be any name you'd like to use; follow the same naming rules used for variables as described on page 44. Finally, you can pass a string containing the settings for the new window (its height and width, for example).

In addition, when opening a new window you usually create a variable to store a reference to that window. For example, if you want to open Google's home page in a new window that's 200 pixels square, you can write this code:

```
var newWin= open('http://www.google.com/', ⏎
'theWin','height=200,width=200');
```

Note: The ⏎ symbol at the end of a line of code indicates that the next line should really be typed as part of the first line. But since a *really* long line of JavaScript code won't fit on this book's page, it's broken up over two lines.

This code opens a new window and stores a reference to that window in the variable *newWin*. The section "Use the Window Reference" on the next page describes how to use this reference to control the newly opened window.

Note: The name you provide for the new window (*'theWin'* in this example) doesn't do much. However, once you've provided a name, if you try to open another window using the same name, you won't get a new window. Instead, the Web page you request with the *open( )* method just loads in the previously created window with the same name.

Window Properties

Browser windows have many different components: scrollbars, resize handles, toolbars, and so on (see Figure 8-1). In addition, windows have a width and height and a position on the screen. You can set most of these properties when creating a new window by creating a string containing a comma-separated list of each property and its setting as the third argument for the *open( )* method. For example, to set the width and height of a new window and to make sure the location bar appears, you can write this:

```
var winProps = 'width=400,height=300,location=yes';
var newWin = open('about.html','aWin',winProps);
```

Warning: Don't include any spaces in the string defining the new window's properties. For example, *var winProps='width = 400,height = 600'* won't work because of the spaces before and after the = signs.

You set the properties that control the size or position of the window using pixel values, while the other properties take either the value *yes* (to turn on that property) or *no* (to turn off that property). In the case of any of the yes/no properties (like toolbar or location), if you don't specify a property value, the Web browser turns that property off (for example, if you don't set the location property, the Web browser hides the location field that normally appears at the top of the window).

- *height* dictates the height of the window, in pixels. You can't specify percentage values or any other measurement besides pixels. If you don't specify a height, the Web browser matches the height of the current window.

- *width* specifies the width of the window. As with height, you can only use pixels, and if you leave this property out, the Web browser matches the width of the current window.

- *left* is the position, in pixels, from the left edge of the monitor.

- *top* is the position, in pixels, from the top edge of the monitor.

- *resizable* specifies whether a visitor can resize the window by dragging.

- *scrollbars* appear at the right and bottom edges of a browser window whenever a page is larger than the window itself. To completely hide the scrollbar, set this property to *no*. You can't control which scrollbar is hidden (it's either both or neither).

- *status* controls the appearance of the status bar at the bottom of the window. Firefox and Internet Explorer normally don't let you hide the status bar, so it's always visible in those browsers.

- *toolbar* sets the visibility of the toolbar containing the navigation buttons, bookmark button, and other controls available to the particular browser. On Safari, the toolbar and location settings are the same: turning on either one displays both the toolbar buttons and the location field.

- *location* specifies whether the location field is visible. Also known as the address bar, this field displays the pages URL and lets visitors go to another page by typing a new URL. Opera, IE 7, and Firefox don't let you hide a page's location entirely. If you don't turn on the *location* property, then the page's URL appears up in the title bar. This feature is supposed to stop nefarious uses of JavaScript like opening a new window and sending you off to another site that looks like the site you just left. Also, Safari displays the toolbars as well as the location field with this property turned on.

- *menubar* applies to browsers that have a menu at the top of their windows (for example, the common File and Edit menus that appear on most programs). This setting applies only to Windows browsers—Macs have the menu at the top of the screen, not the individual window. And it doesn't apply to IE 7, which doesn't normally display a menu bar.

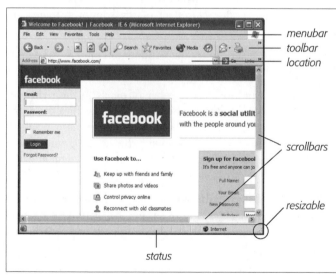

Figure 8-1:
The different properties of a browser window like scrollbars, toolbars, and resize handles are collectively called a browser's "chrome." Each browser has its own take on these properties, and in, general, Web developers have little control over how these work or look. However, when creating a new window using JavaScript, you can turn off some of these features.

Use the window reference

Once you open a new window, you can use the reference to that window to control it. For example, say you open a new window with the following code:

```
var newWin = open('products.html','theWin','width=300,height=300');
```

The variable *newWin*, in this case, holds a reference to the new window. You can then apply any of the browser's window methods to that variable to control the window. For example, if you want to close that window, you could use the *close( )* method like this:

```
newWin.close( );
```

Browsers support many different methods for the window object, but here are some of the most commonly used to control the window itself:

- *close( )* closes the specified window. For example, the command *close( )* closes the current window. But you can also apply this to a window reference: *newWin. close( )*, for example. You can use any event to trigger this close, like a mouse click on a button that says, "Close this window."

Note: If you use any one of these commands by itself, it applies to the window running the script. For example, adding the statement *close( );* to a script closes the window the script is in. However, if you've opened a window and have a reference to that window (for example, a variable that you created when the window was opened like *newWin*) then you can close that window from the page that originally created the window using the reference like this: *newWin.close( )*.

- *blur( )* forces the window to "lose focus." That is, the window moves behind any already opened windows. It's a way to hide an opened window, and Web advertisers use it to create "pop under" ads—windows that open underneath any current windows, so when the visitor closes all of his windows, there's an annoying ad waiting for him.

- *focus( )* is the opposite of *blur( )* and forces the window to come to the top of the stack of other windows.

- *moveBy( )* lets you move the window a set number of pixels to the right and down. You provide two arguments to the method—the first specifies the number of pixels to move to the right, and the second specifies how many pixels to move the window down. For example, *newWin.moveBy(200,300);* moves the window that's referenced by the *newWin* variable 200 pixels to the right and 300 pixels down on the screen.

- *moveTo( )* moves the window to a specific spot on the monitor specified by a left and top values. This command is the same as setting the *left* and *top* properties (page 282) when opening a new window. For example, to move a window to the top-left corner of the monitor, you can run this code: *moveTo(0,0);*.

- *resizeBy( )* changes the width and height of the window. It takes two arguments: the first specifies how many pixels wider to make the window; the second specifies how many pixels taller the window should be. For example, *resizeBy(100,200);* makes the current window 100 pixels taller and 200 pixels wider. You use negative numbers to make the window smaller.

- *resizeTo( )* changes the windows dimensions to a set width and height. For example, *resizeTo(200,400);* changes the current window so it's 200 pixels wide and 400 pixels tall.

- *scrollBy( )* scrolls the document inside the window by the specified number of pixels to the right and down. For example, *scrollBy(100,200);* scrolls the current document down 200 pixels and 100 pixels to the right. If the document can't scroll (in other words, the document fits within the window without scrollbars or the document has been scrolled to the end), then this function has no effect.

- *scrollTo( )* scrolls the document inside the window to a specific pixel location to the right and from the top of the page. For example, *scrollTo(100,200);* scrolls the current document down 200 pixels from its top and 100 pixels from its left edge. If the document can't scroll (in other words, the document fits within the window without scrollbars or the document has been scrolled to the end), then this function has no effect.

Note: The jQuery ScrollTo plug-in provides a simple way to control document scrolling using JavaScript. Find out more about this plug-in at *http://plug-ins.jquery.com/project/ScrollTo*.

Events that can open a new window

In the short history of the Web, pop-up windows have gotten a bad name. Unfortunately, many Web sites have abused the *open( )* method to force unwanted pop-up ads on unsuspecting visitors. These days, most browsers have a pop-up blocking feature that prevents unwanted pop-up windows, so even though you can add the JavaScript code to make a new window open as soon as a page loads, or when the visitor closes a window, most browsers won't let it happen. The visitor will either see a message letting her know that the browser prevented a new window from opening, or maybe get no indication at all that a pop-up window was blocked.

In fact, many browsers won't let you open a browser window using most events like mouseover, mouseout, or keypress. The only reliable way to use JavaScript to open windows is to trigger the action when the user clicks a link or submits a form. To do so, you add a click event to any HTML element (it doesn't have to be a link) and open a new window. For example, say you want some links on a page to open in a new window that's 300 pixels square, has scrollbars, and is resizable, but doesn't have any of the other browser chrome like toolbars. You can add a class name—*popup*, for example—to each of those special links, and then add this jQuery code to your page:

```
$('.popup').click(function( ) {
  var winProps='height=300,width=300,resizable=yes,scrollbars=yes';
  var newWin=open($(this).attr('href'),'aWin',winProps);
}
```

Opening Pages in a
Window on the
Page

Opening Pages in a Window on the Page

Opening new windows can be problematic. Not only do many browsers try to block pop-up windows, but like many designers, you may not like the fact that you can't really control how the browser window looks. What if you just want a clean, simple way to display a new Web page without exiting the current page? Use Java-Script, of course! You can create a window-within-a-page effect by using Java-Script to dynamically add an *iframe* to a page and display another Web page within that iframe. The final effect looks as if the linked page is simply floating above the current page (see Figure 8-2).

The HTML <iframe> tag lets you create something like a window onto another Web page. The <iframe> (short for inline frame) is similar to old-school HTML frames, but you can insert an iframe anywhere in a page's HTML. By setting the dimensions of the iframe and specifying a *src* attribute (a Web page address), you can load another Web page so it looks like it's part of the current page. To make the process easy, you can use a jQuery plug-in called Greybox2 to handle all of the heavy lifting, so you can concentrate on the design.

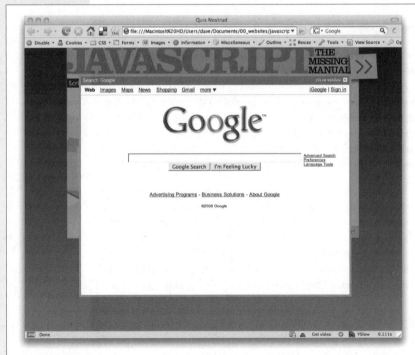

Figure 8-2:
*You can quickly create a
page-within-a-page effect
using the Greybox2
jQuery plug-in. The
original Greybox was
written by the creator of
jQuery, John Resig (see
http://jquery.com/demo/
grey). This book's author
expanded on that
original code and turned
it into an easy-to-use
plug-in.*

Opening Pages in a
Window on the
Page

Note: You can learn more about iframes at *http://www.w3schools.com/tags/tag_iframe.asp*. The <iframe> tag is not valid HTML for HTML 4.01 Strict or XHTML 1.0 Strict. However, the Greybox plug-in uses JavaScript to add the <iframe> tag, so your actual HTML will pass validation. In addition, since HTML 5 supports the <iframe> tag, all major browsers will continue to support it into the future.

To use the Greybox2 plug-in, follow these steps:

1. **Create a Web page with the links that open inside a window-within-the-page.**

   You don't need to apply this effect to every link on a page. Perhaps you want most of the links on the page to work normally (that is, clicking the link simply exits the current page and loads the linked page), with only some links using the window-within-the-page effect. For example, you might want the page listing your company's contact info your site's legal disclaimer to appear on the same page, or page, with external links working the normal way.

   In this case, you need a way to identify those specific links. Since jQuery provides such a flexible way of selecting elements (see page 172 for a refresher), you can achieve this goal in several ways. For example, you can add a class to each link (named something like *pageWindow*, for instance), and then use jQuery to select just those links—with *$('.pageWindow')*, for example. Or, if all of the links are grouped together in one area of the page, you can apply a class to a containing tag like a <div> or <ul> (bulleted list) tag; you can then use a descendent selector with jQuery to select those links—*$('.pageWindow a')*.

Note: The required Greybox2 files are included in the *chapter08* tutorial folder. Page 290 presents a step-by-step tutorial for using the Greybox2 plug-in.

   The Greybox2 plug-in also puts a short caption above the iframe identifying the linked page (see Figure 8-2). The plug-in uses the text inside the link (for example, "Click here to see more info") as the caption, but you can set up a different caption by adding a *title* attribute to the link tag:

   ```
   <a href="more.html" title="More about product XYZ">
   Click here to see more info</a>
   ```

   If the above link had the Greybox effect applied to it, "More about product XYZ" would appear as the caption.

2. **Attach the *greybox2.css* file to the Web page.**

   Attach the file as you would any external style sheet:

   ```
   <link href="greybox2.css" rel="stylesheet" type="text/css">
   ```

   The *greybox2.css* file contains various CSS styles that control the appearance of the effect, including the color of the transparent overlay, the border color and size, and the "loading page" animated GIF. (On page 290, you'll learn which styles you can edit to change the look of the effect.)

3. Attach the *jquery.js* and *jquery.greybox2.js* files to the Web page.

The *jquery.greybox2.js* file contains the code that lets you create the window-in-page effect, but since it uses the jQuery library to perform its magic, you need jQuery as well. Any file that uses jQuery must be linked *after* the jQuery file. Attach the files as you would any external JavaScript file, as described on page 24. For example, assuming the *jquery* and *greybox2* files are in the same folder as the page you're linking them to, add the following code to the <head> region of the page:

```
<script type="text/javascript" src="jquery.js"></script>
<script type="text/javascript" src="jquery.greybox2.js"></script>
```

4. **Add another <script> tag with the jQuery *$(document).ready( )* function.**

To do so, add this code after the <script> tags you added in step 3:

```
1    <script type="text/javascript">
2    $(document).ready(function( ) {
3
4    });
5    </script>
```

The *.ready( )* function is described in detail on page 218. Basically, when using jQuery you always add this function to your page and put all of your JavaScript inside this function (line 3 in this code sample).

5. **Set up any Greybox2 options.**

The Greybox2 plug-in includes just four options, which control the height and width of the in-page window, the height of the caption area, and whether to use a fix that lets the Mac version of Firefox 2 display Flash content inside the window:

- *gbWidth* defines the width in pixels for the in-page window. If you don't specify a value, the window will be 400 pixels wide.

- *gbHeight* sets the window's height in pixels. As with *gbWidth*, if you don't set this option, the window will be 400 pixels tall.

- *captionHeight* specifies the height of the caption area in pixels. The caption area appears above the linked Web page and contains a text caption and a "Close this window" button. If you don't change it, this option is set to 18 pixels, but you'll probably want to change it if you adjust the size of the font used in the caption (see page 290).

- *ffMacFlash*, if set to true, changes how the overlay (the transparent background that covers the Web page while the iframe is visible) is created. You may want to use this setting if the page displayed in the iframe contains a Flash movie and you want that movie to play. Due to a bug in Firefox 2 on

Opening Pages in a
Window on the
Page

the Mac, if you set the opacity of an object on a Web page (the overlay in this case), Firefox 2 can't play a Flash movie in an iframe (now that's a weird bug!). Firefox 3 for Mac doesn't have this problem, nor does any version of Firefox for Windows. (See page 290 for more on this problem.)

To set any of these options, create a variable containing an object literal (see page 188). You can then pass that variable to the *greybox( )* function. For example, say you want to set the width of the window to 600 pixels, the height to 550, the height of the caption to 22 pixels, and turn on the Mac Firefox fix, you can create a variable like this:

```
<script type="text/javascript">
$(document).ready(function( ) {
  var gbOptions = {
    gbWidth: 600,
    gbHeight: 500,
    captionHeight: 22,
    ffMacFlash: true
  };
});
</script>
```

6. **Apply greybox() to links.**

Finally, you apply the *greybox( )* function to the links. You do this by first creating a jQuery selector to select the desired links, and then call the *greybox( )* function passing the options you set in step 5. For example, say you added the class *pageWindow* to each link you want to open in an iframe on the page. You can apply *greybox( )* to the code in bold:

```
<script type="text/javascript">
$(document).ready(function( ) {
  var gbOptions = {
    gbWidth: 600,
    gbHeight: 500,
    captionHeight: 22,
    ffMacFlash: true
  };
  $('.pageWindow').greybox(gbOptions);
});
</script>
```

And that's it! The specified links are now *greyboxed*—meaning that clicking any of them opens the linked page in a nice 600×500 pixel in-page window.

Opening Pages in a
Window on the
Page

Customizing the Look of a Greybox Window

All of the formatting for the Greybox window is controlled by the *greybox2.css* style sheet. To change the look of the window effect, just open the *greybox2.css* style sheet. As shown in Figure 8-3, the top section of the file contains styles that control the look of the following elements:

- The **loading image** is an animated GIF named *loading.gif*. The *#GB_loading* style in the style sheet points to the image file and specifies the background color for the loading area. The CSS file included with the tutorials sets the background to white and assumes that the image is in the same folder as the style sheet. If you wish to move the file or change its name, edit the *#GB_loading* style accordingly.

- The **transparent overlay** is controlled by the *.GB_overlayBG* style. The stock style sheet sets the color to black (#000), and the opacity to 40%. There are two opacity properties—one for IE (*filter:alpha(opacity=40);*) and one for other browsers (*opacity: 0.40;*)—so if you wish to change the opacity, you must change both properties.

- Create an **overlay for Firefox 2 for Mac**. Due to a bug in the Mac version of Firefox 2, Flash movies displayed inside an iframe on a page that also includes transparent elements won't play (this problem doesn't affect Firefox 3 on the Mac). For that browser, you need to create a PNG32 transparent image. (That's just a small file containing a solid color set to a transparency setting of your choosing. You can create one in either Photoshop or Fireworks.)

   The file used in the supplied style sheet is named *macFFBgHack.png*. It's defined in the *.GB_overlayMacFFBGHack* style and is only used if you set the *ffMac-Flash* option to *true* when setting up the Greybox options (see the previous page). If you won't be displaying any Flash movies using the Greybox plug-in, or your audience doesn't use Firefox 2 for Mac, you don't need to even worry about this style or the graphic.

- **Basic window properties** like the background color, border width, and border color are controlled by the *#GB_window* style.

- The **caption area** is defined by the *#GB_caption* style. Edit this style to change the font, font size, background color, or other properties affecting the look of the caption area. In addition, this style puts a background image (named *close.gif* in the stylesheet), which contains the text "Close window" and a small close box. Actually, the entire caption area acts as a close button, so this graphic is merely to inform the visitor that he can close the window by clicking this area (clicking anywhere on the transparent overlay also closes the window).

Tutorial: Opening a Page Within a Page

In this tutorial, you'll take the Greybox2 plug-in for a spin by applying it to a page and customizing its appearance.

**Opening Pages in a
Window on the
Page**

Window border
and background
#GB_window

Caption text
and background
#GB_caption

Close window button
#GB_caption
(graphic file: close.gif)

Figure 8-3:
*You can control the look of a Greybox
window by editing the* greybox2.css *file and
by changing the image files used for the
close window button and loading page
image. The file has CSS comments pointing
out which styles you should edit.*

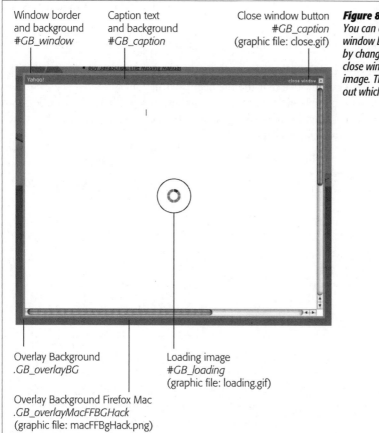

Overlay Background
.GB_overlayBG

Loading image
#GB_loading
(graphic file: loading.gif)

Overlay Background Firefox Mac
.GB_overlayMacFFBGHack
(graphic file: macFFBgHack.png)

Note: See the note on page 27 for information on how to download the tutorial files.

1. **In a text editor, open the file** *8.1.html* **in the** *chapter08* **folder.**

   This file already contains a link to the jQuery file, and the *$(document).ready( )*
   function (page 218). In addition, there's a bulleted list of links on the page.
   These are the links you'll apply the greybox effect to. The first step is to attach
   the *greybox2.css* file to the page.

2. **Click in the empty line after** *<link href="../css/global.css" rel="stylesheet"
   type="text/css">*

   ```
   <link href="greybox/greybox2.css" rel="stylesheet" type="text/css">
   ```

   This CSS file contains the styles that will control the look of the Greybox window. The *greybox2.css* file is inside a folder named *greybox*. That folder holds the
   other files required for the Greybox2 plug-in to work, including some graphic
   files and the Greybox JavaScript file, which you'll attach to this page next.

Opening Pages in a
Window on the
Page

3. Click in the empty line below the <script> tag that attaches the *jquery.js* file and type:

```
<script type="text/javascript" src="greybox/jquery.greybox2.js"></script>
```

This code tells the Web browser to load the plug-in file after it has loaded the *jquery.js* file. You'll notice that the file begins with "jquery"—*jquery.greybox2.js*. Adding *jquery* to the beginning of an external JavaScript file is a convention that jQuery plug-in programmers use as a way to identify a JavaScript file that's dependent on the jQuery library.

Next, you'll define the width and height for the greybox window.

4. Click in the empty line after the *$(document).ready( )* function and add the code listed on lines 3–6 below:

```
1    <script type="text/javascript">
2    $(document).ready(function() {
3      var gbOptions = {
4        gbWidth: 700,
5        gbHeight: 550
6      };
7    }); end ready()
8    </script>
```

The variable *gbOptions* contains a JavaScript object—essentially a list of properties and values. In this case, you've set two properties for the Greybox window—its width (*gbWidth*) and height (*gbHeight*) in pixels. You'll pass these settings to the *greybox( )* function in a moment, but first, you'll tinker with the page's HTML so that you can more accurately target the links you wish to appear inside the iframe created by the Greybox2 plug-in.

5. Locate the <ul> tag (directly below the <h1> tag) that contains the links, and then add a class attribute with the value *inpage*, so the tag looks like this:

```
<ul class="inpage">
```

You probably won't want to trap every link on a page inside the Greybox iframe window. To pinpoint the links you want to apply the effect to, you need a way to uniquely identify them. You could apply a class to each link, but, in this case, since all of the links are inside a single bulleted list, you only have to apply a class to the <ul> tag. Now you'll target those links using JavaScript.

6. Add an empty line below the JavaScript object you created in step 4, and type *$('.inpage a').greybox(gbOptions);* so the completed script looks like this:

```
<script type="text/javascript">
$(document).ready(function() {
  var gbOptions = {
    gbWidth: 700,
    gbHeight: 550
  };
```

**Opening Pages in a
Window on the
Page**

```
    $('.inpage a').greybox(gbOptions);
  }); // end ready( )
  </script>
```

The *$('.inpage a')* is a jQuery selector that simply selects all of the links inside the bulleted list (*.inpage* refers to the class you added to the list in the previous step). The rest of the line applies the Greybox effect to each link while applying the options you set up in step 4.

And that's it. Save the file and preview it in a Web browser. Click any of the links in the main section of the page to see the Greybox effect (see Figure 8-2). If it isn't working, double-check the code you typed.

Next you'll customize the effect a little.

7. **In the *greybox* folder, open the *greybox2.css* file. Locate the *#GB_window* style at the top of the file and change the border color from *#aaa* to *#000*.**

This changes the border color that appears around the iframe from grey to black. You'll next change the caption background color to black as well.

8. **In the style sheet, locate the style *#GB_caption* and change its background property to the following (changes are in bold):**

```
background: #000 url(close2.gif) no-repeat right center;
```

Now the caption's background is black (#000) and you've changed the "Close this window" image (*close2.gif*) to a GIF that matches the black background. Finally, you'll adjust the opacity of the overlay to make it a little less transparent.

9. **Locate the *.GB_overlayBG* style and change its opacity settings to match the style below (changes are in bold):**

```
.GB_overlayBG {
  background-color:#000;
  filter:alpha(opacity=60);
  opacity: .60;
}
```

You need to adjust both the filter and opacity properties. The filter property applies to Internet Explorer, while opacity applies to Firefox, Safari, and other Web browsers. You could, of course, make other changes if you'd like: for example, to add a colorful background, just change this style's *background-color* property.

Save the CSS and HTML files and preview *8.1.html* in a Web browser.

The file *complete_8.1.html* includes the finished JavaScript and HTML, and *complete_greybox2.css* in the *chapter08* folder has the final version of the CSS file for this tutorial.

Tutorial: Making Bigger Links

Most Web usability books (for example, Steve Krug's excellent *Don't Make Me Think*, published by New Riders Press) emphasize that the less you make a visitor think and work, the more likely they'll visit, enjoy, and benefit from your site. And if you haven't read any of these types of books, just think iPod—it's the easiest MP3 player to use, and it's the most successful. The typical HTML link is one of those things that make visitors work—a single, linked word, for example, is a pretty small target that requires good aim to hit. That's one of the reasons Web designers make nice navigation bars with buttons that are bigger than the text inside them.

For really important links, it would be even better to enlarge the clickable area to include an entire block-level tag like a <div>. That way, you could include a lot of information and make the link very easy to follow. For example, in Figure 8-4 four major methods of finding a house are emphasized in four areas of the page. If you mouse over one section (circled), it gets highlighted—thanks to the power of CSS. Unfortunately, clicking anywhere in that section other than the linked text ("value of your home") has no effect. That's because links are inline elements and can't wrap around block-level elements like paragraphs, list items, or divs.

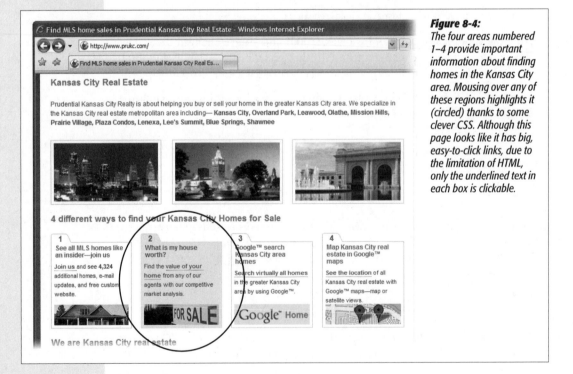

Figure 8-4:
The four areas numbered 1–4 provide important information about finding homes in the Kansas City area. Mousing over any of these regions highlights it (circled) thanks to some clever CSS. Although this page looks like it has big, easy-to-click links, due to the limitation of HTML, only the underlined text in each box is clickable.

Although HTML alone can't turn a <div> tag into a link, JavaScript can. In this tutorial you'll learn how to make any block-level element containing a link into a giant, clickable link (complete with a highlighted rollover effect).

Overview

To turn a block-level element into a clickable link, you bring together HTML, CSS, and JavaScript. The HTML provides a block-level element like a <div> or <li> tag that you wish to turn into a big button-like link. Inside that element go a link and whatever other content you wish; for example, you might add a <div> tag to a page and inside it include the link, a photo, and a descriptive paragraph. The big button's URL comes from the link inside the <div>. Also, you need to identify the block-level element with a class like *bigLink* or *clickable*, so that you can use Java-Script to select those block-level elements that you wish to turn into links.

To provide a *hover* style for the large links, you must add a CSS class style to your style sheet (name it something like *.hoverLink* or *.bigLinkHover*). You can then use JavaScript to dynamically add that class to the block-level element when a visitor mouses over the element. In the style sheet, you can add visual properties to that class that will make the block-level element stand out—like a background color, border, change of text color, and so on. For example, to add a bright yellow background to a <div> when the mouse moves over it, start by creating a style like this:

```
.bigLinkHover {
  background-color: #FF0;
}
```

In addition, you can create descendent selectors based on this class style to format the other tags inside the block-level element. For example, if, when a visitor mouses over the block-level element, you want a paragraph of text to change appearance as well, you can create a descendent selector like this:

```
.bigLinkHover p {
  color: #F20;
}
```

The JavaScript programming breaks down into three steps:

1. **Find each of the block-level elements you wish to turn into a link.**

   As mentioned above, you want to add a special class name to each of these elements' tags (*<div class="bigLink">*, for example) so you can use jQuery's selector functions to access these tags and then manipulate them.

2. **Add a mouseover/mouseout event combination to each element.**

   When the mouse moves over the element, you can apply a special hover CSS style you created. In addition, you can put the URL of the link in the browser window's status bar to simulate what a browser does when you mouse over an <a> tag. When the mouse moves off the element, you want your JavaScript to remove that class and change the status bar back. You can use jQuery's *hover( )* function (page 220) to add the mouseover/mouseout combo.

3. **To each element, add a click event that opens the linked Web page.**

   You need to use JavaScript to first find the URL for the link. This involves searching for the <a> tag inside the block-level element and getting its *href* property. Once you have the URL, you can write a function to open that URL when your visitor clicks the block-level element.

The Programming

Now that you understand the process, it's time to make it happen.

Note: See the note on page 27 for information on how to download the tutorial files.

---

1. **In a text editor, open the file *8.2.html* in the *chapter08* folder.**

   This file contains three <div> tags, which contain a <h2> tag, and a paragraph of text. The <h2> tag contains a link, and the <div> has a class named *bigLink* applied to it. Here's an example of the HTML for one of these divs:

   ```
   <div class="bigLink">
   <h2><a href="http://www.cosmofarmer.com/">CosmoFarmer.com</a></h2>
   <p>Your online guide to apartment farming.</p>
   </div>
   ```

   The goal is to convert this entire <div> into a link that points to *www. cosmofarmer.com* (or whatever link is inside the <div>). Before you jump into the JavaScript, you'll attach a style sheet containing the formatting instructions for these <div>s.

2. **Click in the empty line after *<link href="../css/global.css" rel="stylesheet"type="text/css">***

   ```
   <link href="css/bigLink.css" rel="stylesheet" type="text/css">
   ```

   This CSS file contains the styles that will control the look of the <div>. The first set of styles in the style sheet defines how the <div> tags look, while *.hoverBig-Link* style defines a hover style for the divs. Next, you'll set up a couple of variables for storing basic information for this script.

   The page already has the *jQuery.js* file attached to it and the obligatory *$(document).ready( )* function (see page 218 for more on this).

3. **Click in the empty line inside the *.ready( )* function and add the code in bold below:**

   ```
   $(document).ready(function( ) {
     var target = '.bigLink';
     var hoverClass = 'hoverBigLink';
   });
   ```

The first variable, *target*, defines the CSS selector that jQuery will use to identify which block-level elements to turn into links. In this case, since the class name *bigLink* is applied to each of the <div> tags in this page's HTML, *.bigLink* is the CSS selector that applies to each div. You can use any CSS selector that identifies the block-level element you wish to turn into a link. For example, you want to turn every <li> tag within a <ul> tag with an ID of *links*, you could use this CSS selector: *#links ul li*. Or, in other words, change the variable definition above to:

```
var target = '#links ul li';
```

The second variable, *hoverClass*, sets the name of the class style that will be applied to each block-level element when the mouse moves over it (the CSS selector, *.hoverBigLink*, is defined in the style sheet you attached in step 2). In other words, this class represents a kind of hover style so you can change the appearance of the block-level elements when visitors mouse over them. In this case, the class is named *hoverBigLink,* and it will be applied to the <div> tag when a visitor mouses over it.

4. **Hit Return and type:**

```
$(target).each(function( ) {

    });
```

The first part of this code—*$(target)*—is a jQuery selector. It's a little different from, other jQuery selectors you've seen (like *$('#banner')* or *$('a')*) in that we're passing a variable (*target*) instead of a literal string (*'#banner'*). But ultimately, it works the same way: *$(target)* simply translates to *$('.bigLink')*, since the JavaScript interpreter replaces the variable name with the value stored in the variable (step 3).

The next part of the code taps in the *each( )* function (described on page 193), which lets you loop through each element in a jQuery selection and apply a function to it. You'll start by adding a *hover( )* event.

5. **Add the code in bold below to the script:**

```
$(target).each(function( ) {
  $(this).hover(
    );
});
```

The *hover( )* function, as described on page 220, takes two functions as arguments: the first function runs when the mouse moves over the element, while the second function runs when the mouse moves off the element. You'll start with the mouseover function.

6. **Add the bolded code below (lines 3–6) to your script:**

```
1   $(target).each(function( ) {
2       $(this).hover(
3         function( ) {
4             $(this).addClass(hoverClass);
5         status=$(this).find('a').attr('href');
6           }
7       );
8   });
```

This anonymous function (see page 193 for a definition) does two things. First it adds a class name to each targeted <div> tag—the class (which you set in step 3) represents the *hover* style for the <div>. (The jQuery *addClass( )* function is described on page 185.)

Secondly, line 5 changes the status bar at the bottom of the browser window to display the *href* value for the link. This way, visitors can look down at the status bar and see where they'll go if they click the <div> tag. It replicates what browsers normally do when you mouse over an <a> tag.

Note: Firefox doesn't let JavaScript control the status bar, so line 5 in this step won't have any affect in that browser.

Now, you'll add the *mouseout* function, which essentially undoes the mousever function.

7. **Type a comma, hit Return, and add another anonymous function (lines 6–10 below) so the code for the *each( )* function looks like this:**

```
1    $(target).each(function( ) {
2        $(this).hover(
3          function( ) {
4              $(this).addClass(hoverClass);
5              status=$(this).find('a').attr('href');
6          },
7          function( ) {
8          $(this).removeClass(hoverClass);
9              status='';
10         }
11       );
12   });
```

Note: Don't forget the comma after the first function passed to the *hover( )* function (see line 6). That comma marks the end of the first argument passed to *hover( )*.

This function simply removes the hover class and sets the status bar to an empty string—erasing the URL that the mouseover function added.

Now you'll make the <div> act like a link by making it load a new Web page when clicked.

8. **Add a new *click( )* event to the script immediately between the closing parenthesis of the *hover( )* function (line 11 in the previous step) and the close of the *each( )* function (line 12):**

```
$(this).click(function() {
  location = $(this).find('a').attr('href');
});
```

This code adds a function that runs whenever that particular <div> tag is clicked. To be specific, it loads a new Web page. To understand how it works, you first need to learn about the browser window's *location* object. You probably know that by typing a URL into the location field at the top of a browser window you can go to a new Web page; the same is true when you set the browser's *location* object. This object is programmed into all Web browsers, and you can access it to find out what page the browser is currently displaying or set it to load a new page. For example, to produce an alert box with the current page's URL, you could use this code:

```
alert('You are at: ' + location);
```

Likewise, you can use JavaScript to load a new page like this:

```
location = 'http://www.google.com/';
```

In this case, you're changing the *location* to *$(this).find('a').attr('href')*. In other words, you're changing it to the *href* assigned to the <a> tag inside the <div>. But how does it do that? As you can see, jQuery lets you write very short code that does a lot—unfortunately, that also can make it hard to figure out what the code does. Here's the translation:

- *$(this)* refers to the <div> tag (remember the *each( )* function from step 4 that loops through each element in a jQuery selection). In this case, it loops through each element with a class name of *bigLink*.

- *.find('a')* uses another jQuery function to search for another element inside the current element. This code finds all <a> tags inside the current <div> tag. (See *http://docs.jquery.com/Traversing/find#expr* to learn more about the jQuery *find( )* function.)

- *.attr('href')* retrieves the value stored in the <a> tag's *href* attribute—the URL of the page to load.

Although the code looks confusing, what it does is pretty basic—gets the HREF value of the link and loads that page. In so doing, it lets the visitor click the <div> and go to a page, making the block-level tag behave like an <a> tag!

There's just one last task: currently if you mouse over the <div>, its appearance might change (thanks to swapping in a new CSS class). However, the cursor doesn't change, which may confuse your visitors. When you mouse over an <a> tag, the cursor is supposed to change to a pointing hand—a subtle clue that the page element is clickable. Fortunately, you can fake this with a little CSS.

9. Add one last line of code (right before the end of the *each( )* function), so the finished script looks like this:

```
<script type="text/javascript">
$(document).ready(function() {
  var target = '.bigLink';
  var hoverClass = 'hoverBigLink';

  $(target).each(function() {
    $(this).hover(
      function() {
          $(this).addClass(hoverClass);
          status=$(this).find('a').attr('href');
      },
      function () {
          $(this).removeClass(hoverClass);
          status='';
      });
    $(this).click(function() {
        location = $(this).find('a').attr('href');
    });
    $(this).css('cursor','pointer');
  });
});
</script>
```

This code uses jQuery's *css( )* function (page 186) to simply set a CSS property (*cursor*) to a new value (*'pointer'*). The CSS cursor property lets you assign the type of cursor the browser uses when the mouse is over a particular element. In this case, when a visitor mouses over the <div> tag, the cursor changes to the familiar pointing hand.

Save the file, view it in a browser, and mouse over one of the boxes in the middle of the page (Figure 8-5). The file *complete_8.2.html* is a finished, working copy of the tutorial.

Animated Navigation Menus

As Web sites grow in size, it gets harder and harder to provide access to every section of a site without overwhelming the page (and its visitors) with links. To make navigating a site more manageable, many Web designers use drop-down menu systems to keep links hidden until they're asked for (see Figure 8-6). While there are

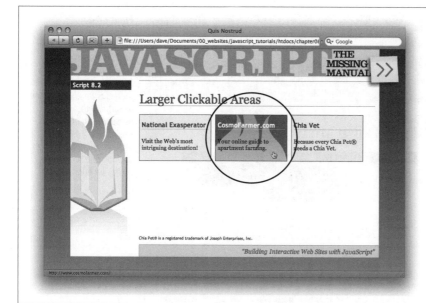

Figure 8-5:
*You can't make block-
level elements like <div>
and <li> tags into links
using HTML. But with a
little JavaScript magic,
you can create large,
block-level links that
make easily clickable
targets.*

CSS-only solutions to this problem, they don't work in Internet Explorer 6. And even though you can kick IE 6 into shape with a little JavaScript, a pure CSS solution isn't ideal. First, CSS-only pop-up menus are temperamental: If you roll off the menu for just a split second, the menu disappears. In addition, CSS doesn't let you add any visual effects, like fading the menu into view or animating it into position.

Fortunately, with just a little JavaScript, you can create an animated menu system that works smoothly for your visitors in all browsers. This navigation menu relies a lot more on HTML and CSS than other JavaScript techniques you've learned in this book so far. You'll use HTML to create a nested set of links, and CSS to format those links to look like a navigation bar and position and hide any submenus. You'll then add some JavaScript to animate the display of menus as the mouse moves over the navigation bar's buttons.

The HTML

The HTML for your navigation menu is a straightforward bulleted list created with the <ul> tag. Each of the top-level <li> tags represent the main buttons on the navigation bar. To create a submenu, you add a nested <ul> tag within the <li> tag the menu belongs to. For example, the HTML for the menu pictured in Figure 8-6 looks like this:

```
<ul class="nav">
  <li><a href="index.html">Home</a></li>
  <li><a href="pages/products.html">Our Products</a>
    <ul>
      <li><a href="pages/books.html">Books</a>
```

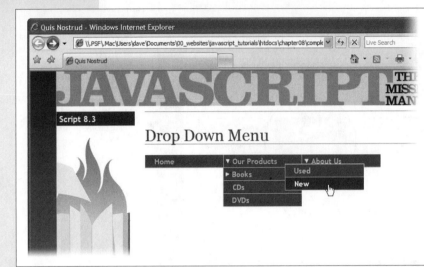

Figure 8-6:
Navigating a Web site filled with many pages and sections can be confusing. A navigation bar with drop-down menus is an elegant way to simplify the presentation of your site's links. It lets you include many navigation options and reduce clutter on your page.

```
      <ul>
        <li><a href="pages/used.html">Used</a></li>
        <li><a href="pages/new.html">New</a></li>
      </ul>
    </li>
    <li><a href="pages/cds.html">CDs</a></li>
    <li><a href="pages/dvds.html">DVDs</a></li>
  </ul>
</li>
<li><a href="pages/about.html">About Us</a>
  <ul>
    <li><a href="pages/contact.html">Contact Info</a></li>
    <li><a href="pages/driving.html">Driving Directions</a></li>
  </ul>
</li>
</ul>
```

The three main navigation buttons are Home, Our Products, and About Us. Under Our Products is a menu, represented by a nested list, which includes the options Books, CDs, and DVDs. The Books button has its own submenu (another nested list) containing the options Used and New. A nested list is just another list that's indented one more level. Visually, the HTML above translates to a list like the following:

- Home
- Our Products
  - Books
  - Used

- New

- CDs

- DVDs

- About Us

- Contact Info

- Driving Directions

Keep in mind that that a nested list actually goes within the <li> tag of its parent item. For example, the <ul> tag containing the list items Used and New above is contained within the <li> tag for the Books list item (if you need a refresher on creating HTML lists, check out *www.htmldog.com/guides/htmlbeginner/lists/*).

Tip: Always make sure that the top-level links (Home, Our Products, and About Us in this section's example) point to a page that links to the subpages in its section (for example, the Contact Info and Driving Directions links under About Us). That way, if the browser doesn't have JavaScript turned on, it can still access the links in the submenus.

The CSS

The style sheet for the navigation menu actually does most of the work. It takes a stack of bulleted and indented list items and converts the first list into side-by-side buttons, an indented list into a menu that appears below its parent button, and a third-level menu that sticks out of the right edge of its parent link.

The file *horz_menu.css* included in the *superfish* folder inside the *chapter08* tutorials folder contains styles to achieve the kind of navigation menu picture in Figure 8-7. Basically, each of the list items in the top-level menu are floated so that they appear side by side (that's defined in the *.nav li* style); each list item in a nested list is *not* floated (so they appear stacked one on top of the other). The pop-up menus are all absolutely positioned so they float above the page (and over any content that appears below the navigation bar).

All of the real style of each link—the text, color, background and so on—is defined for the <a> tags themselves (the *.nav a* style in the style sheet), and the rollover effect is created by the *.nav a:hover* style.

The JavaScript

The basic concept behind using JavaScript to control the display of menus is simple. Mouse over a list item, and if it has a nested list (a pop-up menu), then show that nested list; mouse off the list, and hide any nested lists.

There are a few subtleties that make this basic idea a bit more complicated. For example, pop-up menus that disappear the very instant the mouse moves off of its parent list item require precise mouse technique. It's easy to mouse off a list item

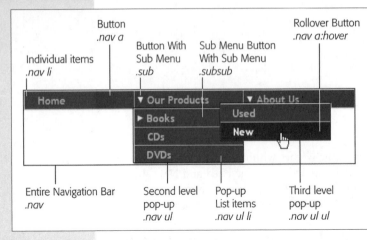

Figure 8-7:
The layout of a navigation menu like this one is controlled almost entirely by CSS. The file horz_menu.css, supplied with the tutorial files, defines the style of this menu. The style names for each part of the menu are listed here. Superfish can just as easily work with vertical menus—to find a style sheet for vertical menus visit http://users.tpg.com.au/j_birch/plugins/superfish/vertical-example.

when trying to navigate to a pop-up menu. If the menu suddenly disappears, your visitor is forced to move the mouse back over the original list item to open the menu again. And when there are a couple of levels of pop-up menus, it's frustratingly easy to miss the target and lose the menus.

To deal with this problem, most navigation menu scripts add a timer feature that delays the disappearance of pop-up menus. This timer accommodates not-so-precise mouse technique and makes the pop-up menus feel less fragile.

In addition, some visitors can't use mice (or don't like to), and use the Tab key to move from link to link in the menu. A good menu script accommodates this method of navigation as well, so that when a visitor tabs onto a link that includes a submenu, the menu pops into view and can also be navigated with the tab key.

The Superfish jQuery plug-in is a lightweight script that makes it easy for you to convert a list of links into an interactive navigation bar. To use Superfish to help create your navigation menu, just add the Superfish JavaScript file to your page, point the *superfish( )* function to the <ul> tag containing the navigation bar, and you're done. The following tutorial takes you through the process.

Note: To learn more about Joel Birch's Superfish jQuery plug-in, visit *http://users.tpg.com.au/j_birch/plug-ins/superfish/*.

The Tutorial

Now that you understand the basics of creating a navigation menu, here's how to make it happen. In this tutorial, you'll add CSS and JavaScript to transform the basic HTML menu list shown on page 301 into a navigation bar.

Note: See the note on page 27 for information on how to download the tutorial files.

1. **In a text editor, open the file *8.3.html* in the *chapter08* folder.**

   This file contains the bulleted list of links that you'll turn into a navigation bar. To see what it looks like without any styling, open the file in a Web browser.

   The first step is to attach the style sheet.

2. **Click in the empty line after *<link href="../css/global.css" rel="stylesheet" type="text/css">*.**

   ```
   <link href="superfish/horz_menu.css" rel="stylesheet" type="text/css">
   ```

   This style sheet controls the placement and look of the nav bar buttons. Next you'll attach the Superfish JavaScript file.

3. **Click in the empty line after *<script type="text/javascript" src="../js/jquery.js"> </script>*.**

   ```
   <script type="text/javascript" src="superfish/superfish.js"></script>
   ```

   The JavaScript file is inside the *superfish* folder in the *chapter08* folder. It contains all of the code to show and hide the pop-up menus. Making it work requires just one line of code.

4. **Click in the empty line inside the *$(document).ready( )* function and add the following code in bold below:**

   ```
   $(document).ready(function( ) {
     $('.nav').superfish( );
   });
   ```

   To activate the menu, you first use jQuery to select the <ul> tag used for the main navigation bar—in this example, that tag has the class *nav* applied to it, so the code *$('.nav')* selects that tag, and the *.superfish( )* applies the Superfish programming to the menu. Save the file, and preview it. You already have a working navigation bar with drop-down menus!

   You may notice that the delay before the drop-down menus disappears is pretty long. That is, once you move your mouse off a link with a menu attached, it takes a while for that menu to go away. Fortunately, you can set a *delay* property for the Superfish function that lets you shorten the time before menus disappear.

5. **Edit the code you just added so that it looks like the code below (additions are in bold):**

   ```
   1    $(document).ready(function( ) {
   2      $('.nav').superfish({
   3        delay: 400
   4      });
   5    });
   ```

At this point, the menu is fully functioning, but there aren't any visual clues as to which buttons contain hidden menus. A nice addition would be arrows on the buttons that include menus, providing visitors a clue about each link. One way is to simply add classes to each <li> tag that includes a nested list, and then create a CSS style for that class that changes the appearance of links inside that <li> tag—for example, adding a background image of an arrow to indicate that mousing over that link opens a menu.

A better approach is to let JavaScript add the class. That way, you don't have to manually add the class names to the appropriate <li> tags.

6. **Add an empty line after the Superfish function call (in other words, insert a blank link) between lines 4 and 5 in the code in step 5. Type:**

```
$('.nav li:has(ul)').find('a:first').addClass('sub');
```

This code really brings out the power of jQuery. There's a lot going on in this one line of code, so here's a breakdown.

The *$('.nav li:has(ul)')* is a jQuery selector. It finds <li> tags inside another tag with the class *nav* applied to it. However, it only selects those <li> tags that have a <ul> tag inside them. The *:has(ul)* part is a clever jQuery filter that lets you select tags (<li> in this case) that contain another specific tag inside them (<ul> in this case). In other words, this filter selects a list item only if it includes a nested (indented) list inside it—that is, an item containing a menu.

Note: You can find out more about the jQuery *:has()* filter at *http://docs.jquery.com/Selectors/has#selector.*

Next, the *.find('a:first')* is a way to search through a selection of elements to find another element. In other words, this code looks through the list of <li> tags selected by the previous code, and selects the first <a> tag it encounters. Finally, the *.addClass('sub')* adds the class name *sub* to those <a> tags. At this point, each navigation button that opens a menu has the specific class; then with a CSS style like *.nav .sub*, you can easily format the look of those buttons differently. In the case of the *horz_menu.css* file used in this tutorial, a *.nav .sub* style adds a down-pointing arrow to those links.

7. **Save the page and preview it in a browser.**

You should now see a down-pointing arrow on all buttons that contain a menu. Mouse over the "Our Products" link and notice that the "Books" link also has a down-pointing arrow. The first level pop-up menus drop down below the main navigation buttons, so the main nav buttons with menus have a down-pointing arrow; however, the second-level menus pop out to the right of their parent buttons, and it makes sense to apply a different style to those buttons, so that they can have a right pointing arrow (see Figure 8-7). The next step is to add another class name for those buttons.

8. Add an empty line after the code you added in the last step, and type: *$('.nav ul
li:has(ul)').find('a:first').removeClass('sub').addClass('subsub');*. The completed
code should look like this:

```
1    <link href="superfish/horz_menu.css" rel="stylesheet" type="text/css">
2    <script type="text/javascript" src="../js/jquery.js"></script>
3    <script type="text/javascript" src="superfish/superfish.js"></script>
4    <script type="text/javascript">
5    $(document).ready(function( ) {
6        $('.nav').superfish({
7        delay: 400
8        });
9        $('.nav li:has(ul)').find('a:first').addClass('sub');
10       $('.nav ul li:has(ul)').find('a:first').removeClass('sub').
     addClass('subsub');
11   });
12   </script>
```

This new line of code is similar to the code in step 6, but it searches one level
deeper, looking for links that live inside of a nested list. It also removes the class
added in step 6, since that class was added to all list items that contained menus,
and then adds a new class named *subsub*. Save the page and try it out in a Web
browser.

In all likelihood, you'll be using a navigation menu like this throughout your
site. To decrease the amount of code per page and make it easier to maintain
the JavaScript that controls the navigation bar, you should move the JavaScript
code into a separate external JavaScript file. This technique is always the way to
go when you use the same JavaScript code on more than one page of a site.

9. Create a new, empty file named *site.js* and save it in the *superfish* folder inside
the *chapter08* folder.

Although you've been working with multiple external files like *jquery.js* and
superfish.js, you'll probably want to create a single JavaScript file that contains
the code used throughout your site, instead of lots of little files for each of your
own programs (like this navigation script). That way you can collect all of your
custom-programmed code into a single file that's easy to find and edit.

Tip: You'll learn even more strategies for external files on page 443.

---

10. Return to the *8.3.html* file. Cut the JavaScript code (lines 5–11 in step 8) and
paste that code into the *site.js* file. Save the *site.js* file and close it.

You've created an external JavaScript file; now you just need to link it to your
page.

11. **Change the last <script> tag on the page so its *src* attribute points to the *site.js* file. The *8.3.html* file should now have the following HTML code:**

```
<link href="superfish/horz_menu.css" rel="stylesheet" type="text/css">
<script type="text/javascript" src="../js/jquery.js"></script>
<script type="text/javascript" src="superfish/superfish.js"></script>
<script type="text/javascript" src="superfish/site.js"></script>
```

Save the file and preview it in a Web browser. If the navigation bar isn't working, you may have either saved the *site.js* file in a different location, or the *src* attribute may not be pointing to it correctly.

CHAPTER

9

Enhancing Web Forms

Since the earliest days of the Web, forms have made it possible for Web sites to collect information from their visitors. Forms can gather email addresses for a newsletter, collect shipping information to complete an online sale, or simply receive visitor feedback. Forms also require your site's visitors to *think*: read labels, type information, make selections, and so on. Since some sites depend entirely on receiving form data—Amazon wouldn't be in business long if people couldn't use forms to order books—Web designers need to know how to make their forms as easy to use as possible. Fortunately, JavaScript's ability to inject interactivity into forms can help you build forms that are easier to use and ensure more accurate visitor responses.

Understanding Forms

HTML provides a variety of tags to build a Web form like the one pictured in Figure 9-1. The most important tag is the <form> tag, which defines the beginning (the opening <form> tag) and the end (the closing </form> tag) of the form. It also indicates what type of method the form uses to send data (*post* or *get*), and specifies where on the Web the form data should be sent.

You create the actual form controls—the buttons, text fields, and menus—using either the <input>, <textarea>, or <select> tags. Most of the form elements use the <input> tag. For example, text fields, password fields, radio buttons, checkboxes, and submit buttons all share the <input> tag, and you specify which one with the *type* attribute. For example, you create a text field by using the <input> tag and setting the *type* attribute to *text* like this:

```
<input name="user" type="text">
```

Here's the HTML that creates the form pictured in Figure 9-1; the <form> tag and *form* elements are shown in bold:

```
<form action="process.php" method="post" name="signup" id="signup">
  <div>
    <label for="username" class="label">Name</label>
    <input name="username" type="text" id="username" size="36">
  </div>
  <div><span class="label">Hobbies</span>
    <input type="checkbox" name="hobby" id="heliskiing" value="heliisking">
    <label for="heliskiing">Heli-skiing</label>
    <input type="checkbox" name="hobby" id="pickle" value="pickle">
    <label for="pickle">Pickle eating</label>
    <input type="checkbox" name="hobby" id="walnut" value="walnut">
    <label for="walnut">Making walnut butter</label>
  </div>
  <div>
      <label for="planet" class="label">Planet of Birth</label>
      <select name="planet" id="planet">
        <option>Earth</option>
        <option>Mars</option>
        <option>Alpha Centauri</option>
        <option>You've never heard of it</option>
      </select>
  </div>
  <div class="labelBlock">Would you like to receive annoying e-mail from
us?</div>
  <div class="indent">
    <input type="radio" name="spam" id="yes" value="yes" checked="checked">
    <label for="yes">Yes</label>
    <input type="radio" name="spam" id="definitely" value="definitely">
    <label for="definitely">Definitely</label>
    <input type="radio" name="spam" id="choice" value="choice">
    <label for="choice">Do I have a choice?</label>
  </div>
  <div>
    <input type="submit" name="submit" id="submit" value="Submit">
  </div>
</form>
```

Note: The <label> tag in this sample is another tag commonly used in forms. It doesn't create a form control like a button, though. It lets you add a text label, visible on the page, that explains the purpose of the form control.

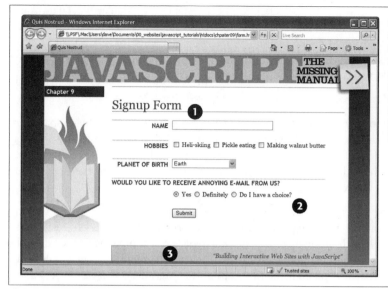

Figure 9-1:
*A basic form can include many
different types of controls
including text fields, radio buttons,
checkboxes, menu lists, submit
buttons, and so on. For a
complete rundown on HTML form
fields and how to use them, visit
www.w3schools.com/html/html_
forms.asp.*

Selecting Form Elements

As you've seen repeatedly in this book, working with elements on the page first
requires selecting those elements. To determine the value stored in a form field, for
example, you must select that field. Likewise, if you want to hide or show *form* elements, you must use JavaScript to identify those elements.

The easiest way to select a single *form* element is to assign an ID to it, like this:

```
<input name="user" type="text" id="user">
```

You can then use the DOM's *getElementById( )* method (page 158) to select that
element:

```
var userField = document.getElementById('user');
```

Or, you could use jQuery's selection function:

```
var userField = $('#user');
```

Once you select a field, you can do something with it. For example, say you want
to determine the value in a field—to check what a visitor has typed into the field,
for instance. If the form field has an ID of *user,* you can use jQuery to access the
field's value like this:

```
var fieldValue = $('#user').val();
```

Note: The jQuery *val( )* function is discussed on page 314.

But what if you wanted to select all *form* elements of a particular type? For example, you might want to add a click event (page 203) to every radio button on a page. The traditional DOM method of selecting elements (page 158) isn't a great help when it comes to forms. For example, the *getElementsByTagName( )* method lets you select all of a form's <input> tags like this:

```
var fields = document.getElementsByTagName('input');
```

However, since the <input> tag is used for radio buttons, text fields, password fields, checkboxes, submit buttons, reset buttons, and hidden fields, the only way you can find all of the fields of a particular type is to select all input fields and then loop through the list checking to see if the *type* attribute matched the element you want (*radio*, for example).

Fortunately, jQuery has taken the burden out of selecting specific types of form fields (see Table 9-1). Using one of the jQuery form selectors, you can easily identify and work with all fields of a particular type. For example, suppose when the visitor submits the form you want to check to make sure all text fields hold some value (you'll see the full code for this example on page 331). You can select all text fields like this:

```
$(':text')
```

Then, you simply loop through the results using the *.each( )* function (see page 193) to make sure there's a value in each field. (You'll learn a lot more about validating form fields on page 330.)

Table 9-1. *jQuery includes lots of selectors to make it easy to work with specific types of form fields*

Selector	Example	What it does
:input	$(':input')	Selects all input, textarea, select, and button elements. In other words, it selects all form elements.
:text	$(':text')	Selects all text fields.
:password	$(':password')	Selects all password fields.
:radio	$(':radio')	Selects all radio buttons.
:checkbox	$(':checkbox')	Selects all checkboxes.
:submit	$(':submit')	Selects all submit buttons.
:image	$(':image')	Selects all image buttons.
:reset	$(':reset')	Selects all reset buttons.
:button	$(':button')	Selects all fields with type *button*.
:file	$(':file')	Selects all file fields (used for uploading a file).
:hidden	$(':hidden')	Selects all hidden fields.

You can combine the form selectors with other selectors as well. For example, say you have two forms on a page, and you want to select the text fields in just one of the forms. Assuming that the form with the fields you're after has an ID of *signup*, you can select text fields in that form only like this:

```
$('#signup :text')
```

In addition, jQuery provides a few very useful filters that find form fields matching a particular state:

- *:checked* selects all fields that are checkmarked or tuned on—that is, checkboxes and radio buttons. For example, if you want to find all checkboxes and radio buttons that are turned on, you can use this code:

```
$(':checked')
```

Even better, you can use this filter to find which radio button within a group has been selected. For example, say you have a group of radio buttons and want to find the value of the radio button that your visitor has selected. A group of related radio buttons all share the same HTML *name* attribute; assume that you have a group of radio buttons that share the name *email*. You can use jQuery's attribute selector (page 177) in conjunction with the *:checked* filter to find the value of the checked radio button like this:

```
var checkedValue = $('input[name=email]:checked').val();
```

- *:selected* selects all selected *option* elements within a list or menu, which lets you find which selection a visitor makes from a menu or list (<select> tag). For example, say you have a <select> tag with an ID of *state*, listing all 50 U.S. states. To find which state the visitor has selected, you can write this:

```
var selectedState=$('#state :selected').val();
```

Notice that unlike in the example for the *:checked* filter, there's a space between the ID name and the filter ('*#state :selected*'). That's because this filter selects the <option> tags, not the <select> tag. To put it in English, this jQuery selection means "find all selected options that are inside the <select> tag with an ID of *state*." The space makes it work like a CSS descendent selector: first it finds the element with the proper ID, and then searches inside that for any elements that have been selected.

Note: You can enable multiple selections for a <select> menu. This means that the *:selected* filter can potentially return more than one element.

Getting and Setting the Value of a Form Element

At times you'll want to check the value of a *form* element. For example, you may want to check a text field to make sure an email address was typed into it. Or you may want to determine a field's value to calculate the total cost of an order. On the other hand, you may want to *set* the value of a *form* element. Say, for example, you have an order form that asks for both billing and shipping information. It would helpful to give your visitors a "Same as billing" checkbox and have the shipping information fields automatically filled out using the information from the billing fields.

jQuery provides a simple function to accomplish both tasks. The *val( )* function can both set and read the value of a form field. If you call the function without passing any arguments, it reads the field's value; if you pass a value to the function, it sets the form field's value. For example, say you have a field for collecting a user's email address with an ID of *email*. You can find the contents of that field like this:

```
var fieldValue = $('#email').val( );
```

Note: The *val()* function even finds the value of a selected option on a menu (the <select> tag). It's cumbersome to use regular DOM techniques to determine which element in a list is selected.

You can set the value of a field simply by passing a value to the *val( )* function. For example, say you have a form for ordering products and you wanted to automatically calculate the total cost of a sale based on the quantity a visitor specifies (Figure 9-2). You can *get* the quantity the visitor supplies, multiply it by the cost of the products, and then *set* the value in the total field.

The code to retrieve the quantity and set the total cost for the form in Figure 9-2 looks like this:

```
1    var unitCost=9.95;
2    var amount=$('#quantity').val( ); // get value
3    var total=amount * unitCost;
4    total=total.toFixed(2);
5    $('#total').val(total); // set value
```

The first line of code creates a variable that stores the cost for the product. The second line creates another variable and retrieves the amount the visitor entered into the field with an ID of *quantity*. Line 3 determines the total cost by multiplying the order amount by the unit cost, and line 4 formats the result to include two decimal places (see page 138 for a discussion of the *toFixed( )* method). Finally, line 5 sets the value in the field with ID *total* to the total cost. (You'll learn how to trigger this code using an event on page 315.)

Determine Whether Buttons and Boxes Are Checked

While the *val( )* function is helpful for getting the value of any *form* element, for some fields, the value is important only if the visitor has selected the field. For example, radio buttons and checkboxes require visitors to make a choice by selecting a particular value. You saw on page 313 how you can use the *:checked* filter to find checked radio buttons and checkboxes, but once you find it, you need a way to determine the status of a particular button or box.

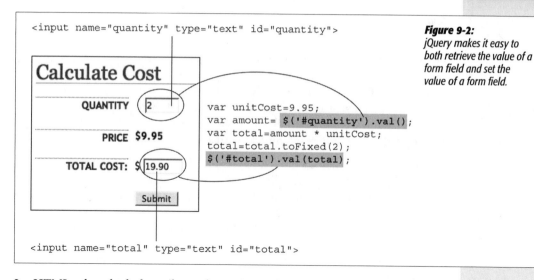

```
<input name="quantity" type="text" id="quantity">
```

Calculate Cost

QUANTITY [2]

PRICE $9.95

TOTAL COST: $[19.90]

[Submit]

```
var unitCost=9.95;
var amount= $('#quantity').val();
var total=amount * unitCost;
total=total.toFixed(2);
$('#total').val(total);
```

```
<input name="total" type="text" id="total">
```

Figure 9-2:
jQuery makes it easy to both retrieve the value of a form field and set the value of a form field.

In HTML, the *checked* attribute determines whether a particular element is checked. For example, to turn on a box when the Web page is loaded, you add the *checked* attribute like this:

```
<input type="checkbox" name="news" id="news" checked="checked" />
```

Since *checked* is an HTML attribute, you can easily use jQuery to check the status of the box like this:

```
if ($('#news').attr('checked')) {
    // the box is checked
} else {
    // the box is not checked
}
```

The code *$('#news').attr('checked')* returns the value *true* if the box is checked. If it's not, it returns the value *undefined,* which the JavaScript interpreter considers the same as *false.* So this basic conditional statement lets you perform one set of tasks if the box is turned on or a different set of tasks if the box is turned off. (If you need a refresher on conditional statements, turn to page 77.)

The *checked* attribute applies to radio buttons as well. You can use the *attr( )* function in the same way to check whether the radio button's *checked* attribute is set.

Form Events

As you read in Chapter 6, events let you add interactivity to your page by responding to different visitor actions. Forms and *form* elements can react to many different events, so you can tap into a wide range of events to make your forms respond intelligently to your visitors' actions.

Submit

Whenever a visitor submits a form by clicking a submit button or pressing Enter or Return when typing into a text field, the *submit* event is triggered. You can tap into this event to run a script when the form is submitted. That way, JavaScript can validate form fields to make sure they're correctly filled out. When the form is submitted, a JavaScript program checks the fields, and if there's a problem JavaScript can stop the form submission and let the visitor know what's wrong; if there are no problems, then the form is submitted as usual.

To run a function when the form's submit event is triggered, first select the form, then use jQuery's *submit( )* function to add your script. For example, say you want to make sure that the name field on the form pictured in Figure 9-1 has something in it when the form is submitted—in other words, a visitor can't leave the field blank. You can do so by adding a submit event to the form, and checking the value of the field before the form is submitted. If the field is empty, you want to let the visitor know and stop the submission process; otherwise, the form will be allowed to go through.

If you look at the HTML for the form on page 310, you can see that the form has an ID of *signup* and the name field has an ID of *username*. So you can validate this form using jQuery like this:

```
1    $(document).ready(function( ) {
2        $('#signup').submit(function( ) {
3            if ($('#username').val( ) == '') {
4                alert('Please supply a name in the Name field.');
5                return false;
6            }
7        }); // end submit( )
8    }); // end ready( )
```

Line 1 sets up the required *$(document).ready( )* function so the code runs only after the page's HTML has loaded (see page 218). Line 2 attaches a function to the form's *submit* event (see page 310 if you need a reminder of how to use events). Lines 3–6 are the validation routine. Line 6 checks to see if the value of the field is an empty string (''), meaning the field is empty. If the field has nothing in it, then an alert box appears letting the visitor know what he did wrong.

Line 5 is very important: it stops the form from being submitted. If you omit this step, then the form will be submitted anyway, without the visitor's name. Line 6 completes the conditional statement, and line 7 is the end of the *submit( )* function.

Tip: You can also stop the form from submitting by using the event object's *preventDefault( )* function, described on page 223.

The *submit* event only applies to forms, so you must select a form and attach the *submit* event function to it. You can select the form either by using an ID name that's supplied in the <form> tag of the HTML, or, if there's just a single form on the page, you can use a simple element selector like this:

```
$('form').submit(function( ) {
    // code to run when form is submitted
});
```

Focus

Whenever someone either clicks into a text field on a form or tabs into a text field, that field receives what's called *focus*. Focus is an event that the browser triggers to indicate that a visitor's cursor is on or in a particular field; you can be sure that that's where your visitor's attention is focused. You probably won't use this event very often, but some designers use it to erase any text that's already present in a field. For example, say you have the following HTML inside a form:

```
<input name="username" type="text" id="username" ↵
value="Please type your user name">
```

This code creates a text field on the form with the text "Please type your user name" inside it. This technique lets you provide instructions as to how the visitor is supposed to fill out the field. Then instead of forcing the visitor filling out the form to erase all that text herself, you can erase it when she focuses on the field, like this:

```
1  $('#username').focus(function( ) {
2    var field = $(this);
3    if (field.val( )==field.attr('defaultValue')) {
4      field.val('');
5    }
6  });
```

Line 1 selects the field (which has an ID of *username*) and assigns a function to the focus event. Line 2 creates a variable, *field*, that stores a reference to the jQuery selection; as discussed on page 194, *$(this)* refers to the currently selected element within a jQuery function—in this case, the form field.

Line 4 is what actually erases the field. It sets the value of the field to an empty string—represented by the two single quote marks—thus removing any value from the field. But you don't want to erase this field every time the field gets the focus. For example, say someone comes to the form and clicks in the form field; the first time, that erases the "Please type your user name" text. However if the visitor then types his name in the field, clicks outside the field, and then clicks back into the field, you don't want his name to suddenly disappear. That's where the conditional statement in line 3 comes into play.

Text fields have an attribute called *defaultValue*, which represents the text inside the field when the page first loads. Even if you erase that text, the Web browser still remembers what was in the field when the page was loaded. The conditional statement checks to see if what is currently inside the field (*field.val( )*) is the same as what was originally inside the field (*field.attr('defaultValue')*). If they are the same, then the JavaScript interpreter erases the text in the field.

Here's an example that explains the entire process. When the HTML on the previous page first loads, the text field has the value "Please type your user name." That's the field's *defaultValue*. So when a visitor first clicks into that field, the conditional statement asks the question "Is what's currently in the field the same as what was first in the field when the page loaded?" In other words, is "Please type your user name" equal to "Please type your user name"? The answer is yes, so that field is erased.

However, say you typed *helloKitty* as your username, then tabbed into another field, and then realized that you mistyped your username. When you click back into the field to fix the mistake, the focus event is triggered again, and the function assigned to that event runs again. This time the question is "Is 'helloKitty' equal to 'Please type your username.'" The answer is no, so the field isn't erased and you can fix your typo.

Blur

When you tab out of a field or click outside of the currently focused field, the browser triggers a *blur* event. This event is commonly used with text and textarea fields to run a validation script when someone clicks or tabs out of a field. For example, say you have a long form with a lot of questions, many of which required particular types of values (for example email address, numbers, Zip codes, and so on). Say a visitor doesn't fill out any of those fields correctly, but hits the submit button—and is faced with a long list of errors pointing out how she failed to fill out the form correctly. Rather than dumping all of those errors on her at once, you can also check fields as she fills out the form. That way, if she makes a mistake along the way, she'll be notified immediately and can fix the mistake right then.

Say, for instance, that you have a field for collecting the number of products the visitor wants. The HTML for that might look like this:

```
<input name="quantity" type="text" id="quantity">
```

You want to make sure that the field contains numbers only (for example 1, 2, or 9, but not One, Two, or Nine). You can check for that after the visitor clicks out of the field like this:

```
1   $('#quantity').blur(function() {
2     var fieldValue=$(this).val();
3     if (isNaN(fieldValue)) {
4       alert('Please supply a number');
5     }
6   });
```

Line 1 assigns a function to the blur event. Line 2 retrieves the value in the field and stores it in a variable named *fieldValue*. Line 3 checks to make sure that the value is numeric using the *isNaN( )* method (see page 137). If it's not a number, then line 4 runs and an alert appears.

Click

The click event is triggered when any form element is clicked. This event is particularly useful for radio buttons and checkboxes, since you can add functions that alter the form based on the buttons your visitor selects. For example, say you have an order form that provides separate fields for both billing and shipping information. To save visitors whose shipping and billing information are the same from having to type their information twice, you can provide a checkbox—"Same as billing information", for example—that when checked hides the shipping information fields and makes the form simpler and more readable. (You'll see this example in action on page 328.)

Like other events, you can use jQuery's *click( )* function to assign a function to a form field's click event:

```
$(':radio').click(function( ) {
  //function will apply to every radio button when clicked
});
```

Note: The click event also applies to text fields, but it's not the same as the focus event. Focus is triggered whenever you click *or* tab into a text field, while the click event is only triggered when the field is clicked into.

Change

The *change* event applies to form menus (like the "Planet of Birth" menu pictured in Figure 9-1). Whenever you make a selection from the menu, the change event is triggered. You can use this event to run a validation function: for example, many designers commonly add an instruction as the first option in a menu, like "Please choose a country." To make sure a visitor doesn't pick a country, then accidentally change the menu back to the first option ("Please choose a country"), you can check the menu's selected value each time someone makes a new selection from the menu.

Or, you could program the form to change based on a menu selection. For example, you can run a function so that whenever an option is selected from a menu, the options available from a second menu change. For example, Figure 9-3 shows a form with two menus; selecting an option from the top menu changes the list of available colors from the bottom menu.

To apply a change event to a menu, use jQuery's *change( )* function. For example, say you have a menu listing the names of countries; the menu has an ID of *country*, and each time a new selection is made you want to make sure the new selection isn't the instruction text "Please choose a country." You could do so like this:

```
$('#country').change(function( ) {
  if ($(this).val( )=='Please choose a country') {
    alert('Please select a country from this menu.');
  }
}
```

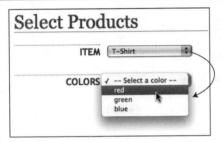

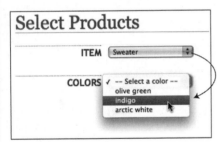

Figure 9-3:
A form menu's change event lets you do interesting things when a user selects an option from a menu. In this case, selecting an option from the top menu dynamically changes the options presented in the second menu. Choose a product from the top menu, and the second menu displays the colors that product is available in.

Adding Smarts to Your Forms

Web forms demand a lot from your site's visitors: text fields need to be filled out, selections made, checkboxes turned on, and so on. If you want people to fill out your forms, it's in your interest to make the forms as simple as possible. Fortunately, JavaScript can do a lot to make your Web forms easier to use. For example, you can hide form fields until they're needed, disable form fields that don't apply, and calculate totals based on form selections. JavaScript gives you countless ways to improve the usability of forms.

Focus the First Field in a Form

Normally, to begin filling out a form, you have to click into the first text field and start typing. On a page with a login form, why make your visitors go to the extra trouble of moving their mouse into position and clicking into the login field before they can type? Why not just place the cursor in the field, ready to accept their login information immediately? With JavaScript, that's a piece of cake.

The secret lies in focus, which isn't just an event JavaScript can respond to but a command that you can issue to place the cursor inside a text field. You simply select the text field, and then run the jQuery *focus( )* function. Let's say, for example, that you'd like the cursor to be inside the name field pictured in Figure 9-1 when the page loads. If you look at the HTML for this form on page 310, you'll see that that field's ID is *username*. So the JavaScript to place the focus on—that is, place the cursor in—that field looks like this:

```
$(document).ready(function( ) {
  $('#username').focus( );
});
```

In this example, the text field has the ID *username*. However, you can also create a generic script that always focuses the first text field of a form, without having to assign an ID to the field:

```
$(document).ready(function( ) {
  $(':text')[0].focus( );
});
```

As you read on page 312, jQuery provides a convenient method of selecting all text fields—*$(':text')*. So in this case, you first select all text fields (which returns an array of elements), then access just the first item in the array—that's the *[0]* part. Finally, you focus that element with *.focus( );*.

If you have more than one form on a page (for example a "search this site" form, and a "signup for our newsletter" form), you need to refine the selector to identify the form whose text field should get focus. For example, say you want the first text field in a signup form to have the cursor blinking in it, ready for visitor input, but the first text field is in a search form. To focus the signup form's text field, just add an ID (*signup*, for example) to the form, and then use this code:

```
$(document).ready(function( ) {
  $('#signup :text')[0].focus( );
});
```

Now, the selector—*$('#signup :text')*—only selects the text fields inside the signup form.

Disabling and Enabling Fields

Form fields are generally meant to be filled out—after all, what good is a text field if you can't type into it? However, there are times when you might *not* want a visitor to be able to fill out a text field, check a checkbox, or select an option from a menu. Say you have a field that should only be filled out if a previous box was turned on. For example, on the 1040 form used for determining U.S. income tax, there's a field for collecting your spouse's Social Security number. You'd fill out that field only if you're married.

To "turn off" a form field that shouldn't be filled out, you can *disable* it using JavaScript. Disabling a field means it can't be checked (radio buttons and checkboxes), typed into (text fields), selected (menus), or clicked (submit buttons). Some browsers also change the color of the form control—dimming it using a light gray color.

To disable a form field, simply set the field's *disabled* attribute to *true*. For example, to disable all input fields on a form, you can use this code:

```
$(':input').attr('disabled', true);
```

You'll usually disable a field in response to an event. Using the 1040 form example, for instance, you can disable the field for collecting a spouse's Social Security number when the "single" button is clicked. Assuming that the radio button for declaring yourself as single has an ID of *single*, and the field for a spouse's SSN has an ID of *spouseSSN*, the JavaScript code will look like this:

```
$('#single').click(function() {
  $('#spouseSSN').attr('disabled', true);
});
```

Of course, if you disable a field, you'll probably want a way to enable it again. To do so, simply set the disabled attribute to *false*. For example, to enable all fields on a form:

```
$(':input').attr('disabled', false);
```

Note: When disabling a form field, make sure to use the Boolean values (page 42) *true* or *false* and not the strings *'true'* or *'false'*. For example, this is wrong:

```
$(':input').attr('disabled', 'false');
```

And this is right:

```
$(':input').attr('disabled', false);
```

Back to the tax form example: If the visitor selects the "married" option, then you need to make sure that the field for collecting the spouse's Social Security number is active. Assuming the radio button for the married option has an ID of married, you can add the following code:

```
$('#married').click(function() {
  $('#spouseSSN').attr('disabled', false);
});
```

You'll run through an example of this technique in the tutorial on page 324.

You'll run through an example of this technique in the tutorial on page 324.

FREQUENTLY ASKED QUESTION

Stopping Multiple Submissions

Sometimes I get the same form information submitted more than once. How can I prevent that from happening?

Web servers aren't always the fastest creatures...and neither is the Internet. Often, there's a delay between the time a visitor presses a form's submit button, and when a new "We got your info" page appears. Sometimes this delay can be pretty long, and impatient Web surfers hit the submit button a second (or third, or fourth) time, thinking that the first time they submitted the form, it simply didn't work.

This phenomenon can lead to the same information being submitted twice. In the case of an online sale, it can also mean a credit card is charged more than once! Fortunately, with JavaScript, there's an easy way to disable a submit button once the form submission process has begun. Using the submit button's *disabled* attribute, you can "turn it off" so it can't be clicked again.

Assume the form has an ID of *formID*, and the submit button has an ID of *submit*. First, add a *submit( )* function to the form, and then, within the function, disable the submit button, like this:

```
$('#formID').submit(function() {
  $('#submit').attr('disabled',true);
});
```

If the page has only a single form, you don't even need to use IDs for the tags:

```
$('form').submit(function() {
  $('input[type=submit]').
attr('disabled',true);
});
```

In addition, you can change the message on the submit button by changing the button's value. For example, the button says "Submit" at first, but when the form is submitted, the button changes to say "...sending information" You could do that like this:

```
$('#formID').submit(function() {
  var subButton = $(this).find(':submit');
  subButton.attr('disabled',true);
  subButton.val('...sending information');
});
```

Make sure to put this code inside a *$(document).ready( )* function, as described on page 218.

Hiding and Showing Form Options

In addition to disabling a field, there's another way to make sure visitors don't waste time filling out fields unnecessarily—just hide the unneeded fields. For instance, using the tax form example from the last section, you may want to hide the field for a spouse's Social Security number when the "single" option is selected and show the field when the "married" option is turned on. You can do so like this:

```
$('#single').click(function() {
  $('#spouseSSN').hide();
});
$('#married').click(function() {
  $('#spouseSSN').show();
});
```

Tip: jQuery's *hide( )* and *show( )* functions (as well as other functions for revealing and concealing elements) are discussed on page 243.

One usability benefit of hiding a field (as opposed to just disabling it) is that it makes the layout of the form simpler. After all, a disabled field is still visible and can still attract (or more accurately, distract) a person's attention.

In many cases, you'll want to hide or show more than just the form field: you'll probably want to hide that field's label and any other text associated with it. One strategy is to wrap the code you wish to hide (field, labels, and whatever other HTML) in a <div> tag, add an ID to that <div>, and then hide the <div>. You'll see an example of this technique in the following tutorial.

Tutorial: Basic Form Enhancements

In this tutorial, you'll add three usability improvements to a basic ordering form composed of fields for collecting billing and shipping information. First, you'll place the text cursor in the first field of the form when the page loads. Second, you'll disable or re-enable form fields based on selections a visitor makes. Finally, you'll hide an entire section of the form when it's not needed (see Figure 9-4).

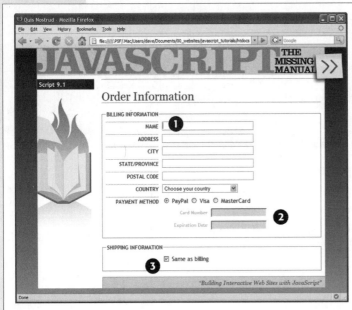

Figure 9-4:
Using JavaScript, you can increase the usability of your Web forms and add interactive features, like hiding fields that aren't needed and disabling fields that shouldn't be filled out.

Note: See the note on page 27 for information on how to download the tutorial files.

Focusing a Field

The first field on this tutorial's order form page collects the name of the person placing the order (see Figure 9-4). To make using the form easier to fill out, you'll place the cursor in this field when the page loads.

1. **In a text editor, open the file *9.1.html* in the *chapter09* folder.**

   This file already contains a link to the jQuery file and the *$(document).ready( )* function (page 218). There's a form that includes two sections—one for collecting billing information and another form collecting shipping information. (Check the page out in a Web browser before continuing.)

   The first step (actually, the only step for this part of the tutorial) is to focus the field.

2. **Click in the empty line after the *$(document).ready( )* function and type *$('#name').focus( );*, so the code looks like this:**

   ```
   $(document).ready(function( ) {
     $('#name').focus( );
   }); // end ready( )
   ```

   The first field has an ID of *name*, so it's a simple matter of applying the *focus( )* function to that field to make a browser place the insertion point in it.

   Save the file and preview it in a Web browser.

   When the page loads, the first field should have a blinking insertion bar—meaning that field has focus, and you can immediately start filling it out.

Disabling Form Fields

That last section was just a warm-up. In this part of the tutorial, you'll disable or enable two form fields in response to selections on the form. If you preview the form in a Web browser (or just look at Figure 9-4), you'll see that at the end of the billing information section of the form, there are three radio buttons for selecting a payment method: PayPal, Visa, and MasterCard. In addition, there are two fields below that for collecting a card number and expiration date. Those two options only apply for credit cards, not for PayPal payments, so you'll disable those fields when the PayPal button is clicked.

The HTML for that section of the page looks like this (the form fields are in bold):

```
1   <div><span class="label">Payment Method</span>
2     <input type="radio" name="payment" id="paypal" value="paypal">
3     <label for="paypal">PayPal</label>
4     <input type="radio" name="payment" id="visa" value="visa">
5     <label for="visa">Visa</label>
6     <input type="radio" name="payment" id="mastercard" value="mastercard">
7     <label for="mastercard">MasterCard</label>
8   </div>
```

```
9    <div id="creditCard" class="indent">
10     <div>
11       <label for="cardNumber" class="label">Card Number</label>
12       <input type="text" name="cardNumber" id="cardNumber">
13     </div>
14     <div>
15       <label for="expiration" class="label">Expiration Date</label>
16       <input type="text" name="expiration" id="expiration">
17     </div>
18   </div>
```

1. **Return to your text editor and the file *9.1.html*.**

   You'll add to the code you created in the previous section. First, assign a function to the click event for the PayPal radio button.

2. **To the script at the top of the page, add the code in bold below:**

```
$(document).ready(function( ) {
  $('#name').focus( );
  $('#paypal').click(function( ) {

  });
}); // end ready( )
```

   The radio button for the PayPal option has an ID of *paypal* (see line 2 in the HTML code), so selecting that field is just a matter of typing *$('#paypal')*. The rest of the code assigns an anonymous function to the click event (if this isn't clear, check out the discussion on assigning functions to events on page 210). In other words, not only does clicking the PayPal radio button select it (that's normal Web browser behavior), but it also triggers the function you're about to create.

   Next, you'll disable the credit card number and expiration date fields, since they don't apply when the PayPal option is selected.

3. **Inside the anonymous function you added in the previous step, add a new line of code (line 4 below):**

```
1    $(document).ready(function( ) {
2      $('#name').focus( );
3      $('#paypal').click(function( ) {
4        $('#creditCard input').attr('disabled', true);
5      });
6    }); // end ready( )
```

   Although you want to disable two form fields, there's a simple way to do that with just one line of code. Both of the form fields are inside a <div> tag with an ID of *creditCard* (see line 9 of the HTML code above). So, the jQuery selector *$('#creditCard input')* translates to "select all <input> tags inside of an element with the ID *creditCard*." This flexible approach makes sure you select all of the input fields, so if you add another field, such as a CVV field, it gets selected as well (CVVs are those 3 numbers on the back of your credit card that Web forms often request to enhance the security of online orders).

To disable the fields, all you have to do is set the *disabled* attribute to *true* (see page 322). However, this doesn't do anything to the text labels ("Card Number" and "Expiration Date"). Even though the fields themselves are disabled, those text labels remain bold and black, sending the potentially confusing signal that the visitor can fill out the fields. To make the disabled status clearer, you'll change the labels to a light shade of gray. While you're at it, you'll also add a gray color to the background of the fields to make them look disabled. (Most browsers already do that, but in Internet Explorer, disabled text fields don't look any different than enabled ones.)

4. **Add the bolded code below to your script:**

```
1    $(document).ready(function() {
2      $('#name').focus();
3      $('#paypal').click(function() {
4        $('#creditCard input').attr('disabled', true)⏎
5        .css('backgroundColor','#E5E5E5');
6        $('#creditCard label').css('color','#CCC');
7      });
8    }); // end ready()
```

Note: The ⏎ symbol at the end of a line of code indicates that you should type the next line as part of the previous line. Since a *really* long line of JavaScript code won't fit on this book's page, it's broken up over two lines.

First, you use the jQuery's *css( )* function to alter the background color of the text fields (note that the code is part of line 4, so you should type it onto the same line as the *attr( )* function. Next, you use the *css( )* function to adjust the font color of any <label> tags inside the <div> tag (the *css( )* function is described on page 186).

If you preview the page in a Web browser at this point, you'll see that clicking the PayPal button does indeed disable the credit card number and expiration date fields and dims the label text. However, if you click either the Visa or MasterCard buttons, the fields stay disabled! You need to re-enable the fields when either of the other radio buttons is selected.

5. **After the *click( )* function, add a new blank line (you're adding new code between lines 6 and 7 in step 5) and then add the following:**

```
$('#visa, #mastercard').click(function() {
  $('#creditCard input').attr('disabled', false) ⏎
  .css('backgroundColor','');
  $('#creditCard label').css('color','');
});
```

CHAPTER 9: ENHANCING WEB FORMS

The selector *$('#visa, #mastercard')* selects both of the other radio buttons (see lines 4 and 6 of the HTML on page 325). Notice that to remove the background color and text colors added by clicking the PayPal button, you simply pass an empty string as the color value: *$('#creditCard label').css('color','');*. That removes the color for that element, but leaves in place the color originally defined in the style sheet.

You're nearly done with this tutorial. In the final section, you'll completely hide a part of the page based on a form selection.

Making It Easier to Select a Date

Whether you're joining a social network site, reserving seats on a plane, or searching a calendar of events, you'll frequently encounter forms that ask you to enter a date. In most cases, you'll see a basic text field into which you're supposed to type a date. Unfortunately, you don't always know what the date is going to be two Fridays from now. In addition, an empty text field means a visitor is free to type a date in any format he'd like: 10-20-2009, 10.20.2009, 10/20/2009, or even 20/10/2009.

The best way to make selecting a date easy and ensuring you'll receive dates in the same format is to use a calendar *widget*—a pop-up calendar that lets visitors select a date by clicking a day on the calendar. Although calendar widgets are useful, they can be hard to program yourself. Fortunately, you can download a jQuery plug-in that makes adding calendar widgets to your forms a piece of cake.

The jQuery UI Datepicker plug-in, by Marc Grabanski and Keith Wood, is a sophisticated date-picking pop-up calendar that you can customize in many ways. To use it, you need to get the plug-in from Datepicker Web site at *http://marcgrabanski.com/code/ui-datepicker/*. Then, on the page to which you want to add the date picker, you have to

attach the *ui.datepicker.css* file (which contains all of the style rules that format the calendar); attach the jQuery library (see page 172); and then link to the *ui.datepicker.js* file (follow the instructions for linking to an external JavaScript file on page 24).

After you set up all of those basic steps, you just need to apply the *datepicker( )* function to a text field. For example, say you have a form and a text field with an ID of *dateOfBirth*. To make it so that when someone clicks inside that field a pop-up calendar appears, add a <script> tag with the basic *$(document).ready( )* function (see page 218 for instructions on this) and invoke the Datepicker like this:

```
$('#dateOfBirth').datepicker( );
```

Of course, *$('#dateOfBirth')* is the old jQuery way of selecting the text field; the *datepicker( )* function then handles the rest. The Datepicker plug-in supports options that include selecting a range of dates, opening the pop-up calendar by clicking a calendar icon, and more. To learn more about this useful plug-in, visit *http://marcgrabanski.com/code/ui-datepicker/*.

Hiding Form Fields

As is common on many product order forms, this tutorial's form includes separate fields for collecting billing and shipping information. In many cases, this information is exactly the same, so there's no need to make someone fill out both sets of fields if they don't have to. You'll frequently see a "Same as billing" checkbox on forms like these to indicate that the information is identical for both sets of fields. However, wouldn't it be even more useful (not to mention cooler) if you could completely hide the shipping fields when they aren't needed? With JavaScript, you can.

1. **Open the file *9.1.html* in a text editor.**

   You'll expand on the code you've been writing in the last two sections of this tutorial. First, add a function to the click event for the checkbox that has the label "Same as billing." The HTML for that checkbox looks like this:

   ```
   <input type="checkbox" name="hideShip" id="hideShip">
   ```

2. **Add the following code after the code you added in step 5 on page 327, but before the end of the script (the last line of code, which reads *}); // end ready( )*):**

   ```
   $('#hideShip').click(function() {

   });
   ```

   Since the checkbox has the ID *hideShip*, the code above selects it and adds a function to the click event. In this case, instead of hiding just a single field, you want the entire group of fields to disappear when the box is checked. To make that easier, the HTML that makes up the shipping information fields is wrapped in a <div> tag with the ID of *shipping*: to hide the fields, you just need to hide the <div> tag.

   However, you'll only want to hide those fields when the box is checked. If someone clicks the box a second time to uncheck it, the <div> tag and its form fields should return. So the first step is to find out whether the box is checked.

3. **Add the code in bold below:**

   ```
   $('#hideShip').click(function() {
       if ($(this).attr('checked')) {

       }
   });
   ```

   A simple conditional statement (page 77) makes it easy to test the state of the checkbox and either hide or show the form fields. The *$(this)* refers to the object being clicked—the checkbox in this case. The element's *checked* attribute lets you know if the box is checked or not. If it's checked, then this attribute returns *true*; otherwise, it returns *false*. To finish this code, you just need to add the steps for hiding and showing the form fields.

4. **Add the bolded code below (lines 14–16) to your script. The completed script should look like this:**

   ```
   1   <script type="text/javascript">
   2   $(document).ready(function() {
   3       $('#name').focus();
   4       $('#paypal').click(function() {
   ```

```
5        $('#creditCard input').attr('disabled', true) ↵
6        .css('backgroundColor','#E5E5E5');
7        $('#creditCard label').css('color','#CCC');
8     });
9     $('#visa, #mastercard').click(function() {
10       $('#creditCard input').attr('disabled', false) ↵
11       .css('backgroundColor','');
12       $('#creditCard label').css('color','');
13    });
14    $('#hideShip').click(function() {
15      if ($(this).attr('checked')) {
16        $('#shipping').slideUp('fast');
17      } else {
18        $('#shipping').slideDown('fast');
19      }
20    });
21  }); // end ready()
22  </script>
```

The *$('#shipping')* refers to the <div> tag with the form fields, while the
slideUp( ) and *slideDown( )* functions (described on page 245) hide and show
the <div> tag by sliding the <div> up and out of view or down and into view.

A finished version of this tutorial—*complete_9.1.html*—is in the *chapter09*
folder. If your version isn't working, compare your code with the finished tutorial and refer to the troubleshooting steps on page 32.

Form Validation

It can be frustrating to look over feedback that's been submitted via a form on
your Web site, only to notice that your visitor failed to provide a name, email
address, or some other piece of critical information. That's why, depending on the
type of form you create, you might want to make certain information mandatory.

For instance, a form used for subscribing to an email newsletter isn't much use if
the would-be reader doesn't type in an email address for receiving the newsletter.
Likewise, if you need a shipping address to deliver a brochure or product, you'll
want to be sure that the visitor includes his address on the form.

In addition, when receiving data from a Web form, you want to make sure the data
you receive is in the correct format—a number, for example, for an order quantity, or a correctly formatted URL for a Web address. Making sure a visitor inputs
information correctly is known as *form validation*, and with JavaScript you can
identify any errors before the visitor submits incorrect information.

Basically, form validation requires checking the form fields before the form is submitted to make sure required information is supplied and that information is
properly formatted. The form's submit event—triggered when the visitor clicks a

submit button or presses Return when the cursor's in a text field—is usually where the validation occurs. If everything is fine, the form information travels, as it normally would, to the Web server. However, if there's a problem, the script stops the submission process and displays errors on the page—usually next to the problem form fields (Figure 9-5).

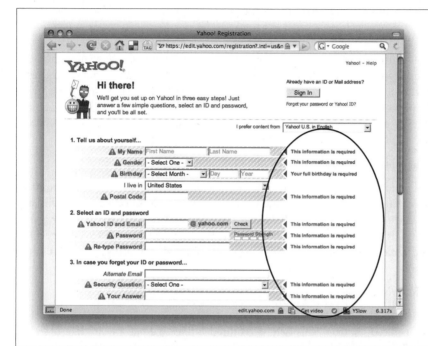

Figure 9-5:
When you sign up for a Yahoo account, you'll be faced with a sea of red error messages (circled) if you fail to fill out the form properly.

Checking to make sure a text field has been filled out is easy. As you read on page 314, you can simply access the form's *value* property (using the jQuery *val( )* function, for example) and if the value is an empty string, then the field is empty. But it gets trickier when you're checking other types of fields, like checkboxes, radio buttons, and menus. In addition, you need to write some complicated JavaScript when you want to check to make sure the visitor submits particular *types* of information, like email addresses, Zip codes, numbers, dates, and so on. Fortunately, you don't need to write the code yourself; there's a wealth of form validation scripts on the Web, and one of the best is a plug-in for the jQuery library.

jQuery Validation Plug-in

The Validation plug-in (*http://bassistance.de/jquery-plug-ins/jquery-plug-in-validation/*) is a powerful but easy-to-use jQuery plug-in created by Jörn Zaefferer. It can check a form to make sure all required fields have been filled out, and check to make sure that visitor input meets particular requirements. For example, a quantity field must contain a number, and an email field must contain an email address. If a visitor doesn't fill out a form correctly, the plug-in will display error messages describing the problems.

Here's the basic process of using the Validation plug-in:

1. **Download and attach the *jquery.js* file to the Web page containing the form you wish to validate.**

   Read "Getting Started with jQuery" (on page 170) for more info on downloading the jQuery library. The Validation plug-in uses the jQuery library, so you need to attach the *jquery.js* file to the page first.

2. **Download and attach the Validation plug-in.**

   You can find the plug-in at *http://bassistance.de/jquery-plug-ins/jquery-plug-in-validation/*. The download includes lots of extra stuff, including a demo, tests, and more. You really only need the *jquery.validate.min.js* file. (You'll also find this plug-in in the *chapter09* tutorial folder, named *jquery.validate.js*—see the tutorial on page 325). This file is just an external JavaScript file, so follow the instructions on page 24 for linking the file to your page.

3. **Add validation rules.**

   Validation rules are just the instructions that say "make this field required, make sure that field gets an email address," and so on. In other words, this step is where you assign which fields get validated and how. There are a couple of methods for adding validation rules: a simple way using just HTML (page 333), and a more flexible but slightly more complicated way using JavaScript (page 336).

4. **Add error messages.**

   This step is optional. The Validation plug-in comes with a predefined set of error messages, like "This field is required," "Please enter a valid date," "Please enter a valid number," and so on. These basic messages are fine and to the point, but you may want to customize them for your form, so that the errors provide more definite instruction for each form field—for example, "Please type your name," or "Please tell us your date of birth."

   There are two methods for adding error messages—the simple way is discussed on page 335, and the more flexible method on page 340.

Note: You can also control the style and placement of error messages as described on page 342.

---

5. **Apply the *validate( )* function to the form.**

   The plug-in includes a function that makes all of the magic happen: *validate( )*. To apply it, you first use jQuery to select the form, and then attach the function to that selection. For example, say you have a form with an ID of *signup* applied to it. The HTML might look like this:

   ```
   <form action="process.php" method="post" name="signup" id="signup">
   ```

   The simplest way to apply validation would be like this:

   ```
   $('#signup').validate();
   ```

The *validate( )* function can accept many different pieces of information that affect how the plug-in works. For example, while you can specify validation rules and error messages in the HTML of the form (see below), you can also specify rules and errors when you call the *validate( )* function. (You'll learn about this method on page 336.)

The entire JavaScript code for a very basic form validation (including the two steps already described in this section) could be as simple as this:

```
<script type="text/javascript" src="js/jquery.js"></script>
<script type="text/javascript" src="js/jquery.validate.js"></script>
<script type="text/javascript">
$(document).ready(function( ) {
  $('#signup').validate( );
});
</script>
```

Tip: Remember to always wrap your script in jQuery's *document.ready( )* function to make sure the script runs after the page's HTML is loaded (see page 218).

Basic Validation

Using the Validation plug-in can be as simple as attaching the plug-in's JavaScript file, adding a few class and title attributes to the form elements you want to validate, and applying the *validate( )* function to the form. The *validate( )* method is the easiest way to validate a form, and may be all you need for most forms. (However, if you need to control where error messages are placed on a page, or apply more than one rule to a form field, or set a minimum or maximum number of characters for a text field, you'll need to use the advanced method described on page 336.)

To add validation, follow the basic steps outlined in the previous sections (attaching the jQuery and Validation plug-in files, and so on), but in addition, you can embed rules and error messages in your form fields' HTML.

Adding validation rules

The simplest way to validate a field using the Validation plug-in is to assign one or more of the class names listed in Table 9-2 to the *form* element. The plug-in is cleverly programmed to scan the class names for each *form* element to determine if one of the validation terms are present, and if so, to apply the particular validation rule to that field.

For example, say you have a text field to collect a person's name. The basic HTML might look like this:

```
<input name="name" type="text">
```

To tell the plug-in that the field is mandatory—in other words, the form can't be submitted unless the visitor types something into this field—add a *required* class to the tag. For example, to make this text field required, add a class attribute to the tag like this:

```
<input name="name" type="text" class="required">
```

Adding a class in this way actually has nothing to do with CSS, even though usually you assign a class to a tag to provide a way of formatting that tag by creating a CSS class style. In this case, you're using a class name to provide the plug-in the information it needs to determine what kind of validation you're applying to that field.

Requiring visitors to fill out a field is probably the most common validation task, but often you also want to make sure the data supplied matches a particular format. For example, if you're asking how many widgets someone wants, you're expecting a number. To make a field both mandatory *and* contain a specific type of value, you add both the *required* class plus one of the other classes listed in Table 9-2.

For example, say you have a field asking for someone's date of birth. This information is not only required, but should also be in a date format. The HTML for that field could look like this:

```
<input name="dob" type="text" class="required date">
```

Notice that the class names—*required* and *date*—are separated by a space.

If you exclude the *required* class and just use one of the other validation types—for example, *class="date"*—then that field is optional, but if someone does type something into the field, it must be in the proper format (a date).

Tip: When you require a specific format for field information, make sure to include specific instructions in the form so your visitors know how they should add their information. For example, if you require a field to be a date, add a message near the field that says something like "Please enter a date in the format 01/25/2009."

Table 9-2. *The Validation plug-in includes methods that cover the most common validation needs*

Validation rule	Explanation
required	The field won't be submitted unless this field is filled out, checked, or selected.
date	Information must be in the format MM/DD/YYYY. For example, 10/30/2009 is considered valid, but 10-30-2009 is not.
url	Must be a full, valid Web address like *http://www.chia-vet.com*. Partial URLs like *www.chia-vet.com* or *chia-vet.com* are considered invalid.

Table 9-2. *The Validation plug-in includes methods that cover the most common validation needs (continued)*

Validation rule	Explanation
email	Must be formatted like an email address: *bob@chia-vet.com*. This class doesn't actually check to make sure the email address is real, so someone could still enter *nobody@noplace.com* and the field would pass validation.
number	Must be a number like 32 or 102.50 or even −145.5555. However, the input can't include any symbols, so $45.00 and 100,000 are invalid.
digits	Can only include positive integers. So 1, 20, 12333 are valid, but 10.33 and −12 are not valid.
creditcard	Must be a validly formatted credit card number.

Adding error messages

The Validation plug-in supplies generic error messages to match the validation problems it checks for. For example, if a required field is left blank, the plug-in displays the message "This field is required." If the field requires a date, then the message "Please enter a valid date" appears. You can, however, override these basic messages and supply your own.

The easiest way is to add a *title* attribute to the form field and supply the error message as the title's value. For example, say you're using the *required* class to make a field mandatory, like this:

```
<input name="name" type="text" class="required">
```

To supply your own message, just add a *title* attribute:

```
<input name="name" type="text" class="required" ⏎
title="Please give us your name.">
```

Normally, Web designers use the *title* attribute to increase a form field's accessibility by providing specific instructions that appear when someone mouses over the field, or for screen-reading software to read aloud. But with the Validation plug-in, you use the *title* attribute to supply the error message you wish to appear. The plug-in scans all validated fields and sees if there's a *title* attribute. If there is, then the plug-in uses the attribute's value as the error-message text.

If you use more than one validation method, you should supply a title that makes sense for either situation. For example, if you have a field that's required and that also must be a date, a message like "This field is required" doesn't make much sense if the visitor enters a date in the wrong format. Here's an example of an error message that makes sense whether the visitor leaves the field blank or enters the date the wrong way:

```
<input name="dob" type="text" class="required date" ⏎
title="Please enter a date in the format 01/28/2009.">
```

Adding validation rules and error messages by adding class names and titles to fields is easy, and it works great. But sometimes you may have more complicated validation needs; the Validation plug-in offers a second, more advanced method of adding validation to a form. For example, you may want to have different error messages based on the type of error—like one message when a field is left blank and another when the visitor enters the wrong type of information. You can't do that using the basic validation method described in this section. Fortunately, the Validation plug-in offers a second, more advanced method that lets you implement a wider range of validation rules.

For example, you must use the advanced method if you want to make sure a minimum number of characters is entered into a field. When setting a password, for instance, you might want to make sure the password is at least six characters long.

Advanced Validation

The Validation plug-in provides another way of adding validation to a form that doesn't require changing the fields' HTML. In addition, the plug-in supports a wide variety of additional options for controlling how the plug-in works. You set these options by passing an object literal (page 188) to the *validate( )* function, containing separate objects for each option. For example, to specify a validation rule, you pass one object containing the code for the rule. First, you include an opening brace directly after the first parentheses for the validation function and a closing brace directly before the closing parentheses:

```
$('idOfForm').validate({
  // options go in here
}); // end validate( );
```

These braces represent an object literal, which will contain the option settings. Using the Validation plug-in in this way gets a little confusing, and the best way to understand how the plug-in's author intended it to work is to look at a simple example, like the one in Figure 9-6.

Note: You can combine the basic validation method described on page 333 and the advanced method described here on the same form. For fields that have just one validation rule and error message, you can use the simple method since it's fast, and just use the advanced method for more complicated validation. The tutorial on page 343, for instance, uses both methods for validating a single form.

The HTML for the form in Figure 9-6 is as follows:

```
<form action="process.php" method="post" id="signup">
  <div>
    <label for="name">Name</label>
    <input name="name" type="text">
  </div>
```

```
<div>
  <label for="email">E-mail Address</label>
  <input name="email" type="text">
</div>
<div>
  <input type="submit" name="submit" value="Submit">
</div>
</form>
```

This form contains two text fields, shown in bold, one for a person's name and one for an email address. This section walks through the process of validating both of these fields using advanced rules to make sure the name field is filled and the email field is both filled in and correctly formatted.

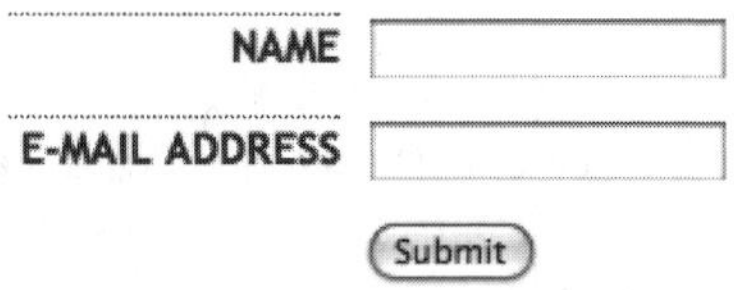

Figure 9-6:
Even with a simple form like this one, you can use the Validation plug-in's advanced options for greater control.

Note: You can find a complete list of options for the Validation plug-in at *http://docs.jquery.com/Plug-ins/Validation/validate#options*.

Advanced rules

The advanced way to specify validation rules involves passing an object (see page 188) containing the names of the form fields and the validation rule or rules you want to apply to the field. The basic structure of that object looks like this:

```
rules: {
  fieldname : 'validationType'
}
```

The object is named *rules*, and inside it you specify the fields and validation types you want to apply to the field. The entire object is then passed to the *validate( )* function. For example, in the form pictured in Figure 9-6, to make the name field mandatory you apply the *validate( )* function to the form as described on the previous page, and then pass the *rules* object to the function like this:

```
$('#signup').validate({
  rules: {
    name: 'required'
  }
}); // end validate( )
```

In this case, the field is named *name* (see the HTML on page 336), and the rule specifies that the field is required. To apply more than one validation rule to a form field, you must create another object for that field. For example, to expand the validation rules for the form in Figure 9-6, you can add a rule that would not only make the email field required, but also specify that the email address must be validly formatted:

```
1   $('#signup').validate({
2     rules: {
3       name: 'required',
4       email: {
5       required:true,
6         email:true
7       }
8     }
9   }); // end validate()
```

> **Note:** According to the rules of JavaScript object literals, you must end each name/value pair except the last one with a comma. For example, in line 3 above, *name: 'required'* must have a comma after it, because another rule (for the email field) follows it. Turn to page 188 for a refresher on how object literals work.

Lines 4–7, shown in bold, specify the rules for the email field. The field's name is *email*, as specified in the HTML (see page 337); *required:true* make the field required; and *email:true* makes sure the field contains an email address.

You can use any of the validation types listed in Table 9-2. For example, say you add a field named *birthday* to the form used in this example. To ensure that a date is entered into the field, you can expand the list of rules like this:

```
$('#signup').validate({
  rules: {
    name: 'required',
    email: {
      required:true,
      email:true
    },
    birthday: 'date'
  }
}); // end validate()
```

If you also want the birthday field to be *required*, adjust the code as follows:

```
$('#signup').validate({
  rules: {
    name: 'required',
    email: {
```

```
        required:true,
        email:true
    },
  birthday: {
   date:true,
   required:true
  }
 }
}); // end validate()
```

As mentioned earlier, one of the most powerful and useful things you can do with advanced validation rules is require visitors' entries to be a certain minimum or maximum length. For example, on a complaint report form, you may want to limit comments to, say, 200 characters in length, so your customers will get to the point instead of writing *War and Peace*. There are also rules to make sure that numbers entered are within a certain range; so if your form isn't easy enough for a caveman to do it, you won't accept birth years earlier than 1900.

- *minlength.* The field must contain *at least* the specified number of characters. For example, the rule to make sure that at least six characters are entered into a field is this:

  ```
  minlength:6
  ```

- *maxlength.* The field must contain *no more* than the specified number of characters. For example, the rule to ensure that no more than 100 characters are entered into the field looks like this:

  ```
  maxlength:100
  ```

- *rangelength.* A combination of both *minlength* and *maxlength*. Specifies both the minimum and maximum number of characters allowed in a field. For example, the rule to make sure a field contains at least 6 characters but no more than 100 is as follows:

  ```
  rangelength:[6,100]
  ```

- *min.* Requires that the field contain a number that's equal to or greater than the specified number. For example, the following rule requires that the field both contains a number and that the number is greater than or equal to 10.

  ```
  min:10
  ```

In this example, if the visitor enters *8*, the field won't validate because 8 is less than 10. Likewise, if your visitor types a word—*eight*, for example—the field won't validate and she'll get an error message.

- *max.* Like *min*, but specifies the largest number the field can contain. To make sure a field contains a number less than 1,000, for example, use the following:

  ```
  max:1000
  ```

- *range.* Combines *min* and *max* to specify both the smallest and largest numbers that the field must contain. For example, to make sure a field contains at least 10 but no more than 1,000, use this:

```
range:[10,1000]
```

- *equalTo.* Requires that a field's contents match another field. For example, on a signup form, it's common to ask a visitor to enter a password and then verify that password by typing it a second time. This way, the visitor can make sure he didn't mistype the password the first time. To use this method, you must specify a string containing a valid jQuery selector. For example, say the first password field has an ID of *password* applied to it. If you want to make sure the "verify password" field matches the first password field, you use this code:

```
equalTo: '#password'
```

Note: The Validation plug-in supports some even more advanced validation methods. To learn about them, visit *http://docs.jquery.com/Plug-ins/Validation#Validation_methods*.

You can use these advanced validation rules in combination. Just take it one field at a time. Here's an example of how they work together: Assume you have a form that includes two fields, one for creating a password, and another for confirming that password. The HTML for those two fields might look like this:

```
<input name="password" type="password" id="password">
<input name="confirm_password" type="password" id="confirm_password">
```

Both fields are required, and the password must be at least 8 characters but no more than 16. And finally, you want to make sure the "confirm password" field matches the other password field. Assuming the form has an ID of *signup*, you can validate those two fields with the following code:

```
$('#signup').validate({
  rules: {
    password: {
      required:true,
      rangelength:[8,16]
    },
    confirm_password: {
      equalTo:'#password'
    }
  }
}); // end validate()
```

Advanced error messages

As you read on page 335, you can easily add an error message for a field by adding a *title* with the error message text. However, this approach doesn't let you create

Validating with the Server

While JavaScript validation is great for quickly checking user input, sometimes you need to check in with the server to see if a field is valid. For example, say you have a signup form that lets visitors create their own username for use on the forums of your site. No two people can share the same username, so it would be helpful if you could inform the person filling out the form if the username he wants is already taken before submitting the form. In this case, you have to consult with the server to find out whether the username is available.

The Validation plug-in provides an advanced validation method, named *remote*, that lets you check in with the server. This method lets you pass both the field name and the value the visitor has typed into that field to a server-side page (like a PHP, JSP, ASP, or Cold Fusion page). The server-side page can then take that information and do something with it, such as check to see if a username is available, and then respond to the form with either a value of *true* (passed validation) or *false* (failed validation).

Assume you have a field named "username" that's both required and must not be a name currently in use on your site. To create a rule for the field (using the advanced rules method described on page 336), you can add the following to the *rules* object:

```
username : {
  required: true,
  remote: 'check_username.php'
}
```

The remote method takes a string containing the path from the current page to a page on the Web server. In this example, the page is named *check_username.php*. When the validation plug-in tries to validate this field, it sends the field's name (username) and the visitor's input to the *check_username.php*, which then determines if the username is available. If the name is available, the PHP page returns the word 'true'; if the username is already taken, the page returns the word 'false', and the field won't validate.

All of this magic takes place via the power of Ajax, which you'll learn about in Part 3. To see a working example of this validation method, visit *http://jquery.bassistance.de/validate/demo/milk*.

separate error messages for each type of validation error. For example, say a field is required and must have a number in it. You might want two different messages for each error: "This field is required", and "Please enter a number." You can't do that using the *title* attribute. Instead, you must pass a JavaScript object to the *validate( )* function.

The process is similar to creating advanced rules, as described in the previous section. The basic structure of the *messages* object is as follows:

```
messages: {
  fieldname: {
    methodType: 'Error message'
  }
}
```

In the above example, replace *fieldname* with the field you're validating, and *method-Type* with one of the assigned validation methods. For example, to combine the validation methods for the password fields and messages for each of those errors, add the following code shown in bold:

```
$('#signup').validate({
  rules: {
    password: {
      required:true,
      rangelength:[8,16]
    },
    confirm_password: {
      equalTo:'#password'
    }
  }, // end of rules
  messages: {
    password: {
      required: "Please type the password you'd like to use.",
      rangelength: "Your password must be between 8 and 16 characters long."
    },
    confirm_password: {
      equalTo: "The two passwords don't match."
    }
  } // end of messages
}); // end validate()
```

Styling Error Messages

When the Validation plug-in checks a form and finds an invalid form field, it does two things: first, it adds a class to the form field; then it adds a <label> tag containing an error message. For example, say your page has the following HTML for an email field:

```
<input name="email" type="text" class="required">
```

If you add the Validation plug-in to the page with this form and your visitor tries to submit the form without filling out the email field, the plug-in would stop the submission process and change the field's HTML, adding an additional tag. The new HTML would look like this:

```
<input name="email" type="text" class="required error">
<label for="email" generated="true" class="error">
This field is required.</label>
```

In other words, the plug-in adds the class name *error* to the form field. It also inserts a <label> tag with a class named *error* containing the error-message text.

To change the appearance of the error messages, you simply need to add a style to your style sheet defining the look for that error. For example, to make the error text bold and red, you can add this style to your style sheet:

```
label.error {
  color: #F00;
  font-weight: bold;
}
```

Since the Validation plug-in also adds an error class to the invalid form field, you can create CSS styles to format those as well. For example, to place a red border around invalid fields, you can create a style like this:

```
input.error, select.error {
  border: 1px red solid;
}
```

Note: Browsers vary significantly in their support for formatting form fields. Some browsers let you use many CSS properties to control the look of fields, while other browsers limit that control. For example, Safari 3 and earlier don't let you put a border around a checkbox. For more information on formatting form fields, visit *www.456bereastreet.com/archive/200705/why_styling_form_controls_with_css_is_problematic.*

Validation Tutorial

In this tutorial, you'll take a form and add both basic and advanced validation options to it (see Figure 9-7).

Note: See the note on page 27 for information on how to download the tutorial files.

Basic Validation

In this tutorial, you'll get started with the Validation plug-in by applying the basic validation methods described on page 333. Then you'll learn more complex validation procedures using the advanced method discussed on page 336. As you'll see, it's perfectly OK to mix and match the two approaches on the same form.

1. **In a text editor, open the file *9.2.html* in the *chapter09* folder.**

   This file contains a form with a variety of form fields, including text fields, checkboxes, radio buttons, and menus. You'll add validation to this form, but first you need to attach the validation plug-in to the page.

2. **On the blank line immediately after the <script> tag that attaches the *jquery.js* file to this page, type:**

   ```
   <script type="text/javascript" src="validation/jquery.validate.js">
   </script>
   ```

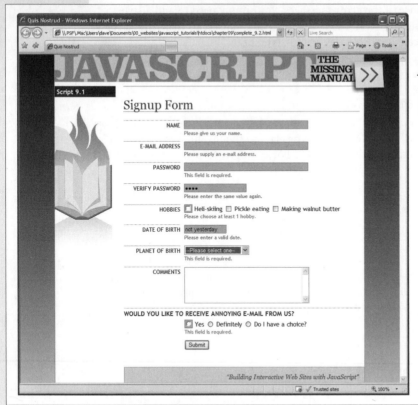

Figure 9-7:
*Don't let visitors submit
your forms incorrectly!
With a little help from the
jQuery Validation plug-in,
you can make sure that
you get the information
you're after.*

The validation plug-in is contained in a folder named *validation* in the *chapter09* folder.

This page already has another <script> tag, complete with the jQuery *ready( )* function. You just need to add the *validate( )* function to this page's form.

3. **In the blank line directly below** *$(document).ready(function( )*, **type:**

```
$('#signup').validate();
```

The form has an ID of *signup*:

```
<form action="process.php" method="post" name="signup" id="signup">
```

So *$('#signup')* uses jQuery to select that form, and *validate( )* applies the validation plug-in to the form. However, the form won't get validated until you specify some validation rules. So first, you'll make the name field required and supply a custom error message.

4. Locate the HTML for the name field— *<input name="name" type="text" id="name">*— and add *class* and *title* attributes, so the tag looks like this (changes are in bold):

```
<input name="name" type="text" id="name" ⏎
class="required" title="Please type your name.">
```

The *class="required"* part of the code lets the Validation plug-in know that this field is mandatory, while the *title* attribute specifies the error message that the visitor will see if she doesn't fill out this field.

5. Save the page, open it in a Web browser, and click Submit.

Since the name field isn't filled out, an error message appears to the right of the field (circled in Figure 9-8).

Congratulations—you've just added validation to your form using the basic method discussed on page 333. Next, you'll add another validation rule for the "date of birth" field.

Tip: If you don't see an error message and instead get a page with the headline "Form Processed," the validation didn't work and the form was submitted anyway. Go over steps 1–4 again to make sure you didn't make any typos.

Figure 9-8:
Don't worry about the appearance of the error message just yet. You'll learn how to format errors on page 352.

6. Locate the HTML for the date of birth field—*<input name="dob" type="text" id="dob">*— and add *class* and *title* attributes so the tag looks like this (changes are in bold):

```
<input name="dob" type="text" id="dob" class="date" ⏎
title="Please type your date of birth using this format: 01/19/2000">
```

Because you didn't add the *required* class, filling out this field is optional. However, if the visitor does type anything into the field, the *class="date"* tells the plug-in that the input must be formatted like a date. You use the *title* attribute again to hold the error message if this field isn't valid. Save the page and try it out in a Web browser—type something like *kjsdf* in the date of birth field and try to submit the form.

Note: If you did want to require that the visitor fill out the date of birth field *and* that they entered a valid date just add *required* to the class attribute. Just make sure *date* and *required* are separated by a space:

```
<input name="dob" type="text" id="dob"
class="date required" title="Please type your date of birth using this
format: 01/19/2000">
```

You can use the same technique for validating a menu (<select> tag).

7. Locate the HTML for the opening select tag—*<select name="planet" id="planet">*—and add *class* and *title* attributes so that the tag looks like this (changes are in bold):

```
<select name="planet" id="planet" class="required" ⏎
title="Please choose a planet.">
```

You can validate menus just like text fields by adding a validation *class* and *title* attribute.

Now it's time to try the advanced validation method.

Advanced Validation

As mentioned on page 333, there are some things you can't do with the basic validation methods, like assign different error messages for different validation problems, or require a specific number of characters for input. In these cases, you need to use the Validation plug-in's advanced approach for creating validation rules and error messages.

To start you'll add two validation rules and two different error messages for the form's email field.

1. In the JavaScript code near the top of the file, locate the line *$('#signup'). validate( );* and edit it to look like this:

```
$('#signup').validate({

}); // end validate( )
```

In other words, add opening and closing braces between the parentheses in *validate( )*, add an empty line between the braces, and add a JavaScript comment at the end. The comment is a note to identify the end of the *validate( )*

function. You'll soon be filling the script with braces and parentheses, so it can get tricky to remember which brace goes with what. This comment can help keep you from getting confused, but like all comments in code, it's optional.

Next, you'll create the basic skeleton for adding validation rules.

2. **In the empty line (between the braces) you added in the last step, type:**

```
rules: {

} //end rules
```

To make the code easier to read, you might also want to put two spaces before the *rules* and *}*. Indenting those lines makes it more visually obvious that these lines of code are part of the *validate( )* function.

This code creates an empty object, which you'll fill with specific field names and validation methods. In addition, a JavaScript comment identifies the end of the rules object. Next, you'll add rules for the email field.

3. **Edit the *validate( )* function so that it looks like this (changes are in bold):**

```
$('#signup').validate({
  rules: {
    email: {
      required: true,
      email: true
    }
  } // end rules
}); // end validate( )
```

Here, you've added another JavaScript object. The first part, *email*, is the name of the field you wish to validate and matches the field's name in the HTML. Next, two validation methods are specified—the field is required (meaning visitors must fill it in if they want to submit the form), and the input must match the form of an email address.

Now you'll add error messages for this field.

4. **Type a comma after the closing brace for the *rules* object (but before the *// end rules* comment), and then type:**

```
messages: {

} // end messages
```

This code represents yet another JavaScript object, named *messages*. This object will contain any error messages you wish to add to your form fields. Again, the comment at the end—*// end messages*—is optional. Now you'll add the actual error messages for the email field.

5. **Edit the *validate( )* function so it looks like this (the additions are in bold):**

```
1   $('#signup').validate({
2     rules: {
3       email: {
4         required: true,
5         email: true
6       }
7     }, //end rules
8     messages: {
9       email: {
10        required: "Please supply your e-mail address.",
11        email: "This is not a valid e-mail address."
12      }
13    } // end messages
14  }); // end validate(),
```

Save the page and preview it in a Web browser. Try to submit the form without filling out the email address field. You should get a "Please supply your e-mail address" error. Now, type something like "hello" into the email field and try to submit the form. This time you should get the "This is not a valid e-mail address" error.

If you don't get any error messages and, instead, end up on the "Form Processed!" page, there's a JavaScript error somewhere in your code. The most likely culprit is a missing comma after the *rules* object (see line 7), or in the *email* message object (see line 10).

Now it's time to add validation rules for the two password fields.

6. **Edit the rules object so that it looks like this (changes are in bold):**

```
1   rules: {
2     email: {
3       required: true,
4       email: true
5     },
6     password: {
7       required: true,
8       rangelength:[8,16]
9     },
10    confirm_password: {
11      equalTo:'#password'
12    }
13  }, //end rules
```

Don't miss the comma on line 5—it's necessary to separate the email rules from the password rules.

The first set of rules applies to the first password field. It makes the field mandatory and requires the password to be at least 8 but not more than 16 characters long. The second rule applies to the email confirmation field and requires that its contents match the value in the first password field (details on how these rules work can be found on page 339).

Tip: It's a good idea to save the file and test it after each step in this tutorial. That way, if the validation stops working, you know which step you made the error in.

These rules also need accompanying error messages.

7. **Edit the *messages* object so that it looks like this (changes in bold):**

```
1   messages: {
2     email: {
3       required: "Please supply an e-mail address.",
4       email: "This is not a valid email address."
5     },
6     password: {
7       required: 'Please type a password',
8       rangelength: 'Password must be between 8 and 16 characters long.'
9     },
10    confirm_password: {
11      equalTo: 'The two passwords do not match.'
12    }
13  } // end messages
```

Don't forget the comma on line 5.

At this point, you should be feeling comfortable adding rules and error messages. Next you'll add validation for the checkboxes and radio buttons.

Validating Checkboxes and Radio Buttons

Checkboxes and radio buttons usually come in groups, and typically, adding validation to several checkboxes or radio buttons in a single group is a tricky process of finding all boxes or buttons in a group. Fortunately, the Validation plug-in takes care of the hard parts, and makes it easy for you to quickly validate this form fields.

1. **Locate the HTML for the first checkbox— *<input name="hobby" type="checkbox" id="heliskiing" value="heliskiing">*— and add *class* and *title* attributes so that the tag looks like this (changes are in bold):**

   ```
   <input name="hobby" type="checkbox" id="heliskiing"
   value="heliskiing" class="required"
   title="Please check at least 1 hobby.">
   ```

   Here, you're using the basic validation technique described on page 333. You could also use the advanced technique and include the rules and error messages as part of the *validate( )* function, but if you only require one validation rule and error message, the basic technique is more straightforward and less error-prone.

In this case, all three checkboxes share the same name, so the Validation plug-in treats them as a group. In other words, this validation rule applies to *all three boxes*, even though you've only added the *class* and *title* attributes to one box. In essence, you've required that visitors checkmark at least one box before they can submit the form.

You'll do the same thing for the radio buttons at the bottom of the form.

2. **Locate the HTML for the first radio button**—*<input type="radio" name="spam" id="yes" value="yes">*—**and add** *class* **and** *title* **attributes so the tag looks like this (changes are in bold):**

```
<input type="radio" name="spam" id="yes" value="yes"
class="required" title="Please select an option">
```

A related group of radio buttons always shares the same name (*spam*, in this case), so even though you've added a rule and error message to just one button, it will apply to all three. Because the field is required, visitors must select one of the three radio buttons to submit the form.

3. **Save the file, preview it in a Web browser, and click Submit.**

You may notice something looks a bit odd: When the error messages for the checkbox and radio buttons appear, they come directly after the first checkbox and radio button (circled in Figure 9-9). Even worse, the messages appear between the form field and its label (for example, between the checkbox and the label "Heli-skiing").

The Validation plug-in places the error message directly after the form field that you apply the validation rule to. Normally, that's OK: when the message appears directly after a text field or menu, it looks fine (as in the earlier examples in this tutorial). But in this case, the message should go somewhere else, preferably after all of the checkboxes or radio buttons.

Fortunately, the Validation plug-in has a way to control the placement of error messages. You can create your own rules for error-message placement by passing another JavaScript object to the *validate( )* function.

4. **Locate the validation script you added earlier, and type a comma after the closing brace for the** *messages* **object (but before the** *// end messages* **comment). Insert a blank line after the** *messages* **object, and then type:**

```
errorPlacement: function(error, element) {
  if ( element.is(":radio") || element.is(":checkbox")) {
    error.appendTo( element.parent( ));
  } else {
    error.insertAfter(element);
  }
} // end errorPlacement
```

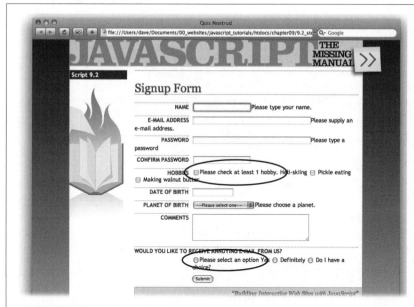

Figure 9-9:
The Validation plug-in places error messages after the invalid form field. In the case of checkboxes and radio buttons, that looks awful. In order to place the error message elsewhere, you need to provide some instruction to the plug-in's validate( ) *function.*

The Validation plug-in is programmed to accept an optional *errorPlacement* object, which is just a JavaScript function that determines where the error message is placed. The function receives both the error message and the *form* element the error applies to, so you can use a conditional statement (page 77) to check whether the form field is either a radio button of a checkbox. If it is, the error message is added to the end of the element containing the button or checkbox. In this page's HTML, a <div> tag wraps around the group of checkboxes, and another <div> tag wraps the radio buttons. So the error message is placed just before the closing </div> tag using jQuery's *appendTo( )* function (see page 182).

You're done with all of the JavaScript programming for this form. Here's the complete script, including the *$(document).ready( )* function:

```
1   $(document).ready(function() {
2     $('#signup').validate({
3       rules: {
4         email: {
5           required: true,
6           email: true
7         },
8         password: {
9           required: true,
10          rangelength:[8,16]
11        },
12        confirm_password: {equalTo:'#password'},
13        spam: "required"
```

```
14        }, //end rules
15        messages: {
16          email: {
17             required: "Please supply an e-mail address.",
18             email: "This is not a valid email address."
19          },
20          password: {
21            required: 'Please type a password',
22            rangelength: 'Password must be between 8 and 16 characters long.'
23          },
24          confirm_password: {
25            equalTo: 'The two passwords do not match.'
26          }
27        }, // end messages
28        errorPlacement: function(error, element) {
29          if ( element.is(":radio") || element.is(":checkbox")) {
30             error.appendTo( element.parent());
31          } else {
32             error.insertAfter(element);
33          }
34        } // end errorPlacement
35      }); // end validate
36   }); // end ready( )
```

Formatting the Error Messages

Now the page has working form validation, but the error messages don't look very good. Not only are they spread around the page, but they don't stand out the way they should. They'd look a lot better if they were bold, red, and appeared underneath the form field they apply to. You can make all of those formatting changes with a little simple CSS.

1. Open the file *form.css* located in the *css* folder in the *chapter09* folder. At the bottom of the file, add the following CSS rule:

```
#signup label.error {
  font-size: 0.8em;
  color: #F00;
  font-weight: bold;
  display: block;
  margin-left: 150px;
}
```

The CSS selector *#signup label.error* targets any <label> tag with a class of *error* that appears inside another element with the ID *signup*. In this case, the <form> tag has an ID *signup*, and the Validation plug-in puts error messages inside a <label> tag and adds the class *error* (see page 342). In other words, this CSS rule only applies to the error message inside this form.

The CSS properties themselves are pretty basic: first, the font size is reduced to .8 em; next, the color is changed to red, and the text is bolded. The *display: block* instruction informs the browser to treat the <label> tag as a block-level element. That is, instead of putting the error message *next* to the form field, the browser treats the error like a paragraph of its own, with line breaks above and below. Finally, to make the error message line up with the form fields (which are indented 150 pixels from the left edge of the main content area), you need to add a left margin.

To make it even clearer which fields have validation problems, you can add CSS rules to change the look of invalid form fields.

2. **Add one final rule to the *form.css* file:**

```
#signup input.error, #signup select.error {
   background: #FFA9B8;
   border: 1px solid red;
}
```

This rule highlights an invalid form field by adding a red border around its edges and a background color to the field.

That's all there is to it. Save the CSS file and preview the *9.2.html* page in a Web browser to see how the CSS affects the error messages (you may need to hit the browser's reload button to see the changes you made to the CSS file).

The final form should look like Figure 9-7. You can find a completed version of the tutorial (*complete_9.2.html*) in the *chapter09* folder, and the final CSS file (*complete_form.css*) in the *css* folder in the *chapter09* folder.

Expanding Your Interface

A Web page can feel like a long one-page brochure. Visitors are overwhelmed if there seems to be acres of text and pictures to scroll through, and they are unable to quickly get the information they need when they need it. It's up to you to provide your visitors tools to find what they're after. Using JavaScript, you can streamline your Web page and make it simpler for visitors to deal with—hiding content until it's required, and providing easier access to information.

In this chapter, you'll learn four common techniques to make your pages easier to read and use. Accordion panels and tabbed panels fit lots of information in a small space and let visitors click a tab to access content in smaller chunks. Tooltips—pop-up windows with additional information about moused-over links, form fields, and other HTML elements—provide supplemental information. Finally, sortable tables make data in your HTML tables more usable—visitors can sort the data right on the page by clicking a column header.

Hiding Information with Accordion Panels

Putting too much information on a page can overwhelm your visitors and make a Web page look crowded. JavaScript gives you many ways to present a lot of information in a small space. One technique is the *accordion* effect. An accordion lets you put content into separate panels, only one of which is visible at a time. When your visitor clicks a tab above a hidden panel, the currently visible panel disappears and the hidden panel rises into place, as Figure 10-1 illustrates.

The jQuery Accordion plug-in is a quick way to add an accordion effect to your site. Thanks to the programming power of this plug-in, creating a complex accordion is just a four-step process:

1. **Attach the Accordion plug-in and several other external JavaScript files to your page.**

   In addition to the jQuery library, you must also link to two additional files: *ui.core.js*, and *ui.accordion.js*. The *ui.core.js* file provides some basic functions that are used by all of jQuery's UI (user interface) plug-ins (see the box on page 361). The jQuery UI components, along with the Accordion plug-in itself, are available from *http://ui.jquery.com/*.

   You attach these files as you would any external JavaScript file, as described on page 24. Just make sure you attach them in order: *jquery.js*, *ui.core.js*, and *ui.accordion.js*. You'll have three <script> tags, something like this:

   ```
   <script type="text/javascript" src="js/jquery.js"></script>
   <script type="text/javascript" src="js/ui.core.js"></script>
   <script type="text/javascript" src="js/ui.accordion.js">
   ```

Note: You're not stuck with the file names supplied by the downloaded JavaScript files. For example, although the programmers of the plug-in named the file *ui.accordion.js*, you're free to rename this file to something else, like *accordion.js*. Just make sure your <script> tags use the new file name.

---

2. **Provide an HTML tag to act as a container for the accordion elements.**

   One HTML tag needs to contain the accordion tabs and panels and nothing else. A simple technique is to wrap the accordion HTML (described in the next step) in a <div> tag with an ID:

   ```
   <div id="accordion">
     <!-- accordion HTML here -->
   </div>
   ```

   Another approach is to build the accordion using a definition list (a <dl> tag), in which each accordion tab is a <dt> tag and accordion panel is <dd> tag. In this case you could add an ID to the <dl> tag: *<dl id="accordion">*. (See *www.htmldog.com/reference/htmltags/dl/* for information on definition lists.)

   You can add more than one accordion to a page. Make sure to provide a unique ID for each accordion's container element.

3. **Structure the HTML for the accordion.**

   The Accordion plug-in expects your HTML to be structured in a specific way. There must be one tag that acts as the *trigger*—the tab that opens an accordion panel. Then, the element following that tab acts as the accordion panel.

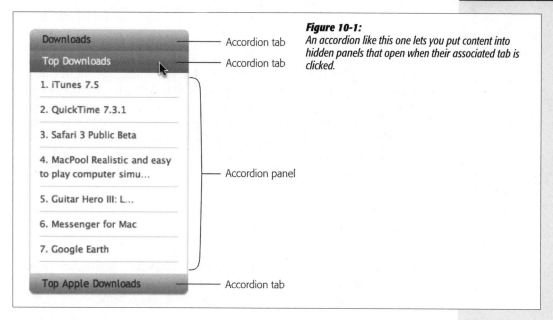

Figure 10-1:
An accordion like this one lets you put content into hidden panels that open when their associated tab is clicked.

One simple way is to use a heading tag for the trigger, followed by a <div> for each accordion element. For example:

```
<div id="accordion">
   <h2>Accordion Tab 1</h2>
   <div>Content for accordion panel 1 goes here</div>
   <h2>Accordion Tab 2</h2>
   <div>Content for accordion panel 2 goes here</div>
</div>
```

In this case, the <h2> tags are the tabs, while each <div> is an accordion panel. You can, of course, put anything you want inside each accordion panel, so you could have photos, paragraphs, and any other element or content inside the <div>.

Another approach is to use a definition list like this:

```
<dl id="accordion">
   <dt>Accordion Tab 1</dt>
   <dd>Content for accordion panel 1 goes here</dd>
   <dt>Accordion Tab 2</dt>
   <dd>Content for accordion panel 2 goes here</dd>
</dl>
```

The <dt> tag can only accept inline content (like the <strong> or <em> tags), but the <dd> tag can accept any block-level element, so you can add paragraphs, headlines, <div>s, and images to the <dd> tag to create an accordion panel that looks like a little Web page of its own.

4. **Apply the *accordion( )* function to the container element, and then identify the tab elements.**

To create the accordion effect, you must use jQuery to select the accordion container and apply the accordion function to it. Of course, you must put this function call inside the obligatory *$(document).ready( )* jQuery function (page 218) to make sure that the page's HTML has loaded first. In addition, you need to tell the accordion function which element acts as the accordion panel tabs. For example, if you use an <h2> tag as the tab (the element's that clicked to show an accordion panel), then the JavaScript code should look like this:

```
$(document).ready(function() {
  $('#accordion').accordion({
    header: 'h2'
  });
});
```

Here, a <div> tag with an ID of *accordion* is the container, and the *accordion( )* function is applied to it. The *accordion( )* function takes a JavaScript object literal (page 188) as its argument—that object holds any options you wish to set for the accordion.

In this case, only the *header* option is needed, and that option requires a string that matches the element to be used as a tab. For example *header: 'h2'* means that the accordion panel tabs are <h2> tags, whereas *header:'.tab'* tells the accordion function to use any tag with the class *tab* as the tab.

Customizing an Accordion

The normal behavior of the Accordion plug-in may be all you need, but you can also change the way the accordion works by setting various options of the *accordion( )* function. In fact, you've already seen an example of that. In step 4 in the previous section, you passed an object literal to the function containing the *header* option to assign the element used as accordion tabs like this:

```
$('#accordion').accordion({
  header: 'h2'
});
```

To customize the accordion further, you can pass additional options (described below) to the function. For example, to make a panel open when the mouse moves over a tab, you'd add the *event* option with a value of *mouseover* to the object literal like this:

```
$('#accordion').accordion({
  header: 'h2',
  event: 'mouseover'
});
```

Note: For more information on object literals and how to create them, see page 188.

- **Accordion height.** Normally, the overall height of an accordion depends on the height of each accordion tab and the height of the tallest accordion panel (in other words, the panel with the most stuff in it). The plug-in displays accordion panels at the same height as the tallest panel, which makes the accordion as a whole a consistent height. So, as a visitor clicks on that accordion's various tabs to reveal new panels, the accordion doesn't continually grow or shrink to fit the different amounts of content in each.

  If you'd rather the accordion change heights when you display panels with varying amounts of content, you can set the *autoheight* option to false:

  ```
  autoheight: false
  ```

Note: There are even more options available to customize the accordion plug-in. Visit *http://docs.jquery. com/UI/Accordion/accordion#options* for details.

- **Triggering event.** Usually, an accordion panel opens when a visitor clicks an accordion tab. In other words, the click event (page 203) triggers the action of opening the panel (and hiding the currently visible panel). You can assign a different event using the *event* option. The most commonly used alternative to the click event for accordions is the mouseover event; in this way, simply mousing over an accordion tab will open its associated panel. You can assign a new event like this:

  ```
  event: 'mouseover'
  ```

- **Initially open panel.** The Accordion plug-in opens the top accordion panel when the page loads. However, you can change this so any of the accordion panels is open, or so no panels are open, when the page loads. A simple way to make sure an accordion panel is open is to first give a class to its tab (for example, the <h2> or <dt> tag that opens the panel):

  ```
  <h2 class="open">Accordion Tab</h2>
  ```

  Then, assign the class selector to the *accordion( )* function's active option:

  ```
  active: '.open'
  ```

  This option is part of the object literal that's passed to the *accordion( )* function. (You'll see this technique in action in the tutorial on page 360.)

  Most Web designers make sure that one accordion panel is open when the page loads, so the visitor doesn't have to click anything to see content; however, it's also possible (if your design warrants it) to start with all accordion panels closed. To do so, set the option to *false*:

  ```
  active: false
  ```

• **Applying a class to the currently selected Tab.** You may want the tab of the currently opened panel to be highlighted—a kind of "you are here" indicator. You can tell the accordion plug-in to assign a particular class to a selected tab, so that when you click the tab to open its panel, the class is applied to the tab element, and when you click on a different tab, the class is removed. To do this, set the Accordion plug-in's *selectedClass* option like this:

```
selectedClass:'current'
```

You can use any class name you'd like (in this example, it's *current*) and create a class style in your CSS that defines the look of that style. That way, when someone clicks the tab, that style is applied to the tab as long as its panel is open. (You'll see this in action in the tutorial.)

The visual appearance of the accordion is controlled entirely by CSS. You just create the appropriate CSS styles to format the accordion tabs and panels. A good approach is to use a descendent selector (see page 176) that lets you control the appearance of just the particular tags inside the accordion. For example, say you created a <div> tag with an ID of *accordion* to hold the accordion tabs and panels. Each tab is an <h2> tag and each panel is a <div> tag. A descendent selector to format the tabs would be *#accordion h2*, while the style for formatting the panels would be *#accordion div*.

Tip: The Accordion plug-in creates tabs that stack vertically, one above the other. Another plug-in, the Horizontal Accordion plug-in, lets you put the tabs side by side. You can find out more about this plug-in at *http://dev.portalzine.de/index.?/Horizontal_Accordion*.

Accordion Tutorial

In this tutorial, you'll take a basic set of headlines and <div>s and turn them into a collapsible accordion, like the one in Figure 10-3. The HTML for the page is very simple: A <div> tag with an ID of *accordion* wraps around all of the elements of the accordion. Each accordion tab (the part you click to see the accordion content) is an <h2> tag, while each accordion fold (the area with the content) is a <div> tag containing one or more <p> tags. Once you add all the code for the accordion, clicking an <h2> tag will reveal the <div> that follows it.

Note: See the note on page 27 for information on how to download the tutorial files.

---

1. **In a text editor, open the file *10.1.html* in the *chapter10* folder.**

   This file already contains a link to the jQuery file, and the *$(document).ready( )* function (page 218). But you also have to link additional files to build the accordion.

2. **Click in the empty line following the <script> tag and add two more <script> tags:**

   ```
   <script type="text/javascript" src="../js/ui/ui.core.js"></script>
   <script type="text/javascript" src="../js/ui/ui.accordion.js"></script>
   ```

The jQuery UI Project

The Accordion plug-in is part of a coordinated effort known as jQuery UI. An official project of the jQuery team, jQuery UI aims to provide plug-ins that solve basic user interface problems: accordions, tabs (page 364), dialog boxes, calendar widgets, and draggable page elements. The project has its own Web site (*http://ui.jquery.com/*), where you can find the latest code, along with demonstrations and a link to documentation on the main jQuery web site.

Each individual plug-in deals with a specific problem—for example, the *ui.accordion.js* plug-in lets you create the type of accordion explained in this section. The UI Web site gives you two ways to download the plug-in files. When getting started, is best to download the "development bundle" from this page: *http://ui.jquery.com/download*. The development bundle contains lots of files, including examples and 3 different versions of the plugins—use the *minified* versions. Each plug-in is a separate file, you need to include the file for each type of user interface element you want to have on a page (tabs, accordion, calendar widget, and so on).

In addition, each plug-in file depends on a basic file named *ui.core.js* that includes functions commonly used by all of the UI plug-ins. In other words, just as a jQuery plug-in depends on the basic *jquery.js* file to work, the UI plug-ins depend on the *ui.core.js* file to work. This simply means that you not only have to link to the main jQuery library file, but also the *ui.core.js* file whenever you want to use a UI plug-in. For example, say you want to add an accordion and a calendar widget to the same page. You need to use two

UI plug-ins, plus the jQuery library file and the *ui.core.js* file. So, in the <head> of your document, you use four <script> tags to link to these files. For example:

```
<script type="text/javascript"
src="jquery.js"></script>
<script type="text/javascript" src="ui.
core.js"></script>
<script type="text/javascript" src="ui.
accordion.js"></script>
<script type="text/javascript" src="ui.
datepicker.js"></script>
```

You can also create one file that contains just the plug-ins you want to use from this page: *http://ui.jquery.com/download_builder*. The download builder lets you hand-pick the plug-ins you use and then creates a single external JavaScript file containing the components you requested. This approach is handy if you know exactly which components you want to use. If you use all of the components, the file is pretty huge (over 200k), and you probably won't find yourself needing all of the different plug-ins on a single site. The best approach is to use the individual plug-in files as you build a site; once you're finished with the site, you can then go to the download builder, create a file with just the plug-ins you're using on your site, and then replace the individual files with that one. (Or you can just leave the individual files, and skip the download builder entirely!)

Check the jQuery UI site often, since you'll probably find more useful user interface plug-ins added as the project grows.

As described on page 356, the first file provides additional programming that the *ui.accordion.js* plug-in needs. Now you're ready to set up another script to turn this page's HTML into an interactive accordion.

3. **Hit Enter (or Return) and add another <script> tag with the *$(document). ready( )* function:**

```
<script type="text/javascript">
$(document).ready(function() {

}); // end ready()
</script>
```

See page 218 if you need a refresher on jQuery's *$(document).ready( )* function. Now you'll call the accordion function.

4. **Inside the *$(document).ready( )* function, add the code below in bold:**

```
$(document).ready(function() {
   $('#accordion').accordion({

   });
});
```

In this case *$('#accordion')* identifies the <div> tag that contains the accordion elements. The accordion doesn't do anything yet—you need to identify which elements will act as the tabs of the accordion. (This example uses <h2> tags, but you can just as easily use an <a> tag or any tag with a particular class applied to it.)

5. **Add *header:'h2'* inside the accordion function, so the script now looks like this:**

```
$(document).ready(function() {
   $("#accordion").accordion({
      header:'h2'
   });
});
```

If you save the file now, and preview it in a Web browser, the top accordion panel should be open and the bottom two closed (Figure 10-2). The Accordion plug-in lets you control which accordion panel is opened when the page loads, but to do that you must first add a class name to the tab of the panel you wish to open. In other words, you need to add a class to a <h2> tag in this page. For this example, you'll make it so the bottom panel is open when the page loads.

6. **In the HTML, locate the *<h2>Accordion 3</h2>* and add *class="open"* to the <h2> tag so that it looks like this:**

```
<h2 class="open">Accordion 3</h2>
```

The class name (here, *open*) simply provides a way of informing the accordion plug-in which panel to show first. You could use any class name. Next, you need to tell the *accordion( )* function which name you used.

7. **In the script, inside the *accordion( )* function add a comma after *header:'h2'*, hit the Enter key, and type:**

```
active:'.open'
```

You don't actually have to use a class name, but you do need to provide a jQuery selector that uniquely identifies which tab to open. In this case, you need to include the period—*.open*—to identify the class selector you're using. Save the file and preview it in a Web browser. Now you'll see that the last panel is open when the page loads.

Figure 10-2:
Adding an accordion to a Web page requires nothing more than some basic HTML, jQuery, the Accordion plug-in, and a few lines of code.

Finally, you'll tell the Accordion plug-in to add a class to the currently selected tab. You can then use CSS to style that tab to give it a unique "I am selected" style.

8. **Add a comma after the line of code you added in the last step (line 5 below), and add the code in line 6 below:**

```
1    <script type="text/javascript">
2    $(document).ready(function() {
```

```
3    $("#accordion").accordion({
4        header:'h2',
5        active:'.open',
6        selectedClass:'current'
7    });
8    });
9    </script>
```

Now, when the page is viewed in a Web browser, the Accordion plug-in adds the class *current* to the <h2> tag when it's clicked. You won't see anything yet, however, since the style for that hasn't been created.

9. **Open the file *accordion.css*, and add the following CSS rule to the bottom:**

```
#accordion h2.current {
    background: #036;
}
```

Save all the *accordion.css* file and the *10.1.html* file, and preview the Web page in a browser. Now the selected tab has a dark blue background (see Figure 10-3).

Organizing Information in Tabbed Panels

Tabbed panels provide another approach to displaying lots of content in a compact space (see Figure 10-4). Each tab has an associated panel; clicking the tab displays the panel and its contents. In other words, tabbed panels achieve the same goal as an accordion, but present the tabs in a different way—straight along the top of the panel. Another jQuery UI component—the Tabs plug-in—makes it easy to add tabbed panels to a page.

Just follow these basic steps:

1. **Attach the necessary external JavaScript files to your page.**

In addition to the jQuery library, you must also link to two additional files: *ui.core.js* and *ui.accordion.js*. As with the Accordion plug-in, you'll need the *ui.core.js* file, which is required by all jQuery's UI plug-ins (see the box on page 361). Finally, the Tabs plug-in (also available from *http://ui.jquery.com/*) provides the tabbed panel functionality.

You attach these files as you would any external JavaScript file (see page 24); just make sure you attach them in order: *jquery.js*, *ui.core.js*, and *ui.tabs.js*. In other words, you'll have four script tags, something like this:

```
<script type="text/javascript" src="js/jquery.js"></script>
<script type="text/javascript" src="js/ui.core.js"></script>
<script type="text/javascript" src="js/ui.tabs.js">
```

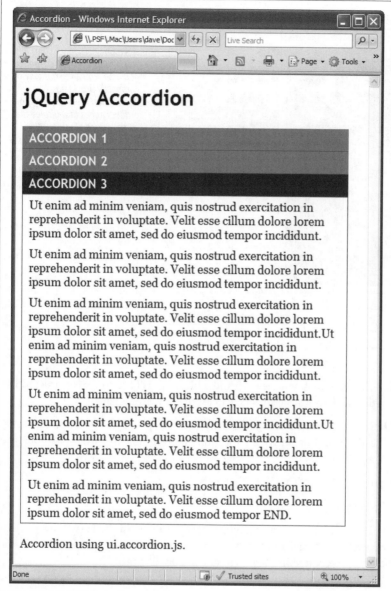

Figure 10-3:
*The Accordion plug-in
provides enough options to
control which accordion panel
displays when the page loads
and apply a style to the
currently selected accordion
tab.*

2. **Structure the HTML for the tabs.**

A group of tabs is represented by a bulleted list (<ul> tag) and each tab is a single list item (<li> tag). The <li> tag should contain the text you want to appear on the tab—for example, the basic HTML for the tabs pictured in Figure 10-4 could start off like this:

```
<ul id="tabs">
  <li>Description</li>
```

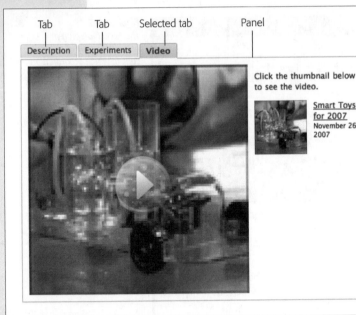

Tab   Tab   Selected tab   Panel

Description   Experiments   Video

Click the thumbnail below
to see the video.

Smart Toys
for 2007
November 26th,
2007

Figure 10-4:
*A tabbed panel (like this one
from www.
stevespanglerscience.com) lets
you display content one panel
at a time. You'll see this way of
compactly providing
information used frequently on
product pages that display the
same groups of information
from page to page, like
"Product Description,"
"Technical Details," and
"Product Options."*

```
    <li>Experiments</li>
    <li>Video</li>
</ul>
```

As you'll see in step 4, you need to add a bit more HTML to this unordered list, but starting with this basic structure helps prevent errors later.

You'll eventually need a way to identify this group of links using jQuery (step 5), so you've supplied an ID for the <ul> tag—*tabs* in this example—but you can use any ID you want.

Next, you'll add the HTML for the panels.

3. **Add the HTML for the panels.**

Each tab should have an associated panel represented in the HTML by a <div> tag, and each <div> needs an ID that uniquely identifies it. So the basic HTML for the tabs you created in the previous step goes like this:

```
<div id="description">
    <!—HTML for panel #1  goes in here -->
</div>
<div id="experiments">
    <!—HTML for panel #2 goes in here -->
</div>
<div id="video">
    <!—HTML for panel #3 goes in here -->
</div>
```

Of course, since a <div> tag can hold any HTML, you can add any content you wish inside each panel—headlines, paragraphs, images, video, and so on.

4. **Add a link from each tab to each panel.**

   Besides being useful for JavaScript and CSS, an ID added to a HTML tag also acts as a linked anchor, which lets you link directly to that element. For example, *<a href="#description">Description</a>* creates a link that, when clicked, scrolls the page to the element that has an ID of *description.* (See *www.w3.org/ TR/html4/struct/links.html#h-12.2.3* for more information, and an example of this technique.) The # symbol is placed before the ID of the element you wish to link to. An anchor is one way to jump to a particular spot in a very long Web page—you usually see them used on Web pages with long glossaries.

   With the Tabs plug-in, you link from a tab to the anchor on the related panel. In other words, each tab gets a link pointing to the panel's ID. So, for example, the list you created in step 3 above gets links like this:

   ```
   <ul id="tabs">
    <li><a href="#description">Description</a></li>
    <li><a href="#experiments">Experiments</a></li>
    <li><a href="#video">Video</a></li>
   </ul>
   ```

   Using linked anchors in this way has one big benefit—if someone doesn't have JavaScript available, the links simply act like anchors normally do. That is, without JavaScript, all of the panels will be visible, and clicking a link on a tab simply makes the browser scroll to the appropriate location on the page.

   Tip: You can actually put the unordered list containing the tabs and links to the panel elements anywhere on the page. The tabs don't have to appear directly on top of the panels.

---

5. **Apply the *tabs( )* function to the <ul> tag containing the tabs.**

   As with all things jQuery, you need to first add the *$(document).ready( )* function, then include the function call:

   ```
   <script type="text/javascript">
   $(document).ready(function( ) {
     $('#tabs').tabs( );
   });
   </script>
   ```

   In this example, *$('#tabs')* selects an element with an ID of *tabs* (see the <ul> tag in step 2 on page 365). You should change this to match your markup, so if you added the ID of *tabGroup* to the <ul> tag, you'd use this jQuery selector: *$('#tabGroup').*

The *tabs( )* function takes care of the rest, but you still need to create a style sheet to format the tabs and panels and also hide the panel groups not currently on display. You'll cover that next.

Formatting Tabs and Panels

After you complete the steps in the previous section, your tabs won't really seem to do anything. In fact, all of the tabbed panels will be visible, and the tabs will still look like a bulleted list of items, not an orderly, side-by-side arrangement of tabs. You must create CSS styles to really make the tabbed panels look right. Fortunately, the Tabs plug-in automatically updates your HTML so when the *tabs( )* function is called, the plug-in adds class names to the different tabs and panel elements. The <ul> tag, the <li> tags for the tabs, and the <div> tags that contain the panel content each have a different class applied to them (see Figure 10-5). Using CSS, you can use these classes to make the tabs and panels look like Figure 10-4.

A required class style

You'll create various styles to format the tabs and panels, but there's one style that you *must* include in your style sheet:

```
.ui-tabs-hide { display: none; }
```

The *ui-tabs-hide* class is applied to every panel (<div> tag) except the currently displayed panel. Unfortunately, the Tabs plug-in doesn't automatically hide those panels, so you need to make the CSS do it. This simple CSS rule hides (*display: none*) any tag with the *ui-tabs-hide* class applied to it. Don't leave this rule out of your style sheet; otherwise, you'll see all of the panels all the time.

The tab group

The Web browser already applies some basic formatting to the <ul> tag that contains the individual tabs; <ul> tags are usually indented and include bullet icons to the left of each list item. If you wish to change the look of the <ul> tags on your page, here's a simple CSS style that eliminates those formatting rules from the group of tabs:

```
.ui-tabs-nav {
    margin: 0;
    padding: 0;
    list-style: none;
}
```

Tabs

Each tab is represented by an <li> tag. You can set the basic look of a tab with the descendent selector *.ui-tabs-nav li*. To make the tabs appear side-by-side, either

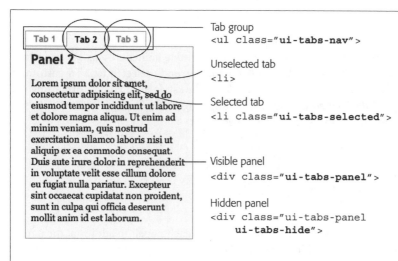

Tab group
`<ul class="ui-tabs-nav">`

Unselected tab
`<li>`

Selected tab
`<li class="ui-tabs-selected">`

Visible panel
`<div class="ui-tabs-panel">`

Hidden panel
`<div class="ui-tabs-panel
    ui-tabs-hide">`

Figure 10-5:
The Tabs plug-in dynamically adds class names to the different tags you use to create tabbed panels. In addition, the plug-in automatically adds an empty <span> at the end of each <a> tag inside a tab. This provides another tag you can attach a style to. For example, you can add a background image to the <a> tag that includes the left side of a rounded corner, and another background image on the <span> to create graphical rounded tab corners. You can create the style .ui-tabs-nav a span to style that <span> tag.

float the *li* elements or use *display:inline* to make the tabs appear in a line. For example:

```
.ui-tabs-nav li {
    padding: 0;
    margin: 0 5px 0 0;
    float: left;
}
```

This style removes any padding around the <li> tag, removes all but the right margin (five pixels, to add a bit of space between each tab), and floats the list items so they appear next to each other.

Another important part of each tab is the <a> tag inside the <li> tag. By removing any padding from the <li> tag and setting the <a> tag to be a block-level element (*display: block*), you can make the <a> tag look like a tab by adding some padding and borders to it like this:

```
.ui-tabs-nav a {
    text-decoration: none;
    display: block;
    padding: 5px 15px 3px 15px;
    border: 1px solid #999;
    border-bottom: none;
}
```

The *text-decoration:none* removes the underline that appears below links, while the other style properties create the border and spacing that make up the tab pictured in Figure 10-5. Of course, you can add additional properties such as a font, font color, background color, and so on to improve the look of the basic tab.

Tip: You can add a rollover effect to the links by creating a style named *.ui-tabs-nav a:hover.*

When a tab is clicked, the Tabs plug-in adds the style named *ui-tabs-selected* to the <li> tag, which lets you create a look for the currently selected tab. To customize the look of that tab, create either a *.ui-tabs-selected* style or, if you're formatting the <a> tag, *.ui-tabs-selected a* style. For example, to add a background color to the links, you could add this style to your style sheet:

```
.ui-tabs-selected a {
  background-color: #FF36A4;
}
```

Panels

The Tabs plug-in adds the class *ui-tabs-panel* to each panel. In addition, the panels that aren't currently visible have the class *ui-tabs-hide* applied to them (see "A required class style" on page 368). To create the look of a visible panel, just add a *.ui-tabs-panel* style to your style sheet. Generally, you'll want to add some padding to the style (to indent the content from the edge of the panel), a border, and perhaps a background color. In addition, if you floated the <li> tags as suggested on page 369, make sure you add a *clear:left* style. Here's an example:

```
.ui-tabs-panel {
    clear: left;
    border: 1px solid #999;
    padding: 10px;
    background-color: #FFC;
}
```

If you want to make the panel a set width, you can add a *width* property to the style (for example *width:500px*).

Customizing the Tabs Plug-in

The Tabs plug-in has many different features—including the ability to load content dynamically from a Web server into a tab panel—and you can set many different options to control how the tabs work. However, Web designers use two options more often than any others: choosing the panel that's initially visible, and assigning a different event to the tab.

Tip: For more examples of tab options, see *http://docs.jquery.com/UI/Tabs/tabs#options.*

Selecting a tab when the page loads

Normally, the Tabs plug-in selects the first tab and panel when the page loads. But you may want to have the second, third, or last panel visible instead. To do this, you just pass an object literal (page 188) to the *tabs( )* function with the option *selected* set to the index value of the tab whose panel you wish to display. For example, say the tabs are contained in an unordered list with the ID *tabs*. The JavaScript code *$('#tabs').tabs( )* will create the tabbed panels, but say you want the second instead of the first panel displayed when the page loads. You can use this code instead:

```
$('#tabs').tabs({
   selected:1
});
```

The *{ selected:1 }* is the object literal, *selected* is the Tabs plug-in option, and *1* indicates the second tab (the first tab is 0). In addition, you can start the page with no panels visible by setting the *selected* option to *null* like this:

```
$('#tabs').tabs({
   selected:null
});
```

When no panels are visible, if a visitor clicks a tab, that panel will pop into view.

Note: You can also "link" to a particular tab by adding the panel's ID to the page link. For example, say you add a tab to a file named *products.html*. On that page, there's a group of tabbed panels, and one of the panels (a <div> tag) has an ID of *panel3*. The link *products.html#panel3* will load the *products.html* page *and* open that panel.

Using a different event to open a panel

You may want to use an event other than the *click* event to open a panel. For example, you can make a panel open when the visitor mouses over a tab, or even double-clicks a tab. To set a new event, you pass the *event* option, along with a string containing the event name, as part of an object literal sent to the *tabs( )* function:

```
$('#tabs').tabs({
   event:'mouseover'
});
```

You can use any of the events commonly used with links (see page 203) such as *click, mouseover, doubleclick,* or *focus.*

Automating the display of panels

A visitor usually accesses a panel by clicking its associated tab, but you may want to create a kind of slideshow effect—displaying each panel in order after a slight delay. For example, perhaps you've created a tabbed panel group, where each tab represents a different part of a portfolio ("Web Design," "Print Design," and so on). Each panel has thumbnails displaying examples of each type of work. You can display a panel, wait a few seconds, and then open the next panel. To create a slideshow like this, you need to call the *tabs( )* function a second time, and pass two arguments to it: the string *'rotate'* and the time, in milliseconds, before the next panel is displayed.

For example, say you want to display each panel for five seconds and then move on to the next:

```
$('#tabs').tabs();
$('#tabs').tabs('rotate',5000);
```

The first line of code creates the tabbed panels, while the second line starts the rotation effect.

Tabbed Panels Tutorial

In this tutorial, you'll take a basic unordered list and a series of <div> tags and create a set of tabbed panels like the one illustrated in Figure 10-6.

Note: See the note on page 27 for information on how to download the tutorial files.

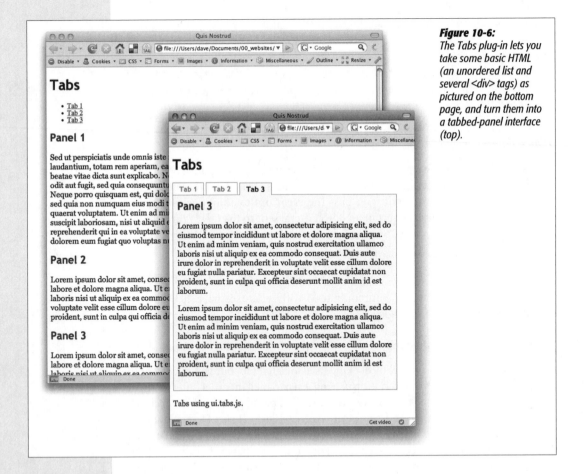

Figure 10-6:
The Tabs plug-in lets you take some basic HTML (an unordered list and several <div> tags) as pictured on the bottom page, and turn them into a tabbed-panel interface (top).

1. In a text editor, open the file *10.2.html* in the *chapter10* folder.

   Before you start adding any JavaScript to this page, you'll modify the HTML a bit. First, you'll add an ID to the <ul> tag so you can later easily use jQuery to select it and use the Tabs plug-in with it.

2. Locate the <ul> tag and add the ID *tabSet* so that it looks like this:

   ```
   <ul id="tabSet">
   ```

   On this page there are also three <div> tags. Each <div> represents one panel and is associated with one of the list items in the bulleted list. Each div also has an ID—for example, *<div id="panel1">*. To make the Tabs plug-in work, you must add links from the list item to each panel.

3. Add a link inside each list item so the unordered list looks like this (changes in bold):

   ```
   <ul id="tabSet">
     <li><a href="#panel1">Tab 1</a></li>
     <li><a href="#panel2">Tab 2</a></li>
     <li><a href="#panel3">Tab 3</a></li>
   </ul>
   ```

   You've just added links to each <div> tag. These links act like anchors, so clicking the link scrolls the page to the proper div. The Tabs plug-in uses this information to know which tab goes with which panel. Now it's time to add some JavaScript.

4. Locate the empty line directly before the closing </head> tag, and add the following code:

   ```
   1   <script type="text/javascript" src="../js/jquery.js"></script>
   2   <script type="text/javascript" src="../js/ui/ui.core.js"></script>
   3   <script type="text/javascript" src="../js/ui/ui.tabs.js"></script>
   4   <script type="text/javascript">
   5   $(document).ready(function() {
   6
   7   });
   8   </script>
   ```

   The first three lines link to the external JavaScript files: the jQuery library, the *ui.core.js* file that all jQuery's UI plug-ins use (see the box on page 361), and the *ui.tabs.js* file that contains all the programming magic to produce the tabbed panels. The last four lines should also look familiar by now: they set up a new script to run when the page's HTML loads.

5. Inside the *$(document).ready( )* function (line 6 in step 4), type:

   ```
   $('#tabSet').tabs();
   ```

If you save the file now and preview it in a Web browser, you won't actually see anything happen. You need to add one crucial CSS style to make the whole thing work.

6. **Open the file *tabs.css*, and add the following style:**

```
.ui-tabs-hide {
   display: none;
}
```

The Tabs plug-in applies the class *ui-tabs-hide* to each of the panels that aren't visible when the page loads. To actually hide those panels, you need to include this CSS rule. Save the page now and preview it in a Web browser, and you'll see that just the first panel is visible. Click the Tab 2 link, and you'll see the second panel pop into view and the first disappear. Next, you'll get rid of the margins around the unordered list, remove the bullets, and make the tabs appear side-by-side.

7. **Add two more styles to the *tabs.css* file:**

```
.ui-tabs-nav {
    margin: 0;
    padding: 0;
    list-style: none;
    zoom: 1;
}
.ui-tabs-nav li {
    padding: 0;
    margin: 0 5px 0 0;
    float: left;
}
```

Most of the properties listed here should make sense (see "Formatting Tabs and Panels" on page 368 for more details). The *.ui-tabs-nav* style applies to the <ul> tag, while the *.ui-tabs-nav li* style applies to the list items (<li> tags) that represent the actual tabs.

Note: You might be wondering about the *zoom:1* style declaration above. It's an IE-only property that's used to fix various Internet Explorer display problems. In this case, without this property IE would take the bottom margin from the <h1> tag above the tabs and place it between the tabs and panels, creating a big empty space between the two. (There's a reason these types of weird problems are called *bugs*.) For more on this workaround, visit *www.satzansatz.de/cssd/onhavinglayout.html*.

Now, it's time to create the actual tab look by formatting the link within each <li> tag.

8. **Add the following style to the *tabs.css* file:**

```
.ui-tabs-nav a {
   font-family: "Trebuchet MS", Arial, Helvetica, sans-serif;
```

```
    font-weight: bold;
    color: #999;
    text-decoration: none;
    display: block;
    padding: 5px 15px 3px 15px;
    border: 1px solid #999;
    border-bottom: none;
}
```

The first three properties just set various font attributes. By setting the *text-decoration* property to *none*, you remove the underline beneath a link. The *display:block* declaration turns the link into a block-level element, which lets you add top and bottom padding as well as treat the entire area of the link (even the space around the text) as clickable. In other words, it lets you create a bigger, clickable area. Finally, the last two properties set a border around the link, and then remove the bottom border. (As you'll see next, the panels also have a border around them, so a bottom border on the tabs would create an unattractive double border line below each tab— the tab's bottom border resting on top of the panel's top border.)

You'll format the panel next.

9. **Add another style to the stylesheet:**

```
.ui-tabs-panel {
    clear: left;
    border: 1px solid #999;
    margin: 0;
    padding: 10px;
    background: #FFC;
    width: 500px;
}
```

Because the tabs are floated to the left, the panels will try to wrap around their right side. The *clear:left* declaration forces the panels to drop below the tabs— exactly where they belong. The *padding* setting adds white space around the inside of the panel so the content doesn't touch the panel borders. This style also adds a background color and sets a width for the panel. If you don't set a width, the panel will grow to fit the available space on the page.

Note: If you're not completely comfortable with floats, you can get up to speed quickly at *http://css.maxdesign.com.au/floatutorial/*.

If you save the CSS file and preview the *10.2.html* page in a Web browser, you should see something like Figure 10-7. Click a tab to display another panel. The tab of the currently visible panel doesn't look any different than the other tabs. The final step is to make that tab look more like the panel, to create a "you've clicked this tab" effect.

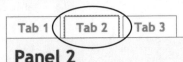

Tab 1 | **Tab 2** | **Tab 3**

Panel 2

Lorem ipsum dolor sit amet, consectetur adipisicing elit, sed do eiusmod tempor incididunt ut labore et dolore magna aliqua. Ut enim ad minim veniam, quis nostrud exercitation ullamco laboris nisi ut aliquip ex ea commodo consequat. Duis aute irure dolor in reprehenderit in voluptate velit esse cillum dolore eu fugiat nulla pariatur. Excepteur sint occaecat cupidatat non proident, sunt in culpa qui officia deserunt mollit anim id est laborum.

Figure 10-7:
Firefox adds a fuzzy outline around a clicked link (circled). That's how that browser shows that the link has the focus. If you want to eliminate that outline, just add the following style to your style sheet: .ui-tabs-nav a: focus { outline: none; }.

10. Finally, add one last style to *tabs.css*:

```
.ui-tabs-selected a {
  color: #000;
  background: #FFC;
  position: relative;
  top: 1px;
}
```

The Tabs plug-in adds the class name *ui-tabs-selected* to the currently selected tab's <li> tag (see page 370). This style applies to an <a> tag inside the current tab. First, the text color is made black and the background color is set to match the background of the panel. In addition, to make the tab appear as part of the panel (as if they're connected), you need to move the tab so that it appears on top of the panel's top border. To do that, you change the position property of the link and set its top position to one pixel. This setting change moves the link down from its current position by one pixel, and stacks the link on top of the border, giving the appearance that the tab and panel are joined.

Save the file and preview the Web page in a browser. The final product should look like Figure 10-6. If it doesn't, you can compare your work to the *complete_10.2.html* page and the *complete_tabs.css* file located in the *chapter10* folder of the tutorials.

Tooltips

Tooltips are common interface elements for desktop applications. When you mouse over a toolbar icon, and you'll often see pop-up box with that tool's name, like the top image in Figure 10-8. Tooltips also appear when you add a *title* attribute to a link (middle image in Figure 10-8). With a little JavaScript magic, you can add tooltips to any HTML element, using any message you like, formatted to match the look of your site, as shown at the bottom of Figure 10-8.

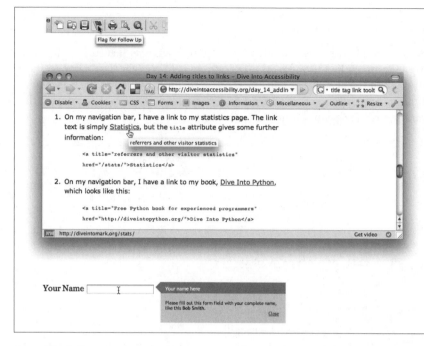

Figure 10-8:
Tooltips are a common user interface enhancement in desktop programs like Microsoft Word (top). Web browsers also display tooltips on links that have their title attribute set (middle). With a little JavaScript, you can add tooltips to any element on a Web page, even a form field (bottom). A JavaScript-generated tooltip also gives you greater control over the tooltip's look and content.

A tooltip is just a message that appears when you mouse over an element. The Cluetip jQuery plug-in, created by Karl Swedberg, offers a full-featured toolkit for adding tooltips to your Web pages.

To use the Cluetip plug-in, visit the Cluetip Web site (*http://plugins.learningjquery. com/cluetip/*) and download the latest version of the plug-in. The plug-in is also included along with the tutorial files for this book. The exact process for using the plug-in depends on how you want to supply the tooltip's content. You can add tooltips using text from a tag's *title* attribute, from another HTML page, or even from a hidden tag (like a <div> tag containing the tooltip text). In addition, you can include images as well as text in a tooltip.

Tooltips Using the Title Attribute

A simple way to add a tooltip is to simply embed the tooltip message in a tag's *title* attribute. The Cluetip plug-in sees a tooltip as composed of two parts—a tooltip title and a tooltip message (see Figure 10-9)—and displays the title above the tooltip's main content. You can put both the title and tooltip text inside a HTML tag's *title* attribute. You just need to use any obscure character to separate the two. For example, using the | (pipe) character, you can add both a tooltip title and content to an <a> tag like this:

```
<a href="http://www.chia-vet.com/" class="tip"
title="Chia-Vet.com|Every Chia pet needs a Chia vet">
Chia-Vet</a>
```

In this case, the | character separates the title (*Chia-Vet.com*) and the tip message ("Every Chia pet needs a Chia vet").

In addition, you'll need a way to identify just those elements that need to have the Cluetip plug-in applied to them. The easiest way is to apply a class name to those HTML tags. In the above example, the class name *tip* is applied to the <a> tag. As you'll see in a moment, you can then use jQuery to select every element with that class and apply the *cluetip( )* function to them.

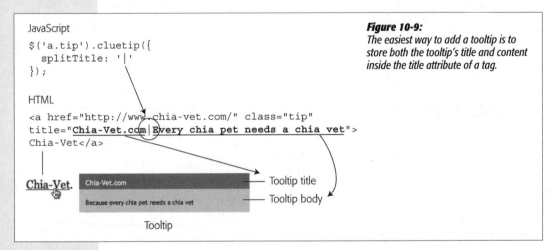

Figure 10-9:
The easiest way to add a tooltip is to store both the tooltip's title and content inside the title attribute of a tag.

```
JavaScript
$('a.tip').cluetip({
  splitTitle: '|'
});

HTML
<a href="http://www.chia-vet.com/" class="tip"
title="Chia-Vet.com|Every chia pet needs a chia vet">
Chia-Vet</a>
```

Chia-Vet.com — Tooltip title
Because every chia pet needs a chia vet — Tooltip body

Tooltip

After you add title tags (and class names) to each tag that will display a tooltip, you can then turn to the JavaScript.

1. **Link to the necessary external JavaScript files.**

   These include the jQuery library and the Cluetip plug-in itself. For example:

   ```
   <script type="text/javascript" src="js/jquery.js"></script>
   <script type="text/javascript" src="js/jquery.cluetip.js"></script>
   ```

   (See page 24 if you need a refresher on how to use external JavaScript files.)

2. **Add another <script> tag and the *$(document).ready( )* function:**

   ```
   <script type="text/javascript">
   $(document).ready(function( ) {

   }); // end ready
   </script>
   ```

   You should know what this function does by now—if not, turn to page 218.

3. **Apply the *cluetip( )* function to the HTML tags you've added the *title* attribute to.**

   For example, if you added the class name *tip* to each tag you wish to display a tooltip, then the JavaScript would look like this:

   ```
   $('.tip').cluetip();
   ```

The Cluetip plug-in isn't set up to work with just the *title* attribute, so to tell it what you want you'll need one more step—pass an option to the function.

4. **Pass an object literal (page 188) to the** *cluetip( )* **function with the** *splitTitle* **keyword and the character you're using to separate the title from the message.**

For example, assuming you use the | character to separate the title and message, your final code would look like this:

```
$('.tip').cluetip({
  splitTitle: '|'
});
```

To set the various options for the Cluetip plug-in, you pass an object literal to the *cluetip( )* function. You'll learn about additional options on page 382.

Tooltips Using Another Web Page

Another way to use the Cluetip plug-in is to put the tooltip's title inside the HTML tag's *title* attribute, and put the body of the tooltip inside a separate HTML file. It's the easiest approach of all, and as a bonus it lets you put other HTML elements like images, tables, and so on inside the tooltip.

The process for using Cluetip this way is similar to the method you learned in the previous section:

1. **Create an HTML file containing the information you want to see in the tooltip body.**

This file can contain any HTML tags, like images, tables, headlines, and so on.

Tip: It's easiest to save the file inside the same folder as the page with the tooltip, but you don't have to. However, due to security restrictions on Web browsers, both the page containing the tooltip text and the page that displays the tooltip must be in the same site.

---

2. **Add a** *title* **attribute and class name to the HTML element. For example:**

```
<a href="http://www.chia-vet.com/" class="tip"
title="Chia-Vet.com">
```

The class name provides a way to use jQuery to identify just the elements you're adding tooltips to. The *title* attribute will act as the title of the tooltip.

3. **Add a** *rel* **attribute to the tag, including a path to the HTML file you created in step 1.**

For example, say the content for the tooltip is stored in a file named *chia.html*. If the *chia.html* file is in the same folder, the HTML would now look like this:

```
<a href="http://www.chia-vet.com/" class="tip"
title="Chia-Vet.com" rel="chia.html">
```

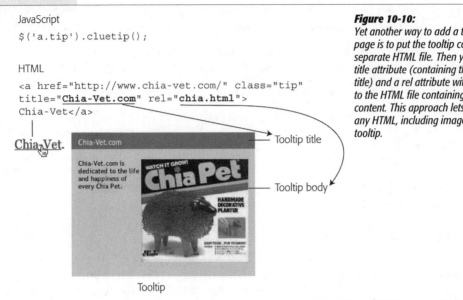

JavaScript

```
$('a.tip').cluetip();
```

HTML

```
<a href="http://www.chia-vet.com/" class="tip"
title="Chia-Vet.com" rel="chia.html">
Chia-Vet</a>
```

Figure 10-10:
Yet another way to add a tooltip to a page is to put the tooltip content in a separate HTML file. Then you add a title attribute (containing the tooltip's title) and a rel attribute with the path to the HTML file containing the tooltip content. This approach lets you use any HTML, including images, inside a tooltip.

Tooltip title

Tooltip body

Tooltip

4. **Attach the external JavaScript files, add another <script> tag, and then add the jQuery $(document).ready( ) function.**

   This step is exactly the same as steps 1 and 2 on page 378.

5. **Apply the *cluetip( )* function to the HTML tags and pass an object literal.**

   For example, if you added the class name *tip* to each tag you wish to display a tooltip, then the JavaScript would look like this:

   ```
   $('.tip').cluetip();
   ```

   And that's it. You don't need to pass any additional settings to make the Cluetip plug-in work—the plug-in is programmed to retrieve the title of the tooltip from the tag's *title* attribute and the content of the tooltip from the Web page referenced in the *rel* attribute if you're using additional HTML files for the tooltip content.

Note: This method is particularly good if you want to dynamically generate tooltips from a database or a server-side program. You don't have to point to a real Web page (*chia.html*, for example). You can point to a dynamic page–*products.php?id=834*, for example.

Tooltips Using Hidden Content

If you don't like the idea of putting the tooltip content into a separate HTML file, you can add the HTML for the tooltip in the page itself. For example, you can create a <div> tag containing the HTML you wish to appear in the tooltip.

The Cluetip plug-in will hide that content when the page loads, then put it into a tooltip when a visitor mouses over the element to which you've added the tooltip.

To use the plug-in this way, follow these steps:

1. **On the page where you're adding the tooltip, create the HTML for the tooltip content.**

   For example, you can have a <div> tag containing paragraphs, images, or any other HTML elements. Make sure to give the <div> tag an ID, so you can associate this <div> with the specific tag that will display the tooltip. Here's a simple example:

   ```
   <div id="nameInfo">
   <p>Please fill out this form field with your
   complete name, like this <strong>Bob Smith</strong>.</p>
   </div>
   ```

   You can place this HTML anywhere on the page—the Cluetip plug-in will hide it when the page loads—though a good place for it would be directly after the element that gets the tooltip (see Figure 10-11, top). That way, if your visitors have JavaScript turned off, they'll still see the content that would have appeared in the tooltip, right near the tag the tooltip goes with.

2. **Add a *title* attribute and ID or class name to the HTML element. For example:**

   ```
   <a href="http://www.chia-vet.com/" class="localtip"
   title="Chia-Vet.com">
   ```

   A class name or ID provides a way to use jQuery to identify the elements you're adding the tooltip to. The *title* attribute acts as the tooltip's title.

3. **Add a *rel* attribute to the tag, with the ID selector for the HTML you added in step 1.**

   For example, if you store the HTML for the tooltip content in a <div> with the ID *nameInfo* (see step 1), your HTML would look like this:

   ```
   <a href="http://www.chia-vet.com/" class="localtip"
   title="Chia-Vet.com" rel="#nameInfo">
   ```

   Make sure to include the # symbol before the ID name. The # represents an ID selector, which lets the Cluetip plug-in identify and pull out the proper content for the tooltip.

4. **Attach the external JavaScript files, add another <script> tag, and add the jQuery *$(document).ready( )* function.**

   This step is the same as steps 1 and 2 on page 378.

---

5. Apply the *cluetip( )* function to the HTML tags you've added the *title* attribute to and pass an object literal (page 188) to the *cluetip( )* function with the *local* keyword set to *true*.

For example, assuming you assigned the class name *localtip* to every tag that gets a tooltip, you'd call the function like this:

```
$('.localtip').cluetip({
    local:true
});
```

The *local* option is just a way to tell Cluetip that the content for the tooltips is contained "locally" on the same page. You can add additional options for this plug-in as described below.

Note: You probably won't use all three techniques discussed here to add tooltips. For simple, one-line tooltips, the *title* attribute method (page 377) is the most straightforward. However, if you want a tooltip that includes images or multiple lines of text, use either the separate HTML file method (page 379) or <div> tags placed on the same page (page 380).

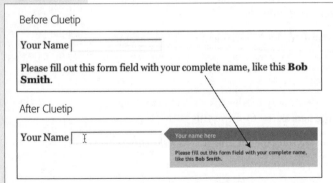

Before Cluetip

Your Name

Please fill out this form field with your complete name, like this **Bob Smith**.

After Cluetip

Your Name

Your name here

Please fill out this form field with your complete name, like this Bob Smith.

Figure 10-11:
Another approach to using the Cluetip plug-in involves adding the HTML for the tooltip directly on the Web page (top). The Cluetip plug-in puts that HTML into a tooltip box (bottom) when the visitor mouses over the correct element (a text box in this case).

Controlling the Display of Tooltips

The Cluetip plug-in provides a lot of flexibility. Not only are there multiple methods of adding a tooltip, as discussed earlier in this chapter, but you can also control the display of tooltips by passing optional parameters to the *cluetip( )* function. You've already seen the *splitTitle* option used to place a tooltip inside a *title* attribute (page 377) and the *local* option to retrieve tooltip content from a <div> on the page. As with many jQuery plug-ins, you can pass optional parameters to a function as part of an object literal (page 188). For example, to set the width of a tooltip, you use the *width* option:

```
$('.tip').cluetip({
    width: 300
});
```

Even More Advanced Interfaces

The power of JavaScript to transform a Web page from a humdrum brochure to an interactive information kiosk is almost unlimited. The plug-ins discussed in this chapter are among the most popular, but they're not by any means the only ones available. Here are a few other jQuery plug-ins you should check out:

- **Coda Slider** (*www.ndoherty.com/demos/coda-slider*) provides a fun, animated approach to tabbed panels. Clicking a tab doesn't merely make a panel appear; it also scrolls the current panel out of view as it scrolls the requested panel into place. Very cool.

- **UI Dialog.** The JavaScript alert box and prompt dialog box you learned about in the first few chapters of this book actually aren't the most professional looking. If you want to create your own dialog boxes to pop up messages, ask questions and take answers in a text field, or confirm actions ("Do you really want to delete that?"), try the UI Dialog plug-in. It's part of the official jQuery UI project (see the box on page 361). You can download it from *http://ui.jquery.com* and find out how to use it at *http://docs.jquery.com/UI/Dialog*.

- **Treeview.** If you want to create the familiar look of a tree view found in many desktop applications, you can turn to Jörn Zaefferer's Treeview plug-in (*http://jquery.bassistance.de/treeview/*). Treeviews are a common way to display a nested list of items, and you'll frequently see them used to display a list of folders and files. They're interactive: when you click a + symbol next to a folder, it opens and a list of files inside it appears.

- **Columnize List.** A long bulleted list of one or two word items usually creates a large empty space on a page. A list of items in side-by-side columns often looks better, but creating one with regular HTML and CSS is an unpleasant task. With jQuery and Ingo Schommer's columnizeList plug-in (*www.chillu.com/2007/9/30/jquery-columnizelist-plug-in*), you'll be able to quickly convert long lists into space-saving columns.

And if that's not enough, you can cruise on over to the jQuery plug-ins repository and check out the "User Interface" category at *http://plugins.jquery.com/project/Plugins/category/21*. As of this writing, there are over 134 different user interface plug-ins available.

You can find a complete list of Cluetip options at *http://plug-ins.learningjquery.com/cluetip/#options*. Here are some of the most useful:

- *width* sets the width of the tooltip in pixels. For example, to make a tooltip 275 pixels wide:

```
width:275
```

- *height* sets the height of the tooltip in pixels. Use this option only if you're certain that the content inside the tooltip won't exceed the height you specify. Otherwise, the tooltip simply clips off the extra content and your visitors won't be able to read it. The normal behavior is to make the tooltip grow to the height of the content inside it.

- *arrows* accepts either the value *true* or *false*. You can skip setting it to *false*—that's what it does normally. However, if you want to add an arrow that points from the tooltip to the element being moused over, set this option to *true*. (See the middle image in Figure 10-13 for an example.)

You can control how this arrow looks, as described on page 388. To add arrows to a tooltip:

```
arrows:true
```

- *dropShadow* determines whether the tooltip has a drop shadow, lending a three-dimensional, professional look. The plug-in is set to always show drop shadows unless you tell it otherwise. However, in real world usage, the Cluetip plug-in frequently has trouble effectively drawing drop shadows. To turn them off:

```
dropShadow:false
```

- *dropShadowSteps* defines how thick the drop shadow is. By default, drop shadows are six pixels wide. To make drop shadows that are 10 pixels wide, pass this option to the *cluetip( )* function:

```
dropShadowSteps: 10
```

- *positionBy* determines where the tooltip is positioned in relation to the element. The normal behavior is to place the tooltip to the element's right; however, if the tooltip won't fit (because the browser window isn't wide enough to display the tooltip to the right), the tooltip appears to the element's left. You can change this positioning and place the tooltip in relationship to where the mouse is. In other words, you can make the tooltip appear directly to the right or left of the mouse when it moves over the element. To get this effect, use the value *'mouse'* like this:

```
positionBy:'mouse'
```

You can also position the tooltip either above or below the element by using the *'bottomTop'* value:

```
positionBy:'bottomTop'
```

With this setting, the plug-in first tries to position the tooltip below the element; but if the tooltip won't be visible below the element (because the element is at the bottom of the browser window), the plug-in will display the tip on top.

- *topOffset* controls how many pixels from the top of the element the tooltip appears. Normally, it's set to 15 pixels, but you can change that. For example, if you want the tooltip to appear over the element, covering it, use a negative value.

- *leftOffset* controls how many pixels from the right edge of the element the tooltip appears. In other words, it adds space on the *left* of the tooltip. Normally, it's set to 15 pixels, but you can change this value. Also, if the Cluetip plug-in displays a tooltip to the element's left because it won't fit on the right, it subtracts the *leftOffset* value from the tooltip position, forcing it further to the right.

Sounds confusing, but you can think of it this way: use a negative value to place the tooltip over the element, a positive value to move it away. For example, to position a tooltip over an element, you can use a value like this one:

```
leftOffset: -20
```

- *sticky* determines whether a tooltip remains open after you mouse off an element. Normally, a tooltip immediately disappears once you mouse off the element with the tooltip. However, you can make the tooltip stick around until a visitor clicks a "close" link. You can use this effect to make a small form appear when a visitor mouses over a "login" link, for instance. The tooltip with the form remains open until the visitor fills out the form.

  You use this option by setting its value to *true*:

  ```
  sticky:true
  ```

  You can control the text and position of the "close" link using the next two options.

- *closePosition* controls where the "close" link appears when creating a "sticky" tooltip (see the *sticky* option above). This option has three settings: *'top'*, *'bottom'*, or *'title'*. The *'top'* setting positions the "close" link at the top of the tooltip's content region, while the *'bottom'* setting positions it at the bottom of the tooltip. The *'title'* option places the link in the right side of the tooltip title bar.

  ```
  closePosition:'bottom'
  ```

- *closeText* specifies the text that appears in the "close" link when using the *sticky* option, as described in the previous two options. Normally, the setting uses the word "close," but you can change the text to, say, "close this tooltip," like this:

  ```
  closeText:'close this tooltip'
  ```

  In addition, you can supply HTML instead of just text, so if you want to use a graphic image as a close button, you can simply supply a valid <img> tag like this:

  ```
  closeText:'<img src="images/close.png" alt="" />'
  ```

- *fx* lets you add "special effects" to the appearance of a tooltip. You can either slide in a tooltip, or make a tooltip fade into view. This option is a bit trickier than the other ones, since it requires another object literal that specifies both the effect and its speed. For example, to make a tooltip fade in over the course of one second, use this code:

  ```
  fx: {
    open:'fadeIn',
    openSpeed: 1000
  }
  ```

  To make a tooltip slide down into view in half a second, use the following:

  ```
  fx: {
    open:'slideDown',
    openSpeed: 500
  }
  ```

  The *fx* option relies on the *slideDown* and *fadeIn* jQuery effects discussed on pages 245 and 244.

You can combine any number of these options to control the way a tooltip is displayed. For example, say you want to use the *title* method of displaying a tooltip (see page 377). You also want the tooltip to fade into view, to not have a drop shadow, to be 200 pixels wide, and to remain open until the visitor clicks a "close" link in the tooltip's title bar:

```
$('.tip').cluetip({
  splitTitle: '|',
  fx: {
    open:'fadeIn',
    openSpeed:1000
  },
  dropShadow:false,
  width:200,
  sticky:true,
  closePosition:'title'
});
```

Formatting Tooltips

The Cluetip plug-in comes with several predefined styles as provided in the *jquery.cluetip.css* file. The basic style is called *'default'*, and there's also a style called *'jtip'*. To define a new style name, you can pass a new value for the *cluetipClass* option to the *cluetip( )* function:

```
$('.tip').cluetip({
  clueTipClass: 'jtip'
});
```

However, you don't really need to go to this bother (unless you like the look of the pre-defined *jtip* styles). To customize the look of the tooltip, it's a lot easier to just edit the styles provided in the *jquery.cluetip.css* file.

To understand how the supplied styles work, you need to understand the structure of the HTML that the Cluetip plug-in produces when it creates a tooltip; take a look at Figure 10-12. Basically there are a series of <div> tags that structure the tooltip:

• The outer container is a <div> tag with an ID of *cluetip-default*. Actually, the "default" part of the ID can change if you set the *clueTipClass* option, discussed on page 393. For example, if you set the *clueTipClass* to *jtip*, then the ID of the tooltip's outer <div> tag will be *cluetip-jtip*.

In the *jquery.cluetip.css* file, you'll find the style *.cluetip-default*. That style formats this <div>.

In addition, a tooltip can appear either to the left, right, top, or bottom of the element. Depending upon the tooltip's placement, a second class name is added to the container <div>: either *clue-right-default*, *clue-left-default*, *clue-top-default*, or *clue-bottom-default*. These different class names are used for formatting arrows (see the *arrows* option on page 383).

- Inside the main tooltip <div> is another <div> with the ID *cluetip-outer*. This <div> contains the tooltip title, the tooltip content, and (if the *sticky* option is turned on) the link to close an open tooltip. The style *.cluetip-default #cluetip-outer* in the *jquery.cluetip.css* file formats this <div>, adding an overall background color to the tooltip.

- The tooltip title is an <h3> tag with the ID *cluetip-title*. The style *.cluetip-default h3#cluetip-title* in the style sheet formats the appearance of the tooltip title. So if you want to change the font, font-size, or background of the title, edit this style.

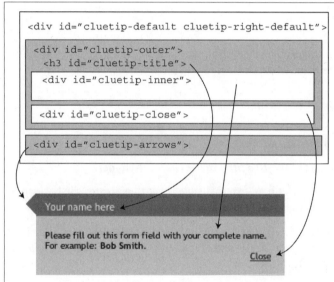

Figure 10-12:
To create a tooltip, the Cluetip plug-in produces a somewhat complex nest of <div> tags to hold the different parts of a tooltip (like the title and tooltip content). Each element has a unique ID that makes it easy to style a tooltip using CSS. The jquery.cluetip.css file includes styles using these IDs. To change the look of the tooltips, just edit the CSS in that style sheet.

- The body of the tooltip is placed into a <div> with the ID *cluetip-inner*. The style supplied in the style sheet, *.cluetip-default #cluetip-inner*, sets 10 pixels of padding on the element, but you can add additional CSS properties to change the look of the content inside.

In addition, you can create descendent selectors to target different elements inside the tooltip. For example, say the tooltip content includes HTML pulled from a HTML file (see page 379 for more on how this technique works). The HTML includes several <p> tags; the following descendent selector will apply to those tags:

```
.cluetip-default #cluetip-inner p
```

• If you're using the *sticky* option (page 385), the close link is contained inside a <div> with the ID *cluetip-close*. The style *.cluetip-default div#cluetip-close* controls the formatting for that <div>. To control the look of the link itself, add the style *.cluetip-default div#cluetip-close a* to the style sheet and add the CSS properties you wish to use.

• A tooltip arrow—displayed if the *arrows* option is turned on—is represented by an empty <div> tag with the ID *cluetip-arrows*. Since the placement of the tooltip dictates where the arrow appears (on the left, right, top, or bottom) of the tooltip, there are four different styles that define which graphics are used in each case. For example, the style *.clue-right-default .cluetip-arrows* assigns the graphic used when a tooltip appears to the right of an element. If you want to replace the images the Cluetip plug-in normally uses with arrows of your own creation, just replace the files *darrowleft.gif*, *darrowright.gif*, *darrowdown.gif*, and *darrowup.gif* in the images folder. You can also rename the images in the *jquery.cluetip.css* file.

Cluetip Tutorial

In this tutorial, you'll use each of the techniques described on page 377 for adding tooltips to a page. The finished product will look like Figure 10-13.

Note: See the note on page 27 for information on how to download the tutorial files.

Adding a tooltip using the title attribute

1. **In a text editor, open the file *10.3.html* in the *chapter10* folder.**

   The Cluetip plug-in relies on an external style sheet that creates the basic tooltip look. You need to attach that file to the page.

2. **Click in the empty line directly below the link to the style sheet *global.css* (just before the first <script> tag), and type: *<link href="jquery.cluetip.css" rel="stylesheet" type="text/css">*.**

   As discussed on page 378, this style sheet provides the necessary style information to display a tooltip.

   This file already has three external JavaScript files linked to the page: the *jquery.js*, *jquery.dimensions.js*, and *jquery.cluetip.js* files. The Cluetip plug-in requires those two other files to work. In addition, the page already has a <script> tag with the *$(document).ready( )* function in place. But before you add any JavaScript, you'll add the necessary HTML to add a tooltip.

3. **A few lines below the opening <body> tag you'll see the HTML *<a href="http://www.sawmac.com/missing/js/">*. Modify that code to look like this:**

   ```
   <a href="http://www.sawmac.com/missing/js/" class="titleTip"
   title="JavaScript: The Missing Manual|The supplemental Web site for this
   book.">
   ```

The class name will come in hand when you need to tell the Cluetip plug-in which tags to add tooltips to. The *title* attribute is used here to supply both the title and content of the tooltip (in other words, you're using the method described on page 377 to create the first tooltip). The | character is used to separate the tooltip's title ("JavaScript: The Missing Manual") from the tooltip's content.

Now you can apply the Cluetip plug-in.

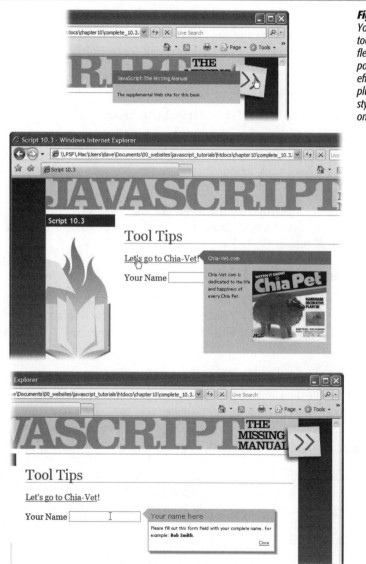

Figure 10-13:
You can use the Cluetip plug-in to add tooltips to any tag on a page. The flexibility of the plug-in lets you position the tooltip (top) and add effects to the tooltip (middle). The plug-in even lets you choose different styles and make a tooltip stay open on a page until it's closed (bottom).

4. **Inside the *$(document).ready( )* function, add the following code:**

```
$('.titleTip').cluetip({
  splitTitle: '|'
});
```

This code starts by selecting every element with the class *titleTip* applied to it. It then calls the *cluetip( )* function and passes an object literal to the function. The *splitTitle* option (see page 379) identifies which character separates the tooltip title from the tooltip content in the tag's *title* attribute.

5. **Save the file and preview it in a Web browser. Move your mouse over the Post-it note in the top right of the page (see Figure 10-13).**

The tooltip should appear—however, it doesn't appear very close to the element you're mousing over. By supplying a couple more options, you can move the positioning of the tooltip.

6. **Edit the code you added in step 4 so that it looks like this:**

```
$('.titleTip').cluetip({
  splitTitle: '|',
  leftOffset: -30
});
```

By changing the *leftOffset* option (discussed on page 384), you can move the tooltip. Using a negative number draws the tooltip closer to and over the element you're mousing over.

Adding a tooltip using another Web page

In this part of the tutorial, you'll load the content of an external Web page into the tooltip's body. In this case, there's a file named *chia.html* containing the HTML elements that you want to display when someone mouses over the "Let's go to Chia-Vet!" link.

First, you'll modify the HTML a bit.

1. **In the *10.3.html* file, locate the code *<a href="http://www.chia-vet.com/">* and change it so that it looks like this:**

```
<a href="http://www.chia-vet.com/" class="tip"
title="Chia-Vet.com" rel="chia.html">
```

You've just added three different attributes to this tag. The first, *class="tip"*, will give jQuery a way to identify this tag as something that should have a tooltip (see step 2 on page 379). Next, the *title* attribute supplies the title that will appear at the top of the tooltip. Finally, the *rel* attribute points to the file—*chia. html*—containing the main body of the tooltip.

Now you just need to add the JavaScript to make it work.

2. Add an empty line after the last *cluetip( )* function you called in step 6 of the previous section of the tutorial, and add this code:

```
$('.tip').cluetip( );
```

That's all you need to do—all of the information for the Cluetip plug-in is in the HTML you added in the previous step.

Note that this one line of code would work for any tag that has the class of *tip* and the proper *title* and *rel* attributes set. In other words, this one line of code could set up tooltips for dozens of different elements—as long as those elements have the proper attributes set up in the HTML.

Now, you'll add an option to display an arrow next to the tooltip's title.

3. Edit the code you created in the last step so it looks like this:

```
$('.tip').cluetip({
  arrows: true
});
```

If you save the file and preview it in a Web browser, you'll now see an arrow pointing from the tooltip title to the link. A fade-in effect might look good here.

4. Once again, modify the JavaScript code so it looks like this:

```
$('.tip').cluetip({
  arrows: true,
  fx: {
    open: 'fadeIn',
    openSpeed: 500
  }
});
```

The *fx* option (see page 385) lets you control how the tooltip appears. In this case, the tooltip will fade into view in half a second (500 milliseconds).

5. Save the page and preview it in Web browser. Mouse over the *Chia-Vet.com* link.

The tooltip fades into view (see Figure 10-13).

Adding a tooltip using HTML on the page

In this final part of the tutorial, you'll learn how to add a tooltip that takes content from a <div> on the current page. This technique is described on page 380.

When you previewed this page earlier in the tutorial, you probably noticed the sentence "Please fill out this form field with your complete name. For example: *Bob*

Smith." The text is inside a <p> tag, which is, in turn, inside a <div> tag. That <div> tag has the ID *nameInfo*. The HTML for this <div> looks like this:

```
<div id="nameInfo">
<p>Please fill out this form field with your complete name. For example:
<strong>Bob Smith</strong>.</p>
</div>
```

The contents of this <div> will end up being the content of the tooltip. First, you need to add some HTML.

1. **Locate the HTML** *<input type="text" name="name" id="name">* **and add two attributes so it looks like this:**

```
<input type="text" name="name" id="name" class="localTip"
title="Your name here" rel="#nameInfo">
```

As with the previous method for adding a tooltip (page 390), the class name provides a way to identify the tags you want to add a tooltip to. The *title* attribute is used to provide the title of the tooltip. The *rel* attribute identifies the selector used to select the <div> tag containing the tooltip content. In this case, it points to the <div> tag with the ID *nameInfo*. You need to include the # symbol—you're essentially providing the selector jQuery needs to select the <div> tag.

Now you just need a little JavaScript to make the tooltip work.

2. **Insert a blank line after the previous code you added (see step 4 on page 391) and type:**

```
$('.localTip').cluetip({
  local: true
});
```

By now this code should be looking familiar—it selects all tags with the class name *localTip* and applies the *cluetip( )* function to them. When you pass the option *local* and set it to *true*, the Cluetip plug-in knows that the content for the tooltip will come from HTML on this page. If you save the page and preview it, you'll see that mousing over the form field opens a tooltip.

Next, you'll make the tooltip "sticky"—meaning it will stay in place until you click a "close" link.

3. **Add two more options for the** *cluetip( )* **function:**

```
$('.localTip').cluetip({
  local: true,
  sticky: true,
  closePosition: 'bottom'
});
```

The *sticky* option makes the tooltip stay open until a "close" link is clicked, while the *closePosition* option dictates where the "close" link goes. Finally, you'll change the style of the tooltip and add an arrow.

4. **Add two final options to the code:**

```
$('.localTip').cluetip({
    local: true,
    sticky: true,
    closePosition: 'bottom',
    arrows: true,
    cluetipClass: 'jtip'
  });
});
```

The *clueTipClass* option (page 386), lets you choose a class name that gets applied to the tooltip. In this case, the *jtip* class refers to a set of styles included with the *jquery.cluetip.css* style sheet, so the finished tooltip will have a new look. At this point, the completed script should look like this:

```
$(document).ready(function( ) {
  $('.titleTip').cluetip({
    splitTitle: '|',
    leftOffset: -30
  });

  $('.tip').cluetip({
    arrows: true,
    fx: {
      open: 'fadeIn',
      openSpeed: 500
    }
  });

  $('.localTip').cluetip({
    local: true,
    sticky: true,
    closePosition: 'bottom',
    arrows: true,
    cluetipClass: 'jtip'
  });
});
```

5. **Save the file and preview it in a Web browser.**

The completed page should have three tooltips that look like Figure 10-13. You can see a completed version of the tutorial in the *complete_10.3.html* file. As mentioned in the Note on page 382, you probably won't use all three of these techniques on a single page—the *title* attribute technique is a quick way to add simple tooltips, while the other two techniques provide a way to create more elaborate tooltips containing different HTML tags.

Creating Sortable Tables

HTML data tables are great for displaying information in a spreadsheet format. However, unlike spreadsheets in a program like Excel, HTML tables don't let you sort the information inside the table. If you want to see all the items in the first column sorted in alphabetical order, for example, you're out of luck—unless you use JavaScript.

The Tablesorter jQuery plug-in, written by Christian Bach, makes an otherwise complex task a simple matter of adding a single line of JavaScript. Then your visitors can view your information sorted any way they like just by clicking a column heading.

1. **Create a HTML data table.**

   If you've been building Web sites for a while, you know that Web designers have used HTML tables for lots of different things, from structuring forms to laying out Web pages. The Tablesorter plug-in depends on having the table's HTML structured in a particular way. Specifically, you must use the <thead> tag to enclose the row containing column headers, and the <th> tag inside the <thead> tag to indicate the cells that provide the header information (like Product, and Cost shown in Figure 10-14).

   You must also use the <tbody> tag around the rows that contain the actual data for the table (<td> tags). If you're unfamiliar with these tags and how to use them, you can find more information at *www.htmldog.com/reference/htmltags/thead/* and *www.htmldog.com/reference/htmltags/tbody/*.

   Here's an example of a basic table using the <thead> and <tbody> tags:

```
<table>
<thead>
<tr>
   <th scope="col">Brand</th>
   <th scope="col">Price</th>
   <th scope="col">Power Source</th>
</tr>
</thead>
<tbody>
<tr>
   <td>Chinook Push-o-matic Indoor Mower</td>
   <td>$247.00</td>
   <td>Mechanical</td>
</tr>
```

```
<tr>
  <td>Sampson Deluxe Apartment Mower</td>
  <td>$370.00</td>
  <td>Mechanical</td>
</tr>
</tbody>
</table>
```

2. **Attach the jQuery file.**

This part should be obvious by now: if you're using a jQuery plug-in, you need to include the jQuery library file first. See page 172 for instructions on adding jQuery to a page.

3. **Attach the Tablesorter file.**

The Tablesorter plug-in is in a separate JavaScript file that you need to include on the page after the jQuery file. You can download the plug-in at *www. tablesorter.com* (how's that for a straightforward domain name?). You can also find it in the tutorial files, in the *js* folder, where it's called *jquery.tablesorter.js*. Of course, you attach this file as you would any external JavaScript file (page 24). For example:

```
<script type="text/javascript" src="jquery.tablesorter.js"></script>
```

4. **Call the *tablesorter( )* function.**

This plug-in is very easy to use. If you don't happen to need any of the plug-in's bells-and-whistles (described in the box on page 396), all you have to do is use jQuery to select the table you wish to make sortable and then call the *tablesorter( )* function. As usual, you add your jQuery code within a <script> tag and within jQuery's *$(document).ready( )* function:

```
<script type="text/javascript">
$(document).ready(function( ) {
  $('table').tablesorter( );
});
</script>
```

Since *$('table')* is jQuery's way of selecting every <table> tag element, the code above assumes that there are only data tables on the page and that you want every table to be sortable. If you want just a specific table to be sortable, add an ID to the table (for example, *<table id="sortable">*), and then call the function like this:

```
$('#sortable').tablesorter( );
```

And that's all there is to it. There are a handful of configuration options that you can try, like sorting the table in a particular order when the page loads (see the box on page 396).

More Ways to Sort Tables

If the information in your HTML table isn't already sorted the way you want it, (hey, manually rearranging data in an HTML table is a pain!), you can force the table to be sorted when the page loads. Say your Web site's been around for a while, and you've added a lot of new products to your catalog page. Adding new ones in alphabetical order to the HTML table is tedious, and a single typo messes up the whole table. It would be much easier to add new items at the bottom of the table and then sort the table using JavaScript. Furthermore, it would be great if you could sort the table by price on one page, and by product category on another.

All you do is pass an object literal (page 188) to the *tablesorter( )* function that includes the key *sortList* followed by an array of sort options. For example, if you want the table to be sorted by the first column in ascending order (A–Z, 0–100), use the following:

```
$('table').tablesorter({
  sortList: [[0,0]]
});
```

In the object literal, *sortList* is the name of the option, while *[[0,0]]* is the value for that option. The first 0 indicates column 1, while the second 0 means sort in ascending order (use 1 to sort in descending order). You need both sets of [ ], because you're actually creating an array where each array element is another array. In this way, you can sort the table on two different columns at once. For example, say column 1 displayed products prices. You might want to sort by column 1 (so you can list items from cheapest to most expensive), then for any products that have the same price, you could then sort by product name, so that all the products that have the same price would be listed in alphabetical order. If column 3 displayed the product names, you could pass the following code to the *tablesorter( )* function:

```
$('table').tablesorter({
  sortList : [[0,0],[2,0]]
});
```

The Tablesorter plug-in has more tricks up its sleeve, although you probably won't need them unless you use lots of data tables on your site. You can learn about them at *http://tablesorter.com/docs/#Configuration*.

Styling the Table

While you don't need to add any formatting to the tables to make the Tablesorter plug-in work, it's a good idea to provide some feedback to let visitors know that they can click on a column header to sort the table. Equally important, you can use formatting to indicate which column is being sorted.

First, you'll want to make sure that a column header looks clickable. Normally, hovering over a <th> tag doesn't make the cursor change into the familiar "you can now click" finger that Web browsers use for links. To make the cursor change, you just need to create a style for the table's <th> tag. Open the style sheet for that page and add a style like this:

```
th { cursor: pointer; }
```

If there are other tables on the page, you may want to pinpoint just the headers for the sortable table. If you added a class name of *sortable* to the <table> tag for any tables you wish to make sortable, you can create a more targeted style like this:

```
.sortable th { cursor: pointer; }
```

In addition, the Tablesorter plug-in adds a class name whenever you click on a column header to sort the row. The first time you click on a column header, the class *headerSortDown* is added to the <th> tag, and the table is sorted using the data in the column in ascending order (A–Z, 0–100, or $1–$100). When you click the header a second time, the table is sorted in descending order (Z–A, 100–0, $100–$0), and the class *headerSortUp* is added to the <th> tag.

You can create styles to change the appearance of these headers when a visitor clicks them. For example, the style *th.headerSortDown* will apply to the <th> tag when it's first clicked and the table is sorted on that column; the style *th.headerSortUp* applies to the <th> tag when it's clicked a second time and resorted. A common technique is to add a background image of an arrow pointing in the direction the data is sorted—you'll see an example in the tutorial.

Using the Tablesorter plug-in to stripe tables

Back on page 30, you learned how to use jQuery to quickly add background color to every other row in a table. If you plan on using the Tablesorter plug-in on a table, you can skip that code you learned earlier—the plug-in has that ability built in.

To stripe a table using the Tablesorter plug-in, just pass this object literal to the *tablesorter( )* function: *{widgets:['zebra']}*. For example, here's how you can rewrite the code from step 6 on page 32 to add the table-striping functionality:

```
$('table').tablesorter({widgets:['zebra']});
```

Adding this code to the call to the Tablesorter function makes the plug-in add the class *even* to every even row in the table and the class *odd* to every odd row in the table. The only other step is creating styles to format the look of those table rows. For example:

```
tr.even { background-color: #F34; }
tr.odd { background-color: #034; }
```

Tablesorter Tutorial

In this tutorial, you'll take a basic HTML table and turn it into an interactive data table that your visitors can sort just by clicking a column heading (see Figure 10-14).

Note: See the note on page 27 for information on how to download the tutorial files.

---

1. **In a text editor, open the file *10.4.html* in the *chapter10* folder.**

   The first step is to link to the required external JavaScript files—the jQuery library and the Tablesorter plug-in file.

2. **Locate the empty line directly before the closing </head> tag, and add the following code:**

   ```
   <script type="text/javascript" src="../js/jquery.js"></script>
   <script type="text/javascript" src="../js/jquery.tablesorter.js"></script>
   ```

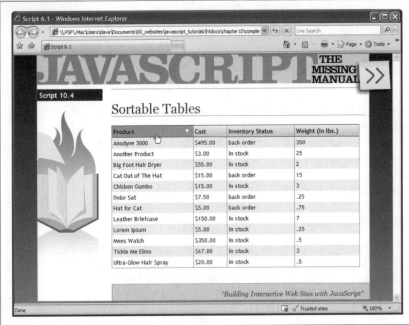

Figure 10-14:
The Tablesorter plug-in is a complicated set of JavaScript programming that's very easy to use.

The first line links to the jQuery library, while the second links to the plug-in. Now you'll add another <script> tag and the now-famous *$(document).ready( )* function.

3. **Add a blank line after the two <script> tags you just inserted, and type:**

```
<script type="text/javascript">
$(document).ready(function( ) {


}); // end ready( )
</script>
```

4. **Click in the empty line inside the *ready( )* function (the third line in the previous step) and type:**

```
$('table.sortable').tablesorter( );
```

The *$('table.sortable')* selects any <table> tag that has the class *sortable* applied to it. Then the *tablesorter( )* function is called. And that's it, really. The table is completely sortable. Preview it in a Web browser and click any of the column headers to sort the table using that column's data.

Tip: You can make more than one table per page sortable. For example, in step 4, every <table> tag with the class *sortable* will have the magic Tablesorter plug-in applied to it.

Although the sorting works, it doesn't provide any feedback about which column was selected. In addition, you can't really tell that you can click on a column header because the mouse pointer doesn't change.

5. **In a text editor, open the file** *tables.css*. **Add the following style:**

```
.sortable th { cursor: pointer;
```

This style changes the cursor to a pointer when the mouse moves over the <th> tag—in other words, it behaves as if the visitor were mousing over a link. Next you'll add two styles to change the way the column headers appear when clicked.

6. **Add two more styles to the** *tables.css* **file:**

```
th.headerSortDown {
    background: #A6B8C2 url(images/down_arrow.png) no-repeat 98% 7px;
}
th.headerSortUp {
    background: #A6B8C2 url(images/up_arrow.png) no-repeat 98% 5px;
}
```

These two styles simply add a background color and image to the header when clicked. Each style is applied based on how the column is sorted (ascending or descending).

Now you'll add the code to stripe the table.

7. **Return to the file** *10.4.html* **and add** *{widgets:['zebra']}* **inside the** *tablesorter( )* **function. The completed script should look like this:**

```
<script type="text/javascript">
$(document).ready(function( ) {
  $('table.sortable').tablesorter({widgets:['zebra']});
});
</script>
```

Although this code makes the plug-in add class names to alternating table rows, you won't see anything until you add a style to the style sheet.

8. **In your text editor, return to the** *tables.css* **file and add one last style:**

```
.sortable tr.even {
```

This style changes the background color of any table row with the class *even* that's also inside another tag with the class *sortable*.

Save the file and preview *10.4.html* in a Web browser. The table should look like Figure 10-14. Notice that the table striping still works when the rows are moved around each time you sort a column. Very slick.

A finished version of this tutorial (*complete_10.4.html* and *complete_tables.css*) is in the *chapter10* folder inside the tutorial folder.

Part Three:
Ajax: Communicating
with the Web Server

3

Introducing Ajax

JavaScript is great, but it can't do everything. If you want to display information from a database, dash off an email with results from a form, or just download additional HTML, you need to communicate with a Web server. For these tasks, you usually need to load a new Web page. For example, when you search a database for information, you usually leave the search page and go to another page of results.

Of course, waiting for new pages to load takes time. And, if you think about it, the concept of a page disappearing and then reappearing is pretty strange in general. Imagine if you were using Microsoft Word and every time you opened a new file the program's menus, panels, and windows suddenly disappeared and then reappeared when the new file opened. Sites like Flickr, Twitter, Google Maps, and Gmail are blurring the line between Web sites and desktop computer programs. If anything, people want Web sites to feel faster and more responsive, like their desktop programs. The technology that makes this new generation of Web applications possible is a programming technology called Ajax.

Ajax lets a Web page ask for and receive a response from a Web server and then update itself without ever having to load a new Web page. The result is a Web site that feels more responsive. When you visit Google Maps, for example (see Figure 11-1), you can zoom into the map; move north, south, east, or west; and even grab the map and drag it around. All of these actions happen without ever loading a new Web page.

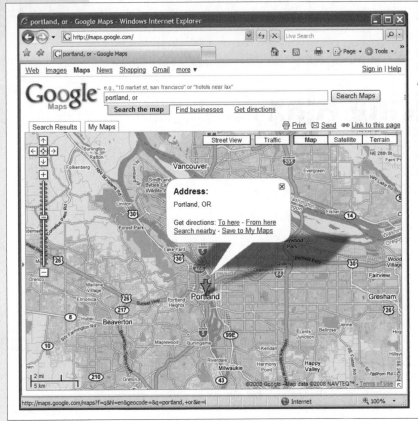

Figure 11-1:
Google Maps (http:// maps.google.com) was one of the first large sites to use Ajax to refresh page content without loading new Web pages. The site's responsiveness is due to the fact that only the map data changes—the other parts of the page such as the logo, search box, search results sidebar, and map controls remain the same even as you request new map information.

What Is Ajax?

The term Ajax was originally coined in 2005 to capture the essence of new Web sites coming from Google—Google Maps *(http://maps.google.com)*, Gmail *(www.gmail.com)*, and Google Suggest *(www.google.com/webhp?complete=1&hl=en)*. Ajax stands for *Asynchronous JavaScript and XML*, but it isn't an "official" technology like HTML, JavaScript, or CSS. It's a term that refers to the interaction of a mix of technologies—JavaScript, the Web browser, and the Web server—to retrieve and display new content without loading a new Web page.

Note: If you want to read the original blog post where the term Ajax was first used, visit *www.adaptivepath.com/ideas/essays/archives/000385.php*.

In a nutshell, current Web browsers let you use JavaScript to send a request to a Web server, which, in turn, sends some data back to the Web browser. The Java-Script program takes that data, and does something with it. For example, if you're on a Google Maps page and click the "north" arrow button, the page's JavaScript requests new map data from the Google server. That new information is then used to display a new chunk of the map.

While you may not create the next Google Maps, there are many simple things that you can do with Ajax technologies:

- **Display new HTML content without reloading the page.** For example, you can use the Tabs plug-in that you learned about in the last chapter (page 364) to request HTML from the server and display it in a tabbed panel. In other words, you can create a lean Web page that loads quickly and only displays content as it's requested. You'll learn how to do this on page 439.

- **Submit a form and instantly display results.** For example, imagine a "signup for our newsletter" form; when someone fills out and submits the form, the form disappears and a "you're signed up for our newsletter" message immediately appears. You'll learn how to make such forms using Ajax on page 426.

- **Log in without leaving the page.** Here's another form-related use of Java-Script—a page with a small "login" form. Fill out the form, hit the "login" button, and you're not only logged in, the page transforms to show your login status, user name, and perhaps other information specific to you.

- **Star-rating widget.** On sites that list books, movies, and other products, you often see a star rating—usually 1 to 5 stars—to indicate how visitors have rated the item's quality. These rating systems usually let you voice your opinion by clicking a number of stars. Using Ajax, you can let your visitors cast votes without actually leaving the Web page—all they have to do is click the stars. There's a cool jQuery plug-in that does just that: *http://plugins.learningjquery.com/half-star-rating/*.

- **Browsing through database information.** Amazon is a typical example of an online database you can browse. When you search Amazon for books on, say, JavaScript, you get a list of the JavaScript books Amazon sells. Usually, there are more books than can fit on a single Web page, so you need to jump from page to page to see "the next 10 items." Using Ajax, you can move through database records without having to jump to another page.

There's nothing revolutionary about any of the tasks listed above—except for the "without loading a new page" part, you can achieve the same basic results using regular HTML and some server-side programming (to collect form data, or access database information, for example). However, Ajax makes Web pages feel more responsive, and improves the user experience of a site. In fact, Ajax lets you create Web sites that feel more like desktop programs and less like Web pages.

Ajax: The Basics

Taken together, the technologies behind Ajax are pretty complicated. They include JavaScript, server-side programming, and the Web browser all working together. However, the basic concept is easy to grasp, as long as you understand all of the steps involved. Figure 11-2 shows the difference between how traditional HTML Web pages and Web pages with Ajax communicate with the Web server.

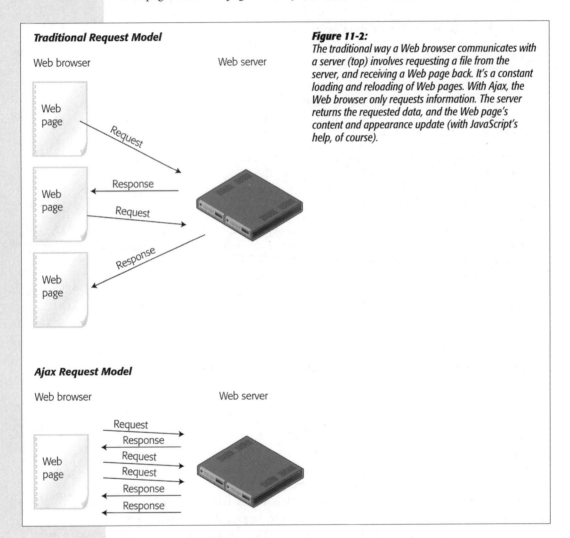

Traditional Request Model

Web browser   Web server

Web page
Request
Response
Web page
Request
Response
Web page

Ajax Request Model

Web browser   Web server

Web page
Request
Response
Request
Request
Response
Response

Figure 11-2:
The traditional way a Web browser communicates with a server (top) involves requesting a file from the server, and receiving a Web page back. It's a constant loading and reloading of Web pages. With Ajax, the Web browser only requests information. The server returns the requested data, and the Web page's content and appearance update (with JavaScript's help, of course).

Pieces of the Puzzle

Ajax isn't a single technology—it's a mixture of several different technologies that work together to make a more effective user experience. In essence, Ajax brings together three different components:

- **The Web browser.** Obviously, you need a Web browser to view Web pages and run JavaScript, but there's a secret ingredient built into most Web browsers that makes Ajax possible: the *XMLHttpRequest object*. This odd-sounding term is what lets JavaScript talk to a Web server and receive information in response.

  The *XMLHttpRequest* object was actually introduced in Internet Explorer 5 many years ago, but has gradually made its way into all the major Web browsers. You'll learn more about it on page 408.

- **JavaScript** does most of the heavy lifting in Ajax. It sends a request to the Web server, waits for a response, processes the response, and (usually) updates the page by adding new content or changing the display of the page in some way. Depending upon what you want your program to do, you might have JavaScript send information from a form, request additional database records, or simply send a single piece of data (like the rating a visitor just gave to a book). After the data is sent to the server, the JavaScript program will be ready for a response back from the server—for example, additional database records or just a simple text message like "Your vote has been counted."

  With that information, JavaScript will update the Web page—display new database records, for example, or inform the visitor that he's successfully logged in. Updating a Web page involves manipulating a page's DOM (Document Object Model, discussed on page 157) to add, change, and remove HTML tags and content. In fact, that's what you've been doing for most of this book: changing a page's content and appearance using JavaScript.

- **The Web server** receives requests from and sends information back to the Web browser. The server might simply return some HTML or plain text, or it might return an XML document (see the box on page 427) or JSON data (page 432). For example, if the Web server receives information from a form, then it might add that information into a database and send back a confirmation message like "record added." Or, the JavaScript program might send a request for the next 10 records of a database search, and the Web server will send back the information for those next 10 records.

  The Web server part of the equation can get a bit tricky. It usually involves several different types of technologies, including a Web server, application server, and database server. A Web server is really kind of a glorified filing cabinet: it stores documents and when a Web browser asks for a document, the Web server delivers it. To do more complicated tasks such as putting data from a form into a database, you also need an *application server* and a *database server*. An application server understands a server-side programming language like PHP, Java, C#, Ruby, or Cold Fusion Markup language and lets you perform tasks that aren't possible with only an HTML page, like sending email, checking Amazon for book prices, or storing information in a database. The database server lets you store information like the names and addresses of customers, details of products you sell, or an archive of your favorite recipes. Common database servers include MySQL, PostgreSQL, and SQL Server.

Note: The term *server* can refer either to a piece of hardware or software. In this book, the terms *application, Web server,* and *database* server refer to different pieces of software that can (and often do) run on the same machine.

There are many different combinations of Web servers, application servers, and database servers. For example, you might use Microsoft's IIS Web server, with ASP.NET (application server) and SQL server (a database server). Or you can use Apache (a web server), PHP (an application server), and MySQL (a database).

Note: The combination of Apache, PHP, and MySQL (often referred to simply as AMP) is free and very common. You'll find that most Web hosting companies provide these servers. This book's examples also use AMP (see the box below).

UP TO SPEED

Setting Up a Web Server

Ajax works with a Web server—after all, its main purpose is to let JavaScript send and retrieve information from a server. While all but one of the tutorials in this and the following chapter will run on your local computer without a Web server, you'll probably want to have access to a Web server if you want to further explore the world of Ajax. If you've already got a Web site on the Internet, one choice is to test your Ajax programs by moving your files to the Web server. Unfortunately, this technique is cumbersome—you have to create the pages on your computer and then move them to your Web server using a FTP program just to see if they work.

A better approach is to set up a *development server*, which involves installing a Web server on your desktop computer so you can program and test your Ajax pages directly on your own computer. This task may sound daunting, but there are plenty of free programs that make installing all of the necessary components as easy as double-clicking a file.

On the Windows side, you can install Apache, PHP, and MySQL using XAMPP (*www.apachefriends.org/en/xampp-windows.html*). XAMPP is a free installer that sets up all of

the required elements needed to simulate a real Web site hosted on the Internet. We've provided complete installation instructions at *www.sawmac.com/xampp*.

For Mac fans, MAMP (*www.mamp.info/en/download.html*) provides an easy-to-use program that includes Apache, PHP, and MySQL. It's also free. You can find installation instructions for MAMP at *www.sawmac.com/mamp*.

The tutorial on page 426 requires AMP; the tutorials on pages 413, 433, and 455 will work without a Web server. So if you want to follow along with that tutorial, you'll need to install AMP on your computer using one of the two programs above. If you already have a Web site that uses a different Web server (for example Microsoft's IIS), you'll probably want to install it on your computer if you plan to create Ajax applications that you'd like to use on your real Web site. There are many resources for installing IIS. If you want to install IIS on Vista, visit *http://learn.iis.net/page.aspx/85/installing-iis7/*. XP Pro users can visit *www.webwizguide.com/kb/asp_tutorials/installing_iis_winXP_pro.asp*.

Talking to the Web Server

The core of any Ajax program is the *XMLHttpRequest* object. Sometimes just referred to as *XHR*, the XMLHttpRequest object is a feature built into current Web browsers that allows JavaScript to send information to a Web server and receive information in return. There are basically five steps, all of which can be accomplished with JavaScript.

1. **Create an instance of the *XMLHttpRequest* object.**

   This first step simply tells the Web browser "Hey I want to send some information to the Web server, so get ready." In its most basic form, creating an *XMLHttpRequest* object in JavaScript looks like this:

   ```
   var newXHR = new XMLHttpRequest();
   ```

   Unfortunately, while that code works in Firefox, Safari, Opera, and Internet Explorer 7, IE 6 uses a different method altogether. In other words, to complete this step so it works in the most common Web browsers, you need *two* different sets of code. In fact, there are enough cross-browser problems with Ajax that is better to use a JavaScript library—like jQuery—to make your Ajax requests. You'll learn the jQuery way on page 411.

2. **Use the XHR's *open()* method to specify what kind of data you'll send and where the data will go.**

   You can send data in two ways using either the GET or POST method—these are the same options as used with HTML forms. The GET method sends any information to the Web server as part of the URL—*shop.php?productID=34*, for example. In this example, the data is the information that follows the *?*: *productID=34*, which indicates a name/value pair, where *productID* is the name and *34* is the value. Think of the name like the name of a field on a form and value as what a visitor would type into that field.

Note: The URL you specify for the *open()* method must be on the same Web site as the page making the request. For security, Web browsers won't let you make Ajax requests to other domains.

The POST method sends data separately from the URL. Usually, you use the GET method to get data back from the server, and the POST method to update information on the server (for example, to add, update, or delete a database record). You'll learn how to use both methods on page 418.

You also use the *open()* method to specify the page on the server the data is sent to. That's usually a page on your Web server that uses a server-side scripting language like PHP to retrieve data from a database or perform some other programming task, and you point to it by its URL. For example, the following code tells the XHR object what method to use (GET) and which page on the server to request:

```
newXHR.open('GET', 'shop.php?productID=34');
```

Note: The POST method also requires you to specify a *request header,* which dictates what type of data the browser is sending to the Web server. But in this book you don't have to worry about this step, since you'll be using jQuery's Ajax tools, which take care of such details automatically.

---

3. **Create a function to handle the results.**

   When the Web server returns a result like new database information, a confirmation that a form was processed, or just a simple text message, you usually want to do something with that result. That could be as simple as writing the message "form submitted successfully," or replacing an entire table of database records with a new table of records. In any case, you need to write a JavaScript function to deal with the results—this function (called a *callback function*) is often the meat of your program.

   Usually, this function will manipulate the page's content (that is, change the page's DOM) by removing elements (for example, removing a form that was just submitted using Ajax), adding elements (a "form submitted successfully" message, or a new HTML table of database records), or changing elements (for example, highlighting the number of stars a visitor just clicked to rate a product).

   You also need to tell the XHR object about the callback function with code like the following:

   ```
   newXHR.onreadystatechange = myCallbackFunction;
   ```

   There are a few other steps involved here, but you'll be using jQuery to handle the details, so the only thing you really need to understand about the callback function is that it's the JavaScript that deals with the server's response.

4. **Send the request.**

   To actually send information to the Web server, you use the XHR object's *send( )* method. Everything up to this point is just setup—*this* step is what tells the Web browser, "We're good to go…send the request!" If you're using the GET method, this step is as simple as:

   ```
   newXHR.send(null);
   ```

   The *null* part indicates that you're not sending any additional data. (Remember, with the GET method, the data is sent in the URL like this: *search. php?q=javascript*, where the *q=javascript* is the data.) With the POST method, on the other hand, you must provide the data along with the *send( )* method like this:

   ```
   newXHR.send('q=javascript');
   ```

   Again, don't sweat the details here—you'll see how jQuery simplifies this process greatly starting in the next section.

   Once the request is sent, your JavaScript program doesn't necessarily stop. The "A" in Ajax stands for *asynchronous*, which means that once the request is sent, the JavaScript program can continue doing other things. The Web browser doesn't just sit around and wait for the server to respond.

5. **Receive the response.**

After the server has processed the request, it sends back a response to the Web browser. Actually, the callback function you created in step 3 handles the response, but meanwhile the XHR object receives several pieces of information when the Web server responds, including the *status* of the request, a *text* response, and possibly an *XML* response.

The status response is a number indicating how the server responded to the request: you're probably familiar with the status number *404*—it means the file wasn't found. If everything went according to plan, you'll get a status of 200 or possibly 304. If there was an error processing the page, you'll get a 500 "Internal Server Error" status report, and if the file you requested is password protected, you'll get a 403 "Access Forbidden" error.

In addition, most of the time, you'll receive a text response, which is stored in the XHR object's *responseText* property. This response could be a chunk of HTML, a simple text message, or a complex set of JSON data (see page 432). Finally, if the server responds with an XML file, it's stored in the XHR object's *responseXML* property. Although XML is still used, it's more common to program server pages to return text, HTML, or JSON data, so you may never have a need to process an XML response.

Whatever data the server returns, it's available to the callback function to use to update the Web page. Once the callback function finishes up, the entire Ajax cycle is over. (However, you may have multiple Ajax requests shooting off at the same time.)

Ajax the jQuery Way

There are enough differences between browsers that you have to write extra code for your Ajax programs to work in Internet Explorer, Firefox, Safari, and Opera. And although the basic *XMLHttpRequest* process isn't too complicated, since you must take so many steps each time you make an XHR request, your Ajax programming will go faster if you turn to a JavaScript library.

The jQuery library provides several functions that greatly simplify the entire process. After all, if you look at the five steps in an Ajax request (page 409), you'll see that the interesting stuff—the programming that actually does something with the server's response—happens in just a single step (step 3). jQuery simplifies all of the other steps so you can concentrate on the really fun programming.

Using the load( ) Function

The simplest Ajax function offered by jQuery is *load( )*. This function loads an HTML file into a specified element on the page. For example, say you have an area of a Web page dedicated to a short list of news headlines. When the page loads, the

Unless you're using jQuery's basic *load( )* function (page 411) to insert HTML from a page on the server into the page in the Web browser, you'll need to have server-side programming to use Ajax. The main point of Ajax is to let JavaScript talk to and get information from the server. Most of the time, that means there's another script running on the Web server that completes tasks JavaScript can't do, like reading information from a database, sending off an email, or logging a user in.

This book doesn't cover the server side, so you'll need to learn how to program using a server-side technology like PHP, .NET, JSP, ASP, or Cold Fusion (or you'll need someone who can program the server side bit for you). If you haven't picked a server-side language yet, PHP is a good place to start: it's one of the most popular Web server programming languages, it's free, and nearly every Web

hosting company offers PHP on its servers. It's a powerful language that's built for the Web, and it's *relatively* easy to learn. If you want to get started learning server-side programming with PHP, you should check out *Learning PHP & MySQL* (O'Reilly), *PHP & MySQL Web Development All-in-One Desk Reference for Dummies* (For Dummies), or *PHP Solutions: Dynamic Web Design Made Easy* (Friends of Ed). Any of these books is a good place to start.

There are also plenty of free online resources for learning PHP. PHP 101 (*http://devzone.zend.com/node/view/id/627*) from Zend (one of the main companies that supports the development of PHP) has plenty of basic (and advanced) information. The W3Schools web site also has a lot of information for the beginning PHP programmer at *www.w3schools.com/PHP*.

five most recent news stories appear. You may want to add a few links that let visitors choose what type of news stories are displayed in this area of the page: for example, yesterday's news, local news, sports news, and so on. You can do this by linking to separate Web pages, each of which contain the proper news items—but that would force your visitors to move onto another Web page (and wouldn't use Ajax at all!).

Another approach would be to simply load the selected news stories into the news headlines box on the page. In other words, each time a visitor clicks a different news category, the Web browser requests a new HTML file from the server, and then places that HTML into the headlines box—without leaving the current page (see Figure 11-3).

To use the *load( )* function, you first use a jQuery selector to identify the element on the page where the requested HTML should go; you then call the *load( )* function and pass the URL of the page you wish to retrieve. For example, say you have a <div> tag with the ID *headlines* and you want to load the HTML from the file *todays_news.html* into that div. You can do that like this:

```
$('#headlines').load('todays_news.html');
```

When this code runs, the Web browser requests the file *todays_news.html* from the Web server. When that file is downloaded, the browser replaces whatever is currently inside the <div> with the ID *headlines* with the contents of the new file.

The HTML file can be a complete Web page (including the <html>, <head>, and <body> tags), or just a snippet of HTML—for example, the requested file might just have a single <h1> tag and a paragraph of text. It's OK if the file isn't a complete Web page, since the *load( )* function inserts only that HTML snippet into the current (complete) page.

Note: You can only load HTML files from the same site. For example, you can't load Google's home page into a <div> on a page from your site using the *load( )* function. (You can display a page from another Web site using an iframe–this is the technique used by the greybox2 plug-in presented on page 286.)

When using the *load( )* function, you must be very careful with file paths. First, the URL you pass to the *load( )* function is in relation to the current page. In other words, you use the same path as if you were linking from the current page to the HTML file you wish to load. In addition, any file paths in the HTML don't get rewritten when the HTML is loaded into the document, so if you have a link or include images in the HTML file that's loaded, those URLs need to work in relation to the page using the *load( )* function. In other words, if you're using document-relative paths (see the box on page 25) and the loaded HTML file is located in another folder on your Web site, images and links might not work when the HTML is loaded into the current page. Here's a simple workaround: just use root-relative links, or make sure the file you load is located in the same directory as the page that's using the *load( )* function.

The *load( )* function even lets you specify which part of the downloaded HTML file you wish to add to the page. For example, say the page you request is a regular Web page from the site; it includes all of the normal Web page elements such as a banner, navigation bar, and footer. You may just be interested in the content from a single area of that page—for example just a particular <div> and its contents. To specify which part of the page you wish to load, insert a space after the URL, followed by a jQuery selector. For example, say in the above example you want to insert the content only inside a <div> with the ID *news* in the *todays_news.html* file. You could do that with this code:

```
$('#headlines').load('todays_news.html #news');
```

In this case, the Web browser downloads the page *todays_news.html*, but instead of inserting the entire contents of the file into the *headlines* <div>, it extracts just the <div> tag (and everything inside it) with an ID of *news*. You'll see this technique in the following tutorial.

Tutorial: The *load()* Function

In this tutorial, you'll use jQuery to replace the traditional click-and-load method of accessing HTML (Figure 11-3, top) with a more responsive method that simply replaces content on the current page with new HTML (Figure 11-3, bottom).

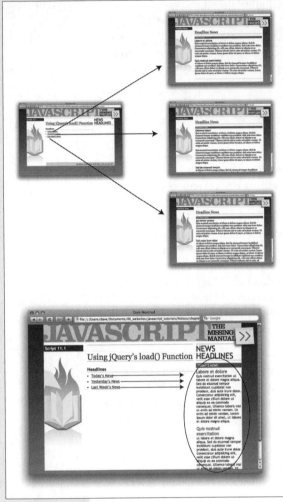

Figure 11-3:
*The top set of images represents the normal method of
accessing additional HTML—links. Click a link on a page
(left) and it loads a brand new page (right). However,
using Ajax and jQuery's load( ) function, you can access
the same HTML without leaving the current Web page
(bottom). Clicking a link loads the HTML content into a
<div> tag (circled).*

Overview

To get a handle on what you'll be doing in this tutorial, you first need to understand the HTML of the page you're about to "Ajaxify." Take a look at Figure 11-4:
The page has a bulleted list of links, each of which points to a different page containing different news headlines. The <ul> tag used to create the list has the ID
links. In addition, there's an empty <div> tag in the right sidebar (below the "News
Headlines" header). That div has an ID of *headlines* and is, at this point, an empty
placeholder. Eventually, once you use jQuery's *load( )* function, clicking one of the
links will load news stories into the <div>.

Currently, clicking a link just opens a Web page with a series of news items. In
other words, this page works the regular HTML way—it has links that point to
other pages. In fact, without the nifty JavaScript you're about to add, the page

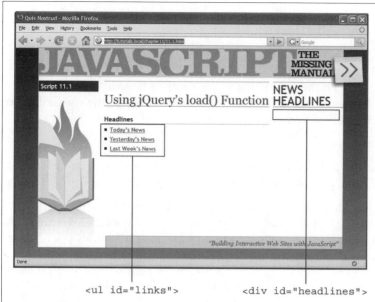

Figure 11-4:
When you want to use JavaScript to add content to a page, it's common to insert an empty <div> tag with an ID. You can then select that <div> and insert content when you want. For example, this page has an empty div (<div id="headlines">) in the right sidebar. With a little Ajax power, it's a simple matter to fill that div with the contents of any of the three linked pages listed in the middle of the page.

```
<ul id="links">                 <div id="headlines">
```

works perfectly fine—it'll get any visitors to the news they're after. That's a good thing, because not everyone has JavaScript enabled in their browsers. In addition, if the only way to get to those news items is through JavaScript, search engines would skip over that valuable content.

Note: You can use the *load( )* function directly from your hard drive without a Web server, so you don't need to set up a server on your computer (see the box on page 408) to follow along.

This tutorial provides an example of *progressive enhancement*—it functions just fine without JavaScript, but works even better with JavaScript. In other words, everyone can access the content, and no one's left out. To implement progressive enhancement, you'll add JavaScript to "hijack" the normal link function, then get the URL of the link, and then download the link to the page and put its contents into the empty <div>. It's as simple as that.

Note: See the note on page 27 for information on how to download the tutorial files.

The programming

1. In a text editor, open the file *11.1.html* in the *chapter11* folder.

   You'll start by assigning a *click* event function to each of the links in the bulleted list in the main part of the page. The bulleted list (the <ul> tag) has an ID of *links*, so you can easily use jQuery to select each of those links and assign a *click( )* function to them.

2. **Click in the empty line inside the *$(document).ready( )* function, and type:**

```
$('#links a').click(function( ) {

});
```

The *$('#links a')* is the jQuery way to select each of those links, and the *.click( )* function lets you assign a function (an event handler) to the *click* event (see page 201 if you need a refresher on events).

The next step is to extract the URL from each link.

3. **Inside the *click( )* function (the blank line in step 2 above) type *var url=$(this). attr('href');* and press Return to create an empty line.**

This line of code creates a new variable (*url*) and assigns it the value of the link's *href* attribute. As you'll recall from page 180, when you attach a function (like the *click( )* function) to a jQuery selection (*$('#links a')* in this case), jQuery loops through each element in the selection (each link) and applies the function to each one. The *$(this)* is just a way to get hold of the current element being worked on. In other words *$(this)* will refer to a different link as jQuery loops through the collection of elements. The *attr( )* function (discussed on page 189) can retrieve or set a particular element for a tag; in this case, the function extracts the *href* property to get the URL of the page the link points to. In the next step, you'll use that URL along with the *load( )* function to retrieve the page's content and display it inside a <div> on the page.

4. **Type *$('#headlines').load(url);* so the script looks like this:**

```
$('#links a').click(function( ) {
  var url=$(this).attr('href');
  $('#headlines').load(url);
});
```

Remember that the empty <div> tag on the page—where the downloaded HTML will go—has an ID of *headlines*, so *$('#headlines')* selects that <div>. The *load( )* function then downloads the HTML at the URL that the previous line of code retrieved, and then puts that HTML in the <div> tag. Yes, there's actually *lots* of other stuff going on under the hood to make all that happen, but thanks to jQuery, you don't have to worry about it.

The page isn't quite done yet. If you save the file and preview it in a Web browser—go ahead, try it—you'll notice that clicking one of the links doesn't load new content onto the page—it actually leaves the current page and loads the linked page instead! What happened to the Ajax? It's still there, it's just that the Web browser is following its normal behavior of loading a new Web page when a link is clicked. To stop that, you have to prevent the browser from following the link.

5. **Add a new empty line after the code you typed in the previous step and type** *return false;* **so the script now looks like this:**

```
$('#links a').click(function() {
  var url=$(this).attr('href');
  $('#headlines').load(url);
  return false;
});
```

This simple step tells the Web browser, "Hey, Web browser, don't follow that link." It's one way of preventing a browser from following its normal behavior in response to an event. You can also use jQuery's *preventDefault( )* function as described on page 223 to achieve the same effect.

6. **Save the file and preview it in a Web browser. Click one of the links.**

Now there's another problem, as you can see in Figure 11-5. The *load( )* function is working, it's just that the downloaded file has a lot of HTML you don't want—like the same banner, layout, sidebar, and footer as the current page. What you really want is only a portion of that Web page—the area containing the news items. Fortunately, the *load( )* function can help here as well.

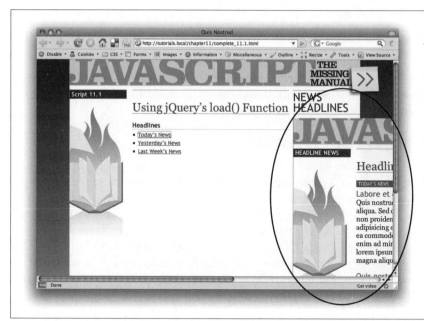

Figure 11-5:
jQuery's load( ) *function will download all of the HTML for a specified file and place it into an element on the current page. If the downloaded file includes unneeded HTML, like a duplicate banner, sidebar, and footer, the result can look like a page within a page.*

7. **Locate the line with the** *load( )* **function and add** *+ ' #newsItems'* **after** *url.* **The finished code should look like this:**

```
$('#links a').click(function() {
  var url=$(this).attr('href');
```

```
$('#headlines').load(url + ' #newsItems');
return false;
});
```

As described on page 413, you can specify which part of a downloaded file you want the *load( )* function to add to the page. To do that, you add a space after the URL followed by a selector that identifies the part of the downloaded page you wish to display.

Here's how the code breaks down into bit-sized chunks: First, on each of the linked pages, there's a <div> tag with the ID *newsItems*. That div contains the HTML you want—the news items. So you can tell the *load( )* function to only insert that part of the downloaded HTML by adding a space followed by *#newsItems* to the URL passed to *load( )*. For example, if you want to load the file *today.html* and place just the HTML inside the *newsItems* div inside the *headlines* div, you can use this code:

```
$('#headlines').load('today.html #newsItems');
```

In this case, you need to combine two strings—the contents of the *url* variable and *' #newsItems'* to get the proper code—so you use JavaScript's string concatenation operator (the + symbol) like this: *load(url + ' #newsItems')*. (See page 49 if you need a refresher on how to combine two strings.)

8. **Save the file and preview it in a Web browser. Click the links to test it out.**

   Now the news items—and only the news items—from each linked page should appear in the right sidebar. Ajax in just a few lines of code! (You'll find a completed version of the tutorial—*complete_11.1.html*—in the *chapter11* file for reference.)

The get( ) and post( ) Functions

The *load( )* function described on page 411 is a quick way to get HTML from a Web server and inject it into a page. But the server may not always return straight HTML—it may return a message, a code number, or data that you then need to process further using JavaScript. For example, if you want to use Ajax to get some database records, the server may return an XML file containing those records (see the box on page 427) or a JSON object (page 432). You wouldn't just insert that data into the page—you first have to get the data and process it in some way to generate the HTML you want.

jQuery's *get( )* and *post( )* functions provide simple tools to send data to and retrieve data from a Web server. As mentioned in step 4 on page 410, you need to treat the *XMLHttpRequest* object slightly differently when using either the GET or POST method. However, jQuery takes care of any differences between the two methods so the *get( )* and *post( )* functions work identically. (So which should you use? Read the box on page 420.)

The basic structure of these functions is:

```
$.get(url, data, callback);
```

Or:

```
$.post(url, data, callback);
```

Unlike most other jQuery functions, you don't add *get( )* or *post( )* to a jQuery selector—in other words, you'd never do something like this: *$('#mainContent'). get('products.php')*. The two functions stand by themselves and aren't connected with any element on the page, so you just use the *$* symbol, followed by a period, followed by either *get* or *post*: *$.get( )*.

The *get( )* and *post( )* functions accept three arguments: *url* is a string that contains the path to the server-side script that processes the data (for example, *'processForm. php'*). The *data* argument is either a string or a JavaScript object literal containing the data you want to send to the server (you'll learn how to create this in the next section). Finally, *callback* is the function that processes the information returned from the server (see the box on page 246 for details on writing a callback function).

When either the *get( )* or *post( )* function runs, the Web browser sends off the data to the specified URL. When the server sends data back to the browser, the browser hands that data to the callback function, which then processes that information and usually updates the Web page in some way. You'll see an example of this in action on page 426.

Formatting Data to Send to the Server

Most of the time when writing a JavaScript program that uses Ajax, you'll be sending some information to the server. For example, if you want to get information about a particular product stored in a database, you could send a single number representing a product. When the Web server gets the number from the XHR request, it looks for a product in the database that matches that number, retrieves the product information, and sends it back to the Web browser. Or, you might use Ajax to submit an entire form's worth of information as part of an online order or a "sign up for our email newsletter" form.

In either case you need to format the data for your request in a way that the *get( )* and *post( )* functions understand. The second argument sent to either function contains the data you wish to send the server—you can format this data either as a query string or as a JavaScript object literal, as described in the next two sections.

Query string

You've probably seen query strings before: they frequently appear at the end of a URL following a *?* symbol. For example, the query string is *www.chia-vet.com/products.php?prodID=18&sessID=1234*. This query string contains two name/value pairs, *prodID=18* and *sessID=1234*. This string does basically the same as creating two variables, *prodID* and *sessID*, and storing two values into them. A query string is a common method for passing information in a URL.

You can also format data sent to the server using Ajax in this format. For example, say you've created a Web page that lets visitors rate movies by clicking a number of stars. Clicking five stars, for instance, submits a rating of five to the server. In this case, the data sent to the server might look like this: *rating=5*. Assuming the name of the page processing these ratings is called *rateMovie.php*, the code to send the rating to the server using Ajax would look like this:

```
$.get('rateMovie.php','rating=5');
```

Or, if you're using the POST method:

```
$.post('rateMovie.php','rating=5');
```

Note: jQuery's *get( )* and *post( )* functions don't require you to define data or a callback function. You only need to supply the URL of the server-side page. However, you'll almost always provide data as well. For example, in this code *$.get('rankMovie.php','rating=5');* only the URL and the data are supplied—no callback function is specified. In this case, the visitor is merely submitting a ranking, and there's no need for the server to respond or for a callback function to do anything.

If you need to send more than one name/value pair to the server, insert a *&* between each pair:

```
$.post('rateMovie.php','rating=5&user=Bob');
```

You need to be careful using this method, however, since some characters have special meaning when you insert into a query string. For instance, you use the *&* symbol to include additional name/value pairs to the string; the = symbol assigns a value to a name. For example, the following query string isn't valid:

```
'favFood=Mac & Cheese' // incorrect
```

The *&* symbol here is supposed to be part of "Mac & Cheese," but when used as part of a query string, the *&* will be interpreted to mean a second name/value pair. If you want to use special characters as part of the name or value in a name/value pair, you need to *escape*, or *encode* them so that they won't be mistaken for a character with special meaning. For example, the space character is represented by *%20*, the *&* symbol by *%26*, and the = sign by *%3D*. So you need to write out the "Mac & Cheese" example like this:

```
'favFood=Mac%20%26%20Cheese' // properly escaped
```

JavaScript provides a method for properly escaping strings—the *encodeURIComponent( )* method. You supply the *endcodeURIComponent( )* method with a string, and it returns a properly escaped string. For example:

```
var queryString = 'favFood=' + encodeURIComponent('Mac & Cheese');
$.post('foodChoice.php' queryString);
```

Object literal

For short and simple pieces of data (that don't include any punctuation symbols), the query string method works well. But a more foolproof method supported by jQuery's *get( )* and *post( )* functions is to use an object literal to store data. As you'll recall from page 188, an object literal is a JavaScript method for storing name/value pairs. The basic structure of an object literal is this:

```
{
  name1: 'value1',
  name2: 'value2'
}
```

You can pass the object literal directly to the *get( )* or *post( )* function. For example, this code uses the query string method:

```
$.post('rankMovie.php','rating=5');
```

To use an object literal, rewrite the code like this:

```
$.post('rankMovie.php', { rating: 5 });
```

You can either pass the object literal directly to the *get( )* or *post( )* functions, or first store it in a variable and pass that variable to *get( )* or *post( )*:

```
var data = { rating: 5 };
$.post('rankMovie.php', data);
```

Of course, you can include any number of name/value pairs in the object that you pass to the *get( )* or *post( )* function:

```
var data = {
    rating: 5,
    user: 'Bob'
}
$.post('rankMovie.php', data);
```

jQuery's serialize( ) function

Creating a query string or object literal for an entire form's worth of name/value pairs can be quite a chore. You have to retrieve the name and value for each form element, and then combine them all to create one long query string or one large JavaScript object literal. Fortunately, jQuery provides a function that makes it easy to convert form information into data that the *get( )* and *post( )* functions can use.

You can apply the *serialize( )*function to any form (or even just a selection of form fields) to create a query string. To use it, first create a jQuery selection that includes a form, then attach the *serialize( )* function to it. For example, say you have a form with an ID of *login*. If you wanted to create a query string for that form, you can do so like this:

```
var formData = $('#login').serialize();
```

The *var formData* part just creates a new variable; *$('#login')* creates a jQuery selection containing the form; finally, *.serialize( )* collects all of the field names and the values currently in each field and creates a single query string.

To use this with either the *get( )* or *post( )* functions, just pass the serialized results to the function as the second argument after the URL. For example, say you want to send the contents of the login form to a page named *login.php*. You can do so like this:

```
var formData = $('#login').serialize();
$.get('login.php',formData,loginResults);
```

This code sends whatever the visitor enters into the form to the *login.php* file using the GET method. The final argument for *get( )* here—*loginResults*—is the callback function: the function that takes the data sent back from the server and does something with it. You'll learn how to create a callback function next.

Processing Data from the Server

Ajax is usually a two-way street—a JavaScript program sends some data to the server and the server returns data to the JavaScript program, which can then use that data to update the page. In the previous pages, you saw how to format data and send it to a server using the *get( )* and *post( )* functions. Now you'll learn how to receive and process the server's response.

As mentioned on page 408, when the Web browser sends off a request to the server using the XMLHttpRequest object, it keeps listening for a response from the server. When the server responds, a callback function handles the server's response. That function is passed several arguments that can be used by the function. First, and most important, the data returned by the server is sent as the first argument.

You can format the data the server returns in any number of ways. The server-side script can return a number, a word, a paragraph of text, or a complete Web page. In cases where the server is sending a lot of information (like a bunch of records from a database), the server often uses XML or JSON. (See the box on page 427 for more about XML; see page 432 for a discussion of JSON.)

The second argument to the callback function is a string indicating the status of the response. Most of the time, the status is "success", meaning that the server has successfully processed the request and returned data. However, sometimes a request doesn't succeed—for example, the request was made to a file that doesn't exist, or there was an error in the server-side programming. If a request fails, the callback function receives an "error" status message.

The callback function processes the information in some way, and, most of the time, updates the Web page in some way—replacing a submitted form with results from the server, or simply printing a "request successful" message on the page, for example. Updating the content of a Web page is easy using jQuery's *html( )* and *text( )* functions described on page 181. Other methods of manipulating a page's DOM are discussed in Chapter 5.

To get a handle on a complete request/response cycle, take a look at a basic movie-rating example (see Figure 11-6). A visitor can rate a movie by clicking one of five links. Each link indicates a different rating. When the visitor clicks a link, the rating and ID of the movie being rated are sent to a server-side program, which adds the rating to the database, and then returns the average rating for that movie. The average rating is then displayed on the Web page.

In order for this page to work without JavaScript, each of the links on the page points to a dynamic server-side page that can process the visitor's rating. For example, the five-star rating link (see Figure 11-6) might be *rate.php?rate=5&movie=123*. The name of the server-side file that processes the ratings is called *rate.php*, while the query string (*?rate=5&movie=123*) includes two pieces

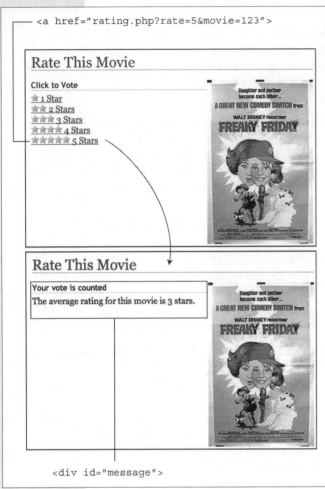

```
<a href="rating.php?rate=5&movie=123">
```

Rate This Movie

Click to Vote

⭐ 1 Star
⭐⭐ 2 Stars
⭐⭐⭐ 3 Stars
⭐⭐⭐⭐ 4 Stars
⭐⭐⭐⭐⭐ 5 Stars

Rate This Movie

Your vote is counted
The average rating for this movie is 3 stars.

```
<div id="message">
```

Figure 11-6:
On this page, a visitor clicks a link to rate the movie (top). By adding Ajax to the mix, you can submit the rating to the server without leaving the page. In fact, using the response from the server, you can update the page's contents (bottom).

of information for the server: a rating (*rate=5*) and a number that identifies the movie being rated (*movie=123*). You can use JavaScript to intercept clicks on these links and translate them into Ajax calls to the server:

```
1   $('#message a').click(function() {
2     var href=$(this).attr('href');
3     var querystring=href.slice(href.indexOf('?')+1);
4     $.get('rate.php', querystring, processResponse);
5     return false; // stop the link
6   });
```

Line 1 selects every link (<a> tag) inside of another tag with an ID of *message* (in this example, each link used to rate the movie is contained within a <div> with the ID *message*). A function is then applied to the click event for each of those links.

Line 2 extracts the HREF attribute of the link—so, for example, the *href* variable might hold a URL like *rate.php?rate=5&movie=123*. Line 3 extracts just the part after the *?* in the URL using the *slice( )* method (discussed on page 117) to extract part of the string, and the *indexOf( )* method (see page 118) to determine where the *?* is located (this information is used by the *slice( )* method to determine where to start slicing).

Line 4 is the Ajax request. Using the GET method, a request containing the query string for the link is sent to the server file *rate.php* (see Figure 11-7). The results will then go to the callback function *processResponse*. Line 5 just stops the normal link behavior and prevents the Web browser from unloading the current page and loading the linked-to page.

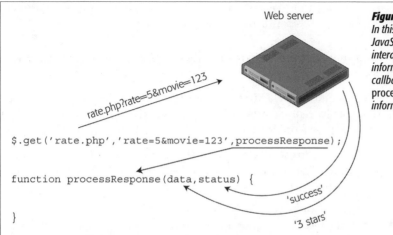

Web server

Figure 11-7:
In this diagram, you can see how JavaScript and the Web server interact. The get( ) function sends information to the server, while the callback function– processResponse( )–handles the information returned by the server.

Note: If you need a refresher on how functions work and how to create them, see page 97.

Finally, it's time to create the callback function. The callback function receives data and a string with the status of the response (*'success'* if the server sent information back). Remember the callback function's name is used in the request (see line 4 of the code on the previous page). So in this example, the function's name is *processResponse*. The code to deal with the server's response might look like this:

```
1   function processResponse(data, status) {
2     var newHTML;
3     if (status=='success') {
4       newHTML = '<h2>Your vote is counted</h2>';
5       newHTML += '<p>The average rating for this movie is ';
6       newHTML += data + '.</p>';
7     } else {
8       newHTML='<h2>There has been an error.</h2>';
9       newHTML+='<p>Please try again later.</p>';
```

```
10      }
11      $('#message').html(newHTML);
12      }
```

The function accepts two arguments—*data* and *status*. Line 2 creates a new variable that holds the HTML that will be displayed on the page (for example, "Your vote is counted"). In line 3, a conditional statement checks to make sure the server responded successfully, and if it did, then the *newHTML* variable is filled with some HTML, including a <h2> tag and a <p> tag. The server's response doesn't come into play until line 6—there the response from the server (stored in the *data* variable) is added to the *newHTML* variable. In this case, the server returns a string with the average rating for the movie: for example, *'3 stars'*.

Tip: If you want to add a star rating system to your site, there's a great jQuery plug-in that handles most of the details available at *http://plugins.learningjquery.com/half-star-rating/*.

The *else* clause simply creates an error message in case the server didn't successfully respond to the request.

Finally, line 11 modifies the HTML on the Web page using jQuery's *html( )* function (see page 181) by replacing the contents of the <div> with the ID of *message* with the new HTML. The result is something like the bottom image in Figure 11-6.

In this example, the callback function was defined outside of the *get( )* function; however, you can use an anonymous function (see page 193) if you want to keep all of the Ajax code together:

```
.get('file.php', data, function(data,status) {
   // callback function programming goes here
});
```

Tutorial: Using the *get( )* Function

In this tutorial, you'll use Ajax to submit information from a login form. When a visitor supplies the correct user name and password, a message will appear letting him know he's successfully logged in. If the login information isn't correct, an error message will appear on the same page—without loading a new Web page.

Note: In order to successfully complete this tutorial, you'll need to have a running Web server to test the pages on. See the box on page 408 for information on how to set up a testing server on your computer.

Overview

You'll start with the form pictured in Figure 11-8. It includes fields for supplying a username and password to the server. When the form is submitted, the server attempts to verify that the user exists and the password matches. If the information supplied matches valid login credentials, then the server logs the visitor in.

Receiving XML from the Server

XML is a common format for exchanging data between computers. Like HTML, XML lets you use tags to identify information. Unlike HTML, you're free to come up with tags that accurately reflect the content of your data. For example, a simple XML file might look like this:

```
<?xml version="1.0" encoding="ISO-8859-
1"?>
<message id="234">
  <from>Bob</from>
  <to>Janette</to>
  <subject>Hi Janette</subject>
  <content>Janette, let's grab lunch
today.</content>
</message>
```

As you can see, there's a main tag (called the *root element*) named <message>—the equivalent of HTML's <html> tag—and several other tags that define the meaning of each piece of data.

When using Ajax, you might have a server program that returns an XML file. jQuery has no problem reading and extracting data from an XML file. When you use the *get( )* or *post( )* functions, if the server returns an XML file, the data argument that's sent to the callback function (see page 423) will contain the DOM of the XML file. In other words, jQuery will read the XML file and treat it like another document. You can then use jQuery's selector tools to access the data inside the XML.

For example, say a server-side file named *xml.php* returned the XML listed above, and you want to retrieve the text within the <content> tag. The XML file becomes the returned data, so the callback function can process it. You can use the jQuery *find( )* function to search the XML to find a particular CSS element using any of the regular selectors you'd use with jQuery. For example, you can find an element, class, ID, or descendent selector (page 172), or jQuery's filters (page 176).

For example:

```
$.get('xml.php','id=234',processXML);
function processXML(data) {
  var messageContent=$(data).
find('content').text();
}
```

The key here is *$(data).find('content')*, which tells jQuery to select every <content> tag within the *data* variable. Since, in this case, the *data* variable contains the returned XML file, this code tells jQuery to look for the <content> tag within the XML.

For learn more about XML, visit *www.w3schools.com/XML*. If you want a little information on how to produce XML from a server, check out *www.w3schools.com/XML/xml_server.asp*. And if you want to read about jQuery's *find( )* function you'll find more information at *http://docs.jquery.com/Traversing/find#expr*.

You'll add Ajax to the form by sending the login information via a *XMLHttpRequest*. The server will send a message to the callback function, which removes the form and displays a "logged in" message if the login information is valid, or an error message if it's not.

The programming

See the note on page 27 for information on how to download the tutorial files. The starting file contains the HTML form, ready for you to add some jQuery and Ajax programming.

1. **In a text editor, open the file *11.2.html* in the *chapter11* folder.**

   The link to the jQuery library file and the *$(document).ready( )* function are already in place. You'll start by selecting the form and adding a *submit* event to it.

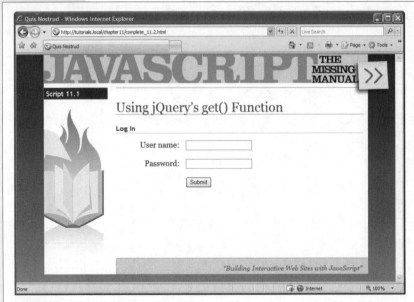

Figure 11-8:
A basic login page is a simple affair: just a couple of fields and a submit button. However, there's really no reason to leave the page when the user logs in. By adding Ajax, you can submit the visitor's credentials, then notify whether he logged in successfully or not.

2. **Click in the empty line inside the *$(document).ready( )* function and type:**

```
$('#login').submit(function() {

}); // end submit
```

The <form> tag has the ID login applied to it, so the jQuery selector—*$('#login')*—selects that form, while the *submit( )* function adds an event handler to the *submit* event. In other words, when a visitor tries to submit the form, the function you're about to create will run.

The next step is to collect the information from the form and format it as a query string to submit to the server. You could do this by finding each form field, extracting the value that the visitor had typed in, then constructing query string by concatenating those different pieces of information. Fortunately, jQuery's *serialize( )* function takes care of all these details in one shot.

3. **Hit return to create an empty line and type:**

```
var formData = $(this).serialize();
```

This line starts by creating a new variable to hold the form data, and then applies the *serialize( )* function to the form. Recall that *$(this)* refers to the current element, so in this case it refers to the login form, and is the same as *$('#login')* (see page 194 for more on how *$(this)* works). The *serialize( )* function (see page 422), takes a form and extracts the field names and values and puts them in the proper format for submitting to the server.

Now you'll use the *post( )* function to set up the *XMLHttpRequest*.

4. **Hit Return to create another empty line and type:**

```
$.post('login.php',formData,processData);
```

This code passes three arguments to the *post( )* function. The first—*'login. php'*—is a string identifying where the data should be sent—in this case, a file on the server named *login.php*. The second argument is the query string containing the data that's being sent to the server—the login information. Finally, *processData* refers to the callback function that will process the server's response. You'll create that function now.

5. **Add another blank line below the last one and type:**

```
1    function processData(data) {
2
3    } // end processData
```

These lines form the shell of the callback function; there's no programming inside it yet. Notice that the function is set up to accept one argument (*data*), which will be the response coming from the server. The server-side page is programmed to return a single word—*pass* if the login succeeded, or *fail* if the login failed.

In other words, based on the response from the server, the script will either print a message letting the visitor know he's successfully logged on, or that he hasn't—this is the perfect place for a conditional statement.

Note: The server-side page used in this tutorial isn't a full-fledged login script. It does respond if the proper credentials are supplied, but it's not something you could use to actually password-protect a site. There are many ways to effectively password protect a site, but most require setting up a database or setting up various configuration settings for the Web server–these steps are beyond this basic tutorial. For a real, PHP-based login script that also uses jQuery, visit *www.chazzuka.com/blog/?p=174*. Once you've complete the tutorial on that site, you will have everything you need to implement a login script like this one.

---

6. **Inside the *processData( )* function (in other words line 2 in step 5) type:**

```
1    if (data=='pass') {
2        $('#content').html('<p>You have successfully logged on!</p>');
3    }
```

Line 1 here checks to see if the information returned from the server is the string *'pass'*. If it is, the login was successful and a success message is printed (line 2). The form is inside a <div> tag with the ID *content*, so *$('#content'). html('<p>You have successfully logged on!</p>')* will replace whatever's inside that <div> with a new paragraph. In other words, the form disappears and the success message appears in its place.

To finish up, you'll add an *else* clause to let the visitor know if he didn't supply the correct login information.

---

7. Add an *else* clause to the *processData( )* function so that it looks like this (additions are in bold):

```
1    function processData(data) {
2        if (data=='pass') {
3            $('#content').html('<p>You have successfully logged on!</p>');
4        } else {
5            $('#content').prepend('<p id="fail">Incorrect ↵
6        login information. Please try again</p>');
7        }
8    } // end processData
```

Line 6 prints the message that the login failed. Notice that the *prepend( )* function is used. As discussed on page 182, *prepend( )* lets you add content to the beginning of an element. It doesn't remove what's already there; it just adds more content. In this case, you want to leave the form in place, so the visitor can try again to log in a second time.

8. **Save the file, and preview it in a Web browser.**

You must view this page through a Web browser using a URL, like *http:// localhost/chapter11/11.2.html*, for this tutorial to work. See the box on page 408 for more information on how to set up a Web server.

9. **Try to log into the site.**

"But wait—you haven't given me the username and password yet!" you're probably thinking. That's the point—to see what happens when you don't log in correctly. Try to log in a second time: you'll see the "Incorrect login information" message appear a second time (see Figure 11-9). Since the *prepend( )* function doesn't remove the first error message, it just adds the message a second time. That doesn't look right at all. You need to add a conditional statement to make sure you print the error message only if it isn't already on the page.

10. **Add another conditional statement (lines 5 and 7 below):**

```
1    function processData(data) {
2        if (data=='pass') {
3            $('#content').html('<p>You have successfully logged on!</p>');
4        } else {
5            if ($('#fail').length==0) {
6                $('#content').prepend('<p id="fail">Incorrect ↵
7                login information. Please try again</p>');
8            }
9        }
10   } // end processData
```

Notice that the error message paragraph has an ID—*fail*—so you can use jQuery to check to see if that ID exists on the page. If it doesn't, then the program writes the error message on the page. One way to check if an element

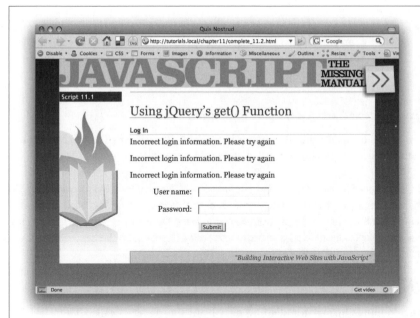

Figure 11-9:
jQuery's prepend( )
*function adds HTML to
an already existing
element. It doesn't delete
anything, so if you're not
careful, you may end up
adding the same
message over and over
again.*

already exists on the page is to try to use jQuery to select it. You can then check
the *length* attribute of the results. If jQuery couldn't find any matching elements, the *length* attribute is *0*. In other words, *$('#fail')* tries to find an ele-
ment with the ID *fail*. If jQuery can't find it—in other words, the error message
hasn't yet been written to the page—then the length attribute is *0*, the conditional statement will be true, and the program writes the error message. Once
the error message is on the page, the conditional statement always evaluates to
false, and the error message doesn't appear again.

Finally, you need to tell the Web browser that it shouldn't submit the form data
itself—you already did that using Ajax.

11. **Add** *return false;* **at the end of the submit event (line 15 below). The finished
script should look like this:**

```
1    $(document).ready(function( ) {
2    $('#login').submit(function( ) {
3      var formData = $(this).serialize( );
4      $.post('login.php',formData,processData);
5      function processData(data) {
6        if (data=='pass') {
7          $('#content').html('<p>You have successfully logged on!</p>');
8        } else {
9          if (! $('#fail').length) {
10           $('#content').prepend('<p id="fail">Incorrect ⏎
11           login information. Please try again</p>');
```

```
12            }
13         }
14      } // end processData
15      return false;
16    }); // end submit
17  }); // end ready
```

12. **Save the file and preview the page once again.**

Try to log in again: the user name is *007* and the password is *secret*. A completed version of this tutorial *complete_11.2.html* is in the *chapter11* folder.

Note: As mentioned on page 418, jQuery's *post( )* and *get( )* functions work identically even though, behind the scenes, jQuery has to do two different set of steps to make the Ajax request work correctly. You can check this out yourself by just changing *post* to *get* in the script (see line 4 in step 11). The server-side script for this tutorial is programmed to accept either GET or POST requests.

JSON

Another popular format for sending data from the server is called JSON, which stands for *JavaScript Object Notation*. JSON is a data format that's written in JavaScript, and it's kind of like XML (see the box on page 427), in that it's a method for exchanging data. However, for an Ajax application, JSON has two major benefits: first, the data is stored as JavaScript, so it's very easy for a JavaScript program to work with. Secondly, you can request JSON data from other domains, so you can, for example, request images from Flickr (*www.flickr.com*) and display them on a page on your own site (as mentioned in the Note on page 409, usually you can only make an Ajax request to your own domain).

You already learned how to create JSON back on page 188. In essence, JSON is simply a JavaScript object literal, or a collection of name/value pairs. Here's a simple example of JSON:

```
{
    firstName: 'Frank',
    lastName: 'Smith',
    phone: '503-555-1212'
}
```

The { marks the beginning of the JSON object, while the } marks its end. In between are sets of name/value pairs: for example, *firstName: 'Frank'*. Every name/value pair is separated by a comma, but don't put a comma at the end of the last pair (otherwise Internet Explorer will cough up an error).

Note: Alternatively, you can put the name in the name/value pair in quotes as well, like this:

```
{
    'firstName': 'Frank',
    'lastName': 'Smith',
    'phone': '503-555-1212'
}
```

You *must* use quotes if the name has a space in it, or other non-alphanumeric characters.

Think of a name value/pair just like a variable—the name is like the name of the variable, and the value is what's stored inside that variable. In the above example, *lastName* acts like a variable, with the string *'Smith'* stored in it.

When the Web server responds to an Ajax request, it can return a string formatted like a JSON. The server doesn't actually send JavaScript: it just sends text that's formatted like a JSON object. It isn't actually real, usable JavaScript until the string is converted into an actual JSON object. Fortunately, jQuery provides a special function, *getJSON( )*, that handles all of the details. The *getJSON( )* function looks and works much like the *get( )* and *post( )* functions. The basic structure looks like this:

```
$.getJSON(url, data, callback);
```

The three arguments passed to the function are the same as for *post( )* or *get( )*—the URL of the server-side page, data to send to the server-side page, and the name of a callback function. The difference is that *getJSON( )* will process the response from the server (which is just a string) and convert it (through some JavaScript wizardry) into a usable JSON object.

Note: PHP 5.2 has a built-in function to make it easy to create a JSON object out of a traditional PHP array. Visit *www.php.net/manual/en/function.json-encode.php* to learn more.

In other words, *getJSON( )* works just like *post( )* or *get( )* but the data passed to the callback is a JSON object. To use the *getJSON( )* function, then, you only need to learn how to process a JSON object with the callback function. For a basic example, say you want to use Ajax to request information on a single contact from a server-side file named *contacts.php*; that file returns contact data in JSON format (like the JSON example on the previous page). A basic request would look like this:

```
$.getJSON('contacts.php','contact=123',processContacts);
```

This code sends a query string—*contact=123*—to *contacts.php*. Say the *contacts.php* file uses that information to locate a single contact in a database and retrieve that contact's information. The result is sent back to the Web browser and handed to the callback function *processContacts*. The basic structure of the callback, then, would look like this:

```
function processContacts(data) {

}
```

The *processContacts( )* function has one argument—*data*—that contains the JSON object from the server. Let's look at how the callback can access information from the JSON object.

Accessing JSON Data

There are two ways to access data in a JSON object: *dot syntax* or *array notation*. Dot-syntax (see page 114) is a way of indicating an object's property—specifically, by adding a period between the name of the object and the property you wish to access. You've seen this in use with properties of different JavaScript objects like strings and arrays. For example, *'abc'.length* accesses the string's *length* property, and, in this example, returns the number of letters in the string *'abc'*, which is *3*.

For example, suppose you create a variable and store an object literal inside it like this:

```
var bday = {
  person: 'Raoul',
  date: '10/27/1980'
};
```

In this case, the variable *bday* contains the object literal, so if you want to get the value of person in the object, use dot syntax like this:

```
bday.person // 'Raoul'
```

To get the birth date:

```
bday.date // '10/27/1980'
```

The same is true with a JSON object that's returned by the Web server. For example, take the following *getJSON( )* example and callback function:

```
$.getJSON('contacts.php','contact=123',processContacts);
function processContacts(data) {

}
```

Assuming that the server returned the JSON example on page 432, that JSON object is assigned to the variable *data* (the argument for the callback function *processContacts( )*), just as if this code had been executed:

```
var data = {
  firstName: 'Frank',
  lastName: 'Smith',
  phone: '503-555-1212'
};
```

Now within the callback function, you can access the value of *firstName* like this:

```
data.firstName // 'Frank'
```

And retrieve the last name of the contact like this:

```
data.lastName // 'Smith'
```

So, let's say the whole point of this little Ajax program is to retrieve contact information and display it inside of a <div> with the ID *info*. All of the programming for that might look like this:

```
$.getJSON('contacts.php','contact=123',processContacts);
function processContacts(data) {
  var infoHTML='<p>Contact: ' + data.firstName;
  infoHTML+=' ' + data.lastName + '<br>';
  infoHTML+='Phone: ' + data.phone + '</p>';
  $('#info').html(infoHTML);
}
```

The final outcome would be a paragraph added to the page that looks something like this:

```
Contact: Frank Smith
Phone: 503-555-1212
```

Complex JSON Objects

You can create even more complex collections of information by using object literals as the values inside a JSON object—in other words, object literals nested within object literals. (Sorry, but don't put down this book yet.)

Here's an example: Say you want the server to send back contact information for more than one individual using JSON. You'll send a request to a file named *contacts.php* with a query string that dictates how many contacts you wish returned. That code may look something like this:

```
$.getJSON('contacts.php','limit=2',processContacts);
```

The *limit=2* is the information sent to the server, and indicates how many contacts should be returned. The Web server would then return two contacts. Say the contact info for the first person matched the example above (Frank Smith), and a second set of contact information was another JSON object like this:

```
{
  firstName: 'Peggy',
  lastName: 'Jones',
  phone: '415-555-5235'
}
```

The Web server may return a string that represents a single JSON object, which combines both of these objects like this:

```
{
  contact1: {
    firstName: 'Frank',
```

```
      lastName: 'Smith',
      phone: '503-555-1212'
    },
    contact2: {
      firstName: 'Peggy',
      lastName: 'Jones',
      phone: '415-555-5235'
    }
  }
```

Assume that the callback function accepts a single argument named *data* (for example, *function processContacts(data)*). The variable *data* would then be assigned that JSON object, just as if this code had been executed:

```
var data = {
  contact1: {
    firstName: 'Frank',
    lastName: 'Smith',
    phone: '503-555-1212'
  },
  contact2: {
    firstName: 'Peggy',
    lastName: 'Jones',
    phone: '415-555-5235'
  }
};
```

Now, you could access the first contact object within the callback function like this:

```
data.contact1
```

And retrieve the first name of the first contact like this:

```
data.contact1.firstName
```

But, in this case, since you want to process multiple contacts, jQuery provides a function that lets you loop through each item in a JSON object—the *each( )* function. The basic structure of the function is this:

```
$.each(JSON,function(name,value) {

});
```

You pass the JSON object, and an anonymous function (page 193) to the *each( )* function. That anonymous function receives the name and value of each item in the JSON object. Here's how the JSON object would look in use in the current example:

```
1    $.getJSON('contacts.php','limit=2',processContacts);
2    function processContacts(data) {
```

```
3      // create variable with empty string
4      var infoHTML='';
5
6      //loop through each object in the JSON data
7      $.each(data,function(contact, contactInfo) {
8        infoHTML+='<p>Contact: ' + contactInfo.firstName;
9        infoHTML+=' ' + contactInfo.lastName + '<br>';
10       infoHTML+='Phone: ' + contactInfo.phone + '</p>';
11     }); // end of each()
12
13     // add finished HTML to page
14     $('#info').html(infoHTML);
15   }
```

Here's how the code breaks down:

1. **Line 1 creates the Ajax request and assigns the callback function**

2. **Line 2 creates the callback function, which accepts the JSON object sent back from the server and stores it in the variable *data*.**

3. **Line 4 creates an empty string. The HTML that eventually gets added to the page will fill it.**

4. **Line 7 is the *each( )* function, which will look through the objects in the JSON data.**

   The *each( )* function takes the JSON object as its first argument (*data*) and an anonymous function as the second argument. The process is diagrammed in Figure 11-10. Essentially, for each of the main objects (in this example *contact1* and *contact2*), the anonymous function receives the name of the object as a string (that's the *contact* argument listed in line 7) and the value for that object (that's the *contactInfo* argument). In this case, the *contactInfo* variable will hold the object literal containing the contact information.

5. **Lines 8–10 extract the information from one contact.**

   Remember that the *each( )* function is a loop, so lines 8–10 will run twice—once for each of the contacts.

6. **Line 14 updates the Web page by adding the HTML to the page.**

   The final result will be the following HTML:

```
<p>Contact: Frank Smith<br>
Phone: 503-555-1212</p>
<p>Contact: Peggy Jones<br>
Phone: 415-555-5235</p>
```

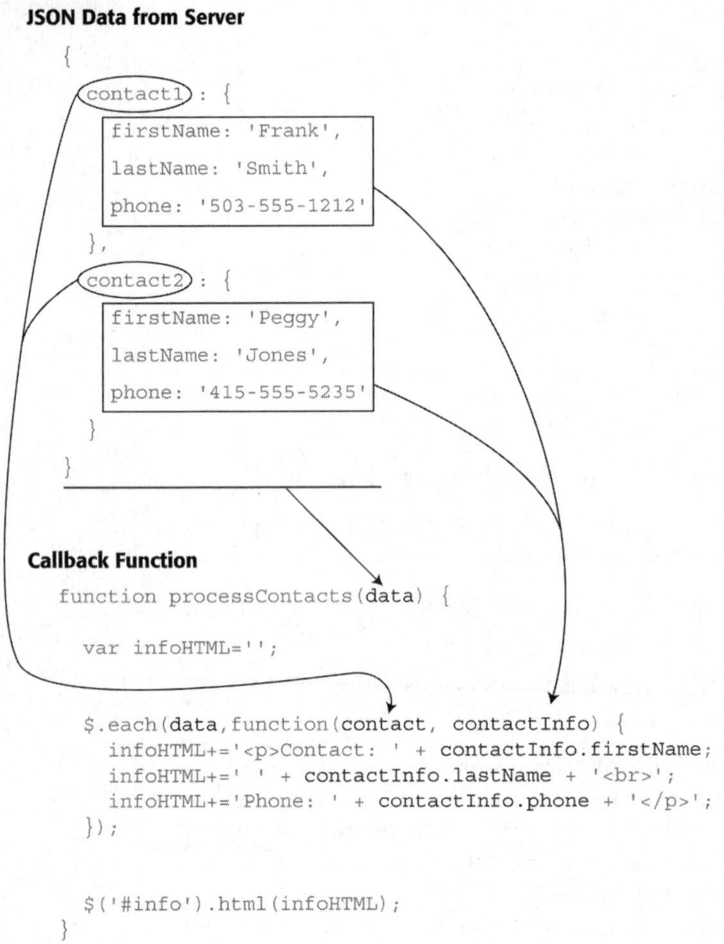

JSON Data from Server

```
{
    contact1 : {
        firstName: 'Frank',
        lastName: 'Smith',
        phone: '503-555-1212'
    },
    contact2 : {
        firstName: 'Peggy',
        lastName: 'Jones',
        phone: '415-555-5235'
    }
}
```

Figure 11-10:
*You can use jQuery's each( )
function to loop through a JSON
object to perform tasks on nested
objects. You can also use the
each( ) function to loop through
arrays. To learn more about this
useful function, visit* http://docs.
jquery.com/Utilities/jQuery.
each#objectcallback.

Callback Function

```
function processContacts(data) {

    var infoHTML='';


    $.each(data,function(contact, contactInfo) {
        infoHTML+='<p>Contact: ' + contactInfo.firstName;
        infoHTML+=' ' + contactInfo.lastName + '<br>';
        infoHTML+='Phone: ' + contactInfo.phone + '</p>';
    });


    $('#info').html(infoHTML);
}
```

CHAPTER

12

Basic Ajax Programming

In the previous chapter you learned the basics of Ajax: what it is, how it works, and how jQuery can simplify the process of Ajax programming. Since Ajax is all about the two-way communication between Web browser and Web server, understanding server-side programming is necessary if you really want to harness Ajax's power. However, you don't need to be a server-side programming guru to use Ajax successfully. To show you how simple and easy it can be to add Ajax to your site, this chapter revisits the Tabs plug-in that you saw in Chapter 10 and introduces a plug-in that makes it easy to add searchable Google Maps to your own Web pages.

Tabs Plug-in

In Chapter 10 you learned how to use the jQuery Tabs plug-in to create tabbed panels that work with already existing Web page content. This plug-in provides a way to divide a lot of content into separate manageable panels. But the Tabs plug-in doesn't just limit you to the content already in the page's HTML; it also has an Ajax mode that lets you dynamically load content from other files on your Web server into panels on the page. In this way, you can have a single page act as a kind of gateway to lots and lots of content on your site, without having to create a single, very large (and slow to download) HTML page. When someone clicks an Ajaxified tab, the data is retrieved from the Web server and displayed in a panel.

Most of the steps on pages 372-376 for creating regular tabbed panels apply to Ajax Tabs, with one big exception. With regular tabs you create separate <div> tags for each panel and insert the content for the panel into its assigned <div>; you then add an anchor link from the tab to the <div>. With Ajax tabs, you don't add those

<div>s, nor do you add the content of the panels—all you need is a bulleted list containing the tab names, along with links to each page containing the content that will be loaded into the panel.

Here are the basic steps for adding Ajax Tabs:

1. **Attach several external JavaScript files to your page.**

   In addition to the jQuery library, you must also link to two additional files: *ui.core.js* and *ui.tabs.js*. The *ui.core.js* file is part of jQuery's user interface library (see the box on page 361), while the Tabs plug-in (available from *http://ui.jquery.com*) provides the tabbed panel functionality.

   You attach these files as you would any external JavaScript file (see page 24); just make sure you attach them in order: *jquery.js*, *ui.core.js*, and *ui.tabs.js*. In other words, you'll have three script tags that look something like this:

   ```
   <script type="text/javascript" src="js/jquery.js"></script>
   <script type="text/javascript" src="js/ui.core.js"></script>
   <script type="text/javascript" src="js/ui.tabs.js">
   ```

2. **Structure the HTML for the tabs.**

   A group of tabs is represented by a bulleted list (<ul> tag) and each tab is a single list item (<li> tag). The <li> tag should contain the text you want to appear on the tab, and the text should link to the Web page you wish to load into a panel. That's the main difference with the regular tabbed panels discussed in Chapter 10, in which, for example, the basic HTML for the tabs pictured in Figure 12-1 may look like this:

   ```
   <ul id="tabs">
     <li><a href="specs.html">Specifications</a></li>
     <li><a href="photos.html">Photos</a></li>
     <li><a href="reviews.html">Reviews</a></li>
   </ul>
   ```

   Notice that this HTML looks like a regular list of links—and it is! For people visiting your site with JavaScript turned off, or for search engines indexing your Web site, these links let them get to your content even if they don't see the fancy tabbed panels.

Note: When creating a bulleted list of links to work with the Tabs plug-in, you can only link to pages on your own site. To enhance security, most browsers won't let you use Ajax to load content from other Web sites.

Keep in mind that you eventually need a way to identify this group of links using jQuery (see step 3 below), so you should supply an ID for the <ul> tag. This example uses an ID of *tabs*, but you could use any ID you want.

Figure 12-1:
An Ajax Tabbed panel looks pretty much like the regular tabbed panel discussed on page 364. However, the content for each panel comes from a separate HTML file that's loaded dynamically. The only visual difference you'll see is the "Loading" text and icon (circled) that indicates the content is being loaded and will appear momentarily in its own panel.

Unlike regular tabbed panels, you don't need to add any additional HTML to your page—no <div> tags and no new content. All you do is apply the *tabs( )* function and the plug-in takes care of the rest.

3. **Apply the *tabs( )* function to the <ul> tag containing the tabs.**

As with all things jQuery, you need to first add the *$(document).ready( )* function, then include the function call:

```
<script type="text/javascript">
$(document).ready(function( ) {
  $('#tabs').tabs( );
});
</script>
```

In this example, *$('#tabs')* selects an element with an ID of *tabs* (see the <ul> tag in step 2 above). You should change this to match your markup, so if you added the ID of *tabGroup* to the <ul> tag, you'd use this jQuery selector: *$('#tabGroup')*.

The *tabs( )* function takes care of the rest. You'll need to create a style sheet that formats the tabs and panels as well as hides the panel groups not currently on display—those details are discussed on page 368.

Changing the Loading Text and Icon

The one visual difference between the tabs in Ajax mode and regular tabs shows up when they're loading. When you click an Ajax tab and the browser starts down-loading the file to display in the panel, some text appears, letting you know the content is loading (circled in Figure 12-1).

You can set the text, and even style the loading message area to include an animated GIF (those spinning dots, lines, and circles used everywhere on the Web to indicate "Please wait…we're getting the information you asked for…"). The plug-in's programmed to display the text "Loading…" unless you tell it otherwise. If you want to change the loading message text, pass an object literal (page 188) containing the name *spinner* and a string as the value. For example, if you want the message to be "Retrieving," you can write this:

```
$('#tabs').tabs({
    spinner: 'Retrieving'
});
```

Note that this option (just like the other tab options discussed on page 370) is set when you call the *tabs( )* function, as described in step 3 on page 441.

If you want to add an animated GIF, you can create a CSS style with a background image. The plug-in adds the class *ui-tabs-loading* to a tab that's downloading content, and surrounds the loading text with an <em> tag. You can use both the class and tag names as handles to create a descendent selector like this:

```
.ui-tabs-loading em {
    background: url(images/loading.gif) no-repeat left center;
    padding: 0 0 0 25px;
}
```

The CSS background property lets you add an image (even an animated GIF) to the background of a tag. To make sure the loading text doesn't overlap the image, add some padding on the side the image appears. For example, in the style above, the image is placed on the left side of the tag, so 25 pixels of left padding is added to make room for the image. This style applies to the tab only when the content is loading—once the content has been downloaded and displayed in a tabbed panel, the plug-in removes the *ui-tabs-loading* class and the loading text from the tab.

Note: You can use the *.ui-tabs-loading em* style to alter the look of the loading text as well. For example, if you wanted to change the text size and color, you could add a *color* and *font-size* property to the rule.

Turning off the "Loading" message

The "Loading" message (and spinning icon if you added one to your CSS) appears every time you click a tab—even if the browser has already downloaded the tabs content. In fact, in Ajax mode, the Tabs plug-in normally re-downloads the content each time you click a tab—a useful feature, if the content in the tab is dynamically generated and changes frequently (for example, providing the scores of an ongoing basketball game, or the current temperature and wind speed).

However, if the tabbed panel's content doesn't change, there's no reason to download the panel's content over and over again. You can instruct the Tabs plug-in to download the content for the panel just once, which has the happy side effect of displaying the "Loading" message only the first time a tab is clicked. To do that, set the *cache* option to *true* when calling the *tabs( )* function:

```
$('#tabs').tabs({
   cache: true
});
```

Ajax Tabs Tutorial

In this tutorial, you'll create a tabbed panel based on an unordered list of links.

Note: See the note on page 27 for information on how to download the tutorial files.

---

1. **In a text editor, open the file *12.1.html* in the *chapter12* folder.**

   Before you start adding any JavaScript to this page, you'll modify the HTML by adding an unordered list of links.

Note: Even though this tutorial uses Ajax, you don't need to have a running Web server to complete it. The tutorial will work just fine running right off your desktop computer.

---

2. **Locate the <h1> tag in the body of the page (<h1>Ajax Tabs</h1>). Click inside the empty line directly below this tag and add:**

   ```
   <ul id="tabs">
     <li><a href="specs.html" >Specifications</a></li>
     <li><a href="photos.html">Photos</a></li>
     <li><a href="reviews.html">Reviews</a>  </li>
   </ul>
   ```

   You've just added a simple list of links, which point to three other pages inside the *chapter12* folder. In addition, the ID *tabs* applied to the <ul> tag will make it easy to turn this list into a set of tabs.

   Now you'll add some JavaScript. First, you'll link to all of the external files needed by this page.

3. **Click in the empty line just *above* the closing </head> tag and type:**

   ```
   <script type="text/javascript" src="../js/jquery.js"></script>
   <script type="text/javascript" src="../js/ui/ui.core.js"></script>
   <script type="text/javascript" src="../js/ui/ui.tabs.js"></script>
   ```

   These three lines of code link the necessary JavaScript files needed for the tabs effect. Next, you'll link to another external JavaScript file.

4. **Add one additional <script> tag below the ones you added in step 3:**

   ```
   <script type="text/javascript" src="myTabs.js"></script>
   ```

What's this *myTabs.js* file? Well, it doesn't exist yet. It's an external JavaScript file that you're about to create. As mentioned on page 24, using external Java-Script files is generally the most efficient way to create and use scripts that are shared on multiple pages of a site. Instead of adding a ton of scripting into the <head> of *each* document on your site, you can create external JavaScript files that include scripts that are shared by multiple pages on the site.

In this case, assume that other pages on the site will have tabbed panels as well, and that they'll be structured similarly (that is, they'll all have a <ul> tag with the ID *tabs*). Every page on the site that has tabbed panels only needs to link to the external JavaScript file you're going to create next.

5. **Create a new file, and save it as *myTabs.js* inside the *chapter12* folder.**

   Make sure you save this file in the *chapter12* folder; if you don't the link to the script you added in step 4 (which points to a file in the same folder as the HTML page), the code won't work. Now, to add the JavaScript:

6. **In the *myTabs.js* file, type:**

```
1    $(document).ready(function( ) {
2        $("#tabs").tabs( );
3    }); // end ready
```

   Note that you don't need any <script> tags—those are just for HTML files. Since this is an external JavaScript file, you add only pure JavaScript to it.

   Lines 1 and 3 should be familiar by now—they're jQuery's function for making sure your code doesn't run until the HTML of the page has loaded.

   Line 2 is the heart of the matter; in fact, it's all you need to do! This one line makes the magic happen.

7. **Save both the *myTabs.js* and *12.1.html* file. Preview the *12.1.html* file in a Web browser. Click each tab.**

   Since you're working off your own computer, you probably won't see the "Loading…" message for long, but it should briefly pop into view. In fact, it should appear over and over again, even if you've already downloaded the content that appears in the panel. Fortunately, you can make the plug-in display the "Loading" message just the first time the content is downloaded.

8. **Edit the code you added in the last step so that it looks like this:**

```
$(document).ready(function( ) {
  $("#tabs").tabs({
    cache: true
  });
});
```

   This option instructs the plug-in to just download the panel content once and display the loading message once per tab (see page 442 for more on this option).

While you're there, why not change the loading message from "Loading…" to just plain "Loading"? (Try it even if the ellipsis doesn't bother you. It's a chance to practice editing the loading message.)

9. **Edit the code one last time to change the loading message:**

```
1   $(document).ready(function( ) {
2     $("#tabs").tabs({
3       cache: true,
4       spinner: 'Loading'
5     });
6   });
```

Don't forget the comma at the end of line 3: it separates the name/value pairs in the set of options passed to the *tabs( )* function.

Finally, you'll add one CSS rule to insert a spinning, animated GIF next to "Loading."

10. **Open the file *tabs.css* and add the following rule to the end of the style sheet:**

```
.ui-tabs-loading em {
    background: url(images/loading.gif) no-repeat left center;
    padding: 0 0 0 25px;
}
```

The *tabs.css* file is the same stylesheet you completed in Chapter 10 (page 374). This final style adds an animated GIF—*loading.gif*—to the background of the loading message.

11. **Save and close the *tabs.css* and *myTabs.js* files. Open the *12.1.html* file in a Web browser and click the tabs.**

The tabs and tabbed panels work as before, but you should notice (very briefly) a spinning icon. It will only appear once per tab, thanks to the cache setting you added in step 8. A completed version of this tutorial—*complete_12.1.html*—is in the *chapter12* folder.

Adding Google Maps to Your Site

Google Maps (*http://maps.google.com*) is an original poster-child for the JavaScript revival. The ability to zoom in and out of a map, move around city streets, and get driving directions in a flash makes Google Maps an incredibly useful site. And thanks to the clever use of Ajax, the site's responsiveness makes it feel nearly like a desktop program.

But Google Maps offers even more power to Web designers: the Google Maps service lets you embed a map in your own site. If you run a brick-and-mortar business (or build sites for businesses), being able to provide an easy-to-understand map and directions can bring more customers through your door. Fortunately,

Going Further with jQuery and Ajax

There are loads of other jQuery plug-ins that can make Ajax development go faster. In some cases, you need to provide the server-side programming—the plug-in just takes care of the JavaScript part. A few other programs supply the basic server-side programming as well. Here are a few good ones:

- **Form plug-in.** The jQuery Form plug-in is a simple way to add Ajax to your form submissions. The plug-in goes far beyond the basics discussed in the previous chapter and includes file uploading ability. It works with form validation as well. For more information, visit *http://plug-ins.jquery.com/project/form*.

- **Ajax chat.** Want to add a live, interactive chat feature to your Web site? You can, using this nifty plug-in (available from *http://plug-ins.jquery.com/project/chat*). It requires some server-side programming to work, but the site provides some basic PHP. For a more hands-on approach, you can follow an article on creating your own Ajax chat with jQuery available from sitepoint.com, at *www.sitepoint.com/article/ajax-jquery*.

- **dirlister.** This plug-in provides an interactive view of folders on a Web server. In other words, you could make a folder of downloadable files on your site into a directory listing—like you'd find on your desktop. It uses Ajax and some cool animations to let you drill into folders and subfolders as well. Find out more about this plug-in at *http://plug-ins.jquery.com/project/dirlister*.

- **Taconite.** Using Ajax, you can receive information from a server and update a Web page. However, you may want to update multiple areas of a page—for example, if a visitor logs in using an Ajax form, you might want to show his login status in one part of the page, a list of the pages he visited last time he was at the site in another part of the page, and display a shopping cart in yet another area of the page. The Taconite plug-in lets you receive a basic XML file from the Web server with simple instructions on what areas of a Web page to update and what information to use. You can find out more about this plug-in at *http://plug-ins.jquery.com/project/taconite*.

thanks to jMaps, a jQuery plug-in, it's easy to add interactive maps directly to your own Web pages (see Figure 12-2).

The jMaps plug-in (*http://jmaps.digitalspaghetti.me.uk*), created by Tane Piper, lets you add a Google map to any Web page, request driving directions between two points on a map, add markers to highlight locations on a map, and much more. The basic steps to using the plug-in are:

1. Get a Google Maps API key from *http://code.google.com/apis/maps/signup.html*.

   API stands for Advanced Programming Interface, and provides the set of instructions for interacting with a complex computer program. In this case, there's an API that lets you communicate directly with Google Maps. Google provides the API key for free, but has a built-in way to limit access to the Google Maps service: if someone starts to misuse the Google Maps service, then Google can revoke their key. A single API key is limited to a single Web site, so if you want to put Google Maps on more than one Web site, you need to get additional keys.

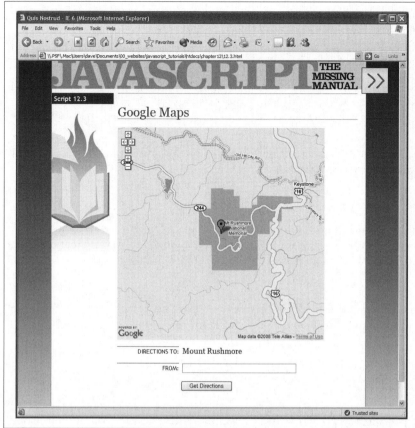

Figure 12-2:
*While a simple picture of
a map is a fine way to
indicate the location of
your (or your client's)
business, an interactive
map like those available
at* http://maps.google.
com *is better. Visitors can
zoom into, zoom out of,
and pan across a Google
Map with ease.
Searching for driving
directions from one point
to another is a piece of
cake. Thanks to the
jMaps jQuery plug-in, it's
easy to add a Google
Map to your Web site.*

Once you sign up, a Google Web page will show you your key: a very long
sequence of numbers and letters like this: ABQIAAAAcodqE5Ud2u_
bV1oo7fjz7BRzIjhvYzTJQihahdS7VPkPLGAtRBRAtUCMgIDrN2B8zAyx6zaz6
RMU. You'll need to use that key when accessing the Google Maps service, so
make sure you save that key information.

Note: For testing Google Maps on your own computer (not on a Web server), you don't need a key at
all. But if you want to move a page that includes a Google Map up to your live Web server, you'll need a
key.

2. **Attach an external JavaScript file from Google Maps.**

   In order to access the maps service, you need to load a script from Google. The
   <script> tag you use looks like this:

   ```
   <script type="text/javascript" src="http://maps.google.com/
   maps?file=api&v=2&key=YOUR_KEY_HERE"></script>
   ```

   You need to replace the "YOUR_KEY_HERE" part with the API key you got
   from Google in step 1.

CHAPTER 12: BASIC AJAX PROGRAMMING

3. **Attach two jQuery files.**

Of course, you need the jQuery library, as well as the jMaps file—*jquery.jmap.js*. The jMaps file is available from *http://jmaps.digitalspaghetti.me.uk*. This file provides all the programming that makes adding a map to your site so easy. So in addition to the <script> tag from step 2, you'll add code that's something like this:

```
<script type="text/javascript" src="js/jquery.js"></script>
<script type="text/javascript" src="js/jquery.jmap.js"></script>
```

Note: You can get the jMaps plug-in file from *http://jmaps.digitalspaghetti.me.uk*. It's also included in the *js* folder with this book's tutorial files.

---

4. **Add an empty <div> tag with an ID to the page.**

jMaps will add a map in this empty tag, so place the <div> where you want the map to appear on the page. Also, you need to provide a way of identifying that tag, so add an ID. The HTML for this might look like this:

```
<div id="map"></div>
```

In addition, you can add a CSS rule to the page's stylesheet to define the height and width of the map on the page. For example:

```
#map {
  width: 500px;
  height: 500px;
}
```

5. **If you want to provide driving directions with the map, add another empty <div> tag.**

As you'll read on page 453, you can use jMaps and Google Maps to provide driving directions from one location to another. For example, if you add a Google Map for your business, you could add a form field that lets a customer type her address and receive directions from her location to your business.

As with the <div> you added in step 4, this <div> should also have a unique ID. For example:

```
<div id="directions"></div>
```

6. **Call the jMaps function.**

Finally, add a new <script> tag, the *document.ready( )* function and call the *jmap( )* function. To use the *jmap( )* function, you select the map <div> using a jQuery selector—*$('#map')*—then add *jmap( )*:

```
<script type="text/javascript">
$(document).ready(function() {
  $('#map').jmap();
});
</script>
```

JavaScript: The Missing Manual

Just calling the *jmap( )* function, though, will give you a map that's centered somewhere in Edinburgh, Scotland. Most likely (unless you're from Edinburgh) you'll want to have the map point to a specific location (such as your or your client's business location). You'll learn how to do that next.

Setting a Location for the Map

A Google Map has a center point as defined by numbers that represent the location's longitude and latitude. If you want to center your map on a place—such as your business's address or the location of your next birthday party—you need to get that location's longitude and latitude. That's easy:

1. **Go to *http://maps.google.com* and search for the location you want.**

   Google Maps lets you type an address, like *123 Main St., Oak Park, IL*, or even a landmark name, like *Mount Rushmore*. Once Google Maps has found the spot you're after, you just need to get the longitude and latitude.

2. **In the browser's location bar, type:**

   ```
   javascript:void(prompt('',gApplication.getMap( ).getCenter( )));
   ```

   Depending on your security settings, in Internet Explorer, a yellow security bar may appear on the browser window. You must click this bar to let the "scriptable window" get the results. A JavaScript prompt window will appear with the latitude and longitude (see Figure 12-3).

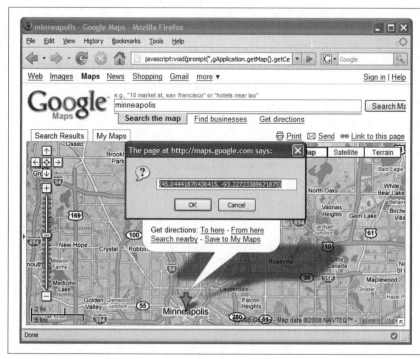

Figure 12-3:
Every Google Map has a center point determined by a longitude and latitude value. For example, here you can see Minneapolis, Minnesota is located at a latitude of about 45° and a longitude of about −93°.

Once you have the proper latitude and longitude values, you can send them to the *jmap( )* function as part of an object literal like this:

```
$('#map').jmap('init',{mapCenter:[43.878946,-103.459824]});
```

In this case, the *jmap( )* function takes two arguments. The first, *'init'*, lets the jMaps plug-in know that you are *initializing* (or creating) a new map. The second argument is an object literal that defines various settings for the new map. The most important setting, *mapCenter*, lets you specify the location the map will display. You supply the *mapCenter* option with an array (page 56) of two values—the longitude and latitude:

```
mapCenter:[43.878946,-103.459824]
```

Note: The code in step 2 opens a dialog box that includes a pair of parentheses surrounding the longitude and latitude values (see Figure 12-3). Don't copy the parentheses—you only need the numbers.

Other jMap Options

In addition to *mapCenter*, you can set many other options when creating a new map. You should incorporate each option into the object literal that's passed as the second argument to the *jmap( )* function. For example, to center the map at a longitude and latitude of 43/–103, set the map so that's zoomed in to show details, and hide the jMap icon from the map, you'd initialize the map like this:

```
$('#map').jmap('init', {
  mapCenter:[43,-103],
  mapZoom: 13,
  mapShowjMapIcon: false
});
```

In other words, the options you're reading about in this section are just passed in as part of an object literal (see page 188 for a recap on object literals).

Here are a few options you can set.

- **Remove the jMaps icon.** Normally, when using the jMaps plug-in, you'll see a little icon in the bottom left of the map—next to the Google Maps icon. If you want to remove the jMaps icon, you must set the *mapShowjMapIcon* option to false:

  ```
  mapShowjMapIcon: false
  ```

- **Control the scale of the map.** Sometimes you want your map focused on the finest details, such as a street-level map. Other times, you might want to have a broader picture and see an entire city or state on the screen. You can control how zoomed-in the map is by providing a number for the *mapZoom* option. A setting of 0 is completely zoomed out (that is, a map of the entire globe), while each number above 0 represents greater zoom. As a general rule, 15 is a good setting if you want to see the names of each street, while 13 is good for more of a bird's-eye view. The upper limit (greatest amount of zoom) depends on how detailed a map Google has for the area and varies anywhere from 17 to 23. Set the option like this:

```
mapZoom:15
```

- **Set the map controller size.** A Google map usually provides a controller that lets you zoom in and move around the map. You can choose from among three settings for the *mapControlSize* option. The *'large'* setting provides arrows for moving around and a zoom slide to let you zoom in tight or zoom out completely to see the whole globe. You see this type of controller at *maps.google.com* and in Figure 12-4. The *'small'* setting provides a controller with arrows to move around and + and – buttons to zoom in and out (Figure 12-2). Finally, you can choose *'none'* if you don't want any controller to appear—but use this option only if you don't want your visitors to be able to zoom in and out. You can set this option like this:

```
mapControlSize: 'large'
```

- **Add a scale marker.** It's common on printed maps to have some kind of scale listed on the map: 1" equals 1 mile, for example. A Google Map can also have a scale marker (see Figure 12-4). To add a small visual scale marker to the lower left of the map, set the *mapEnableScaleControl* to *true*:

```
mapEnableScaleControl:true
```

If you don't want to see the scale marker, you don't need to do anything— jMaps normally doesn't display a scale. If you do add a scale marker, make sure you remove the jMaps icon (see the first item in this list); otherwise, the two will overlap.

Adding Markers and HTML Bubbles

To highlight a point on a map you can add a red pushpin marker like the one in Figure 12-4. These markers are a great way to mark the location of your business or a point of interest on the map. To provide even more information for the marker, you can also add a pop-up bubble with HTML (Figure 12-4). jMaps makes adding these details easy.

To add a marker, you first need to add a map to a page as described above; then to add a marker, you apply the *jmap( )* function a second time, like this:

```
$('#map').jmap('addMarker', {pointLatLng:[43.878946, -103.459824]});
```

When creating a marker, the *jmap( )* function takes two arguments. The first argument, *'addMarker'*, identifies the action you're taking—adding a new marker to the map. The second argument is an object literal, which indicates the longitude

Map controller HTML bubble

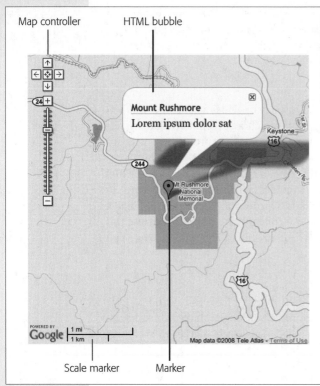

Scale marker   Marker

Figure 12-4:
*Beyond the map itself, a Google Map offers
various controls and information markers that
make it possible to zoom into a map, move the
map within the window, determine the scale of
the map, and pinpoint exact locations on the
map.*

and latitude of the spot where the marker should go. You can determine the longitude and latitude for the marker by following the steps on page 449. You can add
multiple markers by calling the function multiple times:

```
$('#map').jmap('addMarker', {pointLatLng:[43, -103]});
$('#map').jmap('addMarker', {pointLatLng:[43.5, -103.5]});
```

In addition, you can add a pop-up bubble to each marker that appears when the
marker is clicked. To do that, add another item to the object literal containing the
name *pointHTML* and the HTML you wish to display. For example:

```
$('#map').jmap('addMarker', {
  pointLatLng:[43.878946, -103.459824],
  pointHTML: '<h2>Mount Rushmore</h2><p>Lorem Ipsum</p>'
});
```

You can also store the HTML in a variable and access the variable when passing the
object literal to the *jmap( )* function like this:

```
var markerHTML='<h2>Mount Rushmore</h2><p>Lorem ipsum dolor sat</p>';
 $('#map').jmap('addMarker', {
  pointLatLng:[43.878946, -103.459824],
  pointHTML: markerHTML
});
```

You can add any HTML you wish, such as tables, images, and bulleted lists. However, the pop-up bubble doesn't resize when you add content, so you should keep the HTML short—otherwise, it will spill out of the bottom of the HTML bubble.

Tip: To style the HTML inside the HTML bubble, you can use a descendent selector. For example, if you used the name *map* for the ID of the <div> containing the map (see step 4 on page 448), you could create a descendent selector *#map p* to format the look of <p> tags inside the bubble.

Get Driving Directions

One of Google Maps' best features is the ability to get a detailed set of driving directions from point A to point B. For a brick-and-mortar store, providing an easy way for visitors to your site to get directions to your store can translate into more business. The jMaps plug-in lets you print driving directions from any two points on a map directly on your Web page.

To use the jMaps plug-in to get driving directions, you need to add a map to your Web page (as described on page 445), and then follow the steps described below.

1. **Add an empty <div> for the directions.**

   Make sure the <div> has an ID so that you can later target the <div> to place the directions inside it:

   ```
   <div id="directions"></div>
   ```

   This <div> can go anywhere on the page, but below or above the map are common spots.

2. **Add a form to the page.**

   If you know the destination for the directions (for example, you're providing directions to your store or one specific location), then you only need a single text field so the visitor can type his address to get directions to the location you specify. In addition, you should add a Submit button that the visitor can click. Here's some basic HTML that creates a form, a text field, and a Submit button:

   ```
   <form name="getDirections" id="getDirections">
   <p>
    <label for="from">From: </label>
    <input name="from" type="text" id="from">
   </p>
   <p>
    <input type="submit" name="submit" value="Get Directions">
   </p>
   </form>
   ```

   You can also provide driving directions from two locations that the visitor specifies. In this case, add two text fields to the form.

3. **Add a *submit* event to the form and call jMaps.**

   This is the JavaScript code to search for driving directions, so it goes in the <head> of the page within a <script> tag (you should already have added a <script> tag to when you added the original map to the page). You add the event as you would any other browser event (see page 204); for example, if the form has an ID of *getDirections*, add a *submit* event handler like this:

   ```
   $('#getDirections').submit(function() {

   });
   ```

   Inside the event handler you then call the jMap function, and pass the information needed to get driving directions:

   ```
   1    $('#getDirections').submit(function(){
   2      $('#map').jmap('searchDirections', {
   3        toAddress: '123 Main St., St. Paul, MN'
   4        fromAddress: $('#from').val(),
   5        directionsPanel: 'directions'
   6      });
   7      return false;
   8    });
   ```

   Line 2 calls the *jmap( )* function, passing two arguments. The first, *'searchDirections'*, notifies the plug-in that it needs to get driving directions. The second argument is an object literal with all of the information needed get driving directions. For example, in line 3 the option *toAddress* sets the final destination. In this example, it's hard-coded to point to an exact spot (what you'd do if you wanted to just allow visitors to get driving directions to your store).

   Line 4 sets the starting point for the directions using the *fromAddress* option. Since the visitor is supplying this information in a form field, you can extract the address from the field using the *val( )* function as described on page 314. For example, *$('#from').val( )* means "get whatever's been typed into a field with an ID of *from*."

   For the last part of the object literal passed to the *jmap( )* function, you instruct the plug-in where to put the results with the *directionsPanel* option. In this example, an element with an ID of *directions* is specified on line 5.

   Finally, you add *return false* (line 7) to stop the form from being submitted as it normally would—in other words, you want to stop the browser's normal behavior and let JavaScript send the request to Google and handle Google's response (see page 223 for more information on stopping browsers normal response to events).

jMaps Tutorial

In this tutorial, you'll go through the steps necessary to add the jMaps plug-in to a Web page. You'll also add programming so that visitors can request driving directions.

Note: See the note on page 27 for information on how to download the tutorial files.

---

1. **In a text editor, open the file *12.2.html* in the *chapter12* folder.**

    Before you start adding any JavaScript to this page, you'll modify the HTML by adding an empty <div> to hold the map.

2. **Locate the <h1> tag in the body of the page (<h1>Google Maps</h1>). Click inside the empty line directly below this tag and add:**

    ```
    <div id="map"></div>
    ```

    You've just created a placeholder, where the jMaps plug-in will eventually add a Google Map.

    Next, you'll add a CSS style to set the height and width of the map.

3. **Open the file *map.css* in the *chapter12* folder and add a CSS rule at the bottom of the stylesheet:**

    ```
    #map {
      height:500px;
      width:500px;
    }
    ```

    At this point, the map area is 500 pixels square. Now it's time to add some Java-Script.

4. **Click in the empty line just *above* the closing </head> tag and type:**

    ```
    <script type="text/javascript" src="http://maps.google.com/
    maps?file=api&v=2"></script>
    <script type="text/javascript" src="../js/jquery.js"></script>
    <script type="text/javascript" src="../js/jquery.jmap.js"></script>
    ```

    The first <script> tag loads a JavaScript file from Google.com containing the code needed to talk to the Google Maps service. Because you're just testing this page locally on your own computer, you don't need a Google Maps API key (see step 1 on page 446). However, if you wanted to move this page onto your Web server, you'd need to get a key and add it to the URL used to access the JavaScript file at Google.com (see step 2 on page 447).

    The second <script> tag loads jQuery, while the third one loads the jMaps plug-in file. Now, you're ready to create the map.

5. Add one additional <script> tag below the ones you added in step 4, and include jQuery's *$(document).ready( )* function:

```
<script type="text/javascript">
$(document).ready(function() {

}); // end ready
</script>
```

Now, you just need to apply the *jmap( )* function to the empty <div> you created in step 2.

6. Inside the *$(document).ready( )* function, add the following code:

```
$('#map').jmap('init', {
  mapCenter:[37.808445, -122.410161]
});
```

This *initializes* (or creates) the map, displaying a specific longitude and latitude as the center point on the map. (In this case, it's Fisherman's Wharf in San Francisco, but feel free to change these values, as described on page 450, if you want to display a map with a different location.)

7. **Save the file and preview it in a Web browser.**

You can't see the map by viewing the page through a locally running Web browser—as you must with other Ajax-type pages. In other words, don't access this page like this: *http://localhost/chapter12/12.2.html*; you must use a local file path like *C:\Documents and Settings\Dave\Desktop\tutorials\chapter12\12.2.html*. Just use the File → Open command in your Web browser and navigate to and open the *12.2.html* file on your hard drive; or, alternatively, just drag the 12.2.html file into an open browser window.

Provided you're connected to the Internet (so the browser can contact Google.com), you'll see a 500-pixel square map.

Let's zoom in a bit more on the map.

8. **Edit the script by adding a comma after the *mapCenter* option and inserting a *mapZoom* setting (changes are in bold):**

```
$(document).ready(function() {
  $('#map').jmap('init', {
    mapCenter:[37.808445, -122.410161],
    mapZoom: 14
  });
}); // end ready
```

You can zoom completely out (0), or in to street level (17). Feel free to save the page and preview the changes in a Web browser. Next, you'll remove the jMaps icon.

9. Edit the script again. This time add a comma after the *mapZoom* option and insert another line of code:

```
$(document).ready(function( ) {
  $('#map').jmap('init', {
    mapCenter:[37.808445, -122.410161],
    mapZoom: 14,
    mapShowjMapIcon: false
  });
}); // end ready
```

The jMaps icon gets in the way of the next item you'll add to the map—a scale marker. While you're at it, you'll also change the map's controller so that it includes a zoom slider.

10. Edit the *jmap( )* function one last time by adding two more options:

```
$(document).ready(function( ) {
  $('#map').jmap('init', {
    mapCenter:[37.808445, -122.410161],
    mapZoom: 14,
    mapShowjMapIcon: false,
    mapEnableScaleControl: true,
    mapControlSize: 'large'
  });
}); // end ready
```

The basic map is now in place. To highlight the location we've chosen for this map, you'll add a red pushpin marker.

11. After the *jmap( )* function you added earlier, type:

```
$('#map').jmap('addMarker', {
  pointLatLng:[37.808445, -122.410161]
});
```

This sets up a marker at the same location as the center of the map. You can provide different longitude and latitude values, of course, to add a marker elsewhere on the map.

For the last part of this tutorial, you'll add the ability to search for driving directions to Fisherman's Wharf (or whatever you set the map's center to). First, you need to add an empty <div> where the directions will be placed.

12. Locate the closing </form> tag. Immediately after that is a closing </div> tag. In the empty line following add *<div id="directions"></div>*. The code should look like this (the new line is bolded):

```
    </form>
  </div>
  <div id="directions"></div>
</div>
```

When the page loads, that <div> will remain empty. But if someone types an address in the text field and presses the "Get Directions" button, the jMaps plug-in will put the driving directions into that <div>.

Now you need to add a *submit* event handler for the form so that when visitors fill out the "From" field and hit the Submit button, they'll receive driving directions from the location they've specified.

13. **In the <script> tag where you've been adding the programming, insert a blank, empty line after the code you added in step 11 and type:**

```
$('#getDir').submit(function( ){

});
```

The <form> tag on this page has an ID of *getDir* (for "get directions"). So this code selects that form and applies a *submit* event handler (see page 205). In other words, the code you add next will only run when a visitor submits the form.

14. **Inside the *submit* event function, add the code in bold:**

```
$('#getDir').submit(function( ){
  $('#map').jmap("searchDirections", {
    toAddress: 'Fisherman\'s Wharf, San Francisco, CA',
    fromAddress: $('#from').val( ),
    directionsPanel: 'directions'
  });
});
```

This code calls the *jmap( )* function again, but this time tells the plug-in that it wants driving directions (that's the *"searchDirections"* part) to Fisherman's Wharf, from whatever the visitor typed into the "From" field. On this form, there's a text field with the ID *from*, so you can use jQuerys *val( )* function (see page 314) to retrieve the address that was typed in that field. Finally, you'll direct the *jmap( )* function to put the driving directions that Google supplies into the <div> you added in step 12 (that <div> has the ID *directions*).

Note: The backward slash before the ' in Fisherman's Wharf in the code in this step is used to escape the single quote mark, so the JavaScript interpreter doesn't consider it the end of the string. See the box on page 42 for more on escaping quote marks.

Next, you need to stop the Web browser from trying to submit the form information. You've used JavaScript to intercept the submission, so you don't want the browser doing anything.

15. **Insert a blank line directly before the final line of the *submit( )* function and type *return false;* so that the code looks like this:**

```
$('#getDir').submit(function( ){
  $('#map').jmap("searchDirections", {
```

```
      toAddress: 'Fisherman\'s Wharf, San Francisco, CA',
      fromAddress: $('#from').val(),
      directionsPanel:"directions"
  });
  return false;
});
```

As discussed on page 224, you can use *return false;* on *click* and *submit* events to prevent a browser from responding as it would normally to those events. Now you're ready to test this out.

16. **Save the file and preview it in a Web browser. Type an address (like *123 Main St., Boise, ID*), or just a city and state like *St Paul, MN*. Press the Get Directions button.**

The map will zoom out and draw a line from your starting point to Fisherman's Wharf. In addition, a set of written driving directions will appear below the form field (in the empty <div> you added back in step 12, as shown in Figure 12-5).

If you now try to get driving directions from another address, you'll notice that the new directions will appear, but the old directions remain as well. There might be an occasion where you'd like the search function to work that way, but most of the time, you'll just want to replace the old directions with the new ones.

17. **Directly inside the *submit* event, type *$('#directions').empty( );*. The completed code for this page should now look like this:**

```
$(document).ready(function( ) {
  $('#map').jmap('init', {
    mapCenter:[37.808445, -122.410161],
    mapZoom: 14,
    mapShowjMapIcon: false,
    mapEnableScaleControl: true,
    mapControlSize: 'large'
  });
  $('#map').jmap('addMarker', {
    pointLatLng:[37.808445, -122.410161]
  });
  $('#getDir').submit(function( ){
    $('#directions').empty( );
    $('#map').jmap("searchDirections", {
      toAddress: 'Fisherman\'s Wharf, San Francisco, CA',
      fromAddress: $('#from').val(),
      directionsPanel:"directions"
    });
    return false;
  });
}); // end ready( )
```

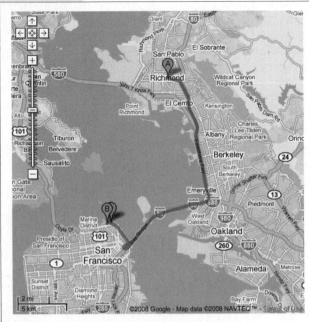

Figure 12-5:
The jMaps plug-in not only lets you add Google Maps to a Web page, but also lets visitors get written driving directions from their location to your store or some other location you specify. To change the appearance of these directions, create descendent selector CSS styles based on the ID of the <div> used to hold the directions. For example, #directions p is a selector that formats all <p> tags inside another tag with an ID of directions.

Directions to: **Fisherman's Wharf, San Francisco**

FROM: Richmond, CA

(Get Directions)

	A	Richmond, CA	

		17.7 mi (about 27 mins)
1.	Head east on Barrett Ave toward 27th St	0.9 mi
2.	Turn right to merge onto I-80 W	7.4 mi
3.	Take the exit onto I-80 W toward San Francisco Partial toll road	6.6 mi
4.	Take the Fremont St exit	0.5 mi
5.	Keep right at the fork, follow signs for Folsom St	489 ft
6.	Turn left at Folsom St	0.3 mi
7.	Turn left at The Embarcadero	1.8 mi
8.	Continue on Jefferson St	0.1 mi

B	Fisherman's Wharf, Jefferson St, San Francisco,. CA

Map data ©2008 NAVTEQ™, Sanbom

jQuery's *empty( )* function removes all of the content inside of the selection. So in this case, the driving directions <div> tag is selected—*$('#directions')*—and then anything inside it (such as previous driving directions) is removed.

Save the page and give it one final check in a Web browser. You'll find a completed version of the tutorial file—*complete_12.2.html*—in the *chapter12* folder.

Part Four:
Troubleshooting, Tips, and Tricks

4

Troubleshooting and Debugging

Everybody makes mistakes, but in JavaScript mistakes can keep your programs from running correctly—or at all. When you first start out with JavaScript, you'll probably make a lot of mistakes. Trying to figure out why a script isn't behaving the way it should can be frustrating, but it's all a part of programming. Fortunately, with experience and practice, you'll be able to figure out why an error has occurred and how to fix it.

This chapter describes some of the most common programming mistakes, and, more importantly teaches you how to diagnose problems in your scripts—*debug* them, as programmers say. In addition, the tutorial will take you step-by-step through debugging a problematic script.

Top JavaScript Programming Mistakes

There are countless ways a program can go wrong, from simple typos to more subtle errors that only pop up every now and again. However, there are a handful of mistakes that routinely plague beginning (and even advanced) JavaScript programmers. Go over the list in this section, and keep it in the back of your mind when programming. You'll probably find that knowing these common mistakes makes it a lot easier to identify and fix problems in your own programs.

Non-Closed Pairs

As you've noticed, JavaScript is filled with endless parentheses, braces, semicolons, quotation marks, and other punctuation. Due to the finicky nature of computers, leaving out a single punctuation mark can stop a program dead in its tracks. One of the most common mistakes is simply forgetting to include a closing punctuation mark. For example, *alert('hello' ;* will produce an error because the closing parenthesis is missing: *alert('hello');*.

Leaving off a closing parenthesis will cause a syntax error (see the box on page 469). This kind of "grammatical" error prevents scripts from running at all. When you give your script a test run, the browser lets you know if you've made a syntax error, but, confusingly, they all describe the problem differently. In the Firefox error console (page 34), you get an error message like "missing) after argument list"; Internet Explorer (page 35) reports this error as "Expected ')'"; and Safari's error console (page 36) gives you the less-helpful message "SyntaxError: ParseError." As mentioned on page 33, Firefox tends to provide the most understandable error messages, so it's a good browser to start with when trying to figure out why a script isn't working (see Figure 13-1).

The syntax error in *alert('hello' ;* is pretty easy to spot. When you've got a nest of parentheses, though, it's very easy to leave off a closing parenthesis and difficult to spot that error at a glance. For example:

```
if ((x>0) && (y<10) {
    // do something
}
```

In this example, the final closing parentheses for the conditional statement is missing—the one that goes directly after *(y<10)*. The first line should really be: *if ((x>0) and (y<10)) {*. Again, Firefox provides the clearest description of the problem: "missing) after condition." Table 13-1 provides a list of Firefox's Error Console syntax error messages.

You'll encounter a syntax error when you forget to include the second quote mark as well. For example, *alert('hello);* produces an error because the final single quote is missing: *alert('hello');*. In Firefox, if you forget to include both quote marks, you'll get an "unterminated string literal" error, while Internet Explorer reports an "unterminated string constant"; Safari again provides the less-than-useful "Syntax-Error: Parse Error" message.

Braces also come in pairs, and you'll use them in conditional statements (page 77), in loops (page 90), when creating JavaScript object literals (page 188), and with JSON (page 432):

```
if (score==0) {
    alert('game over');
```

In this example, the closing } is missing, and the script will produce a syntax error.

One approach to overcome the problem of missing closing punctuation marks is to always add them before adding other programming. For example, say you want to end up with the following code:

```
if ((name=='bob') && (score==0)) {
    alert('You lose (but at least you have a great name');
}
```

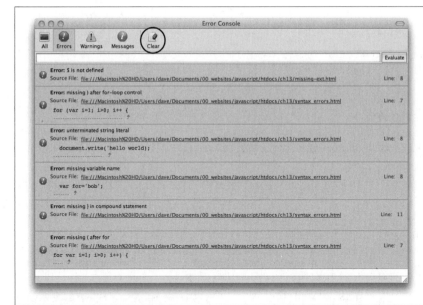

Figure 13-1:
Firefox's Error Console lists all JavaScript errors that the browser encounters. You can display the console by choosing Tools → Error Console. Since the console lists the errors it has encountered on all pages, you'll want to frequently erase the list by clicking the Clear button (circled).

Start by typing the outside elements first, creating a basic skeleton for the condition like this:

```
if ( ) {

}
```

At this point, there's not much code, so it's easy to see if you've mistakenly left out any punctuation. Next, add more code, bit by bit, until the program is in place. The same is true when creating a complex JavaScript object literal like the one used to set the options for the Validation plug-in described on page 331, or like a JSON object described on page 432. Start with the basic structure:

```
var options = {

};
```

Then add more structure:

```
var options = {
  rules : {

  },
  messages : {

  }
};
```

Then finish the object:

```
var options = {
  rules : {
    name : 'required',
    email: 'email'
  },
  messages : {
    name : 'Please type your name',
    email: 'Please type your e-mail address.'
  }
};
```

This approach lets you check your work through various steps and makes it a lot easier to identify any mistakes in punctuation.

Table 13-1. *Firefox's Error Console (discussed on page 34) provides the clearest description of syntax error messages. When a script isn't working, preview it in Firefox and review the Error Console. Here are a few of the most common error messages and what they mean.*

Firefox error message	Explanation

Unterminated string literal	Missing opening or closing quote mark:
	`var name = Jane' ;`
	Error also appears with mismatched quote marks:
	`var name = 'Jane";`

Missing) after argument list	Missing closing parenthesis when calling a function or method: `alert('hello' ;`
Missing) after condition	Missing closing parenthesis within a conditional statement: `if (x==0`
Missing (before condition	Missing opening parenthesis within a conditional statement: `if x==0)`

Missing } in compound statement	Missing closing brace as part of conditional loop:
	`if (score == 0) {`
	`  alert('game over');`
	`    // missing } on this line`

Missing } after property list	Missing closing brace for JavaScript object:
	`var x = {`
	`  fName: 'bob',`
	`  lName: 'smith'`
	`    // missing } on this line`

Syntax Error	General problem that prevents JavaScript interpreter from reading the script.

Table 13-1. *Firefox's Error Console (discussed on page 34) provides the clearest description of syntax error messages. When a script isn't working, preview it in Firefox and review the Error Console. Here are a few of the most common error messages and what they mean. (continued)*

Firefox error message	Explanation
Missing ; before statement	Lets you know when you've run two statements together on a single line, without separating them with a semi-colon. You'll also see this when you incorrectly nest quotation marks:
	`var message='There's an error here.';`
Missing variable name	Appears if you attempt to use a JavaScript reserved word (see page 44) for a variable name:
	`var if="Syntax error.";`
Redeclaration of const	Appears when you try to assign a value to one of the browser's reserved words (see the list on page 45). For example:
	`var document="This won't work.";`

Quotation Marks

Quote marks often trip up beginning programmers. Quote marks are used to create strings of letters and other characters (see page 116) to use as messages on the page, or as variables in a program. JavaScript, like other programming languages, lets you use either *double* or *single* quote marks to create a string. So,

```
var name="Jane";
```

is the same as:

```
var name='Jane';
```

As you read in the previous section, you must include both the opening and closing quote marks, or you'll end up with an "Unterminated string literal" error in Firefox (and all other browsers will give up on your script as well). In addition, as you read on page 41, you must use the same type of quote mark for each pair—in other words, both single quotes or both double quotes. So *var name='Jane"* will also generate an error.

Another common problem can arise with the use of quotations within a string. For example, it's very easy to make the following mistake:

```
var message='There's an error in here.';
```

Notice the single quote in *There's*. The JavaScript interpreter treats that quote mark as a closing quote, so it actually sees this: *var message='There'*, and the rest of the line is seen as an error. In the Firefox Error Console, you'll get the message "Missing ; before statement," because Firefox thinks that second quote is the end of a simple JavaScript statement and what follows is a second statement.

You can get around this error in two ways. First, you can mix and match double and single quotes. In other words, you can put double quotes around a string with single quotes, or you can put single quotes around a string containing double quotes. For example, you can fix the above error this way:

```
var message="There's no error in here.";
```

Or, if the string contains double quotes:

```
var message='He said, "There is no problem here."';
```

Another approach is to *escape* quote marks within a string. Escaping quote marks is discussed in greater detail in the box on page 42, but here's a recap: to escape a character, precede it with a forward slash, like this:

```
var message='There\'s no error here.';
```

The JavaScript interpreter treats \' as a single quote character and not as the symbol used to begin and end strings.

Using Reserved Words

As listed on page 45, the JavaScript language has many words that are reserved for its private use. These words include words used in the language's syntax, like *if*, *do*, *for*, and *while*, as well as words used as part of the Browser object, like *alert*, *location*, *window*, and *document*. These words are not available to use as variable names.

For example, the following code generates a syntax error:

```
var if = "This won't work.";
```

Since *if* is used to create conditional statements—as in *if (x==0)*—you can't use it as a variable name. Some browsers, however, won't generate an error if you use words that are part of the Browser Object Model (see page 45) for your variable names. For example, *document* refers to the HTML document. Firefox alone spits out an error—"Redeclaration of const"—when it encounters code like the following:

```
var document='Something strange is happening here.';
alert(document);
```

You'll get completely different results if you run this code in any other browsers. Internet Explorer, for example, pops up an alert box with the string "Something strange is happening here," since that browser lets you assign a value to that variable name. However, Safari and Opera both pop up alerts with the text "[object HTMLDocument]." Again, Firefox is the best browser to test your scripts in, since it produces real error messages that are easy to understand and fix.

Single Equals in Conditional Statements

Conditional statements (page 77) provide a way for a program to react in different ways depending upon a value of a variable, the status of an element on a page, or some other condition in the script. For example, a conditional statement can display a picture *if* it's hidden or *else* hide it if it's visible. Conditional statements only

Types of Errors

There are three basic categories of errors that you'll encounter as you program JavaScript. Some of these errors are immediately obvious, while others don't always rear their ugly heads until the script is up and running.

- **Syntax Errors.** A syntax error is essentially a grammatical mistake that makes a Web browser's JavaScript interpreter throw up its hands and say, "I give up." Any of the errors involving a missing closing parenthesis, brace, or quote mark generates a syntax error. The Web browser encounters syntax errors immediately, as it reads the script, so the script never has a chance to run. An error message for a syntax error always appears in a Web browser's Error Console.

- **Runtime errors.** After a browser reads a script's code successfully and the JavaScript interpreter interprets it, it can still encounter errors. Even if the program's syntax is fine, other problems might pop up as the program runs—called *runtime* errors. For example, say you define a variable named *message* at the beginning of a script; later in the script, you add a click function (page 203) to an image so an alert box appears when the image is clicked. Say the alert code for this example looks like this: *alert(MESSAGE);*. There's nothing wrong with this statement's syntax, but it calls the variable *MESSAGE* instead of lowercase *message*. As mentioned on page 44, JavaScript is case-sensitive, so *MESSAGE* and *message* refer to two different variables. When a visitor clicks the image, the JavaScript interpreter looks for the variable *MESSAGE* (which doesn't exist) and generates a runtime error.

  Another common runtime error occurs when you try to access an element on a page that either doesn't

exist or the browser hasn't yet read into its memory. See the discussion of jQuery's *$(document).ready( )* function on page 218 for more detail on this problem.

- **Logic errors.** Sometimes even though a script seems to run, it doesn't produce the results you're after. For example, you may have an if/else statement (page 77) that performs step A if a condition is true or step B if it's false. Unfortunately, the program never seems to get to step B, even if you're sure the condition is false. This kind of error happens when you use the equality operator incorrectly (see page 78). From the JavaScript interpreter's perspective, everything is technically correct, but you've made a mistake in the logic of your programming that prevents the script from working as planned.

Another example of a logic error is an infinite loop, which is a chunk of code that runs *forever*, usually causing your programming to hang up and sometimes even crashing the Web browser (see page 91). Here's an example of an infinite loop:

```
for (var i=1; i>0; i++) {
   // this will run forever
   }
```

In a nutshell, this loop will run as long as the test condition *(i>0)* is true. Since *i* starts out with a value of 1 *(var i=1)*, and each time it goes through the loop *i* is increased by 1 *(i++)*, the value of *i* will always be greater than 1. In other words, the loop never stops. (Turn to page 94 if you need a refresher on *for* loops.)

Logic errors are amongst the most difficult to uncover. However, with the debugging techniques described on page 473, you should be able to uncover just about any problem you encounter.

make sense, however, if a particular condition can be *true* or *false*. Unfortunately, it's easy to create a conditional statement that's always true:

```
if (score=0) {
   alert('game over');
}
```

This code is supposed to check the value stored in the variable *score*—if the value is 0 then an alert box with the message "game over" should appear. However, in this case, the alert message will *always* display, no matter what value is stored in *score* prior to the conditional statement. That's because a single equals sign is an *assignment* operator, so *score=0* stores the value *0* in *score*. The JavaScript interpreter treats an assignment operation as *true*, so not only does the code above always pop up the alert box, it also re-writes the value of *score* to *0*.

To avoid this error, make sure to use *double* equal signs when testing whether two values are the same:

```
if (score==0) {
   alert('game over');
}
```

Case-Sensitivity

Remember that JavaScript is case-sensitive, meaning that the JavaScript interpreter tracks not only the letters in the names of variables, functions, methods, and keywords, but also whether the letters are uppercase or lowercase. So *alert('hi')* is not the same as *ALERT('hi')* to the JavaScript interpreter. The first, *alert('hi')*, calls the browser's built-in *alert( )* command, while the second *ALERT('hi')* attempts to call a user-defined function named *ALERT( )*.

You can run into this problem if you use the long-winded DOM selection methods *getElementsByTagName( )* or *getElementById( )*, since they use both upper and lowercase letters. Likewise, if you include both upper and lowercase letters in variable and function names, you may run into this problem from time to time.

If you see an "*x* is not defined" error message (where *x* is the name of your variable, function, or method), mismatched case may be the problem.

Incorrect Path to External JavaScript File

Another common mistake is incorrectly linking to an external JavaScript file. Page 24 discusses how to attach an external JavaScript file to a Web page. Basically, you use the <script> tag's *src* property to point to the file. So in the HTML page, you'd add the <script> tag to the <head> of the document like this:

```
<script type="text/javascript" src="site_js.js"></script>
```

The *src* property works like a link's *href* property—it defines the path to the JavaScript file. As mentioned in the box on page 25, there are three ways you can point to a file: absolute links (*http://www.site.com/site_js.js*), root-relative links (*/site_js.js*), and document-relative links (*site_js.js*).

A document-relative path describes how a Web browser gets from the current page (the Web page) to a particular file. Document-relative links are commonly used because they let you test your Web page and JavaScript file right on your own computer. If you use root-relative links, you'll need to set up a Web server on your own computer to test your pages (or move them up to your Web server to test them).

You can read more about how link paths work on page 25. But, in a nutshell, if you find that a script doesn't work and you're using external JavaScript files, double-check to make sure you've specified the correct path to the JavaScript file.

Tip: If you're using the jQuery library and you get the error "$ is not defined" in the Firefox Error Console, you probably haven't correctly linked to the *jquery.js* file (see page 172 for more).

Incorrect Paths Within External JavaScript Files

Another problem related to file paths occurs when using document-relative paths in an external JavaScript file. For example, you might create a script that displays images on a page (like a slideshow or just a "random image of the day" script). If the script uses document-relative links to point to the images, you can run into trouble if you put that script into an external JavaScript file. Here's why: When an external JavaScript file is loaded into a Web page, its frame of reference for document-relative paths is the location of the Web page itself. So, any document-relative paths you include in the JavaScript file must be relative to the *Web page* and not the JavaScript file.

Here's a simple example to illustrate this problem. Figure 13-2 represents the structure of a very simple Web site. There are two Web pages (*page.html* and *about.html*), four folders (*libs*, *images*, *pages*, and *about*), an external JavaScript file (*site_js.js* inside the *libs* folder) and an image (*photo.jpg* in the *images* folder.) Say the *site_js.js* file references the *photo.jpg* file—perhaps to preload the image (page 235), or display it dynamically on a Web page.

From the *site_js.js* file's perspective, a document-relative path to the *photo.jpg* file is *../images/photo.jpg* (#1 in Figure 13-2). The path tells the browser to exit the *libs* folder (*../*), enter the *images* folder (*images/*) and select the *photo.jpg* file. However, from the perspective of the *page.html* file, the path to the *photo.jpg* file (#2 in Figure 13-2) is just *images/photo.jpg*. In other words, the path to the same photo differs between the two files.

If you want to use the *site_js.js* script within the *page.html* file, then, you have to use path #2 in the *site_js.js* file to reference the location of *photo.jpg* (that is, specify a path relative to *page.html*). By the same token, you can't use the *site_js.js* file in a Web page located in another directory in your site, since the relative path would be different for that file (#3 in Figure 13-2).

There are a few ways around this problem. First, well, you may never encounter it—you may not find yourself listing paths to other files in your JavaScript files. But if you do, you can use root-relative paths (see page 25), which are the same from any page in the site. Alternatively, you can define the path to the files within each Web page. For example, you can link to the external JavaScript file (see page

24), and then, in each Web page, define variables to hold document-relative paths from the current Web page to the correct file.

Finally, you could use an approach like the one used in the slideshow on page 263. The paths come from the Web page and are embedded within links on the page—the JavaScript simply pulls the paths out of the HTML. As long as those paths work in the HTML, they'll work in a script as well.

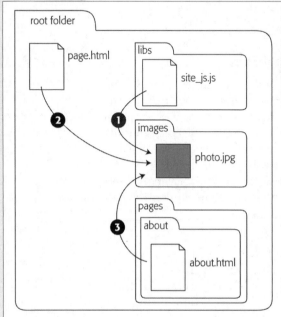

Figure 13-2:
Document-relative paths depend on both the location of the file that path starts at as well as the location of the destination file. For example, the document-relative path from the site_js.js *file to the* photo.jpg *file (#1) is* ../images/photo.jpg; *the path to the same file from the* page.html *file (#2) is* images/photo.jpg; *and the path from the* about.html *file (#3) is* ../../images/photo.jpg.

Disappearing Variables and Functions

You may occasionally encounter an "*x* is not defined" error, where *x* is either the name of a variable or a function you're trying to call. The problem may just be that you mistyped the name of the variable or function or used the wrong case (see page 470). However, if you look through your code and can clearly see that the variable or function is defined in your script, then you may be running into a "scope" problem.

Variable and function scope is discussed in greater detail on page 103, but in a nutshell, if a variable is defined inside of a function, it's only available to that function (or to other functions defined inside that function). Here's a simple example:

```
1    function sayName(name) {
2      var message = 'Your name is ' + name;
3    }
4    sayName( );
5    alert(message); // error: message is not defined
```

The variable *message* is defined within the function *sayName( )*, so it only exists for that function. Outside the function, *message* doesn't exist, so an error is generated when the script tries to access the variable outside the function (line 5).

You may also encounter this error when using jQuery. On page 218, you read about the importance of the *$(document).ready( )* function for jQuery. Anything inside that function only runs once the page's HTML is loaded. You'll run into problems if you define variables or functions within the *$(document).ready( )* function and try to access them outside of it, like this:

```
$(document).ready(function( ) {
  var msg = 'hello';
});
alert(msg); // error: msg is not defined
```

So, when using jQuery, be sure to put all of your programming inside the *$(document).ready( )* function:

```
$(document).ready(function( ) {
  var msg = 'hello';
  alert(msg); // msg is available
});
```

Debugging with Firebug

If you haven't been using Firebug, you've been missing out on one of the best tools a Web designer could have. It's free, easy to install and use, and can help you improve your HTML, CSS, and JavaScript. Firebug is an extension for Firefox that adds a bunch of helpful diagnostic tools to let you pick apart your HTML, CSS, and (most importantly for this book) JavaScript programs.

Installing and Turning On Firebug

You can find the extension at *www.getfirebug.com*. Here's how to install it:

1. **Visit *www.getfirebug.com* using Firefox, and click the Install Firebug button (#1 in Figure 13-3).**

    To protect you from accidentally installing a malicious extension, Firefox stops your first attempt at installing the extension. A yellow banner appears above the page letting you know (#2 in Figure 13-3).

2. **In the yellow warning bar, click the Edit Options button (#3 in Figure 13-3).**

    The Allowed Sites window appears. This window lists all of the sites that you've approved for installing extensions.

3. **Click Allow, and then close the window.**

    You've just added *firebug.com* to your list of approved sites.

Programming Tips to Reduce Errors

The best way to deal with errors and bugs in your programs is to try to stop them as early as possible. It can be really difficult to track down the cause of errors in a program if you wait until you've written a 300-line script before testing it in a Web browser. The two most important tips to avoiding errors are:

- **Build a script in small chunks.** As you've probably figured out by now, JavaScript programs can be difficult to read, what with all of the },), ', ifs, elses, functions, and so on. Don't try to write an entire script in one go (unless you're really good, the script is short, or you're feeling lucky). There are so many ways to make a mistake while programming, and you're better off writing a script in bits.

For example, say you want to display the number of letters typed into a "Comments" box, right next to the box. In other words, as a visitor types into the field, a running total of the number of letters typed appears next to the box. (Some sites do this when they limit the amount a visitor can type into a field—say, 300 letters.) This task is pretty easy JavaScript, but it involves several steps: responding to the keydown

event (when a visitor types a letter in the field), reading the value of that field, counting the numbers of characters in the field, and then displaying that number on the page. You can try to write this script in one go, but you can also write the code for step 1 (responding to a keydown event) and then test it immediately in a Web browser (using the *alert( )* command or Firebug's *console.log( )* function described on the next page, can help you see the results of a keydown event). If it works, you can then move on to step 2, test it, and so on.

As you gain more experience, you won't need to test such small steps. You can write a few steps at once, and then test that chunk.

- **Test frequently**. You should also test your script in a Web browser frequently. At a minimum, test after you complete each chunk of the program, as suggested in the previous point. In addition, you should test the script in different browsers—preferably Internet Explorer 6, 7, and 8; Firefox 2 and 3; Safari 2 and 3; and whatever other browsers you think your site's visitors might be using.

4. **Click the Install Firebug button again (#1 in Figure 13-3).**

Another dialog box appears asking you confirm that, yes, you really, really want to install the extension.

5. **Click Install Now, and Firefox installs the extension. Finally, click the Restart Firefox button to make the Firebug available.**

Even though the extension is installed, there's still one more step to make it available to your Web pages.

6. **Choose Tools → Firebug → Enable Firebug.**

Now you can begin using Firebug to help you debug your scripts.

Viewing Errors with Firebug

Firebug provides an easier and more useful way to view errors than Firefox's built-in Error Console. With Firebug, when you load a Web page with JavaScript errors, you'll see a red X in the lower-right corner of the browser, as well as the number of

❷ Security warning   ❸ Allow site

Figure 13-3:
You have to jump through a series of security hoops to install the Firebug extension, but it's worth it.

❶ Install Firebug

errors encountered (see Figure 13-4). Click the red error button to open the Firebug console, which lists any JavaScript errors.

Note: If there are no errors on the page, the Firebug button in the lower-right corner of Firefox's status bar is a green checkmark.

The errors listed in the console are the same as Firefox's Error Console (Figure 13-1), but Firebug only lists errors for the page you're currently viewing (unlike the Error Console, which lists all errors on all pages Firefox has visited). Because Firebug provides such easy access to error information, you'll probably find yourself skipping the Firefox Error Console entirely once you've experienced Firebug.

Using console.log() to Track Script Progress

Once a script begins to run, it's kind of like a black box. You don't really know what's going on inside the script and only see the end result, like a message on the page, a pop-up window, and so on. You can't always tell exactly whether a loop is working correctly or see the value of a particular variable at any point in time.

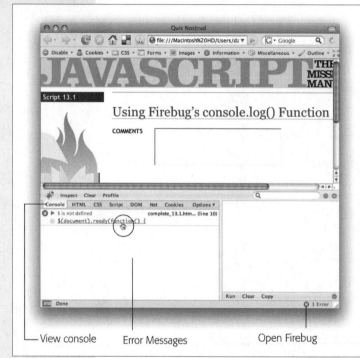

Figure 13-4:
Firebug's console lists any JavaScript errors Firefox has encountered on the current page. To see the exact line of code on which the error was encountered, click the code snippet under the error (circled). Firebug then switches from the console tab to the script tab and highlights the line where the error happened.

View console   Error Messages   Open Firebug

JavaScript programmers have long used the *alert( )* method (page 457) to pop up a window with the current value of a variable. For example, if you want to know what value is being stored in the variable *elementName* as a loop is running, you can insert an alert command inside the loop: *alert(elementName);*. That's one way to look into the "black box" of the script. However, the alert box is pretty intrusive: You have to click it to close it, and in a loop that might run 20 times, that's a lot of pop-up alerts to close.

Firebug provides a better way to look into your program. The Firebug console not only lists errors (see previous section), but can also be used to output messages from the program. The *console.log( )* function works similar to the *document.write( )* function (page 29), but instead of printing a message to the Web page, *console.log( )* prints a message to the console.

For example, you could print the current value of the variable *elementName* to the console using this code:

```
console.log(elementName);
```

Unlike the *alert( )* method, this method won't interrupt your program's flow—you'll just see the message in the console.

Note: Although Firebug only works in Firefox, you can still get the benefit of the *console.log( )* function in other browsers by attaching the Firebug Lite JavaScript file to your page. It works like an external Java-Script file (see page 24), and provides a way to use the console log within Internet Explorer, Safari, or Opera. You can download Firebug Lite from *www.getfirebug.com/lite.html*.

To make the log message more understandable, you can include a string with additional text. For example, if you have a variable named *name* and you want to determine what value is stored in *name* at some point in your program, you can use the *console.log( )* function like this:

```
console.log(name);
```

But if you wanted to precede the name with a message, you can write this:

```
console.log('User name: %s', name);
```

In other words, you first pass a string to the *log( )* function, followed by a comma and the name of the variable whose value should be displayed. The special *%s* is way of saying "substitute the variable value with me." In other words, *%s* gets replaced with the value of *name*, so you'll end up with a message in the console like "User name: Bob."

You can add more than one variable to the message; just include one *%s* for each variable. For example, if you have two variables, *name* and *score*, and want to print both along with a custom log message, you can do the following:

```
console.log('%s has a score of %s', name, score);
```

You can use *%s* for numeric values, but Firebug provides two other tokens—*%d* and *%f*—to represent integers (like 1, 2, and 10) and floating point numbers (like 1.22, and 2.4444). Using one of the two numeric tokens means the numbers are printed in a different color—just an easy way to tell them apart from the rest of the text.

For example, you can rewrite the line of code above to display the number stored in the variable *score*:

```
console.log('%s has a score of %d', name, score);
```

The *log( )* function is merely a way to give you some information about the functioning of your script as you *develop* it. Once your program is finished and working, you should remove all of the *console.log( )* code from your script. Web browsers without Firebug installed (which also includes Internet Explorer, Safari, and Opera) generate errors when they encounter the *log( )* function.

Tutorial: Using the Firebug Console

In this tutorial, you'll learn how to use the *console.log( )* function to see what's going on inside your program. You'll create a script that displays the number of characters typed into a text box on a form.

Note: See the note on page 27 for information on how to download the tutorial files.

To get started, first install Firebug in Firefox using the instructions on page 473 (remember, Firebug only works with the Firefox Web browser).

1. **Open the file *13.1.html* in a text editor.**

   This script uses the jQuery library (page 169). The external *jquery.js* file is already attached to the page, and the opening and closing <script> tags are in place. You'll start by adding jQuery's *$(document).ready( )* function.

2. **Between the <script> tags at the top of the page, add the code in bold below:**

   ```
   <script type="text/javascript">
   $(document).ready(function( ) {

   });
   </script>
   ```

   You learned about the basic *$(document).ready( )* function on page 218, which makes the browser load all of the page's code before starting to run any Java-Script. You'll first use the Firebug *log( )* function to simply print out a message that the script has executed the *.ready( )* function.

3. **Add the bolded code below to the script:**

   ```
   <script type="text/javascript">
   $(document).ready(function( ) {
     console.log('READY');
   });
   </script>
   ```

   The *console.log( )* function runs wherever you place it in the script. In other words, after this page's HTML is loaded (that's what the *ready( )* function waits for), Firebug writes "READY" to the Firebug console. Adding the *ready( )* function is a pretty common and basic move, so you may not always add a *console. log( )* function here, but for this tutorial, you'll add one to see how the *log( )* function works. In fact, you'll be adding a lot of log messages to this page to get the hang of the *console.log( )* function.

4. **Save the file, and open it in Firefox. Click the green checkmark button in the lower-right corner of Firefox's status bar.**

   You can also choose Tools → Firebug → Open Firebug to see the Firebug console.

   The word READY should appear in the console (circled in Figure 13-5). The script you're creating will display the number of characters typed into a form's text field each time your visitor types a character. To accomplish this, you'll add a keyup event (page 207) to that text box. During each step of this script, you'll also add a *console.log( )* function, to clue you in to what's happening.

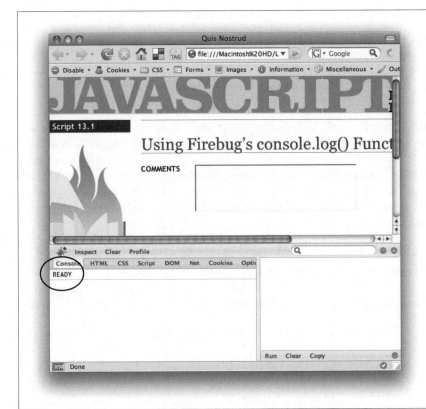

Figure 13-5:
If the Firebug icon in the right corner of the status bar is red instead of green, there's a JavaScript error (probably just a typo). Click the red button, and the console tells you the error.

5. **After the line of code you added in step 3, add the following:**

```
$('#comments').keyup(function() {
  console.log('Event: keyup');
});
```

The <textarea> tag on this page has an ID of comments, so we can select that element using jQuery ($('#comments')) and add a function to the keyup event (see page 207 for a refresher on adding events). In this case, the *console.log( )* function is just printing a status message to the Firebug console telling you each time the keyup event is triggered. This function is an easy way to see whether an event function is actually running or something's preventing the event from happening.

Save the page; reload it in Firefox and type a few characters into the text box. Make sure Firebug's console is open, and you should see several lines (one for each character you typed) of "Event: keyup," Now that the keyup event is working, you might want to retrieve the contents of the text box and store it in a variable. To be sure you're getting the information you're after, you'll print the contents of the variable to the console.

6. **Add lines 3 and 4 below to the code you typed in step 5:**

```
1   $('#comments').keyup(function() {
2     console.log('Event: keyup');
3     var text = $(this).val();
4     console.log('Contents of comments: %s',text);
5   });
```

Line 3 retrieves the value from the text box and stores it inside a variable named *text* (see page 313 for more information on extracting the value from a form field). Line 4 writes a message to the console. In this case, it combines a string 'Contents of comments: ' and the value currently stored in the text box. When a program isn't working correctly, a very common diagnostic step is to print out the values of variables in the script to make sure the variable contains the information you're expecting it to have.

7. **Save the file, reload it in Firefox, and type some text into the comments box.**

The console should now display the contents in the comments box each time you type a letter into the field. By now you should be getting the hang of the console, so you'll add one more message, and then finish this script.

8. **Edit the keyup event function by adding two more lines (5 and 6 below):**

```
1   $('#comments').keyup(function() {
2     console.log('Event: keyup');
3     var text = $(this).val();
4     console.log('Contents of comments %s',text);
5     var chars = text.length;
6     console.log('Number of characters: %d',chars);
7   });
```

Line 5 counts the number of characters stored inside the *text* variable (see page 116 for more on the *length* property) and stores it inside the variable *chars*. Just to make sure the script is correctly calculating the number of characters, use the *log( )* function (line 6) to print a message to the console. Since the variable *chars* holds a number, you use the *%d* token to display an integer value (see page 147).

There's just one last thing to do: finish the script so it prints the number of characters typed so your visitor can see it.

9. **Add one last line to the end of the keyup event function (line 10), so the completed script for the page looks like this:**

```
1   <script type="text/javascript">
2   $(document).ready(function() {
3     console.log('READY');
4     $('#comments').keyup(function() {
5       console.log('Event: keyup');
6       var text = $(this).val();
7       console.log('Contents of comments: %s',text);
```

```
8        var chars = text.length;
9        console.log('Number of characters: %d',chars);
10       $('#count').text(chars + " characters");
11     });
12   });
13   </script>
```

10. **Save the file, and preview it in Firefox.**

Make sure Firebug is open, and the page and console should now look something like Figure 13-6. You'll find a finished version of this tutorial—*complete_13.1.html*—in the *chapter13* folder in the tutorials folder.

Note: As mentioned on page 477, once you have a functioning program, you should remove all *console.log( )* code from your script. The *log( )* function will generate errors in other browsers and in any version of Firefox missing the Firebug extension.

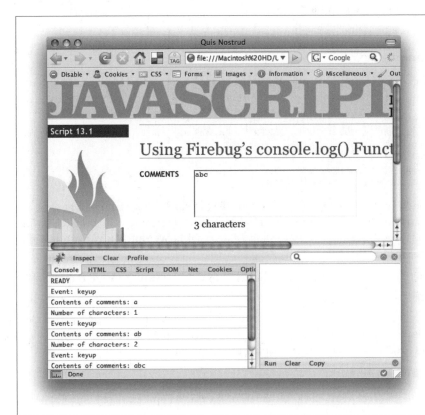

Figure 13-6:
The Firebug console is a great way to print out diagnostic information as a program is running. You can also group together a series of log entries (for example, to group all the log messages printed during a loop) by adding console.group( ) *before the first* console.log( ) *message in the group, and* console.groupEnd( ) *after the last message. You can learn more about console functions at www.getfirebug.com/console.html.*

More Powerful Debugging

The Firebug console is a great way to print out messages so you can see what's going on when a program runs. But sometimes a program zips by so quickly it's hard to see what's going on during each step. You need a way to slow things down. Fortunately, Firebug includes a powerful JavaScript debugger. It lets you step through a script line by line so you can see what's happening at each step of the program.

Debugging is the process of fixing an incorrectly functioning program—getting the bugs out. To really understand how a program is functioning (or malfunctioning), you need to see how the program works, step-by-step.

To use the debugger, you mark certain lines of code as *breakpoints*. A breakpoint is a spot where the JavaScript interpreter stops running and waits. You can then use controls inside Firebug that let you run a program one line at a time. In this way, you can see exactly what's happening at any particular line. Here's the basic process.

1. **Open a Web page in Firefox.**

   You need Firebug installed and enabled as described on page 473.

2. **Open Firebug.**

   Click the Firebug icon (green button in the lower-right corner in the Firefox status bar). Alternatively, press F12 or choose Tool → Firebug → Open Firebug.

Tip: If you don't like the cramped appearance of the Web page stacked directly on top of Firebug, choose Tools → Firebug → "Open Firebug in New Window".

3. **Click the Script tab (see Figure 13-7).**

   The Script tab lists the source code for the file you wish to debug. In the case of a script that's written into a Web page, you see the source code for the entire Web page (including HTML). For an external JavaScript file, you see just the JavaScript in that file.

4. **Select the file with the script you wish to debug from the source menu (see Figure 13-7).**

   It's common to have scripts placed in different files: the Web page itself, or one or more external JavaScript files. If your page uses scripts from multiple files, you need to select the file containing the script you wish to debug.

5. **Add breakpoints.**

   To add a breakpoint, click to the left of the line's number. A red bullet appears indicating a breakpoint.

Note: Adding a breakpoint to a line that only contains a comment has no effect–the debugger won't stop on that line. Only add breakpoints to lines containing actual JavaScript code.

6. **Reload the Web page.**

Since you have to view your Web page in Firefox in order to open Firebug and add breakpoints, the JavaScript you want to debug may have already run (before you added any breakpoints). In this case, you need to reload the page so you can start the JavaScript over again.

If you added a break point in a function that responds to an event (for example, you want to debug the code that runs when you click a button or mouse over a link) then you need to trigger that event—click the button, mouse over the link, or whatever—to reach the breakpoint and start the debugging process.

After the script begins to run, as soon as a breakpoint is reached, the script stops. The program is frozen in time, waiting to execute the line from the first breakpoint.

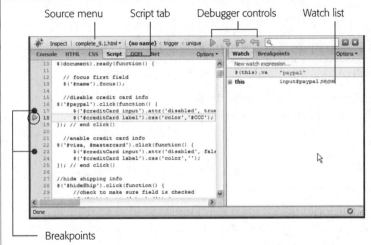

Figure 13-7:
The Firebug debugger lets you set breakpoints (lines where the script stops and waits), control the execution of the script, and watch variables in the Watch list. As the debugger executes the script, the current line (the one that's about to run) has a yellow arrow to its left (circled).

7. **Use Firebug's controls to step through the execution of the program.**

Firebug provides four controls (see Figure 13-7) that dictate how the program runs after stopping at the breakpoint. You can read about these controls on page 484.

8. **Monitor program conditions in the Watch list (see Figure 13-7).**

The point of stepping through a program is to see what's going on inside the script at any particular line. The Watch list provides basic information about the program's condition and lets you add additional variables you want to watch. For example, if you wanted to track the value of the variable score as the script runs, you can do that in the Watch list. You'll find out how to use the Watch list on page 485.

9. **Fix your script in a text editor.**

   Hopefully, in stepping through your script you'll find out what's going wrong—for example, why the value of a particular variable never changes, or why a conditional statement never evaluates to false. With that information, you can then jump to your text editor and modify your script (you'll run through an example of fixing a script in the tutorial on page 486).

10. **Test the page in Firefox, and, if necessary, repeat the above steps to keep debugging your script.**

Controlling your script with the debugger

Once you've added breakpoints to the script and reloaded the page, you're ready to step through the script line by line. If you added a breakpoint to part of the script that runs when the page loads, the script will stop at the breakpoint; if you added a breakpoint to the a line that only runs after an event (like clicking a link), you need to trigger that event before you can get to the breakpoint.

When the debugger stops the program at a breakpoint, it doesn't run that line of code; it stops just *before* running it. You can then click one of the four buttons on the debugger to control what the debugger does next (see Figure 13-8):

- **Play.** The Play button simply starts the script running. The script won't stop again until the JavaScript interpreter encounters another breakpoint, or until the script has finished running. If there's another breakpoint, the script stops again and waits for you to click one of the four debugger controls.

  Use the Play button if you just want run the program through or skip to the next breakpoint.

- **Step Over.** This useful option runs the current line of code, then stops at the next line in the script. It's named Step Over because if the current line of code includes a call to a function, it won't enter the function—it steps over the function and stops at the next line of code. This option is great if you know the function that's being called works flawlessly. For example, if your script calls a jQuery function, you'll want to step over the call to that function—otherwise, you'll be spending a lot of time viewing the scary jQuery programming line by line. You'll choose the Step Over option most of the time.

- **Step Into.** Step Into takes the debugger into a function call. That is, if you're on a line that includes a call to a function, the debugger enters the function and stops at the first line of that function. This option is the way to go when you're not sure if the problem is in the main script or within a function you wrote.

  Skip this option if you're sure that the function being called works—for example, if the function is one you've used dozens of times before. You also want to use Step Over instead of Step Into when you're debugging a line of code that includes a jQuery selector or command. For example $('#button')$, is a jQuery way to select an element on the page. However, it's also a function of the jQuery library, so if you click the Step Into button when you encounter a jQuery function, you'll jump into the complex world of the jQuery library. (And if that happens, you'll know because the script tab will change to show all of the JavaScript code for the *jquery.js* file.)

If, when using the debugger, you find yourself lost within a function, or in the code of a JavaScript library like jQuery, you can use the control described next to get out.

- **Step Out**. The Step Out button gets the debugger out of a function call. You'll usually use it after using Step Into. When you do, the function runs as normal, but you won't stop at each line of the function as you would in normal debug mode. When you click this button, the debugger returns to the line where the function was originally called and then stops.

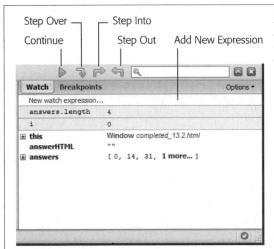

Step Over — Step Into
Continue — Step Out — Add New Expression

Figure 13-8:
Firebug's Watch list shows the value of different variables as the program runs. You can add your own expressions to the list, which appear as grey stripes at the top of the window.

Watching your script

While the buttons at the top of the debugger let you control how the script executes, the whole point of a debugger is to see what's going on inside the script. That's where the Watch list comes in (see Figure 13-8). The Watch list provides a listing of variables and functions within the context of the current executing line of code. All that means is if you put a breakpoint within a function, you'll see a list of all of the variables that are defined within that function; if you put a breakpoint in the main body of your script, you'll see a list of all variables that are defined there. You'll also see any functions that you've created listed in the Watch list.

You can add your own variables and expressions using the yellow bar with the label "New watch expression…". Just click the yellow bar, and a text field appears. Type the name of a variable you'd like to track, or even a JavaScript statement you'd like to execute. For example, since the debugger doesn't keep track of a counter variable in a *for* loop (page 94), you can add this variable, and as you go step by step through the loop, you can see how the counter changes each time through the loop.

You can think of this Watch list as a kind of a continual *console.log( )* command. It prints out the value of a particular variable or expression at the time a particular line of code is run.

The Watch list offers valuable insight into your program, providing a kind of freeze-frame effect so you can find exactly where in your script an error occurs. For example, if you know that a particular variable holds a number value, you can go step by step through the script and see what value gets stored in the variable when it's first created and see how its value gets modified as the program runs. If, after you click the Step Through or Step Into buttons, you see the variable's value change to something you didn't expect, then you've probably found the line where the error is introduced.

Debugging Tutorial

In this tutorial, you'll use Firebug to debug a file that's filled with various types of errors (syntax errors, runtime errors, and logic errors). The page is a simple quiz program that poses three questions and prints quiz results. (Open the *complete_13.2.html* file in the *chapter13* folder in any Web browser to see how the page is supposed to work.)

Note: See the note on page 27 for information on how to download the tutorial files.

To complete this tutorial you'll need run the Firefox Web browser and have the Firebug extension installed and turned on—see page 473 for instructions.

1. **Start Firefox and open the file *13.2.html* from the *chapter13* tutorials folder.**

   Firebug's red error button appears at the bottom of the window (circled in Figure 13-9). You must open the Firebug console to find out what's wrong.

2. **Click the red button to open the console.**

   You should see the error message in Figure 13-9: "Missing] after element list." Square brackets are used for creating arrays (see page 56), so it appears that one of an array's closing brackets is missing. This omission is a syntax error (see the box on page 469) because it represents a "grammatical error" in the code (like a sentence missing a period). You'll notice that to the right of the error message, Firebug lets you know that this error occurred in line 16.

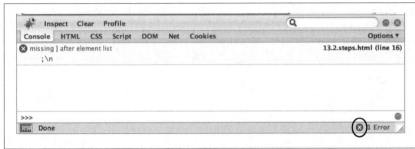

Figure 13-9:
The Firebug console is the
first stop for tracking
down syntax and runtime
errors that bring a script
to its knees.

3. **Launch your text editor and open the file *13.2.html*. Locate line 16 (it's a single ; on a line by itself). Type a closing square bracket before the ; so the line looks like this:**

   ```
   ];
   ```

   This bracket ended a nested array (page 56) that contained all of the questions and answers for the quiz.

4. **Save the file; return to Firefox and reload the page.**

   Another error! This time the error console says "$ is not defined" and points to line 10 containing jQuery's *$(document).ready( )* function. When Firefox reports that something's "not defined," it means the code is referring to something that doesn't exist, which could be the name of a variable or a function that hasn't yet been created. Or you might just have a typo in the code. In this case, the code looks OK. The culprit is actually earlier on the page, in this code:

   ```
   <script type="text/javascript" src="js/jquery.js"></script>
   ```

   A common problem when working with external scripts is accidentally typing the wrong path to the script (see page 470). In this case, the *jquery.js* file is located inside a folder named *js* that's *outside* this file's folder. The code here says that the *js* file should be inside the same folder as this Web page; because Firefox can't find the *jquery.js* file (where jQuery's special *$( )* function is defined), it spits out an error.

5. **Change the <script> tag to read:**

   ```
   <script type="text/javascript" src="../js/jquery.js"></script>
   ```

   The *../* indicates that the *js* folder is outside this folder, and the path is now correctly pointing to the jQuery file. What else could be wrong with this program?

6. **Save the file; return to Firefox and reload the page.**

   No errors! Looks like the page is fixed…or is it?

7. **Click the Start Quiz button.**

   Bam! Another error. This time the console reports that "askQuestions is not defined" and points to line 70 near the end of the the script. Since this error only appears while the program is running, it's called a runtime error (see the box on page 469). The problem appears toward the end of the script, within this conditional statement:

```
if (quiz.length>0) {
  askQuestions();
} else {
  giveResults();
}
```

By now it's probably dawning on you that when something's not defined, it's often just because of a simple typo. In this case, *askQuestions( )* is a call to a function, so take a moment now to look through the code and try to find this function.

Did you find it? While there isn't an *askQuestions( )* function, you should have noticed an *askQuestion( )* function (without an *s*).

8. **Return to your text editor, and then remove the last *s* from *askQuestions( )* in line 70 (near the end of the script). Save the file, reload it in Firefox, and then click the "Start Quiz" button again.**

Now, a quiz question appears along with five multiple-choice options. Unfortunately, the last option has a label of *undefined*. Smells like an error. However, the Firebug console is empty, so technically there's no JavaScript error. Something must be wrong with the program's *logic*. To get to the bottom of the trouble, you'll need to use Firebug's debugger.

9. **In Firebug, click the Script tab and select *13.2.html* from the source menu directly above the Script tab (see Figure 13-10).**

The Script tab gives you access to the page's JavaScript. If the page includes JavaScript and you've linked to other external JavaScript files, the Source menu lets you choose which JavaScript code you wish to debug.

Because the "undefined" radio button seems to be out of place, the code that creates the radio buttons is a good place to start looking for this bug. If you had written this script, you'd probably know just where to look in your code; however, if you were just handed this buggy script, you'd have to hunt around until you found that part of the script.

In this case, the radio buttons are created within a function named *buildAnswers( )*, whose purpose is to build a series of multiple choice options represented by radio buttons. That function is passed an array that includes a list of values for each radio button. When the function is done, it returns a string containing the HTML for the radio buttons. So this function's a good place to start debugging.

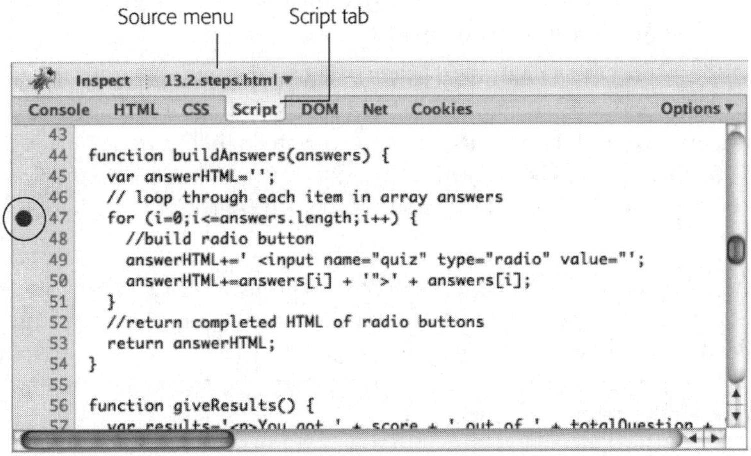

Figure 13-10:
In Firebug, you can debug any scripts that the current page uses. The Source menu lets you select the JavaScript embedded in the current Web page or from any attached external JavaScript file.

10. In Firebug's Script tab, scroll down until you see line 47. Click to the left of 47 to insert a breakpoint (circled in Figure 13-10).

A red dot appears to the left of line 47. The dot indicates a breakpoint, or a spot in the code, where the JavaScript interpreter stops running the script. In other words, when this script runs again, the moment the JavaScript interpreter hits that line, it stops, and you'll be able to step line by line through the code to see what's happening under the hood.

The debugger also lets you look at the values of variables as the program runs, much as you used the *console.log( )* function on page 475. You'll tell Firebug what variables you want to track next.

11. **In the right side of the Firebug window, click the "New Watch Expression" bar, type *i*, and then press the Return (or Enter) key.**

This step adds the variable *i* to the Watch list. That variable is used in the *for* loop as a counter to track how many times the loop runs (see page 90 for more on for loops). As the script runs, you'll be able to see how that value changes. Next, you'll add another variable to watch.

12. **Click the "New Watch Expression" bar again, type *answers.length*, and then hit Return.**

Don't worry about the value Firebug displays at this point (it probably says "answers is not defined"). You can't track the values of variables until you're actually running the debugger and are inside the function. Now it's time to take a look inside the script.

13. **Click Firefox's Reload button or press Ctrl+R (⌘-R). When the page reloads, click the "Start Quiz" button on the Web page.**

The script starts, and the first question is written to the Web page. But when it comes time to create the radio buttons, the debugger stops at line 47 (see the top image in Figure 13-11). Notice that in the Watch tab, the value for *i* is *not defined*. That's because the breakpoint stops the program just before the line is executed. In other words, the loop hasn't started, and the *i* variable hasn't yet been created.

However, the value of *answers.length* is set to 4. The array *answers* is an array of answers that was passed to the function (you can see the array elements listed lower down in the Watch list). An array's *length* property indicates the number of items in the array; in this case there are four, so you should get four radio buttons when the function's completed.

14. **Click the Step Over button (see Figure 13-11).**

This button takes you to the next line in the program. Now you can see that *i* is set to 0. You'll keep clicking through this loop.

Figure 13-11:
When you step through a program using Firebug, red circles to the right of a line number indicate a break point, while yellow arrows indicate the line of code that the JavaScript interpreter is currently stopped at. Click Step Over (or Step Into) to run that line of code and stop at the next line.

15. Click the Step Over button until you see the value of *i* change to *5* in the Watch list (bottom image in Figure 13-11).

    Although there are only four items in the *answers* array, you can see that the *for* loop is actually running five times (the value of *i*). So something's funny about how the loop is terminated. Remember that in a *for* loop, the middle statement in the *for* statement is the condition that must be true for the loop to run (see page 94). In this case, the condition is *i<=answers.length;*. In other words, the loop starts out with *i* containing 0 and continues to run as long as *i* is less than or equal to the number of items in the *answers* array. In other words, *i* will be 0, 1, 2, 3, and 4 before it terminates—that's five times.

16. Return to your text editor, and change the for loop at line 47 to read:

    ```
    for (i=0;i<answers.length;i++) {
    ```

    Now the loop only runs for the number of items in the answers array, creating one radio button for each possible answer.

17. Save the file, and preview it in Firefox.

    You can turn off the breakpoint by clicking its red dot in the firebug script window to see the finished page run without interruption.

The page *complete_13.2.html* contains the completed version of this tutorial. As you can see, finding bugs in a program can take a lot of work. But a debugging tool like Firebug makes it a lot easier to see inside a program's "guts" and find out what's going wrong.

Going Further with JavaScript

This final chapter covers various concepts that can help make you a better Java-Script programmer. You don't need most of the ideas here to write functioning JavaScript programs, so don't worry if you don't understand them all. In fact, aside from the first section, "Putting It All Together" (which contains some good advice for beginners), you can program happily for a long time without needing the information in the other sections in this chapter. But if you want to expand your skills, this chapter can point you in the right direction.

Putting It All Together

So far in this book, you've seen lots of tasks that JavaScript can accomplish: form validation, image rollovers, photo galleries, user interface improvements like tabbed and accordion panels, and more. But you might be wondering, how do you put them together to work with your site? After all, once you start using Java-Script, you'll probably want to use it to improve every page of your site. Here are some tips for how to use multiple scripts on your site.

Using External JavaScript Files

As mentioned on page 24, external JavaScript files are an efficient way to share the same JavaScript code among Web pages. An external file makes updating your JavaScript easier—there's just one file to edit if you need to enhance (or fix) your JavaScript code. In addition, when an external JavaScript file is downloaded, it's stored in the browser's cache, so it doesn't need to be downloaded a second time, making Web pages feel more responsive and load more quickly.

In the case of a JavaScript library like jQuery, external JavaScript files are a necessity—after all, your Web pages would be unnecessarily large and difficult to maintain if you put the actual jQuery JavaScript code into each page. Furthermore, jQuery plug-ins are supplied as external files, so you need to link them to a Web page if you want to use them. As you read on page 24, linking to an external JavaScript file is as easy as this:

```
<script type="text/javascript" src="js/ui.tabs.js"></script>
```

Putting your own JavaScript code into external JavaScript files can also help make your code more reusable and your site feel faster—but only if you actually share that code among Web pages. For example, with the form validation script you created on page 343, it doesn't make sense to put the code used to create the validation rules and error messages into an external file, since all of those rules and error messages are specific to the form elements on that page, and wouldn't work on a form that has different form fields. In that case, it's best to just use the JavaScript to validate the form within the Web page itself.

However, the validation plug-in file you learned about on page 331 can be used for any form, so it makes sense to have that in a separate file. The same is true for any code that you'll use in multiple pages. For example, on page 321 you learned how to focus the first field of a form using JavaScript—that's something you might want to do for every form. Likewise, the box on page 323 presents the JavaScript necessary to prevent a visitor from hitting the submit button multiple times (and thus submitting the form data more than once), which is also useful for any form page. So, you might want to combine these two scripts into a single external file named something like *forms.js*. The JavaScript code would look something like this:

```
1   $(document).ready(function() {
2     // focus first text field
3     $(":text")[0].focus();
4
5     // disable submit button on submit
6     $('form').submit(function() {
7       var subButton = $(this).find(':submit');
8       subButton.attr('disabled',true);
9       subButton.val('...sending information...');
10    });
11  }); //end ready
```

Note that since this code relies on jQuery, you must wrap it inside the *$(document).ready( )* function (lines 1 and 11). In fact, every external file that relies on jQuery must start with the code on line 1 above and end with the code on line 10.

Note: jQuery can handle multiple *$(document).ready( )* functions without any problems. For example, you can have several external JavaScript files that do various things to the page, and each file can have a *$(document).ready( )* function, and you can include a *$(document).ready( )* function within <script> that appears only on that page. That's perfectly fine with jQuery.

Using the same script across multiple pages requires a little planning on your part. For example, line 3 places the cursor into the first text field on a Web page. In most cases, that makes sense—you want the focus to be on the first field so that a visitor can start filling out the form. However, if the page has more than one form, this code might not work as you want it to.

For example, if you have a search box at the top of the page and a separate form for submitting a product order, the code in line 3 will put the focus on the "Search" box and not the first text field in the order form. In this case, you need to think through the problem a bit and come up with a way of making sure the proper text field has the focus when the page loads. Here are two possible solutions:

- Add a class name to the field you want the focus on when the page loads. For example, say you add the class name *focus* to the text field like this:

    ```
    <input type="text" class="focus" name="firstName">
    ```

    You could then you use this JavaScript to make sure that field is focused:

    ```
    $('.focus').focus();
    ```

    To use this code, you just need to make sure that you add the *focus* class to a text field on each form page, and make sure you link the external JavaScript file containing this code to each of those form pages.

- You can get the same effect by adding a class name to the <form> tag itself, using this JavaScript:

    ```
    $('.focus :text')[0].focus();
    ```

    This code automatically focuses the first text field of a form with the class *focus*. The benefit of this approach is that the first text field always gets the focus, so if you reorganize your form (add a few more text fields to the beginning, for example), you know that the first text field will get focus and not some other field (with the focus class) further down the page.

Once you start using JavaScript, you might end up using several scripts on all (or nearly all) of your Web pages. For example, you might have a drop-down navigation menu (like the one discussed on page 300) and some rollover images (page 236), and use JavaScript to make sure links outside your site open in a new window (page 278). In this situation, it's useful to create an external JavaScript file with all of the scripts you share among your site—you could call the file something like *site_scripts.js* or simply *site.js*.

Note: jQuery has a built-in mechanism to protect you from producing unwanted JavaScript errors. Java-Script usually spits out an error if you try to perform an action on something that doesn't exist—for example, trying to select a text field on a page that doesn't have a text field. Fortunately, jQuery ignores these kinds of errors.

Writing More Efficient JavaScript

Programming is a lot of work. Programmers are always looking for ways to do things faster and with fewer lines of code. While there are lots of tips and tricks, the following techniques are especially useful for working with JavaScript and jQuery.

Put Preferences in Variables

One important lesson that programmers learn is how to extract details from scripts so that they are more flexible and easier to update. For example, say you want to change the color of a paragraph of text to orange when a visitor clicks on it. You could do that with jQuery using the *css( )* function (page 186) like this:

```
$('p').click(function() {
  $(this).css('color','#F60');
});
```

In this case, the color orange (#F60) is hard-coded into this step. Say you apply this same color in other steps (maybe to add a background color when the visitor mouses over a table cell). You might be tempted to write #F60 into those steps as well. A better approach is to place the color into a variable at the beginning of your script and then use that variable throughout your script:

```
1   $(document).ready(function() {
2   var hColor='#F60';
3   $('p').click(function() {
4     $(this).css('color',hColor);
5   });
6   $('td').hover(
7     function() {
8       $(this).css('backgroundColor',hColor);
9     },
10    function() {
11      $(this).css('backgroundColor','transparent');
12    }
13  );
14  }); //end ready()
```

In this example, the variable *hColor* now holds a hexadecimal color value—that variable is used both in the *click* event for the <p> tags, and in a *hover* event for the <td> tags. If you later decide orange isn't your thing, you can change the value stored in the variable—*var hColor='#F33';*—and now the script will use that color.

You could make the above code even more flexible by uncoupling the connection between the color used for the <p> tags and <td> tags. Currently, they're both set to the same color, but if you want to make it so that you could eventually assign different colors to each, you could add an additional variable to your code:

```
1   $(document).ready(function() {
2   var pColor='#F60';
3   var tdColor=pColor;
4   $('p').click(function() {
5     $(this).css('color',pColor);
6   });
7   $('td').hover(
8     function() {
9       $(this).css('backgroundColor',tdColor);
10    },
11    function() {
12      $(this).css('backgroundColor','transparent');
13    }
14  );
15  }); //end ready()
```

Now, the *click* and *hover* events the same color—#F60—will be used for both (since the *tdColor* variable is set to the value of *pColor* in line 3 of the code). However, if you later decide that you want the table cells to have a different color, just change line 3 like this:

```
var tdColor='#FF3';
```

When writing a JavaScript program, identify values that you explicitly name in your code and turn them into variables. Likely candidates are colors, fonts, widths, heights, times (such as 1,000 milliseconds), file names (such as image files), message text (such as alert and confirmation messages), and paths to files (such as the path for a link or an image). For example:

```
var highlightColor = '#33A';
var upArrow = 'ua.png';
var downArrow='da.png';
var imagePath='/images/';
var delay=1000;
```

Put these variable definitions at the beginning of your script (or if you're using jQuery right inside the *.ready( )* function).

Tip: It's particularly useful to put text that you plan on printing to a page into variables. For example, error messages like "Please supply a valid email address," or confirmation messages like "Thank you for supplying your mailing information" can be variables. When these messages are grouped together as variables at the beginning of a script, it's easier to edit them later (and to translate the text if you ever need to reach an international audience).

Ternary Operator

It's a common programming task to set the value of a variable based on some kind of condition. For example, say you want to set up a variable that contains text with the login status of a user. In your script there's a variable named *login*, which contains a Boolean value—*true* if the user is logged in, or *false* if she isn't. Here's one way to create a new variable for this situation:

```
var status;
if (login) {
 status='Logged in';
} else {
 status='Not logged in';
}
```

In this case, a basic conditional statement (page 77) sets the value of a variable named *status* based on whether the user is logged in or not. JavaScript offers a shortcut for this common procedure, called a *ternary operator*. A ternary operator provides a one-line approach to creating a simple conditional statement. The basic format of the ternary operator is:

```
(condition) ? A : B
```

Depending upon the result of the condition, either A (if the condition is *true*) or B (if the condition is *false*) is returned. The *?* precedes the *true* result, while the *:* precedes the *false* result. So, for example, the above code could be rewritten like this:

```
var status=(login)?'Logged in':'Not logged in';
```

What was once six lines of code is now a single line of code. Figure 14-1 diagrams how this code works.

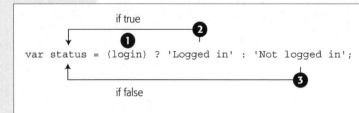

Figure 14-1:
The ternary operator lets you write one-line conditional statements. In this example, 1 is the condition. If it's true, the code immediately following the ? mark is returned (2); if the condition is false, then the code following the : is returned (3).

The ternary operator is simply a shortcut—you don't have to use it, and some programmers find it too dense to easily understand and prefer the easier-to-read if/else statement. In addition, the best use of the ternary operator is for setting the value of a variable based on a condition. It doesn't work for every type of conditional statement; for example, you can't use it for multiple-line statements where many lines of code are executed based on a particular condition. But even if you don't use ternary operators, recognizing how they work will help you understand other peoples' programs, since you'll probably encounter them frequently.

The Switch Statement

There's more than one way to skin a conditional statement. While the ternary operator is great for assigning a value to a variable based on the results of a condition, the *switch* statement is a more compact way of writing a series of if/else statements that depend on the value of a single variable.

For example, say you ask visitors to your site to type their favorite color into a form field, then print a different message based on the color they submit. Here's how you might write part of this code using the typical conditional statement.

```
if (favoriteColor == 'blue') {
 message = 'Blue is a cool color.';
} else if (favoriteColor == 'red') {
 message = 'Red is a warm color.';
} else if (favoriteColor == 'green') {
 message = 'Green is the color of the leaves.';
} else {
 message = 'What kind of favorite color is that?';
}
```

Notice that there's an awful lot of *favoriteColor == 'some value'* in that code. In fact, *'favoriteColor =='* appears three times in just nine lines of code. If all you're doing is testing the value of a variable repeatedly, then the switch statement provides a more elegant (and easy to read) solution. The basic structure of a switch statement is diagrammed in Figure 14-2.

The first line of a switch statement begins with the keyword *switch*, followed by a variable name inside parentheses, followed by an opening brace symbol. Essentially, this code says "let's get the value of this variable and see if it matches one of several other values." Each test is called a *case*, and a switch statement has one or more cases. For example in Figure 14-2, there are three cases, numbered 1–3. The basic structure of a case looks like this:

```
case value1:
   // do something
  break;
```

The *case* keyword indicates the beginning of a case; it's followed by some value and then a colon. This line is shorthand for the longer *if (variable=='value1')*. The value can be a number, string, or Boolean (or a variable containing a number, string, or Boolean), so if you want to test whether the variable is equal to 37, for example, then the case would look like this:

```
case 37:
 //do something
  break;
```

To test whether the variable is true or not, you'd write this:

```
case true:
 //do something
 break;
```

After the first line, you add the statements you want to execute if the variable matches the test case value. Finally, you add a *break;* statement. This step is important—the *break;* statement exits the switch statement. If you leave it out, the JavaScript interpreter will skip to the next test case and see if it matches.

Leaving out the break; statement can cause problems especially if you use the final *default* keyword with a switch statement (number 4 in Figure 14-2). The default statement applies if none of the test cases is true—it's the equivalent of the final *else* clause in a conditional statement. If you leave out the break; statement in one of the earlier test cases, then if one of the cases is true, the JavaScript interpreter will also run whatever code is listed in the default statement

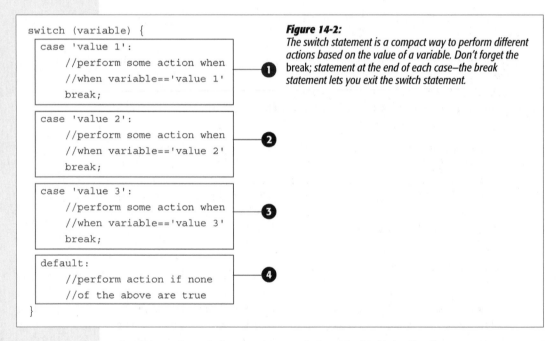

Figure 14-2:
The switch statement is a compact way to perform different actions based on the value of a variable. Don't forget the break; statement at the end of each case—the break statement lets you exit the switch statement.

Here's how the switch statement can help with the *if/else if* code on page 499:

```
switch (favoriteColor) {
  case 'blue':
    message = 'Blue is a cool color.';
    break;
  case 'red':
    message = 'Red is a warm color.';
    break;
```

```
    case 'green':
      message = 'Green is the color of the leaves.';
      break;
    default:
      message = 'What kind of favorite color is that?';
  }
```

This code is the equivalent to the *if/else* if code, but is more compact and easier to read.

In fact, you can also put more than one *case* statement right after one another (and intentionally exclude the *default* keyword) if you want to run the same code for several values. For example:

```
switch (favoriteColor) {
  case 'navy':
  case 'blue':
  case 'indigo':
    message = 'Blue is a cool color.';
    break;

  case 'red':
    message = 'Red is a warm color.';
    break;
  case 'green':
    message = 'Green is the color of the leaves.';
    break;
  default:
    message = 'What kind of favorite color is that?';
  }
```

This is similar to using *if (favoriteColor == 'navy' || favoriteColor == 'blue' || favoriteColor == 'indigo')* in an *if/else* statement.

Using the jQuery Object Efficiently

Every time you call the jQuery object—for example, *$('#example')*—you're asking the jQuery library to find one or more elements on the page. Some jQuery selectors require a lot of work on the part of the library. For example, *$('a[href^=http://]')* tells jQuery to find every link on a page that has an *href* attribute that begins with *http://*. That takes a fair amount of processing power, so don't make jQuery do work it doesn't need to.

If you plan on using the same selector more than once in a script, you should first store it in a variable. The variable will hold the results of jQuery's search throughout the DOM, so you can access that variable any number of times without making jQuery search for those elements again. Storing a reference to an object in a variable is particularly useful when adding an event handler (page 210) or using the *each( )* (page 193) function to perform a series of tasks on page elements.

For example, say you want to locate every link that points outside your site, add a class to those links (so that a CSS style can change their look), and make those links open in a new window when clicked. In other words, you want to find all of those links and then perform two different actions on them. One way to accomplish this task is like this:

```
$('a[href^=http://]').addClass('external');
$('a[href^=http://]').attr('target','_blank');
```

Notice that in the above code, *$('a[href^=http://]')* appears two times. Each time *$('a[href^=http://]')* is encountered jQuery *refinds* the links—this is a waste of processing time, so you could store *$('a[href^=http://]')* into a variable a single time, then access it any number of times without making jQuery go find the elements again:

```
var links = $('a[href^=http://]');
links.addClass('external');
links.attr('target','_blank');
```

Now the variable *links* holds a reference to all of the external links on the page. jQuery has done its job finding those links, and now that they're stored in a variable, jQuery doesn't need to find them a second time.

An even more efficient way to apply multiple commands to a jQuery selection is to use jQuery's *chaining* capabilities (page 180). Every time you run a jQuery command like *addClass( )* or *attr( )*, you can add another command following it to create a chain of commands that are all run on the same object. For example, you can rewrite the above code more succinctly as:

```
$('a[href^=http://]').addClass('external').attr('target','_blank');
```

In this example, both the *addClass( )* and *attr( )* functions are run on the original jQuery object—*$('a[href^=http://]')*. You'll often see a long chain of commands run on a single object, and to make the code easier to read, the long chain is broken up over multiple lines. For example, you can rewrite the above code as follows (and it'll still work):

```
$('a[href^=http://]')
  .addClass('external')
  .attr('target','_blank');
```

Creating Fast-Loading JavaScript

Once you starting using external JavaScript files for your scripts, your visitors should start to feel like your site is faster. Thanks to a browser's cache, once your external JavaScript files download for one page of your site, they don't have to be downloaded a second time for a different page (see page 24 for more detail on this concept). However, there's still another way to make your site download more quickly: compressing your external JavaScript files.

Note: Files sent securely via SSL (secure socket layer) are *never* cached. So if people access the pages of your site using *https://* as the protocol (for example *https://www.sawmac.com*), then any files they download, including external JavaScript files, must be downloaded every time they're needed.

To make a script more understandable, programmers usually insert empty spaces, carriage returns, and comments to explain what the script does. These are all important additions for the programmer, but not necessary for the Web browser, which can happily understand JavaScript without carriage returns, tabs, extraneous spaces, or comments. Using a compression program, you can minimize the space your JavaScript takes up. The version of jQuery recommended in this book, for example, is *minified* (see page 171), and is nearly half the file size of the uncompressed version.

There are several programs aimed at making JavaScript more petite. Douglas Crockford's JSMin (*http://crockford.com/javascript/jsmin.html*) is one example, and Dean Edward's Packer (*http://dean.edwards.name/packer*) is another. However, this chapter uses the same compressor Yahoo uses, because it achieves great file size savings without changing your code (some compressors actually rewrite your code and in some cases can break your scripts!).

Yahoo's JavaScript compressor, *YUI Compressor*, lives at *http://developer.yahoo. com/yui/compressor*. The only downside of YUI Compressor is that it's not really aimed at the average computer user—it's written in Java and doesn't have a simple interface. The steps for using YUI Compressor vary a bit between Windows and Macintosh, so the following tutorials provide separate instructions for each operating system. Here are the basic steps common to all systems.

1. **Download YUI Compressor.**

   Download the latest version of the compressor from *www.julienlecomte.net/ yuicompressor*. It comes in a ZIP file, so you need to unzip it and store it somewhere on your computer. You'll need to know the path to this folder, so put it somewhere easily accessible, like your Desktop or Documents folder.

2. **Move your JavaScript file to the *build* folder inside the *yuicompressor* folder.**

   The build folder has a file named something like *yui-compressor-2.3.4.jar*; it's a file that you can run using a Java virtual machine. You don't have to move your JavaScript file into this folder, but doing so makes it easier when running the compressor to have both the compressor and the script files in the same folder.

3. **Run the YUI compressor.**

   How you run the compressor depends on your operating system, but no matter your operating system, you need to have Java installed on your computer. Most Macs already have Java installed; and, if you're using Windows, you may already have it installed as well. You can download the latest version of Java from *www.java.com/en*.

The compressor works using the command line (don't be scared; it's not that hard), so you need to start up either the Command Prompt (Windows) or Terminal (Mac) program (detailed instructions for starting either of these programs are in the next two sections). With the command line available, you type a command like that pictured in Figure 14-3.

The parts of the command that you'll modify are numbered 1, 2, and 3. It's a little tricky, since it must be a complete path name—the exact location on your hard drive—to each file. The following tutorials cover the steps for each operating system in detail.

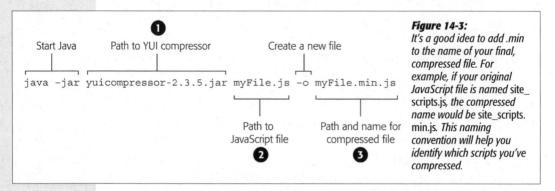

Figure 14-3:
It's a good idea to add .min to the name of your final, compressed file. For example, if your original JavaScript file is named site_scripts.js, the compressed name would be site_scripts.min.js. This naming convention will help you identify which scripts you've compressed.

4. **Move your compressed file to your site.**

The final, compressed file is the one you should use on your site. Link that file to the Web pages that will be using the scripts. Don't throw away the original, uncompressed file, however. It's the one that's easy to read and edit, so when you need to make a change to your scripts, you'll need the original file to work on.

Using YUI Compressor for Windows

Since it's generally easier to learn by doing, let's go step by step through the process of compressing an external JavaScript file for Windows. You'll need to have the tutorial files on hand—see page 27 for instructions on downloading the tutorials.

1. **Move the files *yuicompressor-2.3.5.jar* and *jquery.greybox2.js* from the *chapter14* folder in the tutorials folder to your C:\ drive (or if you can't put them there, to your *users* folder).**

This step isn't absolutely necessary, but it will make it much easier for you to specify the path to the various files on the command line in step 3.

2. **Choose Start → All Programs → Accessories → Command Prompt to launch the Command Prompt program.**

A small window with white text on a black background appears. Here you can type command-line instructions (just like Linux and Unix users—the joy!).

3. **In the Command Prompt window, type:**

```
java -jar "C:\yuicompressor-2.3.5.jar" ⏎
"C:\jquery.greybox2.js" -o "C:\jquery.greybox2.min.js"
```

Depending on where you placed the YUI compressor and greybox files, you may need to change the *C:* part. For example, if you put the files into your user folder, you would replace *C:* with *C:\Documents and Settings\Your UserName*. Or, if you placed them in your My Documents folder, then replace *C:* with *C:\ Documents and Settings\Your UserName\My Documents*.

Note: If you get an error that says that *java* is not a recognized command, then you probably don't have Java installed on your computer. You'll need to download it from *www.java.com/en*.

---

4. **Press the Return key to run the command.**

The compressor does its thing, and you'll find a file named *jquery.greybox2.min.js* in the same folder as the original *jquery.greybox2.js*. This file is your newly compressed JavaScript file.

To compress additional files, just move them into the folder with the *yuicompressor-2.3.5.jar* file, and follow steps 2–4.

Using YUI Compressor for Mac

Since it's generally easier to learn by doing, let's go step by step through the process of compressing an external JavaScript file for a Mac. You'll need to have the tutorial files on hand—see page 27 for instructions on downloading the tutorials.

1. **Move the files *yuicompressor-2.3.5.jar* and *jquery.greybox2.js* from the *chapter14* folder in the tutorials folder to your user folder or Documents folder.**

This step isn't absolutely necessary, but it will make it much easier for you to specify the path to the various files on the command line in step 3.

2. **Launch the Terminal application.**

You'll find this program in Applications → Utilities → Terminal.

3. **In the Terminal window, type:**

```
java -jar ~/yuicompressor-2.3.5.jar ⏎
~/jquery.greybox2.js -o ~/jquery.greybox2.min.js
```

Depending on where you placed the YUI compressor and greybox files, you may need to change the *~/* part. On a Mac (and Unix/Linux), *~/* is a shorthand method of specifying the file path to your Home folder, so *~/myFile.js* indicates the path to the file named *myFile.js* located in the Home folder. If you put the compressor and JavaScript files into your Documents folder, replace *~/* with *~/Documents/*.

4. **Press Return to run the command.**

The compressor does its thing, and you'll find a file named *jquery.greybox2.min.
js* in the same folder as the original *jquery.greybox2.js*; that's your newly compressed JavaScript file.

To compress additional files, just move them into the folder with the *yuicompressor-2.3.5.jar* file, and follow steps 2–4.

Part Five:
Appendix

Appendix A: JavaScript Resources

JavaScript Resources

This book provides enough information and real-world techniques to get your JavaScript career off to a great start. But no one book can answer all of your Java-Script questions. There's plenty to learn when it comes to JavaScript programming, and this appendix gives you taking-off points for further research and learning.

References

Sometimes you need a dictionary to read a book. When programming in Java-Script, it's great to have a complete reference to the various keywords, terms, methods, and other assorted bits of JavaScript syntax. You can find references both in online and book form.

Web Sites

- **Mozilla Developer Center Core JavaScript Reference** (*http://developer.mozilla.org/en/docs/Core_JavaScript_1.5_Guide*) provides a complete reference to Java-Script 1.5 (the version that's best supported by today's browsers).

- **JavaScript Quick Reference from DevGuru** (*www.devguru.com/technologies/javascript*) is a single Web page listing JavaScript keywords and methods. Click a term, and a page explaining the keyword or method appears.

- **Google Doctype** (*http://code.google.com/doctype*) covers JavaScript, DOM and CSS and tells you which features are supported by each browser. It's a kind of encyclopedia for Web developers.

- **MSDN Library** (*http://msdn.microsoft.com/en-us/library/d1et7k7c(VS.85).aspx*) from Microsoft is an excellent resource if you're developing for Internet Explorer only. It's IE- and Microsoft-centric approach can help out intranet developers who are developing internal applications for organizations that have standardized on Internet Explorer. (In other words, if you're developing Web sites for the entire world to enjoy, then skip this resource.)

Books

- **JavaScript: The Definitive Guide** by David Flanagan (O'Reilly) is the most thorough printed encyclopedia on JavaScript. It's a dense, heavy tome, but it has all the details you need to thoroughly understand JavaScript.

Basic JavaScript

JavaScript isn't easy to learn, and it never hurts to use as many resources as possible to learn the ins and outs of programming for the Web. The following resources provide help with the basics of the JavaScript language (which can sometimes be quite difficult).

Articles and Presentations

- **A (Re)-Introduction to JavaScript** by Simon Willison. (*http://simon.incutio.com/slides/2006/etech/javascript/js-tutorial.001.html*). This entertaining presentation provides a slide-based overview of the JavaScript language.

Web Sites

- **JavaScript Cake: Tutorials and Scripts** (*http://jennifermadden.com*) from Jennifer Madden is a Web site with tutorials that cover the basics of JavaScript programming. Simple and to the point.

- **The W3 Schools JavaScript tutorial** (*www.w3schools.com/js*) is a thorough (though not always thoroughly explained) tutorial that covers most aspects of JavaScript programming.

Books

- **Head First JavaScript** by Michael Morrison (O'Reilly) is a lively, highly illustrated introduction to JavaScript programming. It provides lots of information on how JavaScript works and how to program with it, but doesn't provide much in the way of immediately useful Web page examples.

- **PPK on JavaScript** (New Riders) covers all of the JavaScript basics. Written by Peter Paul Koch, an influential JavaScript programmer whose site, *www.quirksmode.org*, contains thoroughly researched information on cross-browser differences. If you want to save a few bucks, you can find most of the content from the book on the author's Web site at *www.quirksmode.org/js/contents.html*.

jQuery

Much of this book covered the jQuery JavaScript library, but there's still lots to learn about this powerful, timesaving, and fun programming library.

Articles

- jQuery Tutorials for Designers (*www.webdesignerwall.com/tutorials/jquery-tutorials-for-designers*) is an article from the well-known Web design blog, Web-Designer Wall, that includes 10 cool, simple things you can do with jQuery.

- jQuery Cheatsheet (*www.gscottolson.com/weblog/2008/01/11/jquery-cheat-sheet*) is a downloadable PDF that puts all of jQuery's functions on a single, printable page.

Web Sites

- **jQuery.com**, the home of the wonderful jQuery JavaScript library, provides access to discussion groups, documentation, plugins, and downloads.

- **jQuery's documentation** is provided via a user-generated Wiki (*http://docs.jquery.com/Main_Page*). Anyone's free to add or edit the descriptions of jQuery's many features on this site, but a core group of people handles most of the documentation. It's the number one place for complete information on jQuery.

- **jQuery for Designers** (*http://jqueryfordesigners.com*) is a site that includes written and video tutorials for creating interesting visual effects, useful interfaces, and generally improving Web sites using jQuery.

- **jQuery HowTo's** (*http://jquery.open2space.com*) includes jQuery tutorials for beginning through advanced JavaScript programmers.

- **Learning jQuery** (*http://www.learningjquery.com*) provides information from some of jQuery's lead developers.

Books

- **jQuery in Action** by Bear Bibeault and Yehuda Katz (Manning) covers jQuery thoroughly with lots of example programming. It assumes some JavaScript and programming knowledge.

- **Learning jQuery** by Jonathan Chaffer and Karl Swedberg (PACKT) was the first book on jQuery. It's short and to the point, covering all of the jQuery basics. It's a little out-of-date, but most of the content still applies.

The Document Object Model

The Document Object Model (DOM) is one of the most important topics in JavaScript programming. It provides the means for adding, deleting, modifying, and accessing a Web page's HTML of using JavaScript. It's so important (and complicated) that you'll find endless resources on the topic. Here are a few of the best.

Note: If you're using jQuery (or pretty much any other JavaScript library), you won't necessarily need this information to program JavaScript successfully. Most JavaScript libraries provide their own functions for accessing and manipulating the DOM, and unless you want to learn the traditional methods of using the DOM, you don't necessarily need to read any of the following resources.

Articles and Presentations

- **An Introduction to the W3C DOM** by Steven Chipman (*http://slayeroffice.com/ articles/DOM*) is an online presentation that covers the basic concepts of the Document Object Model and how to use it.

- **DOM Cheat Sheet** (*www.wait-till-i.com/2007/06/27/dom-javascript-cheat-sheet*) is a PDF that concisely lists the standard DOM methods used for accessing and manipulating the HTML on a Web page.

Web Sites

- **The Document Object Model section of the W3C's Web site** (*www.w3.org/DOM*) provides a detailed, but dense and technical, description of the DOM. But it's from the same people who oversee HTML, CSS, and other technologies the Web depends on, so it gives you definitive information (and you can impress your coworkers when you say you've been "analyzing the W3C's DOM specs").

- **The HTML DOM Tutorial** (*www.w3schools.com/htmldom*) from W3Schools. com is a good overview and hands-on learning tool for gaining a better understanding of the Document Object Model.

Books

- **DOM Scripting** by Jeremy Keith (Friends of ED) is probably the most thorough and easy-to-read bookson the subject of the Document Object Model.

- **Advanced DOM Scripting** by Jeffrey Sambells and Aaron Gustafson (Friends of ED) covers DOM programming with an emphasis on professional programming techniques. It's not the easiest book to wade through, but it teaches valuable programming techniques.

Ajax

Ajax brings together your Web browser, JavaScript, and server-side programming, for triple the fun (and three times the headache). Fortunately, there are plenty of resources to turn to for learning how to use Ajax.

Web Sites

- **Ajaxian** (*www.ajaxian.com*) is a great source for the latest news concerning Ajax, JavaScript frameworks, and useful Web services. The site is aimed at professional JavaScript programmers but is also full of news, tidbits, and often highlights sites that use Ajax in creative ways.

Books

- **Head Rush Ajax** by Brett McLaughlin (O'Reilly) is probably the best introduction to Ajax for those new to both JavaScript and server-side programming. Its playful approach and graphical layout make all of the basic concepts and techniques of Ajax easily understandable.

- **Bulletproof Ajax** by Jeremy Keith (New Riders) is a short read that focuses on how to use Ajax effectively and without alienating visitors who don't have JavaScript enabled.

Advanced JavaScript

Oh yes, JavaScript is even *more* complicated than this book leads you to believe. Once you become proficient in JavaScript programming, you may want to expand your understanding of this complex language.

Articles and Presentations

- **Show Love to the Object Literal** by Chris Heilman (*www.wait-till-i.com/2006/02/16/show-love-to-the-object-literal*) is a short blog post that explains good uses for JavaScript object literals.

- **Object Oriented JavaScript** by Tim Huegdon (*http://nefariousdesigns.co.uk/archive/2006/05/object-oriented-javascript*) provides a short introduction to a complex topic. It's a good place to start learning object-oriented programming with JavaScript.

- **JavaScript Shorthand Tips and Tricks** (*http://blog.reindel.com/2007/11/01/javascript-shorthand-tips-and-tricks*) is a short blog post that offers a few advanced tips on using JavaScript more efficiently.

- **Sorting a JavaScript array using** *array.sort( )* (*www.javascriptkit.com/javatutors/arraysort.shtml*) provides a useful information on how to sort the contents of arrays, including a quick method of randomizing and array (think shuffling a deck of cards).

Web Sites

- **Eloquent JavaScript** (*http://eloquentjavascript.net*) is a JavaScript tutorial site. It's organized well, with creative ways of teaching lessons. Although it's supposed to be a beginner JavaScript tutorial site, the author writes as though he's talking to a bunch of computer scientists, so it's not the best place to start if you're new to JavaScript or programming.

- **Unobtrusive JavaScript** (*www.onlinetools.org/articles/unobtrusivejavascript/index.html*) from Christian Heilmann is a mini-site dedicated to explaining the concept of *unobtrusive JavaScript*—specifically, how to make a Web site accessible to everyone (even those whose browsers don't have JavaScript enabled).

- **The JavaScript section of Douglas Crockfords' World Wide Web** (*http://javascript.crockford.com*) provides a lot of (complex) information about Java-Script. There's a lot of information on the site, some of it requiring a computer science degree just to understand.

- **Yahoo's JavaScript Developer Center** (*http://developer.yahoo.com/javascript*) has more information on JavaScript than nearly any other site on the Web. Much of the information is geared toward Yahoo's own JavaScript library, YUI, as well as the many Web services Yahoo offers (like Yahoo Maps).

Books

- **Pro JavaScript Techniques** (Apress) is written by John Resig himself, the creator of jQuery. Definitely a book for experienced JavaScript programmers, it's filled with lots of helpful programming tidbits.

- **Pro JavaScript Design Patterns** by Ross Harmes and Dustin Diaz (Apress) provides JavaScript programming techniques that help solve common tasks. Note: this is complicated stuff worthy of a computer science major.

- **JavaScript: The Good Parts** by Douglas Crockford (O'Reilly) uncovers the most useful parts of JavaScript, sidestepping bad programming techniques. Douglas should know what he's talking about, since he's a Senior JavaScript Architect at Yahoo. The book is short and dense, but contains a lot of wisdom about how to use JavaScript well.

CSS

If you're tackling this book, you're probably already pretty comfortable with CSS. JavaScript can really take advantage of the formatting power of CSS to control not only the look of elements, but even to animate them across the screen. If you need a CSS refresher, here are a few helpful resources.

Web Sites

- **The Complete CSS Guide** from WestCiv (*www.westciv.com/style_master/academy/css_tutorial*) covers pretty much every part of Cascading Style Sheets. You won't learn a lot of different techniques here, but the basics of what CSS is and how to create styles and style sheets is thoroughly covered.

- **The SitePoint CSS Reference** (*http://reference.sitepoint.com/css*) is another online CSS reference that's easy to use and has a search engine.

- **Selectutorial** (*http://css.maxdesign.com.au/selectutorial*) is a great way to learn CSS selector syntax. Since jQuery is pretty much founded on the idea of using CSS selectors to manipulate the HTML of a page, it pays to have a very good understanding of this concept.

Books

- **CSS: The Missing Manual**, by David Sawyer McFarland (O'Reilly) is a thorough, tutorial-driven book on Cascading Style Sheets. It includes in-depth coverage of CSS as well as real-world examples and troubleshooting tips for making sure your CSS works in a cross-browser world.

- **CSS: The Definitive Guide** by Eric Meyer (O'Reilly). The name says it all; this book covers CSS in such detail that your brain will definitely hurt if you try to read it all in one sitting.

- **CSS Mastery: Advanced Web Standards Solutions** (Friends of ED) is a well-designed book that covers sophisticated CSS-based designs, as well as many techniques for working effectively with CSS.

JavaScript Software

There's really nothing special you need for writing JavaScript programs. Any text editor, the one you're probably using to create HTML and CSS right now, for example, is perfectly fine. There are, however, text editors that can make a JavaScript programmer's life easier. Here are a couple programs with features aimed at making JavaScript programming go faster:

- **Aptana Studio** (*www.aptana.com/studio*). Available in both a free ("Community") and paid ("Pro") version, this Web Development program was written especially with JavaScript programmers in mind. It lets you write HTML, CSS, and JavaScript, FTP files to your server and includes loads of JavaScript-specific tools like JavaScript debuggers, support for popular JavaScript libraries, and (in the paid version) a JSON editor.

- **Dreamweaver CS4** (*www.adobe.com*) has long been a favorite Web design tool. Dreamweaver CS4 has added lots of JavaScript-specific features, such as the ability to view a page "live" within Dreamweaver—meaning you can view how the JavaScript works, freeze the JavaScript as it runs to see how the page looks, and even view the HTML that results when JavaScript manipulates the page's DOM.

Index

I

J